VOID
Davidson College

SUMMA PUBLICATIONS, INC.

Thomas M. Hines
Publisher

William C. Carter
Editor-in-chief

Editorial Board

Benjamin F. Bart
University of Pittsburgh

William Berg
University of Wisconsin

Germaine Brée
Wake Forest University

Michael Cartwright
McGill Universityd

Hugh M. Davidson
University of Virginia

Elyane Dezon-Jones
Washington University

John D. Erickson
Louisiana State University

Wallace Fowlie (emeritus)
Duke University

James Hamilton
University of Cincinnati

Freeman G. Henry
University of South Carolina

Norris J. Lacy
Washington University

Jerry C. Nash
University of New Orleans

Allan Pasco
University of Kansas

Albert Sonnenfeld
University of Southern California

Orders:
Box 20725
Birmingham, AL 35216

Editorial Address:
3601 Westbury Road
Birmingham, AL 35223

Twenty Years of French Literary Criticism

FLS, vingt ans après

Philip A. Wadsworth
(1913–1992)

TWENTY YEARS OF FRENCH LITERARY CRITICISM

FLS, VINGT ANS APRÈS

**A Memorial Volume
for
*Philip A. Wadsworth***
(1913–1992)

Edited
with Foreword and Introduction
by
Freeman G. Henry

SUMMA PUBLICATIONS, INC.
Birmingham, Alabama
1994

Copyright 1994
Summa Publications, Inc.
ISBN 1-883479-02-9

Library of Congress Catalog Number 94-66517

Printed in the United States of America

All rights reserved

CONTENTS

Foreword — xi

Introduction — xvii

I. NARRATIVE: FROM AUTOBIOGRAPHY TO NARRATOLOGY — 1

L'atelier autobiographique de Sartre
Philippe Lejeune — 3

Biographie d'une autobiographie
Bernard Mathias — 17

World War II and the French Novel
Rima Drell Reck — 25

Beyond *Mimesis*: Narrative Modality in *A la recherche du temps perdu*
David R. Ellison — 35

Mimesis et catégories universelles: les limites du réalisme objectif dans le récit
Michel Viegnes — 43

Signifier l'amour: une lecture de Sade
Ralph Heyndels — 53

La rhétorique du silence dans *L'Amour* de Marguerite Duras
Pierre Van den Heuvel — 67

The Emergence of a Poetics
Murray Sachs — 77

Histoire, Fiction, Légende
Robert Champigny — 89

On Narratology (Past, Present, Future)
Gerald Prince — 97

II. PERIODIZATION: FROM THE "DEFFENCE" TO POSTMODERNISM — 109

The *Deffence* and French Humanism
Donald Stone, Jr. — 111

La Fontaine and the Classical Ideal
Philip A. Wadsworth — 123

French Literary Criticism in the Seventeenth Century: Its Nature and Status
Hugh M. Davidson — 137

The Role of the Poet in Eighteenth-Century French Society
John Pappas — 153

Rousseau and Diderot: Education as Politics
Lester G. Crocker — 169

Differing Modes of Myth Expression among the French Romantics: Hugo, Chateaubriand, and Gautier
Richard B. Grant — 185

Texte classique/contexte moderne: l'enjeu des classiques dans la pratique théâtrale entre 1950 et 1970
Laurence Romero — 201

L'essai ou l'anti-genre dans la littérature française du XXe siècle
Edouard Morot-Sir — 213

French Literary Criticism (1945-1975): An Overview
Laurent LeSage — 227

Period Style in the Light of Structuralism, Semiotics, and Catastrophe Theory
Patrick Brady — 241

III. THEMES AND MOTIFS: FROM SOCRATIC IRONY TO "TITROLOGIE" — 251

Ironie socratique, ironie romanesque, ironie poétique
Jean-Pol Madou — 253

The Spirit of Erotic Wit in French Literature
Benjamin F. Bart — 263

The Problematics of Embedded Poems, from *Aucassin* to Artaud
    Laurence M. Porter   277

"J'ai regretté toute ma vie d'être femme": Madame Palatine féministe?
    Dirk Van der Cruysse   291

Marceline Desbordes-Valmore: ni poésie féminine, ni poésie féministe
    Christine Planté   301

Exotisme et vie quotidienne: le cas de la "littérature d'évasion"
    Claude Javeau   315

Ravel's *Trois Poèmes de Stéphane Mallarmé*
    Robert Gronquist   325

The Enchantment of Orpheus: Music and Words in Contemporary French Fiction
    Roland A. Champagne   341

Déictique, énonciatrice et poétique: les fonctions du titre
    Serge Bokobza   347

Index   359

Tabula gratulatoria   367

Foreword

In Memory of Philip A. Wadsworth

When Philip Wadsworth came to the University of South Carolina in 1973, he had already fashioned a distinguished career. Some of our finest universities had recognized his stature by welcoming him into their midst as colleague: Yale (1939–1950), Northwestern (1950–1952, interrupted by recall by the Navy), Illinois (1954–1964), Rice (1964–1972). His arrival in Columbia was viewed as a major event. He brought with him the reputation of a scholar-teacher of the highest caliber. His several books on the French classical tradition had become classics in their own right. It is little wonder, then, that his new colleagues and students alike should be enthused by the prospect of working and learning alongside him.

In fact, enthusiasm had been building for some time among his new colleagues. For all the other dimensions he would lend to the French program at the University of South Carolina—and his gracious gentility was surely not the least of them—one stood out in the minds of a handful of professors who had commited themselves to a new and daring scholarly project: the hosting of an annual literary colloquium and the publication of the acts in the form of a series. Philip A. Wadsworth, they reasoned quite rightly, would bring both recognition and credibility to a fledgling enterprise that was attempting to test its wings during what was hardly the best of times. Indeed, he did that and much more. If Phillip Crant and Maynor Hardee were moving forces behind the founding of the French Literature Conference and the *French Literature Series*, it was Philip Wadsworth's experience and wisdom that provided sage counsel concerning topics, programs, consultants, and logistics. Further, should a difficult decision need to be made about the inclusion of a submission, all eyes turned to Phil. Somehow he knew, whatever the author's approach entailed, whether modifications could satisfy the exigencies of both oral presentation and subsequent publication. Instinctively, he was able to cut through the Gordian knots of literary criticism, to lay problems bare and to find solutions acceptable to contributing scholar, editor and program committee.

Philip Wadsworth was both a "well tempered critic" and a "well tempered man." He was able to appreciate, genuinely, the great diversity of views and methods reflected in the hundreds of studies that came across his desk as member of the editorial board of **FLS**. By the same token, he was always the gentleman's gentleman, an unassuming friend to student and scholar. His quiet demeanor could be deceptive, however; behind the calm, almost serene expression he often wore, his mind was usually abuzz. He would share his ponderings when asked to do so, and those moments are cherished by those of us who had the privilege of listening to the thoughts flow forth, wave upon wave, distilled to a fine liqueur in a language that only a superior mind can articulate.

Phil was sorely missed when he retired from the university in 1979. His death in 1992 was a loss for all of us. This retrospective volume is dedicated to his memory. The essays it contains and the tradition they reflect owe a great deal to him and to those like him who, over the years, have given of themselves so generously and—in Phil's case—so modestly.

Principal Publications

Philip Wadsworth's publishing career spanned forty years. From the very beginning his writings displayed the combination of innovation and scholarly decorum that would become his trademark. His first book, *The Novels of Gomberville* (New Haven: Yale UP, 1942), brought to public and critical attention a major preclasssical novelist whose works had fallen into virtual oblivion. The standard had been set. Subsequent full-length studies on La Fontaine, Tristan l'Hermite and Molière met with similar acclaim. These are books that have indeed passed the test of time; they have become mainstays in the ever-growing annals of seventeenth-century French scholarship. Students and established scholars alike continue to be drawn to them today for their probing insights, their meticulous documentation, their breadth of scope and their eminent readability.

The following bibliography—a partial list of Philip Wadsworth's publications—includes books and major articles.

Books

The Novels of Gomberville. New Haven: Yale UP, 1942.

Selected Works of La Fontaine. New York: Harper, 1950. Revised ed. Carbondale, Illinois: Southern Illinois UP, 1964.

Young La Fontaine. Evanston, Illinois: Northwestern UP, 1952. Reprinted by AMS Press, N.Y., 1970.

Poésies de Tristan l'Hermite. Paris: Seghers, 1962.

Foreword

Molière and the Italian Theatrical Tradition. York, South Carolina: French Literature Publications Co, 1977.

Articles

— "The *Car* Quarrel," *Mod. Lang. Quarterly,* 1 (1940), 527-538.
— "Gomberville: A Bibliographical Sketch," *Yale Romanic Studies,* 18 (1941), 49–100.
— "A formula of Literary Criticism, from Aristotle to La Bruyère," *Mod. Language Quarterly,* 7 (1946), 35–42.
— "La Bruyère Against the Libertines," *Romanic Review,* 38 (1947), 226–233.
— "La Fontaine as a Student and a Critic of Malherbe," *Symposium,* 3 (1949), 130–139.
— "Saint Exupéry, Artist and Humanist," *Mod. Language Quarterly,* 12 (1951), 96–107.
— "An Unpublished MS by La Fontaine," *PMLA,* 66 (1951), 1183–1188.
— "New Views of French Classicism," *The French Review,* 25 (1952), 173–181.
— "La Fontaine and La Rochefoucauld," *Romanic Review,* 46 (1955), 241–249.
— "The Poetry of Tristan l'Hermite," *Kentucky Foreign Language Quarterly,* 4 (1957), 205–211.
— "Artifice and Sincerity in Tristan l'Hermite," *Mod. Language Quarterly,* 74 (1959), 422–430.
— Chapters: "La Fontaine," pp. 114–124 and "Theater: General Studies, Bibliographies, Recueils," pp. 156–159 in *A Critical Bibliography of French Literature* (Seventeenth Century), Syracuse: Syracuse UP, 1961.
— "Malherbe and his Influence," in *Studies in Seventeenth Century French Literature,* Ithaca: Cornell UP, 1962.
— "Form and Content in the Odes of Malherbe," *PMLA,* 77 (1963), 190–195.
— "La Fontaine as a Poet for Women (and Men too)," *The French Review,* 39 (1965), 241–249.
— "La Fontaine and his Views on Marriage," *Rice University Studies,* 51 (1965), 81–96.
— "Malherbe's Youthful Elegy," *L'Esprit créateur* (Winter, 1966), 264-270.
— "Ovid and La Fontaine," *Yale French Studies,* 38 (1967), 151–156.

—"The Composition of *Psyché* by Molière and Corneille," *Rice University Studies*, 53 (1967), 69–76.
—"Montaigne's Conclusion to Book II of his *Essais*," in *Studies in Honor of William L. Wiley*, Chapel Hill: University of North Carolina Press, 1968, 249–260.
—"Exoticism in Molière," *The American Legion of Honor Magazine*, 40 (1969), 73–84.
—"Montaigne's Relation to his Readers," *South Atlantic Bulletin*, 35 (1970), 20–27.
—"La Fontaines's Theories on the Fable as a Literary Form," *Rice University Studies*, 57 (1971), 115–127.
—"Molière's *L'Etourdi* and its Italian Source," *Kentucky Romance Quarterly*, 18 (1971), 319–331.
—"The Art of Allegory in La Fontaine's *Fables*," *The French Review*, 65 (1972), 1125–1135.
—"Scarron's *Nouvelles tragicomiques*," *Rice University Studies*, 59 (1973), 93–100.
—"*L'Interesse* and *Le Dépit amoureux*," *Romance Notes*, 15, supplement 1 (1974), 57–71.
—"Le Douzième Livre des *Fables*," *Cahiers de l'Association Internationale des Etudes Françaises*, 26 (1974), 103–115.
—"Recollections of Cicognini's *Gelosie fortunate* in *Le Misanthrope*," *PMLA*, 89 (1974), 1099–1105.
—"The Prestige of *La Princesse de Montpensier*," *French Literature Series*, 2 (1975), 179–183.
—"From the *Commedia erudita* to Molière," in *Molière and the Commonwealth of Letters*, ed. Johnson, Trail and Neumann, Jackson: University Press of Mississippi, 1975, 443–454.
—"La Fontaine's Poems of Self-Appraisal," *Papers on French Seventeenth Century Literature*, 13 (1980), 291–306.
—"La Fontaine and the Classical Ideal," *French Literature Series*, 7 (1980), 1–15.
—"Smiling with La Fontaine," *Papers on French Seventeenth Century Literature*, 13 (1980), 291–306.
—"Studies of Molière and his Sources," *Oeuvres et Critiques*, 6, 1 (1981), 69–76.
—Chapter: "La Fontaine," pp. 87–97, in *A Critical Bibliography of French Literature*, Vol. III A, Syracuse: Syracuse UP, 1983.

(The primary source of the preceding bibliographical information is *Studies in Honor of Philip A. Wadsworth*, ed. Donald W. Tappan and William A. Mould, Birmingham, Al: Summa Publications, 1985.)

Foreword

FLS 1973-1993

The first French Literature Conference took place in 1973. The initial **FLS** volume appeared the following year, establishing the format and sequence that have endured over two decades: a conference devoted to a pre-announced topic, followed by the publication of the conference papers—usually in expanded essay form—plus scholarly notes and, from 1975 to 1991, a selected bibliography. By the time Philip Wadsworth retired from the University of South Carolina in 1979, **FLS** had already published articles by more than one hundred thirty scholars, including Laurence M. Porter, Rima Drell Reck, Jean Sareil, Murray Sachs, Renée Riese Hubert, François Rigolot, Ronald Tobin, Patrick Brady, Richard Grant, Germaine Brée, Hugh Davidson, Robert Champigny, Philip Duncan, Lester Crocker, Norris Lacy, Marshall Olds, David Rubin, Donald Stone, and John Erickson.

The 1980s witnessed the internationalization of **FLS**. Five European scholars were added to an already distinguished advisory board: Roland Desné (Université de Reims), Henk Nuiten (Katholieke Universiteit, Nijmegen), Ralph Heyndels (Université Libre de Bruxelles), Dirk Van der Cruysse (Universiteit Antwerpen), Pierre Ronzeaud (Université de Provence). Soon essays by scholars from these and other countries were taking their place in **FLS** volumes alongside those of American and Canadian colleagues. Publicity began to reach as far as the pages of *Le Monde*, in which the 1982 conference on eroticism was billed as "érotisme sous les magnoliers." On two occasions, recognized French fiction writers opted to publish original works in **FLS**: Michel Butor (*Bilame ou Diode*, 1984) and Bernard Mathias (*Blasphèmes*, a play performed at the Petit Odéon, 1988).

The year 1992 marked a milestone for **FLS**. Volume XX (*On the Margins of French Literature*)—as well as subsequent volumes—will be published, marketed and distributed on an international basis by Editions Rodopi (Amsterdam/Atlanta). Finally, after twenty years, **FLS** is finding its way systematically into major libraries around the world.

Thanks for this success over the years is due to the support and efforts of numerous individuals. Members of the editorial board have worked tirelessly year after year to organize a colloquium whose goal has been to foster free intellectual exchange in an atmosphere of genteel cordiality. Members of the advisory board have contributed their expertise freely, both as consultants and participants. A. Maynor Hardee, who for many years served as editor, is owed a special debt of gratitude. And the Department of French & Classics of the University of South Carolina has been particularly instrumental in these achievements.

As for the preparation of this retrospective volume, I should like to thank my colleagues James Day, Buford Norman and William Edmiston for their advice and critical acumen. Maynor Hardee has added his proofreading expertise to the process, and for that I am grateful. I am also indebted to both the Office of the Provost and the Research and Productive Scholarship Committee of the University of South Carolina for their generous support.

Freeman G. Henry, Editor

Volumes Appeared

Vol. I, Authors and Their Centuries (1974)
Vol. II, The French Short Story (1975)
Vol. III, Mythology (1976)
Vol. IV, French Literary Criticism (1977)
Vol. V, French Literature and the Arts (1978)
Vol. VI, Authors and Philosophers (1979)
Vol. VII, Manifestoes and Movements (1980)
Vol. VIII, Historical Figures in French Literature(1981)
Vol. IX, The French Essay (1982)
Vol. X, Eroticism (1983)
Vol. XI, The French Novel: Theory and Practice: Michel Butor: *Bilame ou Diode* (1984)
Vol. XII, Autobiography (1985)
Vol. XIII, Exoticism (1986)
Vol. XIV, Irony and Satire (1987)
Vol. XV, Theater and Society (1988)
Vol. XVI, Feminism (1989)
Vol. XVII, Narratology and Narrative (1990)
Vol. XVIII, Poetry and Poetics (1991)
Vol. XIX, Strategies of Rhetoric (1992)
Vol. XX, On the Margins (1993)
Vol. XXI, Discontinuity and Fragmentation (1994)

Introduction

I

In the spring of 1976 Laurent LeSage, who had been following French literary criticism for years as historian and bibliographer, stood before a Columbia, South Carolina audience that included John R. Williams, Hugh M. Davidson, Patrick Brady and Robert Champigny. His was the last presentation of the fourth annual French Literature Conference. His topic: "French Literary Criticism since World War II." He shook his head, appearing to be at a loss. Not for words—not Laurent LeSage—but rather for a sense of what was happening in the field. Roland Barthes had sounded the death knell of structuralism only the year before, had he not? "Structuraliste, qui l'est encore?" he had written in his own "Par lui-même" (*Roland Barthes,* Paris: Seuil, 1975, p. 121), that bantering display of specious self-mockery that seemed for all the world without precedent.

But if structuralism was at last being laid to rest and if there was to be life after semiology, LeSage reasoned, the form or forms after-life would assume should already be observable in the progeny. What he observed, or thought he observed, must have been something like Noah's ark—so many species, some of them quite strange, all housed under the same roof.

The "innovative" journals of the period seemed incapable of charting a common course. "Periodicals like *Tel Quel, Change, Poétique, Communications, Littérature* can scarcely have readers beyond the initiated," he said. The foremost names in the field hardly offered any notion of consensus or common ground: Todorov, Genette, Lacan, Foucault, Culler, Riffaterre, Doubrovsky. And what about Kristeva and Derrida who, each in a different way, were calling for a new freedom in criticism? "In her attempt to break out of the ideology box, Kristeva argues for a shifting norm, as the only concept admissible as basic for poetic analysis, a 'genotype' that is a sort of historical composite. (...) Such speculations lead to affirmations without proof, paradoxes, theory without material support. Derrida asks us to pretend that we are out of the box although he admits we cannot be."

Unknowingly and at a rather early date, LeSage may have arrived at a basic understanding of so-called "poststructuralist" critical theory and practice as it still exists today some. Perhaps the primary difference is that now the ark is more crowded than ever. Barthes's ludic disavowal may be viewed as the point of departure for the many "refusals" to follow. For what is now termed "poststructuralist" criticism has been better known for extolling what it is not rather than what it is or should be. The result is a pluralism that most often prefers to recognize differences, discontinuity, fragmentation, repetition and parody, that tends not to recognize referents, norms, unity, and originality. It is almost always antilogocentric and frequently narcissistically self-referential. It thus may function in much the same way as Barthes's playful yet telling statement: "I don't like strawberries." It can in fact be very entertaining in a self-parodic way. Jean-Jacques Thomas recently published an article in *L'Esprit Créateur* in which he approached the literary text in the following manner: "...je m'autorisais donc à lire un texte selon des critères qui ne répondent qu'aux exigences d'une norme personnelle auto-imposée: mon code postal: 75007" (31, 4 [Winter 1991], 59).

* * *

During the last twenty years French literary criticism has been anything but unicentric or stagnant. The numbers of practitioners and "*praxes*" have multiplied exponentially. Divergent opinions regarding the importance and even direction of the period continue to abound. What is clear is that post-sixties criticism and theory reflect a feeling of disarray or alienation concerning the course of Western civilization. Terms such as crisis, chaos, skepticism, and even anarchism characterize what is perceived as a lack of legitimation, a social, cultural, political and philosophical splintering that recognizes no common origin, that recognizes no dominant discourse.

How has this happened? Explanations often revolve around the notion that capitalism has expanded into daily life in such a way that it has supplanted preexisting value systems. This notion echoes the utilitarian outcries of Gautier, Baudelaire and Flaubert in the nineteenth century, but the phenomenon is more pervasive than they might have imagined, owing to the unforeseeable efficacy of mass media in a technocracy and an interdependence of economies that can be witnessed in virtually every supermarket and department store in the developed world. Infrastructures now stretch tentacularly across oceans, corporate messages traveling at the speed of light on laser beams. Productionism, consumerism, and mass marketing have entered our homes, our institutions, our minds. The consequence, however fortuitous, has been an overriding normatization, the creation of a monolith in which divergent or alternative ideas, codes, or life-styles are not tolerated. A common perception is that there has thus been a commensurate loss of choice, of freedom, in everyday life to be sure, but especially in artistic and intellectual expression.

Reactions have been diverse. Marxism and feminism chose active opposition, often doing battle on similar grounds without recognizing each other's efforts. Cultural or social deconstructionists pointed out the

Introduction xix

fissures in the monolith resulting from the oppression of women and minorities. Narratologists, at least some of them, claimed to have found a new means of cognition that offered hope for the future. Some groups chose to withdraw and to carry on as though the outside world did not exist. Marcuse and the commune movement may be seen as such an attempt. Perhaps this last example provides a key to what many writers, critics and theorists have endeavored to do. By refusing to recognize the referent (or *"pretending"* to do so), by rejecting referentiality other than self-referentiality or interiority—that is the text, the whole text and nothing but the text—they have been able to carry on as though exteriority were of no *signification* and, therefore, no *significance*. On the one hand this concept is exclusionary in that it involves keeping the outside and outsiders out. Only *initiates* are welcomed into the inner circle. On the other hand it is also a means of expressing and proclaiming one's freedom, for the forms of non-normative, non- or self-referential theories may be as numerous as the practitioners themselves. Hence the autonomy of art, literature, theory and criticism is perceived to be maintained in what is otherwise an alien world.

* * *

What role has **FLS** played in all of this? Certainly not a doctrinaire role. Over the years and by design, the very breadth of topics housed by each volume has attracted a wide array of critical approaches to every genre and period of French and francophone literature: medieval, classic, romantic, modern and postmodern. Particular genres have been targeted on occasion: the short story (1975), the essay (1982), the novel (1984), autobiography (1985), theater (1988), poetry (1991). Themes and motifs have not been neglected: mythology (1976), philosophy (1979), history (1981), eroticism (1983), exoticism (1986), irony and satire (1987). Other topics bear witness to a similar scope: criticism (1977), the arts (1978), feminism (1989), narratology and narrative (1990), strategies of rhetoric (1992), marginal literature (1993), fragmentation (1994), values (1995).

Collectively, the first twenty volumes of **FLS** reflect both the evolving trends of literary criticism in general and a changing of the guard in the United States, the emergence of a new generation of scholars equipped with a new set of tools, some of them quite unrecognizable to their ascendants. In the beginning, in the early- to mid-seventies, the seasoned scholars in our major universities were still those who had cut their eye teeth on American new criticism, Wellek and Warren, literary history, genre studies, and Auerbach's notions of *mimesis*. *Les Grands* of French literary criticism in this country had become almost legendary: Germaine Brée, Henri Peyre, Wallace Fowlie, Lester Crocker, Philip Wadsworth. These were people of enormous erudition believed to be equally at ease in their interpretations of Plato or

Dante, Molière or Rousseau, Sartre or Beckett, equally authoritative in their pronouncements on classicism or romanticism, surrealism or the Avant-Garde. If they belonged to any particular school, it was probably the Lansonian school noted for keen readings based on meticulous research, with the added dimension of comparative and interdisciplinary orientations.

Many of the essays **FLS** attracted in the early years, including studies by Brée, Crocker and Wadsworth, are thus of a non-postmodern bent; they are oriented according to pre-structuralist priorities in literary criticism. The referent's function in them, if not unchallenged, is hardly displaced. Hermeneutics and Heideggerian phenomenology, with their propensity for unitive conception or consciousness, underlie several studies; thematics receive due attention; archetypal and genre criticism are present in force; sweeping period or movement studies are common. But *metacriticism*, that is to say the criticism of criticism so rampant in France, is scarcely mentioned.

It was not until the spring of 1976, then, at the Conference of that year and the subsequent publication of the volume on criticism (1977), that the new age of criticism made its full impact on **FLS**. The virulent attack on literary history ongoing at the Sorbonne, historical revisionism based on structuralism, semiotics and catastrophe theory (advanced by Patrick Brady), the revolution being published in the pages of *Tel Quel* and *Change*, all received front-line attention. Armine Kotin of the University of Illinois concluded a study of the critical and theoretical upheavals in France by saying: "Surely it is evident that the revolution has indelibly and necessarily changed the criticism we practice, and that we can't go back again." Indeed, American universities were already at work turning out a new generation of students schooled to accept the challenge of *La Nouvelle Critique*. Henceforth, those students would begin to make their mark throughout the country. And although traditional approaches continued to find their way into **FLS** volumes, the page had been turned. Poststructuralist criticism, whatever it was and whatever it would become, was here to stay.

II

The twenty-nine essays reproduced in *Vingt ans après* have been chosen both for their individual and their collective contributions to this retrospective volume. Although the names of many of the authors are recognizable as belonging to leading American and European scholars, the selection of each essay was based on an interplay of quality, representativeness, and the particular dynamics of the volume itself. Decisions were often difficult, for the total pool of essays exceeded two hundred fifty, excluding creative pieces such as Michel Butor's *Bilame*

Introduction

ou Diode (ten prose poems, **FLS**, Vol. XI, 1984) and *Blasphèmes* (a post-Holocaust play by Bernard Mathias and Geneviève Leymarie, **FLS**, Vol. XV, 1988).

Individually, in addition to shedding new light on particular texts, each essay builds a bridge to an enhanced understanding of literature and criticism within the larger context of human inquiry and expression. Whether it is a matter of Philippe Lejeune or Bernard Mathias on the dichotomy of autobiographer/autobiography, David Ellison or Michel Viegnes on Proustian *mimesis*, Dirk Van der Cruysse or Christine Planté on the "pre-modern feminism" of Madame Palatine or Marceline Desbordes-Valmore, each essay offers insights into the evolving notions of the process and significance of both the production and reception of literary texts. Collectively, given the non-doctrinaire character of **FLS**, the essays constitute a representative sample of French literary criticism in the United States in the last twenty years: the continuing presence of traditionalism, the emergence of the new generation, the swinging of the pendulum, the latest view of the future.

Narrative:
From Autobiography to Narratology

The volume has been divided into three relatively autonomous parts. In many ways narrative has been the "focal point" of French criticism and literature since the 1960s, from the *Nouvelle Critique* to the *Nouveau Roman*. Critic and writer alike have shown a predilection for narrative as both object of and vehicle for innovation and discovery in the postmodern period. Part I, Narrative: From Autobiography to Narratology, has the effect of surveying narrative from the pluralistic perspectives of autobiography and self-referentiality, collaborationist revisionism, new dimensions in mimetic theory, deconstructionist valorizations of emptiness and silence, genre theory past and present, and narratology as beacon in a world of uncertain light.

* * *

It is fitting that this collection of essays should begin with Philippe Lejeune's "L'atelier autobiographique de Sartre." Not only has autobiography been one of France's literary constants since the Second World War—the narrative genre that reflects perhaps better than any other the turning inward (and turning away) produced by the trauma of those difficult years—but also Lejeune's study shares a goal common to this volume: he seeks to re-examine Sartre's autobiographical works "*vingt ans après,*" twenty years after the publication of Sartre's *Les Mots* and in light of the autobiographical interviews the author-philosopher did with Simone de Beauvoir as well as the "shocking" posthumous publication of *Carnets de la drôle de guerre*. Exactly what new light radiates from this new information and how does it reflect on *Les Mots*, thought to be Sartre's final word on his childhood?

Lejeune's reader has the privilege to enter the "atelier" of the author of *L'Autobiographie en France* and *Le Pacte autobiographique*. For what is presented in these pages is not the finished product but rather the various parts that will ultimately constitute it. He proceeds cautiously, meticulously, scholar that he is, being careful not to conclude until all the pieces fit together. And how will they fit together, precisely? The reader can look over his shoulder, so to speak, and witness the first stage of what would culminate in a three-tiered work, "Les enfances de Sartre," published a year later in *Moi aussi* (Paris: Seuil, 1986), pp. 117-163.

* * *

Seeing autobiography from the outside, attempting to understand critically its various dimensions and to evaluate its relationships with other aspects of an author's works, is surely a meaningful endeavor. But what, beyond the obvious, might authors themselves take into account when writing an autobiography? How do family, social, or religious concerns come into play? What influence do editors exert? Which parts are fact, which parts are fiction, and which parts lie somewhere in between? How revealing or accurate is the central persona in reality? Is it even possible that more than one author has contributed to the work? These questions would seem especially relevant to autobiography as fiction, as narrative, as novel. Bernard Mathias, author of the prize-winning *Les Concierges de Dieu* (Grasset, 1982) and of *L'Enfant infidèle* (Grasset, 1988), provides a unique inside look at the process in "Biographie d'une autobiographie"—and there is something foreboding about it.

* * *

The constraints of autobiography are quite real for Mathias, even though the ghosts of the round-ups and deportations that continue to haunt him are some forty years old when he first writes about them. Today nearly a half century has passed since the German Occupation. The way the French treated those who had abetted "the enemy" is understandable: it was a terrible period, the victims too numerous to count. Only a purge would do. If it would not wipe the slate clean, it would help people get on with their lives. The guilty had to pay, all the *collabos*, including the artists, the writers, the intellectuals. And so it went. Sentences were handed out summarily, if assassination or suicide

Introduction　　　　　　　　　　　　　　　　　　　　　　　　xxiii

had not already claimed the accused. Some of the cases are well-known: Louis-Ferdinand Céline spent two years in a Danish prison before returning to France to face yet another year of incarceration; Pierre Drieu La Rochelle took his own life before coming to trial; Charles Maurras's initial death sentence was finally commuted to life in prison; Robert Denoël was struck down by an unknown assailant; Jean Giono had to wait six months in prison to prove his innocence; Georges Suarez was executed in November 1944.

How much the scenario has changed in the intervening years. Germany is no longer "the enemy." As members of the European Community, France and Germany now share political, economic, social, and military policy. French and German soldiers now train side by side, and talk of a truly joint force is commonplace. The evolution has been slow, and sometimes painful, but inevitable. Too, the attitude toward French collaborationist writers has evolved over time. Rima Drell Reck's study of the case of Drieu La Rochelle is in the forefront of this reorienting movement. She first documents the process from inside, through discussions with French university students of the early 1970s—already a generation removed from World War II—and then situates Drieu's thought and writings within a larger, European context. His intentions, as she points out, were hardly without consideration for the welfare of France. Such rectifications have become increasingly common. A humane and insightful revisionism characterizes several full-length studies that have appeared in the last few years: Herbert Lottmann's *The Left Bank* (San Francisco: Halo Books, 1982); Pierre Assouline's *Gaston Gallimard: un demi-siècle d'édition française* (Paris: Balland, 1985) and *L'Epuration des intellectuels* (Paris: Editions Complexe, 1985); Gilles and Jean-Robert Ragache's *Des Ecrivains et des artistes sous l'Occupation, 1940-1944* (Paris: Hachette, 1988).

* * *

In recent years the notion of *mimesis* has been the focus of significant debate. A salient postmodernist position, in part in reaction to the "dogmatic" views of Marxist critics such as Georg Lukács, is that objective reference is both impossible and irrelevant. Yet there is also a significant movement in the opposite direction, a re-evaluation of Erich Auerbach's notion of *mimesis* within a redefined, non-normative context, a rehabilitation of sorts led by Paul Ricoeur (*Temps et récit,* 3 Vols. Paris: Seuil, 1983-1985), Christopher Prendergast (*The Order of Mimesis: Balzac, Stendhal, Nerval, Flaubert.* Cambridge: Cambridge UP, 1986), Mihai Spariosu and Ronald Bogue (*Mimesis in Contemporary Theory: An Interdisciplinary Approach,* 2 Vols. Amsterdam: J. Benjamins, 1984, 1991), and Jerry A. Varsava (*Contingent Meanings: Postmodern Fiction, Mimesis, and the Reader.* Tallahassee: Florida State UP, 1990).

The emphasis has now shifted in the direction of the reader, to reception as opposed to production or intention. The two "readings" by David R. Ellison and Michel Viegnes convey insightful delineations of both the "limits" of *mimesis* and the capacity for going "beyond" *mimesis*.

Proust's referentiality comes into question quite logically, given Derrida's view that he had "tampered with the law of genre." David Ellison elucidates that view in terms of *mimesis* by explaining how the Proustian narrative builds on Balzacian realism only to leave it behind in favor of the self-referentiality that leads to Beckettian experimentation.

Michel Viegnes considers the problematic first historically, from Plato's *cratylism* to the present, and then synchronically through the receptive optic in order to show to what extent text is capable of replicating number, form, matter, space and time. The objective or surface limits are considerable, he concludes, but the pluralistic, subjective dynamics of text—and here the model is again Proust—offer abundant mimetic rewards for the reader.

* * *

Postmodernism is fond of finding in a text that which has been purported not to be there at all. By means of processes of deconstruction, the seals of would-be vacuums of absence are ruptured, allowing signification to come rushing in, forming pockets of presence where only emptiness was once believed to exist. This is how Ralph Heyndels's pluralistic reading of *La Philosophie dans le boudoir* fills love's void in "Signifier l'amour: une lecture de Sade." In order to accomplish his goal, Heyndels calls up a veritable throng of assistants from various camps, ranging from Barthes to Blanchot, from Lacan and Bersani to Bataille, from Merleau-Ponty to Foucault. The results are surely worth the effort: the rhetorics of desire, hatred and Oedipal urges—a fragmentation of self-image—are juxtaposed to form the self-portrait Sade himself never found the words to trace.

* * *

Absence is also the focus of Pierre Van den Heuvel's "La rhétorique du silence dans *L'Amour* de Marguerite Duras." Here Van den Heuvel, author of the seminal study *Parole, Mot, Silence: pour une poétique de l'énonciation* (Paris: Corti, 1985), underscores the vital role of reception in Duras's novel. The rhetorical phenomenon of silence is extremely complex: it signifies at once the breakdown of verbal communication— owing to the insufficiency of language or the referential impotence of the subject—and the means of ideal communication. Decoding silence is the receptive key to Duras's "oeuvre ouverte." The reader is called on to

Introduction

participate dialogically, to "construct by deconstructing," to engage in the performative act of filling in the verbal vacuums.

* * *

Given the displacement of emphasis from production to reception, recent criticism has tended to deny originality, to demonstrate by means of intertextuality or other such textual phenomena that repetition in one form or another dominates present-day culture. Originality is sometimes difficult if not impossible to deny, however, as with the development of a new medium such as cinema. Technological innovation gave birth to a multiplicty of "original" contributions, one must admit, despite debts to photography, the graphic arts, the theater, etc.

The nineteenth century was witness to a birth of another sort, the emergence and coming of age of a new narrative genre in France, the "conte." Murray Sachs examines its debt to the folk art of storytelling and then traces the elaboration of a poetics from Mérimée to Anatole France and beyond, well into the twentieth century, to Gide, Camus, and Sartre.

* * *

The oral tradition of storytelling quite obviously combines history, fiction and legend in a folk art form. Yet when examined semiotically, how do "histoire," "fiction" and "légende" differ in any text—oral or written—and what are their modes of interpretation and valorization? These are all questions the late Robert Champigny set out to answer in the following essay. Champigny elaborates a conciliatory narratological theory that blends the divergent epistemological theories of correspondence and coherence by defining "la correspondance cognitive" as "une cohérence entre des interprétations de signes hétérogènes" and by identifying a zone of intersection between "des interprétations historisantes de divers signes."

* * *

The concept of "coherence" explains in part why, over the last decade, narratology has become a unique, self-perpetuating form of inquiry. Its uses have been probing and pervasive, going far beyond the traditional limits of "literary" narrative to include psychology and cultural analysis, to name only two areas of expansion. Its purview is that of "narrative" redefined as a particular mode of cognition capable of ordering or structuring the possible as well as the extant in individuals or in groups as large as societies. Gerald Prince, author of *Narratology: The Form and Functioning of Narrative* (The Hague: Mouton, 1982) and *A*

Dictionary of Narratology (Lincoln: University of Nebraska Press, 1987), looks to the past before leading an expedition into the future of narratological theory and practice. Will it be primarily this mode of cognition that will reveal the paradigms of the decades to come, and beyond that will it be instrumental in unraveling the secrets of the globe and perhaps the universe? Whatever the answer, narratology continues to reorient itself in relation to changing demands; new paths include especially an increased interest in pragmatics, narrative viewed as act or process, a transaction between two parties. Such explorations need to be multiplied and a clearer sense of imperatives, goals and limitations needs to be articulated in order for narratology to remain vital. While extolling narratology's accomplishments, Prince also issues a formidable challenge to its practitioners.

Periodization: From the "Deffence" to Postmodernism

For many years period studies were a mainstay in **FLS**. It is not surprising that their numbers have diminished substantially, given the emphases of recent critical approaches, including the "deconstructive retrovisionism" represented by the so-called "new historicism." Yet a goodly measure of ink continues to be expended on questions of modernism versus postmodernism versus poststructuralism versus the latest term coined to designate the most current trends in theory and criticism. Too, there is a stable "school" of stalwarts who continue to labor in the Elysian fields of literary history, who continue to produce the annotated editions for the Pléiade series, who continue to root out manuscripts and related documents, who research and write literary biographies. Today the name of Claude Pichois comes immediately to mind. He is heir to a fecund tradition that has spanned five generations of Baudelaire scholars, from Charles Asselineau (the poet's contemporary) to the father-and-son team of Eugène and Jacques Crépet and on to the late W. T. Bandy.

Part II of this volume is devoted largely to the continuation of this tradition. Several of the authors are among those whose critical works helped shape or reshape the basic understanding of diachronic relationships in literature for an entire generation of students: Donald Stone, Phil Wadsworth, Hugh Davidson, Lester Crocker, among others. The studies included here, while focusing on a particular literary or cultural phenomenon, reach out to embrace an entire epoch. The approach, in this sense, is synthetic. It might even be said that it contains elements of what is now being called "constructivism" and, of course, the research orientation is not entirely foreign to Genette's notion of *paratexte*. Finally, as we shall see (especially in the case of Patrick

Introduction

Brady's elaborations), there is something new and vibrant about each of these essays, something quite current and up-to-date.

* * *

Interestingly, the salutary effects of repetition in literature from one age to the next are underscored by Donald Stone in his essay: "The *'Deffence'* and French Humanism." The ludic character often associated with postmodern writers serves as a point of departure as he takes to task the heretofore venerable Johan Huizinga for characterizing the *grands rhétoriqueurs* as having cultivated "literature in the form of an all-round game" and having engaged in stylistic excesses that "by no means give us the feeling of the measure and harmony of the Renaissance." Stone returns to the texts of the period in order to dispel the notion that playful disorder is alien to the writings of the Pléiade. The dynamics of this "new form" literature that would constitute the "new age" canon are far too great to be reduced to such formulas, he insists. Though Stone does not say so in so many words, the key to the matter is intertextuality, the juxtaposition of various texts, as opposed to the purported theoretical prescriptions of Du Bellay's *Deffence* or related pronouncements on intentionality. Indeed, the sixteenth-century reception of literary texts comes into question when both Salel and Peletier du Mans are shown to have read Homer as though the *Odyssey* were a chivalric handbook for would-be warriors. A similar case is made for Erasmus's "Christian reading" of Cicero. Ultimately, Stone returns to the *Deffence* itself to re-read it, "instead of reading into it." What he discovers is of the highest relevance in today's terms: pluralistic independence rather than enslavement to classical models may well have been the moving force in the successful transition from the Middle Ages to humanism.

* * *

Independence and freedom are also key words in Philip Wadsworth's study on "La Fontaine and the Classical Ideal." Using Valéry's aphorisms as springboards ("Classique est l'écrivain qui porte un critique en soi-même" and "Le lion est fait de mouton assimilé"), Wadsworth examines La Fontaine's critical writings with a new eye. La Fontaine held an "eclectic view of literature." His pronouncement—"Mon imitation n'est pas un esclavage"—might even be understood in terms of "originality" or invention defined as the unrestricted production of varieties of repetition, a concept that would find favor among critics today. In addition to the long-recognized ludic qualities of his works, self-analysis and self-criticism are traits common to his prefatory writings as well. One will find no disavowal of intentionality, however. La Fontaine wrote to "please" and to be read by the "honnêtes gens" of Paris and the royal court. There are also elements of moralistic didacticism that create a typically subtle yet unsettling tension in his works. La Fontaine was a man of his times who, Wadsworth concludes, "proved himself to be an independent thinker and at the same time an articulate spokesman for the classical ideal."

* * *

In the following essay Hugh M. Davidson directs his attention to the problematics of literary criticism three centuries removed: its "nature and status" in the seventeenth century. Some of his observations sound quite familiar. "The variety of forms assumed by the discussion of literature in the 17th century," he says, "reflects the confusion that goes with all large-scale and poorly coordinated undertakings." There are distinct differences, however: problems of literature are viewed as a "transaction," that is to say in terms of author-work-audience-aim; art is defined as a "productive discipline"; the rhetoric of "critical consciousness" of the period is dialogical in form, "a dialectical conversation" with the past that, whatever its tenor, tends toward the normative. Yet Davidson, as Wadsworth has done in the preceding essay, emphasizes the concern for independence and diversity voiced by the "critics" of the period themselves. His probings reveal the complex, evolving character of that concern. On the one hand, the primacy of rhetoric is challenged by Descartes, Pascal, Malbranche, and Fontenelle. On the other, and here the message may have particular significance for our own generation, the challenge becomes all the more formidable when it is picked up by the "Creationists" of the time.

* * *

Poetry and values underlie John N. Pappas's study of the role of the poet in eighteenth-century French society. It was a concern for truth that prompted Plato to distrust poets. He banned them from the ideal State because, like Homer, they were thought to reveal truths about the gods and, therefore, rivaled philosophers. They also tended to obnubilate by dealing in contradictions, either without regard for truth or without the ability to discern it. Subsequently, each age has tended to lean toward one position or the other, Pappas says. Societies tend to view the poet as either prophet or jester. The latter notion, reinforced by the ludic frivolity ("élégant badinage") of the *grands rhétoriqueurs*, characterized French society's perception of the poet until the advent of the Pléiade. With Ronsard the concept of divine inspiration again elevated the poet to the position of prestige enjoyed during Plato's day. By the time the eighteenth century was underway, however, the prevalent intellectual view had been voiced by Malherbe: "The poet is no more useful to the state than a good skittle player." Voltaire, La Motte, Fontenelle and d'Alembert soon lined up behind him. But their positions were hardly cut and dried, Pappas informs us. It was a matter of a power struggle — between the court and the *philosophes* as to who would be the "arbiters of French taste" — and a scramble for the spoils. Poetry was alive and well in aristocratic circles, after all; it dwelt in gilded theaters, cloaked in tragedian costume, and was nourished by state pensions. Pappas brings to light the *philosophes'* many inconsistencies and diverse motivations. He conludes that, ultimately (and unwittingly in some cases), the *philosophes* — especially Rousseau and Diderot — helped prepare the way for the *poète mage* of the following century.

* * *

Ironically, if Rousseau and Diderot were both primary contributors to the reformulation of esthetics that culminated in French romanticism, it was despite their antithetical views of the universe and the problems of mankind. Their common literary legacy did not translate into a common philosophical or political legacy. The late Lester Crocker, in his brilliant essay entitled "Education as Politics," comes to some jolting conclusions concerning the ideas they advanced, the means to their realization, and their appropriation by the generations to come.

As in the Pappas study, the notion of values underpins the theories of these two eighteenth-century writers. The primary question is one that is asked in every age: "Where is the highest value? In the individual, which society must serve, or in the community, which the individual must serve so that it can best serve him?" Rousseau opts for the latter. His goal is to remold the community, to establish "true society" by changing the individual into an altruistic enactor of the common good. Thus dedicated, Rousseau rejects the concept of individual civil liberties as we now know them in favor of "collective" liberties. Diderot chooses the opposite interpretation. His concern is for individual freedom and the preservation of diversity as a means to individual happiness.

This dichotomy is reflected clearly in the theories of education elaborated by the two men. Rousseau's precepts and methods are issue of the primacy of order and system; Diderot's stem from the idea of the "inviolable sanctity" of "individual as individual." Archetypally, Crocker asserts, these divergent attitudes not only culminate politically and socially in antithetical societies — Western liberal societies or Marxist societies — they also determine the educational philosophies and practices common to each.

* * *

This political and social dichotomy has obviously undergone a metamorphosis in the 1990s. Marxist socialism has disintegrated. First phase capitalism has moved in to take its place. And so the monolith grows, some would say, ever hardening at the core and flowing outward irrisistibly like so much molten lava. Hence the simultaneous disintegration of two myths: social utopianism, on the one hand, and free market idealism on the other. This phenomenon, the disintegration of myth, may in part explain the fragmentation and discontinuity that characterize postmodern intellectual and artistic expression. The reaction may have been fostered by Sartre for whom myth is a falsehood, an inauthentic principle people invoke to lend structure and coherence to their lives.

If such is now a common concept, myth was alive and well at the end of the nineteenth century, according to Richard B. Grant's study of "Differing Modes of Mythic Expression among the Romantics." Grant identifies four basic modes of mythic expression used to varying degrees by authors such as Chateaubriand, Gautier, Hugo, Flaubert, Maupassant and Zola: direct myth, displaced myth, hybrid myth and fantastic myth. His conclusion that myth *has not* and *will not* disappear from literature might not go unchallenged today. But such a challenge would meet ardent opposition. Given the etymology of the Greek word *mythos—story* or *narrative*—it can be argued that narratologists, in their quest for coherence, are today's myth-seekers. Could they be tomorrow's myth-makers as well?

* * *

We have seen how the *philosophes* endeavored to undermine both the role of poet as it was perceived in the eighteenth century and the very lucrative monopoly the nobility held on the theater (Pappas). The post-World War II program of decentralization in France involved similar concerns, we may conclude from Laurence Romero's essay "L'enjeu classique dans la pratique théâtrale entre 1950 et 1970." In this instance the "animateurs" were controversial directors such as Jean Vilar and Roger Planchon, thanks to whom a revitalization of the "classics" was accomplished. Though viewed as a coup d'état by "establishment" critics, as a subversion of authenticity and intentionality, their goals and processes were in fact democratic in principle. They entailed at once a *mise en pratique* of the concept of reception as performance and the revalorization of theater as "popular" culture.

* * *

The freedom to "reconstitute" Racine or Molière for a "reconstituted" audience is an inherent right, supporters of Vilar and Planchon would argue. It is a means of keeping theater viable within a

Introduction

changing cultural context, a means of projecting the past into the future, however uncertain that future may be. It emanates from an initial refusal, as we have noticed so often. In this case the refusal is of origin and authorial intentionality. The "genre" *par excellence* that has survived throughout the ages by dint of refusal, by maintaining its congenital non-normative status, the late Edouard Morot-Sir asserts quite steadfastly in the following study, is the essay.

The essay predates genre, he maintains, that is to say it predates order; it emerges directly from the primal pre-language anarchy or chaos. Its very nature is that of *anti-genre*, a freedom from normatization. If it has been falsely viewed as subservient to other genres, it is only because its forms are so multiple. In reality, its very existence is contingent upon its absolute independence. In the twentieth century, literary genres themselves have attempted to attain that independence, becoming what Morot-Sir calls "essais polarisés." In his usual meticulous and sustained fashion, Morot-Sir sounds the depths of this phenomenon both conceptually and linguistically.

* * *

Separate notions of *chaos* characterize the final two essays of this section. In Laurent LeSage's survey of French literary criticism in the thirty years following World War II, the author of *The French New Criticism* (University Park: Penn State UP, 1967) discerns no dominant or unifying trends, as we have noted earlier. To the contrary, he sees a crisis for American universities which in years past have tended to teach foreign culture through literature. The generation of Ph.D. students schooled in structuralist and "poststructuralist" critical theory and methods, he fears, will not be able to accomplish that task. Perhaps they should not be asked to do so, but if not, who will fill the vacuum in the attempt to attain the newly formulated objectives of diversity and multiculturism?

* * *

Finally, Patrick Brady points to the future and a means of bridging such gaps in his essay on "Period Style in the Light of Structuralism, Semiotics, and Catastrophe Theory." After having taken Foucault to task for postulating "arbitrary *ruptures*... although his method allows for no such postulates," and offering Piaget's "genetic structuralism" as an alternative response to the need to deal with diachronics, Brady turns to René Thom's "catastrophe theory," a "branch of the mathematical discipline of topology... devoted to the description and analysis, and ultimately the prediction, of processes which are 'abrupt' or discontinuous." What could be more attuned to postmodernist concerns? Indeed, what Brady was calling for in 1977 has come to be known as "chaos theory," a new interdisciplinary perspective which redefines "chaos" as "low-dimension deterministic non-linear dynamics." Brady has further delineated the approach in three very recent articles: "Chaos Theory, Control Theory, and Literary Theory..." (*Modern Language Studies*, Fall 1990); "Chaos and Revolution in Art and Literature: Zola's *L'Oeuvre* (*Nineteenth-Century French Studies*, Fall–Winter 1991–1992); and "From Feminism to Chaos Theory: Nonlinearity in Lucette Desvignes" (*Discontinuity and Fragmentation. French Literature Series XXI*. Amstrdam/Atlanta: Rodopi, 1994).

Themes and Motifs: From Socratic Irony to "Titrologie"

Part III of this volume contains nine large-scope essays. Each study, whether dealing with one or more authors or periods, uses thematics to explore the dynamics of repetition in literary and artistic expression, the function of the variable within a text and its interrelationship with other texts, other genres, other arts. In their explorations these studies call on intertextuality, of course, but also psychocriticsm, sociocriticsm, stylistics or pragmatics as well.

* * *

It was Socratic irony that gave rise to dialectics, Jean-Pol Madou states at the outset of his essay entitled "Ironie socratique, ironie romanesque, ironie poétique." Yet if such is the case, how does Socrates reconcile the ludic chiaroscuro of irony and the laborious clarity of dialectics? He does not, in fact. Rather, he practices such an artful blend of the two that it is virtually impossible to determine which is the product of the other. Consequently, irony becomes the liberating force in Socratic dialectics that fosters both the transcendence of opposites within the context of ethics and esthetics and the "allegorical" conceptualization of *le Vrai, le Beau* and *le Bien*.

From the Renaissance through the eighteenth century in France, this allegorical tradition is continued in aphoristic writings. It is not until the advent of romanticism that irony becomes a means and an end unto itself: absolute, infinite, unbridled in its freedom and its subjectivity, at once *"souffle divin"* and *"bouffonnerie transcendantale."* In poetry, romantic irony acquires the aura not of *le Bien Suprême* but rather of its ultimate denial: *l'Illusion Suprême*. Irony in narrative is more complex, Madou explains. A descendant of the Socratic dialogues, the ultimate romantic narrative ("Livre romantique") is an all-encompassing medium radiating *le Beau Suprême*. Such is the Flaubertian ideal: perfection out

Introduction

of nothingness. But in Flaubertian narrative that perfection also includes *la Bêtise universelle*, "*l'intégrale* ironie de toutes les fausses perspectives suscitées ironiquement par le Destin."

* * *

Where does wit fit in this scheme of things? Benjamin F. Bart addresses one aspect of this question in a masterful panorama entitled "The Spirit of Erotic Wit in French Literature." For a definition of the erotic, Bart returns to Aristotle's *Nicomachaen Ethics* and *Poetics*, according to which eroticism may be perceived as a "mean" between the non-literary poles of banality and pornography. Yet the distinction of "titillating" vs. "banal" and "erotic" vs. "pornographic" is truly a complex reader-response phenomenon which varies from period to period and from individual to individual.

It is esthetic distance that characterizes literary eroticism. Through careful selection of passages from Balzac and Flaubert, Bart provides revealing examples of the sophistication and subtlety that mark the most accomplished forms of "high literature" eroticism. From there he turns to what is known traditionally as "l'esprit gaulois" and its omnipresence in French erotic literature. Again it is a matter of esthetic distance, of the ludic presence of "esprit" in the dynamics of reception. Calling upon a variety of texts, both prose and poetry, Bart categorizes, hierarchizes and analyzes these multifarious processes of distanciation, including "mocking the classics" and "black humor."

* * *

Both intertextuality and intratextuality are instrinsic to the following essay by Laurence M. Porter, "The Problematics of Embedded Poems, from *Aucassin* to Artaud." This seminal study examines the lyric and narrative hybrid from its obscure medieval Latin origins into the twentieth century and the pages of writers such as Patchen, Nabokov, and Artaud.

Definition is once again an important matter. Neither "reduplication" nor *mise en abyme* qualify as embedded poetry, Porter explains, for both are "same genre" phenomena. The embedded lyric involves a transformational code switching that "deconstructs the illusion of a unitary social nexus" and functions as "a metaphor of metaphor." When contextualized, such transformations may generate a "totalizing impulse" that conveys an "overarching truth," they may create the "dialogic interaction of a tonal dissonance," or they may "connote psychic disintegration," among numerous other possibilities.

Porter moves deftly from Boethius to *Aucassin et Nicolette* to *Le Voir Dit* and then to Villon, Rabelais, La Fontaine, Blake, Rimbaud, and the twentieth century, with several other stops in between. Barthes's notion of oppositional text is everywhere present. In each instance it is a question of embedded poems that serve either to "foreground opposition *intra*textually" or to allow "oppositionality to be inferred from its *inter*textual relationships."

* * *

The 1988 French Literature Conference on feminism produced some of the liveliest discussions in all the years of its existence. The debate revolved around the historical notion of feminism. Though the systematic oppression of women appears to be as old as civilization itself, feminism as a movement is a "modern" phenomenon dating from the nineteenth century. Feminist criticism and the idea of feminist literature, recognized as such, have developed within the context of the present century. What meaning do the terms *feminism* and *feminist* have, then, for prior periods? Should identical standards be applied equally to all women writers throughout the ages? Should there be any mitigating or orienting considerations such as social or political relativity? In terms of the appreciation of the literary work itself, what criteria should be preeminent and how should they differ from those applied to male writers?

Two essays published in volume XVI of **FLS** (1989) address these questions quite specifically, each of them focusing on a woman writer from a different era. In the first essay Dirk Van der Cruysse, author of the monumental *Madame Palatine, princesse européenne* (Paris: Fayard, 1988), contextualizes the epistolary writings of the sister-in-law of Louis XIV, a woman smitten with "scribo-manie." Spouse of the king's "homosexual" brother—known as "Monsieur" at court—Elisabeth-Charolotte ("Madame" Palatine) wrote thousands of letters in both French and German depicting her life as a princess and as a woman. As for the latter, Van der Cruysse tells us, she was always "très mal à l'aise dans sa peau de femme." As a child she considered herself a "garçon manqué" who preferred swords and guns to dolls. Later her preferences for masculine activities such as the hunt and a predilection for masculine attire raised more than one eyebrow. Her letters are a telling account of the oppression she experienced both despite her social position and because of it. Therein she confides that she had always regretted being female. She protested this "injustice" of fate the only way the social and political context of the time would allow. Since the idea of emancipation or overt contestation was unthinkable, she turned to the process of writing both to express her regret and as a means to self-actualization.

* * *

Introduction

The second essay belongs to Christine Planté, who has also produced an important full-length study entitled *La Petite Soeur de Balzac: essai sur la femme auteur* (Paris: Seuil, 1989). Planté calls into question the criteria used to anthologize women writers. Her immediate concern centers on Domna Stanton's anthology *The Defiant Muse: French Feminist Poems from the Middle Ages to the Present* (New York: The Feminist Press at the University of New York, 1986). Planté wonders what determined certain exclusions, why such well-known women writers as Louise Labé, Marie de France, Anna de Noailles and Marceline Desbordes-Valmore are not represented in its pages. Rather than conducting a systematic inquiry about each of these writers, she focuses on the writings of Marceline Desbordes-Valmore.

Planté's approach is binary in structure; it examines Desbordes-Valmore's works from the traditionally oppositional perspectives of "poésie féminine" and "poésie féministe." Her conclusions are revisionist in nature, for she demonstrates convincingly how Desbordes-Valmore has been misread and misunderstood over the years. Her poetry is at once a good deal more "feminist" in character than has been thought and a good deal less "feminine." Yet, according to Planté, these terms are quite inadequate to characterize anyone's writings: "...le couple féministe/féminin ne peut fonctionner, ni pour désigner une opposition dans les pratiques d'écriture, ni pour instaurer une périodisation littéraire." In the final analysis such categorizations (and resultant groupings) are detrimental, Planté asserts. They lend themselves all too readily to stereotype and further misreading; they deny the literary work the recognition it and its author deserve for "individuality," "subjectivity" and "creativity." Such recognition, she adds, should be a paramount requirement in the elaboration of a theory of feminist literary criticism.

* * *

Of course reading also consitutes a means of escape, of self-projection and cerebral displacement. In the next essay the sociocritic Claude Javeau studies the "exoticism" of the form of popular fiction most often associated with "feminine" readers, that is to say the Harlequin romance whose slogan in France is "tout un monde d'évasion."

Adopting a phenomenological approach to sociology that combines concepts common to Edmund Husserl and Max Weber, Javeau views both the production and the reception of this "literary genre" in terms of the technocratic culture of which it is part. He distinguishes three stages in this process: (1) the creation of the literary "object," (2) the institutional mediation which brings the public into contact with it, and (3) the "consumption" of the "object."

Since it is a matter of literature produced for and consumed by the masses, Javeau concentrates on the group dynamics inherent in this process. The appropriation of mass readership depends on a very particular "relevance" formula: the problematics of passionate love plus the esthetic interplay of alterity and similarity, dissidence and order. The key is "relevance" for the masses. The result is what might be termed a *typical* postmodern *contresens*: typification or normatization of the exotic.

* * *

The terms *logocentrism* and *phonocentrism* are readily recognizable as belonging to Derrida's vernacular. The second is privileged over the first, Derrida explains, because the immediate and simultaneous act of emitting and hearing sound and words—as process and as opposed to writing—entails a greater cognitive consciousness. Sound, then, constitutes an important and, one may infer, enhancing element in this medium. If such is the case, what could possibly be the effect when sound becomes music? And, following this same line of reasoning, what could be the further effect should that music also be poetry? The answer may be given in three words: Mallarmé, Debussy, Ravel. The next two essays are closely related, for both involve the interdimensionality of music, words and literature. The first, by Robert Gronquist, probes with meticulous scrutiny the transpositional processes at work in the Ravel composition *Trois poèmes de Mallarmé*.

In an incredible coincidence in 1913, both Debussy and Ravel set to music quite independently Stéphane Mallarmé's "Soupir" and "Placet futile." Today Ravel's *Trois poèmes*—the two mentioned as well as "Surgi de la croupe et du bond"—are recognized as "supreme examples of Ravel's compositional art, difficult to perform" and "among his most original, subtle, and recondite achievements." Gronquist follows the genesis of these songs, beginning with Ravel's fascination with Stravinsky's *Poèmes de la lyrique japonaise* and the coloristic possibilities of the scoring: voice, piano, string quartet, piccolo, flute, clarinet, and bass clarinet. By this time Ravel was no stranger to setting poems to music; he had already done so for pieces by Verlaine, Leconte de Lisle, Verhaeren and one for Mallarmé ("Sainte" for voice and music).

Yet how can a composer set to music that which, according to Mallarmé himself, already *is* music? Gronquist accomplishes an admirably complex transpositional synthesis. He interposes words and sounds, Mallarmé's poems and Ravel's score, bringing both to life in a merging of Mallarmé's "new poetics" and Ravel's "modern song." He shows how the musical and poetic lines are not composed of words or notes at all but

Introduction xxxvii

rather, and again according to Mallarmé's original design, of "intentions," "effects" and "sensations." In "Surgi de la croupe et du bond," Gronquist relates, "Ravel's setting... is a perfect distillation of the poet's 'music of silence' and is paradigmatic of the text's cancellation of rhetoric, eloquence, and formalism."

* * *

The following essay may be viewed as a sequel to the preceding one; in it, Roland Champagne undertakes an overview of this interdimensionality in contemporary French fiction. The "music of silence" may call to mind Pierre Van den Heuvel's study of the role of silence in Marguerite Duras's prose fiction. Champagne considers the "enchantment of Orpheus" (which includes silence) in her works and many others as well. His point of departure is Barthes's notion of *écriture* as it has been related to music by people such as Claude Lévi-Strauss, Pierre Boulez and Umberto Eco. Contemporary writers have tended to displace "the center of verbal communication" just as Debussy had displaced the center of musical structure, his whole-tone scale obscuring "the musical train of thought like a tonal fog." Sollers's *verbal orchestration* is a prime example with its associative word patterns and neological projections. Duras's fragmented dialogues in *Moderato cantabile, Détruire* and *Dit-elle* "provide horizontal cohesion by giving rhythm to the work in songlike fashion." *Ciné-roman, Musica* and *India Song* add other dimensions (visual, olfactory and tactile) "beyond words" to this polyphonic and often contrapuntal "musical aura." Other fiction writers such as Claude Simon, Robbe-Grillet and Butor are viewed in terms of consonance or dissonance; Beckett's "dramaticules" may be understood as contemporary atonal music, the "primitivistic gropings" of his characters may imitate "a primitive sense of nonverbal music." Moreover, Champagne points out, music according to Butor is quite capable of providing the medium in which a truly "new literature" can germinate and mature.

* * *

Michel Butor's *Les Mots dans la peinture* evokes a related interdimensional phenomenon: the role of title or signature in painting. Christian Moncelet's later study, *Essai sur le titre littéraire et dans les arts* enlarges the scope to include music. Serge Bokobza, in the final essay of this volume, narrows the scope again to "la titrologie romanesque," an area of critical inquiry he considers quite neglected. If titles have been the object of study on occasion, Bokobza states, only now is an efficacious procedure in the process of being formulated.

In order to consider the problematics of this endeavor, Bokobza turns to the history of the title and its etymology. *Titulus* becomes associated with *volumen* at an early date for the sake of identification and classification. With regard to books, the title is habitually placed at the beginning and with the advent of printing is accorded a page unto itself. Titles begin to appear on the jacket only when leather becomes too expensive owing to the French Revolution. The functions of the title as we know them today date from the mass merchandising of the novel in the nineteenth century.

Those functions are multiple; they may be labeled apellative, designative, enunciative, conative, poetic, publicitary, referential, and/or deictic, depending on the terminology selected by the particular critic (Grivel, Duchet, Barthes, for example). The problematics cannot be reduced to mere terminology, however; for if, primarily, the title fosters the perception of novel as object—deictically—there is a good deal more involved. Beyond dictionary meanings, successive connotations expand the "sens commun" to the point that the title becomes a "signe à contenu 'flottant'" akin to the proper noun. The title may thus be viewed as one of the vacuums critics are so fond of pointing out today. It acquires a non-deictic value only when "concretized" or "contextualized," and it does so by becoming "l'abstraction du texte, sa métaphore ou sa métonymie." Further, marketing strategies come quite prominently into play, the enticement factor being of prime importance. The title is thus the product of a product that serves also as what Derrida calls an "archonte," a "conducteur de texte"—unless of course, as Bokobza explains, it is the other way around, as in the case of Giono and Ricardou.

Freeman G. Henry

I. NARRATIVE: FROM AUTOBIOGRAPHY TO NARRATOLOGY

L'atelier autobiographique de Sartre

Philippe Lejeune
Université de Paris XIII

Cela pourrait s'appeler, comme chez Alexandre Dumas, *Vingt ans après*. En 1964, le Sartre en culottes courtes des *Mots* a surpris, en même temps que le texte lui-même donnait au lecteur une impression éblouissante de maîtrise et de totalisation. Il était "irréfutable," en deux sens: qu'on la trouvât admirable ou artificielle, l'interprétation collait au récit; d'autre part le lecteur n'avait sur cette enfance aucune autre information, puisque c'était la première fois que Sartre la racontait. Le livre lui-même, sans préface, sans mode d'emploi (si l'on excepte l'interview donnée au *Monde* en avril 1964), se présentait comme un bloc, à prendre tel quel.

En 1984, vingt ans après, le livre reste aussi éblouissant, mais la perspective a changé complètement. Pendant les quinze dernières années de sa vie, Sartre a continué à évoluer politiquement, et à envisager d'autres projets autobiographiques. En même temps, il s'est généreusement abandonné à la curiosité biographique de ses proches, acceptant de parler sa mémoire. Après sa mort, la publication de ses lettres de jeunesse et surtout des *Carnets de la drôle de guerre* ont révélé que, contrairement à ce qu'on pensait, les *Mots* n'étaient nullement son premier essai d'écriture autobiographique. Si bien qu'ils apparaissent aujourd'hui comme un *moment* dans une entreprise autobiographique qui est coextensive à la vie de Sartre.

Mon propos sera ici de dresser un tableau, une vue cavalière, de cette entreprise singulière et exemplaire.

Pour moi, comme pour bien d'autres lecteurs, le choc a été la publication des *Carnets de la drôle de guerre* en 1983. On pouvait s'attendre à des journaux ou des brouillons, textes mineurs, scories, comme on en trouve dans les papiers d'un écrivain après sa mort. Or les *Carnets* sont une véritable oeuvre, originale et autonome, et même peut-être le chef-d'oeuvre de Sartre. Il y a inventé une forme pratiquement inédite, aussi bien dans l'histoire de la philosophie que dans celle de l'autobiographie, en articulant l'exploration de son vécu et l'élaboration d'une théorie, et en faisant de l'autoportrait le moyen d'une conversion.

Les *Carnets* ne sont nullement l'"avant-texte" des *Mots*. Sur beaucoup de points, les deux textes s'opposent. Les *Carnets* sont un journal de recherche authentique, recherche de quelque chose que Sartre ne sait pas d'avance, et que nous le voyons découvrir; les *Mots*, eux, sont une oeuvre fortement composée à la lumière d'une vérité déjà acquise. Les *Carnets* sont entièrement tendus vers l'avenir, d'un nouvel homme en train de naître; les *Mots* accouchent d'un vieil enfant. Les *Carnets* sont écrits sans rature, sans relecture, d'un jet, avec une liberté d'allure, une allégresse, un bonheur d'expression très communicatifs; les *Mots* ont un style travaillé, brillant, constamment parodique, c'est une oeuvre d'apparat. Même si les *Mots* sont une oeuvre plus achevée, les *Carnets* donnent peut-être une meilleure idée de ce qu'est...la liberté.

Mais ce bref parallèle qui, dans l'enthousiasme de la découverte, donne l'avantage aux *Carnets*, est injuste. Difficile de comparer deux moments si différents d'une évolution, dans deux situations différentes: l'élan de 1939 ("Il me semble que je suis en chemin, comme disent les biographes aux environs de la page 150 de leur livre, de 'me trouver,' " jubile Sartre[1]), le bilan de 1963 ("Depuis à peu près dix ans je suis un homme qui s'éveille, guéri d'une longue, amère et douce folie..."[2]). Surtout les deux textes n'appartiennent pas au même genre. Les *Mots* sont un récit biographique, les *Carnets*, eux, articulent tous les genres: journal, autoportrait, récit biographique, discours théorique,—et même poésie...,—ce qui est sans exemple dans tout le reste de l'oeuvre de Sartre. Tout se passe comme s'il avait réalisé lui-même, dès 1939, le projet qu'ont eu la plupart de ses interviewers à la fin de sa vie, de capter un Sartre total, "producteur," en action, au centre de son système. Mais ici ce n'est pas un spectacle, c'est la réalité.

***

L'activité autobiographique de Sartre est donc dominée par les *Carnets* et les *Mots*. Mais les publications récentes nous permettent de la suivre depuis sa jeunesse (1926) jusqu'aux toutes dernières années (1975). Le tableau ci-après récapitule ces différents "actes" autobiographiques, tels que nous pouvons aujourd'hui les connaître.

****

**L'Atelier autobiographique de Sartre
1926-1975
Points de repère**

A. 1926

Autoportrait, *écrit pour Simone Jollivet, qui lui reprochait de n'être "ni simple, ni vrai"* (Lettres au Castor..., 1983, p. 9-11 et 14): *"J'ai un fond de caractère très hétéroclite...." Cet autoportrait peut être considéré comme un* spécimen du travail d'introspection auquel Sartre dit s'être essayé avec ivresse "*entre 17 et 20 ans*" (Carnets, p. 175). *Après quoi, dégoûté: "je suis resté plus de quinze ans sans me regarder vivre. Je ne m'intéressais pas du tout"* (Ibid., p. 174).

B. 1939-1940

Dès avant la déclaration de guerre, Sartre essaie une "nouvelle méthode" pour raconter sa vie (des "explications psychanalytico-marxisto-historiques," lettre à Louise Védrine, 4 août 1939, in Lettres au Castor, *p. 245). Il lit* L'Age d'homme *de Leiris.*

Mobilisé en Alsace, il va tenir des carnets de manière pratiquement journalière du 14 septembre 1939 jusqu'en avril 1940 (il s'interrompt seulement pendant ses deux permissions). Quinze carnets, de tailles très différentes. Cinq carnets seulement ont été conservés (n° 3, 5, 11, 12 et 14). Ils ont été publiés chez Gallimard en 1983 par Arlette Elkaïm-Sartre: Les Carnets de la drôle de guerre, *novembre 1939-mars 1940.*

Ces carnets sont à la fois journal de la vie quotidienne, journal de lectures, tentative d'autoportrait "aussi complet que possible" se fondant souvent sur des pans d'exploration autobiographique, et essais d'élaboration d'une nouvelle philosophie (ébauche de ce qui sera l'Etre et le Néant). *Le travail de conversion personnelle et la construction théorique sont étroitement associés: "Je suis en train d'apprendre, au fond, à être une personne"* (p. 394).

C. 1953-1956

Sous le coup d'une nouvelle conversion (son rapprochement avec le parti communiste en 1952), Sartre décide d'écrire son autobiographie. "Je voulais écrire toute ma vie d'un point de vue politique, c'est-à-dire mon enfance, ma jeunesse et mon âge mûr, en lui donnant ce sens politique d'arrivée au communisme (...). Je voulais me montrer constamment pressé de changer, mal dans ma peau, mal avec les autres et puis changeant et devenant enfin le communiste qu'il devait être au début" (La Cérémonie des adieux, *1981, p. 274-275).*

On connaît les intentions de Sartre à l'époque par ses interviews (voir Les Ecrits de Sartre), *et par ses déclarations à S. de Beauvoir en 1974 (citées ci-dessus). Le problème est de savoir quel rapport il y avait entre ces intentions et la réalité.*

Le livre devait s'appeler Jean-sans-terre. *Sartre a écrit entre 1953 et 1956 un premier jet, couvrant l'enfance. C'est à proprement parler, l'avant-texte des* Mots. *Il ne l'a pas vraiment abandonné, comme il l'a prétendu, il y a retravaillé, mais n'a jamais pu dépasser le point atteint par le récit en 1956.*

D. 1963

Pressé par des besoins d'argent, Sartre reprend ce début et le transforme en une oeuvre achevée, Les Mots. *Il a atténué, prétend-il, la sévérité avec laquelle en 1954 il condamnait sa névrose littéraire: "Entre temps, je m'étais rendu compte que l'action aussi a ses difficultés et qu'on peut y être conduit par la névrose"* (interview au Monde, *18 avril 1964). Il évoque en raccourci, à la fin, son évolution ultérieure, et laisse la porte ouverte à une éventuelle suite: "J'ai changé. Je raconterai plus tard..." (p. 211, Folio).*

E. 1970

    Sous le coup d'une nouvelle conversion (son rapprochement avec les gauchistes après 1968), Sartre annonce qu'il n'écrira pas la suite des Mots, *mais qu'il pense plutôt à écrire un testament politique: "Je raconterai ce que j'ai fait dans ce domaine, quelles erreurs j'ai commises et ce qui en est résulté. En faisant cela j'essaierai de définir ce qui constitue la politique aujourd'hui, dans la phase historique que nous vivons" (interview à* New Left Review, *26 janvier 1970). Vers 1971 il abandonne ce projet d'autobiographie politique et envisage de faire passer son "testament" politique indirectement dans une nouvelle, dont la part de fiction serait mince (*Situations X, *p. 145-148). Mais à partir de 1973, il n'est plus capable d'écrire. Ce projet de "testament politique" est néanmoins à l'arrière-plan des entretiens avec ses amis maos (*On a raison de se révolter, *1974), du film fait avec Astruc et Contat, et du projet d'émissions télévisuelles sur l'histoire du siècle (1974-1975), qui n'aboutira pas.*

F. 1972-1975

    Sollicité par son entourage, Sartre se met à parler sa vie, soit devant des caméras, soit devant un magnétophone:

1972: en février-mars, A. Astruc et M. Contat tournent pendant neuf heures une interview de Sartre, interrogé par ses proches (Groz, Pouillon, Bost) en présence de S. de Beauvoir. Le montage du film a été fait seulement en 1976. Il sort fin 1976 sous le titre Sartre par lui-même. *Une transcription de la bande sonore est publiée en 1977 chez Gallimard sous le titre* Sartre. *En 1983 le film est édité en vidéocassette par Cinéthèque.*

1973: 17 juin. Sartre accorde un entretien à Francis Jeanson, sur son adolescence qu'il avait jusque-là "mise sous la cendre" L'entretien est publié en 1974 par Jeanson dans sa biographie de Sartre, Sartre dans sa vie, *Seuil, p. 289-299.*

1974: pendant l'été 1974 à Rome, et à l'automne à Paris, Simone de Beauvoir interroge Sartre au magnétophone, systématiquement, sur tous les aspects de sa vie. Ces entretiens ont été publiés par elle après la mort de Sartre: ils forment la seconde partie de La Cérémonie des adieux, *Gallimard, 1981, p. 161-559. Vingt et un chapitres thématiques dont voici à peu près la suite: Ecrits de jeunesse, littérature et philosophie, La Rochelle / La violence, Province-Paris, Nizan / L'idée de salut, la mission, la gloire / Philosophie, carnets, lettres, théâtre / Les lectures, la littérature,* Les Mots */ Lectures actuelles, musique, peinture / Voyages / La lune / Egalité, hiérarchie / Orgueil / Les groupes, l'amitié / Rapports avec les femmes / Rapports avec le corps / La nourriture / L'argent / La liberté / La politique / Socialisme et liberté / Rapports avec le temps / Bilan de vie / L'approche de la mort.*

1975: *"Autoportrait à soixante-dix ans,"* interview par *Michel Contat publiée dans le* Nouvel Observateur *en juin-juillet.* Texte intégral dans Situations X, *1976, p. 133-226.*

* * * * * * * * * * * *

Comme tout tableau, celui-ci simplifie. Il est incomplet: je n'ai gardé que les étapes principales (mais on pourrait ajouter les textes biographiques sur Nizan et Merleau-Ponty, en 1960-1961, qui ont précédé la mise au point définitive des *Mots*, ou s'interroger sur le statut à accorder à la correspondance). Le tableau, d'autre part, isole la production autobiographique des autres productions (fictionnelles, philosophiques, ou biographiques), alors que, les *Carnets* le montrent bien, l'essentiel c'est l'articulation de ces différents types d'écriture. Enfin le tableau suggère qu'il y a continuité et homologie entre ces différents actes, ce qui n'est pas tout à fait exact.

Est-ce d'ailleurs vraiment un "atelier"? Le mot "chantier" serait peut-être plus juste: idée d'une vaste entreprise inachevée, d'un travail qui n'a pas effacé ses traces. Bien sûr il est difficile de voir en Sartre un Rembrandt accumulant tout au long de sa vie les autoportraits. Mais je puis, malicieusement, m'appuyer sur les dires de Sartre lui-même pour montrer le caractère central du projet autobiographique dans son oeuvre. A l'en croire *Jean-sans-terre* aurait été, vers 1952, en même temps qu'une critique du mythe biographique, son accomplissement:

> S. de B. — Comment est-ce venu la première idée des *Mots* et puis pourquoi est-ce que c'est resté en rade?
> J.-P. S. — J'ai toujours eu l'idée, à dix-huit ans, d'écrire ma vie quand je l'aurais faite, c'est-à-dire à cinquante ans.
> S. de B. — Vous avez toujours pensé à écrire sur vous.
> J.-P. S. — Oui.
> S. de B. — Et alors vers 1952?
> J.-P. S. — Eh bien je me suis dit: voilà, je vais écrire.[3]

Déclaration en face de laquelle je puis mettre celle de Simone de Beauvoir elle-même:

> Je souhaitais à quinze ans que des gens, un jour, lisent ma biographie avec une curiosité émue; si je voulais devenir "un auteur connu", c'était dans cet espoir. Depuis, j'ai souvent songé à l'écrire moi-même. L'exaltation avec laquelle je caressais ce rêve m'est aujourd'hui bien étrangère; mais j'ai gardé au coeur l'envie de le réaliser...[4]

Mais le parallèle est trompeur. Si Sartre, en 1952, renoue apparemment avec son projet d'enfance, c'est à la faveur d'une rupture (sa "conversion" au marxisme). Et il découvre bien vite que tout converti qu'il soit, sa vie n'en est pas pour cela "faite," si bien que l'autobiographie ébauchée est restée en rade. Tandis que Simone de Beauvoir, en dehors de toute crise, en toute tranquillité, sera fidèle à son rêve d'adolescente, qu'elle réalisera dans les formes les plus classiques: elle a composé une longue chronique que nous lisons avec une curiosité émue.

Le rythme de l'activité autobiographique de Sartre est très différent, comme le montre mon tableau: une série de *crises*, séparées par de longues périodes de désengagement ou de latence. Rien n'est plus loin de Sartre que l'idée d'une "autobiographie permanente." Quoiqu'il ait tenu, à certains moments, des carnets ou des journaux, il a horreur de l'idée de s'engluer dans l'introspection, de devenir esclave d'une écriture répétitive et fétichiste. En 1939, dans les *Carnets*, il a esquissé une analyse de ce rythme, auquel il est resté fidèle par la suite. D'abord, de 17 à 20 ans, il s'est essayé avec ivresse à la psychologie d'introspection: on peut supposer que la lettre à Simon Jollivet (1926) témoigne de cette passion. Mais cette introspection n'est nullement stagnante: c'est celle d'un adolescent qui est en train de "construire son propre caractère." Une fois le caractère construit, il se dégoûte de l'introspection et, s'il faut l'en croire, reste quinze ans sans se regarder vivre.[5] Il faut une nouvelle crise, en 1939, pour qu'il revienne à lui. Mais il sent bien qu'une fois ce travail de transformation de soi accompli, il renoncera de nouveau à fixer son regard sur lui-même:

> Une fois lancé dans cette entreprise, je m'y acharne par esprit de système, goût de la totalité, je m'y donne tout entier par manie. Je veux faire un portrait aussi complet que possible, comme j'ai voulu, étant petit, avoir toute la collection des *Buffalo Bill* et *Nick Carter*, comme j'ai voulu, un peu plus tard, tout savoir sur Stendhal, etc., etc. Il y a certainement chez moi un manque de mesure: indifférence ou acharnement maniaque, c'est l'un ou l'autre. Mais je ne pense pas qu'il y ait avantage à s'épouiller toute sa vie. (CDG, p. 175)

Effectivement, les *Carnets*, commencés en septembre 1939 seront abandonnés en avril 1940, avant l'attaque allemande. Sartre ne reviendra à lui-même qu'à l'occasion d'une nouvelle conversion, au marxisme, en 1952. De 1953 à 1959 il annoncera, dans ses interviews, qu'il travaille à une grande autobiographie totalisante, politique, exemplaire: en fait il ébauche un récit d'enfance dans lequel il reste bloqué en 1956. Il le reprendra, cette fois hors crise, dans une période de relative stabilité, en 1963, pour en faire les *Mots*, dont la "suite" ne viendra jamais. Nouvelle conversion après 1968, gauchiste cette fois, et nouveau projet autobiographique. De crise en crise, donc, mais sans que jamais la production autobiographique qui naît de la crise et aide à la résoudre ait la même forme ni la même fonction.

En temps "ordinaire," Sartre dit n'avoir aucune des caractéristiques d'un autobiographe: il ne s'intéresse pas à lui-même, il n'a pas bonne mémoire, il passe son temps à se désolidariser de son passé et à se projeter dans l'avenir. Le moment autobiographique, pour lui, ne correspond pas à un ralentissement, à une retombée contemplative vers le passé, mais au contraire à une *accélération:* il n'est possible de voir le passé que lorsqu'on s'arrache à lui.

C'est pourquoi il s'est si peu intéressé à une question pourtant inévitable: dans quelle mesure l'autobiographie est-elle *possible?* Très tardivement, en 1971, il reconnaîtra l'impossibilité de faire sur soi le genre de travail qu'il a fait sur Flaubert.[6] Comme il accomplit en général ses actes autobiographiques dans un moment de rupture, cela lui donne l'impression d'échapper à l'adhérence à soi. Dans les *Carnets,* il appelle cela une "mue": ses écrits autobiographiques, ce sont des peaux mortes qu'il laisse derrière lui (CDG, p. 175). Dans *l'Etre et le Néant,* il fait un portrait enthousiaste de l'instant libérateur, il exalte "le surgissement fréquent de 'conversions' qui me font métamorphoser totalement mon projet original."[7] On lâche pour saisir, on saisit pour lâcher. En 1957, à un interviewer qui lui demande si, tout de même, écrire une autobiographie n'implique pas plus de contradictions qu'écrire une biographie, il répond:

> C'est vrai, mais il y a des moments où on peut le faire. Soit qu'on ait atteint une crise, un point d'arrivée—ce qui est plutôt rare—ou un point de départ; ou qu'un changement de situation soudain vous découvre votre vie dans une nouvelle perspective. On peut bien sûr objecter qu'il n'y a pas de raison pour que ce nouvel aspect soit plus réel que le précédent. Mais une autobiographie doit chercher à saisir l'individu comme un objet autant que comme un sujet. Cependant, s'examiner soi-même n'est pas suffisant pour s'étudier—on ne fait que tourner en rond.[8]

En dehors des périodes de crise, une introspection autobiographique ne peut avoir qu'une fonction d'hygiène: consolider les acquis de la crise en achevant de déraciner le passé.[9]

Bien sûr, au moment où, en pleine crise, Sartre cherche à saisir sa vie comme un tout, son travail totalisateur, constructeur, ressemble à celui d'un biographe. Il exprime souvent son projet de saisir toute une vie dans ses "arguments" lapidaires: "C'est l'histoire d'un homme qui...", "Je veux retracer l'histoire assez curieuse d'une génération...", "Je voudrais montrer comment un homme en vient à la politique...", "Ce qui m'intéressait c'était d'essayer d'expliquer ce que c'est qu'un intellectuel, comment il pense et sent les choses, comment une vie d'intellectuel peut s'interpréter...", etc. Arguments forcément assez simplificateurs, et qui font craindre que l'autobiographie ne tourne au roman à thèse ou au récit didactique.

Mais bien sûr aussi, l'acte autobiographique qui cherche à construire le passé et à englober la vie, est lui-même un moment de cette vie et se trouve englobé par elle. Ce que fait réellement Sartre est assez différent de ce qu'il prétend faire: sa volonté totalisatrice aboutit à une série de textes ambigus, contradictoires et inachevés. J'ai employé constamment ici l'adjectif "autobiographique," mais le terme "autoportrait" conviendrait mieux pour définir l'ensemble de pratiques regroupées dans mon tableau. Chaque fois, c'est le présent qui est le centre: la reconstruction historique n'est qu'un moyen de se définir aujourd'hui. Qu'aujourd'hui devienne hier, et l'autobiographie perd sa valeur historique générale pour devenir l'autoportrait de son auteur hier. Voici comment en 1976 il juge le film autobiographique tourné en 1972:

> Il s'est passé beaucoup de temps entre le moment où les entretiens ont été tournés—c'est-à-dire en 1972—et le moment où le film a été terminé. J'ai changé, aujourd'hui, je ne parlerais pas tout à fait de la même façon que je faisais en 1972. De telle sorte que je vois ce film comme un moment de mon évolution, un film sur Sartre en 1972.[10]

D'un acte de reconstruction à l'autre, il n'y a pas vraiment continuité, même s'il y a réutilisation des mêmes matériaux. Certes le lecteur, placé à l'extérieur de ce système, peut penser (comme parfois, lucidement, fugitivement, Sartre le pense aussi...) qu'il y a une part d'illusion dans cette impression qu'il a eu de toujours changer. Reste que ces textes ne s'ajoutent pas, ne se referment pas une totalité.

De 1926 à 1975, nous pouvons donc suivre les regards qu'il a portés sur sa vie. Non pas, banalement, comme chez ceux qui tiennent leur journal intime et reflètent leur présent au fur et à mesure. Mais en comparant, de l'adolescence à la vieillesse, une série de reconstructions de la même vie, du même "projet original."

Cette série, ce n'est pas Sartre qui l'a constituée. On peut même dire qu'il a fait tout son possible pour qu'elle n'existe pas... Sa lettre de 1926, était-elle faite pour être conservée? Ses carnets de 1939-1940, perdus par un ami, il n'a rien fait pour les récupérer quand cela a été possible.[11] Eparpillés, les manuscrits de *Jean-sans-terre* et des *Mots*.[12] Quant aux interviews de la période 1972-1975, ce n'est jamais lui qui en a eu l'initiative, même s'il a étroitement collaboré avec ses interviewers.[13] Dans cette série, le seul acte autobiographique vraiment assumé et authentique, ce sont les *Mots,* dont la publication a d'ailleurs d'une certaine manière figé un pan de son passé. Sartre a été aussi insoucieux de ses autobiographies passées que de son passé. C'est ce relatif désengagement qui lui a permis de recommencer. Et c'est sous notre regard biographique à nous que cette série diachronique d'autoportraits trace à la fois la trajectoire d'une vie et l'histoire d'une mémoire.

Auteur (ou co-auteur) de chaque élément de la série, Sartre n'est donc pas l'auteur de la série elle-même: c'est ce qui oppose son atelier à d'autre ateliers célèbres, où l'autobiographe, par exemple, a essayé d'intégrer dans son texte l'image même du temps qui s'est écoulé entre le début et la fin de la rédaction, de reprendre prise sur flux de la vie, de redevenir par l'écriture maître du temps. Maîtrise imaginaire, donnée en spectacle au lecteur, qui du coup perd accès à la réalité des changements. Je pense bien sûr aux *Mémoires d'outre-tombe:* Sartre ne peut être que du côté de Stendhal contre Chateaubriand, il laisse ses autobiographies s'effondrer dans le passé, accepte l'inachèvement, pratique parfois le "brouillon," et quitte la vie en faisant des projets d'avenir... La stratégie Chateaubriand, c'est Malraux qui l'a réalisée, intégrant par des séries de réécritures dans *Le Miroir des Limbes* une vie au moins aussi contradictoire que celle de Sartre.[14]

La conduite de Sartre s'oppose à celle d'autres autobiographes contemporains luttant pour échapper au temps. Je pense moins à Leiris, dont l'écriture est tendue dans une sorte de "course contre la mort," mais perdue d'avance, qu'à la tentative extraordinaire de Claude Mauriac dans le *Temps immobile:* sept volumes de montage d'un journal intime tenu pendant cinquante ans.[15] Claude Mauriac construit un va-et-vient entre les différentes couches du journal (et de la vie), qu'il tresse avec le journal du va-et-vient lui-même, orchestrant échos et analogies, pour se découvrir *le même* dans le temps, et—qui sait—hors du temps... Peut-être n'est-ce pas le temps, mais l'écriture, qui est ici immobile: fabriquant, jour après jour, le même... Du moins est-ce l'effet produit sur le lecteur. C'est ce qui permet à Claude Mauriac d'enchaîner comme dans une même phrase une journée de 1982 avec une journée de 1932. Rien de gratuit dans ces exercices de virtuosité. Comme dirait Sartre: "Une technique autobiographique renvoie toujours à la métaphysique de l'autobiographe." Technique et métaphysique diamétralement opposées à celles de Sartre: fuite hors de l'histoire à la recherche d'une fixité, hors de l'existence vers une essence.

Mais je pensais à Mauriac (Claude) parce qu'au fond Sartre a réussi, sans le vouloir quelque chose d'analogue—et de contraire—à ce que Mauriac visait: jalonner sa vie, montrer son relief temporel, au lieu de l'abolir. Le lecteur de Claude Mauriac n'a rien d'autre à faire que de suivre l'auteur dans ce labyrinthe un peu monotone: il est difficile d'imaginer une autre règle du jeu, de redistribuer les cartes autrement. Le lecteur de Sartre, placé en face de la série de ses autoportraits, a, lui, tout à faire: il doit répondre à un véritable défi. Il n'est pas devant des bouts de "vécu," enregistrés et redistribués: il est devant des interprétations construites, mais ces interprétations, plurielles, contradictoires, provisoires, n'aboutissent à aucune somme, à aucune certitude, même si, à la fin de sa vie, les interviewers de Sartre ont essayé de le faire jouer au jeu du "bilan de vie."

Qui était Sartre? Aujourd'hui les informations ne manquent pas: à celles qu'il a données s'ajoutent la chronique de sa vie tenue jusqu'au dernier soupir par Simone de Beauvoir et un nombre croissant de témoignages. Les interprétations non plus, fournies par lui-même. Mais ce trop plein de faits et de sens donne le vertige et laisse tout de même le sentiment d'un manque,—le sentiment que Sartre était débordé par sa vie et ne la maîtrisait pas. Il a laissé les maquettes d'un certain nombre de "Sartre" possibles, maquettes qui lui ont été utiles à telle ou telle étape de sa vie; dans un autre coin de son atelier, il travaillait à élaborer une *méthode* biographique, sur un autre, Flaubert. Il est mort, il a tout laissé en plan, à nous de nous débrouiller.

Voici quelques-unes des surprises que j'ai éprouvées en m'aventurant dans cette structure mobile, évolutive, instable qu'est l'autobiographie sartrienne. Chacun pourra ajouter les siennes à cette liste.

Je n'ai jamais compris vraiment la fin des *Mots,* cette incompréhensible "folie," qui lui ferait transformer sa névrose en "caractère."

Jusqu'en 1973, il a soigneusement caché les drames essentiels de sa vie (le remariage de sa mère, la violence subie au lycée de La Rochelle). Il en a parlé, mais jamais écrit (sinon peut-être dans des Carnets perdus).

Maniaque de liberté, persuadé d'être translucide, il a essayé d'intégrer la psychanalyse et le marxisme à sa philosophie du sujet.

Peu de temps avant de mourir, l'auteur de la *Nausée* déclare: "Je n'ai jamais eu d'angoisse."[16]

Dans ses engagements politiques, il avoue s'être parfois trompé, tout en revendiquant avoir eu toujours raison.

Mais j'arrête là: car fait si vite, l'inventaire de violentes contradictions risque de tourner à la trop facile satire. Ou plutôt je continue en enchaînant des impressions de lecture. Lire les *Entretiens* de 1974 après avoir lu les *Mots,* c'est à peu près comme redécouvrir la contingence dans la rue en sortant d'une salle de cinéma. A la maquette exemplaire succède le fouillis, la prolifération molle, l'incertitude d'une vie où resurgissent des "illusions" jadis dénoncées. Jean-Paul Sartre, quelle est la plus grande chance de votre vie? D'être né dans une famille universitaire, ça m'a donné un bon point de départ pour écrire. Mais on y découvre aussi des Sartre étonnants (quand il fait l'analyse de sa sexualité), et tout de suite après des Sartre étonnés (quand Simone de Beauvoir veut le faire remonter à sa toute petite enfance, à des questions de servage, à des questions vraiment tout à fait infantiles,—il ne voit pas), fluctuant entre des accès de maîtrise et d'incertitude.[17] Je saute cinquante ans en arrière: stupeur de découvrir qu'il était vraiment translucide! A Simone Jollivet il décrit l'essentiel de ce qu'il appellera plus tard sa "névrose littéraire," dont on croyait qu'il n'avait pris conscience qu'en 1939... Il le savait déjà! Mais cela n'empêchait rien, au contraire. On le croit d'abord critique, alors qu'il serait plutôt triomphant. C'est qu'il décrit tout, mais n'explique rien: lucidité n'est pas connaissance. Mais comment expliquer? Je redescends jusqu'en 1939 et je le vois, dans les *Carnets,* en train d'élaborer la notion de "projet" et même de "projet original": il met au point, à propos de Guillaume II, sa méthode biographique, et cela *contre* toutes les doctrines déterministes. Il a identifié le noyau de son projet originel à lui, et voici comment il le présente dans une alternative où la décision qu'il prendra est déjà marquée:

> (...) Si cette attitude contemplative avait pour origine ma fonction contemplative de gardien de la culture au sein de la société, comme le déclarerait sans ambages un marxiste, ou si elle représente un projet premier de mon existence (on y trouve en effet l'orgueil, la liberté, la désolidarisation de soi-même, le stoïcisme contemplatif et l'optimisme qui font certainement partie de mon premier projet) c'est ce dont je ne veux pas décider ici. (CDG, p. 392)

L'idée même de "projet" ne serait-elle pas une manière de transformer la description en explication? Avoir une origine, ou être l'origine: that is the question. Mais permanence et origine, est-ce la même chose? A la recherche du premier projet, Sartre, pour la première fois en 1939, explore son enfance. Mais ce n'est pas la même enfance que dans les *Mots*! Enfin, pas tout à fait. Il parle avec tendresse de ses premiers essais de création littéraire![18] Et des mots eux-mêmes, en particulier du verbe "pulluler," qui lui inspire un développement plus proche du Leiris de *Biffures* que du Sartre des *Mots*! Il ne dit pratiquement rien de sa mère, très peu sur ses grands-parents, le tableau familial manque. Il dit avoir été "soustrait de très bonne heure à l'influence familiale" (CDG, p. 356). Alors je retourne aux *Mots*. J'y vois un narrateur, d'une grande violence satirique, se féliciter de n'avoir pas de surmoi; il stagmatise avec force la violence que les pères font subir aux enfants, tout en s'attribuant un Oedipe fort incomplet. Comment le croire? Quant à son indéracinable optimisme, le tient-il de la lecture de *Cri-Cri* et de *l'Epatant*, comme il le dit dans les *Mots,* ou du fait que sa mère l'a *aimé,* ce qui est plus probable, mais aussi plus difficile à dire?[19]

Une vie, "c'est une enfance mise à toute les sauces," même si, ce qui n'est pas contradictoire, "je ne crois pas que l'histoire d'un homme soit inscrit dans son enfance."[20]

J'arrête cette dérive. Les "contradictions" ne sont pas signes d'incohérence ou de versatilité, mais de la complication d'un réel (la vie d'un homme) que Sartre a exploré avec plus... d'énergie que d'autres.

Le problème est de savoir comment les lecteurs de Sartre vont réagir devant ce chantier abandonné, quel profit ils tireront de ces contradictions. Ces autobiographies inachevées *appellent* inéluctablement la biographie. C'est aux lecteurs d'achever ce geste suspendu par la mort, de trouver ce sens, ou cette unité, qui se dérobent, d'écrire ce texte impossible... On s'y emploie déjà, pendant que Sartre, disparu mais effervescent, continue à produire des textes: correspondances, que l'on commence à publier, et qui infléchissent la connaissance qu'on a de sa vie privée (phénomène classique, c'est le sort de tout "grand écrivain"); moins classique, la résurgence d'inédits plus géniaux peut-être que les textes publiés. Les cinq *Carnets de la drôle de guerre* ne doivent pas faire oublier qu'il en reste dix autres qui ne sont peut-être pas tout à fait perdus: les biographes sartriens écriront sous la menace, ou dans l'espoir, de leur réapparition. En même temps qu'ils écriront à l'ombre de *l'Idiot de la famille*... De quelle méthode se serviront-ils? De quel point de vue construiront-ils l'image de Sartre? Arriveront-ils à une vie plus compréhensive que la sienne? Selon Michel Contat, il existe déjà au moins quatre biographes (dont lui-même) qui se sont, chacun de leur côté, lancés dans l'entreprise, et dont les productions verront le jour dans les années qui viennent. Déjà différents textes de polémique ou d'essai ont commencé à occuper le terrain: Michel-Antoine Burnier a rédigé à la place de Sartre son "Testament politique," ce texte-fantôme des années 1970. Médiocre sur le plan du pastiche stylistique, c'est un pamphlet fort bien informé (puisque Burnier fut un compagnon de route de Sartre...), qui met habilement en lumière, par des jeux de citations, les aveuglements et les palinodies de Sartre depuis qu'il s'est "engagé" politiquement dans le monde réel.[21] Plus subtilement, Denis Hollier joue à tracer de longs circuits à travers les textes les plus divers de Sartre moins pour traquer, ce qui est trop facile, des incohérences, que pour dessiner de nouveaux réseaux de cohérence....[22]

La question biographique sera d'autant plus centrale qu'il est difficile de séparer la pensée de Sartre de sa personne. Dans les *Carnets*, à la fin d'une longue analyse sur le désir de possession d'autrui, Sartre note:

> Ça n'en a pas l'air, mais je me suis peint en pied dans cette description métaphysique. J'essaierai demain de me décrire plus simplement dans mes rapports avec autrui. (CDG, p. 318)

C'est d'ailleurs le mouvement général des *Carnets* que ce va-et-vient entre la théorie et l'autoportrait. Cette coïncidence fait preuve pour Sartre: mais le lecteur peut la percevoir plutôt comme un cercle dans l'évidence duquel Sartre est enfermé. Une biographie faite d'un autre point de vue que le sien, selon d'autres modèles, pourrait alors prétendre expliquer son système. D'autant que l'on peut être frappé par une autre coïncidence: certaines des positions fondamentales de Sartre (qui ont été les plus contestées) coïncident avec postulats (eux aussi les plus contestés) de la pratique autobiographique: le refus de l'idée d'inconscient, l'idée de la liberté de l'homme dans son projet fondamental, et, au fond, l'idée (croyance ou désir) d'être... source de soi-même.

Pour moi je n'entends point contribuer à cette approche biographique autrement qu'en continuant à explorer les formes et les stratégies de son autobiographie. Ecrivant en 1972 sur les *Mots*, j'avais eu une formule conclusive qui aujourd'hui me semble bien imprudente: je voyais formule conclusive qui aujourd'hui me semble bien imprudente: je voyais dans les *Mots* le seul livre de Sartre "à avoir réussi, par sa forme même, à totaliser une vie."²³ A bien lire Sartre, une telle chose était-elle possible? Aujourd'hui, c'est la mobilité de l'ensemble du système qui me fascine, et que, peut-être aussi imprudemment, je surestime... Entre 1977 et 1980, j'ai essayé d'analyser la métamorphose de l'autobiographie de Sartre après les *Mots*.²⁴ Il me reste donc à reprendre les choses au début: l'étude à laquelle cet exposé sert de préambule présentera rapidement l'autoportrait de 1926, longuement les *Carnets de la drôle de guerre,* et, pour conclure, ce qu'on sait aujourd'hui de *Jean-sans-terre* et des avant-textes des *Mots*.

La lecture des *Carnets* m'a d'autre part donné l'envie d'étudier la mémoire de Sartre, du moins ce qu'on en peut appréhender à travers des textes qui obéissent à des stratégies divergentes. Sartre a toujours présenté la mémoire comme une reconstruction,—ce qui apparemment le rapproche de Freud. Mais à la différence de Freud, il n'a jamais été très soucieux de regarder pourquoi, comment, et quand, la mémoire reconstruisait. L'idée de reconstruction semble avoir été pour lui une manière de se débarasser des théories de la mémoire-trace et du déterminisme qui les accompagnent, et de s'autoriser à ne pas se poser de problème sur ses propres souvenirs... Peut-on, d'ailleurs, hors d'une situation analytique, observer sa propre mémoire? En tout cas Sartre qui, dans les *Carnets,* met souvent sa théorie à l'épreuve de son vécu, s'en abstient totalement quand il aborde le problème de la mémoire (CDG, p. 256-264). Une manière comme une autre, pour le lecteur, de s'introduire dans l'atelier de Sartre, serait donc, par une étude comparative des souvenirs d'enfance dans les *Carnets,* les *Mots* et les *Entretiens* de 1974, d'essayer d'entrevoir ce qu'il n'a jamais vu: sa mémoire.

---

[1] Lettre à Simone de Beauvoir, 6 janvier 1940, *Lettres au Castor* (Paris: Gallimard, 1983), II, 21.

[2] *Les Mots*, collection "Folio," 1972, p. 212.

[3] *Entretiens avec Jean-Paul Sartre*, in *La Cérémonie des adieux (Paris: Gallimard, 1981)*, p. 274.

[4] Simone de Beauvoir, *La Force des choses* [1963] (Paris: Livre de Poche, 1969), II, 132.

[5] *Les Carnets de la drôle de guerre* (Paris: Gallimard, 1983), p. 174; dans le Carnet XII, p. 329-331, il décrit comment il a vécu pendant cette période "translucide" et totalement "public" dans ses relations amicales, ce qui était manière de tuer le "psychologue"... Toute autre référence à cette édition sera faite dans le texte, entre parenthèses, par l'abbréviation CDG suivie par le numéro de page.

[6] "Sur *L'Idiot de la famille*" (entretien avec M. Contat et M. Rybalka, *Le Monde*, 14 mai 1971), *Situations X*, (Paris: Gallimard, 1976), p. 103-105.

[7] *L'Etre et le Néant*, (Paris: Gallimard, 1943), p. 555. Le "je" de Sartre n'est pas ici autobiographique, mais pédagogique.

[8] "Jean-Paul Sartre on His Autobiography: an Interview with Oliver Todd," *The Listener* (June 6, 1957). Ma traduction.

[9] *Plaidoyer pour les intellectuels* [1965] (Paris: Gallimard [Collection "Idées"], 1972), p. 47-49.

[10] Interview de Sartre, recueillie le 1er mai 1976, reproduite dans le press-book du film *Sartre par lui-même*, p. 2: "Sartre parle du film."

[11] Cf. Michel Contat et Michel Rybalka, *Les Ecrits de Sartre* (Edition Gallimard), p. 84 et p. 226.

[12] Les parties actuellement accessibles de l'avant-texte des *Mots*, notamment l'ensemble de manuscrits que la Bibliothèque Nationale a acheté au début de 1984, seront présentées dans l'étude à laquelle le présent texte sert d'introduction.

[13] Je n'ai fait figurer dans mon tableau que les interviews actuellement publiées. A quoi s'ajouteront sans doute plus tard les entretiens (une centaine d'heures enregistrées) que Sartre a accordées à John Gerassi en vue de la biographie qu'il prépare (voir Sartre, *Oeuvres romanesques*, Bibliothèque de la Pléiade, 1981, p. CXI).

[14] Voir la présentation que Jacques Lecarme a donnée de la stratégie autobiographique de Malraux dans l'*Encyclopédia Universalis*, Supplément, tome II, 1980, p. 908-910.

[15] Claude Mauriac, *Le Temps immobile*, sept volumes publiés chez Grasset entre 1974 et 1983, à quoi il faut ajouter, publié chez Belfond en 1977, *L'Eternité parfois*.

[16] Entretien avec Benny Lévy, *Le Nouvel Observateur*, 10 mars 1980, p. 92.

[17] *Entretiens*, dans *La Cérémonie des adieux*, respectivement p. 539-540, p. 370-392, et 401.

[18] CDG, p. 193-194 (écriture de "Pour un papillon") et p. 320-322 (ses premières pièces pour marionnettes).

[19] *Les Mots* ("Folio"), p. 66, et *Situations X* (Paris: Gallimard, 1976), p. 97 ("sur *l'Idiot de la famille*).

[20] *L'Idiot de la famille* (Paris: Gallimard, 1971), I, 56, et *Situations X*, p. 175 ("Autoportrait à soixante-dix ans").

[21] Michel-Antoine Burnier, *Le Testament de Sartre* (Paris: Olivier Obran), 1982.

[22] Denis Hollier, *Politique de la prose, Jean-Paul Sartre et l'an quarante* (Paris: Gallimard, 1982).

[23] "L'ordre du récit dans les *Mots* de Sartre," *Le Pacte autobiographique* (Paris: Seuil, 1975), p. 243.

[24] Cf. "Ça c'est fait comme ça," *Poétique*, 35 (septembre 1978), 269-304 (sur le film *Sartre par lui-même*), et "Sartre et l'autobiographie parlée," *Je est un autre* (Paris: Seuil, 1980), p. 161-202.

Biographie d'une autobiographie

Bernard Mathias

Notre époque voit apparaître en librairie un foissonnement d'autobiographies. Si chacun ne se sent pas le don d'un romancier, chacun, par contre, se sent capable de rédiger une autobiographie, encouragé par l'idée qui court: "Nous portons tous un roman en nous. Celui de notre vie. Il suffit de l'écrire."

Ce n'est certes pas cette seule motivation qui m'a poussé à enterprendre mon roman autobiographique.[1] En vérité le complexe, très français, de la "pudeur" en littérature, a, longtemps, censuré en moi un tel projet. Mais j'aimais l'art: cinéma, peinture.... J'ai commencé par être peintre—et, il m'est arrivé, je l'avoue, de faire mon autoportrait. Par la suite—pour vivre avec ma femme, écrivain, l'aventure de l'écriture—je me suis mis à un premier roman, une fiction où personnages et situations étaient aussi éloignés de ma vie que possible. Ainsi, contrairement à une idée préétablie chez les critiques, la première oeuvre d'un romancier n'est pas forcément autobiographique.

Mais en chaque artiste vit, on le sait, un exhibitionniste. Cet exhibitionnisme, je l'ai éprouvé dès ma plus tendre enfance où je rêvais que quelque coup de "sunlight" magique (une fée... une star?) me transportât sur les plateaux des studios de Hollywood (auxquels je fais souvent allusion dans mon ouvrage). Vivant un enfermement assez oppressant dans une antique synagogue aux contraintes religieuses rigoureuses, je rêvais, comme le personnage incarné par Al Jolson dans *The Jazz Singer* de voir mon nom "inscrit" quelque part, hors les murs étriqués de mon décor quotidien. Représentant, dès mon plus jeune âge, toute une communauté, et jugé par elle si je me rendais coupable de manquement à la Tradition, mon désir grandissait de me disculper, de m'expliquer, prendre ma revanche, prendre le large.

Revanche, libération, désir de déplacer son image dans un cadre plus large: tels me semblent les impulsions de base de toute entreprise autobigraphique. La première—et non la moindre—fut assurément les *Confessions* de Jean-Jacques Rousseau.

* * *

Ce souci de revanche sur un destin que l'on vous désigne et que vous déviez en un acte frondeur est un acte d'écriture violent. Plus que jeter le masque, c'est montrer, selon une expression populaire, "de quel bois l'on se chauffe."

"Mais à qui profite le crime?" tenterait-on de s'interroger comme dans un roman policier. Car c'est en effet un délit que l'autobiographie puisqu'elle met en cause situations et personnages "ayant réellement existé," et, ce qui est plus grave, existant souvent encore. A un critique qui avait cru voir dans *Les Concierges de Dieu* une autobiographie pure, j'ai répondu: "Autobiographie? Impossible tant que les parents sont vivants. Essayez, vous verrez."

Ce qui complique l'affaire, c'est que le romancier-autobiographe répond au double besoin—en cela très différent du simple romancier— d'écrire à la fois pour un vaste public et de répondre à son entourage immédiat. Des conflits naissent alors avec les personnages de ce livre où l'on sert si directement d'eux: Rousseau s'est fait passer pour un affabulateur doublé d'un paranoïaque. Simone de Beauvoir, plus récemment, a choqué les lecteurs de Jean-Paul Sartre car elle le montrait comme un vieil homme diminué par la maladie et mourant sur son lit d'hôpital.

Mon expérience personnelle fut à la fois agréable et surprenante. J'avais tout à craindre de la réaction d'un père dont le personnage pouvait passer pour très dur. Effet de catharsis que lui et moi croyions jusqu'alors voué à l'échec? Désir de sa part à lui, de sortir de l'anonymat, quelle que soit l'image qu'on donnât de lui?... Par contre, le personnage de la soeur que j'avais considérablement adoucie, angélisée dans le livre, fut très mal reçu par "l'original" qui s'est au contraire, trouvée très noircie—alors que beaucoup de jeunes lectrices s'identifièrent au personnage, l'ont trouvé "poétique," voire "sublime."

**

Toutefois, la nécessité autobiographique va bien au-delà du simple règlement de comptes. Elle est avant tout la manifestation en littérature de se démarquer de la masse ou de l'idéologie dominante. Les pays totalitaires voient naître bon nombre d'autobiographes plus ou moins clandestins. C'est le cas des dissidents de tous bords. L'autobiographie: acte de liberté. C'est ainsi qu'elle ambitionne de porter un message universel. Mais se libérer, se démarquer—et, en particulier d'une communauté culturelle—ne va pas sans arrachements. A ce propos, un critique m'écrivit gentiment que: "si on sait ce qu'on y gagne, on ne sait pas toujours ce que l'on perd."

**

Il serait bien sûr trompeur d'envisager l'autobiographie comme un acte spontané, sans retouches, sans auto-censure. D'abord en raison de cette fameuse mémoire défaillante et sélective. Ensuite, parce qu'en écrivant son autobiographie, l'auteur pense, plus encore peut-être que pour un roman, au *lecteur*... Il apparaît assez rapidement qu'il est indispensable de composer, voire mentir et affabuler. Le premier jet des *Concierges de Dieu* fut une fresque dense, brouillonne, où je n'avais fait ni coupe ni finitions dans le tissu de ma vie. Aussi le ton de cette première mouture s'avéra-t-il dur, rageur, illustrant quelque peu le "Famille, je vous hais" d'Arthur Rimbaud.

Il me fallut donc retravailler mon texte plus pour me prouver que je savais me "dominer" littérairement, que par simple pudeur.

D'abord, le décor: la synagogue, pauvre, délabrée, offrit un aspect sordide qui eût rebuté le lecteur—et même le lecteur juif, hyper-sensible, craignant toujours une utilisation antisémite de toute image "juive" aussi peu avilissante soit-elle. Il est vrai qu'en Europe, on n'a toujours pas bien mis à clair les consciences depuis la dernière guerre mondiale. Si un Phillip Roth peut, aux Etats-Unis, écrire un roman autobiographique où ses personnages juifs ont droit, comme tout individu sur terre, à des défauts ou des vices, en Europe, toute description trop libre dans ce domaine peut produire un scandale. Il me fallut donc "poétiser" lieux et personnages, un peu comme s'ils sortaient d'un tableau de Chagall. A ce propos, il fut reproché à la comédie musicale *A Fiddler on the Roof* de baigner dans une larmoyante mièvrerie d'un ghetto aseptisé par Hollywood. Mais comment aurait-elle été accueillie, et particulièrement de ce côté de l'Atlantique, en une version réaliste, fatalement prosaïque?

Pour mon roman, il ne fut pas aisé d'éviter le sordide sans tomber dans la mièvrerie, de trouver le biais, ainsi que mon personnage l'exprime à son amie Pascale (page 218): "Expliquer. Comment ne pas donner une fausse image trop poétique, ce qui serait faux, ou trop sordide, ce qui serait inexact, ou poético-sordide, ce qui serait un mensonge?" Ma démarche fut, en fait, l'inverse de celle de Céline dans *Mort à crédit* où l'auteur a, au contraire, accentué le sordide, le trivial, la misère au sein d'une famille qui, dans la réalité, était trop pâlote, trop "France profonde," pas assez folklorique...

Le folklorisme justement, et en sens inverse, fut une autre de mes préoccupations. Dieu sait s'il y avait matière dans ma vie pour un livre quasi ethnologique des us et coutumes d'un peuple... Mais pour traduire, précisément, mon "overdose" de folklore, il m'a semblé indispensable d'éviter cet écueil, d'autant plus que ce genre était devenu un peu trop à la mode ces dernières années. De plus, comme tout autobiographe, je voulais que ce microcosme que je décrivais eût, pour intéresser un public élargi, un caractère universel... Star-mania ou mégalomania? Mais aussi Montaigne oblige: "Tout homme porte en soi un exemplaire de l'humaine condition."

Quant à l'aspect anecdotique, c'est un lieu commun de le rappeler, mais c'est un fait: la vie est plus incroyable que la fiction. Pour que l'on croie à mon autobiographie, il me fallut donc inventer des épisodes ou des personnages plus vraisemblables que les vrais. Cette résolution, je l'avais prise à la suite d'une expérience littéraire qui advint à ma femme[2]: elle avait écrit un roman intimiste, un huis-clos assez oppressant au sein d'une famille "comme les autres," où elle n'avait pas craint de décrire les personnages dans leur crudité, leur férocité naturelle—chacun fait de son côté, au mieux, pour sauver sa propre peau. Rien de plus quotidien, mais qui fut décrit avec une lucidité impitoyable. Auteurs et éditeurs louèrent, enthousiastes, les qualités du roman. Ils craignirent cependant que le public ne soit "traumatisé" par ce trop fidèle reflet de sa vie la plus secrète. Or, pour corser l'intrigue, et aussi pour rompre avec la sobriété presque insoutenable du récit, ma femme décida d'y ajouter un meurtre: celui du père par sa fille. Et c'est cet épisode, séduisant pour un éditeur, qui les fit en même temps hésiter: comment publier le témoignage d'une adolescente meurtrière? Ainsi étaient-ils persuadés que, dans ce roman, seul le meurtre fût authentique, alors qu'il était pratiquement le seul élément non-autobiographique du livre!

De la même façon, certains épisodes de ma vie auraient été jugés "intolérables"—ou invraisemblables. Ainsi, le "pèlerinage" de mon personnage, Daniel, en Transylvanie, berceau de mes ancêtres, passa le plus souvent comme une méditation lyrique. Or, c'est le passage le plus "vécu" et le plus fidèlement rapporté de mon livre.

J'aurais pu regretter d'avoir été contraint à tous ces compromis. Il s'avéra pourtant par la suite que le récit, même édulcoré et simplifié, restituait auprès du lecteur une réalité aussi dense et dure que celle que j'avais vécue. Pour cette fois, du moins, je ne trouvai pas que "traduction" soit nécessairement synonyme de "trahison."

* * *

La réception du manuscrit par les éditeurs me donna une nouvelle occasion de réfléchir sur le genre autobiographique.

Aux éditions Grasset où le manuscrit arriva par la poste, on l'accepta très rapidemment sans paraître devoir se préoccuper de l'aspect autobiographique du texte—seule entrait en ligne de compte la "qualité littéraire." On ne m'y demanda point d'en changer un mot.

Des éditions Gallimard, le contrat me parvint pratiquement le même jour (j'eus en fait la chance, pour un premier roman, de pouvoir "choisir"). Mais là, on me proposait d'écarter la dernière partie (là où mon personnage s'évade de sa synagogue et tente une aventure avec une jeune fille d'un autre milieu). De l'avis de Simone de Beauvoir (qui avait proposé le manuscrit) la fin pouvait être ressentie comme "rupture de ton" et "trop happy end." Opinion parfaitement respectable, et intéressante en ce que, tout en reconnaissant l'aspect autobiographique du livre, on exigeait une unité, une ligne générale, comme si la vie elle-même n'était pas un "patchwork." D'autre part en jugeant le dénouement "trop happy end," on agissait avec cet ouvrage comme s'il se fût agi d'une fiction qu'il fallait bien "ficeler et nouer." Or ce type de critique ne saurait se prévaloir pour un récit de vie, puisque dans une autobiographie, l'auteur, moins que quiconque, n'en connaît la fin, encore moins ne décide si oui ou non, il y a "happy end."

* * *

Au moment de sa parution, de nouvelles questions se présentèrent, et surtout celle-ci: comment allaient réagir les critiques diverses par rapport au thème, et au milieu décrit?

Là encore, je fus assez surpris, et agréablement, le plus souvent. Ce roman que je craignais malgré tout pas assez élargi, trop rattaché—et donc limité—à une supposée école juive de littérature, fut accueilli par les journaux "laïques" comme un roman typiquement et profondément français, par sa langue, sa structure, sa sensibilité. Ainsi le compara-t-on à *L'Enfant* de Jules Vallès (*Le Monde* du 10 octobre 1982).

J'avais, de même, pas mal d'appréhension quant à la presse religieuse. Or, la critique chrétienne le salua comme un roman qui en disait "bien plus long" que d'autres ouvrages épais et ardus (*Télé 7 Jours*, novembre 1982) sur la question juive, mais aussi sur la relation entre les deux cultures. La dernière partie avait donc jeté un pont et permettait à mon autobiographie de délivrer un "message" au-delà de ma communauté, au-delà aussi, de la simple anecdote.

Mais cette communauté dont je m'étais "servie"? Bonne réaction, là encore. Je récoltai des témoignanges bienveillants (enfin!). Après tout, les gens étaient-ils peut-être heureux de se voir mis en scène dans une histoire grave, certes, mais qui ne larmoyait pas sur sa fatalité. Plus inattendue fut la sensibilisation des lecteurs juifs sur le problème du mariage mixte que je n'avais pourtant qu'ébauché dans les dernières pages. Les lecteurs me questionnèrent comme s'ils étaient eux-mêmes des personnages de cette histoire. Il leur fallait des preuves: avais-je réussi mon expérience? Quand leur donnerais-je la suite pour qu'ils puissent voir comment "ça s'est passé"? Et, puisque ça semblait tenir, pourrait-on rencontrer cette femme qui... Ainsi, ma femme, personnage de mon autobiographie fut souvent sollicitée pour s'expliquer, en personne, sur cette question.

On voit comme une autobiographie, même atténuée, interpelle le lecteur. J'avais eu peur d'un procès: je fus au contraire approuvé, et même présenté comme témoin sincère et authentique de la "conscience juive lucide et blessée" (*L'Arche*, sept-oct 1982).

L'autobiographe veut à la fois prendre sa revanche et gagner l'approbation de ceux à qui il s'est opposé: j'avais donc eu la chance d'atteindre ces deux buts contradictoires.

Avais-je bien eu raison, malgré tout, d'entrer "en littérature" par une autobiographie? Le critique dira oui: le premier livre (publié) est naturellement autobiographique. Puis l'auteur doit faire ses preuves en produisant des fictions.

Au fait: n'est-il pas plus logique de rédiger son autobiographie en fin de parcours où l'on peut prendre du recul, où, comme l'a dit Jean-Paul Sartre, "on a sa vie derrière soi"?

En réalité, nombreux sont les auteurs qui, pour mettre la touche finale à leur carrière, brossent le tableau de leur vie personnelle, mondaine, intellectuelle. Comme ils sont célèbres, cela s'intitulera tout simplement: "Mémoires." Et ces autobiographies connaissent souvent un plus grand succès que l'oeuvre romanesque du même auteur: de Simone de Beauvoir, le grand public citera *Les Mémoires d'une jeune fille rangée*, *La Force de l'âge*, *La Force des choses*. De l'oeuvre de Jean-Paul Sartre, on se réfère de plus en plus souvent aux *Mots*, et la parution, posthume, en 1983, de ses *Carnets de la drôle de guerre*, puis des *Lettres au Castor*, ont connu un grand retentissement. De même pour les *Mémoires* de Raymond Aron. Fait plus étonnant: Nathalie Sarraute, chef de file du Nouveau Roman des années 60, courant littéraire connu pour sa sécheresse, son goût pour l'abstraction et l'impersonnel, vient de donner une autobiographie qui a touché tous ses lecteurs par sa chaleur humaine, et modestement intitulée: *Enfance*.

* * *

Car c'est bien de chaleur humaine, de confidences: d'autobiographies, en somme, dont le public actuel ressent le besoin. Lassé par les terribles "happenings" de l'époque, c'est encore la réalité—ou ce qu'il croit telle—qui l'émeut et l'étonne le plus.

Par ailleurs, influencé par le cinéma et la télévision, dont le principe est essentiellement voyeuriste, le lecteur ne veut plus rêver, imaginer, mais "apprendre": "votre livre m'a beaucoup appris" est une phrase que j'eus souvent le plaisir d'entendre.

Cependant, il est normal que le romancier se méfie un peu de cette intimité lecteur/auteur, et qu'il veuille s'éloigner vers la fiction. Mais c'est surtout à cause de la critique qui fait pression sur lui pour qu'il dépasse le "je" autobiographique. Ce certificat du créateur pur: le passage du "je" au "il"... Et pourtant, est-il vraiment possible de "dépasser" l'autobiographie, puisqu'écrire sa propre vie est déjà en quelque sorte un acte extrême. Et où se dépasse-t-on le plus: dans le "mentir-vrai," selon l'expression d'Aragon, ou plutôt dans la superbe indécence d'un Jean Genet ou d'un Michel Leiris?

Malgré tout, l'écrivain qui veut se faire reconnaître comme tel proteste: "Mon livre n'est pas autobiographique, malgré les apparences. Ou alors, tous les livres le sont. Ou bien encore: l'autobiographie, ça n'existe pas."

Ainsi naissent actuellement quantité d'autobiographies qui faussent un peu la piste en faisant inscrire "roman" en page de couverture. Je ne puis cacher que tel fut mon cas, d'autant plus qu'en effet, à mesure que je "récrivais ma vie," j'avais de plus en plus de mal à discerner le "vrai" du "faux."

En fait, aucun écrivain aujourd'hui n'échappe à l'autobiographie, ou plutôt: l'autobiographie échappe à chacun, un jour ou l'autre. Si le XXe siècle marque le triomphe de ce genre littéraire, c'est peut-être parce que, plus que jamais en cette époque où les hommes se multiplient et se trouvent, fatalement, gommés dans la foule, ils ont le besoin de se sentir vivre en tant qu'être unique porteur d'une Histoire qui lui est propre. Il n'y a pas que l'auteur qui a besoin de crier son moi. Le lecteur se rassure maintenant à l'idée que, grâce à l'autobiographie, l'individualité a encore ses chances.

---

[1] Bernard Mathias est l'auteur du roman primé *Les Concierges de Dieu* (Paris: Grasset, 1982): Prix Hermès (décerné à un premier roman par les lauréats Goncourt, Académie Française, Renaudot, Femina, Médicis); Prix Bonardi (Académie Française). Son deuxième roman, *L'Enfant infidèle*, a paru chez Grasset en 1989.

[2] Geneviève Leymarie-Mathias. Dans une autre communication à ce sujet Monsieur Mathias explique davantage: "En ce qui concerne mon roman, évoqué par moi dans ma communication, j'ai justement expliqué que le sujet, bien que séduisant, a fait en quelque sorte peur aux éditeurs. Le roman n'a donc pas été publié à ce jour, mais a été examiné aux comités de lecture sous le titre: *Une famille comme les autres*" —Editeur.

World War II and the French Novel

Rima Drell Reck
University of New Orleans

The novelist creates his fictions out of a need to restate, reshape, even totally to escape the real world. In all its forms the work of fiction is directly related to *le monde actuel,* even when quotidian existence appears to be deliberately ignored. I do not believe that fiction is historically determined, any more than I believe that a painting is a product of price fluctuations in tubes of pigment or of scientific developments in the manufacture of brushes and canvases. But it is indeed true that technical matters enter into the choice of *materials* the painter will use in the act of externalizing an inner vision and that the novelist, whose material is language and whose subject is *experience in time,* as Proust so clearly put it, must reflect in his writing the historical moment in which he lives. The *roman à clef* is no less or more a historical object than the purest of literary fantasies. In any study of a given period in the development of the novel or of a particular novel seen within the context of the era in which it was written, we must attempt to understand the relationship between the novelist and his time.

My subject, "World War II and the French Novel," can be approached in a number of ways. For the purpose of clarity and also to explain what I have chosen *not* to discuss, let me enumerate some of the possibilities this subject suggests. First and most obviously, we have the instance of novels written about the French experience of the Second World War—Sartre's trilogy, *Les Chemins de la liberté,* Céline's *Nord,* Aragon's *Les Communistes,* Malraux's *Les Noyers d'Altenburg* (in part, that is), to name some striking examples. In these works the intense and special human experience of participating in a continent-wide military conflict which has engulfed the writer's own land is given fictional form; the writer's personal reactions and judgments on this cataclysmic experience are embodied in the creation of fictional beings living *in the time of the event.* In such works of fiction the relationship between a major historical event and the work of fiction is clear and unmistakable. World War II is in fact part of the subject of the novels.

Second, we have the instance of novels written about the aftermath of the event, ones which attempt in retrospect to assess the impact of that terrible war on the lives of men and women who lived through it and its impact on France, a country whose legal and moral position during the war was particularly charged with emotional and moral ambiguities. It is perhaps difficult for us, and in this we are fortunate, to imagine the long-range impact of having lived in a nation whose official government decided to collaborate with the occupying enemy; and where a large percentage of the population did not protest this apparent shift of loyalties. The moral reassessment this fact demanded within the French conscience once the war ended was incalculable in its scope. It is still going on today. Countless novels deal with this problem, from novels about the period which led to the fall of France such as Drieu la Rochelle's *Gilles* to Camus' *La Chute,* which dealt in allegorical form with the fundamental issue of moral choice raised by the Vichy regime and its aftermath. It is also enlightening to view, in part at least, the major *nouveaux romans* of Robbe-Grillet, Nathalie Sarraute, and Michel Butor as reflections of a reaction to the war years. The deliberate conscious turning away from the traditional novel of psychological analysis and moral penetration was in fact a reaction against the turn French fiction inevitably took after the Second World War—one might call the *nouveau roman* a negation in retrospect.

The third major way one may approach my general subject is by examining the effect the Second World War had on the development of the novel and critical theory. From this viewpoint, one would have to examine in detail the major critical fashions which assumed their hegemony after the war and how these fashions shaped the fiction of the post-war era and even shaped retroactively the critical history of the novel before that war ever took place. I have examined this aspect of the subject in some detail in my book, *Literature and Responsibility*.

The *moral* aspect of the Second World War remains a vital subject in contemporary France. The theft of Pétain's tomb this year by Frenchmen who wanted him to be buried alongside the soldiers he led in World War I, rather than in a prison cemetery as a punishment for his activities as head of the Vichy regime, brought home once again, even to those of us who have been working for some time on the subject of the Collaboration, that the battle over the morality of that era is far from finished. We had begun to see a diminishing in everyday French life of the omnipresent division of all Frenchmen into *anciens résistants* and *anciens collabos*. The under-30s long ago tired of what they considered an outmoded and highly exaggerated way of viewing the world on the part of their elders. In the summer of 1971 I delivered a paper on a collaborationist writer at the International Comparative Literature Association meeting in Bordeaux. The greatest revelation of that trip came out of talks with students at the University there. They had come to regard the *collabos* as fellow outsiders, young men who had bucked the Establishment of their day and been made to suffer for their rebellion. The attitude of these students was most enlightening—they were committing the same historical error as the spokesmen of the French national conscience during the late 40s and early 50s had, but in a different direction. The presence of the intentional fallacy in almost all discussions of that crucial period in French life and history is in fact quite depressing.

Which leads me to the fourth manner of approaching the subject of World War II and the French novel, the one I have chosen to deal with here—the circumstances of creation, the moral dilemmas, the practical problems confronting a French writer who during the Second World War chose to side with the occupying enemy. We know a great deal about the moral and artistic situations of writers such as Sartre, Beauvoir, and Camus during the period of the Occupation, from a number of sources—Beauvoir's *La Force de l'âge,* Camus' *Carnets* and journalism, Sartre's *Situations.* What we lack is a clear view of the other side of the coin. This view has been deliberately obscured for many years by those French writers who became the *directeurs de conscience* of post-war France. It is easy enough to understand *why* the immediate post-war period necessitated a clarification which in fact amounted to an oversimplification.

Only by dividing the world into *anciens résistants* and *anciens collabos* could the French once again give their nation the image the French psyche then demanded—the image of a strong nation, torn between the powers of good and the forces of evil, which had managed to make the good prevail. The great gray reality was that the majority of Frenchmen simply managed to survive the Occupation with as little damage to their personal lives as possible. This was not a reality from which to forge ringing maxims, not one to inspire moral firmness and effective political activism. We can understand the practical necessities of the late 40s and early 50s in France, and why it was perhaps inevitable that some writers who had vacillated during the war, or indeed collaborated, came to be expunged for a time from the national consciousness. What is surprising, however, is the fact that the process of rewriting literary history to protect a moral viewpoint should have gone on so long—perhaps the most vivid testimony one can find to the inner sense of disgrace felt by the French people.

But a great many years have passed. The lions of the French literary 40s and 50s have grown old and their voices now seem shrill and just a trifle anachronistic. I say this with regret, because no new writers have come along to play the moral role that Sartre in his time played with supreme literary talent in several genres. Changes in Europe have made France and Germany economic allies, even political ones. In the light of the present era, it is most ironic to examine the emotional and political evolution of Pierre Drieu la Rochelle, editor of the *Nouvelle Revue Française* for several years under the German occupation, an ardent antimilitarist who dreamed of a federated Europe, a gifted writer of fiction and superb essayist, a man who came to be disillusioned with the Germans as well as the French. After several unsuccessful suicide attempts, he at last died by his own hand in March, 1945.

"Thirsty for speculation, passionate about that perilous and misleading art called the philosophy of history, intimately involved in the necessary evil of prophecy, I have spoken many truths and made many mistakes," Pierre Drieu la Rochelle wrote in his *Chronique politique,* published in Paris in 1943 under the German occupation.[1] A member of the same literary generation as Louis Aragon, Georges Bernanos, and Céline, eight years older than André Malraux, Drieu la Rochelle was one of a small but significant number of French writers and intellectuals who chose the German side during the Second World War. Like Céline and Aragon he saw action on the battlefield in the First World War and like them he became violently convinced that universal military conflict was the most destructive experience his country could undergo. His antimilitarism changed the direction of his life and his writing. From a sensitive young poet before his service in the army, Drieu was transformed into an acerbic polemicist and pamphleteer. He gave up writing poetry to concentrate on prose fiction. His novels revealed an increasing ideological discontent and an ever deepening pessimism. As he reflected on what was happening to France after the First World War, he began to think that the root of the problem lay in a kind of moral and physical laziness which tended to reinforce the country's fundamentally weak political and economic situation.

Drieu began to look toward Germany. There he thought he saw a growing strength of national character and unity of purpose which would eventually make that country the future leader in Europe. To Drieu, Germany represented health while France grew ever sicker. The eyes of a disillusioned poet saw an answer for France in the German way, a model in German leadership. Fundamentally out of touch with current artistic movements such as Surrealism, which assumed the artist's ability to isolate himself from historical and political concerns, Drieu found that he could not ignore the larger world around him. He began to worry about the total European situation in the twenties.

In *Le Jeune Européen,* an essay written in 1927, he confessed, "I am not simply a writer. I am a man prey to the total problem." Drieu's essay was written the same year as André Malraux's "D'une jeunesse européenne," another telling personal document on the complex issues which confronted French intellectuals in the twenties. Eight years younger than Drieu and of an entirely different temperament, Malraux suggested that the crisis of European youth was due primarily to a failure of *aesthetic vision* rather than *moral vision.* Malraux had not fought in the First World War. His training in art history and archeology, his relatively privileged youth and his basic aesthetic optimism enabled him to transmute his uneasiness about the world as it was into symbolic images. He concluded that the road to the salvation of Western culture, and of France along with it, lay in broadening the field of consciousness of European art. In answer to the Spenglerian negation which haunted his generation, Malraux began in 1927 to limn his huge vision of world art as proof of man's divinity and of his self-continuity throughout history. Drieu's essay, on the other hand, expressed his sense of total physical involvement in the European historical and political situation; in this situation he found the roots of France's deepening decline. And he saw no hope in aesthetic solutions. For Drieu possible solutions seemed exclusively political.

Only by understanding Drieu's acute awareness of the choice he was making in the twenties and early thirties can we hope to understand what Germany came to mean to him and why he collaborated fifteen years later. It is evident that his ultimate choice was an entirely voluntary one, the natural outcome of a growing disillusionment with France and its future which had begun during Drieu's First World War experiences. When he became an active collaborator during the Occupation and served for several years as editor of the *Nouvelle Revue Française* under the Germans, he was for a time firmly convinced that his choice was right.

It is not my aim here either to justify or condemn this choice. It appears to have been an honest if misguided one, one which eventually condemned Drieu to a premature suicide and to the destruction of his literary reputation. What does concern me is the extent to which the choice may have been more a *literary* than a *political* one. In all of Drieu's writings up to the time of the Second World War, it was the *image of Germany* which moved him, rather than the reality, which he knew only slightly. This image ultimately affected his writing, as Drieu experienced a phenomenon peculiar to many nineteenth- and twentieth-century writers. His purely literary grasp of fundamentally unliterary realities, such as political struggles and military conflicts, changed the very shape of his literary production.

Critics often cannot avoid the pitfalls of extra-literary involvement, as they evaluate and judge in the context of their own total experience. For example, in recent years we have witnessed a striking phenomenon in France. There has been a considerable rebirth of interest in French collaborationist writers. Historians such as Robert Aron and Paul Sérant have undertaken a reassessment of the immediate post-war period. The same vague sense of moral culpability over the treatment of collaborationist writers at the war's end, which inspired the historians to better examine what really happened during the troubled years after the Second World War, now infects the critics. They are trying to right the balance and to correct some of the injustices committed in the name of morality upon literary figures who had the bad luck or the bad judgment to choose the losing side in a political conflict. Some of these reappraisals are balanced, well reasoned, and justified by the works being evaluated.

Others are overly favorable and motivated more by bad conscience than by sound literary judgment. The gradual rehabilitation of Céline's reputation, for example, has only been possible with the detachment brought about by the passage of time and a gradual dying down of rancor. Céline, the great underground giant of the French novel in this century, to whom even Sartre has acknowledged his infinite debt, is finally being read and appreciated again, despite the nature of his political pronouncements between 1936 and 1945. There is, however, a great difference between *le cas Céline* and *le cas Drieu*. Although accused, hounded out of France, and long persecuted, Céline was never convicted of collaborationist activity. There was not enough evidence. He did for a time think that the Germans were better than the French—in the Célinian scale of values that was indeed faint praise. The treatment he suffered at German hands and the insights into the German nation he gained during the long months spent there during the last year of the war on his way to what he hoped would be a safe haven in Denmark (vividly recounted in his novel *Nord*) led Céline ultimately to rank the Germans with all other men—*vache et miteux*. Drieu, on the other hand, made a vocal political and literary choice by which he lived for several years and which he repeated and defended countless times, in full awareness that what he was doing could lead him to defeat both in politics and in literature.

Perhaps any careful reappraisal will reveal what some of us already suspect, that neither Drieu la Rochelle nor Robert Brasillach (also presently being "revaluated" in the critical canon) was of the stature of Céline. They were, however, at least as talented and as important in the development of the style and shape of French literature in the mid-twentieth century as many of their more fortunate contemporaries who chose the winning side in the Second World War.

The *literary* results of the *épuration*, "the settling of accounts" which took place during the liberation of Paris in 1944, were effective and long lasting. Some of the more important older writers who had taken the wrong side were either hounded out of the country or buried alive critically by being totally ignored for the rest of their productive lives. This clearing of the decks facilitated the meteoric rise to prominence of many deserving young writers such as Camus and Sartre. It also badly imbalanced the diversity of literary styles and possible choices of subjects for a number of years. Gruesome moments of *épuration*, such as the public execution of Robert Brasillach before many obviously delighted spectators, have begun to seriously trouble the French literary conscience. (Not all were troubled, obviously; Simone de Beauvoir describes in her autobiography her immense sense of righteous satisfaction on that day.) It is not surprising that the attempted reassessment has often "rehabilitated" literary reputations far beyond their intrinsic merit. The counterswing has often been too strong.

Pierre Drieu la Rochelle was indeed a better than average novelist. He was not a great one. *Gilles,* written in 1939 and republished under the German occupation, is an important novel and frequently a very well written one. It is important above all for what it shows us of France in the period between 1918 and 1938. However, despite the claims of critics eager to forgive themselves for having perhaps contributed to Drieu's suicide in 1945, *Gilles* is a highly defective work. Drieu's polemical spirit often totally undermines his art. In this he is not unlike another far greater French novelist, Georges Bernanos. Bernanos managed in at least one novel, the *Journal d'un curé de campagne,* to find a form ideally suited to his temperament and his talents. Drieu never wrote a great novel. He was aware of this, lucid as he was about the polarities in his life and work which continually undermined his fiction. In his preface to the 1942 edition of *Gilles,* Drieu explained what happened to him. He found himself divided, both in energies and in spirit, between his novels and his political essays. He called this phenomenon, which he found present both in his era and in himself, decadence, and proudly asserted that alone he and Céline were truly aware of it and willing to face it without evasion. He faced it, he wrote, "by means of systematic observation and satire."[2] It is difficult to ascertain whether in Drieu's mind these two modes of facing reality were divided between the two literary genres he practiced most extensively, the essay and the novel. One can find systematic observation and satire in both. Indeed some of Drieu's greatest stylistic moments occurred not during the writing of his novels but in the essays written to defend the novels after their publication.

Drieu's preface to the 1942 edition of *Gilles* traces his evolution as a novelist and outlines with perfect clarity how the shifting emphasis in his fiction paralleled his deepening sense of political involvement. At that moment in 1942 Drieu was already able to foresee dimly the end result of his choices. He clearsightedly admitted that every choice he had made up to that time was the result of deliberate assessment of factors available to him and a willingness to act without assurances or total knowledge of the situation or its ultimate consequences. Drieu's *défense et illustration* in the preface to *Gilles* shows him to be one of the true forerunners of engaged literature. It is ironic that in good faith he chose the wrong side and that *le cas Drieu* was later to be cited as an outstanding example of bad faith by his more fortunate contemporaries. In 1937 Drieu wrote, "The most penetrating definition of fascism is this: it is the political movement which is moving the most directly and most radically toward that great revolution of manners and morals, in the direction of the restoration of the body—health, dignity, plenitude, heroism—in the direction of the defense of man against the big city and against the machine (CP, p. 50). Drieu's growing fear of Communist power in France led him to see the German way as the only solution. Drieu represents a mode of rightist thought in France which is an offshoot of Maurras and the Action Française movement, but one which substituted for an emphasis on extreme French nationalism the hope for a united Europe (see CP, pp. 309, 373). During the Occupation Drieu compared the conflicts between *résistants* and *collabos* to a drama common on the European scene, the basic drama of national consciousness: nationalism vs. a larger internationalism (an article in *La Gerbe,* March 26, 1942, reprinted in CP, p. 343). He urged his countrymen to make the most of the Occupation: "The French community has not lost everything; the only ones among us who have lost everything are those who related their ideas of life and happiness too closely to transitory and inevitably outmoded forms of national continuity" (CP, p. 246). He continued, "Germany is moving with the century, Germany is the incarnation of the necessity of the century" (CP, p. 249).

Drieu loved politics. He called it "the spirit, quite simply the life of the spirit" (CP, p. 286). Elsewhere he defined politics as "the meeting place of the material and the spiritual" and asserted that "if one is a leader in any domain at all one cannot avoid politics" (CP, pp. 268-269). From these remarks we see that for Drieu politics was actually a fusion of consciousness and the desire to act. And all forms of action, even purely intellectual ones he had pointed out in *Socialisme fasciste,* always reveal a political tendency.[3] Drieu was perhaps better aware than any of his contemporaries of the ambiguities of action and political choice; "There is something deeply representative," he wrote in *Socialisme fasciste,* "in the ambiguity of the intellectual's attitude. In this ambiguity he demonstrates his similarity to the masses, who never surrender themselves, who nourish and tolerate (at least on the surface) all kinds of partisan viewpoints and extremisms, but who never really become engaged except from time to time, and then only for a brief period... And the mass of men share the depth and ambiguity of nature itself.... In the same way, the intellectual is part of the mysterious misleading indifference of animals and of plants" (SF, pp. 236-237). Drieu's reverence for natural forces and his effort to explain the intellectual's attraction to political action as a kind of unconscious natural affinity is an excellent example of what the historian Paul Sérant has aptly termed "fascist romanticism."

In 1934 Drieu wrote, "Politics does not exhaust all there is to the human being. But because I am more engaged than most intellectuals and more dangerously (dangerously, for my artistic work), I have the right to say so and to shout warnings to others.... I do not desire neutrality; besides, I don't believe it's possible. I believe that from the work of an intellectual or an artist a deep political tendency always emerges (SF, p. 237). Drieu makes this statement in an essay entitled "Itinéraire" and included in *Socialisme fasciste*. In "Itinéraire" Drieu traces his intellectual and political odyssey from his first years as a writer to that precarious midpoint in the thirties which was a watershed for many French intellectuals and artists. They had at that moment to decide which way they were going to turn. Many of them visited Russia, attracted by an image they had of a socialist Utopia being built upon the European continent. Among these were Céline, Gide, Aragon, Malraux. Their reactions to Russia were varied. Céline returned convinced that the Russian menace, the growing power of Communists in France, and a swelling pro-war sentiment were far more dangerous than any threat from Germany.

Drieu was among those who began to define their political positions around a *counter-image,* an image of Germany as the sole defense against growing Soviet power and as a model for France. The Germany Drieu dreamed of was a Germany of the mind, a kind of pre-Socratic Greece along the lines of Nietzsche's fantasies, where men were young, healthy, free, and unspoiled by the debilitating rational tradition which had undermined France. Drieu's Germany of the mind is the most visionary, the most patently poetic to be found in the literature of the thirties in France. It is an obvious triumph of desire over reality.

For this reason, Drieu is one of the most interesting of the collaborationists writers. Convinced that political engagement was inevitable, he was willing to assume the risks of involvement. Isolated by the intensity of his choice, he soon had time to regret it at leisure as he saw the side he had chosen lose. We may ask, at this moment more than twenty-five years later, whether an existential choice *avant la lettre,* made in full consciousness of the responsibility, is any more condemnable than another choice, made with no fewer guarantees, which happens ultimately to fall on the winning side? Is the choice to be judged solely by its results? This has been the basis for judging collaborationist literature until very recently. Older Frenchmen still tend to divide the world between *résistants* and *collabos.* The younger generation in France at this moment no longer much cares about what happened during the Second World War; they have battles of their own to wage. They have in fact encouraged the work of revisionist critics by tending to view writers such as Drieu and Brasillach as fellow "outsiders" of another time, men out of step with an out-of-joint era who became martyrs to lost causes. There is some measure of truth in this over-simple interpretation.

Drieu was not a great sinner; neither was he a sainted martyr. If we can avoid elevating him beyond his merits or condemning him utterly because we disagree with his political preferences, we are able to see him for what he was—a kind of eternal romantic, a man who wanted things to be other than they are. In some eras this desire has made men long for the pastoral life. In others it has fired them to undertake bloody crusades. In our century, this desire has made political activists out of men fundamentally unsuited to the life of politics. Never at home in any party, regarded cautiously by rightists and Communists alike, Drieu confessed that dedicated political activists were correct to view the intellectual's engagement with suspicion. He wrote, "If the intellectual chooses action, it is because he has yielded to some totally momentary and futureless impulse. This is why men of action who belong to a political party see [in the intellectual] a haggard man who tries to use the same words they do, the words of a language which is indeed foreign to him. They welcome him with ingenuous or feigned emotion. Then one day the intellectual goes away as suddenly as he came" (SF, p. 241).

The curious admixture of passions and ideas which characterizes Drieu's political writings makes it very difficult to judge him in political terms. Aware of the pitfalls of action and yet convinced that no artistic existence could remain totally detached from the artist's historical moment, Drieu was as he himself said " laboratory experiment," a living crucible in which the dilemmas of the period between the two world wars in France produced some of the era's finest prose and some of its most touching contradictions. Unlike André Malraux, whom Drieu called "the archangel of permanent revolution," Drieu was never buttressed by an aesthetic certainty powerful enough to enable him to live easily with the contradictions inherent in action. Nor did Drieu have the poetic optimism which made his contemporary Louis Aragon a staunch Communist who found no conflict between a party line and a long creative life.

Always too much aware of all the possibilities, paralyzed by an excessively honest consciousness of the ambiguities of engagement, Drieu could never live comfortably with any choice he made. In the long run he could not live with the images he had created. He probably could not have lived without them, either. His passion for truth and for poetry could not free him from another passion, a passion characteristic of his time and of ours—the desire to become involved in a shifting political world in order to change it in some way. When Drieu stuck his head in an oven in 1945, he had realized that his dreams had been based on a poetic illusion, an image infinitely greater than the reality that inspired it.

And so, as has always been the case, writers have willingly or unwillingly been caught up in their historical moment. From such involvement and the conflicts it produces literature is born. The novel in particular flourishes in times of moral anguish and historical change. It is the characteristic literary form of the modern era, from *Don Quixote* to the present. And one of the richest periods in modern fiction began when France, weakened from within and without, fell to the Germans in 1940.

---

[1] Pierre Drieu la Rochelle, *Chronique politique, 1934-1942* (Paris: Gallimard, 1943), pp. 9-10. Hereafter cited in the text as CP. All translations from the French are mine.

[2] Pierre Drieu la Rochelle, *Gilles* (Paris: Gallimard, 1939; reprinted in Livre de Poche, 1967), p. 5. Hereafter cited in text as G.

[3] Pierre Drieu la Rochelle, *Socialisme fasciste* (Paris: Gallimard, 1934), p. 237. Hereafter cited in the text as SF.

Beyond *Mimesis*: Narrative Modality in *A la recherche du temps perdu*

David R. Ellison
Mount Holyoke College*

The inclusion of Marcel Proust's work in a discussion of the theory of the modern French novel appears natural, logical, almost inevitable. First: because Proust himself theorizes about artistic representation, in the sections of the *Recherche* devoted to Elstir, Bergotte, and Vinteuil, and in the long speculative conclusion of *Le Temps retrouvé*. Second: because structuralist and post-structuralist criticism have found in Proust's writings a convenient and rich *matière première* from which to mine discoveries on the nature of fictionality of which the author may have been unaware at the time he was composing his novel. From our postmodernist perspective, Proust can be seen both as the concluder of Balzacian realism and as the precursor of Beckettian experimentation. There will never be a dearth of critical literature on the subject "Proust and theory" or "Proust and representation" since we cannot be sure whether the *Recherche* is a novel or an autobiography, or a strange hybrid of the two forms.[1] Since Proust, to paraphrase Derrida, has "tampered with the law of genre,"[2] we can be reasonably certain that his text will continue to inspire differing interpretations and scholarly debate.

In recent years, the best-known French critics have, in fact, almost exclusively concentrated on the problem of representation in Proust, whether it be Genette on "indirect language," metaphor and metonymy, or *naming;* Deleuze on "signs;" Ricardou on textual "self-representation" or "anti-representation;" Barthes on Proust and "photography," etc.[3] In each case, the presupposition of the critic is that Proust's work is "really" a reflection on literary language as such, or at least (more modestly) that certain passages of the *Recherche* turn away from the representation of a given social or historical reality, and in this turning or textual troping reveal an underside of the text that is self-referential and self-contained. No one is quite audacious enough to affirm that there is no *mimetic* Proust or no "Balzacian" Proust, that there are no pages in the *Recherche* that lay claim to traditional *vraisemblance:* it is just that "this Proust" is no longer discussed as much as he used to be—he has faded into the background. I will immediately assure you that it is *not* my purpose here to resuscitate Proust in the adopted and perhaps badly-fitting garb of the nineteenth-century realist, but rather to raise the following question, in the overly rapid style the context of this brief essay requires: namely, is there an inner evolution, within the pages of the *Recherche,* through which Proust passes beyond mimetic realism, toward something else? If so, how can we characterize this something else? In the final pages of this study, we shall have a look at a crucial passage from the conclusion of *Sodome et Gomorrhe* which, in my view, depicts the turning away from or beyond *mimesis,* but first, I would like to examine briefly the reasons usually given for Proust's modernist or "post-Balzacian" status as a novelist.

Perhaps the easiest place to begin is André Maurois' preface to the Pléiade edition of *A la recherche du temps perdu.* In order to more clearly affirm the greatness of Proust's novelistic enterprise, Maurois compared it explicitly to Balzac's encyclopedic work:

> *La Comédie humaine* avait eu pour domaine le monde extérieur; elle avait annexé la finance, les salles de rédaction, les juges, les notaires, les médecins, les marchands, les paysans; Balzac s'était proposé de peindre, et avait peint en fait, une société tout entière. L'un des aspects originaux de Proust est, au contraire, son indifférence au choix des matériaux. Il s'intéresse bien moins à l'action d'observer qu'à une certaine manière d'observer toute action. Par là il opère, comme quelques philosophes de son temps, "une révolution copernicienne à rebours." L'esprit humain se trouve replacé au centre du monde; l'objet du roman devient de décrire l'univers réfléchi et déformé par l'esprit.
>
> Définir Proust par les événements et les personnages de son livre serait aussi absurde que définir Renoir: un homme qui a peint des femmes, des enfants et des fleurs. Ce qui fait Renoir, ce ne sont pas ses modèles, c'est une certaine lumière irisée dans laquelle il place tout modèle. Proust lui-même a montré, à propos de Bergotte, que la matière de l'oeuvre n'entre guère dans la composition du génie. C'est le génie qui transfigure toute matière.[4]

What matters to Proust, therefore, is not the objects one sees, but the way in which one sees (and "transfigures") the outside world: Proust is a novelist-phenomenologist or a novelist-Impressionist. The passage from Balzac to Proust would seem to be a movement from outside to inside, from a naïve confidence in the writer's ability to represent reality by analyzing it into its socially given constituent parts, to a radical subjectivism and temporal relativism: just as society changes under the pressures of the Dreyfus Affair or the Great War, similarly, Charlus and Albertine metamorphose through time in such a way as to be never "the same essence," never completely *knowable*.

However persuasive these analogies (of the *Recherche* to phenomenology or Impressionism) may seem at first glance, there is one major problem with assimilating a fiction to other forms of representation: namely, the matter, so difficult to define yet so easy for all readers to intuit, of *tone*. And tone is by no means based on what Maurois calls "indifference to content." The Proust-Renoir comparison works best in the earlier parts of the novel, especially *A l'ombre des jeunes filles en fleur,* in which an impressionist esthetic prevails, coupled with the happy luminosity characteristic of its school. But what do we do with the more somber "colors" that emanate from the scenes in which Charlus and Albertine play a major role? Yes, Charlus and Albertine are "deformed" and "transfigured" in the eyes of the narrator, but not always in the same way or according to the same mood. The dramatic progression of the novel is from spectral luminosity to a certain drab *grayness,*[5] and it is this grayness and especially its connotative richness that is hardly ever discussed by Proust critics. The latter sections of *Sodome et Gomorrhe* and the entirety of *La Prisonnière* and *La Fugitive* may in some ways incorporate aspects of Impressionism or phenomenology, but these purely formal aspects in no way help us to understand the *meaning* of Proust's text at its most enigmatic.

The same kind of interpretive problem raised by Maurois emerges in no less a critic than Edmund Wilson, whose *Axel's Castle*[6] was at one time the acknowledged Bible of Modernism. Wilson prefers the designation Symbolist to Impressionist or Phenomenologist, and he has no trouble seeing Proust as "the first important novelist to apply the principles of Symbolism to fiction" (*Axel's Castle,* p. 132), but he accuses Proust of being inconsistent in his adherence to Symbolist theory. In short, Wilson finds that Proust was unable to decide between Balzacian *mimesis* and the Symbolist esthetic: "Proust's novel as a whole, superb as are the qualities of objective dramatic imagination which have gone into it, was never quite disengaged from his sick-room. 'That work which I was bearing inside me,' he calls it in *Le Temps retrouvé*—he never entirely got it out. Is he telling us his own case-history with symbols? Is he presenting the world as he believes it to be? He is never perhaps quite sure himself" (p. 185). What disturbs Wilson most in Proust is not merely esthetic indecision, however; he is bothered by the novel's "gloom" (p. 164) and by the strangeness of the Albertine episode:

> This episode with Albertine, upon which Proust put so much labor and which he intended for the climax of his book, has not been one of the most popular sections, and it is certainly one of the most trying to read. Albertine is seen in so many varying moods, made the subject of so many ideas dissociated into so many different images, and her lover describes at such unconscionable length the writhings of his own sensibility, that we sometimes feel ourselves going under in the gray horizonless ocean of analysis and lose sight of the basic situation, of Proust's unwavering objective grasp of the characters of both the lovers which make the catastrophe

> inevitable. Furthermore, the episode of Albertine does not supply us with any of the things which we ordinarily expect from love affairs in novels: it is without tenderness, glamour or romance—the relation between Albertine and her lover seems to involve neither idealism nor enjoyment. (153)

I would now like to examine briefly one of the novel's major transitions, the point at which we turn from the sociability of Balbec to the anerobic void of the prison-room in which Marcel will keep Albertine. My purpose will be to suggest that the passage *inside,* toward radical subjectivism, involves the development of an anti-mimetic narrative modality, and that there is nothing "indecisive" or haphazard in this highly conscious strategic shift of perspective.

Sodome et Gomorrhe (II, 1126-31)

The final pages of *Sodome et Gomorrhe* describe Marcel's decision to "marry" Albertine. The episode as a whole is under the aegis of agony and despair, since the protagonist makes his decision immediately after learning of Albertine's lesbian relationships. As Wilson suggests, there is no "enjoyment" in Proustian love: this is because, for Proust, to love is to desire an impossible possession, impossible because Marcel can never fully penetrate the mysteries of homosexual *otherness*. Furthermore, as the narrator says in the penultimate paragraph of *Sodome,* the loving subject and the beloved object can never merge completely, since the object is really the idolized *projection* of subjective desire:

> Au reste, les maîtresses que j'ai le plus aimées n'ont coïncidé jamais avec mon amour pour elles... elles avaient plutôt la propriété d'éveiller cet amour, de le porter à son paroxisme, qu'elles n'en étaient l'image... On aurait dit qu'une vertu n'ayant aucun rapport avec elles leur avait été accessoirement adjointe par la nature, et que *cette vertu, ce pouvoir simili-électrique avait pour effet sur moi d'exciter mon amour,* c'est-à-dire de diriger toutes mes actions et de causer toutes mes souffrances... J'incline même à croire que dans ces amours..., sous l'apparence de la femme, c'est à ces forces invisibles dont elle est accessoirement accompagnée que nous nous adressons comme à d'obscures divinités. (my emphasis; II, 1126-27)

Albertine is, for Marcel, an object of *taboo*. She is both loved and hated, sacred and forbidden. She is surrounded by a magical aura and possesses the formidable powers that Freud attributes to all taboo objects:

> The source of taboo is attributed to a peculiar magical power which is inherent in persons and spirits and can be conveyed by them through the medium of inanimate objects. *Persons or things which are regarded as taboo may be compared to objects charged with electricity;* they are the seat of a tremendous power which is

transmissible by contact, and may be liberated with destructive
effect if the organisms which provoke its discharge are too weak to
resist it (my emphasis).[7]

The "electric charge" transmitted from Albertine to Marcel is the revelation of her Lesbianism, which causes the protagonist to see the world in a different light. For our purposes here, Marcel's change of perspective on reality corresponds to a change in narrative modality: we pass beyond the depiction of the real toward a dream-like, hallucinatory, hypothetical construct. Proust emphasizes this passage in two descriptive sections in *Sodome et Gomorrhe* which I would now like to analyze:

I (II, 1128)

Je n'avais jamais vu commencer une matinée si belle ni si douloureuse. En pensant à tous les paysages indifférents qui allaient s'illuminer et qui, la veille encore, ne m'eussent rempli que du désir de les visiter, je ne pus retenir un sanglot quand, dans un geste d'offertoire mécaniquement accompli et qui me parut symboliser le sanglant sacrifice que j'allais avoir à faire de toute joie, chaque matin, jusqu'à la fin de ma vie, renouvellement solennellement célébré à chaque aurore de mon chagrin quotidien et du sang de ma plaie, l'oeuf d'or du soleil, comme propulsé par la rupture d'équilibre qu'amènerait au moment de la coagulation un changement de densité, barbelé de flammes comme dans les tableaux, creva d'un bond le rideau derrière lequel on le sentait depuis un moment frémissant et prêt à entrer en scène et à s'élancer, et dont il effaça sous des flots de lumière la pourpre mystérieuse et figée.

The peculiar power of this evocation resides in the relation of the self to nature or reality. It is evident that Marcel is projecting his own feeling onto the scene, and in this sense, the passage is an example of what John Ruskin called the "pathetic fallacy." The mechanical movement of the "golden egg of the sun" that bursts forth from behind a curtain contrasts with the gradual, sequentially even emergence of the sun in nature. The scene is doubtlessly stylized: it is like a reproduction of medieval paintings that depict the crucifixion with the sun in the background, "barbed with tongues of flame," and it is theatrical, in that the lifting of the curtain reveals the protagonist's own "passion." The religious vocabulary ("offertoire," "sacrifice," "sang de ma plaie") merges with the drama of the self in such a way as to make of the protagonist the Lamb of God who has assumed the guilt of the world. But underneath the coherent sacramental/sacrificial symbolism is a more hidden level of allusiveness that reintroduces into the passage the logic of natural processes. The words "sanglant sacrifice," "renouvellement solennellement célébré," "sang de ma plaie," and especially "l'oeuf d'or du soleil...propulsé par la rupture d'équilibre qu'amènerait au moment de la *coagulation* un changement de densité" contain an unconscious reference to menstruation. In swallowing or interiorizing Albertine, in transgressing the prohibition that keeps her, *as* taboo object, separate from him, Marcel has become a woman [in Freud's terms, he has "acquired the characteristic of being prohibited—as though the whole of the dangerous charge had been transferred over to him"—*Totem and Taboo,* p. 22] and is condemned to the "curse" of renewable, repetitious bleeding.

In the final moments of the episode, the force of the hallucination and illusion replaces the visible evidence of natural phenomena. When, after Marcel has begun to cry in desperation, his mother enters the room to comfort him, she appears not as herself but as the ghostly apparition of the grandmother. In becoming the grandmother, she assumes the latter's physical and moral traits—her kindness, her permissive attitude toward the weakness of the protagonist, and, most importantly, her love for physical exercise and participatory immersion in the beautiful spectacle of concrete reality. For the mother now, as was the case for the grandmother in the early pages of "Cambray," the rising of the sun is a natural event that one should contemplate with an almost prayerful admiration. To observe the unfolding of such a spectacle is to become integrated into the cosmic order of things. Marcel, on the other hand, cannot perceive the reality of the sunrise as such. Instead, he sees "derrière la plage de Balbec, la mer, le lever du soleil, que maman me montrait...la chambre de Montjouvain où Albertine, rose, pelotonnée comme une grosse chatte, le nez mutin, avait pris la place de l'amie de Mlle Vinteuil et disait avec des éclats de son rire voluptueux: 'Hé bien! si on nous voit, ce n'en sera que meilleur. Moi! je n'oserais pas cracher sur ce vieux singe [M. Vinteuil]?' C'est cette scène que je voyais derrière celle qui s'étendait dans la fenêtre et qui n'était sur l'autre qu'un voile morne, superposé comme un reflet" (II, 1129). In this passage and in the description that follows, Proust's text is a perfect illustration of what Freud calls the "omnipotence of thoughts," where the "reflection of the internal world is bound to blot out the other picture of the world—the world which *we* [i.e., the "normal" person and the psychoanalyst] seem to perceive" (*Totem and Taboo,* p. 85):

II (II, 1130)

Dans le désordre des brouillards de la nuit qui traînaient encore en loques roses et bleues sur les eaux encombrées des débris de nacre de l'aurore, des bateaux passaient en souriant à la lumière de leur beaupré comme quand ils rentrent le soir; scène imaginaire, grelottante et déserte, pure évocation du couchant, qui ne reposait pas, comme le soir, sur la suite des heures du jour que j'avais l'habitude de voir le précéder, déliée, interpolée, plus inconsistante encore que l'image horrible de Montjouvain qu'elle ne parvenait pas à annuler, à couvrir, à cacher—poétique et vaine image du souvenir et du songe.

Proust's description adds an element of complexity to Freud's conception of the omnipotence of thoughts. It is true that what Marcel sees is a projection of his mind's conflicts and that this projection involves an *inversion* of natural reality: what appears to him is not the moment of transition between the end of night and the rising of the sun, but the opposite—a "pure evocation of the sunset" that is not linked in any way to the predictable movement of solar circularity. This completely artificial spectacle, associated by the protagonist with coldness and isolation, is said to be even more "inconsistent" than the image of Montjouvain that it is unable to hide or negate. In fact, there are not two but three levels of descriptive appearance here: the purely natural, which has been effectively eliminated by the projective power of Marcel's anguish; the artificial ("a scene imaginary, chilling and deserted"); and the moral (Montjouvain). In terms of literary representation, we are moving from realism (the domain of Balzac and Marcel's grandmother) to an abstract narration of moral conflict, an *allegory*[8] of the combat between virtue and vice—in other words, the "plot" of *La Prisonnière* and *La Fugitive*.

To read the novel's penultimate volumes—those long chapters that Wilson described as a plunge into the "gray horizonless ocean of analysis"—is to discover the way in which Proust progressively distanced himself from the natural world, or what Romantic esthetic theory called the "symbolic/organic" order of things. Proust was an allegorist of the first order, in that he, like Prudentius, conceived of eros as a mental struggle, a *psychomachia*. What is important to Marcel is not that Albertine "love" him in the usual sense of the word, but that she not escape his jealous investigations, that she remain always *knowable*. The message of the *Recherche* is, however, that Albertine is never entirely knowable, and that the tabooed object is not to be possessed. The impossibility of possession-taking is the infinitely repeatable narrative pattern of the novel, a hypothetical construct incompatible with the conventions of nineteenth-century realism. The Albertine episode has not been particularly popular with most readers, but this is because the radical impossibility of the happy merging of subject and object, lover and beloved, is too powerfully negative for most of us to accept or enjoy. Proust's modal shift from the logic of *mimesis* to that of allegory[9] is a challenge to the greatest of esthetic presuppositions: the idea that, beyond all obstacles, is some form of ultimate reconciliation, and end to suffering, a way out of anxiety. The esthetic revelations of *Le Temps retrouvé* are less a conquering of anxiety than a forgetfulness of its permanence. Perhaps the only way to put an end to allegory—its monotony and its negative truth—is to repress it.

* Professor Ellison presently teaches at the University of Miami.

[1] On the subject of the generic identity of the *Recherche* see Gérard Genette, *Figures III* (Paris: Seuil, 1972), pp. 225-267, and Philippe Lejeune, *Le Pacte autobiographique* (Paris: Seuil, 1975), pp. 19-35.

[2] See Derrida's analysis of Blanchot's *La Folie du jour*. "The Law of Genre," in *On Narrative*, ed. W.J.T. Mitchell (Chicago: The University of Chicago Press, 1981), pp. 51-77.

[3] Gérard Genette, "Proust et le langage indirect," *Figures II*, (Paris: Seuil, 1969), pp. 223-294. "Métonymie chez Proust," *Figures III*, pp. 41-63; "L'Age des Noms," *Mimologiques* (Paris: Seuil, 1976), pp. 315-328. Gilles Deleuze, *Proust et les signes* (Paris: PUF, 1979). Jean Ricardou, *Nouveaux Problèmes du roman* (Paris: Seuil, 1978), pp. 89-139. After *La Chambre claire: Note sur la photographie* (Paris: Cahiers du Cinéma, 1980) Barthes had begun a seminar on "Proust et la photographie" before he was killed crossing the street from the Collège de France.

[4] André Maurois, Preface to *A la recherche du temps perdu* (Paris: Pléiade, 1954), Vol. 1, vii-xix. All further references to the *Recherche* will be drawn from the Pléiade edition.

[5] See Marcel's analysis of Albertine's metamorphosis, expressed as the change from color to grayness, in the early pages of *La Prisonnlère:* "C'est parce que je l'[Albertine] avais vue comme un oiseau mystérieux, puis comme une grande actrice de la plage, désirée, obtenue peut-être, que je l'avais trouvée merveilleuse. Une fois captif chez moi l'oiseau que j'avais vu un soir marcher à pas comptés sur la digue, entourée de la congrégation des autres jeunes filles pareilles à des mouettes venues on ne sait d'où, Albertine avait perdu toutes ses couleurs...je pouvais très bien diviser son séjour chez moi en deux périodes: la première où elle était encore, quoique moins chaque jour, la chatoyante actrice de la plage; la seconde où, devenue grise prisonnière, réduite à son terne elle-même, il lui fallait ces éclairs où je me ressouvenais du passé pour lui rendre ses couleurs (III, 173).

[6] Edmund Wilson, *Axel's Castle: A Study in the Imaginative Literature of 1870-1930* (New York: Charles Scribner's Sons, 1969).

[7] Sigmund Freud, *Totum and Taboo*, trans. James Strachey (New York: W. W. Norton and Company, 1950), p. 20.

[8] My use of the term here is closest to that of Paul de Man in "Proust et l'Allégorie de la lecture," in *Mouvements premiers: études critiques offertes à Georges Poulet* (Paris: Corti, 1972), pp. 231-250. [translated into English and reprinted in *Allegories of Reading* (New Haven: Yale University Press, 1979), pp. 57-78]. For a more general (and semiologically less complex) treatment of the question of allegory in Proust, see J. Theodore Johnson, Jr., "Proust and Giotto: Foundations of an Allegorical Interpretation of *A la recherche du temps perdu*," in *Marcel Proust: A Critical Panorama* (Urbana, Ill. 1973).

[9] For further justification of the term *allegory* in the overall narrative configuration of the *Recherche*, see Hans-Robert Jauss, *Zeit und Erinnerung in Marcel Proust's 'A la Recherche du temps perdu': En Beitrag zur Theorie des Romans* (Heidelberg: 1955), and David R. Ellison, *The Reading of Proust*, fifth chapter (Baltimore: The Johns Hopkins University Press, 1984).

Mimesis et catégories universelles: les limites du réalisme objectif dans le récit

Michel Viegnes
Indiana University

Depuis la *République* de Platon et la *Poétique* d'Aristote, la notion de *mimesis* revient constamment dans le débat sur la littérature. Erich Auerbach, dans son étude classique, *Mimesis: la représentation de la réalité dans la littérature occidentale,* a essayé, au prix d'une synthèse colossale, de retracer le parcours et l'évolution des instances mimétiques dans le récit, d'Homère à Virginia Woolf. On se souvient qu'il établit une liste de cinq points pour donner un modèle narratif du réalisme moderne. Est réaliste, selon Auerbach, un texte:

1. sérieux
2. mêlant les registres stylistiques
3. n'excluant la représentation d'aucune classe sociale
4. recréant un maximum de cohésion logique, et enfin,
5. intégrant l'histoire dans l'*Histoire*.

Après lui, de nombreux théoriciens se sont efforcés de raffiner ce modèle pour cerner les outils narratifs qui permettent à l'auteur de transformer un texte en miroir de la réalité objective. Philippe Hamon, dans son article "Un Discours contraint," va jusqu'à énumérer une quinzaine de points en vue de définir la *mimesis* caractéristique des réalistes français du dix-neuvième siècle. En fait, dès que l'on impose au récit cette esthétique du miroir—comme le voulait Stendhal, et avant lui Saint-Réal—on se heurte de plein fouet à des problèmes soulevés dès l'origine de la pensée occidentale.

Mettons entre parenthèses la problématique interne de la notion de littérature, qui selon Todorov, ne possède que des définitions fonctionnelles, mais non structurales ("La Notion de littérature," in *Les Genres du discours*). Dans le cadre de cette courte étude, je compte seulement faire référence au problème quasi-incontournable de l'arbitraire du signe linguistique, tel que l'a défini Saussure. En fait, chacun sait que Platon avait déjà abordé cette question dans le *Cratyle,* où apparaît le grand mythe de la langue motivée, une langue où l'écart tragique entre les mots et les choses n'existerait pas, et qui serait donc une nomenclature parfaitement transparente de l'univers. Malheureusement, le rêve de

Cratyle n'est qu'une chimère, puisqu'il n'existe aucun rapport motivé entre le signe et son référent, sauf dans certains cas: au niveau de la simple unité linguistique, l'onomatopée est le seul signe vraiment "cratyléen"; au niveau de la phrase, Philippe Hamon cite comme cas unique de réalisme total la citation au style direct, où l'on voit du langage reproduit par du langage. En effet, le langage est le seul "objet" susceptible d'être reproduit tel quel par lui-même. Le problème est donc bien, comme le pose Philippe Hamon, de savoir comment il est possible de "reproduire une immédiateté non-sémiologique au moyen d'une médiation sémiologique" (in *Littérature et Réalité,* p. 124). La tâche apparaît impossible, le mot restant, dans toute son opacité sémantique, l'unité de base de la phrase. On se souvient néanmoins qu'Aristote, dans sa *Logique,* déplace le problème, en désignant la phrase, et non plus le mot, comme le *locus* de la *mimesis*; la phrase grammaticale, en effet, reproduit par sa structure même les relations logiques qui unissent entre eux les divers éléments du réel. Cette idée est d'ailleurs reprise, sous une forme différente, par Wittgenstein, dans son *Tractatus,* et elle est très intéressante par rapport à notre thème de réflexion.

Il est vrai, comme le démontre l'expérience courante, que la véritable *mimesis* ne saurait passer par l'unité linguistique de base, le mot n'étant pas, sauf exception, un signe *iconique* du réel, pour reprendre la terminologie de C.S. Peirce. En revanche, la phrase et le texte, se déployant dans le temps (de la lecture) et l'espace (du support matériel), peuvent beaucoup mieux se prêter à une réduplication de la réalité objective, telle qu'elle est perçue par les sens. Je voudrais ici étudier les limites de la représentation dans le texte, en considérant les cinq catégories ontologiques fondamentales: trois "catégories-contenu," le nombre, la forme et la matière, puis ces deux "catégories-contenant" que sont l'espace et le temps. En effet, il est manifeste que l'ensemble de la réalité objective nous apparaît comme une combinaison indéfiniment complexe de ces cinq conditions universelles. Précisons que ces catégories sont ontologiques, elles n'ont donc aucun rapport avec celles d'Aristote, qui, elles, sont liées à la cognition.

1. NOMBRE, FORME, MATIERE

A. NOMBRE. La réalité physique que nous percevons se présente à nous, le plus souvent, sous un aspect de multiplicité. Hormis certains points de référence qui se signalent par leur caractère isolé et unique, comme le soleil ou la lune, la quasi-totalité des objets de la perception sont pluriels. En marchant dans la rue, nous voyons *des* maisons, *des* voitures, *des* passants. Une promenade dans la campagne nous met en présence de fleurs, d'arbres, etc... Comment le texte écrit rend-il cette multiplicité des objets du monde? Première constatation: le nombre grammatical n'a aucun rapport motivé, ontologique, avec le nombre réel, puisque le signe linguistique, même affecté des marques du pluriel, n'en demeure pas moins unique. Que je dise *un* arbre ou *des* arbres, je n'utilise dans les deux cas qu'un seul substantif. Certaines tentatives expérimentales, notamment dans le cadre du Nouveau Roman, ont été effectuées pour circonvenir cette limitation inhérente à la syntaxe. Prenons par exemple ce passage de *Dans le labyrinthe,* de Robbe-Grillet (Paris: Editions de Minuit, 1959):

> L'enfant se met à reculer progressivement, à s'éloigner vers le fond de la scène...dépassant l'une après l'autre les fenêtres du rez-de-chaussée: quatre fenêtres identiques, suivies d'une porte à peine différente, puis quatre fenêtres encore, une porte, une fenêtre, une fenêtre, de plus en plus vite à mesure qu'il prend de la distance, devenant de plus en plus petit, de plus en plus incertain, de plus en plus brouillé dans le crépuscule, soudain happé vers l'horizon et disparaissant alors d'un seul coup, en un clin d'oeil, comme une pierre qui tombe. (pp. 107-108)

Ici, Robbe-Grillet, s'inspirant des techniques de l'écriture cinématographique, qu'il a explorées aussi minutieusement que celle de l'écriture narrative, transpose dans son texte le procédé du *traveling,* en nous montrant son personnage se déplaçant régulièrement vers l'arrière-fond du champ de vision du protagoniste. Chaque porte et chaque fenêtre jalonnant la progression arrière de l'enfant se trouvent mentionnées l'une après l'autre, recréant ainsi, d'une façon saisissante et "hyperréaliste" la pluralité de ces éléments du décor. Malgré tout, il est clair que le texte écrit ne peut guère *reproduire* de façon motivée une pluralité d'objets coexistant au même moment dans l'espace. En revanche, le texte reproduit très bien la pluralité des apparitions successives d'un objet ou d'un être dans le temps. Pour paraphraser la première phrase de *L'Etre et le néant,* il s'avère que le texte d'un récit réduit l'être "à la série de ses apparitions" (p. 9). Vautrin, pour prendre un exemple célèbre, disparaît et reparaît dans le texte du *Père Goriot* exactement comme il le ferait dans la réalité, telle qu'elle pourrait être saisie subjectivement par Rastignac.

B. FORME. La forme physique des objets de la perception n'est généralement pas *mimée* dans l'espace du texte, sauf encore dans des cas expérimentaux rarissimes. La tentative d'Apollinaire dans ses *Calligrammes,* où le poème épouse la forme de la colombe, du jet d'eau et de la pluie, semble réservée de préférence au domaine de la poésie, comme on le voit dans la tradition de la poésie concrète. La raison en est sans doute que le poème lyrique, non épique, est par nature plutôt statique; c'est un instant du monde, saisi comme un instantané dans sa fragilité suggestive. Le texte narratif, au contraire, épouse le dynamisme de la durée. Il y aurait donc une multiplicité de formes à reproduire, si l'on voulait tenter une représentation iconique des formes dans la diégèse. En théorie, pourtant, rien ne s'opposerait à ce que le texte imite visuellement la forme de tel ou tel objet central dans l'univers du récit. L'expérience a été tentée par Claude Ollier dans *Fuzzy Sets,* où le texte, dont la mise en page constitue un tour de force typographique, épouse la forme du satellite triangulaire ou reproduit visuellement, par un vide en forme de trou de serrure, le regard du narrateur considérant l'intérieur d'une chambre.

En fait, si le texte narratif reproduit des *formes*, ce ne sont pas généralement des formes physiques, mais des "formes" au sens de structures de perception, telles que Merleau-Ponty les analyse dans sa *Phénoménologie de la perception*. La division en chapitres et paragraphes, qui sont des *formes* textuelles, traduit la structuration opérée par la pensée sur le donné brut de l'information narrative. A moins que cette structuration elle-même ne soit dénoncée comme fallacieuse: depuis Joyce, de nombreux auteurs évitent délibérément de circonscrire le courant de conscience dans un cadre rigide de divisions textuelles. Aussi voit-on dans le Nouveau Roman des textes comme *Histoire,* de Claude Simon, qui ne sont plus, à la limite, qu'une longue phrase unique, donc une négation de toute forme textuelle.

C. MATIERE. Par rapport à d'autres modes de représentation, comme les arts plastiques, la littérature est particulièrement pauvre sous le rapport de son *medium*. Alors que la statue figurative est un composé matière-forme, au même titre que son référent, et que même la peinture, au moyen des grattages et des empâtements, peut posséder un certain relief et imiter la consistance brute de tel ou tel objet, le texte, quant à lui, ne possède guère de matérialité en dehors de son support. L'expression dérisoire de "pattes de mouches" pour désigner l'aspect des lettres sur le papier, traduit bien le sentiment d'évanescence et d'immatérialité que l'on éprouve devant l'écriture comme medium de la représentation. Certains auteurs, dans la mouvance du Nouveau Roman, ont voulu, sinon résoudre, du moins soulever le problème de cette immatérialité propre au texte écrit, et la pauvreté de moyens mimétiques qu'elle implique: ainsi, par exemple, de Michel Butor, dans *La Modification*. Au cours du voyage en train qui le mène de Paris, où réside sa femme qu'il a décidé de quitter, vers Rome, où vit la femme qu'il aime et qu'il espère rejoindre, Léon Delmont revit en esprit, d'une manière plus ou moins discontinue, les étapes de la double vie qu'il mène depuis plusieurs années. Il en vient à se remémorer une visite du Louvre, au cours de laquelle il n'a prêté que peu d'attention aux chefs-d'oeuvre les plus en vue, pour se laisser envoûter par deux tableaux assez médiocres:

> Ce que vous avez amoureusement détaillé...ce sont deux grands tableaux d'un peintre italien de troisième ordre, Panini,

> représentant deux collections imaginaires exposées dans de très hautes salles où des personnages de qualité, ecclésiastiques ou gentilshommes, se promènent parmi les sculptures entre les murs couverts de paysages, en faisant des gestes d'admiration, d'intérêt, de surprise, de perplexité, comme les visiteurs de la Chapelle Sixtine, avec ceci de remarquable qu'il n'y a aucune différence de matière sensible entre les objets présentés comme réels et ceux représentés comme peints, comme s'il avait voulu figurer sur ses toiles la réussite de ce projet commun à tant d'artistes de son temps: donner un équivalent absolu de la réalité. (p. 55)

Ce court passage, en fait, décrivant une peinture représentant de la peinture, peut être vu comme une *mise en abyme* de tout le texte, car il reflète le projet de l'auteur lui-même. En effet, à la fin de ce "roman," si l'on peut accepter ce terme, Butor nous présente son personnage arrivé en gare de Rome, ayant modifié peu à peu son projet initial au point d'y renoncer: il ne verra pas sa maîtresse, et retournera à Paris pour reprendre la vie commune avec sa femme. Il a décidé d'écrire un livre, où il relatera minutieusement les étapes de ce cheminement intérieur, de cette modification:

> Le mieux serait... de tenter de faire revivre sur le mode de la lecture cet épisode crucial de votre aventure, le mouvement qui s'est produit dans votre esprit accompagnant le déplacement de votre corps d'une gare à l'autre à travers tous les paysages intermédiaires, vers ce livre futur et nécessaire dont vous tenez la forme dans votre main.

Cet extrait, qui constitue l'avant-dernière phrase de *La Modification,* suggère clairement que dans le projet idéal de Butor son propre livre ne serait que la copie exacte et "l'équivalent absolu" du livre écrit par son personnage, abolissant ainsi toute différence de matière sensible, à l'instar du peintre. On se trouverait alors dans la seule situation possible de "réalisme total" relevée par Philippe Hamon, situation où nous aurions un texte reproduisant un autre texte.

2. ESPACE ET TEMPS

A. ESPACE. L'écriture, en ce qui concerne l'espace et le temps, est loin d'être aussi pauvre en capacités mimétiques. En premier lieu, comme les arts plastiques, le texte possède son propre espace, dans lequel il se déploie. Certes, comme le rappelle Jean Rousset, "l'espace pictural [ou sculptural] n'est pas l'espace du livre" ("Les Réalités formelles de l'oeuvre," in *Chemins actuels de la critique,* p.107). D'une part, on a l'espace extérieur, cette étendue du monde physique que Kant définissait comme une condition *a priori*, c'est-à-dire indubitable, de la perception externe; même si au vingtième siècle les conceptions d'Euclide et de Kant ont été remises en question, l'espace vécu, existentiel, demeure pour nous tous une expérience intime et immédiate. Comment le texte narratif recrée-t-il cette étendue? L'espace proprement textuel, en effet, est d'une nature tout autre: c'est d'abord un espace à deux dimensions seulement; dans les langues indo-européennes, il est orienté horizontalement selon l'axe de la phrase, et verticalement selon la succession des lignes et des paragraphes. Il existe pourtant une certaine correspondance entre l'espace référentiel et l'espace du texte, dans la mesure où deux objets du monde, séparés par une certaine distance, apparaîtront aussi séparés dans le texte par l'intervalle des mots.

Reportons-nous à la plus classique des topographies, celle de la pension Vauquer au début du *Père Goriot:*

> Le rez-de-chaussé se compose [d'une première pièce] éclairée par les [croisées de la rue], et où l'on entre par une [fenêtre]. Ce salon communique à [une salle à manger] qui est séparée [de la cuisine] par [la cage d'un escalier] dont les [marches] sont en bois et les carraux en couleurs et frottés.

Dans cette description topographique de la pension, nous voyons une certaine analogie proportionnelle entre l'espace textuel et l'espace référentiel, puisque les intervalles très courts qui séparent *dans le texte* les divers substantifs de lieu reflètent les distances également courtes qui sépareraient ces objets dans l'espace physique de la maison. La structure même et le rythme de la phrase topologique peuvent d'ailleurs accentuer cette faculté que possède le texte de mimer l'espace. Prenons comme exemple l'incipit de *Soeur Philomène* des frères Goncourt, qui décrit l'intérieur de la salle d'hôpital:

> La salle est haute et vaste. Elle est longue, et se prolonge dans une ombre où elle s'enfonce sans finir.

Dans ces deux phrases, la quantité spatiale est plus que représentée; elle se trouve *mimée* par une répétition sonore: les quatre [õ] qui ponctuent la seconde phrase à intervalle régulier matérialisent pour ainsi dire l'étendue obscure de la salle d'hôpital, que l'oeil perçoit comme un enfoncement régulier et monotone dans les ténèbres. Autre correspondance directe, et quasiment iconique, entre l'espace longitudinal de la salle et l'espace de la phrase, toute la partie postérieure à "longue" est clairement perçue dans une lecture à haute voix ou même simplement mentale, comme une suite parfaitement symétrique de deux octosyllabes blancs, ce qui dénote encore la régularité géométrique de la salle, dont on ne distingue pas la fin dans la pénombre. On a donc, très curieusement, une structure sonore et rythmique utilisée comme reflet iconique de l'espace référentiel.

Cependant, de tels procédés sont très limités; de toute évidence l'espace physique, tridimensionnel, est beaucoup trop complexe pour pouvoir être reflété dans celui du texte. Contrairement à l'exemple tiré de Balzac cité plus haut, il apparaît dans la plupart des cas que l'écart entre les intervalles textuels et les distances physiques joue selon une extrême mobilité, comme on peut le voir dans cette description polytopique:

> Tout près de sa cabane se trouvait le bureau colonial; au-delà, passées les limites de la ville, s'étendait la brousse; plus au nord, la mer; et de l'autre côté de la mer, ce pays étrange et barbare, la France.

Pour un intervalle textuel à peu près identique, le texte distribue des lieux référentiels séparés par des distances fabuleusement inégales. On ne peut même pas, pour cette topographie, invoquer le parallélisme avec les lois de la perspective en peinture, puisque la mer et les côtes françaises, selon toute vraisemblance, se situeraient très au-delà du champ visuel de l'observateur. Le texte suit non pas un regard physique, mais un regard mental, qui se joue des distances, et envisage le monde dans une sorte de simultanéité spatiale, que la peinture elle-même ne saurait reproduire, à moins de briser l'homogénéité du tableau.

B. TEMPS. Des cinq conditions d'existence énumérées dans ces pages, le temps est sans aucun doute celle qui a été analysée le plus en profondeur par les théoriciens du récit. On peut penser à Harold Weinrich, auteur d'une étude capitale sur *Le Temps,* à Georges Poulet, avec ses monumentales *Etudes sur le temps humain,* et surtout à Gérard Genette, qui a consacré de nombreuses pages au temps diégétique dans *Discours du récit (Figures III).* Mais la plupart des théoriciens ont étudié la représentation et le sentiment du temps *dans* le récit, et non pas le temps *du* récit lui-même, qui se confond en fait avec le temps de lecture. Seuls Genette et l'Allemend Günther Müller ont examiné les rapports entre la durée représentée (le temps référentiel) et la durée de représentation (temps nécessaire à la lecture, ou à la réception, sous n'importe quel mode, du récit lui-même). Les deux auteurs utilisent les termes suivants pour distinguer les deux durées:

Durée représentée	**Durée de représentation**
Müller: *Erzahlte Zeit*	*Erzahlzeit*
Genette: Temps de l'histoire (TH)	Temps du récit (TR)

Pour plus de commodité, je reprends ici la terminologie de Genette. Ce dernier regroupe en quatre cas de figure principaux les rapports qui peuvent s'établir entre TR et TH:

1. Pause: TR=variable TH=0
2. Scène: TR=TH
3. Sommaire: TR<TH
4. Ellipse: TR=0 TH=variable

Eliminons le cas 1, au profit des seuls cas où nous avons une diégèse effective: le cas des digressions personnelles du narrateur ou des descriptions atmosphérielles ne nous retiendra pas ici. Il apparaît d'abord que l'on pourrait envisager une autre possibilité, le cas où le temps du récit est supérieur au temps de l'histoire (TR>TH), ce qui nous donnerait, pour le récit, l'équivalent du *ralenti* cinématographique. En fait, le rapport proportionnel entre TR et TH joue selon une trop grande mobilité pour être aisément systématisé. Le cas 2, de la scène, où TR=TH, est extrêmement rare. Seuls des passages particulièrement *dramatiques* au sens propre du terme peuvent en offrir des exemples, telle la scène du suicide de Boris à la fin des *Faux-Monnayeurs*, où Gide s'est efforcé de coller le plus près possible à la durée référentielle:

> Le coup partit. Boris ne s'affaissa pas aussitôt. Un instant le corps se maintint, comme accroché dans l'encoignure; puis la tête, retombée sur les épaules, l'emporta, et tout s'effondra.

Le cas où TR>TH, cette forme de ralenti diégétique, encore plus rare, se trouve par exemple dans le dernier chapitre du *Chaos et la nuit*, de Montherlant, où nous voyons le protagoniste tué de quatre coups de poignard, scène qui, dans la réalité, ne prendrait pas la dixième partie du temps qu'il faut pour la lire dans le récit: le temps se trouve alors dilaté dans la conscience de l'homme à l'agonie, qui fait en quelques secondes un retour sur toute son existence passée.

En somme, le temps est une dimension trop complexe pour pouvoir être réduite à une donnée quantifiable et constante; en effet, le temps diégétique confond deux dimensions distinctes du temps, qui n'ont que peu de rapports: d'une part le temps dit "objectif" qui est celui des horloges et du comput astronomique, et d'autre part le *Geistzeit*, cette durée subjective qui est le flux même de la conscience. Pour compliquer encore davantage le problème, le temps de lecture lui-même ne saurait être considéré comme totalement invariable: l'expérience courante suffit à nous montrer que deux personnes ne lisent pas le même texte à la même vitesse; de même, un lecteur unique n'aura pas forcément, devant deux textes différents, la même vitesse de lecture.

En effet le temps diégétique, même s'il ne possède pas la complexité du temps référentiel, est néanmoins élastique et réversible. Elastique: contrairement aux images cinématographiques, qui imposent au récepteur une vitesse constante de projection, une scène lue peut défiler dans l'esprit du récepteur à une vitesse variable. Réversible: contrairement au cinéma ou au théâtre, le récepteur d'un texte écrit possède une très grande liberté par rapport au medium de représentation; il peut à son gré relire, revenir en arrière, sauter des pages, lire en diagonale. C'est de lui, lecteur, que dépend la durée de représentation, plus que de l'auteur.

Ceci nous amène à considérer le paradoxe suivant: le temps diégétique, ou *Erzahlzeit* dans la terminologie de Müller, n'est rien d'autre, en dernière analyse, que la vitesse de lecture, et celle-ci est basée sur le déplacement du regard du lecteur dans l'espace textuel. Or l'oeil parcourt l'étendue des signes de l'écriture plus ou moins vite, selon:

1. l'intérêt du texte (rapport affectif), et
2. la richesse et la complexité de l'information narrative (rapport intellectuel).

Il est ironique de penser qu'une grande vitesse de lecture peut avoir deux causes opposées: intérêt passionné ou désintérêt total, qui amène à parcourir le texte en diagonale, d'un oeil distrait. Quant à la richesse de l'information textuelle, il est évident que nous lisons plus rapidement un article de *Paris-Match* qu'un passage de Proust. Finalement, quelle que soit la relation affective et intellectuelle entre texte et lecteur, il apparaît que le temps et l'espace textuels tendent à se confondre entièrement. Raccourcir la durée du récit, c'est parcourir plus vite son étendue, et inversement, figer le temps du récit consiste à s'arrêter en un point de son espace. De tous les mediums de la représentation (couleurs, formes, matériaux solides, sons), l'écriture est le seul dont l'espace et le temps propres constituent un seul et unique *continuum*. Dans le texte, le temps *est* de l'espace et vice-versa.

Ces considérations sur les cinq conditions de l'existence physique et leurs doubles dans l'univers parallèle du texte nous permettent de mieux mesurer les limites du réalisme objectif en littérature. Privée de signifiants iconiques, la littérature est l'un des moins mimétiques de tous les modes de représentation. Le monde physique ne se trouve pas reflété au niveau des signifiants eux-mêmes, comme dans les arts plastiques, ou même dans certains cas la musique, mais seulement au niveau plus profond des signifiés. En définitive, ce réalisme subjectif, non objectif, est peut-être la grande force du texte, puisque, comme y insiste le narrateur de la *Recherche* dans *Le Temps retrouvé,* une littérature qui limiterait son domaine à la seule surface de la réalité n'aurait aucune raison d'être, le réel, à proprement parler, se situant au-delà de l'univers physique et de ses conditions d'existence.

*Professor Viegnes currently teaches at Bryn Mawr College

Ouvrages Cités

Auerbach, Erich. *Mimesis: The Representation of Reality in Western Literature.* Traduction Willard Trask, New York: Doubleday Anchor Books, 1957.

Genette, Gérard. *Figures III*. Paris: Seuil, 1972.
Hamon, Philippe. "Un Discours contraint," in *Littérature et Réalité*, textes recueillis et présentés par G. Genette et T. Todorov. Paris: Seuil, 1970.
Merleau-Ponty, Maurice. *Phénoménologie de la perception*. Paris: Gallimard, 1945.
Müller, Günther. "Erzahlzeit und Erzahlte Zeit," in *Feschrift für Paul Kluckholn und Hermann Schneider*. Thubingen: J.B.C. Mohr, pp. 195-212.
Rousset, Jean. "Les Réalités formelles de l'oeuvre," in *Les Chemins actuels de la critique*, colloque présidé par Georges Poulet. Paris: Plon, 1970.
Todorov, Tzvétan. *Les Genres du discours*. Paris: Seuil, 1974.
Sartre, Jean-Paul. *L'Etre et le néant*. Paris: Gallimard, 1943.
Saussure, Ferdinand de. *Cours de linguistique générale*. Paris: Payot, 1916.
Weinrich, Harald. *Le Temps*. Paris: Seuil, 1973.
Wittgenstein, Ludwig. *Tractatus Logico-Philosophicus*. Texte allemand avec traduction anglaise de D.F. Pears et B.F. McGuiness: Londres, 1966.

Signifier l'amour: une lecture de Sade

Ralph Heyndels
Université Libre de Bruxelles*

> Il en résulte (chez Sade) que tout ce qui est dit est clair, mais semble à la merci de quelque chose qui n'a pas été dit, qu'un peu plus tard ce qui ne s'est laissé dire se montre et est resaisi par la logique, mais à son tour obéit au mouvement d'une force encore cachée et qu'à la fin, tout est mis au jour, tout arrive à l'expression, mais que tout est aussi replongé dans l'obscurité des pensées irréfléchies et des moments non formulables.
>
> M. Blanchot, *Lautréamont et Sade*

A l'ouverture de *La philosophie dans le boudoir* (1795), Madame de Saint-Ange demande au chevalier de Mirvel, son frère, de lui tracer le portrait de ce libertin d'élite dont il lui a promis la très active présence pour l'instruction particulière que va subir l'exquise et naïve Eugénie:

> Peins-moi ton Dolmancé, je t'en conjure, afin que je l'aie bien dans la tête avant de le voir arriver; car tu sais que je ne le connais que pour l'avoir rencontré l'autre jour dans une maison où je ne fus que quelques minutes avec lui. (40)[1]

On a dit de la description à laquelle se livre alors le chevalier qu'elle désignait peut-être l'auteur lui-même, tel qu'il aurait été (ou aurait voulu être) aux environs de ses trente-six ans.[2] On a souligné aussi le caractère tout à fait conventionnel du patron discursif utilisé, comme représentant d'ailleurs un aspect dominant de la rhétorique de Sade, "incapable"[3] d'atteindre à un véritable effet d'illusion référentielle lorsqu'il s'agit de *représenter* un personnage. Si l'on veut bien considérer d'un seul tenant l'assertion biographique et le "jugement littéraire" (dont le bien fondé douteux ne nous importe pas *hic et nunc*), on peut suggérer l'hypothèse herméneutique suivante—nous tenterons, par la suite, de mesurer son opérativité pour une approche de la "signification" du texte sadien—: pas plus qu'il ne parvient (ou qu'il ne vise) à "donner vie" aux êtres qui peuplent son univers imaginaire, pas plus qu'il ne réussit (ou ne s'efforce) à nous les *donner à voir*, Sade ne les voit "réellement"[4] et, sans doute, ne se voit lui-même.[5] Une défaillance originelle affecterait donc son *schéma corporel*, la connaissance réflexive de son propre corps représenté et l'*éprouvé vital* de celui-ci dans son rapport avec l'espace et l'environnement.⁶ La structuration incomplète d'un tel schéma signale et signifie une fixation infantile phantasmatique et perturbe l'ensemble des relations affectives. Si l'on accepte "l'observation de maints psychanalystes sur la corrélation existant entre l'image du corps, la sexualité et les problèmes d'identité (...)"⁷ cette *insuffisance* empêche notamment le passage du *corps vécu* au *corps perçu* et au *moi imagé*.⁸

Il plaît, à cet égard, à notre propos (qui est peut-être une fable: mais cela, c'est une autre histoire), de rappeler que nous ne disposons, comme par un hasard signifiant, d'aucune figuration de Sade, qui reste pour nous un de ces écrivains sans visage. De toute manière, l'image demeure ici abstraite; *elle ne parle pas*—et nous aurons l'occasion de revenir sur ce *déficit* du langage; elle se contente de renvoyer à une stéréotypie précodée: elle se fige en *topos*. Pourtant, les quelques lignes consacrées à Dolmancé paraissent, relativement, un tout petit plus originales (ou un peu moins vite expédiées) que ce qu'on rencontre généralement chez Sade. Il suffit, pour s'en tenir à l'ouvrage référé, de les comparer au degré zéro de la représentation qui affecte Eugénie—dont nous saurons seulement qu'il n'y a rien "d'aussi délicieux au monde" (47).

> (...) il est grand, d'une fort belle figure, des yeux très vifs et très spirituels, mais quelque chose d'un peu dur et d'un peu méchant se peint malgré lui dans ses traits; il a les plus belles dents du monde, un peu de mollesse dans la taille et dans la tournure, par l'habitude, sans doute, qu'il a de prendre si souvent des airs féminins; il est d'une rare élégance, une jolie voix, des talents, et, principalement beaucoup de philosophie dans l'esprit. (41)

Certes, comme d'habitude, ce pourrait être à peu près n'importe qui. Mais, du point de vue général de la poétique descriptive de Sade, on se trouve ici devant une espèce de *formulation intermédiaire* entre le "portrait typologique" qui désigne (souvent par une certaine forme, ici absente, de laideur) les libertins et le "portrait rhétorique" qui caractérise les victimes.⁹ Une impression, en effet, semble se dégager, serait-elle très incomplète; une perception devrait pouvoir opérer, même ténue—ce qui est particulièrement rare dans une oeuvre où "l'on n'en finirait plus de compter le retour des mêmes mots, banals et usés par la répétition," fixés dans "le registre (...) du spectacle de l'enchantement" maléfique.¹⁰ Ce bref passage présente en fait un statut contradictoire: placé sous l'obédience du *convenu*, il acquiert une pertinence relative. Il semble que l'image s'efforce de s'arracher, au moins l'espace d'un bref sursis, à sa condition inéluctable, à cette espèce de destin qui la marque du sceau de l'abstraction. C'est en appréhendant cette abstraction non comme une nécessité fatale (dont le "bénéfice secondaire" d'ordre esthétique fut sans doute une certaine affirmation de *singularité*) mais comme un choix d'écriture que l'on passe peut-être à côté de la spécificité du travail textuel sadien. Notre intervention, autant, contrairement au projet de Bataille,[11] elle entend "prendre Sade *à la lettre*, au sérieux" (sur le plan éthique et politique), voudrait se situer *entre le déni de valeur* (au nom d'une norme de la représentation) et la *valorisation de fait* (du point de vue des phantasmes modernistes de la "textualité"): là où s'effectue, en un procès éminement paradoxal, *une tentative de signifier qui signifie précisément par son incapacité même à signifier*. Dès lors, on retiendra de l'extrait cité qu'il essaie d'éveiller un intérêt, de provoquer une attente, de déclencher un besoin: celui de réaliser davantage une *teneur concrète*, de ressentir l'effet de substance d'un référé signifié. Voulant peut-être mettre en scène—Dolmancé, génie du mal accompli, médiatisant le philosophe dans le dialogue—Sade tenterait de se voir en se rendant visible, sensible, perceptible au regard de l'autre et à sa propre conscience (ce qui supposerait le remplacement, au demeurant *inadmissible* en "bonne théorie" sadienne, du *moi-ça* par le *moi-toi*).[12] Mais l'intérêt est vite éteint, l'attente déçue, le besoin incompris. Madame de Saint-Ange ne tient pas compte de ces détails physiques, et peu lui importe une apparence que d'ailleurs elle connaît *par avance*— puisqu'elle a déjà aperçu l'ami du chevalier, et qu'elle a pu en noter instantanément la taille, les principaux traits du visage, le maintien, le vêtement. En fait: la fiche signalétique, qui nous est ainsi tracée (on l'aura deviné) pour de strictes raisons fonctionnelles liées à l'enclenchement diégétique. C'est bien pourquoi ce qui la retient, l'excite et l'anime, ne concerne en rien le corps de Dolmancé.[13] Ce qui l'"échauffe," ce qui va la faire "raffoler de cet homme," c'est qu'il ne croit pas en Dieu, qu'il est "le plus immoral..., la corruption la plus complète et la plus entière, l'individu le plus méchant et le plus scélérat qui puisse exister au monde" (41), et que ses goûts sont pervers. Dolmancé l'excite donc *par principe*, non en tant que véritable entité charnelle. Le personnage se dissout de cette façon dans sa *valeur d'échange pour un usage*, dans l'immédiateté d'un *être pour un faire* (ce qui est bien le sens de l'effectuation perverse).[14]

Pour faire quoi? La réponse semble aller de soi: *pour faire jouir*. Et son écho s'entendra ici doublement, car la jouissance sera à la fois intellectuelle et organique, qui, sans trêve, tout au long des milliers de pages d'une textualité toujours recommencée, produit du discours et tente de se reproduire par le discours. Celui-ci n'est pas *restrictivement* référable à un pur "érotisme de tête"[15] et peut provoquer une espèce d'orgasme mental qui migre dans les voies les plus intimes du sexe:

> Ah cher amour, comme ces discours séducteurs enflamment ma tête et séduisent mon âme...Je suis dans un état difficile à peindre...,

s'écrie Eugénie à Mme de Saint-Ange lorsque celle-ci fait le panégyrique, systématique et magistral, de l'existence la plus débridée. Visant à cet effet—effectuer la jouissance dans et par les mots—, tout en maintenant son objectif didactique (on se souvient du sous-titre: "Les instituteurs immoraux"), la démarche scripturale de Sade se situe entre la redondance d'une continuité obsessionnelle et l'inévitabilité d'une irruption du discontinu[16] toujours conjurée: le totalisme n'épuise pas la somme des virtualités concevables, le désir ne s'apaise jamais, la jouissance conserve le goût de sa propre insuffisance. Il lui faut donc inlassablement boucher les trous d'un édifice sans cesse prêt à s'effondrer (celui de l'individualisme radical le plus forcené), réalimenter un plaisir condamné à sa perte, mettre de l'ordre dans une anarchie partout menaçante et jaillissant de la liberté souveraine *prétendument* accordée aux pulsions:

> Mettons, s'il vous plaît, un peu d'ordre à ces orgies, il en faut même au sein du délire et de l'infamie." (111)

Pour faire jouir vient donc Dolmancé. Mais il ne dispose pas d'une autre réalité que celle de la projection phantasmatique, elle-même dépendante, *in fine*, d'une pensée du mal sombrement fanatique et presque dérisoirement répétitive. La réitération trahit le manque, la peur que quelque chose n'échappe (au discours, à la mémoire, au désir), que quelque chose ne s'oublie. Ce manque, cette échappée, cet oubli porte ici trois noms qui se répondent (montrer comment et pourquoi nous ferait par trop sortir des limites imposées à cet exposé): le corps (plus spécifiquement: le *corps* de la femme), l'*amour* (plus spécifiquement: l'amour de la mère), le *langage* (plus spécifiquement: le langage de la jouissance).

Car ce théâtre pornographique du *comme si*—où l'on suppose à la fois la résistance des victimes, leur manipulation absolue et leur "coopération inconsciente,"[17]—ne met aux prises que des fantômes et/ou des "bagnards de la sexualité."[18] Et si le boudoir ici "symbolise le lieu d'union de la philosophie et de l'érotique,"[19] c'est un lieu où, dans et malgré une frénésie violente qui y augmente en *crescendo*, ne se mirent que des images insaisissables, où ne se croisent que des ombres, où ne s'investissent l'un dans l'autre que des corps absents, où ne s'échangent que des signes vides. Or à lire (ou à relire) Sade dans une herméneutique du soupçon, à l'écoute d'un aveu implicite et dans la direction d'une vacuité qui se pare de tous ornements de la plénitude, un malaise nous saisit, un vertige nous aspire. Et, quelque part, une détresse inconsolable nous étreint, une *angoisse impensable*,[20] dont il faudra bien sonder le message. Celle-ci résulte notamment de l'*abstraction* même du "paradis infernal" sadien, espace onirique de compensation pour qui n'a pas renoncé à la fusion originelle ni réussi à la surmonter dans le symbolique, qui n'a pas accepté d'être "incomplet, clivé, habité par le négatif," qui refuse d'admettre "que le paradis est perdu, en somme, qu'il nous hante comme nostalgie, comme regret, comme désespoir."[21]

L'amour est ici mis au banc des accusés (172 sv). Mais c'est par peur d'une *folie d'aimer* contre laquelle le divin marquis fait appel à une très cartésienne maîtrise de soi. Mais c'est par déception d'un abandon fondamental (réactivé sans doute par la relation manquée avec Mlle de Lauris). Mais c'est par négation dogmatique d'une atttraction dangereuse pour une intégrité ressentie dans toute sa fragilité. Sade fut amoureux, avec passion, avec excès. De cet événement de sa vie nous ne voulons retenir, par delà les considérations strictement biographiques, que le signe: celui d'un amour très "fatidiquement" *échoué* sur les rivages incontournables de l'échec. Là s'inscrit cependant ce qui aurait pu être et ne sera pas ("un bonheur durable [...] que rien ne pourra troubler"): la *reconnaissance,* la *réappropriation*, l'*adoption* de soi dans la relation à l'autre ("Quel objet suis-je à tes yeux? D'horreur? d'amour? dis? *Comment me vois-tu?*"); le renoncement en vain conjuré et le risque de mort à soi-même comme condition de vie[22] ("Je te perds, je perds mon existence, ma vie, je meurs..."; "ne m'abandonne pas, je t'en supplie"); la nostalgie de la mère ("J'ai besoin d'être consolé, d'être rassuré, de recevoir des preuves de ta constance....") L'amour est donc ici rejeté, et pourtant c'est bien le sentiment *opaque* qui parfois réunit nos protagonistes, lorsqu'ils se donnent mutuellement du plaisir et s'embrassent avec ravissement. La jouissance est ici survalorisée. Mais elle demeure toujours *en attente.* Mais elle ne s'émancipe jamais de la *ratio*, et il convient d'en user "avec sagesse" (172). Mais elle *n'a rien à voir* avec ce dont le besoin fait frémir chaque espérance. Mais elle est, de toute façon, une "sensation impossible à peindre" (63), et ne se prononce que dans la lacune du langage:

> ...la crainte d'être monotone nous empêche de rendre des expressions qui, dans de tels instants, se ressemblent toutes. (155)

Or notre auteur, faut-il le rappeler?, n'a jamais craint la monotonie que pour mieux s'essayer à la surmonter... Ce qui motive dès lors l'empêchement énoncé est bien plutôt l'impossibilité de retrouver, dans et par la jouissance, l'*antériorité à jamais non dite*, souverainement "sémiotique" (au sens de J. Kristeva), le lieu pulsionnel où se resource l'imaginaire et où s'origine la signification (qui toujours déstructure, déchire le symbolique, le codifié, le cela-va-de-soi du sens institué), "le chaos d'où tout ordre est issu, l'anarchie qui précède fatalement toute loi."[23]

Voilà maintenant que Mme de Saint Ange, après n'avoir prêté aucune attention à l'ébauche esquissée par le chevalier, requiert à nouveau "un peu de détails (...) et sur le physique de cet homme et sur ses plaisirs...." L'insistance apparaît pour le moins paradoxale, quand on songe au peu de cas qui vient d'être fait des quelques phrases que nous avons citées. Mais le chevalier, lui, a bien entendu de quoi il s'agissait, qui répond en décrivant son propre membre viril et en indiquant combien

Dolmancé présente pour celui-ci un réceptacle digne des plus vifs éloges... L'image s'abolit définitivement. Et le corps réifié devient pur instrument d'un plaisir prétendument illégitime—l'érotisme rejoignant l'impératif philosophique de la subversion de la Norme (donc précisément celui de sa consolidation la plus figée, la plus structurale et la plus signifiante en tant que "figuration familialiste d'une coercition culturelle acceptée comme loi anthropologique"[24])—dans cette ellipse de toute actualisation *vivante*. Eugénie, elle, se trouve immédiatement ramenée à son rôle:

> Ce serait en vain, mon ami, que j'essaierais de te la peindre: elle est au-dessus de mes pinceaux,

déclare Mme de Saint-Ange à Mirvel.

On remarque combien le recours au *topos* de la beauté convenue, "l'exigence de surenchère et d'excès,"[25] permet à Sade de faire l'économie du portrait. Dans cette apologie de la *libido*, le corps, décidément fait problème. Or ce problème du corps rejoint pour nous celui de la signification: dans une oeuvre où rien ne peut se faire sans lui, le corps est absent, scotomisé, insaisissable; et pourtant, en même temps, il est doté d'une espèce de "présence" particulière (*il est nécessairement là* dans son absence même). Précisément: le corps, c'est-à-dire le *concret indicible* qui ne se dit nulle part en dehors du désir,[26] *signifie l'absence qui signifie*. Mais de quel désir s'agit-il? Peut-être bien de celui qui veut rejoindre fusionnellement la mère—celle qui, pour Sade, *ne fut jamais là*, ni comme *interprète*, ni comme *contenant,* ni comme *protection*[27] contre la violence de soi—et en "repartir" enfin, mais sans déperdition fatale: désir de l'enfant-roi qui veut vivre dans le présent même le souvenir d'une joie hors d'atteinte, d'une jouissance exceptionnelle et parfaite (Leclaire, *Démasquer...*, 54-62). Or un tel désir, pour se dire, doit trouver, dans la langue commune, son discours propre: *le langage de l'impossible* (qui est littérature). Opération seulement réalisable si le manque s'y reconnaît comme l'aveu à surmonter, l'oubli à remémorer, et, toujours, par avance, en vain. Certes, l'initiation d'Eugénie commence par une *leçon d'anatomie*. Mais ce préliminaire didactique efface cela même sur quoi il repose, en même temps qu'il révèle, par l'emphase de son didactisme insistant, la déficience de l'*auto-somatognosie* du personnage concerné.[28] On a fait remarquer que pour Sade "la victime n'existe pas en tant que corps mais en tant que victime. Elle doit être vivante, et douée de goûts et de répulsions, et en même temps n'accéder jamais à l'épaisseur d'existence du corps...."[29] Mais ce qui nous retient plutôt ici est le sens même du paradoxe: au moment où Eugénie devrait prendre conscience de son corps (on le lui "apprend"), celui-ci s'évanouit, perd toute consistance et toute singularité. Vidé de son intériorité, il est situé hors de toute *discrimination perceptive*.[30] Le voilà bientôt remplacé par une machine sophistiquée dont on dénombre les utilisations possibles, dont on démonte les rouages sexuellement efficaces et dont on calcule le rendement érotique supposé. Le point de visée est évidemment constitué par le désir phallocentrique: le corps de l'autre est avant tout là où le phallus se dispose et explose comme une petite bombe à retardement plus ou moins retenu; donc: *là où je me place sans savoir ce qui s'y passe* autrement que sur le mode du mimétisme pour lequel la femme est un homme qui s'ignore (songeons à Juliette).... Lors même que l'identification (au sens freudien) est défaillante, la "réception" de l'image de l'autre sans cesse échappe: c'est bien pourquoi *l'image a toujours déjà fui,* avant même que ne s'exerce une évocation par avance condamnée à la vanité. Le sadisme sera, devant ce risque insupportable du vide[31]—devant la terreur de disparaître à soi-même dans l'évanouissement de l'autre—une *parade rituelle*[32] s'efforçant de conserver, malgré tout, et ne fût-ce qu'illusoirement dans un espace fermé, bouclé, muré—château de Lacoste et château de Silling, château de l'esprit, forteresse mentale, phantasme carcéral, prison intérieure[33]—une intégrité psychosomatique, une *intersegmentation* qui fait cruellement défaut[34] afin de *se sentir être* même d'une façon déceptive. Et l'écriture sadienne sera, quant à elle, par son effort perpétuel de *reconstruction*, par son classicisme de la page "bien écrite" (Laborde, 9), par son obstination aussi à faire coexister l'irréconciliable mais sans payer le prix d'un tel pari esthétique—ce prix serait: la *modernité*, l'illisibilité au sens de Barthes: ce serait Artaud[35]—, par la règle de l'ordre, l'opération de camoufler par le "mal" cet autre mal qu'aucune médecine ne peut guérir, castration que rien ne peut compenser, blessure qu'aucun fétichisme du signifiant ne peut fermer; la mise en texte d'une certitude forte seulement de ses coulées de béton verbal pétrifié; l'étalement convulsé des mots qui s'enchaînent sur la feuille blanche comme pour éviter ce que Serge Leclaire appelle "la débandade devant la jouissance."[36]

D'où le recours à l'homosexualité, directe ou non, qui est ici comme ailleurs "présentée comme l'idéal du rapport érotique" (Molino), mais se trouve en fait elle-même envisagée en dehors de l'effective *vivance* du désir. "*Si l'on ne peut se voir soi-même, si l'on ne se reconnaît pas dans les yeux troublés de la victime,* on ne pourra tenter de s'atteindre que dans l'être qui nous offre la plus grande ressemblance avec nous-même, c'est-à-dire non pas dans n'importe quel complice, mais un complice qui sera un double, donc du même sexe"(Molino, 149):

> Quand il s'agit de pollution, un homme s'y entend, pour un homme, infiniment mieux qu'une femme. Comme il sait ce qui lui convient, il sait ce qu'il faut faire aux autres....

Or Dolmancé vient, rappelons-le, *pour faire jouir*—l'autre (Mme de Saint-Ange) comme il a déjà fait jouir le chevalier. Comment dès lors transcoder cette altérité qui s'affirme par delà sa négation? Sans doute par la prétention de l'identité absolue (ton *foutre* égale le mien), qui suppose, notamment, la sémiotisation visuelle du plaisir et l'adéquation rigoureuse de celui qui s'éprouve dans la féminité à celui qui se décharge au masculin; ou (seconde variante), par le refus pur et simple de la question (je ne me soucie guère de ta jouissance, obnubilé que je suis par la mienne, car "l'homme qui bande est loin du désir d'être utile aux autres" [260]). La deuxième solution équivaut d'ailleurs à la première, manifeste le même aveuglement. Mais cette conjonction, justement, signifie autre chose que le triomphe éclatant du règne phallocentrique: la crainte de sa défaite imminente, la phobie de l'impuissance et la nostalgie des délices ignorés pour lesquels on manque d'assurance effective, d'authentique *souveraineté*, et de temps, et de mots. Une écriture fébrile et compulsive mime sans doute cette finalité tyrannique: conjurer, avec toutes les ruses polymorphes de *la peur d'avoir peur*, le manque et l'insuffisance "à peindre." Pour Yvon Belaval, le texte sadien "est un monologue masculin qui ne se soucie guère du plaisir de l'autre, le monologue unisexe d'un prisonnier qui fantasme ses dialogues" (Préface, 14). Prisonnier assurément. Mais pas seulement dans la contingence dramatique d'une vie; surtout, peut-être, dans l'enfermement d'un *isolisme* radical, un "unicisme" (Bataille), une "solitude absolue" (Blanchot), dont, avec Jean-Jacques Brochier,[37] nous trouvons les contradictions plus fécondes que la volonté totalisante en elle-même. Ces contradictions, cependant, il faut les décrypter. Car elles tendent à recouvrir ce qu'elles trahissent: l'insatisfaction fondamentale, la souffrance finalement insurmontable, la désilluson aiguë et intenable.

> Ne naissons-nous pas tous isolés? je dis plus, tous ennemis les uns des autres...,

s'écrie le porte-parole de celui qui, de ses prisons bien réelles, ailleurs, dans des missives désespérées envoyées à ses proches, déclare:

> Ne me réduisez pas au désespoir..., je ne puis tenir à cette horrible solitude, je le sens....[38]

L'une des sources ultimes de ce terrible *manque à gagner* est du côté du corps; plus précisément, pour reprendre une expression de N.O. Brown: du *corps d'amour*.[39] Et, assurément, du corps de la femme où s'instaure l'inacceptable *désordre amoureux*.[40] L'une des conséquences majeures de cette inévitable *ellipse* réside dans la nécessité de se (ré)approprier ce corps de la femme comme possibilité d'exister dans son propre corps; donc dans l'appel forcené à la domination brutale; dans l'adhésion à ce *despotisme* dont le divin marquis a pourtant tellement souffert et que sa conscience politique républicaine,[41] opposée à l'absolutisme, à la peine de mort, à la guerre..., repousse avec horreur.

> Il n'est point d'homme qui ne veuille être despote quand il bande...,

affirme Sade. Mais il ajoute en note:

> *La pauvreté de la langue française* nous contraint à employer des mots que notre heureux gouvernement réprouve aujourd'hui avec tant de raison; nous espérons que nos lecteurs éclairés nous entendront et ne confondront pas l'absurde despotisme politique avec le très luxurieux despotisme des passions du libertinage.

Peut-être l'un peut-il aller *sans* l'autre. Et sans doute une telle dichotomie nous interdit-elle de penser le sadisme soit comme une *conduite conceptuelle* déplacée (faute de mieux) dans l'imaginaire, soit comme une *inversion* de la philosophie des lumières faisant de la Nature le Mal; soit comme la conséquence néfaste d'un excès dans la logique rationaliste des Philosophes, à partir de la mort de Dieu; soit encore comme une abolition du sujet et de l'éthique dans une théorie de l'apathie.[42] Croyons donc Sade. Encore faut-il découvrir, dans le rapport du phallocentrisme au politique, et dès lors ailleurs que dans l'utopie *explicite* (telle celle que développe "Français encore un effort..."), *comment s'idéologise* dans la *libido* une signification appelée, attendue et parfois approchée dans les *effets d'implication* du texte.[43] Signification nostalgique et désolée dont la mise à jour fait reconsidérer l'ensemble du rituel scriptural sadien, en son origine existentielle, en son insertion historique, en sa dimension sociologique, en sa portée politique: le mal, la révolution, le "peuple," la "république" comme *parade* de la souffrance, de l'impossible, de l'absence, de l'ennui. A cet égard, une fois encore, l'intertexte de l'amour nous éclaire. Car la négation sadienne de l'amour "répond" à toute l'inauthenticité du discours de la passion occidentale moderne devenue le système de la désillusion et bientôt, sous les figures de la séduction, du bovarysme et de l'anaphrodisie, la complaisance au "mal du siècle." Si l'amour, chez Sade, est imprononçable, c'est à partir du constat de son anéantissement effectif. A la fin du XVIIIe siècle, dans la situation de dégradation globale de la passion qui s'annonce, Sade ne peut qu'admettre la protestation violente du négatif, pour, paradoxalement, revendiquer une place "vide" en attente pour un amour devenu inconcevable. De même quant au politique: Sade entend, d'une certaine façon, transgresser l'Ancien Régime par le républicanisme, mais dans une "attitude," un "comportement mental" qui renvoie à une *posture* aristocratique. Peu importe, ici et maintenant, le statut "réel" d'un tel paradoxe: ce qui compte pour nous est la nécessité qui en procède, nécessité significative de *rendre cohérente une pensée impossible centrée sur une évidence qui demeure hors champ*. Rien d'étonnant, dès lors, aux hésitations de l'auteur lui-même:

Que suis-je à présent? Aristocrate, ou démocrate? *Vous me le direz, s'il vous plaît, ...* car pour moi *je n'en sais rien.* (*Correspondance,* 301-302)

Dis-moi *qui* je suis, je ne me vois pas, je m'ignore, je n'en sais rien: tout dépend de toi. Mais il n'y a nulle part de "toi," *je* et *tu* nulle part ne font *nous.* Ce qui se prononce est bien une *exigence insensée.* Il y a de quoi devenir fou, et seule une rationalisation abstraite développant un systémisme implacablement continu, peut "contre-effectuer" le risque d'une telle folie. Encore faut-il, d'autre part, s'interroger, et profondément, jusqu'à la racine, sur cette solidarité du phallocentrisme et du pouvoir, dont le mérite incontestable de Sade est de faire surgir les implications mutuelles et de découvrir la portée symbolique. Or devant un tel questionnement, le texte sadien se taît. Ou plutôt: il se perd dans un vaste silence bavard. Par là, il répond *négativement.* Une somatisation paradoxale se donne ici à déchiffrer, car c'est encore avec des corps assemblés que Sade tente de clôturer son univers (Laborde, 143), de combler les failles, de résoudre les doutes. Et, en même temps, c'est l'expulsion du corps "réel"—"les bras et mains d'amour, lèvres d'amour, pouce phallique d'amour, seins d'amour, ventres pressés et collés l'un à l'autre par l'amour" (Walt Whitman)—, du corps concret (non *machiné*[44])—"charmes érotiques de la voix," "communauté complice, égalitaire, dans le partage du toucher" (Belaval, 15)—qui symptomatise tout le non dit lancinant dont l'accumulation scripturale et la relance phantasmatique doivent absolument étouffer la *voix blanche,* et le cri indéfiniment contenu. *Tout l'expulsé du texte*: la parole qui dirait la main tendue, la tiédeur d'une épaule, le refuge de la chevelure, la senteur de la peau; la parole qui dirait l'absence de tout cela, et l'échec, et la mortification, et l'anxiété, et la rage. Non, l'indifférence n'est pas "le véritable nom de l'unique passion de Sade,"[45] mais la hantise à refouler par un travail intellectuel/imaginaire infatigable.

Travail infatigable *pour donner corps au texte,*[46] pour l'unifier, le cohérencifier, l'organiser. Labeur pour *faire corps* avec cela même qui se dérobe lorsque sa perception machiniste s'effondre devant le *déjà défait, déjà ruiné.* Et précisément, en son apparence si bien "construite" comme l'*action de présence d'une chose absente,*[47] le corps se défait, se fragmente, éclate sous l'illusion idéologique du discours homogénéisant—corps textuel, corps réel.[48] L'un, esclave du repli narcissique, où se complaît son onanisme rageur, jamais vécu dans sa complétude assumée (donc dans la conscience de sa fragilité inévitable et de son indifférenciation essentielle toujours menaçante...), jamais conquis à travers des *expériences praxiques globales.* L'autre toujours trop lisiblement figé dans son unité hors d'atteinte. Car "nul texte ne peut mettre en jeu ce que sa texture même est faite pour colmater" (Leclaire, *Démasquer...,* 22). L'un fragmenté comme dans une scène des glaces de *La Philosophie* (59). L'autre jamais arrivé au terme de l'ultime dépassement dans "la rigueur même de son ordonnance qui ne dément ni ne voile sa fonction de vêture" (59). Travail infatigable aussi de n'avoir pas pu rendre *ce qui devait être;* et de n'avoir pas voulu nommer *ce qui n'allait pas.* De cela—de cet immense effet de refoulement textuel si complaisant aux mille défoulements de l'apparence physique...—est née la haine, la haine du prochain si étranger, de l'autre devant moi qui me fonde dans mon être propre *mais au risque de ma perte* (du moins: je l'imagine, et je le crains). Mais une haine finalement toute rhétorique de n'avoir pas trouvé les mots qu'il fallait "pour le dire." *Une langue a manqué à Sade pour dire le manque*; et pour avouer l'incommensurable joie[49] qu'aucun livre, aucune suite de livres, aucun torrent de mots, aucune effervescence des théories conceptuelles, aucune frénésie des postures érotiques ne peut venir remplacer. Il n'est pas innocent que cette haine soit prioritairement tournée vers la mère vertueuse,[50] celle qui a originellement séparé l'amour de la jouissance, et dont l'action inconsciente continue d'empêcher la réconciliation du plaisir et du bonheur; mère au corps sublime, vierge mère phantasmatiquement épargnée par le sexe, mère de tous les interdits[51]—"menaces, exhortations, devoirs, vertus, religion, conseils," "tout ce qui ne tend qu'à nous renchaîner" (84)—, mère prohibitrice dont le silence seul suffit à couper le flux de la jouissance à peine née.[52] Mère vertueuse dont *La philosophie dans le boudoir* opère la dégradation et la mise à mort,[53] mais dont le texte occulte aussi le renversement en son contraire (Mme de Saint-Ange devenant pour Eugénie la *bonne "mauvaise" mère*), l'ouverture sur le désir permis, le sexe que l'on peut toucher, avec lequel on peut jouer, jouir. Il s'agit alors de cette mère érotisée où se fixent à la fois, dans le rêve incestueux, l'amour *et* la transgression "permise": Mère-Laure aux yeux de feu, parée de l'amour qui la rend "plus belle encore" et qui "tourne la tête" par "l'éclat de ses charmes," telle qu'elle apparaît dans le rêve de la nuit du 16 au 17 février 1779, en même temps qu'elle échappe à toute espérance de fusion:

> "Pourquoi gémis-tu sur la terre? m'a-t-elle dit. Viens te joindre à moi. Plus de maux, plus de chagrins, plus de troubles, dans l'espace immense où j'habite (...)" A ces mots, je me suis prosterné à ses pieds, je lui ai dit: "O ma Mère...." Et les sanglots ont étouffé ma voix (...) Alors, absorbé par mon désespoir et ma tendresse, j'ai jeté mes bras autour de son col pour la retenir, ou pour la suivre, et pour l'arroser de mes larmes, mais le fantôme a disparu. *Il n'est resté que ma douleur.*[54]

Travail infatigable du texte qui laisse dès lors ce sentiment si particulier où se mêlent la froideur de l'abstraction et l'incandescence d'une noire fureur, où le délire ne se libère jamais de la maîtrise, et où, bien que pourchassée sous de faux noms (la vertu, l'honneur, le respect des lois), une innommable tristesse hante les abords de la luxure et envahit des lendemains qui déchantent. En ce sens, à la fois structural et thématique, l'oeuvre de Sade, qui mine l'idéologie mécaniste du bonheur sans parvenir à signifier pleinement son contraire s'inscrit dans l'échec d'une forme tragique où la division fondamentale règle les diverses actualisations d'un style voué à l'unification. "Et l'expérience dernière de Sade, sa volonté d'écrivain, tient tout entière dans ce frémissement."[55]

---

* Professor Heyndels presently teaches at the University of Miami.

[1] Les références renvoient à l'édition *Folio*, préfacée par Yvon Belaval, qui est la plus aisément accessible (Paris: Gallimard, 1976).

[2] Voir, parmi d'autres, J.J. Brochier, *Sade* (Paris: Ed. Universitaires, 1966), p. 57.

[3] Les guillemets sont, évidemment, de rigueur. Sur la description du personnage chez Sade, lire Roland Barthes, "L'arbre du crime," in *Tel Quel*, 28 (1967), 22-37, 27 sv.

[4] Il faut par là entendre ce que L. Bersani nomme "la peur du réel."

[5] Cette absence de l'image dans le miroir a été traitée sur le plan imaginaire par Aragon dans *La mise à mort*.

[6] Cf. J. Lacan, "Le stade du miroir comme formateur de la fonction du *je*," in *Revue Française de Psychanalyse* 13, 4 (1949), 449-455.

[7] H. Lichtenstein, "Identity and Sexuality," in *Journal of the American Psychoanalytical Association* (1961), p. 9.

[8] Voir M. Merleau-Ponty, *La phénoménologie de la perception* (Paris: Gallimard, 1945), pp. 515 sv; et le chapitre VIII ("Corps et Métaphore") du livre de J. McDougall, *Théâtres du je* (Paris: Gallimard, 1978).

[9] Voir Barthes (art. cit.).

[10] Jean Molino, "Sade devant la beauté," in *Le marquis de Sade* (Paris: Colin, 1968).

[11] G. Bataille, *La littérature et le mal* (Paris: Gallimard [Idées], 1957), pp. 120-148.

[12] Voit L. Crocker, "Au coeur de la pensée de Sade," in R. Trousson, éd., *Thèmes et figures du siècle des Lumières. Mélanges offerts à Roland Mortier* (Genève: Droz, 1980), pp. 59-71, p. 61.

[13] Voir G. Deleuze, *Logique du sens* (Paris: Minuit, 1969), p. 378.

[14] Cf. P. Aulagnier-Spairani, *Le désir et la perversion* (Paris: Seuil, 1967), notamment pp. 123-124.

[15] L'expression est de Pierre Fédida. Voir Mellor-Picart, "Le corps savant et l'érotisme de tête," *Topique*, 27 et "Représentation du corps et appel au persécuteur dans la problématique perverse," *Topique*, 28.

[16] Voir R. Heyndels, "Problématicité de la réception du texte discontinu," in *Acta Universatis Wratislaviensis, Romanica Wratislaviensa*, 20 (1983), 156-169.

[17] M. Kahn, *Figures de perversion* (Paris: Gallimard, 1981), pp. 31 sv.

[18] L'expression est de G. Mendel dans "Sade et sadisme," *La révolte contre le père* (Paris: Payot, 1968), pp. 102-110.

[19] Belaval, Préface à *La philosophie dans le boudoir*, p. 8.

[20] W. Winnicott, *Jeu et réalité* (Paris: Gallimard, 1975).

[21] R. Gentis, *Leçons du corps* (Paris: Flammarion, 1980), p. 188.

[22] Voir S. Leclaire, *On tue un enfant* (Paris: Seuil, 1975) et *Démasquer le réel* (Paris: Seuil, 1971).

[23] Ph. Sollers, *Logiques* (Paris: Seuil, 1968), p. 94.

[24] F. Gaillard, "Au nom de la Loi," in *Sociocritique*, éd Cl Duchet (Paris: Nathan, 1979), pp. 11-33.

[25]Molino, art. cit., p. 149.
[26]Voir S. Leclaire, *Démasquer le Réel*, pp. 54-62.
[27]P. Aulagnier, *La violence de l'interprétation* (Paris: PUF,1975); Bion, W., *Elements of Psychoanalysis* (Londres: Heinemann, 1962); et M. Fain, *L'enfant de son corps* (Paris: PUF, 1974), respectivement.
[28]Voir C. Camilli, *Psychothérapie corporelle et psychosomatismes* (Paris: Maloine, 1979).
[29]J. Brochier, *Sade* (Paris: Ed Universitaires, 1966), p. 109. On a remarqué que cette caractéristique ne concernait *pas exclusivement* les victimes.
[30]Dr Le Boulch, *L'éducation par le mouvement* (Paris: Editions E.S.F., 1976).
[31]Voir le remarquable n° de la *Nouvelle Revue de Psychanalyse* consacré aux "figures du vide" (11, 1975).
[32]Alice M. Laborde, *Sade romancier* (Neuchâtel: La baconnière, 1974). Voir surtout le chapitre IV sur le "rituel sadique."
[33]Voir M. Foucault, *Histoire de la folie* (Paris: Gallimard, 1972), pp. 380-382. Voir aussi A. M. Dardigna, *Les châteaux d'Eros* (Paris: Maspero, 1980).
[34]P. Schilder, *Image du corps* (Paris: Gallimard, 1968).
[35]Voir F. Tonelli, "Artaud et Sade," *Comparative Drama*, 6 (1969).
[36]*On tue un enfant*, p. 47.
[37]*Le marquis de Sade et la conquête de l'unique* (Paris: Losfeld, 1966).
[38]D.A.F. Sade, *Correspondance. Oeuvres complètes* (Paris: Cercle du Livre Précieux), 11-12, 119.
[39]*Le corps d'amour* (Paris: Denoël, 1967), trad. R. Dadoun.
[40]On reprend l'expression au titre du livre de P. Brückner et A. Finkielkraut, *Le nouveau désordre amoureux*.
[41]Pour une étude nuancée de la dimension politique de Sade (dans une perspective dont la discussion est ici hors de propos), voir J.M. Goulemot, "Lecture politique d'Aline et Valcour," dans l'ouvrage collectif *Le marquis de Sade* (Paris: Colin, 1968), pp. 115-140.
[42]Voir P. Klossowski, *Sade, mon prochain* (Paris: Seuil, 1967 [1947]), notam. pp. 90 sv; ainsi que son étude "Sade, ou le philosophe scélérat," in *Tel Quel*, 28 (1967), 3-22.
[43]Sur ces points, voir R. Heyndels, "L'idéologie. Critique d'une notion," in *Cahiers Internationaux de Sociologie* 70 (1981), 157-168; et du même auteur: "L'improbabile imprevedibilità," in C. Bordoni, éd., *La pratica sociale del testo* (Bologne: CLUEB, 1982), pp. 101-122.
[44]Voir R. Heyndels, "Le *voyage du Monde de Descartes*, du Père Gabriel Daniel," in *Annales de l'Institut de Philosophie*, 1976, 1977; réimpr. 1991.
[45]Selon une expression de G. Picon.
[46]Voir l'étude de C.L. Hart-Nibbrig sur le "Corps du texte," in C. Reichler, *Le corps et ses fictions* (Paris: Minuit, 1983), pp. 97-107.
[47]La formule est reprise à Paul Valéry.
[48]On *ne recouvre pas* l'un par l'autre, mais on les *juxtapose*.
[49]Lire le beau livre de Clément Rosset, *La force majeure* (Paris: Minuit, 1983). Voir aussi. R. Heyndels, "Vision de misère et de joie," in *Rev. Univ. Bruxelles*, 1, 2 (1984), 199-215.
[50]Voir P. Klossowski, "Le Père et la mère dans l'oeuvre de Sade," dans *Sade, mon prochain* (appendice III).
[51]On songe à la figure de la belle-mère de Sade.
[52]Voir l'étude sur "Le conflit masculin," in N. Friday, *Les fantasmes masculins* (Paris: Laffont, 1981), pp. 9-21.
[53]Voir J. Lacan, "Kant avec Sade," in *Ecrits* (Paris: Seuil, 1966).

[54] Nous soulignons. Voir G. Lely, *Vie du marquis de Sade*, pp. 309-310.
[55] J.J. Brochier, p. 259.

La rhétorique du silence dans *L'Amour* de Marguerite Duras

Pierre Van den Heuvel
Université de Nimègue

1. *Duras: vers un discours du silence*
   Toute l'oeuvre littéraire de Marguerite Duras, dans son ensemble comme dans chacune de ses élaborations romanesques, repose sur un va-et-vient entre deux pôles, celui du silence et celui du cri. De toute évidence, les mots disponibles dans le langage commun ne permettent pas de rendre compte, de manière adéquate, de ce qui est en cause et qui veut être dit. Dans l'évolution de l'oeuvre durassienne, cette prise de conscience s'aggrave progressivement. Au niveau de l'énoncé narratif où s'introduisent de plus en plus souvent des manques graphiques et des silences descriptifs, l'identité du narrateur premier s'estompe peu à peu. En se multipliant ou en se camouflant, l'instance de parole s'efface pour n'être plus que pure voix venant on ne sait d'où. Parallèlement, le discours des personnages se réduit pour faire place au langage du corps. Au niveau de l'énonciation, le sujet de l'écriture chez qui la méfiance des mots s'accroît visiblement éprouve de plus en plus de difficultés à se situer. La narration devient hésitante et le récit lui-même, lacunaire et fragmentaire, n'a plus guère de consistance, ne sert plus qu'à véhiculer une parole incertaine. Ainsi, les mots de l'énoncé et la parole énonciative se confondent, le discours se minimalise et le texte acquiert le statut d'une "référence sans référent."[1] Cette tendance réductrice s'observe jusque dans le volume des textes dont les derniers constituent des mini-romans qui ne comptent plus que quelques dizaines de pages.[2]
   Cette déconstruction de la narration et de la représentation romanesque traditionnelles se fait principalement, chez Duras comme chez Beckett, par l'instauration du *silence* dans le texte. Non seulement ces vides accordent une nouvelle valeur aux mots environnants, à ces quelques paroles qui restent, ils exercent aussi une fonction capitale sans la communication littéraire puisqu'ils appellent l'instance interlocutrice à la collaboration. On peut même dire que la technique du vide transforme le lecteur de Duras en co-producteur du texte. Dans ce sens, les silences textuels doivent être considérés comme de véritables *figures rhétoriques*.

Cette substitution du mode non-verbal au mode verbal de la communication est devenue la marque principale de l'oeuvre durassienne où le silence est "sans cesse questionné, menacé par une parole qui ne vient pas."[3] Son origine se trouve dans la conception même du langage: dans cette "ère du soupçon," on est de plus en plus convaincu de la pauvreté de la communication verbale, de la déficience du langage inapte à dire la vérité, voire même, en tant que cause de malentendus, obstacle à la communication humaine.

Pour saisir le fonctionnement de la figure du silence comme moyen de communication, j'observerai sa présence dans *L'Amour*,[4] texte qu'on a défini comme "un récit du silence entrecoupé de paroles."[5] Il va de soi que cet exposé ne rendra que très sommairement compte de la complexité du phénomène et qu'il a surtout pour but de souligner l'urgence de l'élaboration d'une rhétorique générale du silence.

Dans le cadre de l'élaboration d'une "poétique de l'énonciation," j'ai proposé, il y a quelques années, d'accorder une attention particulière à "la *puissance latente* des mots et des structures qui, dans le langage, réfèrent au niveau sous-jacent de l'énonciation, aux éléments qui sont chargés d'une énergie capable de transformer les mots et les *vides* de l'écrit en paroles."[6] Ainsi, j'ai tenté d'esquisser une approche théorique et méthodologique pour l'étude du silence qui peut se définir comme "la non-réalisation d'un acte d'énonciation qui pourrait ou devrait avoir lieu dans une situation donnée."[7] Totalement absent en linguistique, cet aspect a été également négligé par la recherche littéraire qui ne l'a observé que rarement, tantôt comme une figure rhétorique dans le discours oratoire, tantôt comme une "structure d'appel" dans le langage poétique (les *Leerstellen* chez Roman Ingarden et Wolfgang Iser). Aujourd'hui, face aux textes "troués" de Beckett, de Robbe-Grillet, de Duras et de tant d'autres, l'analyse littéraire se contente encore trop souvent de remarques occasionnelles, disparates et hétérogènes.

En appliquant ici la poétique du silence à *L'Amour* de Duras,[8] mon but est de montrer comment dans un tel discours discontinu les non-dits constituent des figures de construction tout aussi constitutives d'un sens — ou plus — que les éléments textuels visibles. Je partirai de l'étude de l'énoncé, des mots *in praesentia* qui, au fond, ne semblent servir qu'à créer un acte énonciatif lequel produit, grâce à la causalité contextuelle du dit, un discours *in absentia*, un discours non-verbal qui renferme l'essentiel de ce qui s'exprime. Ainsi, devenant signe au même titre que le mot écrit, le silence parle et, chose étonnante, son éloquence l'emporte même sur celle des paroles actualisées.

2. *Silences typographiques*

Dans l'énoncé, les silences s'inscrivent d'abord d'une façon éclatante par le procédé des blancs typographiques. Dans l'oeuvre de Duras, les effets de ces silences visibles sont de plus en plus systématiquement exploités, surtout à partir du cycle de *Lol V. Stein* et du *Vice-consul*. En général, ces vides sont produits par l'emploi de phrases inachevées se terminant par un blanc ou par des points de suspension. Dans *L'Amour* s'y ajoute un autre procédé, celui des blancs excessifs qui séparent des groupes de phrases lesquels apparaissent alors comme des "paragraphes" quasi indépendants du reste. En pratiquant la stratégie paratactique qui efface au maximum les relations de cause à effet, l'auteur se sert de cette technique du blanc pour obliger le lecteur à ralentir sa lecture et à s'investir dans les manques. Il en est de même des vides créés à l'intérieur d'une phrase composée de bribes d'un discours caduc, pratique qui transforme le texte en exercice à trous ou à choix multiple. Il importe d'observer comment de telles césures typographiques dans l'énoncé rapporté s'accompagnent d'interprétations de la part des allocutaires intradiégétiques:

—Ce parcours toujours égal... Ce pas si régulier... on dirait...
Elle fait signe: Non. (p. 24-25)

La manière dont les personnages donnent sens au non-dit sert manifestement d'exemple au lecteur du texte lacunaire. Figure spéculative, cette économie de la phrase inachevée montre aussi qu'aux yeux de l'auteur la communication réussie n'a guère besoin de mots— ceux-ci sont même dangereux—et que, dans sa réalisation idéale, elle aurait même intérêt à se fonder sur un silence absolu.

3. *Silences descriptifs*

Dans l'énoncé textuel, l'importance du silence se manifeste aussi par sa fréquence d'emploi sur les plans du lexique et de la représentation romanesque. Le terme *silence/silencieux* apparaît régulièrement (10 occurrences), non pas pour s'attacher à un personnage,[9] mais pour désigner un état général, un univers silencieux, indéfini, où évoluent des personnages eux aussi muets, n'évoquant que rarement leurs souvenirs. Ces silences descriptifs appliqués à la nature servent avant tout à exercer une fonction symbiotique par rapport au mutisme des interlocuteurs textuels. En outre, ils constituent des moyens pour faire progresser le discours: en tant que pauses de réflexion ils facilitent l'avènement des paroles difficiles et la continuation du récit précaire. Dans tous les cas, le silence de l'univers produit un effet positif.

Quand il s'agit de silences humains, c'est le verbe d'action *se taire* qui apparaît le plus souvent (18 fois) avec ses synonymes *ne pas parler* (3) et *ne rien dire* (2). Le mutisme, surtout celui de la femme, est alors la conséquence directe de la difficulté de parler:

—Je ne sais pas le mot pour dire ça.
Ils se taisent. (p. 65)

Rompant le dialogue en cours, il met l'accent sur la nature des quelques mots qui viennent d'être dits et dont l'emploi même semble imposer le silence aux locuteurs tant est infirme leur sens. Comme les blancs, ces silences exercent une fonction métadiscursive: à l'exemple des personnages, le lecteur est amené à juger de la valeur de l'énoncé produit, toujours imparfait et impropre, exigeant une formulation meilleure mais irréalisable.

Sur le plan technique, on peut distinguer quatre procédés qui servent à mettre en place ces silences descriptifs:

Il y a d'abord la *pause* qui interrompt un discours rapporté, généralement marquée par le verbe *arrêter* entre tirets:

> —De partout—il s'arrête—ils étaient nombreux: des millions—il s'arrête encore—tout est dévasté. (p. 30)

C'est ensuite l'*attente* située tantôt à l'intérieur d'une phrase, tantôt après un énoncé manqué:

> —Non, mais lui—elle attend—lui quelquefois, il se perd. (p. 29)
> Ils se taisent, ils attendent en se taisant. (p. 28)

Le troisième type est celui de la description *physique* du locuteur réduit au silence:

> L'immobilité éclate, la bouche ouverte, aucun son ne sort, il fait encore l'effort de parler, n'y arrive pas... (p. 72)

La dernière catégorie comprend les *descriptions* proprement dites du silence humain:

> La phrase reste ouverte, elle n'en connaît pas la fin. (p. 62)
> La phrase reste suspendue un instant, puis elle se termine. (p. 107)

Dans tous les cas, ces descriptions de silences humains réfèrent à un silence involontaire, à une parole désirée mais irréalisable. Cette impuissance verbale cause l'arrêt, produit l'attente et conduit à des efforts physiques résultant en un "énoncé silencieux" qui devient objet de la description. Dans les deux premiers cas, il s'agit de silences de réflexion qui désignent la difficulté de la verbalisation, donc de références à l'activité prélangagière qui précède l'actualisation d'un énoncé. Dans les deux autres cas, où l'effort énonciatif est vain, ce sont des silences suggestifs qui sont chargés de "dire" l'indicible, de "nommer" l'innommable, non pas par des moyens linguistiques mais par la mobilisation de l'émotivité et de l'imaginaire. Ce sont donc toujours des silences qui "parlent" ou qui "font parler."

A ces fonctions comunicative, réflexive et spéculative du silence descriptif s'ajoute une fonction métadiscursive dans la mesure où l'ensemble de ces silences de l'énoncé réfère à des silences semblables au niveau de l'énonciation où le sujet se trouve confronté à la même difficulté de parole. Sur le plan de la technique romanesque, il s'agit donc d'une mise en place volontaire, dans l'énoncé narratif, de silences qui, ensemble, se rapportent à un silence involontaire chez un sujet impuissant de dire par des paroles ce qu'il aimerait dire.

4. *Les substituts du langage*

Comme je l'ai déjà signalé, l'impuissance langagière n'est pas seulement concrétisée, au niveau diégétique, par le silence, mais aussi par le *cri*—parole sauvage inarticulée—qui se substitue lui aussi à la parole impossible.[10] Dans *L'Amour*, c'est par un cri que commence le récit:

> Et puis il y a un cri... L'histoire, elle commence. (p. 12-13)

Dans la suite, le cri est lié aux thèmes de l'enfance et de la digue (p. 52, 53, 68). Comme dans *Le Vice-consul*, il est ici le plus souvent poussé par un homme, le voyageur dont il annonce "la mort émotionnelle" (p. 12, 24, 57, 61; cf. le cri d'Anne dans *Moderato Cantabile*). Le cri féminin, si fréquent chez Duras, provient surtout de la femme du voyageur qui n'occupe qu'une place réduite dans le récit (p. 89-100 où elle crie 6 fois). Ce sont des cris énoncés dans une situation de désespoir et de colère par une femme qui ne parvient pas à communiquer avec l'homme qui l'a abandonnée.

Comme les silences, les cris apparaissent toujours à des moments de forte émotivité où l'on ne peut s'exprimer par le verbal commun, en général au début ou à la fin d'une crise. Cri et silence sont donc étroitement liés: le cri supprime le silence et donne accès à la narration; le silence donne naissance au cri, le précède ou le suit. Entre ces deux extrêmes qui se touchent, des mots tentent de suggérer le contexte situationnel qui, excluant le recours à la parole normative, provoque la non-parole du silence et la parole primitive du cri.

Un langage constitué de silences et de cris étant impossible, Duras recourt ainsi à d'autres moyens de communication pour remédier à la déficience du langage.[11] Elle trouve un autre substitut du verbal dans le langage du corps. Dans *L'Amour*, le corps lui-même, notamment le corps féminin, est marqué par l'immobilité, non par une immuabilité définitive, mais par une fixité virtuellement dynamique comme s'il était saisi sur un cliché photographique ou simplement endormi:

> Mains à moitié enfouies dans le sable, immobiles comme le corps. Force arrêtée, déplacée vers l'absence. Arrêté dans son mouvement de fuite. L'ignorant, s'ignorant. (p. 10)

Faisant partie d'un "ensemble," subjugué aux éléments naturels de l'univers qui l'entoure, ce corps, dans sa totalité, n'exerce aucune fonction sur le plan de la communication. Il en est tout autrement de certaines parties du corps comme les *mains* et les *yeux* dont les mouvements expressifs se substituent à la communication verbale. A la page 72, l'homme qui n'arrive pas à parler "tend la main vers le voyageur," son interlocuteur. Au lieu de parler, il se sert de la main pour "montrer," pour "faire signe" (cf. p. 30, 45-46, 64, 80). La main aide même le locuteur à formuler des phrases:

> Dans l'impossibilité de répondre, le voyageur lève la main et montre autour de lui, l'espace. Le geste fait, il parvient à avancer dans la réponse. (p. 18-19)

Très souvent aussi, la position de la main exprime, dans une représentation behaviouriste, l'état psychologique d'un personnage réduit au silence.

Le regard est un moyen de communication non-verbale encore bien plus efficace. Sa fréquence dans *L'Amour* est surprenante: sur les 143 pages du texte, 88 mentionnent *regarder/regard* et 41 *voir/vue*. Ces occurrences concernent généralement le personnage du voyageur qui est progressivement chargé de la focalisation dans les descriptions. En résumant fortement, on peut dire que le regard nous renseigne sur l'état psychologique d'un personnage ("l'égarement" ou la "violence" d'un regard), qu'il précède la prise de parole (le regard scrutateur qui examine la situation dialogique et détermine le choix des paroles) et que, dans certains cas, il va jusqu'à remplacer la communication verbale ("elle l'interroge du regard"). L'action de regarder ne constitue donc pas seulement une activité complémentaire qui provoque la parole ou la rend superflue, elle peut aussi se substituer au verbal, aux pages 47 et 115 par exemple où le regard remplit les mêmes fonctions phatique et communicationnelle que les paroles. C'est pourquoi *voir* et *regarder* sont maniés comme le verbe *parler*, mais dans une situation de silence:

> Ils se regardent. Ils se voient...
> Elle se met à regarder avec méfiance...
> Elle regarde comme forcée de le faire...
> Elle recommence à ne plus regarder rien... (p. 118-121)

C'est donc grâce au cri et au langage du corps que le discours du silence peut fonctionner et que l'histoire peut être racontée.

Mais on sait que ces silences explicites, inscrits dans un énoncé narratif fictionnel, ont avant tout pour tâche de référer à un silence implicite, situé au niveau sous-jacent de l'énonciation.

5. *Silence et énonciation*

Le silence que l'écriture instaure dans la communication littéraire entre l'instance productrice et l'instance réceptrice, toutes deux extradiégétiques, est évidemment bien plus difficile à saisir que celui qui est inscrit dans l'énoncé. J'ai proposé ailleurs des procédures analytiques qui permettent de capter et de circonscrire, dans une mesure nécessairement limitée, bien entendu, l'activité du sujet de l'énonciation.[12] En étudiant minutieusement les éléments déictiques et modalisants, les figures métadiscursives et réflexives, les repères intertextuels, le rapportage des discours internes et quelques autres particularités de l'énoncé, on peut mettre à jour la situation contextuelle de cette instance. Dans le cas du silence dans les textes durassiens, seul un tel travail permet d'expliciter les rapports qui relient les silences de l'énoncé à un silence semblable, fondamental, qui est à la base de la forme qu'a prise le texte. Je tracerai rapidement les grandes lignes d'une telle analyse.

Dans le domaine de la déictisation,[13] certaines irrégularités ébranlent le statut du mode narratif de *L'Amour*. A première vue, il semble s'agir d'une narration impersonnelle: un narrateur invisible décrit les faits et gestes de quelques vagues personnages par des phrases courtes, d'une extrême sobriété. Une observation attentive révèle cependant qu'il ne s'agit pas d'un narrateur omniscient, hétérodiégétique, puisque quelques détails dans la pronominalisation s'y opposent ("*Nous* nommerons cet homme le voyageur,"p. 13). D'autres éléments, d'ordre modalisant et à effet subjectif, réfèrent encore à une vague présence (l'impératif "Ne les appelle pas," p. 68; "*En effet*, l'homme passe...*Oui*. Les pas s'arrêtent," p. 10). L'incertitude est encore rehaussée par quelques déictiques démonstratifs qui limitent la perspective du locuteur ("A *cette distance* son visage est indistinct," p. 7). Mais son identité reste obscure. Il s'agit avant tout d'une *voix* issue d'une instance primaire qui ne se définit que par sa parole parcimonieuse. C'est surtout l'emploi du pronom personnel *nous* qui, en situant l'instance narrative au même niveau extradiégétique que l'instance de parole, réfère au sujet d'énonciation et à sa situation. Reliant l'acte de lire à l'acte d'écrire, cette déictisation curieuse vise à intensifier la subjectivité du discours tout en passant sous silence—le code littéraire l'exige—l'identité de la "personne" qui parle. La primauté accordée à la voix est également instaurée par l'absence de noms propres, par l'omission régulière de l'article défini et du pronom personnel de la troisième personne ainsi que par l'emploi du passif. Dans la rhétorique durassienne, de telles figures subvertissent la situation traditionnelle du narrateur implicite et rapprochent la lecture de l'écoute. C'est pourquoi, dans cette oeuvre, les silences "s'entendent" d'abord.

La déictisation temporelle et spatiale renforce encore ces effets. Si dans les romans précédents le temps était encore conçu, même vaguement, dans sa linéarité, dans *L'Amour* cette chronologie a disparu pour faire place à un temps psychologique et poétique.[14] Ce qui est de l'ordre du temporel est ici rendu par le passage du jour à la nuit, de l'ombre à la lumière, du bruit au silence, métaphorisation qui crée un temps circulaire. Dans ce déroulement indéterminé, où l'action des personnages est réduite à l'extrême et où la progression concerne essentiellement celle du texte et de sa lecture, les silences occupent une place privilégiée: ils marquent aussi bien la durée—de l'écrire et du lire— que l'action—l'inaction, le vide du récit—d'un temporel cyclique indéfini, toujours exprimé au présent, n'admettant ni l'intrusion du passé ni la prédiction de l'avenir. Ce n'est qu'à la clôture du texte qu'apparaît le futur qui désigne la continuité implacable d'un pareil discours qui se répétera éternellement, mais en silence, après le point final qu'impose la facture du livre.

Ainsi, dans *L'Amour*, le temps vide permet d'exploiter pleinement la thématique de la mémoire humaine vidée de sens, de l'oubli et de la léthargie:

> Il faut que je dorme ou je vais mourir. (p. 39)

Cette thématique douloureuse accorde à l'écriture une valeur thérapeutique. Elle semble aussi vouloir présenter une "morale" fondée sur le silence bienfaisant qui nous entoure et sur le silence impitoyable et effrayant qui nous habite. Grâce à l'ambiguïté des déictiques temporels, à leur double référentiation, interne et externe, cette morale dépasse les limites de la diégèse et s'étend au domaine de l'énonciation où elle constitue l'intentionnalité textuelle et où se réalise l'interaction dialogique qui engage le lecteur.

La même ambiguïté est appliquée au cadre spatial de l'énoncé narratif. L'espace du récit réfère sans cesse à l'espace scriptural et psychologique du sujet (ici/là, dedans/dehors, près/loin, devant/derrière, à la surface/au fond, voici/voilà, les démonstratifs, les présentatifs, les domaines de la mer et de la terre, la figure symbolique de la digue, etc.). Prisonnier de l'espace restreint où règne le silence, le sujet met son espoir dans "l'enchaînement continu de l'espace" (p. 107), dans une écriture qui "monte, ouvre, montre l'espace qui grandit" (p. 142).

L'extension de cette référentiation temporelle et spatiale au domaine de l'énonciation est favorisée par l'emploi de certains verbes performatifs et modalisants qui subjectivisent le discours. La fréquence de ces formules ("il semblerait," "on dirait," "il a dû entendre," etc.) force le lecteur à relier les références à un sujet parlant, à sa situation et à son contexte. Cette orientation est soutenue par l'emploi d'expressions modalisantes ("en effet," "peut-être," "sans doute," "oui," "non," etc.) et par des figures syntaxiques autoréférentielles (l'interrogation, l'affirmation, la négation, l'impératif, etc.).

Dans ce contexte, j'ai déjà mentionné le rôle très important que jouent les références métadiscursives et les figures réflexives ou spéculaires qui dans le récit, renvoient indirectement à l'instance de parole. Quant aux figures réflexives, deux sont assez précises pour qu'on puisse parler d'une mise en abyme ou d'un véritable métadiscours explicatif (p. 13-14 ou le sujet de l'écriture expose clairement sa fonction productrice et p. 68 où il donne une leçon de lecture à l'allocutaire).

Dans la plupart des cas, le sujet ne se manifeste que très indirectement, par exemple par la manière dont il rapporte le discours des personnages: le métadiscours attributif et commentatif qui accompagne ces "citations" renseigne le lecteur non seulement sur la position du narrateur premier, mais aussi, grâce à l'ambiguïté et à l'implicite, sur celle du sujet caché, sur son activité productrice:

> La phrase reste ouverte, elle n'en connaît pas la fin. Elle se fermera plus tard, elle le ressent, ne précipite rien, attend; (p. 62)

et sur la nature de son langage:

> La sincérité de la réponse fait peur. Elle recule. (p. 91)
> Sa voix est claire, d'une douceur qui effrayerait. (p. 15)

De semblables références métadiscursives se trouvent aussi insérées dans le discours rapporté, comme dans la lettre que le voyageur écrit à sa femme et dans laquelle il demande de mettre leurs enfants au courant de la situation:

> Si vous n'arrivez pas à leur expliquer, laissez-les inventer. (p. 42)

De tels conseils enchâssés stimulent l'imagination à laquelle fait appel, chez le lecteur, la totalité de ce texte troué où manquent les références habituelles et où dominent les silences.[15] Il va de soi que ces instructions de lecture proviennent du sujet de l'écriture qui "construit sa lisibilité en la déconstruisant."[16] Leur inventaire montre qu'elles apparaissent aux moments difficiles de l'interprétation, surtout là où se creusent les silences. C'est pourquoi on peut affirmer que le texte contient son propre "mode d'emploi": il apprend au lecteur à lire les silences, à se rendre compte qu'à l'origine de la perte du verbal il y a la perte de l'identité, mais que ces pertes peuvent engendrer un langage nouveau et créer une identité nouvelle.

Ainsi, le silence durassien est complexe: il signifie en même temps le blocage de la communication verbale, par la référence à l'impuissance du sujet ou à l'insuffisance du langage, et le moyen de la communication idéale. Substitut du langage, chargé d'une fonction phatique très efficace et d'une force suggestive remarquable, il est *parole* et fait partie intégrante du discours où il engage l'interlocuteur à la participation dialogique. Enfin, sur le plan de la communication littéraire, il exerce une fonction poétique de première importance: figure historique fondamentale, emprunté à l'oral, ce silence du recueillement, de l'écoute et de l'attente transforme le texte en "oeuvre ouverte" où chaque lecteur peut investir sa subjectivité propre et apprendre à donner sens à ses silences à lui.

[1] M. Collot, "La Dimension du diétique," in *Littérature*, 38 (1980), 75.

[2] *L'Homme assis dans le couloir*, 1980; *L'Homme atlantique*, 1982; *La Maladie de la mort*, 1982. (Tous aux Editions de Minuit à Paris).

[3] D. Bajomée et R. Heyndels éd., *Ecrire, dit-elle. Imaginaires de Marguerite Duras*, (Bruxelles: Editions de l'Université de Bruxelles, 1985), p. 66.

[4] (Paris: Gallimard, 1971). Edition utilisée 1986.

[5] J. Kristeva, *Soleil noir: dépression et mélancolie* (Paris: Gallimard, 1986), p. 234.

[6] Pierre Van den Heuvel, *Parole, mot, silence: pour une poétique de l'énonciation* (Paris: José Corti, 1985), p. 115.

[7] Van den Heuvel, *Parole, mot, silence*, p. 67. Pour le cadre théorique et méthodique de l'étude du silence, voir p. 65-85 et pour les applications l'index analytique.

[8] Je remercie Mariska van den Hove, lectrice assidue de Marguerite Duras, pour ses remarques judicieuses qui m'ont aidé à mieux apprécier les effets des silences à la lecture.

[9] Ce n'est que dans deux cas, aux pages 80 et 96, que le mot *silence* s'applique à des personnages.

[10] Cf. F. Drykoningen, "Les cris dans *Moderato Cantabile*," in *Het Franse Boek*, 2 (1970), p. 133-140. Pour le statut du *cri* dans la théorie de l'énonciation, voir mon ouvrage cité, p. 59-60

[11] Le "livre sur rien" que Flaubert aimait tant écrire a été réalisé par le pataphysicien Latis en 1964: son *Organiste athée* est un livre aux pages vides... Les écrivains préfèrent généralement se limiter aux blancs excessifs (Mallarmé), aux pages pointillées (Bataille) ou à l'insertion d'une page blanche (les cas fameux de la page vide dans *L'Après-midi de Monsieur Andesmas* de Duras et dans *Le Voyeur* de Robbe-Grillet qui, dans ses *Romanesques*, vient de souligner l'importance capitale de la "technique des trous" dans son oeuvre).

[12] Op. Cit., 1985, Première partie. Pour la manière dont certains auteurs, comme Duras, mélangent aujourd'hui les plans de l'énoncé et de l'énonciation dans la "Nouvelle Autobiographie," voir mes études "L'Espace du sujet: la Nouvelle Autobiographie," in *Proceedings of the XIIth Congress of the ICLA*, Vol. V (München: Iudicium Verlag, 1990), p. 85-90, et "L'Attitude énonciative dans la Nouvelle Autobiographie," in *Enonciation et parti pris*, Actes du Colloque d'Anvers, 1990 (à paraître chez Rodopi à Amsterdam).

[13] Pour les résultats parfois surprenants que l'observation des déictiques peut donner, voir mes articles "Révélations d'un discours mensonger: les déictiques temporels dans *La Symphonie pastorale* d'André Gide," in *Neophilologus*, 72, 3 (1988), 366-375, et "A la recherche du sujet perdu *In Our Time* d'Ernest Hemingway," in *Neophilologus*, 73, 2 (1989), 189-206.

[14] Cf. V. Guers-Villatte, *Continuité/Discontinuité de l'oeuvre durassienne* (Bruxelles: Editions de l'Université de Bruxelles, 1985).

[15] Pour ces "leçons de lecture" dans l'oeuvre d'Alain Robbe-Grillet, voir mon ouvrage cité, chap. V, et mon étude "L'aide au lecteur en péril: les *Romanesques* d'A. Robbe-Grillet," in *French Literature Series, Narratology and Narrative*, Vol XVII (Columbia, South Carolina, University of South Carolina, 1990), 26-34.

[16] L. Dällenbach, "Réflexivité et lecture," in *Revue des Sciences Humaines*, 177 (1980), 23-37.

The Emergence of a Poetics

Murray Sachs
Brandeis University

In his pioneering study of the early development of the French short story, Professor Alfred Engstrom flatly declares: "The first formal short story in French literature is Prosper Mérimée's *Mateo Falcone*, which appeared in the *Revue de Paris* for May, 1829."[1] The assured precision of that statement may arouse suspicion, since it designates no less a cultural phenomenon than the start of a new literary genre, about which we are not accustomed to be so exact. However, those investigators who have since gone over the same ground have been led to the same conclusion.[2] It would therefore seem to be settled historical fact that Mérimée's famous *conte* is an authentic literary landmark which pinpoints the first appearance of a new art form in French literature.

Now genuinely new art forms are rare phenomena in modern western cultures—film is, for example, the only instance that we can point to in the twentieth century—and a new art form whose birth we can date as precisely as we apparently can the French short story, invites particular inquiry into its essential nature. Our curiosity is aroused simply because we can see it whole, as we cannot view the older, established forms whose beginnings are hidden from us. Our natural impulse to try to analyze the nature of the literary genre inaugurated by Mérimée's *Mateo Falcone* is surely akin to the impulse which must have moved Aristotle to try to analyze the nature of Athenian tragedy, a genre of impressive achievement in his culture, and whose origins were familiar to him. Aristotle's famous efforts at analysis supply a model for this kind of critical enquiry. One examines a corpus of the best literary works of a particular kind in order to discover and describe how they are made, i.e., upon what theoretical principles of composition they are constructed, and what rules might seem to govern their style, forms, and choice of subject—in order to determine their poetics. Recent though the scholarly interest in the French short story is, the groundwork for a critical enquiry into its poetics is already being laid: the work of a number of individual authors has been carefully scrutinized from this point of view, and general historical overviews of this material have revealed interesting themes, subjects, and techniques, and some helpful hints about the forces which spawned the genre.[3] But the study of the French short story remains in its infancy, because the genre itself is so young; and little has in fact so far been done to elucidate the *theory* of its forms, the underlying principles which govern its existence—which is the heart of any poetics—even though significant progress has been achieved in defining it as a genre.[4]

Of course, the short story did not suddenly blossom into a fully developed genre with the publication of *Mateo Falcone*. If that story was recognizably superior to, and different from, the many specimens of brief narrative that preceded it, it also resembled its predecessors in many ways. It was by no means a strange and alien composition to the readers of 1829, for it was, after all, a story recounted in its normal chronology, like most stories. Its basic achievement was to give intimations of artistic possibility to the ancient and familiar entertainment of storytelling. But there was a long way still to travel before that kind of storytelling would be able to boast of an organic body of aesthetic principles defining its art. Its poetics would have to develop slowly out of that promising start, against entrenched literary habits and rival forms—not only the various long-established dramatic and poetic genres, but also the new and closely-related narrative genre of the novel, just then coming into its own. It is a central point of interest, when one has the rare opportunity to study a newly emerging literary form, to observe how it distinguishes itself from the existing forms, and how it establishes the uniqueness of its claim on public attention as a form of artistic expression. In the literary world of nineteenth-century France, we must remember, the short story was in the role of "the new kid on the block," trying to establish its own identity, yet inevitably needing to draw on local customs in order to be recognized. So it need not surprise us that *Mateo Falcone*, for example, clearly shows the influence of the techniques of classical tragedy in its structure: there is but a single action confined to one locale, which proceeds with such inexorable speed that it seems to require hardly more time to happen than it takes to recount it; the story falls naturally into five segments: exposition, Fortunato and the bandit, Fortunato and the police, Fortunato confronts his parents, Fortunato is executed; even the narrative form gives way almost completely to dialogue on the last two pages. Not for nothing did Mérimée begin his career as a dramatist. Nevertheless, in spite of such influences, *Mateo Falcone* is a work of fiction which planted the small seed of a literary idea, an idea which proved capable of growth and development, and ultimately of independent vitality.

As it happens, the evolution to full maturity of this fragile new art required the better part of the remainder of the nineteenth century, and the collaboration of a number of gifted writers, to come to fruition. It would be of value to trace the unfolding of the whole process by which the poetics emerged, with a detailed analysis of each new advance in theory along the way. But such a project is obviously beyond the scope of this study. The best that can be attempted here is to suggest a preliminary outline of the subject, emphasizing two major breakthroughs which permitted a poetics specific to the short story to emerge, and impress itself on the consciousness of writers and public alike. This outline will, I hope, stimulate others to undertake the detailed analysis we need to have, if we are to understand and appreciate fully both what the genre of the short story is, and how it got that way.

It must not be supposed that the instant success and acclaim which greeted *Mateo Falcone* in 1829 signified knowing public joy over the birth of a new genre. There was much that was not new but excellent of its kind to admire in the composition: a tense and unforgettably shocking plot, the impact of which was heightened by the spare, matter-of-fact narrative tone; fascinatingly exotic setting and characters; vivid realism of detail; exciting narrative pace. Most readers who appreciated those qualities in the story would likely have given no thought to any underlying artistic theory which may have shaped it. But there were surely those who must have recognized, or at least sensed, the special power imparted to this story by the manner of its composition, and for those readers it was a revelation, as it seems to have been for Mérimée himself. Its success inspired him to write more stories, in rapid succession, and to abandon further experiments with the theatre, verse, and the novel. He had discovered his true vein—the short story became his literary vocation thereafter. The four stories which appeared immediately after *Mateo Falcone*, still in 1829, were each strikingly—almost defiantly—different, as though Mérimée feared being accused of repeating his original success. And the skein of widely disparate creations continued into 1830 with two more stories quite unlike any of the others. Though each of these first seven stories had a quite different setting and theme, Mérimée was nevertheless able to publish them together in a volume whose title, *Mosaïque*, clearly suggested some interconnected design, as though they were various-shaped tiles arranged in a mosaic. There were, in fact, two elements common to all the stories: an overarching theme, and a technique. Each story offered a different instance of the irrational violence man perpetrates on his fellow man, and the structure of each narrative obeyed the principle of composition which Mérimée knew had given *Mateo Falcone* its impressively concentrated power. That principle was the imposition of a disciplined unity on its every part. The secret of artful storytelling, which the success of *Mateo Falcone* had revealed to him, was to select as subject a single, simply stated action, and to exclude rigorously from the telling of it any sentence or any detail which was not directly relevant to that subject. Thus the opening description of the wild and inaccessible *maquis* in *Mateo Falcone* is not mere local color, but prepares the way for the primitive violence which is the story's basic subject matter; and the group of apparently irrelevant details in the second paragraph about Mateo Falcone's background and reputation, which seem to delay the start of the action, all turn out to have a specific point in the unfolding narrative. There are no superfluous elements in *Mateo Falcone*. The same carefully controlled unity can be found in all of Mérimee's short stories, even though the stories vary considerably in mood and tempo, and even in length. His later stories, *Carmen* and *Colomba* for example, tended to be three or more times as long as the stories in *Mosaïque*, approaching the dimensions of a short novel in some cases. But the principle of unified structure around a single subject he always observed scrupulously, in part because the principle ensured a quality in his stories that would clearly distinguish them from novels. And while the principle restricted him to subjects of suitable scope and simplicity, and constrained him to the discipline of pruning and shaping each new story so as to focus relentlessly on its single animating subject, he accepted those limitations gladly, for they were what made his stories art.

Mérimée's creative vein proved thin—he wrote only nineteen short stories in all—but with that handful of stories he made a major contribution to the genre he founded. He not only left a legacy of stories with a consistently high level of literary skill, which attracted a public, but he also discovered a first principle for a theory of the short story, a principle which helped to establish the credentials of the short story as different in kind from the novel. It was in part Mérimée's success with the form which tempted his contemporary, Balzac, in 1829, to try his hand at it also. The temptation was brief, but it lasted long enough to enable Balzac to produce some excellent specimens of the form, and at the same time to add significantly to the theory of the genre which Mérimée had begun to formulate. For Balzac, who always took the art of literature seriously,[5] was able to see more than a financial opportunity in the sudden success which the short story began to have in 1829. He saw certain aesthetic possibilities as well. Because the most obvious characteristic of the form was brevity, Balzac recognized that its most basic requirement, from the reader's point of view, was that it concentrate its effects and provide a strong emotional impact. The greater length of a novel permitted a novelist to engage his reader's emotions many times and in various ways within the same novel, and to accumulate his effects. The short story writer had only one chance at his reader's emotions, and he had to make it a strong effect. Only the most tense and dramatic story material, therefore, seemed to Balzac to be suited to the short story form. Moreover, he sensed, as a matter of aesthetics, that merely to provide a random emotional shock was not justification enough for the existence of a short story, for it risked leaving the reader dazed but unsatisfied. The shock should be of the meaningful kind—those which suddenly reveal, and inspire reflection about some large philosophical or moral question. Balzac's approach thus extended and refined further Mérimée's discovery of the importance of the single subject, by specifying that the subject have both extraordinary intensity and philosophical implications. Balzac's recipe for a short story is clearly exemplified in such a well-known anthology piece as *Une Passion dans le désert*, in which the strange story of a man's love for a panther raises the question of whether animals have souls. A more persuasive example might be *Le Chef-d'oeuvre inconnu*, because it is artistically superior and more typically Balzacian in theme, and because its extended passages on the theory of art will convince us that it is not unreasonable to see underlying theoretical principles in the way this particular story is constructed. What dominates the story is the passion for art, expressed in the long discussions of Part I, then focused suspensefully in Part II on the symbol of the mysterious masterpiece which Frenhofer has been working on for ten years. The final shock is that the canvas is a meaningless jumble of paint, its masterpiece obliterated by Frenhofer's obsessive perfectionist retouching. The shock is enough to kill Frenhofer, and to leave the reader meditating about the nature of art and genius, and man's self-destructive drives. Passion for art is announced as the theme in the opening paragraph, as the young Poussin arrives worshipfully at the door of the studio belonging to an established master, Porbus. Frenhofer's masterpiece is mentioned soon after, and all the strands of the story then begin to move toward that one centre of attention: what is on the canvas? Not only the three painters, representing three generations of devotion to art, but also Poussin's mistress, Gillette, the only other character in the story, come to have their destinies directly linked with the mysterious masterpiece. Balzac's unmistakable purpose is to build enormous tension and meaning into the climactic moment when Frenhofer consents to uncover his canvas. Everything in the story is geared to that moment, including the relationship between Poussin and his mistress, who fall out over the issue of her posing for Frenhofer. Thus Balzac's underlying design in *Le Chef-d'oeuvre inconnu* is to converge the destinies of all his protagonists on a single moment of maximum intensity and transcendent meaning. In its way, it is as effective a story as *Mateo Falcone*, and from the point of view of the principles of composition, it is very close kin.

Balzac produced some thirty short stories between 1829 and 1832, some of them authentic masterpieces of the genre. But he chafed under the inherent constraints of the form, for he was temperamentally a novelist and preferred those subjects which allowed expansive social analyses and character portrayals for which the short story form was quite unsuitable. After 1832 his output ran heavily to novels, interspersed with only occasional short stories. But with his early group of stories he had made his contribution to the genre and to its aesthetics. His insistence on focusing his stories on a moment of high intensity and moral revelation extended and clarified the principle of controlled unity of subject and structure which Mérimée had developed, and thereby helped to make the short story still more definably distinct from the novel. Taken together, the contributions of Mérimée and Balzac to the short story between 1829 and 1833 were enough to establish the validity of the genre, to provide it with a solid corpus of achievement, and to forge the first principles of an effective poetics on which it could grow.

The 1830's witnessed an immense vogue for the short story, in fact, but Mérimée and Balzac were not joined by any other practitioners who were capable of bringing new theoretical concepts to bear upon the genre. The major Romantic poets, who might have been expected to bring a special sensibility to the new form, produced nothing of distinction in the few tries they made. In mid-century, Gautier and Nerval experimented interestingly with private fantasies as a basis for short fiction, which extended the genre's thematic range but not its technical capabilities, or its theoretical underpinnings. In Barbey d'Aurevilly's *Les Diaboliques* and Villiers de l'Isle-Adam's *Contes cruels* we find the darker side of human emotions being systematically exploited, in an intriguing cultural phenomenon, but we encounter no formal innovations in their work. As the Second Empire moved towards its end, one striking talent in the short story appeared: Alphonse Daudet, who for a few years before and after 1870 was perhaps the most popular *conteur* in France. He can be credited with one technical contribution to the genre, perhaps: he revitalized the role of the narrator, by emphasizing stylistically the charm and oral immediacy of storytelling, and giving the story a personal, rather than an objective, narrative tone. The *Lettres de mon moulin*, for example, were all composed as though the author were in direct personal communication with a single reader, and the personality of the author contributes importantly to the pleasure one takes in these stories. But Daudet had no theoretical conception of the essential nature of the short story as a genre, and his stories mark no advance in its poetics, though their high quality contributed to the growing public interest in the form.

It was, in fact, nearly half a century after the groundwork was laid by Mérimée and Blazac that the short story again received a notable impetus in the development of its poetics. The impetus came with the publication of Flaubert's *Trois Contes* in 1877, and of the Naturalist collection, *Les Soirées de Médan* in 1880. With these two publications, the short story attained confident artistic maturity as a medium of expression, and offered fully-realized models of a coherent, integrated art form. Flaubert's famous trilogy, in particular, seemed to confirm that in half a century's time the genre of the short story had come of age.

Flaubert was an unlikely source for a volume of three tales that could serve as a textbook for the study of the art of the short story. He was, after all, a novelist who had never previously published a single short story, when he began work on the *Trois Contes*. Nevertheless these three compositions — the only specimens of the genre he ever published — are of an exemplary formal perfection, so far as the art of the short story is concerned. Each story is of a different type, one a realistic portrait, one a legend, one a historical evocation, and each therefore requires different techniques of composition and a different style. But the common artistic principle which they all share is the harmonious integration of techniques within each story. In *Un Coeur simple*, for example, the simple, self-effacing character of the protagonist is echoed in the simple, direct prose, the short sentences, the even pace of events, the placid rhythms, and the virtual disappearance of plot. In *Hérodias*, on the other hand, the volatile character of the title figure is echoed in the nervous prose rhythms, the dense paragraphs, the erudite vocabulary, and the complicated movements of the plot. In each story, every technical aspect seems to be deliberately suited to the nature of the theme and characters being treated, every word seems to be selected with care, every detail calculated in its relation to every other detail. The overall effect is one of the author's total mastery over his material, and of a finished product whose every element had been shaped by an artistic sensibility, in the manner of a disciplined lyric poem. Such a manner of composition is perhaps only Mérimée's principle of a unified structure carried to the ultimate degree, but Flaubert's performance set a standard of aesthetic excellence for the short story which made it the equal of any art. It must be added, however, that Flaubert's brilliantly executed stories do not have, implicit in their structures, any really new theoretical concept about the short story as a genre. It is clear from the *Trois Contes* that Flaubert subscribes to Merimée's principle of the unity of subject, but rejects Balzac's notion that an intense emotion and philosophical import are inherent in the form. Beyond that, however, it is hard to see any evidence that Flaubert considered the short story to be different in kind from the novel, or to be governed by a different poetics. Except for the nature of the subjects, the *Trois Contes* are not significantly different as compositions from his novels. The *Trois Contes* make a major and significant contribution to the aesthetics of the short story, but not to the theory of the genre.

The collection of stories about the Franco-Prussian War which Zola and his young disciples published in 1880 under the title *Les Soirées de Médan* achieved greater public acclaim than the intrinsic merit of its contents might suggest. The success, of course, had largely to do with its polemical character as the manifesto of a new literary school, and with the scandal of its uniformly antimilitarist and anti-war bias. For both political and literary reasons, in other words, its timing was felicitous. But some of the success is attributable also to the fact that the quality of the stories was unusually high, and two of them were plainly masterpieces. At the very least, it seems significant for the development of the short story genre that in 1880 a collection of stories could arouse enough interest to be counted an important landmark in the history of Naturalism.

That suggests how securely the genre had become established in public favor as reading matter, a bare half century after its invention.

Of the two stories in *Les Soirées de Médan* which were instantly recognized as masterpieces, one, Zola's *L'Attaque du moulin*, an exciting and superbly handled narrative, has nothing to contribute to the emergence of the short story's poetics, the movement of its plot, and its five-part structure, suggesting much more the poetics of tragedy, indeed. But the other, Maupassant's *Boule de Suif*, revealed a major new talent to the literary world who would make the short story his vocation and permanently transform its poetics. Although *Boule de suif* was Maupassant's first published story, he was thirty years old in 1880, and had already learned a great deal about the art of fiction from his mentor, Flaubert. The story thus bore no trace of the novice, but showed instead a remarkably clear-sighted command of the medium of short fiction.

Boule de suif is a good deal longer than most short stories, but its unity of conception and composition is no less rigorous. The opening pages, which convey the atmosphere of Rouen as the routed French army passes through and the Prussian conquerors arrive, also state the theme: the horror of human behavior when normal life is disrupted. Maupassant does not hesitate to point out the moral of his story, in his own words, before the story proper gets under way: "Car la même sensation reparaît chaque fois que l'ordre établi des choses est renversé, que la sécurité n'existe plus, que tout ce que protégeaient les lois des hommes ou celles de la nature se trouve à la merci d'une brutalité inconsciente et féroce."[6] The author then introduces "l'ordre établi des choses," in the condensed form of ten travelers, of varied social status, who abruptly find themselves at the mercy of "une brutalité inconsciente et féroce" in the person of a Prussian officer. Far from undercutting his story, Maupassant's bold early statement of both his theme and its moral serves to pique the curiosity of the reader and to rivet his attention on the crisis and its consequences, which is the central subject to which every detail of the story is made to lead. The story is a tightly controlled, unified structure, uniquely directed to a vivid illumination of an aspect of human conduct.

This clearly-intended purpose in the story is surely the most significant extension of short story theory which *Boule de suif* embodies. The story is deliberately organized to say something, to communicate a meaning. That idea goes well beyond Mérimée's principle of unity, and Balzac's concern for intense emotion and moral resonance. Maupassant seems to suggest that a story must have, not only a single subject on which to concentrate, not just a subject of strong emotional impact which vaguely "makes you think," but a subject which has a concrete point, which reveals a truth about man or nature or society. For Maupassant, it was the very genius of the short story form, with its compression and concentrated focus, that it forces both writer's and reader's attention primarily to the end, to the purpose or objective which the whole structure is designed to reach. To organize a story around a point or a meaning was the only logical way to take full advantage of the form's primary characteristics: totality, and constraint.

Boule de suif launched Maupassant's career, giving him both the financial freedom and the courage to devote his talent primarily to the short form. His output in the 1880s, both qualitatively and quantitatively, became a legend, and certainly far exceeds that of any other major writer of his day. There is no doubt that, by the course of his career alone, Maupassant established the literary and artistic respectability of the short story writer as a professional man of letters. A reader of the stories which poured from his pen after *Boule de suif* would have been struck by the growing tendency of the endings of his stories to usurp attention, and gradually to become their dominant feature. Instead of a climactic event or situation somewhere in the middle, to focus the story, Maupassant began merging the climax and the ending until they became one. The tendency is hardly surprising, given his theoretical approach to the genre, but those who complain of Maupassant's contrived surprises or his trick endings are surely missing the point. At least in the best stories (there are, of course, many trashy formula stories which he churned out to order, and which are beneath critical notice) the ending neither tricks nor surprises the reader, but is its only possible outcome, because the whole story has been conceived with that ending in mind to reveal the story's full meaning. The famous instance of *La Parure* illustrates the point nicely. Some readers have always felt that the revelation that the lost necklace was paste, at the end of the story, is a last-minute contrivance which makes the reader feel tricked rather than enlightened, and a twist of the plot which the story does not require. Yet one need only reflect on what the story would be without that ending to see why it is in fact an organic necessity for that story. Had Madame Loisel never learned the truth about the necklace, her fate would of course have been just as pathetic, but she herself would not have understood her fate, the reader would not have fully grasped the shallowness of the aspirations for which her life went down the drain, and the story would lack a dimension and the satisfying sense of closure. The reader would feel that the story had stopped before it was over, had Maupassant simply omitted the last sentences, in which Mme Loisel—and the reader—accidentally learn the truth. For the truth about the story, and its meaning, is inseparable from that ending.

Maupassant provided the richest and most varied specimens of the short story genre of any writer in the nineteenth century, and displayed a mastery of its various technical requirements as well as a profound understanding of its nature. Recognizing that brevity was essential to the form, Maupassant developed to a high art the technique of suggestive notation to portray a place or a character or a mood with just a very few words. He learned that the successful subjects, for the short story, were not just simple, or intensely dramatic, or shocking, but rather a combination of the unique and the obscure, the kind of uncommon subject only an artist might spot, and the kind whose interest and meaning will at once be apparent when revealed, without further explanation or analysis. It was for the novel to treat subjects which need analysis to be understood, which undergo change and development, which can only be adequately known in a context of extended time and space. The brevity of the short story permits only the disclosure of a reality, not its dissection or its history. And because the nature of the medium is revelation and exposure, the ending, and the meaning it could convey, took on paramount importance in the economy of a story's organization and structure.

It is clear that Maupassant's understanding of the medium, as implied in his practice of the genre, was both theoretically and aesthetically advanced, and amounted to the fullest poetics of the short story yet developed. His influence on the genre, both in France and elsewhere, has been profound and continues to affect what is written today. Almost all our contemporary short story writers admit freely to having learned their craft by studying Maupassant. But in his time, Maupassant was unique. There was no contemporary of his in France who did work of equal significance in the short story during the 1880s. When his powers declined, after 1890, the genre's development was carried forward principally by Anatole France, who ushered it into the twentieth century enriched with at least one important technical innovation which extended its range. That innovation was to found his creations not on observation, not on imagination, but on ideas. The starting point of any Anatole France story is a particular thought or concept, not necessarily an original one with him, and often suggested by his reading. He then invents or selects the characters and actions which will best express the idea he wishes to communicate. Anatole France simply had too little interest in the unusual characters, piquant situations, or violent actions which were the standard stuff of short fiction in his day. He was absorbed by books and ideas, and he succeeded in the unlikely enterprise of making books and ideas a source of fiction. Every reader of the famous story, *Le Procurateur de Judée*, for example, realizes from the way the story is written that the author is not primarily interested in Herod or Jesus or Roman civilization, but in the ironic ambiguities of history. *Crainquebille* is often admired as a comment on the Dreyfus Affair, but that is information brought in from outside the text of the story. The careful reader will notice that the vital center of the story is not current events or politics, nor even a generalized outcry against injustice. The story concerns the inherent absurdities of the law as an institution for dealing with truth. Thus Anatole France suggests that a short story is no more than an idea—

often an abstraction—made concrete with carefully selected characters and events. Interestingly enough, his method happens to correspond—so far as I am aware, by pure chance—with the famous, now classic, definition which Edgar Allan Poe offered of how a short story should be composed: "A skilful literary artist has constructed a tale. If wise, he has not fashioned his thought to accommodate his incidents; but having conceived, with deliberate care, a certain unique or single *effect* to be wrought out, he then invents such incidents—he then combines such events as may best aid him in establishing this preconceived effect."[7] I think it might have amused Anatole France to know just how "classic" his procedures in the making of short stories are by American standards. By French standards, where the genesis of a story seemed almost always before to be in an observed or imagined character or event or situation, Anatole France's habit of beginning with an idea represented a new departure. But it was an innovation that seemed promptly to win acceptance into the poetics of the short story by those twentieth century writers who have made distinguished use of the form—though they would be unlikely to credit Anatole France with that influence. Do not the most famous stories of Gide, and Sartre, and Camus, for example, tend to be about the transcendent moral issues of our time, rather than about people, places and events? And is that tendency so very remote from what Anatole France was doing at the turn of the century?

In the development of the French short story, Anatole France must be considered a transitional figure, embracing what his nineteenth-century predecessors had discovered about the form, and handing it on to the next century enriched, but little changed in its essence. That essence seems to have attained full maturity with Maupassant, whose work implies a well-rounded, organic poetics at its base. The emergence of that poetics was a gradual development which, having gone unrecorded, has to be traced, deduced and reconstructed from the work of those who practised the genre over the years. There is no doubt that Mérimée and Maupassant, the two writers who made a vocation of short story writing, were the key architects of that poetics, with important assists from Balzac and Flaubert. But the challenging task which scholars interested in the short story need to undertake is to fill in the exact details of the history of that emerging poetics, the first faint outlines of which are, I hope, at least dimly discernible in this essay.

---

[1] Alfred G. Engstrom, "The Formal Short Story in France and its development before 1850," in *Studies in Philology*, 42, No. 3 (1945), 634.

[2] See, for example, Albert J. George, *Short Fiction in France: 1800-1850* (Syracuse: Syracuse U P, 1964), p. 9. Others who take the same view include Robert Lewis, in his unpublished Hopkins dissertation of 1952, "The Development of the French Short Story 1795-1850," and more recently, Maxwell Smith, in his Twayne study of Mérimée (New York, 1972).

[3]Albert George is especially helpful on the historical reasons for the rise of the short story. See especially chapter III of his *Short Fiction in France*. P. G. Castex's study of the fantastic tale (Paris, 1951) is an outstanding example of a theme study in short fiction. Pierre Trahard has studied Mérimée's short stories in a small volume (Paris, 1952), Edward Sullivan has examined Maupassant's short stories (London, 1962), and most recently there is my own study of the short stories of Anatole France (London, 1974). René Godenne has published the first volume of a history of the nouvelle (Geneva, 1970), and volume two is expected to deal with the nineteenth century. It promises to be the best tool so far made available to researchers in this field.

[4]Alfred Engstrom's article, previously cited, and even more his University of North Carolina dissertation (1941), "The Artistic Short Story before Maupassant," makes a serious effort to delimit the genre by means of the phrase "formal short story," and to define its characteristics. Marcel Raymond's essay, "Notes pour une histoire et une poétique de la nouvelle," in *Vérité et Poésie* (Neuchatel, 1964), is helpful on this subject too, though there is more "histoire" than "poétique" in his discussion.

[5]See Pierre Laubriet, *L'Intelligence de l'art chez Balzac* (Paris: Didier, 1961), passim, but especially pp. 145-252.

[6]Emile Zola, et al., *Les Soirées de Médan* (Paris: Fasquelle, 1955), p. 53

[7]Robert L. Hough, editor, *Literary Criticism of Edgar Allan Poe* (Lincoln: University of Nebraska Press, 1965), p. 136. The passage originally appeared in Poe's review of Hawthorne's *Twice-Told Tales*, in *Graham's Magazine* for May, 1842.

Histoire, Fiction, Légende

Robert Champigny
Indiana University †

A. *Préliminaires*

A1. Toute expérience est expérience de signes. Toute expérience est interprétative. Il n'y a pas d'interprétation sans signes et les signes ne signifient pas par eux-mêmes.

A2. Le sens est signification et valeur. On éprouve des significations selon certaines valeurs. On éprouve aussi des antisignifications selon certaines antivaleurs. On éprouve enfin les phénomènes (qui signifient), des fonds de nonsens qui peuvent être dits absurdes ou absolus.

A3. Les types d'interprétation, de compréhension, de signification, et donc d'antisignification, sont à distinguer selon des types de valeurs et d'antivaleurs: valeurs cognitives et morales d'une part, ludiques et esthétiques de l'autre. Les principaux types de signification verbale et nonverbale sont les mêmes; les catégories métasémantiques et métasémiotiques sont les mêmes.

A4. Les types verbaux de signification et d'interprétation sont des genres sémantiques. Les moyens qu'offre une langue ne sont pas suffisamment distincts et cohérents pour contraindre les interprètes à adopter un certain type d'interprétation. Il y a du flou entre stylistique et sémantique. Les divers styles ne peuvent qu'inciter, incliner.

A5. La base sémantique du genre philosophique est conceptuelle. Les concepts et leurs relations sont intemporels. La base sémantique des autres proses est temporelle, c'est-à-dire spatiotemporelle. Leur logique individue et peut personnifier ce qui est signifié. La poésie pure se compose en effaçant les catégories prosaïques. Elle tente d'homogénéiser les qualités phonétiques et sémantiques. Elle signifie qualitativement.

A6. Les proses temporalisantes sont historisantes ou fictivantes, proverbiales ou narratives. L'historisation ne se limite pas au passé, à des individus humains, à des événements jugés collectivement importants. Le genre narratif signifie des événements, des états de choses et des processus singuliers. Le genre proverbial, ou nomique, signifie ces entités génériquement. Il pose des corrélations répétitives. Les lois scientifiques sont des proverbes mathématisés.

Le genre narratif a une version historisante et une version fictivante. Le genre proverbial n'a pas de version fictivante. Le terme d'historiographie sera réservé à des écrits à base historisante et narrative. Il couvrira, entre autres, biographies et autobiographies.

A7. Les interprétations historisantes sont cognitives: elles tiennent des narrations ou proverbes pour plus ou moins vrais ou faux. Une interprétation fictivante considère une narration comme ni-vraie-ni-fausse. Dans ce cas, au lieu d'assertions, on a affaire à des axiomes narratifs. On n'ira pas dire qu'un romancier a menti ou a fait erreur, s'il a écrit: «Il pleuvait», à moins qu'on ne veuille parler d'une contradiction intérieure au texte.

La question du vrai et du faux étant éliminée, les compositions de philosophie ou de fiction s'orientent sur des valeurs ludiques et esthétiques. Un essai philosophique tel que celui-ci s'appuie sur mainte présupposition historisante; mais il ne prouve cognitivement rien et ne résout aucun problème cognitif. Un concept du vrai-faux ne peut être tenu ni pour vrai ni pour faux.

La distinction entre historique et fictif ne coïncide pas avec celle entre perception et imagination. Les signes sensoriels peuvent signifier du joué, du fictif. Les signes imaginatifs ne signifient pas toujours de l'imaginaire.

B. *Histoire et fiction*

B1. Les significations, ou interprétations, historisantes demandent une triple réciprocité entre signe et signifié, entre interprétation et signifié, entre les interprètes.

B2. Des signes signifient historiquement s'ils sont eux-mêmes interprétés comme événements historiques situés par rapport à ce qu'ils signifient. Je dois ainsi situer dans le domaine historique les paroles «Il pleut», «Il a plu avant-hier», «Il pleuvra demain». Au contraire, dans le cas d'une interprétation fictivante, l'événement historique de la parole ou de l'écriture n'est pas situé par rapport à l'événement fictif qui est signifié. Car il n'y a pas de relations spatiales et temporelles entre événements historiques et fictifs. Une interprétation, ou signification, fictivante doit être distinguée d'une interprétation, ou signification, fictive. A l'intérieur d'un domaine fictif, des interprètes fictifs interprètent des signes fictifs.

B3. Une interprétation historisante doit elle-même être historisée comme événement situé par rapport à l'événement de la parole ou de l'écriture et aux événements qu'elles signifient. En revanche, une interprétation fictivante n'est pas un événement fictif situé par rapport aux événements fictifs signifiés par la parole ou l'écriture.

B4. Historiquement, je ne peux me personnifier seul. Je me personnifie par rapport à d'autres interprètes. Fictivement, je peux me personnifier seul, me placer en seul interprète fictif dans un domaine fictif, par exemple si je joue seul. Il peut y avoir des romans ou des drames à un seul personnage, lequel personnage ne personnifierait rien d'autre. Même si une historiographie ne met qu'une seule personne en scène, cette personne est au contraire située par rapport aux autres interprètes historiques, en particulier l'auteur et les lecteurs.

B5. Il y a beaucoup de domaines fictifs, verbalement établis ou non: domaines romanesques, dramatiques, filmiques; domaines sportifs; domaines rêvés. Il n'y a en théorie qu'un domaine historique; c'est là un postulat de la possibilité de la connaissance: on n'ira pas vérifier dans un univers ce qu'on a cru constater dans un autre. Ainsi peut-il y avoir des contradictions entre assertions cognitives. En revanche, il ne peut y avoir de contradiction entre des axiomes narratifs appartenant à deux romans. Il peut simplement y avoir contradiction entre des axiomes considérés comme devant contribuer à la composition d'une même séquence d'événements fictifs. Dans ce cas, ou bien la contradiction est une faute, ou bien elle est reconnue comme impossibilité et finalement abolie (romans à énigme). Le terme de roman ne couvre donc pas ici des textes, appelés jadis «nouveaux romans», qui ne respectent pas la logique narrative et qui, de ce fait, seraient plutôt à étiqueter «antiromans» ou «poèmes en prose».

B6. La diversité des signes, l'hétérogénéité des phénomènes éprouvés permettent des vérifications. Elles permettent aux significations historisantes de nettement se détacher des interprétations fictivantes. Le signal verbal «Il pleut» est vérifié par des interprétations de signaux nonverbaux: tactiles (gouttes sur la peau), visuels (averse dehors), auditifs (pluie sur le toit). «Il a plu hier» serait à vérifier sur l'appui de signaux mémoriels, de traces extérieures, de divers autres témoignages verbaux. Au contraire, s'ils sont interprétés comme fictivants, si la valeur recherchée est esthétique, la zone des signes doit se restreindre, fournir une certaine homogénéité. Othello est signifié verbalement (et auditivement); il est aussi signifié visuellement (et nonverbalement). Mais on peut toucher un acteur, non Othello. Un chirurgien peut opérer un acteur, non Othello.

La théorie présentée ici concilie les théories de la vérité comme cohérence et comme correspondance. Toute expérience est expérience de signes. La correspondance cognitive est une cohérence entre des interprétations de signes hétérogènes. La dichotomie entre signifié et référent se trouve du même coup rejetée. Le référent est le signifié cognitif, l'intersection entre des interprétations historisantes de divers signes. Ce n'est pas une chose-en-soi.

C. *Légende*

C1. Par mythes, j'entends des indistinctions entre des significations cognitives-morales et ludiques-esthétiques. Les deux types principaux d'indistinction mythique sont l'allégorie (indistinction entre historique et conceptuel) et la légende (indistinction entre historique et fictif).

C2. Un rêve nocturne vécu sans conscience d'être en train de rêver est un exemple d'interprétation légendante. Si l'on rêvasse sur son passé au lieu de s'appuyer sur des souvenirs pour prévoir et agir, on légende. Il convient de distinguer entre émotion utilitaire et émotion jouée. Un acteur qui joue Othello joue la jalousie. Mais il peut se laisser prendre à son rôle. Les spectateurs n'ont pas l'idée qu'ils pourraient porter secours à Desdémone. Mais j'ai lu (c'est vrai ou c'est faux, peu importe ici, car l'exemple est philosophique, non scientifique) qu'un spectateur, outré de voir un moricaud marié à une blanche et occupé de surcroît à la tuer, avait fait usage de son revolver. Il ne distinguait pas entre l'acteur et le personnage.

D'un côté, comme le montre cet essai, une langue telle que le français offre des moyens de distinguer en théorie entre historique et fictif. D'un autre côté, elle ajoute des occasions d'indistinction légendaire. Elle n'offre pas en effet de distinctions morphologiques entre les mots employés pour historiser et pour fictiver: «Il pleuvait» peut être interprété cognitivement ou non. De plus, une certaine partie de ce que l'on tient pour vrai ou faux repose purement sur des indications verbales.

C3. C'est sur l'appui de témoignages verbaux que je crois être né en un certain lieu à une certaine date. Lisant ce que je prends en gros pour une autobiographie plutôt que pour un canular, je n'ai pas l'intention de vérifier ce qui est dit. Pour bien des passages, je ne vois pas d'ailleurs comment je m'y prendrais. Ce qui reste invérifié risque de se confondre avec ce qui n'est pas de nature à être vérifié, c'est-à-dire ici avec le fictif.

C4. Les historiographies tendent à légender en ceci que, sur la base de faits vérifiables, elles brodent des interprétations psychologiques invérifiables. Elles légendent aussi en ce qu'elles choisissent des faits discrets pour les rassembler plus ou moins élégamment en un collage global qui n'applique pas de lois causales expérimentalement vérifiables.

C5. Les personnages dramatiques parlent en discours direct. De même certains personnages romanesques. En quelle langue parle Rodrigue? En français du dix-septième siècle? Une langue historique déborde chacun de ses emplois particuliers. Au contraire, la langue que parlent les personnages dans une pièce ou un roman est limitée aux mots qu'ils emploient. Mais à quel point tel ou tel spectateur distingue-t-il entre la langue dans laquelle Corneille écrivit (passé historique) et la langue dans laquelle parle Rodrigue (présent fictif)?

On légenderait si l'on disait que le fictif imite l'historique ou l'historique le fictif. Car ce qui est imité précède ce qui imite; et l'on aurait ainsi l'air de placer historique et fictif dans le même domaine spatiotemporel, lequel ne pourrait être que légendaire. Disons plutôt qu'à un certain moment historique, un romancier a employé des mots d'une manière qui ressemblait à d'autres, historisantes, fictivantes ou légendantes.

C6. «‹Si j'étais riche›»; «‹si le nez de Cléopâtre avait été plus long›»; «si on mettait Paris en bouteilles (parfum d'égouts ou *Soir de Paris*?)». Les conditionnels dits irréels légendent. Ils agglomèrent une signification historisante et une signification fictivante. La Cléopâtre au nez plus long que la Cléopâtre historique est fictive. En termes de rhétorique, on a donc affaire à une antonomase non reconnue: «Cléopâtre» est à analyser comme nom commun.

On parle de romans historiques et d'histoire romancée. Mais les écrits appelés romans tout court se servent souvent eux aussi de raccords qu'on pourrait dire historisants: dates, lieux dits (villes, rues, pays), noms de personnes, d'objets, d'événements, d'institutions et de groupes (Napoléon, Tour Eiffel, révolution de février, religion catholique, parti communiste). Les indistinctions risquent ainsi, sans nécessité, de s'étendre aux noms propres.

Dans *La Condition humaine*, Tchen projette de tuer Tchang-Kaï-Chek à Changhai. Dans *Le Sursis*, Daladier débarque de l'avion qui le ramène de Munich en 1938. Dans *La Nausée*, Roquentin prend le train dans une ville fictive et se retrouve à Paris. Ce train fait des prodiges ontologiques. De même, apparemment, le service des postes pour les épistoliers historiques qui adressaient des missives à Sherlock Holmes, Baker Street.

Pour transplanter les ingrédients historiques, leur accorder droit de cité romanesque, on peut ici encore faire appel à l'antonomase. Il y a des villes historiques nommées «Paris»; il y a eu au moins une personne historique nommée «TchangKaï-Chek». D'autre part, il y a des villes et personnages fictifs de même nom, qui ressemblent à l'une de ces villes ou personnes historiques par certains traits. Mais, ici encore, comme dans le cas des langues historiques et fictives, les villes et personnages fictifs sont limités à ce qui est dit d'eux, le reste demeurant irréductiblement indéfini.

Tout lecteur de roman réagit-il ainsi? Ai-je toujours réagi ainsi? Dans quelle mesure y a-t-il transposition au fictif, dans quelle mesure contamination et indistinction de légende? Cela dépend des textes, des circonstances, des interprètes, de leur culture et de leurs expériences passées. Comment s'en rendre compte? La science des cerveaux ne nous dit pas encore grand chose concernant les questions de psycho-linguistique. Et si je fais de l'introspection, ce qui se passe dans ma tête s'évanouit comme Eurydice.

C7. Victor Hugo était un fou qui se prenait pour Victor Hugo. Nul besoin d'être célèbre pour cela; nul besoin d'être officiellement classé fou. Nous nous légendons nous-mêmes en nous légendant les uns les autres, et autre chose que des humains (villes, pays, objets). Pourquoi, au-delà de ce qui est inévitable?

En légendant, on peut chercher à profiter des avantages de la fiction sans la reconnaître pour telle. Les axiomes fictivants ne sont pas à vérifier. Ils peuvent passer pour certains et complets. Ainsi réaliseraient-ils l'idéal de la connaissance, de l'historisation. Et l'on oublie que ce serait en irréalisant. Moralement d'autre part, l'ingrédient fictif permet d'esthétiser le mal. On jouit de la compassion.

Les folies collectives offrent un refuge, un remède, aux folies personnelles. Elles apportent l'appui d'un accord verbal entre des interprètes. Des couples aux multitudes, les objectifs des groupements sociaux ne se limitent pas à des buts, soit utilitaires, soit ludiques, bien déterminés. En devenant collectives, les allégories et légendes deviennent religieuses.

C8. D'un côté, la littérature a tendu à saper la religiosité. Même si elle n'est pas critique, la prolifération fictive émiette les dieux et héros, humains ou non, qui aident les membres d'un groupe à se légender. D'un autre côté, la production littéraire est demeurée contaminée. Les épopées, pièces et romans ont jeté des ponts illogiques entre historique et fictif; et les métaphysiques entre intemporel et temporel, concept et individu. D'où des personnages allégoriques tels que l'Homme, l'Amour, la Vérité, Dieu. *Le Roman de la Rose* résume tout cela.

C9. Pourquoi, maintenant encore, dans des pièces et des romans, continue-t-on à insérer tant de pseudo-identités entre des entités historiques et des entités fictives? Pour attaquer directement des légendes? Parfois; mais on ne peut ainsi que proposer des contre-légendes, des contre-mythes. La complicité religieuse demeure.

On Narratology (Past, Present, Future)

Gerald Prince
University of Pennsylvania

Within the past few years, many volumes devoted to the presentation and discussion of narratological principles, achievements, and goals and just as many volumes devoted to the narratologically inspired study of particular aspects of narrative have appeared.[1] The abundance of this production may be due to a greater awareness of the importance of narrative in human life, a greater awareness that, in large part, springs from narratology itself. After all, the latter has underlined the extent to which narrative inhabits not only literary texts and ordinary language but also scholarly or technical discourse; and narratological tools and arguments have been used in domains far exceeding the bounds of "literary studies proper": in musicology, art criticism, and film studies, for instance, to investigate compositional and representational practices; in cultural analysis, to trace the ways in which various forms of power legitimate themselves through narrative; in psychology, to explore memory and comprehension.[2]

Narratology has made it clear that, while narrative can have any number of functions (entertaining, informing, persuading, diverting attention, etc.), there are some functions that it excels at or is unique in fulfilling. Narrative always reports one or more changes of state but, as etymology suggests (the term *narrative* is related to the Latin *gnarus*—"knowing," "expert," "acquainted with"—which itself derives from the Indo-European root *gnâ*, to know"), narrative is also a particular mode of knowledge. It does not merely reflect what happens; it discovers and invents what can happen. It does not simply record events; it constitutes and interprets them as meaningful parts of meaningful wholes, whether the latter are situations, practices, persons, or societies. As such, narrative can provide an explanation of individual fate as well as group destiny, the unity of a self as well as the nature of a collectivity. By showing that disparate situations and events compose one signifying structure (or vice versa) and, more specifically, by giving its own form of order and coherence to a possible reality, narrative supplies models for that reality's transformation or redescription and mediates between the law of what is and the human desire for what may be. Above all, perhaps, by instituting different moments in time and establishing links between them, by finding significant patterns in temporal sequences, by pointing to an end already partly contained in the beginning and to a beginning already partly containing the end, by exposing the meaning of time and imposing meaning on it, narrative reads time and teaches how to read it. In other words, narratology has helped to show how narrative is a structure and practice that illuminates temporality and human beings as temporal beings. Indeed, to speak most generally, narratology does have crucial implications for our self-understanding. To study the nature of narratives, to examine how and why it is that we can construct them, memorize them, paraphrase them, summarize and expand them, or organize them in terms of such categories as plot, narrator, narratee, and character is to study one of the fundamental ways—and a singularly human one at that—in which we *make* sense.

The abundance of recent narratological production may also be due to the undeniable usefulness of narratological instruments for the description, classification, and interpretation of literary narratives. On the one hand, of course, narratology is not mainly or primarily a handmaiden of literary analysis and hermeneutics. Its very origins (Propp's investigation of the Russian fairy tale, say, and Lévi-Strauss's exploration of the logic of myth),[3] its domain and ambitions as delineated by some of its practitioners (narratology is a theory of narrative; it studies its nature, form, and functioning and tries to characterize narrative competence; rather than being concerned with the history, meaning, or purpose of particular narratives, it examines what all and only possible narratives have in common as well as what enables them to differ from one another *qua* narratives and it aims to describe the narratively pertinent system of rules presiding over narrative production and processing),[4] and many of the criticisms directed at it (narratology has been taken to task for its universalizing ambitions, its scientific bias, its reductionism, the cumbersomeness of the apparatus it needs to account for even the simplest narratives, and the reductiveness of its models)[5]— all of these could imply that any (fruitful) narratological focus on individual literary texts would be quite problematic. Indeed, through its concerns for the governing principles of narrative and through its attempt to characterize not so much the particular meaning of particular narratives but rather what allows narratives to have meanings, narratology has proven to be an important participant in the assault against viewing literary studies as devoted above all to the interpretation of texts. On the other hand, though it aspires to be an autonomous branch of poetics rather than a foundation for critical commentary, narratology has fostered an important body of narratological criticism, two main forms of which can be distinguished.

In the first place, narratological description can not only help to account for the uniqueness of any given narrative, to compare any two (sets of) narratives, and to institute narrative classes according to narratively pertinent features, but it can also help to account for certain responses to texts (if *L'Etranger* is esthetically powerful, perhaps it is partly because of the way Camus makes it impossible to situate the narrating instance in time and space), to support certain interpretive conclusions (the switch from first-to third-person narration in *Madame Bovary* underscores Flaubert's rejection of subjective narrative), and even—by providing certain points of departure—to devise (new) interpretations (François Mauriac's *Le Noeud de vipères*, for example, features a first-person narrator addressing a series of different narratees: it could mean, perhaps, that the novel is ultimately about a human being in search of an understanding audience; or again, to argue like Mieke Bal, the multiplication of causes and effects at the beginning of the *Iliad* indicates how the life of human beings is "determined by powers beyond them;" the continual embedding of important events into banal ones that function as their causes can signal "the impotency of man against the world;" and an abundance of temporal anticipations, of flashforwards, may "express a fatalistic vision of life").[6] Indeed, as Gérard Genette's outstanding "Discours du récit" and a long tradition of (para-narratological) Anglo-American and Germanic criticism centered on narrative technique demonstrate, any narratologically descriptive statement can become a springboard for a reading, any technical feature can lead to the construction of meaning, any "how" can give rise to a "why."[7]

In the second place, by characterizing the elements necessary to any and all narratives, by determining the principles governing their production and processing, by studying the ways in which they can reflect themselves, the *mises en abyme* of the code, the enunciation, and the enunciated, by specifying that there is, in a narrative text, an autonomous layer, a system constituting that which in the text is "properly" narrative, a configuration instituting events as such, fixing their beginning and their end, and dictating the itinerary linking them, narratology facilitates the choice of narrative as thematic frame and its influence explains in part the extraordinary popularity recently enjoyed by that frame.

During the past twenty years, the theme of narrative has been exploited intensively and has given rise to countless "narrative" readings of well-known texts (I mobilized it myself to study *Candide* and *Le Moyen de parvenir, Bel-Ami, Le Noeud de vipères*, and *Journal de Salavin*). It has been said to be the theme privileged by any great narrative, the theme indispensable to any narrative (I read in Jean Ricardou that great narratives are recognizable by the sign that the fiction they propose is nothing else than the dramatization of their own functioning; in Tzvetan Todorov, that narrative is the essential theme of the *Quête du Saint Graal* just as it is the essential theme of any narrative, but always in a different way; in Roland Barthes, that "in exemplary narratives, narration is the theory of narration" and that "ultimately, there is no *object* of narrative: narrative discusses only itself: *narrative tells itself*").[8] In (re)discovering and (re)inventing narrative, narratology allows us better to (re)discover and to (re)invent narrative as theme. Narrative consists of a certain number of sequences combined through simple conjunction, embedding, or alternation; it features narrations, narrators, and narratees; it implies a (partially ordered) series of transformations; it is both product and production, structure and structuration, object and act; it settles in repetition, moves through the desire for an end and its deferral deciphers temporality and memory. These narratologically-specified traits (and numerous others!) constitute so many entrance and reference points in the domain covered by the theme of narrative and they even provide a basis for the following preliminary articulation of that theme. Narrative is an act and it is an object. This act and this object have a certain value (what they are or could be exchanged for, what they represent or could represent) that (1) can be underlined by entities or practices constituting the contradictory, the contrary, the intensification, or the diminution of narrative; (2) can be modalized in terms of the will, the duty, the knowledge, the power from which narrative springs or which it implies; and (3) can be positive or negative with regard to the circumstances in which narrative appears and to the participants which it involves.[9]

Finally, the abundance of recent narratologically-centered volumes may constitute a mere end-of-century symptom (stock-taking activities are particularly common at certain temporal junctures)[10] or, more ominously (?), this abundance may be an indication that narratology (perhaps because of its very triumphs) can no longer progress very much. If, from a more strictly critical point of view, one could multiply profitably readings, taxonomies, and typologies based on narratological features or exploring more systematically the concrete manifestations of narrative as theme, from a more theoretical point of view, about the only thing that could be done would be to provide ever more lucid, more systematic, and more self-conscious characterizations of work already accomplished.

This last assessment, however, would not be quite adequate. To begin with, the very domain of narratology is in constant flux and the discipline keeps on changing as its boundaries are (re)drawn. If narratology is a theory of narrative, its corpus and scope depend, first of all, on the definition of narrative.[11] When the latter is viewed primarily as a verbal mode of representation (the telling of events by a narrator as opposed to, say, the enacting of them on stage), the narratologist (e.g. Gérard Genette) pays little or no attention to the story, the narrated, the "*what*" that is represented and concentrates instead on the discourse, the narrating, the *way* in which the "what" is represented. This view may well have tradition on its side: the Latin term *narrare* designated a *language* act and the opposition between *diegesis* and *mimesis*, recounting and representing, epic and drama, narrative and theater goes back to Plato and is still very common. Furthermore, this view may well capture the specificity of a purely verbal representation of events by a narrator and, in particular, account for the many ways in which the same set of events can be told (cf. "Mary ate before she slept" and "Mary slept after she ate"). But it neglects the fact that non-verbal or mixed modes of event representation (e.g. movies or comic strips) are often taken to *tell* stories, to *recount* them, and are often referred to as narratives; besides, it forgets that the story too makes narrative whatever it is (without story, no narrative). When, on the contrary, narrative is defined not so much in terms of mode (a narrator narrating) or substance (linguistic as opposed to non-linguistic) but rather, as in Paul Ricoeur's *Temps et récit,* by its object (events), the narratologist focuses on the structure of represented events and their possible combinations. But she or he would then be unable to account for the various forms a given story can take.[12] There is a third possibility. Since both story *and* discourse, narrated *and* narrating make up narrative, a number of narratologists (e.g. Jean-Michel Adam) define the latter as the *representation* (verbal or non-verbal, with or without a narrator) of one or more events and they attempt to integrate the study of the "what" and the way.[13]

Of course, even if all narratologists agreed on a definition of narrative, they would still have to determine what in narrative is specific or relevant to narrative. Narratology is not so much a theory of narrative as it is a theory of narrative *qua* narrative: it tries to account for all and only possible narratives to the extent that they are narrative. Now, if plot structure, say, and temporal relations are clearly pertinent to narrativity and if psychological insight, comic power, or philosophical force are not, the relevance of certain other elements or aspects of narrative texts to the study of narrativity is much more difficult to fix. Think of *style,* for instance, which can help to characterize and differentiate narrator and characters; or think of *tone,* which can affect the very way a novel or a tale *makes* sense. Though neither of these elements constitutes a *differentia specifica* of narrative, the same can be said of character, description, or even focalization; and only much further study can determine the narrative and narratological pertinence of stylistic or tonal qualities.[14] To summarize—and to put it bluntly—narratology is still a very young discipline whose limits and limitations are problematic.

Besides, much narratological investigation is needed (and much is going on) both in areas that are already considerably developed and in areas that have been overly neglected or that have proven particularly thorny. Even in the area of discourse—the one in which the advances of narratology have been the most spectacular—many problems still confront the narratologist (what, for example, are the links between speed and frequency? what is the relationship, if any, between person and point of view? what are the constraints on the possible combinations of given features of the narrating?). In the area of story, much work remains to be done on such categories as "narrative space" (following the lead of Philippe Hamon, Helmut Bonheim, or Gabriel Zoran) and "character" (Thomas Docherty, Uri Margolin, and—once again—Philippe Hamon suggest several interesting avenues of research).[15] Furthermore, narratological models of plot and its syntax (from Propp to Greimas and to my own grammars) have too often proved overly static: they have tended to ignore—or have been unable to characterize—the progressive logic of stories;[16] they have disregarded the motor forces that drive a narrative forward to an end; they have not made enough room for temporal dynamics. More recent modeling attempts have begun to rectify the situation. Thus, the latest narrative grammar I know, that of Thomas Pavel, underlines the primacy of action and transformation and sketches the system of energies, tensions, and resistances that plot constitutes. Similarly, Marie-Laure Ryan has been developing an artificial intelligence inspired model that gives its due to the moments of suspense and surprise, advance and delay, trickery and illumination, to the samba-like movement emblematic of plot.[17]

If interest and work in the syntactic dimension of narratives have not diminished, the study of their semantic dimension has made important advances. We know that, in the 1960s and 1970s, narratologists often ignored the question of narrative meaning or, at the very least, attempted to place it temporarily within brackets. The enormous prestige of linguistics as the "hardest" and most successful of the human sciences led many narratologists to pattern their work first on structural linguistics then on (early) transformational grammar, that is, on theories of language that had little to say about meaning (and context). Moreover, that which is most specific to narrative, that which is most narrative in it, is the syntax and the discourse: a poem or an essay may, after all, have the same subject, develop the same themes, and occur in the same context as a narrative. Narratologists therefore concentrated on the syntactic and "discursive" traits distinguishing narratives from other signifying systems and on the modalities of these traits. Finally (and candidly!), questions of meaning are rather difficult to solve and to formalize. Granted, quite a few narratologically important texts were much more semantics-bound than I have just made it seem. Propp's *Morphology of the Folktale*, which stresses syntagmatic rather than paradigmatic structures, develops only an elementary syntax and relies heavily on semantic operations to isolate and name the thirty-one functions constituting the basic components of any fairy tale; Greimas's most important contributions to narrative theory can be found in his *Sémantique structurale* and *Du sens* (both titles are revealing); and the short-lived offshoot of transformational grammar known as generative semantics did inspire at least one model of narrative in which the rules generating deep structures are principles and constraints providing for semantic coherence and correct logical form.[18] Still, until recently, achievements in narrative semantics proper did not match those in narrative discourse and narrative syntax. The situation has been changing, thanks to the work of Lubomír Dolezel on modality, for example, to that of Pavel and Ryan on narrative domains and narrative worlds, and to that of researchers in cognitive psychology and artificial intelligence who view stories as problem-solving schemata.[19]

Many narratologists now consider that a story can be characterized as a universe consisting of one or more worlds. There are actual worlds, which have an absolute or autonomous existence, may or may not be similar to our own "real" world, and comprise the current state of affairs, its predecessors, the laws defining the range of possible future changes from the current state of affairs, and those changes that are actualized. These actual worlds may be ontologically flat (governed by one set of laws) or salient (split into two or more autonomous spheres—e.g. sacred and profane—each governed by its own set of laws) and they may contain beings with a flat or salient private ontology (think of Joan of Arc in *Saint Joan* or of Don Juan in the myth). There are also relative worlds (representations of actual worlds or of other relative worlds, "idealized" models of them, and alternatives to them), each set of which pertaining to the same character constitutes that character's domain. For example, there are epistemic or knowledge-worlds (what a character knows or believes), wish-worlds, moral worlds (specifying what a character considers good, bad, or indifferent for all the members of a particular group), obligation-worlds (specifying the values of a group as opposed to those of an individual), and alternate worlds (creations of the mind: dreams, fantasies, hallucinations, fictions, counterfactual statements, and so on). In terms of this semantic characterization, plot is a function of the relations between and within worlds in the global narrative universe. It moves from one set of relations to another through events aiming for, producing, affecting, or resolving conflicts in these relations. Such conflicts (and their motivations) vary in kind and can occur, for instance, between the worlds of two different characters (John wants X but Mary wants Y), between the worlds of one character's domain (Jane must not do X according to her society but Jane wants to do X), or within one of the worlds of a given character (Peter must do Y and must also do its contrary).

So acute has been the interest in problems of narrative meaning that narratologists have even begun to investigate such notions as "theme" (!), the possible affinities between certain kinds of narrative structures and certain families of themes (Aarne-Thompson's so-called *unfinished tales*, for instance, may be linked to the theme of narrative as trap and their *endless tales* to that of narrative as deferral), and the thematic content of given plot articulations.[20] Particularly suggestive in this regard and potentially fruitful for criticism is the work of Pavel on the meaning of plot architecture. At the basis of any narrative, there can be said to be a balance to (re)establish, a lack to liquidate, a need to satisfy, or, in other words, a state of affairs calling for a certain mobilization of energy. Following the recent work of Peter Brooks, who attempted to link the form and progression of a plot with the turns and detours of desire which found the narrative enterprise, and prolonging Aristotle, Hegel, and Northrop Frye, Pavel analyzed some of the (signifying) relations between narrative dynamics and energetic investment and he sketched a typology of plot based on the energy of the protagonist and the obstacles she or he must overcome to reach a particular goal.[21]

But perhaps the most striking difference between what might be called the classical narratology of the 1960s and 1970s and what might be designated as modern narratology is the increased attention paid to pragmatics. Again, I do not mean to say that pragmatic factors were entirely ignored by classical narratologists. After all, in "Introduction à l'analyse structurale des récits," Roland Barthes suggested that perhaps the most powerful motor of narrativity is the *post hoc ergo propter hoc* fallacy.[22] Yet the allegiance to strategies and arguments inspired by structural linguistics or generative-transformational grammar, the concern for capturing the *differentiae specificae* of narrative, the difficulty of incorporating contextual factors into a systematic description, and the "scientific" ambitions of narratology (its desire, in particular, to isolate narrative universals, which transcend context) resulted in the narratologists' reluctance to make pragmatics part of their domain of inquiry and in their neglect of the contextual dimensions of meaning production and processing. During the last few years, because of the repeated (sociolinguistic) reminders about the importance of communicative contexts, because of the great interest among literary critics in receivers and their decoding strategies, because of the increasing number of cognition-oriented studies, and because of the growing awareness that narrative must be viewed not only as an object or product but also as an act or process, as a situation-bound transaction between two parties, as an exchange resulting from the desire of at least one of these parties, a number of narratologists have begun to address explicitly questions pertaining to narrative pragmatics.

Thus, Susan Sniader Lanser and Robyn Warhol, in attempting to develop a feminist narratology, have stressed the advantages for narrative theory of being socially sensitive and of considering the role of gender in narrative production and processing. Ross Chambers has insisted on the importance of reading *in* narratives the situation they produce as giving them their point and on the equal importance of reading narrative meaning as a function of the situation in which narratives occur. In *Le Texte narratif*, Jean-Michel Adam has tried to build a model that takes into account the contract between sender and receiver underlying an act of narration. Similarly, I have argued that one way of accounting for the multiple interpretations that a single narrative (or non-narrative) can yield is to consider the context of that narrative (or non-narrative) as part of its text; I have further argued that a multiplicity of contexts results in a multiplicity of points; and I have stressed that narratological models of narrative ultimately should include—along with a syntactic, a semantic, and a discursive component—a pragmatic one.[23]

Moreover, some narratologists have attempted to isolate the factors affecting the value of a narrative *qua* narrative, the properties accounting for tellability. Ryan, for example, has argued that some configurations of events make better narratives than others: her formal model of plot predicts that tellability is a function of unrealized strings of events (unsuccessful actions, broken promises, crushed hopes, etc.), that it increases as the narrative goes back and forth between the competing plans of (different) characters, and, most generally, that it depends on the functioning of "virtual embedded narratives" (any story-like representations produced in the mind of a character).[24]

Likewise, I had myself underlined the importance for tellability of such elements as discreteness and specificity of events, hierarchical structuring, conflictual plans, and wholeness.[25] I have also started to explore the tellability function of what I call the disnarrated: all those terms, phrases, and passages in a narrative that refer to what *does not* take place ("this could have happened but didn't;" "this didn't happen but could have") whether they pertain to the vision of a narrator ("You will suppose that it was the people from the inn, their servants, and the brigands of whom we spoke.... You will suppose that this little army will set upon Jacques and his master, that there will be a bloody skirmish...and it lies entirely within my power to make all of that happen; but farewell the truth of the story") or whether they spring from the views of a character ("How easy and unexpected it had been! Until then, he had imagined that, to approach and conquer one of these creatures he so much desired, infinite attentions were required, interminable waits, a skillful siege made up of gallantries, words of love, sighs, and presents. And suddenly, after the slightest of attacks, the first one he met gave way to him so quickly that it left him dumbfounded"). The disnarrated, which helps to make explicit the logic at work in narrative whereby every narrative function opens an alternative, a set of possible directions, and every narrative progresses by following certain directions as opposed to others, can, of course, fulfill a number of functions (becoming a rhythmical instrument, for example, contributing to the development of a theme, its designation, focalization, and individualization, depicting a character, or foregrounding the links between narrator and narratee). But its most important function is probably a rhetorical/interpretive one. When it refers back to a narrator's vision, it underlines certain ways of fabricating a world, of making up a situation, of exploiting a norm or refusing a convention, and it conveys something like the following message: "This narrative is valuable because it develops in terms of different and more interesting narrative strategies." When it refers back to a character's views, it emphasizes the qualities of the very world represented rather than that of the representation: "this narrative is worth telling because '*it*' could have been otherwise, because '*it*' is usually otherwise, because '*it*' is precisely what happened and not something else." In other words, the disnarrated institutes an antimodel in terms of which the narrative text defines itself and underlines the values which it elaborates and to which it aspires.[26]

Beside the shifting nature of narratology's domain and the (need for further) work in (well-developed and not so well-developed) narratological areas of inquiry, there is a third factor that has affected the development of the discipline and that will, I think, insure its liveliness for some time to come: narratological criticism itself. If narratology provides tools and ideas for investigations of specific texts, these investigations, in turn, test the validity of narratological categories, distinctions, and arguments, they identify (more or less significant) elements that narratologists (may) have overlooked, underestimated, or misunderstood, and they (can) lead to basic reformulations of models of narrative. Even a quick study of Giraudoux's *Bella*, for example, is enough to make it clear that there is no essential contradiction between a first-person narration and an omniscient point of view; similarly, an energy-centered analysis of the interaction between the plot architecture of Maupassant's *Bel-Ami* and the world view that it conditions and is conditioned by brings out the importance of an element narratology has overly neglected and should take into account: that of the length of the narrative text;[27] and a careful examination of Robbe-Grillet's *La Jalousie*—which involves temporal distinctions and represents events while resisting chronological ordering—shows that narratologists would be wrong to assume that the fundamental order of narrative sequencing is bound to chronology.

To recapitulate and conclude very quickly, narratologists still have a lot of work to do. They should make the imperatives, goals, and limitations of their discipline clearer to others and to themselves; they should multiply their explorations of those factors and principles that underlie narrative form, meaning, and functioning; and, with the help of other students of narrative, they should endeavor to perfect the fit between their theory of narrative and the narrative texts for which that theory strives to account.

---

[1] See, for instance, Jean-Michel Adam, *Le Récit* (Paris: Presses Universitaires de France, 1984) and, by the same author, *Le Texte narratif* (Paris: Nathan, 1985); Mieke Bal, *Narratology: Introduction to the Theory of Narrative* (Toronto: University of Toronto Press, 1983); Anne Hénault, *Narratologie, sémiotique générale: les enjeux de la sémiotique 2* (Paris: Presses Universitaires de France, 1983); Thomas Pavel, *The Poetics of Plot. The Case of English*

Renaissance Drama (Minneapolis: University of Minnesota Press, 1985); and Shlomith Rimmon-Kenan, *Narrative Fiction. Contemporary Poetics* (London: Methuen, 1983).

[2] See, for example, Anthony Newcomb, "Schumann and Late Eighteenth Century Narrative Strategies," *19th-Century Music*, IX (1987), 164-174; Wendy Steiner, *Pictures of Romance: Form against Context in Painting and Literature* (Chicago: University of Chicago Press, 1988); Christian Metz, *Essais sur la signification au cinéma* (Paris: Klincksieck, 1968); Fredric Jameson, *The Political Unconscious: Narrative as a Socially Symbolic Act* (Ithaca: Cornell University Press, 1981); Christine G. Glenn, "The Role of Episodic Structure and Story Length in Children's Recall of Simple Stories," *Journal of Verbal Learning and Verbal Behavior*, XVII (1978), 229-247; Nancy L. Stein, "The Definition of a Story," *Journal of Pragmatics*, VI (1982), 487-507.

[3] Vladimir Propp, *Morphology of the Folktale* (Austin: University of Texas Press, 1968); Claude Lévi-Strauss, *Anthropologie structurale* (Paris: Plon, 1958).

[4] See, for instance, Gerald Prince, "Narratological Illustrations," *Semiotica*, LXVIII (1988), 355-366 or, by the same author, *Narratology. The Form and Functioning of Narrative* (Berlin: Mouton, 1982).

[5] Cf., e.g., Wayne C. Booth, *The Rhetoric of Fiction*, 2nd ed. (Chicago: University of Chicago Press, 1981) or Barbara Herrnstein Smith, "Narrative Versions, Narrative Theories" in W. J. T. Mitchell, ed., *On Narrative* (Chicago: University of Chicago Press, 1981), pp. 209-232.

[6] Mieke Bal, *Narratology*, op cit., pp. 21, 55, and 63.

[7] Gérard Genette, "Discours du récit" in *Figures III* (Paris: Seuil, 1972), pp. 65-282. See also Wayne C. Booth, *The Rhetoric of Fiction*, op cit.; Eberhart Lammert, *Bauformen des Erzählens* (Stuttgart: J. B. Metzlersche Verlag, 1955); and Franz Stanzel, *Narrative Situations in the Novel: "Tom Jones," "Moby Dick," "The Ambassadors," "Ulysses"* (Bloomington: Indiana University Press, 1971).

[8] Jean Ricardou, "L'Histoire dans l'histoire" in *Problèmes du nouveau roman* (Paris: Seuil, 1967); Tzvetan Todorov, "La Quête du récit" in *Poétique de la prose* (Paris: Seuil, 1971); Roland Barthes, *S/Z* (Paris: Seuil, 1970), pp. 96 and 219.

[9] On the theme of narrative, see Gerald Prince, "Le Thème du récit," *Communications*, no 47 (1988), 199-208.

[10] Cf., e.g., Gerald Prince, *A Dictionary of Narratology* (Lincoln: University of Nebraska Press, 1987).

[11] Cf. Michel Mathieu-Colas's outstanding "Frontières de la narratologie," *Poétique*, no 65 (1986), 91-110.

[12] Paul Ricoeur, *Temps et récit* (Paris: Seuil, 1983).

[13] Jean-Michel Adam, *Le Texte narratif*, op. cit.

[14] Cf. Susan Sniader Lanser, "Shifting the Paradigm: Feminism and Narratology," *Style*, XXII (1988), 52-60.

[15] See Helmut W. Bonheim, *The Narrative Modes: Techniques of the Short Story* (Cambridge, England: D. S. Brewer, 1982); Thomas Docherty, *Reading (Absent) Character* (Oxford: Clarendon, 1983); Philippe Hamon, *Introduction à l'analyse du descriptif* (Paris: Hachette, 1981) and, by the same author, *Le Personnel du roman* (Geneve: Droz, 1983); Uri Margolin, "Characterization in Narrative," *Neophilologus*, LVII (1983), 1-14; and Gabriel Zoran, "Towards a Theory of Space in Narrative," *Poetics Today*, V (1984), 309-335.

[16] A notable early exception is Claude Bremond, *Logique du récit* (Paris: Seuil, 1973).

[17] See Thomas Pavel, *The Poetics of Plot*, op. cit. and Marie-Laure Ryan, "Embedded Narratives and Tellability," *Style*, XX (1986), 319-340.

[18] A. J. Greimas, *Sémantique structurale* (Paris: Larousse, 1966) and *Du sens* (Paris: Seuil, 1970); Marie-Laure Ryan, "Linguistic Models in Narratology," *Semiotica*, XXVIII (1979), 127-155.

[19]See, for example, John B. Black and Gordon Bower, "Story Understanding as Problem Solving," *Poetics*, IX (1980), 223-250; Lubomír Dolezel, "Narrative Semantics," *PTL*, I (1976), 129-151; Thomas Pavel, "Narrative Domains," *Poetics Today*, I (1980), 105-114; and Marie-Laure Ryan, "The Modal Structure of Narrative Universes," *Poetics Today*, VI (1985), 717-755.

[20]See *Poétique*, no 64 (1985). The entire number is devoted to the question of theme.

[21]Thomas Pavel, "Le Déploiement de l'intrigue," *Poétique*, no 64 (1985), 455-461 and *The Poetics of Plot*, op. cit. See also Peter Brooks, *Reading for the Plot. Design and Intention in Narrative*. (New York: A. A. Knopf, 1984).

[22]Roland Barthes, "Introduction à l'analyse structurale des récits," *Communications*, no 8 (1966), 1-27.

[23]Thomas Pavel, "Le Déploiement de l'intrigue," *Poétique*, no 64 (1985), 455-461 and *The Poetics of Plot*, op. cit. See also Peter Brooks, *Reading for the Plot. Design and Intention in Narrative* (New York: A. A. Knopf, 1984).

[24]Marie-Laure Ryan, "Embedded Narratives and Tellability," op. cit.

[25]Gerald Prince, *Narratology*, op. cit., chapter V.

[26]Cf. Gerald Prince, "The Disnarrated," *Style*, XXII (1988), 1-8.

[27]See Gerald Prince, "Architecture et thématique dans Bel-Ami," *Littérature*, no 71 (1988), 59-66.

II. PERIODIZATION: FROM THE "DEFFENCE" TO POSTMODERNISM

The *Deffence* and French Humanism

Donald Stone, Jr.
Harvard University

When Johan Huizinga published *The Waning of the Middle Ages*[1] and traced in its final pages "the advent of the new form," that is, the coming of the Northern Renaissance, the Dutch critic effectively summarized the thoughts of a great many scholars of the day. For example, in his last chapter Huizinga characterizes the *grands rhétoriqueurs* as cultivating "literature in the form of an all-round game" (p. 329) and as being responsible for stylistic excesses which "by no means give us the feeling of the measure and harmony of the Renaissance" (p. 330). Interestingly enough, Huizinga groups *rhétoriqueurs* and humanists together in these judgments and declares that neither classicism nor paganism would provide the essence of Renaissance literature. The "moderns" of the fifteenth century are, he says, Villon, Charles d'Orléans, "just those who kept most aloof from classicism and who did not strain after over-nice forms" (p. 332). They merit the label "modern" by the "spontaneity of their expression" (ibid.) and signal to what degree writers had begun "to grasp . . . the spirit [of antiquity]" (p. 335), to what extent "the incomparable simpleness and purity of the ancient culture, its exactitude of conception and of expression, its easy and natural thought and strong interest in men and in life,—all this began to dawn upon men's minds" (p. 338).

Since these lines were written, the profession has revised many of their assumptions. Following the lead of Paul Kristeller, who maintains that "Renaissance humanism must be understood as a characteristic phase in what may be called the rhetorical tradition in Western culture,"[2] more and more scholars have pointed out the crucial importance of the theory and practice of antiquity's "art of speaking well" for an accurate evaluation of Pléiade poetry.[3] We are now aware also of the fact that whatever the shortcomings of the *rhétoriqueurs* may have been, we can no longer in good conscience reduce their poetry to "literature in the form of an all-round game.[4] Techniques and theories that pervade French humanist writing throughout the sixteenth century appear already in the works of the *rhétoriqueurs*. Well before the publication of the *Deffence* in 1549, Jean Robertet speaks about divine inspiration and the poet's gift of immortality to those about whom the poet chooses to sing. Barthélemy Aneau and Pierre Saliat defend French against Latin. Saliat even alludes in a work of 1537 to "plusieurs nobles espritz de ce temps, lesquelz chescun [sic] jour s'efforcent d'ennoblier et enrichir notre langue Francoyse."[5]

It is very possible that had one confronted Huizinga with such a reassessment, he would not have changed the basic outlines of "the advent of the new form." Maintaining with considerable firmness that "Nothing is more erroneous than to identify classicism and modern culture" (p. 335), he shows his determination to distinguish between mere familiarity with ancient forms and a process which caught the "spirit" of antiquity. By this notion he seems to describe both a philosophical and a literary awakening. On the one hand, the Renaissance writers began to grasp antiquity's "strong interest in men and in life"; on the other, "the incomparable simpleness and purity of the ancient culture, its exactitude of conception and of expression." These views have been with us so long in Renaissance studies and have been repeated in so many various ways that it may appear to some as foolhardy to consider them worthy of reevaluation. Yet no less than older remarks on the *rhétoriqueurs*, such claims too prove subject to question when we explore the texts of the period.

The sixteenth century saw many ancient works translated into French for the first time. The authors of these translations inevitably justify their efforts in some liminary statement printed with the new French text. Thus, Amyot speaks at length about Heliodorus' *Histoire Aethiopique* and Peletier du Mans writes several lines of poetry to introduce his rendering of Homer's *Odyssey*. What we learn from their remarks is not easily described by the phrase "the spirit of antiquity," however. Amyot praises in Heliodorus "oultre lingenieuse fiction, ...quelques lieux de beaux discours tirez de la Philosophie Naturelle, & Morale: force dictz notables, & propos sentencieux: plusieurs belles harengues, ou l'artifice d'eloquence est tresbien employé."[6] The presence of these qualities is so important that it directs the movement of the entire preface. To underscore the worth of the *Histoire Aethiopique*, Amyot points out that the "truth" of history is to some too austere "to please sufficiently,"[7] and medieval romances, in addition to being poorly structured, possess "nulle erudition, nulle cognoissance de l'antiquité, ne chose aucune (à brief parler) dont on peust tirer quelque vtilité" (printer's flower 2ᵛ).

Peletier, too, admires the style of the author he has translated and admits to having tried to omit nothing:

> Mais il conuient garder la maiesté,
> Et le naif de l'ancienneté,
> Pareillement exprimer les vertuz
> Des adiectifz dont les motz sont vestuz,

Et biengarder en son entier l'obiet
De son Autheur, auquel on est subiet.[8]

Addressing the King, Peletier stresses also that with both the *Iliad* and the *Odyssey* now translated into French, one can contemplate how by a merging of Achilles' bravery and Odysseus' cleverness, a stronger and more resourceful knight would emerge.

> Certainement cela est bien possible:
> Car si on voit en deux liures traduictz
> Fidellement tous les deux introduictz,
> Les Cheualiers nobles de ton Royaume
> Qui sont appris à l'espée & au heaume,
> Quand par escrit les deux contempleront,
> Facilement les deux ressembleront. (ff. 3ᵛ-4ʳ)

That the *Iliad* and the *Odyssey* are seen as textbooks of chivalry is an interesting idea in itself, but the interpretation becomes even more intriguing when compared with the words of Hugues Salel (d. 1533) regarding his translation of the *Iliad*:

> Je diray bien, & ne m'en sçaurois taire,
> Que le plus beau de tout l'art militaire,
> Est tellement à son ouurage espars,
> Que l'on le peult cueillir de toutes pars.[9]

In other words, Peletier du Mans conceives of Homer in ways no different from the thinking of Hugues Salel, a contemporary and friend of Marot. Given, moreover, that Salel, like Amyot, is sensitive to the capacity of his classical text to improve our general knowledge —

> Il n'est passage en la Philosophie,
> Tant soit diuers, qui ne se fortifie,
> Par quelque dict, ou sentence notable,
> De ce Poete (sig. ã3ʳ) —

these collective statements accentuate more than once a continuity in attitude from the early sixteenth century to "the advent of the new form." We are experiencing anew the lesson learned from recent studies on the *grands rhétoriqueurs*.

Since we have now moved a great distance away from Huizinga's thesis, it might be useful in our deliberation to turn for a moment to the *Deffence*, *the* text of the period which has been associated with "the advent of the new form."

What do we actually find in this manifesto, however? Here is how Du Bellay expresses himself on the central issue of the creation of a new literature for France: "j'ay tousjours estimé notre poësie Francoyse estre capable de quelque plus hault & meilleur style que celuy dont nous sommes si longuement contentez."[10] The emphasis could not fall more squarely upon style. Later, when we encounter Du Bellay's list of the new genres to be used, only an occasional slap at contemporary French poets or reference to appropriate subject matter interrupts the flow of concern for a show of erudition and the well-placed use of the *copia* of rhetoric. So engrained, in fact, is this equation of art with the manipulation of rhetorical devices, that on occasion Du Bellay reshapes his classical source. Quoting supposed critics of his contemporaries, Du Bellay says that one finds fault with a poet who does not know that "le commencement de bien ecrire, c'est le scavoir" (p. 95). A footnote by Chamard reveals that Du Bellay has here misconstrued Horace's "Scribendi recte sapere est ea principium et fons." Horace, observes Chamard, meant by "sapere" "good judgment," not "knowledge." Fair enough, but he neglects to add that Du Bellay was directed in his thinking by the testimony of the ancient rhetoricians. Noting that "the material of rhetoric is composed of everything that may be placed before it as a subject for speech," Quintilian sustains and quotes Cicero to the effect that "no one can be an absolutely perfect orator unless he has acquired a knowledge of all important subjects and arts."[11]

If, for these many reasons, Huizinga's remarks concerning the humanists and the "spirit" of antiquity prove to be problematic, so, too, is his implied equation of Renaissance poetry with simplicity and "exactitude of conception and expression." To be sure, we will always remain aware that Du Bellay wrote "Heureux qui comme Ulysse" and Ronsard, "Mignonne, allons voir," but there is also an inescapable similarity between those excesses of fifteenth-century "classical" verse that Huizinga disliked and the neologisms and other learned innovations of Pléiade poetry which made Boileau speak of Ronsard's muse as "en françois parlant grec et latin." Moreover, contrary to the evolution from *rhétoriqueurs* to the "new form" as traced by Huizinga, the Pléiade and its friends did not eschew poetical word games. Du Bellay and Jodelle both wrote sonnets in *vers rapportés*, two of which Etienne Pasquier considered worthy of publication in *Les Recherches de la France*. Pasquier's admiration is all the more interesting since in addition to writing a chapter on "Vers François tant rapportez que retournez" (Book VII, xiv), he includes another entitled "De quelques jeux Poëtics, Latins & François" (VII, xii) which speaks enthusiastically of the epigrams of a *rhéoriqueur*, Guillaume Crétin.

We must also confront the evidence of texts which, if different from the works of the *rhétoriqueurs*, still do not conform to the notions of "simplicity" and "exactitude." Whether or not one accepts the concept of a French Baroque or the validity of the term "mannerism," new work on Ronsard has reminded us of that poet's preoccupation with metamorphosis and movement, and of noticeable tensions in his attitude toward love, beauty, reality, and myth.[12] His universe is far from stable or simple; his longer poems, often nervous and complex in their development. A famous example is his "Elégie à Marie Stuart" whose opening movements have been studied by Marcel Raymond,[13] although the work, taken as a whole, reveals itself to be fully as intriguing as its initial section.

Two portraits—those of Mary Stuart and of Charles IX of France—are evoked and described. The portrait of the Queen recalls to Ronsard the way she looked on the day of her departure for Scotland, an event twice suggested within the description of Mary through a comparison of her garments to ships' sails. On contemplating the King in his picture, Ronsard writes, "Chacun diroit qu'il aime vostre Image," (that is, the portrait of Mary Stuart).[14] Ronsard so develops what appears to be evident in the King's face that the poet eventually makes a long speech in Charles' name. At the close of the poem, Ronsard steps back, reflects again on the two portraits, and tells us how Charles seems to sigh and she to accept and appreciate the King's adoration. But alas, the two sovereigns are separated by the sea, like Hero and Leander. Indeed, Ronsard adds, Venus was born of the sea to show how cruel and bitter love can be. Consequently, to the very end, the poet mixes fact (the portraits, Mary's departure, the location of the sovereigns' respective kingdoms) and poetry (the image of her billowing garments, Ronsard's "reading" of the expressions in the portraits, his association of the "lovers'" separation with myths and a moral). All is done with great control, but the "simplicity" and "purity" of the usual anthology pieces representing the Pléiade prove utterly inadequate when we attempt to explicate this poem, and on one occasion at least Ronsard warns us of that fact. When the Geneva preachers said that his muse wandered uncontrolled wherever inspiration led,[15] Ronsard's answer made no claim to classical simplicity but rather to something quite different. The poet's art, according to Ronsard, is not that of the preacher, "Où tousjours l'orateur suit le fil d'une chose" (II, 614); it has its own method, following, "D'une libre contrainte où la Muse le meine" (ibid.) .

Thus, to discuss the "advent of the new form" in the light of contemporary documents is to recognize that Huizinga's phrases explain little of the triumph of the Pléiade. These poets shared ideas on style and imitation with a humanistic movement already well defined before 1549. Their appreciation of antiquity, if real enough, does not mean that, like Winckelmann, they saw in classicism above all simplicity and purity. Such was not the vocabulary they used with reference to antiquity nor the manner in which they composed many of their works. And yet, fixed for so long on phrases like "the spirit of antiquity" or "interest in men and in life," we have been led away from an objective examination of how exactly classical culture was appreciated and interpreted by the sixteenth century. Taking for granted that there was an invasion of French minds by classical culture has postponed the moment when we would seek to ask what the sixteenth century said about antiquity and against what background .

Many of the preceding remarks assure us that the canons of rhetoric constitute one significant part of that background. It may just be possible that chivalry, too, has its role to play. Once believed dead and thus relived in the Renaissance in the most artificial of ways, chivalry has been taken more seriously by critics of English literature in recent years[16] and perhaps should be so treated by us. Can it be of no consequence, for example, that the early years of the sixteenth century in France see the publication, three times over, of a translation of Ramon Llull's *Book of the Order of Chivalry* (Paris, 1504, 1505; Lyons, 1510) or that Christine de Pisan's translation / adaptation of Vegetius' *Epitoma rei militaris* was printed in 1488 by Anthoine Vérard who also oversaw the Paris editions of the Llull volume, and that in 1527 Philippe le Noir brought out a copy of the Vérard edition? It might be added that over the same period Latin editions of Vegetius were printed in Paris in 1515, 1532 (a Budé edition), 1535, 1553 and that yet another French translation of the *Epitoma* appeared in Paris in 1536 under the title *Du fait de guerre et fleur de chevalerie*, a copy of which bearing Montaigne's signature still exists at the Bibliothèque Nationale. However we decide to explain these phenomena, they and the comments by Salel and Peletier du Mans on Homer would seem to belong to a world that retained a firm interest in the warrior knight.

The way in which Salel and Peletier du Mans read Homer is all the more intriguing since it appears to be rather unique. The ancients were of two minds about the blind poet. In the *Republic*, Plato dismisses him but Horace speaks of Odysseus as "the tamer of Troy, who looked with discerning eyes upon the cities and manners of many men, and while for self and comrades he strove for a return across the broad sea, many hardships he endured, but could never be o'erwhelmed in the waves of adversity" (*Epistles*, I, ii).[17] The Church Fathers took the next small step and made Odysseus everyman, sailing through the sea of life, beset by temptations and trials. Thus, St. Basil recounts how he heard the *Odyssey* described as a hymn to virtue in which the character of Odysseus symbolizes the virtue that avoids shipwreck. On the interpretation, St. Basil adds: "C'est bien cela."[18] Renaissance humanists were well aware of these ancient commentaries on the *Odyssey* and readily accepted the moral inherent in its protagonist's trip.[19] Neither Horace nor St. Basil suggest that Homer is a handbook for would-be warriors, however. Nor does Cicero, who in the *Tusculan Disputations* includes "aspect or form of combat" and "marshalling of battle" among the phenomena vividly depicted by the poet.[20]

The fact that both Salel and Peletier du Mans make their observations on Homer in a poem addressed to the King may provide a valuable clue to the particular nature of their assessment of the epics of Homer.

The humanists' involvement with the court takes diverse forms but the chivalric ideal constitutes a thread running through many of those forms, from the Galerie François I at Fontainebleau to Du Bellay's verses for a 1559 tourney. However much critics disagree on the overall scheme of the Galerie, by common accord one fresco portrays the King as warrior, ready to leave lady and learning when battle calls. The tourney verses predictably stress social as well as military values. Still, the lines spoken to explain how the knights in question intend to win their wives—

> Non point vsant de fraudes & rapines
> Dont Romulus vsa vers les Sabines,
> Mais par vertu, par proësse & valeur,
> Par courtoisie & noblesse de cœur[21]—

show courtesy well outnumbered by stouter qualities.

Examined in isolation, the prefatory statements by Salel and Peletier du Mans have the decided ability to surprise. Seen in the light of these further contacts between humanism and the court, they bear the unmistakable stamp of the noble class's capacity to influence even the most dedicated of Calliope's minions.

Of another part of the background against which the sixteenth century studied antiquity there can be no doubt. I speak of Christianity, about whose impact on the "new form" Huizinga remains quite silent. Yet in one of Erasmus' *Colloquies* a speaker exclaims: "It is possible that the spirit of Christ is spread more widely than we realize and that many belong to the company of the saints, even though they are not in our catalogue. I confess before my friends that I cannot read Cicero's words on old age and friendship or his *De Officiis* and *Tusculan Disputations* without kissing the book many times over and venerating that pious soul infused with the divine breath."[22] Here is discovery, to be sure, but dare we state that Erasmus has reached back and caught the "spirit" of antiquity?

Previous reference to the reaction of the Church Fathers to Homer should suffice to underscore the fact that Erasmus was not the first to see Christian messages in classical texts and we may well conclude that Erasmus' familiarity with patristic writings encouraged him in this practice. Yet he was prepared to defend and develop it in the light of very immediate concerns. How, for example, does Erasmus explain the inability of the scholastic theologians to match the exegetical powers of St. Augustine or Origen? Here are his reasons, as set down in the *Enchiridion*:

> For one thing, it is impossible for the mystical sense not to be dull or trivial when it is not seasoned with skill in eloquence and a certain charm of language, something the older divines excelled in but which we do not even approach. For another thing, present-day theologians, devoted solely to Aristotle, shut out the Platonists and

> Pythagoreans Augustine prefers, not only because they hold a
> great many views fully harmonious with our religion, but also
> because their very manner of using a language figurative and, as I
> have said, appropriate to allegory, comes closer to the style of the
> Holy Scriptures. So it is not to be wondered at that theological
> allegory was handled more perceptively and that, by their
> copiousness of language, any subject you please, even one dry and
> commonplace could be enriched and made attractive by those who
> were the most learned men of all antiquity and who had already
> practiced on the books of Plato and the poets the skill which they
> were to exercise later on in the interpretation of holy mysteries.[23]

Because so much of Erasmus' writing is devoted to biblical exegesis and to defining the Christian life, it may seem only too obvious to expect that he will exemplify the impact of Christianity on Renaissance minds. Yet a great many elements in "the advent of the new form" come together in this passage. Du Bellay's emphasis on style is already here; so, too, a fascination with allegorical meanings, a fascination that carries through Rabelais' novel, Pléiade poetry, even French humanist tragedy.

When, in the *Quart Livre*, Pantagruel holds up the mast of the ship during the storm at sea, Rabelais comes remarkably close to reproducing the posture of Odysseus, saved from the songs of the Sirens by having been lashed to the mast of his ship, and there is every likelihood that Pantagruel's activity was meant to be read as the Church Fathers read the gesture of Odysseus: an image of seeking survival through cleaving to the cross.[24] Similarly, various poems of the century inspired by the *Metamorphoses* recast Ovidian material to accentuate moral commonplaces through the behavior of the characters depicted. Daphne fleeing Apollo shows how virtue flies from vice; Adonis' death reminds us that pleasure is always mixed with pain.[25] When we delve farther into the less well-known corners of sixteenth-century verse, we find Jean Passerat comparing stags and lovers:

> O Cerfs à quatre pieds, nous sommes vos parens,
> Nous les Cerfs à deux piés qu' Amour a rendu bestes.

Judging by the close of the poem, "bestes" is a play on words. Love renders us both "animals" and "fools."

> Mais vous faites tomber vos cornes tous les ans,
> Nous n'auons pas ce bien, dont plus heureux vous est[es]
> Car depuis qu'vne fois sont cornus les Amans,
> Iamais ne font tomber les cornes de leurs testes.[26]

The overall tone is light, but not so light that we cannot discern the vestige of a familiar technique.

French humanist tragedy gladly fulfilled its didactic function by calling attention to the broad lessons contained within the actions of its characters. Although such explication usually falls to the chorus, on occasion, the reader was alerted even before the first act commenced. Jean Godard had his tragedy *La Franciade* printed with his comedy *Les Déguisés* in order to underscore the distinct, yet related message of each genre, to wit:

> Que la fortune peut ses longues mains estendre
> Aussi bien sur les grands, comme sur les petits,
> Qui ne soulent pas tant ses cruels appetits
> Comme font les grands Roys, les princes monarques,
> Qu'elle marque tousiours de ses sanglätes marques:
> Au lieu qu'elle se iouë, & que par passetemps
> Les petits elle estonne, & puis les rend contens.[27]

Robert Garnier more than once draws a parallel between his plays and the events of war-torn France and his best known tragedy, *Les Juives*, presents a moment in Jewish history whose gloss—provided within the play's closing pages—concerns the inscrutable and independent ways of the Lord.

These facts about the century are slowly being absorbed by literary historians and there are definite signs that criticism on the sixteenth century has now begun to approach its subject differently. The distance that separates Pierre Villey's *Les Sources et l'évolution des Essais de Montaigne* from Michaël Baraz' *L'Etre et la connaissance selon Montaigne* is one of time and attitude. It is the difference between seeing the development of the *Essais* against a background of significant source material and seeing that development as an existential event, influenced to some degree, of course, by the author's readings, but rooted above all in his perceptions of himself and his world. Gilbert Gadoffre's recent *Du Bellay et le sacré* not only insists (and demonstrates) that the poet's writings reflect essential political and intellectual issues of the day but also asks whether we can be completely clear about Du Bellay's frame of reference in his poems:

> L'Ulysse des *Regrets* sort-il de l'*Odyssée* ou d'un apologue patristique? Le Romulus gravé en creux dans les *Antiquitez* est-il un personnage de légende ou la figure de Caïn? L'histoire romaine qui se profile derrière les ruines est-elle issue de Tite-Live ou de saint Augustin?[28]

Thanks to such new work we should be better prepared to read the *Deffence* (instead of reading into it) and to appreciate the relevance of observations from the period such as a singular judgment on Jodelle by his friend and editor Charles de La Mothe in which La Mothe affirms that although Jodelle read and understood the ancients, nevertheless, he never desired to follow them, but rather always pursued his own inspiration.[29] Grounded in the theories and precepts of classical rhetoric,

French humanism could not help but involve its followers in an intense study of the style of the ancients and we would be foolish, especially in the face of the *Deffence*, to believe that such study had no role in the subsequent success of the Pléiade. Yet is such success to be equated with dependence (infusion of "the spirit of antiquity") or with independence of the kind that La Mothe refers to? Is it more accurate to refer to an awakening or to a subtle combination of talent, training, and tradition? Huizinga and his generation apparently once thought they knew the answer. Today it grows harder and harder to share their confidence.

The more we appreciate to what degree the curriculum called the *studia humanitatis* involved its students in the serious pursuit of linguistic and exegetical excellence, the more we see how determined were the humanists to rise to the challenge. They learned the classical languages, they explicated the classical texts and became acquainted with those "mots propres... metaphores, alegories, comparisons, similitudes, energies, & tant d'autres figures & ornemens" without which, according to Du Bellay in the *Deffence*, all speeches and poems are "nudz, manques & debiles" (pp. 35-36). They made these "figures & ornemens" an integral part of their own style quite as Quintilian and the *Deffence* said they should. In this connection, Du Bellay even uses the phrase "quasi comme se transformer en luy" to describe the relationship that should pertain between the young French poet and his classical model. Huizinga appears to have believed that just such a series of metamorphoses occurred. But it is always helpful to keep in mind how, in a remarkable review of medieval philosophy, Etienne Gilson took pains to remind his reader that however often the scholastics refer to Plato and Aristotle, when such Christian principles as "God is being," "God is one" were introduced into the corpus of classical philosophy, that system of thought was profoundly altered.[30] Does not this kind of study impress upon us all the difficulties in talking about the "advent of the new form" in France in terms of classical notions that "began to dawn upon men's minds" (as if those minds brought nothing to their reading)?

In all fairness to Huizinga, he does open his last chapter with a statement to the effect that the transition from the Middle Ages to humanism was "far less simple than we are inclined to imagine it" (p. 323). The thrust of his conclusion remains, nonetheless, that over time fifteenth-century classicism gave way to "modern culture," to an aesthetic of simplicity infused with the "spirit" of antiquity.

Evidence provided here as well as the wealth of new texts from the sixteenth century that have been studied and edited in the past few decades suggests rather that the complexity of fifteenth-century humanism as espied by Huizinga did not disappear so neatly. As with the period examined in *The Waning of the Middle Ages*, the sixteenth century in France proves to be a world in which writers read and employ the works of antiquity against a backdrop of values, preoccupations, and perspectives which interact with the message of those classical works. How else but through reference to such interaction can we explain that the Renaissance, not antiquity, created the emblem book, that the sixteenth century became the heyday of the mythographers (both phenomena that underscore again the fascination in the century with allegorical meanings). How else do we explain the perplexing richness of works like the *Praise of Folly* or Rabelais' novel in which antiquity and St. Paul, irony and commitment to the Holy Word are made to share center stage. Many times over modern readers have doubtlessly wanted these works to display "the incomparable simpleness and purity of the ancient culture" but to no avail. They come to us in a quite different form and we must respect that fact.

---

[1] First published in 1919. We quote from the Doubleday Anchor edition (New York: Doubleday, 1956).

[2] *Renaissance Thought* (New York: Harper Torchbooks, 1961), p. 11.

[3] See for example, Robert Griffin, *Coronation of the Poet: Joachim Du Bellay's Debt to the Trivium* (Berkeley and Los Angeles: University of California Press, 1961).

[4] A succinct review of contemporary reassessment of the *rhétoriqueurs* is provided by Pierre Jodogne's "Les 'Rhétoriqueurs' et l'Humanisme," in *Humanism in France*, ed. A. H. T. Levi (New York: Barnes and Noble, 1970), pp. 150-75. See also my "Octovien de Saint-Gelais's *Le Séjour d'honneur* and French Humanism," *French Studies* 28 (1974), 272-281.

[5] J. Chocheyras, "En marge de La '*Deffence et Illustration*,' Pierre Saliat: Une Préface critique de 1537," *BHR* 28 (1966), p. 677. On Robertet, see C. M. Zsuppan, "An Early Example of the Renaissance Themes of Immortality and Divine Inspiration: The Work of Jean Robertet," *BHR* 28 (1966), 553-563; on Aneau, John L. Gerig, "Barthélemy Aneau: A Study in Humanism," *Romanic Review* 1 (1910), 203.

[6] *L'Histoire aethiopique de Heliodorus* (Paris, 1559), printer's flower 2ᵛ.

[7] "pour suffisamment delecter" (printer's flower 2ᵛ).

[8] *Premier et Second Livre de l'Odissee d'Homere* (Paris, 1571), f. 4ᵛ.

[9] *Les xxiiii. Livres de l'Iliade d'Homere* (Paris, 1580), sig. ã5ʳ .

[10] Joachim Du Bellay, *La Deffence et illustration de la langue francoyse*, ed. Henri Chamard (3rd. ed. Paris, 1966), p. 91.

[11] *Institutio Oratoria*, 11, xxi, 4, 14 (Loeb Classical Library translation). The passage referred to in Cicero occurs in the *De Oratore*, I, vi, 20.

[12] See in particular the excellent articles contained in *Ronsard the Poet*, ed. Terence Cave (London: Methuen, 1973).

[13] Marcel Raymond, *Baroque et Renaissance poétique* (Paris, 1955), p. 144.

[14] Ronsard, *Oeuvres complètes*, ed. Gustave Cohen (Paris: Gallimard, 1950), II, 295.

[15] The poem is his "Response aux Injures et Calomnies de je ne sçay quels Predicantereaux et Ministreaux de Genève."

[16] See Rosemond Tuve, *Allgorical Imagery* (Princeton: Princeton University Press, 1966), p. 341.

[17] *Satires, Epistles, and Ars Poetica*, ed. and trans. H. Rushton Fairclough (London: Heinemann, 1970), pp. 263, 265.

[18] *Aux jeunes gens*, ed. and trans. F. Boulenger (Paris: Les Belles Lettres, 1952), p. 48.

[19] Raphael Volaterranus (Raffaele Mattei) mentions both in his prefatory remarks to a Latin translation of the *Odyssey* (*Odissea Homeri per Raphaelem Volateranum in Latinum conversa*, Rome, 1510, sig. A2ʳ).

[20] Cicero, *Tusculan Disputations*, ed. and trans. J. E. King (London: Heinemann, 1966), V, xxxix, 114.

[21] Du Bellay, *Oeuvres françoises*, ed. Ch. Marty-Laveaux (Paris: Lemerre, 1867), II, 443.

[22] *Desiderii Erasmi Roferodami Opera omnia* (Lugduni Batavorum, 1703), 1, 682.

[23] *The Enchiridion of Erasmus*, ed. and trans. Raymond Himelick (Gloucester, Mass.: Peter Smith, 1970), p. 107.

[24] Hugo Rahner devotes an entire chapter to the Christian interpretation of Odysseus tied to the mast in his *Greek Myths and Christian Mystery*, trans. Brian Battershaw (London: Burns and Oates, 1963).

[25] See, for example, my "The Sixteenth Century and Antiquity: A Case Study," *L'Esprit Créateur*, XVI (1976), 37-47.

[26] *Les Poésies françaises de Jenn Passerat*, ed. Prosper Blanchemain (Paris: Lemerre, 1880), I, 20-21

[27] *Les Oeuvres de Jean Godard* (Lyon, 1594), II, 101.

[28] (Paris: Gallimard, 1978), p. 247.

[29] "L'auteur auoit bien lue, & entendu les anciens, toutesfois par vne superbe asseurance ne s'est oncques voulu assuiettir à eux, ains a tousiours suiui ses propres inuentions." From "De la poesie francoise, et des oeuvres d'Estienne Jodelle," in *Les Oeuvres et meslanges poetiques d'Estienne Jodelle* (Paris, 1574), sig. elᵛ. Compare also this remark by Raymond on Ronsard's "Elégie à Marie Stuart": "Sans doute est-ce l'étude des Anciens qui a permis un tel épanouissement. Mais cette poésie, en ces caractères les plus originaux, n'a rien de spécifiquement gréco-latin . . ." (*Baroque et Renaissance*, p. 144).

[30] See *The Spirit of Medieval Philosophy*, especially chapter III.

La Fontaine and the Classical Ideal

Philip A. Wadsworth †
University of South Carolina

In 1669, when La Fontaine published his novel, *Les Amours de Psyché et de Cupidon*, he unwittingly helped to generate the legend of a French classical school. The framework of the novel shows four men of letters, all close friends, visiting Versailles and strolling through the gardens, then pausing while one member of the group, Poliphile, reads to the other three his latest composition, the story of Cupid and Psyche. The legend, of course, is that the four friends were the famous "quartet" of classical literature—La Fontaine, Boileau, Molière, and Racine—and that their appearance in the novel was meant to pay tribute to their intimacy and collaboration as a literary group. Twentieth-century scholarship has finally destroyed this durable and appealing legend. None of the friends in *Psyché* can be positively identified. And the great classical writers were by no means a close-knit group that got together regularly for discussions of literary matters.

To be sure, there was a movement that has come to be called classical, a movement or, at least, a phenomenon, when a constellation of artistic geniuses matured and flourished in the sixteen sixties and seventies, at a time when social, cultural, and political conditions happened to be particularly favorable. It is not my purpose to retrace the history of French classicism but I should perhaps point out that classical doctrine belongs to an earlier period. The various principles and rules were the product of many forces and personalities, with contributions from such men as Malherbe, Balzac, Chapelain, and Vaugelas; the doctrine was well established by 1650 and no longer needed defending. Classical literature, when it arrived on the scene, was a movement without a manifesto. Also, it was a movement without a leader. Boileau came to have great prestige as the "législateur du Parnasse," but actually his *Art poétique* was a summing up, a popularization and a reaffirmation in eloquent verse of literary ideas that were already quite familiar to men of letters.

Although the great writers associated with the first decades of Louis XIV's reign belonged to no school, although they usually avoided pedantic discussions of doctrine, they shared certain attitudes or ideals which we can all sense and which have been labeled as classical. It is good to remember that they were the *avant-garde* of the sixteen sixties, innovative, competitive, and eager to attract attention. At the same time they were respectful toward the ancient classics, impatient of mediocrity, guided by the highest artistic aims, dedicated to the study of man and society, and inclined for the most part to express themselves in rather simple, concentrated language. There is no need to define or describe the key characteristics of French classicism; many scholars and critics have already done so, with considerable brilliance.[1] It may be useful, however, to quote a famous aphorism by Paul Valéry, since it is pertinent to our subject: "Classique est l'écrivain qui porte un critique en soi-même, et qui l'associe intimement à ses travaux."[2] Classical writers did tend to be self-critical in the sense that they kept their work under careful control; they were acutely conscious of problems of form and style.

The word classical does not provide an adequate description of any individual artist, and perhaps La Fontaine least of all. His case is particularly slippery because of his many inconsistencies, his wide ranging literary tastes, and his ventures in a variety of styles and genres. Although not always easy to understand he offers much material for study. One of his deepest needs, apparently, was to justify everything he published, and he has left us numerous prefaces, *avertissements*, and explanatory prologues, the fruit of his constant meditation on artistic questions. There are certain aspects of classical esthetics to which he returned again and again. One was the broad topic of originality, which can be subdivided into the traditional concepts of imitation and invention. Another of his important preoccupations was the purpose or usefulness of poetic art, which in seventeenth-century rhetorical terms also had two categories, pleasure and instruction, "plaire et instruire." My plan is to take a brief look, a fresh and rather personal one, at La Fontaine's treatment of these themes in some of his critical texts. I shall deal mainly with the prefatory statements that accompany certain early works and also with *Clymène*, a comedy on the subject of poets and poetry.

La Fontaine's first published work, in 1654, was *L'Eunuque*, an adaptation in French verse of Terence's *Eunuchus*, slightly revised so as to conform to seventeenth-century standards of decency. With the French play there appeared a brief "Avertissement au lecteur," about two pages long (*OD*, 263-64) in which the poet makes excuses for his work but suggests that it may be worth reading because of the high quality of its source. The *Avertissement* begins "Ce n'est ici qu'une médiocre copie d'un excellent original," then goes on to express La Fontaine's great admiration for all the superior features of Terence's comedy: simplicity, a well-organized plot, economy of expression and style, an easy manner, "bienséance," "médiocrité," i.e. moderation, "vraisemblance" in the presentation of characters, and finally "la nature" or naturalness. Clearly La Fontaine was well-versed in contemporary dramatic theory, particularly the rules inherited from the *Ars poetica* of Horace, and he may have been showing off his knowledge to forestall objections from pedantic critics. After further praise for Terence, and Menander too, he offers some comments on the composition of his own work. The project was probably a mistake, he says, and he would have abandoned it except that some friends urged him to finish it and have it published. He insists that he is not trying to influence the judgment of the reader, since the "Etat des belles-lettres" is a democracy where everyone is free to cast a vote. Finally, the only reason for his writing this *Avertissement* is to declare his indebtedness to Terence for the subject of his play and to several distinguished but unnamed persons to whom he has turned for help "pour les vers et pour la conduite."

La Fontaine's prefatory statement reveals some genuine timidity or lack of confidence, quite natural in an author who is presenting his first book, yet it is obviously rather devious and self-serving. Like most other writers, then and now, he was eager to advertise his wares. His particular approach in these matters, in the case of *L'Eunuque* and in later volumes also, was to take the reader into his confidence, or to appear to do so, emphasizing the difficulty of his task and his struggle to solve various literary problems. He was modest and deferential, yet always called attention to his high professional standards. The subtlety of his attitude should not cause us to lose sight of the basic truth. He did love the comedies of Terence and he did labor to compose a French imitation of the *Eunuchus*. This was a major enterprise, even though it turned out rather badly, and its 1,800 alexandrins made it the longest poetic work that he would ever write.

La Fontaine declared his admiration for Terence on several subsequent occasions, and also for a host of ancient masters including Homer, Plato, Horace, Virgil, Ovid, and Cicero. He read very widely in the literature of antiquity but, like his contemporaries, he seldom imitated it at all closely. After *L'Eunuque* his next major work, presumably, was the long mythological poem, *Adonis*, quite freely adapted from some stories in Ovid's *Metamorphoses*. *Adonis* made its first appearance in a beautiful manuscript presented to Nicolas Fouquet in 1658 and then, much revised, was finally published in 1669.

In the *Avertissement* that accompanies the printed version of *Adonis*, La Fontaine speaks nostalgically and rather cryptically of his younger days when his imagination was more active and when he devoted much study to a type of poetry which he calls "héroïque," "fleuri," rich in "ornements" and in "figures nobles et hardies," and which he sums up as "la langue des dieux." He then says of all these readings: "Le fonds que j'en avais fait, soit par la lecture des anciens, soit par celle de quelques-uns de nos modernes, s'est presque entièrement consumé dans l'embellissement de ce poème..." (*OD*, 3). Thus, he claims to have steeped himself not only in Ovid but in many other poets as well. We are not concerned here with the identity of all these models, a question which scholars have studied quite laboriously, but rather with his description of the imitative process. For one thing, it included selected modern sources of inspiration—both Italian and French, in fact—as well as his cherished Greeks and Romans. This eclectic view of literature is one he maintained in other critical prefaces, in *Clymène*, and as an important theme in his *Epître à Huet*, published in 1687 at a time when battle lines were drawn in the Quarrel of the Ancients and the Moderns. In *Adonis* the story from Ovid is enriched by many memories of Virgil, and these voices are joined by echoes that seem to come from Marino and Ronsard. Similarly, the dry little fables of Aesop and Phaedrus take on new life because La Fontaine has embellished them with details that he recalled from authors as diverse as Horace, Voiture, and Rabelais.

This kind of imitation in which he stored up knowledge and consumed it creatively ("Le fonds... s'est... consumé") is like taking nourishment to improve one's strength. We are reminded of another of Paul Valéry's reflections on the artist's craft, expressed in fable-like language: "Rien de plus naturel, rien de plus soi que de se nourrir des autres. Mais il faut les digérer. Le lion est fait de mouton assimilé."[3] La Fontaine expressed a similar idea on several occasions. In the *Epître à Huet* he mentions adapting or even translating favorite passages from ancient writers and incorporating them in his own poems, trying to make them his own, "Tâchant de rendre mien cet air d'antiquité" (*OD*, 648). The process of assimilation or fusion goes beyond the mere use of quotations or reminiscences and I shall return to it a little later. It is sufficient at the moment to note that this concept was fundamental to the classical belief in imitation as the mother of invention.

With *Adonis* La Fontaine began to allow himself ever-increasing freedom in the handling of sources. He discussed this matter several times, always praising his models but also insisting on his own originality. After some hesitation in launching Part I of his *Contes et Nouvelles en vers* (1664-65), which turned out to be a great success, he showed great confidence when he published Part II, in 1666. The preface to Part II is his declaration of imitative independence. It develops his esthetic theories for the tale in verse and it proclaims his right to borrow from any sources, whether famous or obscure, and to revise them in any way he likes. He says that he has added or subtracted materials and has drastically revised certain plots, with the result that "ce n'est plus la même chose, c'est proprement une nouvelle nouvelle." He makes this same point again in the prologues to several individual tales in verse, such as *La Servante justifiée* (II, 6) or *La Fiancée du roi de Garbe* (II, 14). Similarly for his fables—both in the preface to the volume of 1668 and in some prologues—he boasts quite rightly that, in spite of his many precursors, he is the inventor of the fable as a French poetic genre. In

Clymène Apollo denounces imitators as sheep who follow one another stupidly from place to place (OD, 34) and in the *Epître à Huet*, speaking in his own name, La Fontaine uses the sheep image again for those who try to emulate Virgil (*OD*, 648). It is in this latter text that he makes his famous statement, "Mon imitation n'est pas un esclavage."

The preface to *Psyché* is particularly important for an appreciation of La Fontaine's concept of originality (*OD*, 123-26). He has much to say in praise of the myth as told by Apuleius, but notes that he has taken his usual liberties with the plot, changing certain episodes and adding some new ones. But he also says that subject matter was not the real problem: "Apulée me fournissait la matière; il ne restait que la forme, c'est à dire les paroles...." Nothing but the words! This charming understatement is really a claim that he created everything that counts, the language in which the novel is told. He then mentions several types of narrative style that were too simple or too ornate and did not seem appropriate for this mythological love story. Because of the strict rule of stylistic uniformity he had to devise a new style having "un caractère nouveau." It would involve a mixing of tones—*l'héroïque, le galant, le plaisant*—in what he called "un juste tempérament." His goal was not the assimilation of passages from multiple sources but rather a new blend of language. I am not convinced that the result was a homogeneous fusion, but the mixture turned out well. Readers of *Psyché* have been troubled by some of its structural features but they have seldom found fault with the novel's style.

The problem in *Psyché* was to create a suitable prose style. Usually La Fontaine's medium was verse, but he approached it in the same way. Prefaces to his tales and fables invariably dwell on questions of style, in particular the need to find the most appropriate style—right for the genre and right for his own gifts as a poet. His expression of these views can be seen best in *Clymène* (*OD*, 20-46), a mysterious work that is partly a precious love story, partly a comedy involving the inhabitants of Mount Parnassus, and at the same time La Fontaine's closest approach to an *art poétique*. *Clymène* was published in 1671 but its themes suggest that it may have been composed some years earlier, perhaps concurrently with the first fables and *Psyché*. The subject is very simple. Apollo, who serves as master of ceremonies, asks each of his Muses to show her skill in celebrating Acante's love for Clymène. ("Acante" is a poetic name often used by La Fontaine for himself but "Clymène," if a real woman, has never been identified.) The Muses take turns in a series of performances, praising Clymène in various poetic genre and styles or taking the part of Acante and Clymène in dramatic scenes. After seven of these recitals, interspersed with critical comments made by Apollo and some of the performers, the whole group goes to find Acante himself. He closes the comedy by recounting ardently the progress of his love, an adventure in which he received some help from Cupid and some encouragement from Clymène.

The importance of *Clymène* as a literary document is widely recognized.[4] Collinet has even called the work a manifesto, although in a rather limited sense of this word: "le manifeste individuel d'un poète parvenu désormais à la pleine possession de ses moyens" (p. 292). That is correct; La Fontaine does seem to make a confident announcement of his own special talents. Without attempting still another study of *Clymène* I do want to offer some reflections on features of it which I think have been neglected and which can help to illuminate La Fontaine's theory and practice as a poet.

The reader of the work is likely to be struck by the banality of its subject, Acante's courtship of Clymène, and the elaborate mechanism to blow it up and view it from so many different angles. This is indeed much ado about nothing or, more accurately, a virtuoso demonstration of the primacy of manner over matter. One may be reminded of Racine's argument in the preface to *Bérénice*, defending the simplicity of its action: "...toute l'invention consiste à faire quelque chose de rien...." But La Fontaine had neither the vision nor the discipline to be a creator of tragedies. In *Clymène* he weaves together a miscellany of small compositions representing different poetic veins. In this respect *Clymène* resembles a volume of fables or tales. La Fontaine could succeed only in brief works, as he often admitted, but he knew how to treat them with superb craftsmanship. I think that the trivial subjects of tales and fables offered him an advantage. These were minor genres, traditionally written in prose. They were not subject to any rules and did not require sustained uniformity of style. They gave him boundless freedom for his playful imagination and versatile technique.

In their presentation of various styles and genres the Muses of *Clymène* try to echo some of La Fontaine's favorite poets: Marot, Malherbe, Horace, and Voiture. They do not imitate specific texts but rather certain types of poems, such as the ballad and the ode, and the manner or tone of each poet. La Fontaine's gifts for mimicry and *pastiche*, which help to account for the rich and wide-ranging musicality of his fables, may indeed raise the question whether he possessed any style that was fully and authentically his own. In a recent article on his introspective poems I have pointed out his dependency on models, expressed in self-reproachful images of trying too many paths or missing the right goals and going astray.[5] In his *Epître à Huet* (*OD*, 648) there is a famous passage where he recalls that he once became the disciple of the wrong kind of poet. Fortunately, he adds, Horace opened his eyes and, incidentally, became one of the masters he cherished the most. I think this is the point of *Clymène*, that La Fontaine could not limit himself to a single guide, or doctrine, or school, or type of poetry. His mind contained an encyclopedia of models and styles, and it was his nature to move ceaselessly from one to another, assimilating them, mixing them, and putting them together in new combinations. *Clymène* is the expression of what Collinet has called "une esthétique de la diversité," a personal style that was a mosaic of variegated colors and tones.

The unifying force in *Clymène*, as in *Psyché* and many other works, is that of a winning personality whose presence can be felt on every page. Among other things, *Clymène* is La Fontaine's first major effort at what is called nowadays the creation of an image. As a character in the comedy, Acante is partially a representation of the author; he is described as a poet, ardently in love with Clymène, overly serious and full of sighs. Clio mentions that he tends to be oblivious to everything around him when preoccupied with some "rêverie agréable et profonde," and another Muse speaks of him as hard to know, changeable, and "inégal": "Inégal en amour, en plaisir, en affaire;/Tantôt gai, tantôt triste..." (*OD*, 32). But this moody poet-lover does not express La Fontaine's ideas on literature. In this area it is mainly Apollo who seems to speak for the author, lamenting the decline of love poetry, occasionally expressing boredom and a need for something new, praising Horace and several other poets, and explaining the concept of free imitation of favorite styles and genres. Apollo is surrounded by the Muses and they also contribute some opinions attributable to La Fontaine: Calliope complains that Malherbe and Voiture are very difficult to imitate, Erato points out that even a trifling poem requires hard work, and Uranie joins Apollo in the complaint that true poetry, the language of the gods, has gone out of style, yielding to the work of shallow versifiers.

This composite portrait of an eccentric poet with likable human failings and total dedication to his art remains largely unchanged whenever La Fontaine indulges his taste for self-analysis. Some of the same traits are to be found in various prefaces, in the *Hymne à la Volupté*, in the *Epître à Huet*, in the *Discours à Madame de La Sablière*. And most of his fables and tales contain some interjection of opinion or feeling. His self-expression tends to be playful rather than deeply emotional and more calculated than spontaneous. La Fontaine seems to use himself as a sounding board to stimulate reverberations in his reader. Although carefully manipulated, this is a kind of lyricism and it distinguishes him from the other great writers of the classical period.

In our remarks on imitation and originality we have moved from sources to style to questions of tone and manner, but have said very little about the poet's justification for his work. Like most classical writers La Fontaine claimed that his art was intended to provide pleasure and instruction for his readers. And, by "readers" he of course did not mean pedants, rulemakers, or literary critics; he had in mind, very much like Molière and Racine, the fairly cultivated "honnêtes gens" of Paris and the royal court. To give pleasure, first and foremost, was the goal he ascribed to his tales in verse (Preface of 1666) and also to his fables. His most memorable comment on pleasing the public occurs in the preface to the fables of 1668: "On ne considère en France que ce qui plaît: c'est la grande règle, et pour ainsi dire la seule." Molière's defender, Dorante, had used almost the same words, "plaire" as "la grande règle de toutes les règles," in the *Critique de l'Ecole des femmes* (scene 6). Various authors made similar declarations, even declaring or implying that public acceptance, or rejection, would determine the value of their work. Whether he liked it or not La Fontaine saw the necessity of accepting the verdict of his readers. He said so at the outset of his career in his comments on *L'Eunuque* and also in several later publications.

We should not view such statements as the whole and literal truth. There is always a process of adaptation, a pulling back and forth, between writers and readers, a matching of artistic talents and crafts, on the one hand, and on the other the likes and dislikes, or changing tastes, of the literary public. In his critical writings La Fontaine often justified his approach to a subject, or his choice of a style, as a response to the tastes of his potential readers. He rushed to publish the *Contes et Nouvelles* of 1665, as he frankly admitted, "afin de ne pas laisser refroidir la curiosité de les voir, qui est encore en son premier feu." For the fables of 1668 he said that he deliberately sought to give these old stories "un certain charme" in order to please the public: "...on veut de la nouveauté et de la gaieté." *Psyché* also required a careful diagnostic effort so that he could satisfy "le goût du siècle" and, after some hesitation, he decided that "ce goût se porte au galant et à la plaisanterie." Sometimes he registered a complaint about changing times, regretting that the long "poème" and the elegant manner of Malherbe had gone out of style (*Adonis*, *Clymène*) or commenting in a letter to Racine that people at court preferred ignorant poets to those who showed any trace of erudition (*OD*, 657). But on the whole he remained, or at least gave the impression of remaining deferential to the demands of his readers.

La Fontaine had a modern flair for market research and, to give his books every chance for success, he liked to test the reaction of readers before risking publication. The practice of obtaining advice from friends, as he had done for *L'Eunuque*, served him again when he was preparing his fables. In the preface of 1668 he said that he showed some of his manuscript pieces to unspecified men of letters and that their encouragement led him to publish the whole collection. Most admirers of La Fontaine are acquainted with the public opinion poll he conducted when launching his tales in verse. In 1664 he brought out a small booklet containing only two tales, one written in mixed meters and the other in regular lines but with old-fashioned language. This was an experiment to learn "lequel caractère est le plus propre pour rimer des contes." Readers were invited to make their choice and the author promised to be guided by the majority opinion (*Avertissement* of 1664). It would seem, from his subsequent production of tales, that both poetic manners were well received. It is less well known that La Fontaine conducted a similar test in 1671 in an attempt to salvage several fragments of *Le Songe de Vaux*, composed some ten years earlier. In his *Avertissement* (*OD*, 78) he said that he needed to know the reaction of his audience before attempting to complete his work: "Selon le jugement qu'on fera de ces trois morceaux, je me résoudrai: si la chose plaît, j'ai dessein de continuer; sinon, je n'y perdrai pas de temps davantage." In this instance the probe must have given negative results, since other fragments of *Le Songe de Vaux* remained unpublished during the poet's lifetime.

My reason for dwelling on the publication history of these books is that La Fontaine shows the same pattern of thought in some of his works themselves. His choice of a subject, then his treatment of it, often take the form of an opinion test or a competition. To enliven *Le Songe de Vaux* he invented a contest in which four fairies—the protectors of architecture, painting, gardening, and poetry—made speeches boasting of each art and its contribution to the beauty of the palace of Vaux (*OD*, 84-96). The structure of *Clymène* is of course quite similar, with the Muses vying to praise the heroine in their characteristic poetic styles. Some of the tales present numerous variations on a given sexual theme (I, 1 and II, 14). In *Psyché* Poliphile reads his manuscript to obtain the reaction of his companions, and the four of them offer some comments on the novel and related literary matters. I think that the same artistic tendency can be discerned in the paired fables, such as *Le Héron* and *La Fille* (VII, 4) where fastidiousness is duly punished, first in an animal and then in a human, or in the two renderings, based on different sources, of the story about the peasant who called upon Death to end his sufferings (I, 15 and 16).

La Fontaine's extraordinary efforts to please his readers and his vulnerability to their opinions would seem to be one of his fundamental characteristics as a poet. Without attempting a psychological explanation of his attitudes I think that we can all feel, at least in his early works, a certain dread of failure, a need for advice and approval, and an extreme sensitivity to criticism. But we must not expect him to be consistent. He obviously liked to demonstrate his stylistic skills and he was well aware of his literary accomplishments. At the head of Book II of his fables he placed a sort of prologue, *Contre ceux qui ont le goût difficile*, in which he provided samples of epic and pastoral verse and brushed aside the complaints of some perhaps imaginary critics. This confidence in his ability to win the approbation of readers became stronger as his career progressed and can be seen in the authoritative tone of later declarations about his tales and fables.

As a critical thinker La Fontaine had much more to say about poetic pleasure than about instruction. Although he insisted on the moral usefulness of his fables he tended to express his theories in a fragmentary and disjointed manner. When he published his collection of 1668, for which he provided a long preface and two flowery dedications to the six-year-old *dauphin*, he had to justify his work as a teaching aid in the education of children. Hence his rather ridiculous claim that his fables could teach children what they needed to know about wild animals. He frequently made vague statements to the effect that the fables contained "des vérités importantes" or "un sens très solide." He of course recognized the poetic potentiality of fables but perhaps his own moral ambivalence made it hard for him to treat artistically the lessons that are an inherent feature of the genre. Or perhaps these precepts, usually proverbs or bits of folk wisdom, amounting to a sort of survival kit for use in a cruel world, didn't lend themselves to poetic handling. Whether the reason was the "incapacité de son esprit" or "celle de sa matière" (*Preface* of 1668), he felt obliged to abandon some of the lessons of Aesop.

Aesopic fables are based on the existence of resemblances between men and various animals and on the assumption that animal stories may serve as examples applicable to mankind. La Fontaine was well aware of this principle, and in the preface of 1668 he dwelled on it with a show of erudition: Prometheus created man as a microcosm, he said, with qualities taken from different species of animals. "Ainsi, ces fables sont un tableau où chacun de nous se trouve dépeint." Our poet kept coming back to the animal-man parallel, looking at it from points of view that ranged from the literary to the philosophical.

La Fontaine's most elaborate esthetic statement on this subject occurs in the prologue to a fable, *Le Bûcheron et Mercure* (V, 1), the passage that reaches its climax in the lines: "Une ample comédie à cent actes divers,/ Et dont la scène est l'univers." This much quoted formula so aptly suggests the dramatic quality and diversity and humor of the fables that it casts a shadow over the equally important preceding lines that deal with moral instruction. The poet says that he is not particularly gifted to carry out Aesop's main purpose, which is teaching, but nevertheless:

> Je tâche d'y tourner le vice en ridicule,
> Ne pouvant l'attaquer avec des bras d'Hercule.
> C'est là tout mon talent; je ne sais s'il suffit.

His weapon is mockery and he points out certain human vices which he has satirized in specific fables, such as vanity and envy in the frog who tried to make himself as big as a steer (I, 3), and the contrasts he has drawn between vice and virtue in *Le Loup et l'Agneau* (I, 10) or *La Mouche et la Fourmi* (IV, 3). In his "ample comédie" most of the actors are animals, but he adds that he sometimes makes use of gods or men. They all represent character types or traits, usually some widespread folly or excess. Thus, they teach us about mankind, and about ourselves, not through moral pronouncements but simply by acting out their parts on

La Fontaine's small, brightly lighted stage. This theory should of course remind us of Molière, who expressed the same view whenever he had to defend the usefulness, or at least the innocence, of his comedies.

The idea of fables as a theater where the actors provide portraits of men and women like ourselves is conveyed again in the image of a mirror which La Fontaine develops allegorically in *L'Homme et son image* (I, 11). You will recall that this fable, an ingenious tribute to La Rochefoucauld, tells of a man who thinks of himself as handsome but is really very ugly. He avoids mirrors, hoping never to see his face, but he comes upon a clear stream that shows him a perfect reflection of all his blemishes. The poet explains his riddle in detail:

> Notre âme, c'est cet homme amoureux de lui-même;
> Tant de miroirs, ce sont les sottises d'autrui,
> Miroirs, de nos défauts les peintres légitimes;
>   Et quant au canal, c'est celui
>   Que chacun sait, le livre des *Maximes.*

Although the text stresses *l'amour-propre,* quite naturally, La Fontaine must have realized that his fables had the same didactic function as the *Maximes*, indeed that he was in his own way, a *moraliste* like La Rochefoucauld. Or like Molière. It is interesting to note that in *La Critique de l'Ecole des femmes* (scene 6) Uranie had used the mirror metaphor rather ironically, telling Molière's critics that they should not feel personally offended by the playwright's satire of manners: "Ces sortes de satires...sont miroirs publics où il ne faut jamais témoigner qu'on se voie...."

On many occasions La Fontaine spoke of *mensonge* and *vérité* in connection with his fables, i.e. fictions which contained some truth or lesson. He was much interested in the ways that fables communicate their truth, their useful message. In 1668 he tried to demonstrate that stories can teach children better than history books (*Préface*) and argued that Aesop had discovered a way to plant the seeds of virtue in a young mind ("âme"), "sans qu'elle s'aperçoive de cette étude" (Dedication in prose). One could learn without conscious study because the pill of knowledge was sugar-coated. The metaphor of the theater returns with a new emphasis in the second collection of fables, in 1678-79, when the poet looks back at his accomplishments. He has put on stage many types of characters, he says, endowing them with the gift of poetic speech and the ability to express truth "sous les habits du mensonge" (*Le Dépositaire infidèle*, IX, 1). The "acteurs en mon ouvrage" are the subject of the same boast in the epilogue at the end of Book XI. In this farewell piece he invites other poets to follow his example, giving lessons that are wrapped up or concealed ("envelopper") in this kind of story ("ces inventions"). In all these comments he says little or nothing about maxims and precepts. He is stating—but perhaps not forcefully enough since scholars have tended to misunderstand him—that the didactic value of his fables lies in the characters and the way they act. They teach us to understand the nature of man. And of course he views mankind lucidly and pessimistically, very much in the manner of La Rochefoucauld or Racine.

It is the charm of the fables that makes their teaching so palatable, but this word has different meanings in the two collections. In 1668 (*Préface*) La Fontaine spoke of "un certain charme" as a synonym for "gaieté" or "un air agréable," i.e. his humorous treatment of the material. Ten years later the dedication for the second collection stresses another kind of *charme*, a magic spell. La Fontaine says of the art of telling fables ("ce bel art"):

> C'est proprement un charme: il rend l'âme attentive,
>   Ou plutôt il la tient captive,
>   Nous attachant à des récits
> Qui mènent à son gré les coeurs et les esprits.

Here the hidden lesson and the actor's costume are replaced by a mysterious power with which the artist can hypnotize his readers. These various comments and their imagery are all related to the art of suggestion, of saying much in a few words, or somehow implying more than the literal meaning that words express. La Fontaine, who often praised brevity, also made one specific comment on the goal of understatement; it occurs, rather significantly, I think, in the poem addressed to La Rochefoucauld in the fables of 1678-79. In this *Discours* the poet describes two cases of similar behavior in animals and men and then announces that he could provide many further examples but that his poem would lose its effectiveness if he made it much longer:

> En cela j'ai pour guide
> Tous les maîtres de l'art, et tiens qu'il faut laisser
> Dans les plus beaux sujets quelque chose à penser. (X, 14)

These lines on the art of suggestion are in themselves suggestive; they may lead us to think of a sense of proportion, of modesty in the expression of feelings and ideas, of subtle evocations, or of any of the components of classical restraint.

In his comments on imitation and invention, and again in discussing pleasure and instruction, La Fontaine pursued different trains of thought but reached similar conclusions. Questions of style and manner were of paramount importance to him. He relied on sources but claimed complete freedom to mix them and change them. In *Clymène*, especially, he stressed the many ways of treating a subject and the necessity of making choices that would satisfy the public and allow him to take advantage of his artistic virtuosity. *Plaire* was an instinctive activity but *instruire* did not come naturally. He was not a preacher and was often ill at ease with Aesop's moral lessons but he saw that his fables could convey to us, poetically, what he knew about man and society. Content was not to be despised but it had to be expressed in the most attractive form. Again he emphasized technical questions such as poetic diction, manner, tone and suggestion.

As a writer on the art of writing La Fontaine possessed unusual gifts. He did not aspire to be a professional critic and, unlike Boileau, he did not have a belligerent spirit or a sense of moral outrage. His main concern was to further the acceptance and appreciation of his own works. The essence of his genius was his mastery of poetic styles and many of his esthetic inquiries were devoted to, or became reduced to, stylistic problems. The medium outweighed the message. In the realm that interested him so much he proved himself to be an independent thinker and at the same time an articulate spokesman for the classical ideal.

---

[1] It is a pleasure to acknowledge my indebtedness to the major interpreters of French classicism, in particular E.B.O. Borgerhoff, Jules Brody, Hugh M. Davidson, and Henri Peyre. I wish also to express my gratitude to Pierre Clarac for his many studies of La Fontaine and to Jean-Pierre Collinet for his impressive thesis, *Le Monde littéraire de La Fontaine* (Paris: Presses Universitaires de France, 1970). My page references, using the abbreviation OD, apply to Pierre Clarac's edition of La Fontaine's *Oeuvres diverses* in the Bibliothèque de la Pléiade, 2nd ed. (Paris: Gallimard, 1958).

[2] Paul Valéry, "Situation de Baudelaire," in his *Oeuvres*, ed. Jean Hytier, Bibliothèque de la Pléiade, I (Paris: Gallimard, 1957), 598.

[3] Paul Valéry, *Tel Quel*, in his *Oeuvres*, ed. cit., II (1960), 478.

[4] See my *Young La Fontaine* (Evanston: Northwestern University Press, 1952), pp. 167-78, and Collinet, pp. 286-93.

[5] "La Fontaine's Poems of Self-Appraisal," *Papers on French Seventeenth Century Literature*, Nos. 4-5 (Summer 1976), 57-74.

French Literary Criticism in the 17th Century: Its Nature and Status

Hugh M. Davidson
University of Virginia

Literature is in part what it is, and in part what it is said to be. To anyone interested in what happens to literature when it is brought into discourse about itself, the 17th century in France is a rich source of data. In polite society people talked a great deal about literature and also wrote a great deal about it. What remains of their literary criticism, as we should call it, comes in all sizes and shapes: *commentaires, pensées, entretiens, lettres, examens, arts poétiques, satires, épîtres, comédies, parodies, préfaces, romans, traités, sentiments, factums, dialogues, éloges, mémoires, anecdotes, sonnets, remarques, discours, maximes, récits, nouvelles, parallèles, divertissements, gazettes, journaux, doutes, bibliothèques, poèmes, observations, réflexions, conversations, comparisons, dissertations, digressions.*

The line we follow as we try to discover and reconstruct the meaning of the data is to some extent a matter of choice. I have decided on what might be called a *problematic* approach. To save time and space, I shall simply state my premises and then do what I can with them. Perhaps the results will provide some justification for them.

1. The variety of forms assumed by the discussion of literature in the 17th century reflects the confusion that goes with all large scale and poorly-coordinated undertakings; the unity it has, nonetheless, bears witness to a constant effort of invention that takes place within a widely-held framework of ideas, facts, and values.

2. The dominant discipline for both literary and critical activity in the 17th century is *rhetoric*, but not exactly the so-called "traditional rhetoric" that amounts to little more than an eclectic summary of notions and precepts found in Cicero and Quintilian; I mean something more fundamental: a persistent tendency to pose all problems of literature in terms of four interrelated factors, author-work-audience-aim, or, to say it in a word, in terms of a transaction.

3. Rhetoric is, in fact, a common 17th-century matrix within which both literary and extra-literary activities may be specified; here are four examples: (a) it regulates the exchanges of discourse among the characters of a play; (b) it regulates the exchanges that occur when an author offers his play to an audience in a theatre; (c) as a comprehensive code of language and behavior it regulates the interactions in real life of those who belong to polite society; (d) it underlies the conduct of the prince when he undertakes to present to his subjects, as d'Aubignac says, *divertissements* worthy of his crown.[1]

4. Given that, within the matrix of rhetoric, literature emerges as language used in ways that move us, give us pleasure, and cause us to think, then the fact that some obviously do that better than others may be explained in terms of *nature* and *art*, of what is given in the way of talent, and of what is acquired in the way of technique: without this distinction 17th-century criticism could not live or breathe.

5. Art here is not primarily a product but a productive discipline; although it involves knowledge, it is not primarily erudition or science; it may be defined, rather, as a habit of judgment and execution, to be fixed in the powers of human nature and used freely according to reason, its immediate concern being language and its expressive and impressive possibilities.

6. For some grasp of the ambiguous divisions of literary art in the 17th century, we may turn to the program that the French Academy set for itself in 1635: to assemble a dictionary, to prepare a grammar, and to compose two treatises, one on rhetoric and the other on poetics; and thus to cover the entire range of problems from choice of vocabulary to arrangement of words and to composition in prose to the writing of poetry.

With that set of assumptions, we can leave the broad focus for a time and concentrate on those problem areas.

*
* *

It was an ambitious program. By great labor the Academy did manage to publish its dictionary almost sixty years later, in 1694. The grammar took longer, more like three centuries, for its first edition came out in 1935. If we pause to think that half the program was finished in

300 years we may, by extrapolation, expect to see the rhetoric and the poetics by the year 2235 A.D., though that may be a conservative guess. The real point is that one-third of the way through the 17th-century literature a group of verbal arts began to reflect and to affect each other in a very close way. Four sets of topics involving literary language came into view, and it was thought self-evident that they needed disciplined treatment. The Academy could, as a body, produce a dictionary. But writers and critics and consumers of literature were in the meantime going back and forth over the whole ensemble of problems, and so the main discussions—in private, in public, in conversations, and in print— gather about the poles of lexicography or diction, grammar, rhetoric, and poetics. Under these headings I believe one can bring together some typical views that throw light on the nature and status of French literary criticism in the 17th century. For this occasion I have decided not to lengthen an already long paper with treatments of the first two. I shall limit myself to saying that the important dictionaries and grammars are obviously not intended for foreigners so that they may translate French accurately and speak it correctly, but for natives so that they may bring into being a new body of literature. Richelet, Furetière, and the Academy as dictionary makers, and Malherbe, Vaugelas, and Bouhours as grammarians must definitely be counted among the motive forces at work in 17th-century critical discourse.

Rhetoric

In turning to the third verbal art I must make clear the two senses in which I am using the term rhetoric here. (1) It refers to the pervasive framework within which writers, critics, and commentators work during most of the 17th century, and, as I have suggested, it supplies a social as well as a literary *thématique*. (2) But it refers on a lower level of analysis to a particular art of language that is brought to bear on the process of composition. In the light of the second, narrow sense, the main discussions start from the topics of invention, expression, and effect or judgment, three easily recognizable points on the line along which an author moves as he composes his work and presents it to his audience for a response. I can best show something of the characteristic turn taken on these topics by establishing some contrasts with ancient theories.

1. Invention has always had an essential role in rhetoric. And one approach to it has been through imitation—imitation of the master, imitation of the work. Horace advised his readers to thumb Greek texts assiduously and to imitate them; this advice moves on into the Renaissance and the 17th century in France, modified by the fact that Latin and Italian as well as Greek models are available. Into this ensemble

come, on the theoretical side, vestiges of Aristotle's *Poetics*, where the imitation of models is raised in tone by attending to the serious and philosophical aspects of poetry, and traces of Plato's dialectic, where imitation is of the ideal (or should be). Invention in the 17th century takes its flavor from the faith, by moments pedantic, naive, or subtle, in the validity of this paradox, namely, that invention has its origins in imitation. La Fontaine's experience, for example, led him from mistaken imitation of Voiture back to the ancients: "Horace, par bonheur, me dessilla les yeux."[2] He finds everything he needs in the distant past: "Arts et guides, tout est dans les Champs-Elysées." And yet he does not renounce his own intuitions:

> Souvent à marcher seul j'ose me hasarder.
> On me verra toujours pratiquer cet usage:
> Mon imitation n'est pas un esclavage.

2. As for expression, that other essential link in the rhetorical chain, we see again a continuation of the Horatian habit. Literary works, which may be kinds of things (as in the analysis of Aristotle), become in Horace's view kinds of speeches. He looks at poems and asks not, "what are the causal aspects of made objects?" but rather, "what are the *res*, the subjects, the contents?"; and, "are they effectively conveyed by the *verba*, the words, the figures, and the levels of style?" There is much evidence of this sort of redefinition in the 17th century. For d'Aubignac in his *Pratique du Théatre*, the task of the dramatic poet is to produce discourse; and to him that means to adjust words to a conceived action having strict limits of place and time. In the first section of his *Art Poétique*, as Boileau gives general advice to his reader-poet, he moves back and forth from one of the poles to the other, from what is thought to how it is expressed and back. One phase of the cycle is contained in the familiar couplet, "Ce qui se conçoit bien s'exprime clairement,/ Et les mots pour le dire arrivent aisément." Moreover, his way of distinguishing one genre from another is based, as we shall see in a moment, on the possibility of taking his principle and applying it to specific pairings of subject matters and styles.

3. Effects are sought by authors, defined by critics, and reported by audiences. Once more, in the effort to recover the force of 17th-century positions, we do well to make some distinctions in the tradition toward which those who discuss literature in the 17th century almost invariably turn. In an early chapter of the *Poetics* Aristotle speaks very generally: the origins of poetry lie in our natural aptitude and taste for imitation, which is an occasion for knowing and a source of pleasure. Then he becomes very specific: the effects of poetry differ widely and we must determine them in particular for each poetic species. Horace, at times alleged to be his prophet, tends to be unspecific. Poets wish, he says, to

edify us or to please us—"aut prodesse aut delectare"—and that poet wins all votes who does both. It is obvious that he is telescoping the three generally stated aims of rhetoric—*conciliare* or *delectare*, *docere*, and *movere*—into two, *docere* giving the idea of instruction and the other two infinitives tending to coalesce or to be closely linked. "Le secret est d'abord de plaire et de toucher," writes Boileau.

In the 17th century we find endless variations on *plaire* and *instruire* and on how the two are related. To these trump cards is added a third, *les règles*. The relative value of the cards depends on who is talking. Corneille, in his first *discours* on dramatic poetry, does a virtuoso turn: of course the poet must please, but to do that he must pay attention to the rules, and whoever follows the rules (as Corneille formulates them) will certainly achieve *utilité* in his play. "Cette dispute même serait très inutile," he says, "puisqu'il est impossible de plaire selon les règles sans qu'il ne s'y rencontre beaucoup d'utilité" (p. 38).[3] Molière knows that pleasing comes first; he makes light of rules, which are a few observations based on common sense; but in more than one place he assumes a serious moral attitude, for he is re-presenting the members of his audience to themselves for self-recognition and self-judgment. Racine keeps his rules mostly to himself; it is impossible to imagine him publishing anything like Corneille's *discours* and *examens*. In his last works he is concerned with the theater as an educational force, but in the earlier ones, he seems to have rediscovered and sought a specific tragic effect along Aristotelian lines when he set as his aim the arousing of what he calls in the preface to *Bérénice* "cette tristesse majestueuse qui fait tout le plaisir de la tragédie."

It is clear, then, that the 17th-century interest in rhetoric as an art or technique explains the place that certain questions have in critical consciousness (as we might say). One sees a steady play of continuity against innovation: the thought of critics and writers turns to the past for examples and advice, and then they find themselves obliged, by the unique facts of life in their century, to enter into a dialectical conversation with that past. The upshot is that their urge to imitate often leads them away from obvious features of ancient works to insights into possibilities of which the classics were simply one realization.

Poetics

We could have said much more about audiences and, especially, about kinds of audiences in the preceding section. Poetics, as a discipline, leads in another direction, toward an understanding of kinds of works. D'Aubignac shows in the opening pages of the *Pratique du théatre* one way to proceed on this topic. By a series of distinctions, comparisons, and contrasts we arrive finally at what is our real object of attention. (1)

He begins with the idea of a body politic, composed of a prince and his subjects who engage in wars, sciences, arts, and commerce but seek—as the end of all that busy-ness—leisure and diversions. (2) These amusements are not only ends but also means to ends, such as showing the greatness of a state, or inspiring virtue, or simply remedying idleness ("l'un des plus grands maux qui puissent être dans un état," p. 10). (3) The theater is one item on a long list of public spectacles and games, but it has fallen into decline, and it deserves to be restored to something like its ancient status. (4) Plays differ from epic poems and novels; and yet, in spite of limits imposed by dramatic rules, it is possible to render indirectly complex actions, panoramic scenes, and long time-perspectives. (5) The technique of painting throws light on what should be the *pratique du théâtre*: "Je prends ici la comparaison d'un tableau, dont j'ai résolu de me servir souvent dans ce traité" (p. 34). This takes us into an analogy of action/representation to content/expression. (6) Beyond this point d'Aubignac concerns himself mainly with ways of achieving coherence and *vraisemblance* in the total discourse that constitutes the play. He moves out of poetics and into rhetoric. But his shrewd and detailed analyses, dotted with examples from Greek, Latin, Italian, and French sources, give us authentic insight into one of the best minds among the *doctes*.

D'Aubignac often mentions Corneille's plays in making his points and is usually complimentary in his remarks. Corneille, though, is perfectly capable of writing his own *pratique du théâtre*. He had read, to say the least, the *Sentiments de l'Académie sur le Cid*; he knew d'Aubignac and his work; he could read Aristotle and Horace and their commentators as well as anyone else; and he had been a successful playwright. And so, he published in 1660 his own poetics in the form of three prefatory *Discours* for the three volumes of his collected works. Then he went on to consider and judge, in a series of *Examens*, each of his plays in the light of his own views. These remarkable essays and pieces of practical criticism illustrate for us very well how Corneille conceived the structure of literary discussion. A continuous line of reasoning flows from the ancient critics and authors and the impersonal tradition they have inspired to a synthesis—personal but not idiosyncratic, modern, but not revolutionary—of productive principles; these principles yield norms; and particular plays result from free activity based on knowledge of these principles and norms. It is not possible to describe this structure without making it sound mechanical—to us, who are not playwrights. In the hands of Corneille and in his mind, this way of seeing literary composition has a vitality and openness that keeps it from being academic. (Of course one must add that it comes *ex post facto*: he did not write according to this theory as such and *a priori*; still, it was surely germinating and growing and affecting his practice as he went along.)

There is a curious feature in Corneille's "poetics" that remains to be noted. It goes considerably beyond the scheme just presented. In the first *Discours* he recalls Aristotle's list of the six parts of tragedy, which he translates as *sujet, moeurs, sentiments, diction, musique,* and *décoration du théatre.* He continues:

> De ces six il n'y a que le sujet dont la bonne constitution dépende proprement de la poétique; les autres ont besoin d'autres arts subsidiaires: les moeurs, de la morale; les sentiments, de la rhétorique; la diction, de la grammaire; et les deux autres parties ont chacune leur art. (p. 45)

The poet's equipment includes in effect if not in fact poetics *plus* three quite sizeable subsidiary arts: morality, rhetoric, and grammar.

I like the valedictory near the end of the third *Discours.*

> Quoiqu'il en soit, voilà mes opinions, ou si vous voulez, mes hérésies touchant les principaux points de l'art; et je ne sais point mieux accorder les règles anciennes avec les agréments modernes.

He cannot resist adding a sentence that has in it a scarcely veiled challenge:

> Je ne doute point qu'il ne soit aisé d'en trouver de meilleurs moyens, et je serai tout prêt de les suivre lorsqu'on les aura mis en pratique aussi heureusement qu'on y a vu les mieux. (p. 148)

With Boileau the scope of the discussion widens again, and he continues more directly than Corneille the thought of d'Aubignac and Horace. We have already seen how he analyzes expression. In the second and third *chants* of the *Art poétique* he proceeds in a very similar way. Without exception but with a lot of variation to avoid monotony he defines the minor and major poetic genres in terms of content and style. In general content, fixed by example, convention, or by "what oft was thought but ne'er so well expressed" determines the words to be used, and the choices made by the poet may be judged by reference to the criterion of appropriateness.

All that is quite familiar—and rather unjust to Boileau. He knows that no amount of correctness can excuse a poet who leaves us cold, uninterested. For a poem may also be judged by its immediate effect: does it, to use three of his favorite verbs, *attacher, plaire, toucher*? Moreover, his views regarding *genres* are less static and less dogmatic than we might suppose. Less static, because he has a thesis regarding the evolution of genres. Reason, that is, poetic good sense, is a moving principle that causes poets to go from ignorance to knowledge, from crude experiments to better works. The phrase "Enfin, Malherbe vint" applies strictly to diction and grammar in poetry, but Boileau utters a similar sigh of relief more than once in treating the history of genres, as he indicates gropings in forms, then mature states, then the need for vigilance in preserving what has been gained. His views are less dogmatic, I suspect, then we usually think. He thought very highly of Longinus and his treatise *On the Sublime*. But Longinus has no theory of genres; his examples come pêle-mêle from oratory, poetry, history, and philosophy. What he prizes is a quality of writing that occurs in short passages: it has nothing to do with generic rules. Longinus adds also a corrective influence against attaching too much weight to the verdicts of particular, historically-determined audiences. The soul of the poet counts most of all. If it is great, it leads audiences where it will. We may doubt that Boileau saw all the revolutionary consequences that the treatise of Longinus might have on his own critical thinking, but he certainly saw some of them.

One final and more general point here. As we try to discern some typical themes and variations in the views of d'Aubignac, Corneille, and Boileau, we must keep in mind that poetic considerations are not free and independent. The position of Aristotle helps us to see what has happened. There is no doubt in his mind that rhetoric and poetics are distinct arts, dealing with different sets of causes. There is nothing, however, that prevents later thinkers from importing terms, outlines, and sequences from poetics into a framework that is fundamentally rhetorical. That step was taken early in the history of Western literary criticism; and that decision, with its allied habit of mind, is resumed almost without question in France in the 16th century and continued into the 17th century.

History and Philosophy as Rhetoric

This paper is about the discussion of literature. We think that we understand what literature is, but does our notion do justice to our 17th-century data? And do we see clearly enough the nature of the "discussion"? Perhaps not. Here is the title of a work by Rapin: *Réflexions sur l'éloquence, la poétique, l'histoire et la philosophie....* Of the four sets of reflections, that on éloquence comes first, because Rapin thinks art to be the foundation of all the others. How far he is willing to go in promoting rhetoric strikes us forcibly as we read through the whole series. The vocabulary he uses for analyzing or commenting on eloquence reappears with slight adaptations in all the other reflections. We have come to expect it in the discussion of poetry, but there it is again in what he says about two new disciplines, history and philosophy: the venerable triad of author-work-audience, the starting points in nature, to which art is added; the adjustment of styles to content; the two aims of pleasing and instructing (history and philosophy must do more than simply the latter); the tendency to fall back on examples and attractively-framed precepts instead of technical precision.

And now here is the rest of that title: *Réflexions sur l'éloquence, la poétique, l'histoire et la philosophie, avec le jugement qu'on doit faire des auteurs qui se sont signalés dans ces quatre parties des belles-lettres.* "Ces quatre parties des belles-lettres"—note the emergence of something like an encyclopedia of liberal arts and the subject matter on which one may exercise them. I say liberal arts, but I have just shown their subordination to the first, *éloquence*, so in a real sense, there is a single method as well as a single subject matter ("...les auteurs qui se sont signalés..." etc.). Rapin is something of an evangelist: all of us need to be acquainted with those parts of *belles-lettres*:

> ...parce que l'on trouve dans le commerce de ces sciences tous les plaisirs de l'âme et que l'on ne peut parvenir presque à aucun degré de politesse, ni de cette honnêteté qui fait le commerce le plus doux de la vie, que par quelque teinture de ces facultés et par quelque connaissance de ceux qui y ont excellé.[4]

Arts of Words, of Things, of Creatures

Such self-assurance, such imperialism on the part of one intellectual discipline does not go unchallenged. If rhetoric can determine the status of history and philosophy, historians and philosophers can return the compliment and say some things about the nature and competence of rhetoric. In fact, as the intellectual and artistic life of the century proceeds, one sees more and more evidence of resistance and counterattack from people who have quite different views of literature, art, and the status of rhetoric.

1. In 1637, two years after the founding of the Academy and in the year of *Sentiments de l'Académie sur le Cid*, Descartes published his *Discours de la méthode pour bien conduire sa raison et chercher la vérité dans toutes les sciences*. In reviewing his studies at La Flèche he draws up a list of disciplines and judges each item on the list. He comes quickly to poetry and eloquence. "J'estimais fort l'éloquence et j'étais amoureux de la poésie; mais je pensais que l'une et l'autre étaient des dons de l'esprit plutôt que des fruits de l'étude." In case we missed the point, he goes on to show that he meant exactly what he said:

> Ceux qui ont le raisonnement le plus fort, et qui digèrent le mieux leurs pensées, afin de les rendre claires et intelligibles, peuvent toujours le mieux persuader ce qu'ils proposent, encore qu'ils ne parlassent que bas breton, et qu'ils n'eussent jamais appris de rhétorique.

So much for that discipline.

> Et ceux qui ont les inventions les plus agréables, et qui les savent exprimer avec le plus d'ornement et de douceur, ne laisseraient pas d'être les meilleurs poètes, encore que l'art poétique leur fût inconnu.[5]

So much for the art of poetry. In those two symmetrical sentences Descartes provides a strong antidote against rules and rationalized technique in poetry and prose. It is not that he distrusts completely the power of art: far from it. For what is his method if not an intellectual art? However, it is an art not of words but of things, and of the ideas by which we know things.

2. In 1662 the Port-Royalists published the first of many editions of *La Logique ou l'art de penser*. It buckles onto their *Grammaire générale et raisonnée* published two years earlier. In other words logic, not rhetoric, follows as the natural sequel of grammar. There can, indeed, be no doubt from the many disparaging remarks made about rhetoric in the *Logique* and from the many claims made regarding the usefulness of their *art de penser* that the Port-Royalists intended to destroy the prestige of rhetoric and to eliminate the need for it as a technique.

3. In the second edition of the *Logique* there is a footnote that pays tribute to Pascal as "feu Mr Pascal qui savait autant de véritable rhétorique que personne avait jamais su."[6] Something invidious is meant by that adjective *véritable*, I think. For Pascal, as is clear from his fine pages on *l'art de démontrer* and *l'art de persuader* (in spite of complications due to what he calls "l'art d'agréer"), these two arts are one and the same: to persuade is to demonstrate, or at least to prove. From judgments expressed in the *Pensées* and from his practice, we know that he was one of the anti-Ciceronians. When he read, he looked for the man and not the author. When he wrote, he approached his readers in terms of fundamental needs and not with an eye to their tastes in *divertissements*. He accepts in the *Provinciales* and in the *Pensées* the triadic rhetorical situation, but the decisive weight is displaced from the audience to the author, the one who has the truth and intends to communicate it, putting behind it wherever possible and suitable the force of reasoning.

4. In his *De la Recherche de la vérité* Malebranche analyzes at length the styles of Tertullian, Seneca, and Montaigne. The Cartesian theme of distrust of the imagination, which had been orchestrated in a famous fragment by Pascal, is joined to the theme of the distrust of rhetoric. Most men value what they do not understand, and the arts of

language, as they play on men's imaginations, cause them to fly in the face of reason. Thus, for example, the rhetoric of Tertullian consists in part in making himself unintelligible.

5. The next in this series of voices who wish to cut rhetoric down to size is Fontenelle. His *Digression sur les Anciens et les modernes* of 1688 sets up a contrast between physics, medicine, and mathematics, on one side, and on the other, poetry and eloquence. The former are capable of unlimited progress in the number of their "views"; the latter reach their perfection in a relatively short time, and consist of only a small number of "views." The sciences are incontestably useful; as for poetry and eloquence: "...elles ne [sont] pas en elles-mêmes fort importantes."[7] Rhetoric once led—in Greece and Rome—to honors, and had at least then a practical excuse for being. "La poésie au contraire n'était bonne à rien, et ç'a été toujours la même chose dans toutes sortes de gouvernements; ce vice-là lui est bien essentiel."[8] Fontenelle likes to tease, but like Descartes he means what he says, I think.

6. There is another current in 17th-century thought that opposes the claims of the rhetoricians and partisans of belles-lettres. In fact these voices were raised against Cartesian rationalism as well. Here is an example:

> Tous les grands divertissements sont dangereux pour la vie chrétienne, mais entre tous ceux que le monde a inventés, il n'y en a point qui soit plus à craindre que la comédie....[9]

That is taken from fragment 764 of Pascal's *Pensées*. And everyone knows the sentence from the *Visionnaires* of Nicole:

> Un faiseur de romans et un poète de théâtre est un empoisonneur public, non des corps mais des âmes des fidèles.

That was published in 1667, the year of *Andromaque*. Racine recognized the consequences of that statement; it was surely one of the immediate causes of his rupture with his teachers and friends at Port-Royal. A moment ago, apropos of their grammar and their logic, I was drawing attention to the intellectual polemic carried on by the group: now we see how they argue on the theological terrain. Curiously enough Bossuet came in his later years to sound more and more like the Jansenists. In 1694 he published his *Maximes et réflexions sur la comédie*, which are a merciless condemnation of the theater. He spares no one: not Racine, not Corneille, not Molière. He saved his most terrible words for Molière.

> La postérité saura peut-être la fin de ce poète comédien qui, en jouant son malade imaginaire ou son médecin par farce, reçut la

dernière atteinte de la maladie dont il mourut peu d'heures après, et passa des plaisanteries du théâtre, parmi lesquelles il rendit presque le dernier soupir, au tribunal de celui qui a dit «Malheur à vous qui riez, car vous pleurerez.»[10]

Incidentally, as that sentence reminds us, Bossuet, though he criticizes often the artifices of rhetoric, knew something about their uses. If he had not said so himself, one would not always be aware of the fact that his ideal in eloquence was Saint Paul.

Pascal, Nicole, and Bossuet represent for us the numerous groups in the 17th century who saw in literature, and especially in dramatic literature a threat to piety and to the Church.

A Complex Situation

I have not tried to give a narrative account of French literary criticism in the 17th century, but to sketch the problematic background against which such a narrative might be written. As I analyze this complex situation, three attitudes, conceptions of literature, and intellectual techniques confront each other more or less continuously.

1. The first attitude arises from concern with an order of language and action. It leads to a culture (in the sense of a mental habit) that lives mainly in the present, but cares about rules, precedents, *bienséances*, and so looks backward to the ancients in ways sometimes superstitious, sometimes discerning. In this framework literature emerges as an exploration of human nature and behavior in beautiful and appealing language. The favored method of discussing it moves up and down a line from casual affirmations based on taste to elaborate arts of words into which such judgments may finally be resolved. Corneille and Boileau represent this approach. *Rhetoric* has the architectonic role; it widens its scope to matters that otherwise would be reserved to poetics, and comes at last to say what history and philosophy must do if they wish to be effective. This tendency dominates the scene from, say, 1635 to 1685. It inspires most of what we think of as literary criticism in the 17th century.

2. But it is challenged by another attitude and concern, this time with an order of things, of physical nature and of human nature as part of that order. The mental habit here is inclined to discard ancient advice and models (except for a few exemplary contributions to mathematics), to take a fresh look at all that may be known and then, starting from the present, to look to the future, when definitive works of mechanics, medicine, and morality will supply the bases of life and action. In this framework literature appears as an agreeable element in society, one that is not without value in education, but its ties to imagination and feeling

distinguish it from serious intellectual activity. Literature, like everything else, tends to be discussed in the context of science, where the favored method is an art of things; and questions are settled usually by analyzing things into their elements. Descartes and Malebranche represent this approach. Scientistic *metaphysics* has the architectonic role, and claims its jurisdiction over rhetoric, poetics, and history. It freely judges their principles; it puts them in their proper and modest places. This tendency grows throughout the century; its partisans become progressively surer of themselves, and of their lease on the future.

3. Finally, there is an attitude, by no means negligible—though we sometimes neglect it in studies of 17th-century criticism—that is based on a concern with things and men (as before) but with this difference: they are parts of creation, and men in particular are destined one day to face their Creator. The mental habit in this case sees the world from an outside vantage-point, as a great train of events moving toward eternity: man fell; his Redeemer came; and all live in the city of man that is preparing the way for the City of God. In this framework literature shows up as a repertory of ideas and models that leave much to be desired. At worst they are morally poisonous; at best they are distractions. Here literature is continually measured against eternal values in a dialectic of words, things, and thoughts designed to purify hearts and to change lives. Pascal and Bossuet are champions of this approach. The architectonic role falls to *theology*. Its scope is without limit; in the light of divine wisdom it relativizes and on occasion pulverizes rhetoric, poetics, history, and philosophy (along with its developing brood of natural sciences).

Thus I cannot show a serene picture of "doctrine classique," reached after a period of struggle among diverse tendencies. The facts suggest instead a continuing contest and a cycle of refutation that has no real end, at least not on the plane of intelligence alone. It is clear that great disciplines like rhetoric (and its company of verbal arts), history, philosophy, and theology—when they are pursued with enthusiasm and on a high level of competence—can, all of them, make strong claims to universal relevance in life and art. The final decline of rhetoric and of theology in the discussion of literature would seem to be due not so much to flaws in the analyses proposed as to the absence of first-rate proponents in the younger ranks and to an obscure but massive decision to think about something else, and in a different way.

And yet, the main documents of 17th-century criticism are much more than museum pieces. My conviction on this point arises from two facts: (1) that it is very easy to show their links with the best ancient discussions of literature; and (2) that it is not hard to connect them with some of the liveliest recent criticism (here I do not mean simply that they provide a classical "sujet" and "écriture" for new criticism to react to).

With that conviction in mind, I shall conclude with a few adventurous questions. Is it not true that we can see about us a habit of analysis strikingly similar in some ways to the main one I have been describing? Is there not now a broad orthodoxy according to which theology and metaphysics are *out*, while studies of language and human behavior are *in*? Somewhat further along in the argument can we not see a great distinction looming before us: that of *subject matter* and *science*, corresponding to *nature* and *art* in the 17th century? Still lower down, just before we begin to read books and articles now appearing, do we not see the term *science* dividing up four ways, to form the quartet of "human sciences"—linguistics, psychology, sociology, and anthropology—with the *beau rôle* being assigned this time not to rhetoric but to a new version of grammar: linguistics and sign-theory? We note an important difference in that contemporary criticism tends to place itself under the aegis of science and the investigation of literature, rather than of art and the production of literature; but if we look at 17th-century word-study, grammar, rhetoric, and poetics, paying special attention to their premises, may we not see in them family resemblances to present-day concerns with signs and codes, with elements subject to combination or found by deconstruction, with strategies for debunking bourgeois myths, and with levels of poetic structuration?

A number of needed adjustments or of objections or even of rebuttals to these suggestions come into our minds. But some such attempt has the advantage of drawing things into a synoptic view that allows us to glimpse a terrain on which we may understand each other better, and where duels between critical modes that are sometimes opposed may give way to joint work in the light of permanent possibilities.

---

[1] See *La Pratique du théatre*, in the edition of P. Martino (Paris: Champion, 1927), p. 10. Elsewhere in this paper, when I quote from d'Aubignac, page indications referring to this edition are given in parentheses in the text.

[2] *Oeuvres de J. de la Fontaine*, ed. H. Régnier (Paris: Hachette, 1892), IX, 203, 1. 48, of the "Epître" to Huet. The two following quotations are from the same work, 11. 34 and 24-26.

[3] This quotation and all others from Corneille's discours refer to the edition by L. Forestier, *Pierre Corneille: Trois discours sur le poème dramatique* (Paris: Société d'édition d'enseignement supérieur, 1963).

[4] From R. Rapin, *Les Comparaisons des grands hommes de l'antiquité... Les Réflexions sur l'éloquence, la poétique, l'histoire et la philosophie*, in two volumes (Paris: 1684), 1, pp. iii-iv. For further details concerning this influential work, see my *Audience, Words, and Art* (Columbus: The Ohio State University Press, 1965), pp. 27-55.

[5] Descartes, *Discours de la méthode...*, edited by E. Gilson (Paris: Vrin, 1947), p. 7.

[6] A. Arnauld and P. Nicole, *La Logique ou l'art de penser*, second edition (Paris, 1664), p. 341.

[7] Fontenelle, *Digression sur les Anciens et les Modernes*, edited by R. Shackleton (Oxford: Clarendon Press, 1955), p. 167.

[8]Ibid., p. 168.

[9]Blaise Pascal, *Pensées sur la religion et sur quelques autres sujets*, edited by L. Lafuma, in three volumes (Paris: Editions du Luxembourg, 1951), 1, 412.

[10]Quoted in *Dictionnaire des lettres françaises: Le XVIIe siècle*, G. Grente, et al. (Paris: Fayard, 1954), *s.v. Bossuet*, p. 188.

The Role of the Poet in Eighteenth-Century French Society

John N. Pappas
Fordham University

Since antiquity, the poet has been alternately viewed as either a divinely inspired visionary who, as Rimbaud phrased it, "est vraiment voleur de feu. Il est chargé de l'humanité," and therefore is responsible for bringing truth to the masses; or he has been considered a mere entertainer or practitioner of a frivolous art which has no real value to society. It is this latter attitude which is reflected in Malherbe's dictum: "Un bon poète n' [est] pas plus utile à l'état qu'un bon joueur de quilles,"[1] or in Newton's dismissal of poetry as "ingenious fiddle-faddle."[2]

In order to understand the role of the poet in the Eighteenth Century therefore, it will be necessary to review historically the philosophical and sociological factors which led to contemporary attitudes toward that role; and our quest begins with Plato and his times. If Plato banned poets from his ideal State, it was because poets like Homer were not mere tellers of tales but were viewed as revealing truths about the gods. They were authorities not only in theology, but in the arts and sciences. Thus poets were rivals of philosophers, who also aspired to being the legislators of the nation. Since Plato saw reason and philosophy as the surest guides for mankind, he found himself obliged to attack the veneration accorded to poets and to Homer in particular. In the *Apology*, Socrates' scorn of poets as ignorant of the meaning of what they themselves have written is followed by Plato's conclusion that poetry is inartistic and unscientific, and the poet therefore no fit guide for society: "I presently recognize this, what they compose they compose not by wisdom, but by nature and because they were inspired, like the prophets and givers of oracles; for these also say many fine things, but know none of the things they say."[3]

This irrational source, explains Plato in the *Laws*, compels the poet "often to contradict himself, when he creates characters of contradictory moods; and he knows not which of these contradictory utterances is true." The true artist is the just lawgiver, the philosopher king, he concludes: It is not possible for the lawgiver in his law thus to compose two statements about a single matter.... He must always publish one single statement about one matter."[4]

We can recognize in the poet's contradictions, pointed up by Plato, Diderot's propensity for and defense of paradoxes and poetic analogies and it is no coincidence that in the beginning of the Eighteenth Century, the Quarrel of the Ancients and the Moderns revolves around Homer and the nature of poetry; with such defenders of the Moderns as La Motte and Fontenelle extolling the philosopher over the poet: these classicists were quite familiar with the Platonic arguments, and they were siding with him for rationality against the irrationality of poetic fervor.

In the history of French poetry, this ancient struggle between the inspired poet and the rational philosopher can be seen as determining to an extent the place of the poet in society. In the Middle Ages, aside from the renegade Villon and a few like him, the Platonic definition of art as the exercise of intelligence rather than emotional spontaneous utterances led to the intricate poetry of the Grands Rhétoriqueurs. And poetry became an intellectual game—Newton's "ingenious fiddle-faddle"—while the poet became nothing more than a witty court jester. This role continued during the Renaissance with a poet such as Marot, whose poetry becomes an "élégant badinage," as Boileau put it, which served to amuse the king and his courtiers. More importantly for our subject, this position led to a dependence of the poet on the aristocracy—and above all the king—for his success and material sustenance. The need for pensions from powerful and wealthy protectors, and the servitude which this implies, will remain throughout the Eighteenth Century one of the chief complaints of men of letters. The *Encyclopédie* article "Poète couronné," for example, laments the fact that poets are indifferent to the honor of being named poet laureate: "Les faveurs de nos rois," explains Jaucourt, "et les récompenses qu'ils accordent aux poètes...leur inspirent sans doute de l'indifférence pour une vaine couronne.... Il n'est donc pas surprenant que nous ayons parmi nous des poètes...qui se soient glorifiés du titre de poète du roi, tandis que nous n'en connaissons aucun qui ait pris celui de 'poète lauréat.'" We need only read Marot's numerous *Epîtres au roi*... begging for favors while having to amuse the king with his verse to recognize the humiliating condition of poets and men of letters in general under the Old Régime. In his *Essai sur les grands et les gens de lettres*, d'Alembert will speak out harshly against such wealthy noblemen who are accustomed to "commander durant leur digestion, du sublime à un poète, ou des découvertes à un savant..." and he will call for a declaration of independence for men of letters.[5]

With the advent of Ronsard and the Pléiade, the pendulum swings to the side of the inspired poet as a prophet for society. With the *Défense et illustration de la langue française*, we have the poet asserting his role as a reformer and leader of the masses in a socially meaningful campaign. His *Discours des misères de ce temps*, as with d'Aubigné's *Les Tragiques*, treats serious subjects like the religious wars and voices his indignation against them. For Ronsard, poetry becomes an elevated art. His is a return to the Platonic concept of the divinely inspired poet, not as a reason for banning him, but to give poetry the prestige it deserves and had in Plato's time (1550 Préf. of *Oeuvres*). Divine inspiration, for Ronsard, makes the poet a participant in divinity and gives him immortality. If inspiration is a divine grace, technique is not; and Ronsard will insist on a rigorous training for the would-be poet. It is this latter aspect of his theories we emphasize today as a kind of preparation for the theories of Malherbe.

We may say that with Malherbe, the history of Eighteenth-Century poetry begins. Boileau's "Enfin Malherbe vint" is echoed by d'Alembert in the "Discours préliminaire" of the *Encyclopédie* when he declares: "Malherbe...répandit le premier dans notre poésie une harmonie et des beautés auparavant inconnues" (I, 58). In criticizing Ronsard and the Pléiade, Malherbe first attacked as pretentious their claim to being divinely inspired prophets. Poetry is only a diversion and has no social utility except as an amusement. His already-quoted statement that a good poet is no more useful to the state than a good skittle player is close to Voltaire's declaration to Sir George Lyttleton that "a poet is just above a fiddler."[6] For Malherbe, poetry should address itself to man's reason—not to his feeling as had done Ronsard; and here too Voltaire echoes Malherbe when he writes: "Je n'estime la poésie qu'autant qu'elle est l'ornement de la raison."[7]

Thus the emphasis on technique—on rules deduced by reason, on the removal of whatever is unessential to the idea—the emphasis on clarity and simplicity, principles codified by Boileau, became the basis for Eighteenth-Century poetics. The article "Poète Lyrique" in the *Encyclopédie* testifies to the preponderant role of Malherbe when Jaucourt attacks the "galimatias" of his predecessors who had only "génie" and "feu," and adds: "Malherbe réduisit ces muses effrénés aux règles du devoir; il voulut qu'on parlât avec netteté, justesse, décence.... Il fut en sorte le père du bon goût dans notre poésie: et les lois prises dans le bon sens et dans la nature, servent encore de règles, comme l'a dit Despréaux, même aux auteurs d'aujourd'hui."

An esthetic which insists that "tout ce qui n'est pas clair n'est pas français" can have a devastating effect on poetry which tends to be affective rather than rational. We can find no better proof of this than to point to the Eighteenth-Century phase of the Quarrel of the Ancients and Moderns. As I suggested at the beginning of this study, the quarrel revolved around Homer: a choice of target rich in allusion to the Platonic argument against poets. What is ironic in the argumentation of the period is that in order to uphold Homer before the arguments of Plato and the partisans of the Moderns, i.e., those whose models were Boileau and Racine, is the fact that they sought to transform Homer into a paragon of clarity and "bienséances." Mme Dacier's translation of the *Iliad* systematically eliminated what Sainte-Beuve calls Homer's "souffle, véhémences, torrent, abondance, grandeur, feu et richesse,"[8] in order to make him speak the cultivated language of the salons. Her adversary, and the attacker of Homer, La Motte, had done the same in his translation of the same work aimed at correcting and improving the poet. Despite his ideological affinities with the Moderns, Voltaire in the article "Epopée" of his *Dictionnaire philosophique* showed his recognition and appreciation of Homer's poetic qualities when he writes:

> On doit répéter ici que ce fut une étrange enterprise, dans Lamotte, de dégrader Homère, et de le traduire; mais il fut encore plus étrange de l'abréger pour le corriger. Au lieu d'échauffer son génie en tâchant de copier les sublimes peintures d'Homère, il voulait lui donner de l'esprit: c'est la manie de la plupart des Français...[9]

Already in 1746 he had written on the same subject: "Quel malheureux don de la nature que l'esprit, s'il a empêché M. de Lamotte de sentir ces grandes beautés de l'imagination…. Ceux qui ne peuvent pardonner les fautes d'Homère en faveur de ses beautés sont la plupart, des esprits trop philosophiques, qui ont étouffé en eux-mêmes tout sentiment."[10] This could easily apply to La Motte's spiritual disciples, Fontenelle and d'Alembert, as we shall presently see.

If reason, clarity and directness are the criteria to be extolled, what exactly is the justification for the artificial barriers to direct communication imposed by poetry? This was really the question aroused by the quarrel over Homer. And among Frenchmen, being cartesian rationalists at heart, there were not lacking theoreticians who made the logical application of this consequence and decided that the best thing to do would be to eliminate poetry altogether. La Motte had suggested as much when he wrote in his *Discours sur la poésie*: "Le but du discours n'étant que de se faire entendre, il ne paraît pas raisonnable de s'imposer une contrainte qui nuit souvent à ce dessein et qui exige beaucoup plus de temps pour y réduire sa pensée qu'il n'en faudrait pour suivre simplement l'ordre naturel de ses idées."[11] His disciple, the abbé de Pons, nicknamed "le bossu de La Motte," pushed the idea to its logical conclusion: "Je crois donc que l'art des vers est un art frivole; que si les hommes étaient convenus de les proscrire, non seulement nous ne perdrions rien, mais que nous gagnerions beaucoup."[12] Fontenelle is not far from this position when he writes in his *Traité sur la poésie*: "Que serait-ce si l'on venait à découvrir...qu'il y a de la puérilité à gêner son langage uniquement pour flatter l'oreille, et à le gêner au point que souvent on en dit moins ce qu'on voulait et quelquefois autre chose?"[13] Prose is the natural means of communication, he pursues, and the natural beauty of speech consists in ideas précisely and forcefully expressed through a judicious choice of words. "A tout cela," he concludes, "l'Art de la Poésie ajoute sans aucune nécessité, sans aucun besoin pris dans la chose, les rimes et les mesures. Les voilà devenues une beauté par ce seul caprice de l'Art, et par la seule raison qu'elles gêneront le Poète, et que l'on sera bien aise de voir comment il s'en tirera. Si cette nouvelle sujétion fait dire au Poète des choses forcées ou inutiles, comme elles sont contraires à la beauté naturelle du discours, on en est plus choqué que l'on n'est touché de ce qu'il a satisfait à la contrainte de la rime. Mais si malgré cette contrainte, il pense et s'exprime aussi bien que s'il eût été entièrement libre; alors, au plaisir naturel que fait la beauté du discours, se joint le plaisir artificiel de voir que la contrainte n'a rien gâté."[14]

I have already exposed at greater length d'Alembert's view on poetry in my article "La Poétique de d'Alembert," so I will only say here that his view is close to that of La Motte and Fontenelle. The only justification for poetry, he held, is if it contains philosophical ideas and makes it easier to retain them. He rejects poetic imagery as childish. In a public speech made as Secretary of the Académie Française, d'Alembert announced "la loi rigoureuse, mais juste, que notre siècle impose aux poètes; il ne reconnaît plus pour bon en vers que ce qu'il trouverait excellent en prose.... Cette manière de penser...dirigera dans la suite plus que jamais le jugement de l'Académie Française sur les pièces de poésie qu'on lui adresse pour le concours" (IV, 294).

Thus poetry—and by extension poets—is tolerated grudgingly by the *philosophes* of the Eighteenth Century as a means of spreading ideas. Even Voltaire, who was considered the great poet by his contemporaries, often shows a disdainful attitude toward poets who would do better to engage in more philosophical, thus more important, matters. In trying to dissuade a correspondent from becoming a poet, for example, he advises: "Je prendrais la liberté de vous prier de regarder la poésie comme un amusement qui ne doit pas vous dérober à des occupations plus utiles."[15] And Rousseau was later to rail against poets and men of letters in general, as useless—and sometimes even harmful—to society. Further, in an age when metaphysics was taboo, the view of the poet as a Prometheus revealing divine truths to mankind could only be regarded as the worst superstition and could only lower him even more in the *Philosophes*' estimation, as it had for Plato. Certainly poets are not conveyors of truth, Jaucourt makes clear in his article "Liberté des poètes." Such liberty, he explains, "consiste à ôter des sujets qu'ils traitent, tout ce qui pourrait y déplaire et à mettre tout ce qui peut y plaire, sans être obligé de servir la vérité." And elsewhere he calls poetic style a "style de fiction." And, not without a grain of irony, he concludes: "Le style poétique abandonne les termes naturels pour en emprunter d'étrangers: il parle le langage des dieux dans l'Olympe." As it was for Plato, this is an argument against the poet. Indeed, in his article "Poète," Jaucourt quotes Plato and Democritus to the effect that one cannot be a poet "sans un grain de folie," and he speaks of the scorn of the emperor Philippe, who refused to grant poets the same immunities accorded to professors in the Sciences.

With poetry and poets so little appreciated by the *philosophes*, one might ask with Voltaire: "On demande comment la poésie étant si peu nécessaire au monde, elle occupe un si haut rang parmi les beaux-arts."[16] The answer must be sought in the sociological considerations promised earlier in this study. If a young writer wished to become celebrated as rapidly as possible in salon society and at the court, his surest means was to become a successful playwright—with top honors going to writers of tragedies. It is in this genre that Voltaire achieved his high position in the arts; and more than one mediocre author was elected to the Académie Française on the basis of one or two now-forgotten tragedies. Other than the minor salon verse such as the madrigals or fashionable bucolic or "bergerie" pieces, poetry in the Eighteenth Century usually referred to the alexandrin used in tragedy; and treatises on poetics generally dealt with the rules for tragedy, which Voltaire declared to be not merely French rules but natural laws applicable to English or any other theater. It is on this basis that he attacked Shakespeare, and even Homer—despite his grudging concession that both those authors had occasional "éclairs" in all that darkness. But in comparison with the views of the Encyclopedists, Voltaire proved to be an aristocratic conservative when it came to esthetics.

One of the ambitions of Diderot and d'Alembert in the *Encyclopédie* was to supplant the aristocracy as the arbiters of good taste. We recall Molière's satire in *Les Précieuses ridicules* when he has Mascarille, speaking as a Marquis, brag that he intends to make a new play succeed, explaining: "C'est la coutume ici qu'à nous autres gens de condition les auteurs viennent lire leurs pièces nouvelles, pour nous engager à les trouver belles, et leur donner de la réputation; et je vous laisse à penser si, quand nous lisons quelque chose, le parterre ose nous contredire. Pour moi, j'y suis fort exact: et quand j'ai promis à quelque poète, je crie toujours: 'Voilà qui est beau,' devant que les chandelles soient allumées." Molière of course exaggerates for comic effect, but Lancaster has amply proved in his study of French tragedy that the theatergoers who set the standards were the nobles, with the king and his court chief among them. There are even anecdotes describing the audience waiting quietly until the king applauded in order to know whether to approve or disapprove a play.

In *La Nouvelle Héloïse*, Rousseau's Saint-Preux attacks the monopoly of the theater by aristocratic tastes when he says of the noblemen: "Ils sont comme les seuls habitants de la terre; tout le reste n'est rien à ses yeux. Avoir un carosse, un suisse, un maître d'hôtel c'est être comme tout le monde.... Ceux qui vont à pied ne sont pas du monde; ce sont des bourgeois, des hommes du peuple. Il y a comme cela une poignée d'impertinents qui ne compte qu'eux dans tout l'univers.... C'est pour eux uniquement que sont faits les spectacles."[17] This is basically the complaint Diderot makes in his *Entretiens sur le fils naturel* when he argues for his drame bourgeois. The weapon the Encyclopedists used to wrest this power from the court were "reason" and "philosophy," as opposed to what they termed an uninformed taste based on whim or caprice. Here too Fontenelle had led the way when he had enjoined all men "qui aiment la raison" to go back to the origins of the beautiful in order to "réduire sous l'empire de la Philosophie les choses qui en paraissent les plus indépendantes et que l'on croit communément abandonnées à la bizarrerie des goûts."[18] Thus, while Diderot was developing his concept of poetry as hieroglyphics and preaching a theory of the inspired genius-poet in some of his other writings, in the *Encyclopédie* he followed the *philosophe* party line as enunciated by d'Alembert and praised, in the article "Encyclopédie," "La Motte, Terrason, Boindin, Fontenelle, sous lesquels la raison et l'esprit philosophique ou de doute a fait de si grands progrès..." D'Alembert, in the "Discours préliminaire" to the *Encyclopédie*, had defined art thusly: "On peut en général donner le nom d'*arts* à tout système de connaissance qu'il est permis de réduire à des règles positives, invariables et indépendantes du caprice ou de l'opinion" (I, 40). Thus, it was the rational philosopher and not the ignorant aristocracy who knew best how to deduce these rules for all the arts. That is why in his *Discours sur la poésie* he assumes the role of legislator of good taste and enunciates the "principes incontestables" which must guide poets.

Despite his appeal elsewhere for greater freedom for the genius and his superiority to any rules, Diderot as Encyclopedist echoes d'Alembert and affirms in his article "Encyclopédie": "... il y a bien de la différence entre enfanter à force de génie un ouvrage qui enlève les suffrages d'une nation qui a son moment, son goût, ses idées et ses préjugés, et tracer la poétique du genre, selon la connaissance réelle et réfléchie du cœur de l'homme; de la nature des choses et de la droite raison, qui sont les mêmes dans tous les temps. Le génie ne connaît point les règles; cependant il ne s'en écarte jamais dans ses succès. La philosophie ne connaît que les règles fondées dans la nature des êtres, qui est immuable et éternelle."

The attack against aristocratic taste was waged in every domain of literary and artistic endeavor. During the Querelle des Bouffons, for example, when the *philosophes* attacked the aristocratic preference for French opera and sought to substitute for it the more earthy Italian opera, Grimm made it quite clear that this was really part of the general power struggle between the court and the *philosophes* as to who would be the arbiters of French taste. "En fait de goût la cour donne à la nation des modes et les philosophes des lois. Il ne leur faut que le courage, qu'ils n'ont pas toujours, d'affronter les opinions les plus généralement reçues et souvent les plus absurdes, de les attaquer avec toute la force de la raison, de les exterminer partout où ils les trouvent. Le philosophe qui a fait le Discours préliminaire de *l'Encyclopédie* leur a donné le signal."[19]

If the status of tragedy was high in the Eighteenth Century, that of men of letters, as I have already suggested, was not. Whereas under Louis XIV authors had gained a measure of prestige because of the king's protection (we recall his intervention when *Tartuffe* had been banned), and were therefore more content with their role as courtiers, Louis XV showed little concern for, and at times even antipathy toward, authors. Their bolder writings and the ensuing intensification of censorship after the Regency further alienated them from the court. But even on the purely literary plane, there was a marked decline in royal attendance at the Comédie Française during Louis XV's reign, as Lancaster's *French Tragedy in the Time of Louis XV and Voltaire* attests. It is small wonder that Voltaire viewed the age of Louis XIV as the golden age for writers, and his excessive praise of the Sun King was in part an attempt to teach his successor his responsibilities toward men of letters. But his exile to England revealed that the situation that had prevailed under Louis XIV was not the ideal. In his *Lettres philosophiques* Voltaire revealed to his compatriots the honored position enjoyed by men in the arts and sciences in England—even to being granted influential governmental posts—whereas in France they and the *Bourgeoisie* in general were scorned. His own experience of being beaten by the servants of the Chevalier de Rohan to teach him that it was beneath a nobleman's dignity to duel with a commoner, proved that despite his being received in the salons of high society as the author of *Oedipe*, he was really there as a court jester for the amusement of the greats. He was later to learn the same lesson from his trip to the court of Frederick the Great. In a subtle way, his correspondence reveals, he was being told what Jacques's master in Diderot's novel said: "Vous ne savez pas ce que c'est que le nom d'ami donné par un supérieur à son subalterne." In this respect, an episode from Book III, Chapter xi of Lesage's *Gil Blas* is particularly revealing of the plight of men of letters. At a mundane *salon*, the valet approaches the mistress of the house and announces: "Madame, un homme en linge sale, crotté jusqu'à l'échine, et qui, sauf votre respect, a tout l'air d'un poète, demande à vous parler.— Qu'on le fasse monter, répondit Arsénie. Ne bougeons pas, messieurs, c'est un auteur."

Beginning with the *Lettres philosophiques* wherein Voltaire urges kings to take men of letters into their councils, the *philosophes* persistently fought to acquire a greater appreciation and respect from their society, and, as Diderot's article "Encyclopédie" puts it, to "changer la façon commune de penser." Even Rousseau, in his *Discours sur les sciences et les arts*, ends with an appeal to kings: "Que les rois ne dédaignent donc pas d'admettre dans leurs conseils les gens les plus capables de les bien conseiller; qu'ils renoncent à ce vieux préjugé inventé par l'orgueil des grands, que l'art de conduire les peuples est plus difficile que celui de les éclairer...que les savants du premier ordre trouvent dans leurs cours d'honorables asiles; qu'ils y obtiennent la seule récompense digne d'eux, celle de contribuer par leur crédit au bonheur des peuples à qui ils auront enseigné la sagesse..."[20] Diderot and Saint Lambert did not appeal to the king as had Rousseau and Voltaire. In their *Encyclopédie* article "Luxe" they proclaimed that "la seconde classe des citoyens," that is, the *Bourgeoisie*, are destined to enlighten the great, who have been corrupted by luxury, and "ce sera d'elle que partiront des lumières qui tomberont sur le peuple et remonteront vers les grands."

I began this essay with a quotation from d'Alembert's *Essai sur les grands et les gens de lettres* which decries the aristocratic custom of asking poets to be sublime during their digestion. The fact is that, despite his low opinion of poetry, d'Alembert, and the *philosophes* in general, saw the plight of the poet as one with all men of letters; and in the struggle for emancipation from the tyranny of the nobility, their cause was one. The "signal" referred to by Grimm is this very *Essai* of d'Alembert. It is a veritable manifesto for men of letters. In daring language he strikes out against "ces hommes orgueilleux et vils, qui regardent les gens de lettres comme des espèces d'animaux destinés à combattre dans l'arène pour le plaisir de la multitude." The only way to break their chains, he insists, is for writers to imitate Diogenes and refuse to be courtesans—an idea Diderot later adopts in *Le Neveu de Rameau* when Moi declares that the philosopher must refuse to dance "la vile pantomine." "Liberté, vérité et pauvreté," exclaims d'Alembert, "voilà les trois mots que les gens de lettres devraient toujours avoir devant les yeux" (IV, 367). They must not "se prosterner aux genoux de ceux qui devraient être à leurs pieds." It was not at the Hôtel de Rambouillet that Descartes discovered the application of algebra to geometry, he pursues, nor at the court of Charles II that Newton discovered universal gravity. In other words, "ce n'est pas dans une antichambre que l'on apprend à penser" (IV, 363). In spite of this truth, the aristocracy looks upon the man of letters as "un Etat inférieur; comme si l'art d'instruire et d'éclairer les hommes n'étaient pas, après l'art si rare de bien gouverner, le plus noble apanage de la condition humaine" (IV, 360).

How can men of letters improve their condition? By enhancing their own reputations with the general public, thus forcing the nobility to their views by the weight of public opinion, and by uniting in a common cause: "Heureux au moins les gens de lettres, s'ils reconnaissent enfin que le moyen le plus sûr de se faire respecter, est de vivre unis...et presque renfermés entre eux; que par cette union ils parviendront sans peine à donner la loi au reste de la nation sur les matières de goût et de philosophie" (IV, 372) . In this general movement toward emancipation, d'Alembert sought to transform poetry—and literature in general—into a "littérature engagée." If poetry, particularly in the theater, was so popular (a fact he learned when he proposed tragedies in prose and called Racine monotonous—everybody, including Voltaire, jumped on him for that), then it must be made to serve useful ends; and Voltaire's philosophic poetry became d'Alembert's model. Thus, while attacking poetry, d'Alembert, with the aid and example of Voltaire, nevertheless transformed the poet's role to that of educator and leader of the masses, along with that of men of letters in general. So that we now witness a curious reversal of the situation; poetry becomes less and less esteemed for its own sake, but the poet regains a certain respectability insofar as he to is serving the cause of philosophy.

But without realizing it, the very philosophy d'Alembert and the *philosophes* were preaching was paving the way for a greater appreciation of the poet and the poetic method. All of them espoused the empirical method which limited the area of man's concerns only to what the senses could grasp directly, that is, to matter. The Eighteenth-Century *philosophes* sought to apply the scientific method to all domains of human inquiry. Locke had shown the way by applying what Voltaire called "le flambeau de la physique" to the human soul, leading Voltaire to declare: "Je suis corps et je pense; je n'en sais pas davantage." With metaphysics eliminated, the area of inquiry for man's reason was suddenly stunted. Any attempt to go beyond sensation was "vaine spéculation": and Descartes' rationalism suddenly becomes the promotor of "l'esprit de système," to be avoided at all costs. Rousseau's decision to trust "sentiment" rather than reason is a logical application of this Lockean approach. In his *Profession de foi* he writes: "Je sais seulement que la vérité est dans les choses et non pas dans les jugements que j'en porte, et que moins je mets du mien dans les jugements que j'en porte, plus je suis sûr d'approcher la vérité." But Rousseau remains Cartesian enough to want his position to appear reasonable, so he adds: "Ainsi ma règle de me livrer au sentiment plus que la raison est confirmée par la raison meme."[21]

Diderot shares Rousseau's insistence on sentiment in the moral realm. In his play *Le Père de famille*, he has Cécile declare: "mon coeur me dit que cela est mal; et il ne m'a jamais trompée." Voltaire, too, will put the moral law on a non-rational basis when in his *Poème sur la loi naturelle* he likens conscience to the instinct of animals and insects. What is more germane to our subject, however, is that Diderot will apply this principle to the realm of esthetics. While the Cartesian d'Alembert was insisting that good taste is formed through a knowledge and application of rules deduced through reason, Diderot, following the abbé du Bos, postulated a theory that the superior man judges "par sentiment"—this, at the very time that he was proclaiming the reign of reason in his article "Encyclopédie." Voltaire, too, shows the ambivalence of the age when he writes in the article "Goût" of his *Dictionnaire philosophique* that literary taste "est un discernement prompt, comme celui de la langue et du palais, et qui prévient comme lui la réflexion.... Il ne suffit pas, pour le goût, de voir, de connaître la beauté d'un ouvrage; il faut la sentir, en être touché." This is exactly what Diderot had written about the simplicity found in Sedaine's play *Le Philosophe sans le savoir*: "Il faut être un ange en fait de goût, pour sentir le mérite de cette simplicité-là. J'ai quelquefois eu hier la vanité de croire, au milieu de deux mille personnes, que je le sentais seul; et cela parce qu'on n'était pas fou, ivre comme moi, qu'on ne faisait pas des cris."[22]

Since all knowledge comes from the senses, it follows that the more our senses are keen and active, the greater is our knowledge. And we have here in embryo the whole theory of the Romantic genius, superior to other men precisely because he is more strongly moved by his passions and sensations. Already in 1730, abbé Prévost had suggested it in his novel *Manon Lescaut*, when he has Des Grieux declare: "Le commun des hommes n'est sensible qu'à cinq ou six passions, dans le cercle desquelles leur vie se passe, et où toutes leurs agitations se réduisent.... Mais les personnes d'un caractère plus noble peuvent être remuées de mille façons différentes. Il semble qu'elles aient plus de cinq sens, et qu'elles puissent recevoir des idées et des sensations qui passent les bornes ordinaires de la Nature...et qui les élèvent au dessus du vulgaire...."[23]

This principle permeates the century. Strong passions and sensations, and not reason, become the source of man's greatness. Even Voltaire who, with Helvétius, called the passions "les vents qui font mouvoir la barque," shows the superiority of his interplanetary traveler Micromégas over the inhabitant of Saturn by endowing him with almost a thousand senses, whereas the Saturnian has only 72. The latter complains of it, saying: "nous sommes trop bornés..., malgré toute notre curiosité et le nombre assez grand de passions qui résultent de nos soixante-douze sens."[24]

Diderot was the chief exponent of this concept of genius. In his *Entretiens sur le fils naturel*, he shows us the genius Dorval overcome by his sensations to the point that when he awakens from his creative trance, he cannot recall what he said. We are back to Plato's claim that poets are like prophets or givers of oracles: they know not what they say. Already, in *De l'Interprétation de la Nature*, Diderot had expounded a concept of the genius who arrives at truth through a poetic vision based on analogies which goes beyond rational methods. In Pensée XXXI, he says that if the genius who possesses this gift attempted to explain it, "ce serait une histoire fidèle de toutes les extravagances qui lui ont passé par la tête. Je dis extravagances; car quel autre nom donner à cet enchaînement de conjectures fondées sur des oppositions ou des ressemblances si éloignées, si imperceptibles que les rêves d'un malade ne paraissent ni plus bizarres, ni plus décousus?"[25] We can see in the reference to the dreams of a sick man an anticipation of the poetic evocation of "le grand Tout" which Diderot will give us in *Le Rêve de d'Alembert*, and which he will describe as "de la plus haute extravagance, et tout à la fois de la philosophie la plus profonde." In the introductory part of that work, Diderot defends the method of argumentation which he will use in the *Rêve*, the method of poetic analogies. Analogy, he explains, "est une quatrième corde harmonique et proportionnelle à trois autres dont l'animal attend la résonance qui se fait toujours en lui-même, mais qui ne se fait pas toujours en nature. Peu importe au poète, il n'en est pas moins vrai."[26]

In his article "Encyclopédie," Diderot returns to his theory of the intuitive genius and explains that through the method of analogy, he arrives at "de nouvelles vérités spéculatives." While in the article "Génie," the superior man is depicted as one who "jette sur la nature des coups d'oeil généraux et perce ses abîmes.... Il s'élève d'un vol d'aigle vers une vérité lumineuse, source de mille vérités auxquelles parviendra par la suite en rampant la foule timide des sages observateurs." Diderot viewed himself in this role: he is the poet-prophet who can declare with Rimbaud's *Bateau ivre*: "J'ai vu ce que l'homme a cru voir." In a letter to Grimm, he makes precisely such a claim: "Je sens bien, je juge bien; et le temps finit toujours par prendre mon goût et mon avis. Ne riez pas. C'est moi qui anticipe sur l'avenir, et qui sais sa pensée."[27]

Thus d'Alembert's campaign to make men of letters the legislators of the nation in matters of taste and philosophy, coupled with Diderot's theory of the superior poet-genius, laid the foundation for the Nineteenth-Century theories of the superior Poet-prophet. Already on the eve of the French Revolution, the emancipation and the prestige of men of letters, in large measure thanks to the *philosophe* campaign articulated by d'Alembert, had reached such proportions that the Comte de Ségur, in his *Mémoires*, describes how he and the young noblemen courted, not the king, but men of letters: "La cour seule conservait son habituelle supériorité, mais, comme les courtisans en France sont encore plus les serviteurs de la mode que les serviteurs du prince, ils trouvaient de bon air de descendre de leur rang, et venaient faire leur cour à Marmontel, à d'Alembert, à Raynal, avec l'espoir de s'élever, par ce rapprochement, dans l'opinion publique.... Jamais il n'y eut à la cour plus de magnificence, de vanité, et moins de pouvoir. On frondait les puissances de Versailles, et on faisait sa cour à celles de *l'Encyclopédie*. Nous préférions un mot d'éloge de d'Alembert, de Diderot, à la faveur la plus signalée d'un prince."[28]

In the preface to *La Comédie humaine*, Balzac insisted that the man of letters "doit se regarder comme un instituteur des hommes"; and in his *Essai sur les gens de lettres*, he acknowledged the debt he owed to the *philosophes* of the previous century by giving, in effect, a résumé of d'Alembert's doctrine: "Réunis nous sommes au-dessus des lois, car les lois sont dominées par les moeurs. Ne constatons-nous pas les moeurs?

La civilisation n'est rien sans expression. Nous sommes les nouveaux pontifes d'un avenir inconnu, dont nous préparons l'œuvre. Cette proposition, le XVIIIe siècle l'a prouvée. Réunis nous sommes à la hauteur du pouvoir qui nous tue individuellement."[29]

Critics of the Eighteenth Century are accustomed to accusing the *philosophes* of having killed poetry through an excessive rationalism, and manuals note that we had to wait for the Nineteenth Century to see true lyric poetry. This may be so, but what the critics fail to add is that much of Eighteenth-Century poetry, as the aristocracy conceived of it and demanded, may have deserved to be killed. As we have seen, the poet under the Old Régime was no more than a court jester—even when he wrote tragedies, as Voltaire painfully learned when he tried to act the equal of de Rohan. Despite his habitual hyperbole, Rousseau is not far from wrong when he asks, in his *Discours sur les sciences et les arts*, what an artist seeking the approbation of his society must do to obtain it: "Ce qu'il fera messieurs? Il rabaissera son génie au niveau de son siècle, et aimera mieux composer des ouvrages communs qu'on admire pendant sa vie, que des merveilles qu'on n'admirerait que longtemps après sa mort. Dites-nous, célèbre Arouet, combien vous avez sacrifié de beautés mâles et fortes à notre fausse délicatesse et combien l'esprit de galanterie, si fertile en petites choses, vous en a coûté de grandes!"[30] The debate between Diderot and the sculptor Falconet is an example of the artist's prostitution of his art to cater to his public. When Diderot urged him to create what his inspiration dictated and put his faith in posterity to appreciate it, Falconet replied that he was well paid for the terra cotta shepherds making love, so much in vogue at the time, and that was the appreciation that counted. Later, Diderot was to give us a reminder of the quarrel when, in the *Rêve de d'Alembert*, as he is about to pulverize a statue, he has d'Alembert object that it is a masterpiece by Falconet. "Cela ne fait rien à Falconet," he replies, "la statue est payée, et Falconet fait peu de cas de la considération présente, aucun de la considération à venir."[31] The same is true for the painter Boucher. Diderot calls him the hypocrite of the arts, and he notes: "Il a de vieux portefeuilles pleins de morceaux admirables qu'il dédaigne. Il en a de nouveaux, farcis de moutons et de bergers à la Fontenelle sur lesquels il s'extasie. Cet homme est la ruine de tous les jeunes élèves en peinture. A peine savent-ils manier le pinceau et tenir la palette, qu'ils se tourmentent à enchaîner des guirlandes d'enfants et à se jeter dans toutes sortes d'extravagances..."[32] He makes a similar criticism of French opera in *Le Neveu de Rameau*. The aristocratic defenders of the traditional French musicalized tragedies, after seeing the more realistic Italian opera, had convinced themselves, he says, that "ils ne s'ennuieraient pas de leur féerie, de leur insipide mythologie, de leurs petits madrigaux doucereux qui ne marquent pas moins le mauvais goût du poète, que la misère de l'art qui s'en accommode. Les bonnes gens! Cela n'est pas et ne peut être. Le vrai, le bon, le beau ont leurs droits. On les conteste, mais on finit par admirer. Ce qui n'est pas marqué à ce coin, on l'admire un temps; mais on finit par bâiller. Bâillez donc, messieurs; bâillez à votre aise. Ne vous gênez pas."³³ It is interesting to note that in attacking the poetry of his age, d'Alembert had complained of the boredom felt at the interminable mythological clichés like "Flore" and "Zéphyre" with which it was filled. Even a staunch defender of classical tragedy like Voltaire had to admit that the countless imitations of the classic authors were beginning to tire the public; and he introduces innovations in *Zaïre*, he says, in its "Epître dédicatoire," in the hopes that it might lead to "un genre de tragédie qui nous est inconnue jusqu'ici et dont nous avons besoin."³⁴

In his *De la poésie dramatique*, Diderot makes the same accusation as had Rousseau against the stultifying effects of the "bienséances" on poets, and he complains that they are prevented from being true to nature. "O peuple plaisant et léger!" he exclaims, "quelles bornes vous donnez à l'art! quelle contrainte vous imposez à vos artistes! et de quels plaisirs votre délicatesse vous prive.... Malheur à l'homme né avec du génie, qui tentera quelque spectacle qui est dans la nature mais qui n'est pas dans vos préjugés."³⁵ What can the poet do in a society "dont les moeurs sont faibles, petites et maniérées.... Il tâchera de les embellir." And in a well-known passage in which he seems to be predicting the resurgence of poetry after the French Revolution, he concludes: "Quand verra-t-on naître des poètes? Ce sera après les temps de désastre et de grands malheurs; lorsque les peuples harassés commenceront à respirer. Alors les imaginations, ébranlées par des spectacles terribles, peindront des choses inconnues à ceux qui n'en ont pas été les témoins."³⁶

In his unpoetic way, d'Alembert attempted to transform poetry from the frothy salon tidbits concocted for the palate of frivolous noblemen, to a more meaningful, elevated state in which the poet, along with all men of letters, would be the educators of the masses. If Balzac and the Romantic and Symbolist poets could view themselves as superior to ordinary men and as the guides for the nation, it is in large measure, as Balzac himself admitted, thanks to the Eighteenth-Century *philosophes* and their campaign for freedom and prestige for the creative artist. And if today writers are treated with a certain respect and awe even when they speak on political or economic matters, they are enjoying a position which the Eighteenth-Century *philosophes* earned for them. Today the poet is no longer viewed simply as an entertainer or a clown, but as one who expresses profound truths concerning the inner man and the human condition. We can thank men like Diderot and d'Alembert for such an exalted view of the poet and man of letters.

---

[1]*Poésies de F. Malherbe*, Becq de Fouguières ed. (1874), p. xxiv.
[2]Quoted by Blair and Chandler, *Approaches to Poetry* (New York, 1935), p. 3.

[3] Quoted by Gilbert and Kuhn, *History of Aesthetics* (Bloomington, 1954), p. 25.
[4] Ibid., p. 26.
[5] D'Alembert, *Oeuvres complètes*, Belin, ed., IV, 364. Further quotations from this work will be cited directly in the text with volume and page numbers in parenthesis.
[6] Voltaire, *Correspondence*, Besterman ed., XVIII, 69.
[7] *Oeuvres complètes*, Moland ed., XXIII, 497.
[8] *Causeries du Lundi*, XIII, 154.
[9] *Oeuvres complètes*, Moland ed., XVIII, 568.
[10] Ibid., VIII, 349.
[11] Quoted by Lagarde and Michard, *XVIIIe siècle* (Paris, 1960), p. 353.
[12] Ibid.
[13] *Oeuvres de Monsieur de Fontenelle* (Paris, 1766), VIII, 315-316.
[14] *Ibid.*, III, 200.
[15] *Correspondence*, Besterman ed., III, 170.
[16] *Oeuvres complètes*, Moland ed., XX, 232.
[17] Rousseau, *Oeuvres complètes*, Pléiade ed., II, 252.
[18] *Oeuvres de Monsieur de Fontenelle* (Paris, 1766), III, 206.
[19] *Correspondance littéraire*, XVI, 301-302.
[20] *Oeuvres complètes*, Pléiade ed., III, 29-30.
[21] Ibid, IV, 573
[22] *Correspondance de Diderot*, Roth & Varloot eds., V, 205.
[23] *Manon Lescaut*, ed. Paul Vernière, Paris, 1957, p. 100.
[24] *Oeuvres complètes*, Moland ed., XXI, 108.
[25] Diderot, *Oeuvres philosophiques*, Garnier ed., pp. 197-198.
[26] Ibid., p. 280
[27] *Correspondance de Diderot*, Roth & Varloot eds., V. 206.
[28] *Mémoires, souvenirs et anecdotes* par M. le comte de Ségur (Paris: 1859), Vol. XIX of Barrière's *Mémoires*, pp. 97-99.
[29] Quoted by Louis de Royaumont, *Balzac et la société des gens de lettres*, p. 25.
[30] *Oeuvres complètes*, Pléiade ed., III, 21.
[31] *Oeuvres philosophiques*, Garnier ed., p. 263.
[32] Oeuvres esthétiques, Garnier ed., p. 453.
[33] *Oeuvres romanesques*, Garnier ed., 467.
[34] *Oeuvres complètes*, Moland ed., II, 542.
[35] *Oeuvres esthétiques*, Garnier ed., p. 263.
[36] Ibid., p. 262.

Rousseau and Diderot: Education As Politics

Lester G. Crocker †
University of Virginia

Rousseau and Diderot present a curious and significant instance, for the interpretation of the Enlightenment, of two men working within a common context and sharing certain assumptions and goals—both were devoted to happiness, justice and virtue—but who conceived of the universe and the problems of man in totally dissimilar terms and consequently reached antithetical conclusions.

Rousseau tells us in both the *Confessions* and *Emile* that everything belongs to the realm of politics.[1] By that I take him to mean that everything men do, or that is done to them, relates to their behavior, and that men's behavior is the realm of politics. Problems and solutions must therefore be approached as politics, if meaningful goals are to be set and to be met.

Although Diderot, like all Enlightenment thinkers, recognized the influence of legislation on behavior, and exaggerated it with typical naiveté, he never made any statement similar to Rousseau's, nor did he think along those lines. For him, the individual and his creative potentialities remained an unassailable center of value; such an attitude automatically imposes limits on the encroachments of political and social forces.

Diderot's viewpoint is likely to be more appealing to twentieth-century men of the West who share it. Yet, however we may judge Rousseau's ideas, both fairness to him and my own claim to objectivity require me to emphasize the fact that he was more totally committed than Diderot to finding a resolution to the human predicament. It is difficult not to remember that while Rousseau was thinking constructively about a new nation in Poland, Diderot turned his back to what was going on in that country. The brutal rape of Poland did not prevent him from journeying to Saint-Petersburg, to pay homage to one of the predators, content with the price she had paid to buy him, lulling his enlightened conscience with the delusion that he would direct the Semiramis of the North toward peace and reform in the spirit and letter of the Enlightenment.[2] It was for her that he later formulated his educational ideas. But even as he wrote them, his disillusion was by then complete, and he knew that he was writing only for himself, or for a vague posterity, and at the end, he had the courage to tell her what he really thought. Rousseau, having no illusions, was never disappointed, embarrassed or ashamed. At least he told the world about *his* brave new world.

But all this is only background to our study.

The essential fact, in my view, is that both Rousseau and Diderot have the same starting point, if I may use that expression in the sense of logical priority. Both assert that man's predicament arises from the divisions and tensions caused by his peculiarly human duality. Man is impelled by "natural" forces to live as an egocentric individual, to realize certain satisfactions (pleasure, power, importance) at the expense of other similarly motivated individuals. At the same time, the satisfaction of these drives and survival itself require him to live in a society, which in turn cannot survive without the imposition of contrary, so-called "artificial" restrictions that hinder or prevent his self-centered satisfaction.

Diderot's phrases in the *Supplément au Voyage de Bougainville* are often quoted "Voulez-vous savoir l'histoire abrégée de presque toute notre misère? La voici. Il existait un homme naturel: on a introduit au-dedans de cet homme un homme artificiel; et il s'est élevé dans la caverne une guerre continuelle qui dure toute la vie."[3] Rousseau's two *Discourses* are an explication of the same idea in terms of the effects— inner and outer—on the psyche of the individual and on social relations among men. In *Emile* he insists on this contradiction and calls it the source of all other contradictions (*Emile*, pp. 280, 93). But the formulation in one of his fragments is particularly striking by its similarity to that of Diderot. "Ce qui fait la misère humaine est la contradiction qui se trouve entre notre état et nos désirs, entre nos devoirs et nos penchants, entre la nature et les institutions sociales, entre l'homme et le citoyen. Rendez l'homme un, et vous le rendrez aussi heureux qu'il peut l'être."[4] Without this cardinal theme, it is not possible not to misinterpret the educational system of *Emile*, where Rousseau writes at the outset "Forcé de combattre la nature ou les institutions sociales, il faut opter entre faire un homme ou un citoyen: car on ne peut faire à la fois l'un et l'autre" (*Emile*, p. 9).

The basic assumption, then, is common to both men. But they will react to it in antithetical ways. The character of this reaction will determine their political and consequently, their educational ideas.

The revelation of what was wrong came to Rousseau in his famous "crise de Vincennes." The solution dawned on him less dramatically, but with a logical certainty that to him was absolute. Not only absolute, but obvious. The split which caused the alienation of man from himself and from other men must be overcome, healed. From that came all that was wrong: the hypocrisy, the shams, the predatory lusts and exploitation, the degenerative luxury, in a word, the ruthless competition that makes each man the enemy of all others, that makes each seek his good at the expense of others. We are neither natural men, living with the innocent *amour de soi* of the state of nature, nor social beings. Social animals, as nature has created them in some species, are by definition those who put the welfare of the community above their good as individuals; or more precisely, a social animal is one who has no personal interest other than the general interest.

Time's arrow flies in one direction; history cannot be undone. The state of innocence is not recoverable. But it is possible to conceive of a different history, or more exactly, of a state in which history can be avoided. History, after all, is only unguided nature, which in man, because he is "perfectible" (free from the fixity of instinct, capable of reflective as well as reflexive responses) produces that which the eighteenth century called "the artificial"—that domain, including society itself, which conflicts with the natural. But nature can be guided. It is not solely a given, but a virtual form contained in what is given, to be realized or created, as the tree is in the acorn. This human verity follows from the same powers, distinctive of man, that have made us what we are. We can be made into something different from what we are. Such is the meaning of what I have always considered to be Rousseau's basic statement in *La Nouvelle Héloïse*, the parable of Julie's garden, in which nature is guided and shaped by the unperceived and demiurgic gardener (read lawgiver, guide, leader, educator), by his "main cachée," made to correspond to a *human* idea of what nature is, or ought to be. In metaphysical terms, which are not Rousseau's terms, the implicit assumption is that the "true" or "real" world is specific to a species; that is, the work of the brain is to create a model of a possible world rather than to transmit to the mind a world that is metaphysically true.

It follows that men as they are, and their societies—so-called societies—as they are, are not viable. The futilities of proposed Enlightenment reforms cannot remedy the malady, for they do not touch its root causes, which will only continue, whatever the retouching, to blossom into new flowers of evil. Rousseau, a man of absolutes, declares his solution to be the only one. If a society cannot be created in which laws are above men (that is, in which the general interest supersedes the individual interest), the only alternative way to control men's disorderly unsocial behavior is "le despotisme arbitraire, et le plus arbitraire qu'il est possible... car le conflit des hommes et des lois, qui met l'Etat dans une guerre intestine continuelle, est le pire de tous les Etats politiques."[5]

Rousseau does not offer a program for action—though he will apply his theories, as far as possible, in programs of action for Poland and Corsica. He proposes a concept of another way of life. The answer is for men to form a true society, instead of "ce troupeau qu'on appelle société."[6] But since men have formed and perpetuated all the jungle societies, the only ones we know, we must change men. Rousseau criticizes the abbé de Saint-Pierre, "de chercher toujours un petit remède à chaque mal particulier, au lieu de remonter à leur source commune, et de voir qu'on ne les pouvait guérir que *tous à la fois*" (*Emile*, p. 599, italics added).

The great demiurge, modeled on the great lawgivers of the past, the fictitious gardeners of Rousseau's own pages, Wolmar in Clarens, Emile's tutor, the guides of his political writings, are designed to show us how to accomplish the desired end. The demiurge needs to have a grasp of two factors: the human psyche and what can be done with it; the concept of a true society and the institutions that can indefinitely perpetuate it. To create them is insufficient; equally difficult is to preserve them. For nature's nature is always ready to reassert itself against the gardener's, the great cleft is always ready to be reopened, and mankind ready again to "fall" into history.

The concept of a true society is set forth with perfect clarity in Rousseau's article, "Economie politique." It is the antithesis of bourgeois liberalism, as developed by the Physiocrats, with its tenets of free competition, private rights, and unlimited inequality. This is the model of the non-society, or disorder. For Rousseau, order is the unique fundamental value, which makes other values possible. Thus, to cite an important instance, there must be no mobility of roles in society; to aspire to change one's place is to recreate competition and disorder.[7] Rousseau's society is aristocratic and élitist; there are the leaders or guides, and those who are led and guided. The true society, he explains, is patterned on the living body. The parts must function, in orderly and harmonious fashion, as elements of the whole. All centrifugal forces, which would disrupt the health of the body, must be eliminated. Dissident or self-centered individuals are the analogues of diseased organs. Already, at this time, Rousseau states in a fragment what will become the leitmotiv of his political and educational system:

> Celui qui se croit capable de former un peuple doit se sentir en état de changer, pour ainsi dire, la nature des hommes. Il faut qu'il transforme chaque individu, qui est par lui-même un tout parfait et solitaire, en partie d'un plus grand tout, dont cet individu reçoive en quelque sorte sa vie et son être; qu'il mutile, pour ainsi dire, la constitution de l'homme.... Donnez-le tout entier à l'Etat, ou laissez-le tout entier à lui-même. Mais si vous partagez son coeur, vous le déchirez." (Vaughan, I, 324, 326)

This remedy is perfectly consistent with the diagnosis.

The true society is a different kind of alienation, that of self to society, an "alienation" which ends alienation, since the self is lifted out of the discordant sphere of the nature-society dichotomy into a realm of interpersonal harmony, one in which liberty and self-realization are attained, but in transmuted forms.[8] This state is as essentially different from what we now call the social order as the latter is from the state of nature; it is the secular equivalent of Pascal's order of grace, while the other states are analogous to the two lower orders, each discrete and irreducible to the other.

The goal can be reached only by the draconian yet subtle methods of Julie's gardener, by the total mobilization of the forces available. On the purely political level, they include the substitution of the general will for private or group wills, as solely constitutive of justice and law; the participation of all citizens in the ratification of such formulations of the general will as are presented to them by their leaders; the elimination of opposition, and as far as possible, of privacy; delegation to the government of vast powers to mould, control and punish both the behavior and the thinking of the social components in various ways detailed by Rousseau. To these relentless pressures there can be no end in time, for nature can be moulded but not extirpated. What Rousseau calls the "detestable human self," "the vile human self," "the abject human self," is ever lurking, ready to reassert itself against the manufactured social self ("le moi commun"). What would happen to Julie's wonderful garden if its gardener relinquished his constant surveillance and control?

Rousseau's ideas on education are the complement and extension of his political ideas, no more and no less. They are, as he says, a system, and the system is one unit of the larger system. Superficially, they seem to be two-faced, with *Emile* on the one hand and the mass education of the political writings on the other. This apparent dichotomy is, however, only the result of a difference in the postulated situation. Rousseau wishes to show how Emile can be made into "a man and a citizen," but because his subject is to live in our kind of society, the development takes place in isolation, abstracted from a political context and from the theoretical problem of the individual and society.

Despite their different character, the educational writings form a single, coherent doctrine in method and in aims; both method and aims are integrated into the universal sphere called politics—the art of governing men. To govern men, Rousseau had written in "Economie politique," it is necessary to make them "tels qu'on a besoin qu'ils soient." There is only one way—to capture their wills.[9] In short, reflexive response, the result of conditioning, is required to give artificially to men what nature failed to give them—social behavior, without which there can be no true society. No one is *naturally* a citizen. We must see "dans l'art perfectionné, la réparation des maux que l'art commencé fit à la nature."[10]

This, then, is the end that education must serve. The end is a possible one because of the malleability of man. As Rousseau explains in Book IX of the *Confessions*, he had developed a theory for controlling behavior, which he called "la morale sensitive." In *Emile* (p. 135) he declares, "Je n'imagine rien dont, avec un peu d'adresse, on ne pût inspirer le goût, même la fureur, aux enfants." The elements of the theory are in Locke, but it was Hartley (*Observations on Man*, 1749) who developed it. I do not know whether Rousseau had read Hartley, but the idea was taken up by Helvétius. At best, these men provided a conceptual framework, but not a model for praxis. This was to be Rousseau's great work, in the formative processes applied to Saint-Preux and Julie, to Emile, and to an abstract entity, "the citizen."

If politics is the art of controlling men's behavior—which is to "govern" them—their education, like all else, religion, the arts, public opinion, must be considered a means to that end.[11] ll It is not possible for there to be objective truths that contradict useful political ends (*Emile*, pp. 180, 214). It can be easily demonstrated that Rousseau's precepts follow exactly this course. His ideas on raising children are identical in theory and practice in *La Nouvelle Héloïse* and in *Emile*. He is educating an élite, men who will always keep their distance from the common people, and who will know how to manage them. Emile will learn (we are never told how) to manage them without their being aware of it, even as he has been managed "sans croire obéir, ils obéiront" (*Emile*, p. 389). Rousseau frequently insists that his plan for Emile's education follows "nature"; but the methodology reinforces the idea, which he repeats five times, that nature is not what is originally given. It becomes something different, indeed something opposite, in the conditions required by a society. To think otherwise, he warns, will only prolong the present state of man, "toujours en contradiction avec lui-même." The "natural order" contains a "gradation directement opposée à celle qu'exige l'ordre social," that is to say, it makes each individual put himself first.[12] Man "ne peut tendre à la fois à deux buts opposés" (*Emile*, pp. 3, 356). As in Julie's garden, Emile's nature will be the nature designed by someone else. "On façonne les plantes par la culture et l'homme par l'éducation" (*Emile*, p. 6). But the job must be done thoroughly: "notre espèce ne veut pas être façonnée à demi" (Emile, p. 4). The use of education for the political end is made explicit at the outset

> Les bonnes institutions sociales sont celles qui savent le mieux dénaturer l'homme, lui ôter son existence absolue pour lui en donner une relative, et transporter le *moi* dans l'unité commune; en sorte que chaque particulier ne se croie plus un, mais partie de l'unité, et ne soit plus sensible que dans le tout. (*Emile*, p.9)

How is this great and grandiose end to be accomplished? Passions cannot be eliminated, but they can be modified, guided; "il est aisé de voir comment on peut diriger au bien et au mal toutes les passions des enfants et des hommes."[13] Rousseau's educational theories are precisely a manual for doing this, by association, conditioning,[14] and above all by trickery, for everything must be done without the subject's ever realizing that he is being manipulated and molded. "On l'enchaîne, on le pousse, on le retient, avec le seul bien de la necessité, sans qu'il en murmure: on le rend souple et docile par la seule force des choses" (*Emile*, pp. 52, 80, 273).

The purpose is clearly set forth: "c'est de substituer la loi à l'homme, et d'armer les volontés générales d'une force réelle, supérieure à l'action de toute volonté particulière" (*Emile*, p. 70; also p. 305). This requires total control of the subject. But control will not work unless the pupil, like the citizen of the *Contrat social*, has the illusion of being free. Freedom is doing what one wants, and what one can, writes Rousseau (*Emile*, p. 69). Both of these factors must be surreptitiously controlled. The tutor constantly leads the child to think that what is really the tutor's will is the force of necessity (*Emile*, pp. 79-80), thus controlling what he *can*. He also leads Emile to think that he is doing what he wishes to do, when he is really doing what the tutor wishes him to do. He thus controls what he *wants*. Rousseau hits this point hard and repeatedly.[15]

Again, education rejoins politics, for Rousseau tells us more than once that any one can enforce laws but the art of the great leader is to capture wills and minds ("opinions"). The methods, including secret manipulation, spying and denunciation, and the redirection of the natural passions, are designed to make education *politically* effective.[16] The connection is summarized in *Emile* (p. 70): "Si les lois des nations pouvaient avoir, comme celles de la nature, une inflexibilité que jamais aucune force humaine ne pût vaincre. . . on joindrait à la liberté. . . la moralité . . ." The same idea was already formulated in "Economie politique."[17] It is omnipresent in *Emile*. We can grasp Rousseau's concept of liberty: to be free to do, and to want to do what the community, or those who direct it, decide what one ought to will and what one has been induced to will. A man is free when he is in this way a part of the sovereign functioning of the collective body—a citizen.

So much for the education of the élite, the supposed leaders of men. What about the common people, the masses of citizens? Emile is in a quite exceptional and hypothetical ideal situation. Rousseau knows that his wise rulers cannot educate the individual without educating the community, since the content of the conscience is influenced by public opinion. To weld the disparate units into an organic body, to maintain the complete supremacy of the *moi commun* over the ever-dangerous *moi humain*, education is the most important amongst a battery of weapons.

This view is outlined in "Economie politique":

> Or, former des citoyens n'est pas l'affaire d'un jour, et pour les avoir hommes, il faut les instruire enfants.... Si, par exemple, on les exerce assez tôt à ne jamais regarder leur individu que par ses relations avec le Corps de l'Etat, et à n'apercevoir, pour ainsi dire, leur propre existence que comme une partie de la sienne, ils pourront parvenir enfin à s'identifier en quelque sorte avec ce plus

grand tout, à se sentir membres de la patrie, à l'aimer de ce sentiment exquis que tout homme isolé n'a que pour soi-même ... et à transformer ainsi en une vertu sublime cette disposition dangereuse d'où naissent tous nos vices. (Vaughan, I, 255-56)

Education is *exercise*—habituation, conditioning. So indeed it always is; but Rousseau makes it absolutely clear what the *goal* and the degree or thoroughness are to be, and they are strangers to the open or liberal society.

Once again, the operation must be begun as soon as the children are born, while they can still be "taken out of themselves," before the *moi humain* has developed. (I cannot help thinking of the words of Fidel Castro, who was greatly influenced by Rousseau: "We have to create this [Communist] consciousness in man from the time he starts to talk, from the time he starts to say mama and papa.") Therefore the upbringing of children must be taken away from the family and entrusted to the State, or more exactly, to the Government, to which Rousseau in the *Contrat social* will give vast powers of surveillance and thought control. In this way alone can children be taught to will properly, that is, "à ne vouloir jamais que ce que veut la société" (Vaughan, I, 257). They will be citizens.

These ideas will be more fully developed in Chapter IV of the *Considérations sur le Gouvernement de Pologne* (1772), on education. It begins with a simple statement: "C'est ici l'article important" (Vaughan, II, 437). After the theory, the practice. Physical training is paramount. The children may not play freely, only together and in public, "de manière qu'il y ait toujours un but commun auquel tous aspirent, et qui excite la concurrence et l'émulation." The aim is to teach them to live, not in private, but "sous les yeux de leurs concitoyens" and to desire public approbation. The citizenry will be expected to attend their games.

Rousseau stops short at this point. But if his program of schooling is vague, he had defined the essential aims, and he has also specified the necessary supplements. Schooling is only part of education. It is carried on by other means: the pomp and majesty of public ceremonies, which inspire confidence in the leaders (Vaughan, II, 435); a national religious cult (which, we are told elsewhere, must be followed, on the pain of being labelled "le perturbateur de l'ordre et l'ennemi de la société,"[18] public ceremonies to reward virtuous citizens (Vaughan, II, 433); and, as in the *Lettre à d'Alembert sur les spectacles*, games and festivals to excite patriotic zeal—"De l'effervescence excitée par cette commune émulation naîtra cette ivresse patriotique qui seule sait élever les hommes au-dessus d'eux-mêmes...." (Vaughan, II, 492). In *Emile* (p. 406) Rousseau had said, "On n'a de prise sur les passions que par les passions." In the *Projet de Constitution* he declares that we must reach untapped passions, excite and develop them, in order to win hearts

(Vaughan, II, 478, 426). Without this, the best of laws are useless for the grand design.

Diderot's evolving political theories are in a sense more difficult to describe, though they are simpler and less abstruse. Rousseau's ideas constitute a coherent political philosophy, one reason why their influence has been so vast. Diderot's ideas display three facets: the earlier, Encyclopedic period, apparently moderate and in some ways rather close to the Physiocrats; the secret writings, in which he appears as the radical, sometimes the rebel; the mature thought of the papers written for Catherine, these in turn divided into the prudent early reflections and the hard-hitting plain talk of the last.

Again we cannot in this study be concerned with institutional proposals, but only with the response to what I have defined as a common *point de départ*—the fundamental cleavage of individual and society, similarly formulated by both men and doubtless discussed together when Diderot was advising Jean-Jacques in the early fifties about the *Discours sur l'origine de l'inégalité*.

Like Rousseau, Diderot was deeply concerned with the problem of order in society. He, too, would have liked a harmonious society in which men are virtuous, altruistic, public-spirited. And like Rousseau again— though he expressed himself quite differently and in closet writings only—he described the jungle society and the rewards of clever unsocial behavior.

However, several factors made it impossible for him even to entertain the type of solution embodied in Rousseau's ideal society. In entirely different ways, both men were committed, at least as an ideal, to progress, to a better state of things. Diderot was committed to progress in its manifold forms envisioned by the Enlightenment. On the other hand, he thought progress to be bounded in its possibilities and felt a great aversion to all utopian plans such as Rousseau's. His later political writings are marked by a striking pessimistic tinge about the possibility of the good or just society. Third, his idea of nature was different from Rousseau's. It was less abstruse, but rather confused and not well thought out. This is obvious in his ill-conceived if brilliantly executed *Supplément au Voyage de Bougainville*. The Old Man of Tahiti declares, "nous sommes innocents. . . nous suivons le pur instinct de la nature" (OP, p. 466). And Diderot thinks, or writes as if he thinks, that nature and society could be reconciled, if only society's laws did not contradict those of nature: "la loi civile ne doit être que l'énonciation de la loi de nature" (OP, p. 505). He will repeat the idea in his political writings. Rousseau, on the other hand, knew that there was no innocence once man left his hypothetical state of nature and entered into the social, therefore moral state. In his major works he makes it clear and explicit that our original nature, in the social state, is the enemy. But Diderot's idea of nature is not even that simple. Not only would he have society's laws confirm nature's, he will have it both ways, and have nature's laws confirm those of society! As Orou puts it, "Sa volonté éternelle est que le bien soit préféré au mal, et le bien général au bien particulier" (OP, p. 482). Again, Rousseau said that the contrary was true.

The three considerations I have just mentioned may be considered as either tangential or as background to the major conclusions expressed in Diderot's writings for Catherine.[19] It is in these that he seriously confronts the basic problem he shared with Rousseau. Where is the highest value? In the individual, which society must serve, or in the community, which the individual must serve so that it can best serve him? The philosophical decision must be made, even if in real life it never works out in pure and clean terms. Diderot never doubted that the first alternative was his, even as Rousseau never doubted that the second alone was valid. From among many statements of Diderot I select only one:

> ... toute philosophie contraire à la nature de l'homme est absurde, ainsi que toute législation où le citoyen est forcé continuellement de sacrifier son goût et son bonheur pour le bien de la société. Je veux que la société soit heureuse; mais je veux l'être aussi; et il y a autant de manières d'être heureux qu'il y a d'individus. Notre propre bonheur est la base de tous nos vrais devoirs.[20]

This view is antithetical to Rousseau's. That Rousseau places the locus and primacy of value in the community rather than the individual follows from his consistent organic concept of the political. It may be argued that—as I have just stated—the community is for him an instrumental value; however, it is so essential, in his scheme, so all-pervasive, that it becomes, or cannot be differentiated from an inherent value or finality. It would be difficult to explain otherwise a statement such as the following: "Pour empêcher la pitié de dégénérer en faiblesse, il faut donc la généraliser et l'étendre sur tout le genre humain. Alors on ne s'y livre qu'autant qu'elle est d'accord avec la justice... Il faut par raison, par amour pour nous, avoir pitié de notre espèce encore plus que de notre prochain..." (*Emile*, 303). It follows, too, that whereas Diderot stresses "droits inaliénables" and individual liberties (*Observations*, pp. 354-55), Rousseau insists that rights be totally alienated at the outset and rejects what we would call the liberal conception of individual or civil liberties. The basic difference is right here. Diderot is against all who think it necessary to enclose citizens in a prefabricated system in order to ensure their happiness. Rousseau thinks that there is no other way to make them happy. Both respect the dignity of man as man; but for Diderot that dignity inheres in each individual as individual, as inviolable sanctity, else it has no meaning.

Despite occasional anarchic speculations or temptations, Diderot was no anarchist or revolutionary, but a bourgeois and to an extent a part of the Establishment. He earnestly wanted men to be good citizens and to obey the laws, which ought to be good laws, in a representative form of government. Here again he was perplexed by the problem of disobedience to unjust laws, for contrary to Rousseau, he did not believe that law as the expression of the general will necessarily defines justice. The general interest is indeed the rule of right and wrong, but laws are imperfect and the situation is always changing in the dynamics of a social system.

Diderot, too, held that order is an essential value. Again the difference is clear: he did not believe that social order can be perfect or perpetual, or that it is worth buying at any price, certainly not if the price is regimentation. Such an order is a false order, for it suppresses or eliminates one half of man's being, the "natural" half, in favor of the other, "the social." He would rather accept the imperfect state of tension and war, in which the evildoer can often profit at the expense of others (*Observations*, p. 352). Within such a state, great improvements can still be made over the unacceptable status quo, and men can become better citizens. In fact, order for Diderot is less a state than a process, or a stage in a process, one which has no ideal or final terminus. At best we can speak of a multiplicity of orders, among which some are more disorderly than others. No law or constitution, he says, is good everywhere or for all time (*Observations*, p. 353). Society, which came about naturally to satisfy needs and to combat the disorders arising from biological drives, has created its own forces of disorder, which both Rousseau and Diderot recognized as the product of psychological drives. There is, then, no ideal or final form of political organization and Diderot's preference is for one that holds options and uncertainties, one that maximizes individual freedom and opportunities while minimizing the abuses of power. Imperfection is man's fate, and Diderot might have applied Pascal's aphorism, "qui veut faire l'ange, fait la bête."

Diderot's educational ideas are in perfect accord with his political preferences. Rousseau had argued that because social roles must be fixed, the individual talents of the man with the hoe must remain undeveloped, like gold mines which if exploited would produce an excess disruptive of the social body's organic harmony. Diderot declares that the individual talents of each child are the very point of education. "Ce n'est point du tout de faire du premier enfant communément bien organisé ce qu'il plaît à ses parents d'en faire, mais de l'appliquer constamment à la chose à laquelle il est propre."[21] And he gives examples. In the university, too, each is to choose the course that suits his tastes and talents.[22] In the *Plan d'une université* (1776), he puts it this way: the university must be open to all, "parce qu'il serait aussi cruel qu'absurde de condamner à l'ignorance les conditions subalternes de la société."[23] Teaching must not concentrate on the élite of best students.[24]

In educating children the purpose is first of all to develop character, justice and "fermeté."25 Second, it is to develop a mind that reasons clearly and correctly ("la justesse de l'esprit"). "Il faut plus de raison, plus de lumières et de force qu'on ne le suppose communément pour être vraiment homme de bien" (*Plan*, III, 433). All the arts must be cultivated, to accomplish a third objective, to form a man of broad culture and good taste. Fourth, the social graces are requisite for "l'art de plaire." Fifth, since one cannot learn everything, preference should be given to those studies that will be useful in the social rank or role that the child is likely to occupy. Sixth, physical culture and good health are basic to all else. In sum, education's purpose is this: "leur dérober sans cesse leurs lisières, afin de conserver en eux le sentiment de la dignité, de la franchise, de la liberté, et de les accoutumer à ne reconnaître de despotisme que celui de la vertu et de la vérité.... Je ne sais ce que c'est que l'éducation libérale...." The parent will say: "Je l'éleverai donc pour l'instant de son existence et de la mienne. Je préférerai donc mon bonheur et le sien à celui de la nation."

Despite this emphasis, education has a political function. "Instruire une nation, c'est la civiliser.... L'ignorance est le partage de l'esclave et du sauvage. L'instruction donne à l'homme de la dignité." Such are the liminary words of the *Plan d'une université*. Education is the source of the ideas of honor and fame, of civilized living and discourse. In an apparently direct challenge to Rousseau, he adds "J'oserais assurer que la pureté de la morale a suivi les progrès des vêtements depuis la peau de la bête jusqu'à l'étoffe de soie" (*Plan*, III, 430). We are very far from the *Supplément au Voyage de Bougainville*! Quite consistently, then, Diderot's plan of university studies is remarkable for the breadth of culture that he tries to combine with professional specialization. He stresses the value of Greek and Latin, of the arts, philosophy, and the sciences.

To be sure, there are certain superficial similarities with Rousseau's plans. Diderot advises a catechism of morals and politics, containing the duties of citizens, for all children.26 He emphasizes "connaissances utiles," the study of things, and the mechanical arts (*Plan*, III, 421). Utility is a basic consideration: "L'objet d'une école publique n'est point de faire un homme profond en quelque genre que ce soit, mais de l'initier à un grand nombre de connaissances dont l'ignorance lui serait nuisible dans tous les états de la vie" (*Plan*, III, 444-45). Depth will come at the higher level of studies. Like Rousseau, Diderot would have public offices filled by public competitions; but whereas for Rousseau a prime purpose is the inculcation of public spirit, stimulated by the reward of public approbation, Diderot, recognizing the importance of public recognition, emphasizes two other aims: the stimulus to study and the remedy to inequalities of birth and fortune.27 He, too, would build an élite, but by a process of open opportunities for all classes, with money and birth as no bar. Natural inequality should function freely in this regard at least.

The differences, as we have seen, are deeper. Whereas Rousseau relies on a crude advocacy of dissimulation ("la main cachée"), Diderot declares that "pour le grand nombre, l'exacte vérité, qui est presque toujours sans fâcheuse conséquence, est à préférer à la dissimulation" (*Plan*, III, 432). And while Rousseau emphasizes what can be done to mould behavior to a desired social end, Diderot, it is well known, takes issue with Helvétius on just this point. This idea is generalized in the *Supplément au Voyage de Bougainville*: "L'empire de la nature ne peut être détruit: on aura beau le contrarier par des obstacles, il durera" (OP, p. 510). These words are a denial of Rousseau's whole project of turning man into a social being, into what he called "the citizen," who thinks of himself only as part of a whole. "Il faut dénaturer l'homme," Rousseau had cried. And Diderot replies: "Mais ce coeur indocile ne cessera de réclamer. . . vous deviendrez féroces, et vous ne réussirez point à me dénaturer."

Clearly, Diderot's insistence on national free education as a political instrument is entirely different from Rousseau's. Its purpose, never perfectly realized, is emancipation, not, to quote Rousseau's terms, "submission to the yoke" and "docility;" it is the reflective, not the reflexive. Both men shared the century's scorn for the intellectual and political capacities of the common people. Both were ambivalent about them. Rousseau saw them as the seat of moral goodness, but politically they were children requiring constant guidance. Diderot, in his last work, *Claude et Néron*, wrote, "l'homme peuple est le plus sot et le plus méchant des hommes" (*Oeuvres*, III, 263). Yet in his writings for Catherine, in the insertions into Raynal's *Histoire des Deux Indes*, and in the *Apologie de l'abbé Raynal*, he seems to pose as the tribune of the people. Both men thought the common people to be within natural limits educable; but the character and purpose of that education were antithetical. For Rousseau, education for the masses was not "enlightenment," but conditioning, and this kind of "education" he held to be attainable with almost all men. For Diderot, education was, precisely, enlightenment.

Both wanted men to be happy. Diderot realized that happiness has certain common human dimensions, but thought that as an individual experience, its character depended on individual character. The government could do no more than provide external conditions; education could do no more than develop the best and minimize the worst of innate dispositions. Happiness is individual self-realization, within acceptable limits. Rousseau thought of the individual as primarily part of a community. The condition of happiness is not the race for individual self-realization, but integration into a just social order, such integration being the requisite condition of order. He thought happiness attainable in his "true" society, with men remade into his definition of citizens, led and directed like the eternally irresponsible children they are. "Vous promettez d'être docile, et moi je promets de n'user de cette docilité que pour vous rendre le plus heureux des hommes" (*Emile*, p. 406). That is why he wrote, "le pauvre n'a pas besoin d'éducation" (*Emile*, p. 27) — in Diderot's sense of that word. In his sense, it was conditioning and indoctrination; in Diderot's sense, it was expansion and fulfillment.

Both men wanted a just society. Rousseau confronted and "solved" the problem of a just society. Diderot considered such absolutes as hopelessly beyond men's reach. He never wrote, "Donnez-le tout à l'Etat, ou laissez-le tout entier à lui-même," because despite his occasional anarchistic or primitivistic longings, he knew that the split between "natural" man and social man is irresolvable and that our lot is an eternal struggle between order and disorder. The ambiguity of man's nature cannot be suppressed without dehumanizing him.

With Diderot's return from Russia, writes Furio Diaz, "l'illuminismo francese raggiunge forse la sua punta piu avanzata e coerente, sul piano di un programma liberale di governo."[28] In Holland, Diderot wrote at the time, "chacun est maître chez soi; la liberté civile y met tous les habitants au niveau; les petits ne peuvent être opprimés par les grands, ni les pauvres par les riches. . .la liberté de penser, de parler et d'écrire est presque illimitée" (*Oeuvres*, XVII, 406). Rousseau was equally ferocious in his hatred of oppression, but the remedy was precisely not to have that freedom, but to substitute for personal power, always selfish and exploitative, the omniscient, omnipotent impersonal power of the so-called general will, which enabled each to obey only himself, insofar as that self was transposed into the general will — and *that* was the purpose of education. But his writings show his basic realism: he knew that power is always exercised by men, by an élite of leaders. That is why he said that to make a government in which laws and not people are superior is to find the square of the circle.[29] How impressive is his constant awareness that even his reprocessed men could never be trusted not to backslide. He never believed that the people could be trusted with real political power, but he taught the world how to utilize the show of direct democracy. Diderot, on the other hand, would surely have taken as his the words of Thomas Jefferson, "I know of no safe depository of the ultimate powers of the society but the people themselves, and if we think them not enlightened enough to exercise their control with a wholesome discretion, the remedy is not to take it from them but to inform their discretion by education." Rousseau also wants his "guides," in the *Contrat social*, to "inform" the assembled citizenry. But the difference between to "inform" as indoctrination and to "inform" as enlightenment is epitomized right here.[30]

Western liberal societies have followed Diderot's path, and Marxist societies, in varying degrees, that of Rousseau. I am not referring to influences, but to archetypal models. This has long been my contention, and I have based it on political theory. What I now suggest is that if my contention is correct, then the educational philosophies and practices of those types of society should basically correspond to the educational models of Diderot or Rousseau, respectively. If you consider educational theory and practice in both types of state, a subject I cannot undertake here, I am sure you will find that they do.

---

[1] *Confessions, Oeuvres*, Pléiade, I, 404 ("j'avais vu que tout tenait radicalement à la politique"); *Emile*, R. Richard, Garnier, p. 179. Further references to the Pléiade edition will be indicated in the text by *Oeuvres*, volume and page number. Further references to Richard's edition of Emile will be indicated in the text by *Emile* and page number.

[2] He did protest later, in the *Essai sur les règnes de Claude et de Néron*: "une societé d'hommes n'est pas un troupeau de bêtes; les traiter de la même manière, c'est insulter à l'espèce humaine" (*Oeuvres*, Assézat-Tourneux, III, 264).

[3] Diderot, *Oeuvres philosophiques*, ed. P. Vernière, Paris, Garnier, n.d., pp. 510-511. Further references to this edition in the text will be indicated by OP.

[4] *The Political Writings of Jean-Jacques Rousseau*, ed. C. E. Vaughan, Cambridge, 1915, I, 326. Further references to this work will be inserted in the text.

[5] Rousseau to Mirabeau, le 26 juillet 1767.

[6] *Discours sur les sciences et les arts*, ed. G. R. Havens, New York, 1946, p. 106.

[7] Both *La Nouvelle Héloïse* and *Emile* make this explicit: "assigner à chacun sa place et l'y fixer," he urges in *Emile*, p. 63.

[8] See my forthcoming article, "Order and Disorder in Rousseau's Social Thought," *PMLA*, March 1979.

[9] "L'autorité la plus absolue est celle qui pénètre jusqu'à l'intérieur de l'homme, et ne s'exerce pas moins sur la volonté que sur les actions... Formez donc des hommes, si vous voulez commander à des hommes; si vous voulez qu'on obéisse aux lois, faites qu'on les aime, et que, pour faire ce qu'on doit, il suffise de songer qu'on le doit faire." (Vaughan, I, 248.)

[10] Vaughan, I, 454 (*Première Version du Contrat Social*).

[11] In the *Projet de constitution pour la Corse*, the most "Maoist" or "Cambodian" of Rousseau's writings, the arts are not tolerated.

[12] *Emile*, pp. 10, 593; also pp. 239-40, 306, 514; "Economie politique," pp. 240-41.

[13] *Emile*, p. 249; also, pp. 256-57, 406.

[14] *Emile*, p. 43, 87 and throughout.

[15] "Jusqu'ici vous n'en obteniez rien que par force ou par ruse... il fallait le contraindre ou le tromper... Je lui laisse, il est vrai, l'apparence de l'indépendance, mais jamais il ne me fut mieux assujetti, car il l'est parce qu'il veut l'être. Tant que je n'ai pu me rendre maître de sa volonté, je le suis demeuré de sa personne.... Sans doute il ne doit faire que ce qu'il veut; mais il ne doit vouloir que ce que vous voulez qu'il fasse" (*Emile*, pp. 392, 414, 121; also, p. 110). This process must start from infancy "Sitôt qu'il naît, emparez-vous de lui, et ne le quittez plus qu'il ne soit homme" (Ibid., pp. 22, 41).

[16] For spying in *Emile*, see pp. 217, 219.

[17] "En un mot, les abus sont inévitables et leurs suites funestes, dans toute société où l'intérêt public et les lois n'ont aucune force naturelle et sont sans cesse attaqués par l'intérêt personnel et les passions du chef et des membres" (Vaughan, 1, 239).

[18] Vaughan, II, 429; *Emile*, p. 481.

[19]*Entretiens avec Catherine II, Observations sur le Nakaz*, in *Oeuvres politiques*, ed. P. Vernière, Paris, 1963.
[20]*Observations*, ibid., p. 404.
[21]*Réfutation d'Helvétius, Oeuvres*, A.-T., II, 3 74-75.
[22]*Essai sur les études en Russie*, ibid., III, 422-23.
[23]*Plan d'une université*, ibid., III, 433. Subsequently referred to as *Plan*.
[24]*Réfutation*, ibid., II, 451.
[25]*Lettre à Madame la Comtesse de Forbach*, ibid., III, 540-44 (c. 1772).
[26]*Essai sur les études en Russie, Plan.*, III, 418.
[27]*Réfutation*, ibid., ll, 417-18. J. M. Dolle's thesis, *Politique et pédagogie: Diderot et les problèmes de l'éducation* (Paris Vrin, 1973), useful in many ways, is insufficiently analytical and contains a number of unacceptable statements, e. g. "Ainsi se fonde l' éducation naturelle comme essence même de l'*organisation* politique" (p. 65, italics mine); all acts of individuals should be open to public view (p. 86), a statement that would be accurate for Rousseau but anathema to Diderot. More important, Dolle simply ignores the whole humanistic aspect and intent of Diderot's ideas on education.
[28]Furio Diaz, *Filosofia e politica nel Settecento francese*, (Torino, 1962), p. 563.
[29]*Considérations*, Vaughan, II, 426.
[30]Diderot would have also endorsed Jefferson's argument for public education: "By that part of our plan which prescribes the selection of youths of genius from among the classes of the poor, we hope to avail the State of those talents which Nature has sown as liberally among the poor as among the rich, but which perish without use" (Quoted in H. S. Commager, *The Empire of Reason*, Garden City, N. Y., 1977, p. 125). Again, the antithesis with Rousseau is obvious.

Differing Modes of Myth Expression among the French Romantics: Hugo, Chateaubriand, and Gautier

Richard B. Grant
University of Texas at Austin

When one has the pleasure of discussing myth in the works of Hugo, Chateaubriand, and Gautier, it is tempting to plunge directly into the texts. But when dealing with mythic literature, prudence is advisable. The very term "myth" is a slippery one, one used today in different ways and with different meanings. To pause first to establish a working definition suitable for the literary critic is not an exercise in pedantry, but a wise precaution.

Our first task, to distinguish between myth and mythology, is simple enough. Mythology consists of a body of individual myths, but when we move on to the nature and function of these separate myths, the matter becomes enormously complicated. What, for instance, do we do with so-called "modern myths," which appear in phrases like "the myth of the state" or "the myth of the family"? The present popularity of this usage in all likelihood stems from the philosophy of Jean-Paul Sartre. Sartre, we recall, used the term "myth" to apply to any principle that we invoke in an attempt to organize our lives and give them meaning and coherence, and for Sartre, of course, all these myths are equally inauthentic, merely efforts to keep us from understanding that existence is as absurd as the universe. French literary critics in particular have often adopted this meaning of the word and have created titles like "le mythe de la société chez Balzac" or "le mythe de la femme chez Lamartine" to imply that society or woman is so central to these writers that it forms an organizing principle for their work. But it is not my purpose today to deal with myths of this kind. Rather, I am interested in the continuing vitality of the older tradition.

For the Greeks, the word *mythos* was simply a traditional story, and as many of their old traditional stories were about their gods, Greek mythology became thought of as being stories about the Olympians. In practice, of course, the Greeks were more eclectic in their choices. In the Oedipus and Perseus tales, for instance, we find human beings, not divinities, at the center of the narratives. But ultimately the term dropped any sense of nuance—at least in reference to the Greek tradition—and came to apply generally to stories about the extinct gods of Greece. Hence the idea in popular language that myth is something false.

Even when a more scholarly approach to the subject began to develop in the nineteenth century, this idea that myth consists of stories about dead religions and their gods was still central to an understanding of the field. Georg Creuzer's *Symbolik und Mythologie der Alten Volker* (1810-1823) is a classic example of such thinking. The twentieth century, however, has gone beyond this limited understanding and has totally revolutionized the subject. But if modern scholars have widened our understanding of the origins, nature, and function of myths in culture, they have also caused problems. By arriving at widely divergent conclusions, they have left non-specialists in a state of considerable confusion. For example, there is one group of scholars who take the religious content of myth seriously. Bronislaw Malinowski believed that in primitive cultures myths were not merely old tales intended for the entertainment of the tribe, but rather dynamic statements of a primeval reality, of happenings and events that took place before the dawn of history, and which legitimize and justify sacred ritual.[1] His follower Mircea Eliade insists even more strongly on the centrality of the sacred, seeing a divine dimension in the myths of all primitive societies, whatever may be their cultural divergences.[2] A larger group of scholars, on the other hand, is more secular in attitude, considering myths to be expressions of natural or cultural phenomena, and nothing more. But these secularists or positivists cannot agree among themselves. We can hardly go into this complex matter in detail here, but an example or two will prove the point. At the turn of the century Sir James Frazer in *The Golden Bough* explained dying and resurrecting gods as metaphors for the annual death and rebirth cycle of vegetation. More recently, we find Claude Lévi-Strauss, who has little or no interest in ritual for itself, seeing myths only as attempts to "mediate" the contradictions latent in any culture. There is also a third group, more eclectic than the previous two. G.S. Kirk, for instance, views with suspicion attempts to reduce myths to any one pattern, claiming that they have many origins and many functions, and he adds that the word myth cannot in fact be carefully defined.[3] Even Eliade, who enjoys simplification, has had to admit that "myth is an extremely complex cultural reality."[4]

Faced with the uncertainties of definition and realizing that specialists disagree among themselves, literary critics, normally not trained in the study of primitive cultures, tend to hesitate. They should not despair, however. The literary critic must realize that he is not an anthropologist and that he does not necessarily have to become one. As a literary critic he has his own field and needs his own tools, that is, he must derive his definition from his own field and not from that of the anthropologists. To explain this point, an analogy will serve. In modern science, the discoveries of Copernicus, Newton, and Einstein have relegated to the dustbin the Ptolemaic three-tiered universe of Heaven, Earth, and Underworld; yet in literature we find the old concept still dynamic and a purveyor of truth. To take but one example, in Camus' *La Chute* the canals of Amsterdam are used in a Dantean sense of the circles of Hell. The cosmology is scientifically outmoded, but the images are alive and well, and if the literary critic is to penetrate into the text, he must not discard Ptolemaic cosmology. Similarly, whatever conclusions may be reached by the squabbling anthropologists, the literary critic should not be unduly concerned. He needs to derive his understanding of the word myth from the field of literature itself, the fictions of early cultures. Hence, for him the old idea that myth consists of stories about gods still makes sense: it is not only a useful, it is a vital concept. Indeed, Northrop Frye has based much of his *Anatomy of Criticism* on this assumption.[5]

If we can accept this definition of myth for our purposes as critics, we find that in France myth has operated primarily out of Celtic lore, Greco-Roman mythology, and the Biblical and Christian traditions. Whereas Celtic myths lost much of their vigor after the Middle Ages, the Biblical and Christian tradition has remained a more vital presence in French, and indeed in all European literature. As for Greco-Roman mythology, by the time Western Europe emerged from the ruins of the Roman Empire, no one believed literally that Jupiter was lord of the universe. So each age, each generation chose to adapt the Greek, and indeed other myths, to the needs of their own day. For instance, Apollo appears in *La Chanson de Roland* startlingly linked with Mahomet and Tervagant as one-third of an evil Sarracen Trinity. In the Renaissance, D'Aubigné selected Apocalyptic visions borrowed from the Bible and adapted them to the Religious Wars. Even the seventeenth century, which later Romantics thought had merely continued the banalities of Greek mythology, reworked the old tradition. Frequently in French Classical literature, the Greek gods were a serious expression of that century's belief in Providence, and we know that Louis XIV and many of his court felt that he was in some measure divine. Apollo was not merely a literary metaphor at Versailles. By the end of the eighteenth century, however, there was once again the feeling that the tradition had become sterile. André Chénier expressed his dissatisfaction with the old mythology when he wrote: "Il faut que j'invente entièrement une sorte de mythologie *probable* et poétique avec laquelle je puisse remplacer les tableaux gracieux des anciens."[6] Like Chénier, the Romantics felt the need to renew literary forms. As a result, they reduced their dependence on Greek mythology, which they associated with worn-out Classicism. But a considerable amount of direct mythic literature is nonetheless to be found in the first half of the century. It is true that some of it was sterile. Such figures as Simon Ballanche and Edgar Quinet wrote vast epico-mythic tales that are of interest to anyone studying the impact of the French Revolution on the doctrine of progress, but I do not intend to discuss these in this study. Herbert J. Hunt long ago studied them in his

The Epic in Nineteenth-Century France.[7] From a literary point of view, they were something of a dead end. They continued an essentially neoclassical esthetic in which an abstract or generalized idea was the point of departure, and the episodes of the narrative were illustrative of a priori ideas. In the works of Ballanche and others, the fictional characters failed to come alive because their authors could not resist turning them into allegorical abstractions. These figures suffered the same fate as in the field of painting, where we find innumerable mythological canvases painted for the official academies by candidates for the Prix de Rome.

But the major Romantic writers suffered from no such sterility. No doubt this fact was due in considerable measure to their genius as writers, but their success can also be attributed to their temperament. They tended to feel that they were lonely and superior, even god-like beings who stood above the average man: sometimes it was a matter of social class, as with Chateaubriand and Vigny; sometimes it was an awareness of heightened sensibility, as with Lamartine and Musset; sometimes a feeling of power, vision, and leadership, as in the case of Hugo. But diverse in nature as they were, they all at times used myth to communicate their visions. Yet, if they all used it, they all used it differently. For this presentation I have chosen texts by Hugo, Chateaubriand, and Gautier, texts designed to show the very different ways in which myth could be treated, even by authors whom we think of belonging to the same literary "school"—Romanticism.

If I have chosen to violate chronology and begin with Victor Hugo, it is because he was—despite his claim of having wrought a revolution in French letters—a poet very conscious of literary tradition, and was at home with some of the techniques of neoclassical French art. Hugo had no hesitation in using the traditional ode in the 1820s and he never abandoned the standard alexandrine. Like seventeenth-century writers, he tended to assume that tragedy should be written in verse. It is not surprising that he would find older literary forms, such as traditional myth, congenial to his vision. But there was nothing sterile about his use of it; in fact, so brilliant and powerful was his manipulation of myth, that he infused it with new life. The following passage is taken from the opening section of *La Fin de Satan*. The scene is Lucifer's fall from Heaven.

> L'abîme s'effaçait. Rien n'avait plus de forme.
> L'obscurité semblait gonfler sa vague énorme.
> C'était on ne sait quoi de submergé; c'était
> Ce qui n'est plus, ce qui s'en va, ce qui se tait;
> Et l'on n'aurait pu dire, en cette horreur profonde,
> Si ce reste effrayant d'un mystère ou d'un monde,
> Pareil au brouillard vague où le songe s'enfuit,
> S'appelait le naufrage ou s'appelait la nuit;
> Et l'archange sentit qu'il devenait fantôme.
> Il dit:—Enfer!—Ce mot plus tard créa Sodome.

> Et la voix répéta lentement sur son front:
> —Maudit! autour de toi les astres s'éteindront.—
>
> Et déjà le soleil n'était plus qu'une étoile.

In this direct recreation of the old myth, Hugo does not mention Lucifer's pride, but otherwise he accepts the tradition that the archangel is a rebel against God and that he has been expelled from Heaven. The landscape through which he falls is real within the context of the myth, the beginning of his spatial Hell.

Obviously, there is more to this episode than mere narrative. Because God is by definition the unquestioned seat of legitimate authority, Lucifer must feel guilty. Because God is also by definition not only the creator but the One who orders and gives form to the cosmos, the exile, who finds himself outside this divine order, is by the very nature of things engulfed by chaos. On the psychological level, this chaos is itself a metaphor for the total loss of orientation that comes with the crumbling of one's values and sense of belonging. Ultimately, Lucifer will lose his old identity and become another under the impact of banishment. In this passage the beginning of the loss of identity is made explicit: —"Et l'archange sentit qu'il devenait fantôme."

Against this threat of obliteration of the self, the individual reacts strongly, trying to reaffirm his being in all its concreteness. In this way a tension is set up between dissolution of forms into nothingness on the one hand and a desperate attempt to create concrete reality on the other. The passage works out this dialectic in intricate detail. It opens with a statement of total chaos: "L'abîme s'effaçait. Rien n'avait plus de forme." Here the poet has taken a place by definition without form or outline (the void) and then has dared to compound the horror by adding that this abyss becomes blurred and fades away. But having initially insisted on total dissolution of familiar reality, the poet then begins to restore the equilibrium. Line three juxtaposes the affirmative *c'était* to the vague, formless *on ne sait quoi*, and in the next line the repetition of *ce qui* proclaims that something *is* even at the very moment when, in the very same clauses, *n'est plus, s'en va, se tait*, suggest the disappearance of anything tangible. But the imagery of formlessness dominates through the use of words like *vague, brouillard, songe, nuit, fantôme*, and others. So Lucifer, desperate, must react radically against the threat to his being. He screams "Enfer," and from this word, this *logos*, Sodom, a precise, contoured place on earth is literally brought into being. Sodom is an evil place, of course, but to the human psyche affirmation of being is so vital that anything is preferable to annihilation. But God, too, creates from the word. He announced that the stars will go out, and Lucifer's last sun—his last link with his previous, ordered existence—shrinks to a distant star. Against God, the guilty one cannot win; he must become

Satan and spend his time in Hell before there can even be a possibility of redemption. Hugo has used direct myth very successfully to communicate the psychology of the outcast.

Up to this point we have dealt with the text independently of its author, but one detail compels us to realize that there is a personal, biographical element at work here that gives the poetry an extra dimension and makes us realize that Lucifer-Satan has much in common with Victor Hugo himself. On the most superficial level, we might suspect this parallel because when Hugo wrote this passage he was an exile from France just as Lucifer is from Heaven, but the rapprochement goes deeper than that. The idea of creating something real from a word is a common motif of creation myths, but it is also an example of the task of the poet, who creates his poetic world from the raw material of language. In a poem from *Les Contemplations*, entitled "Suite," Hugo sees the word, the *logos*, as alive. "Car le verbe, qu'on le sache, est un être vivant," he writes, and since the word is alive, it can procreate. But the greatest of all poets is not Victor Hugo, but God himself. That same poem, "Suite," closes with the ringing proclamation: "Car le mot, c'est le Verbe, et le Verbe, c'est Dieu." The poet tries to create order out of the chaos of words by relying on syntax and the subtle interaction of separate words and by channeling his vision within the structuring walls of the regular alexandrine,[8] but compared to God, the poet always falls short as creator. Nowhere is this sense of inferiority to the divine more aptly expressed than at the end of Hugo's own monumental creation, *La Légende des siècles*. God surveys Hugo's immense seven-hundred page universe and says very simply in the last line: "Je n'aurais qu'à souffler, et tout serait de l'ombre." God has the last word in the creation and dissolution of forms.

Once we have recognized the identification of Hugo with Satan (one that has of course been recognized by critics for some time), we are in a position to explain the most fundamental pattern of the passage. If Hugo is Satan, then Hugo must feel guilt, and we know that he did. Some of his guilt was due to his early rejection of his father after his parents' divorce, but the main guilt was sexual. Hugo felt that his conquest of Adèle Foucher was responsible for driving his jealous brother, Eugène, to madness and early death, and in later years Hugo's erotic obsessions were deeply disturbing to him. Now Hugo associated woman's sexuality with non-contour or formlessness, for the obvious reason that a woman's sex adapts to the man's presence. He also saw woman in terms of the sea. Water has always been considered a feminine element, and as an image of liquid non-contour a very appropriate one. Hugo was very much afraid of women. As he put it once: "Quand la femme se fait, l'ange s'en va."[9] The most spectacular example in Hugo's work of this fear of feminine sexuality associated with water and viscous forms is to be found in *Les Travailleurs de la mer* in the episode in which the octopus seizes Gilliatt in an underwater grotto. The octopus is formless and absorbing like woman's sexuality, and Gilliatt's phallic knife is his only defense, but it is a defense that is also an encounter.

If we now revert to our passage, we note immediately the threat of the engulfing wave as well as marine images like *submergé* and *naufragé*, but behind these words there is the more fundamental structure of the fall of the male into the formless void, and the horror that he experiences. Obviously, there is no direct sexual content to this passage; the images have been displaced from sexuality to theology, but there can be little doubt as to their origin.

To conclude: This passage shows Hugo taking an old myth and using it directly with remarkable profundity. It has meaning in itself, of course, but the poet enriched it with his personal concerns. We find his preoccupation with the limits of his poetic creativity and his anguish over his sexual guilt. These private obsessions are not merely added on in mechanical fashion. They are worked into the deepest levels of the literary structure. Hugo's achievement was a remarkable one and proves the flexibility of the ancient mythic forms. There is no reason to assume, in fact, that direct myth will ever become outmoded, because although in one sense the gods may seem obsolete, we find that these gods always lead us to an understanding of man.

Not every author succeeded as brilliantly as Hugo. If Vigny's Jesus in "Le Mont des oliviers" stresses the human almost exclusively, there is good reason for it in a poem that repudiates divinity; but even in *Eloa* where the mythic content is "real," Eloa and Satan seem to the reader only young human beings play-acting at being angel and demon. If direct mythic expression was not easy in verse, in prose the problem was even more acute. Prose was falling increasingly under the domination of a realistic esthetic, with the result that direct mythic expression in fiction seemed less and less appropriate. In realistic prose one cannot have Venus or Apollo walking around the streets of a modern French town. If myth was to continue as a major presence in prose fiction, it had to go underground, so to speak, to be disguised or displaced into imagery. This development was made possible by a basic shift that was taking place in Western European esthetics. Neo-Classicism, in theory at least, began with a universal concept and then proceeded to the particular example which illustrated that concept. To use the language of scholasticism: *universalia ante rem*. The nineteenth century increasingly began with the centrality of a particular object, which was then expanded into a universal through symbolism: *res ante universalia*. In this new esthetic system, the object is real, but the author can, if he chooses, infuse myth into it through metaphor.

Chateaubriand's *René* may not be real realistic fiction by some standards, yet it is set in what claims to be the real world. Hence the mythic dimension must be disguised. From his work I have chosen two passages. The first of these is well known to every student of the field. René, vainly seeking permanence and beauty in life, finds himself in Sicily:

> Un jour, j'étais monté au sommet de l'Etna, volcan qui brûle au milieu d'une île. Je vis le soleil se lever dans l'immensité de l'horizon au-dessous de moi, la Sicile resserrée comme un point à mes pieds, et la mer déroulée au loin dans les espaces. Dans cette vue perpendiculaire du tableau, les fleuves ne me semblaient plus que des lignes géographiques tracées sur une carte; mais, tandis que d'un côté mon oeil apercevait ces objets, de l'autre il plongeait dans le cratère de l'Etna, dont je découvrais les entrailles brûlantes entre les bouffées d'une noire vapeur.

As if we could not guess, Chateaubriand is quick to add: "Quoi que vous puissiez penser de René, ce tableau vous offre l'image de son caractère et de son existence." The details are first real, then symbolic, by the author's own admission. Obvious, of course, is the inner fire of the volcano as an exteriorization of the hero's inner turmoil. The fact that the fire is subterranean and gives off black smoke permits us to glimpse through the imagery the fires of Hell. René's being on a mountain-top adds another dimension to the scene. He can feel demonically superior to the masses below. One thinks of the devil lifting Jesus onto a mountain-top in Luke IV: 5-7, in order to tempt him with earthly riches and power.

Set in opposition to René is his sister Amélie. Her task in the story is to overcome her incestuous desires for her brother and to find salvation. She writes to René from the convent where she has finally found peace:

> Quand j'entends gronder les orages et que l'oiseau de mer vient battre des ailes ma fenêtre, moi, pauvre colombe du ciel, je songe au bonheur que j'ai eu de trouver un abri contre la tempête. C'est ici la sainte montagne, le sommet élevé d'où l'on entend les derniers bruits de la terre et les premiers concerts du ciel; c'est ici que la religion trompe doucement une âme sensible: aux plus violentes amours elle substitue une sorte de chasteté brûlante où l'amante et la vierge sont unies; elle épure les soupirs, elle change en une flamme incorruptible une flamme périssable, elle mêle divinement son calme et son innocence à ce reste de trouble et de volupté d'un coeur qui cherche à se reposer et d'une vie qui se retire.

This passage contains more than one example of generally mythic language. Immediately obvious are such phrases as the *sainte montagne* and the *concerts du ciel*. But the most interesting use of myth in this passage lies in the image of the dove, interesting because of the manner in which direct myth has been disguised or displaced. By 1802, the date of *René*, the term dove probably meant in normal usage any innocent and frail creature, but if we trace the image back through history we find more. For the Christian Church, of course, the dove had long been a symbol of the Holy Spirit. If we go back to the Old Testament, we find the dove that Noah sent from the ark to see whether the floods had receded. When it came back bearing the olive branch, both plant and bird became associated with peace, and later by extension to the Holy Spirit which brings God's peace to mankind. On the symbolic level, Amélie, too, has ultimately found peace. All this is clear enough, but there is more. The passage stresses purification and transformation, and in the Old Testament (Lev. XII: 6-7; XVI: 25) we find the Jewish ritual that doves are to be offered in purification rites after any sexual defilement. Again this fits Amélie. Finally, we may note that the dove image antedates the Bible. In the fertility cults of the Eastern Mediterranean region the dove was sacred to Venus (or Aphrodite, or Astarte, or Ishtar) because the bird was reputed to be especially erotic. Slowly, through history, the dove has become transformed from a sexual symbol into one of purity and peace. Like Amélie. So the imagery tells us that René is a lonely, self-centered and tormented Satan in Hell, while his sister, beginning as an unwilling servant of the goddess of lust, a dove of Venus, is transformed into a Christian angel. Where direct mythic literature centered on the god and moved to the human by extension, in displaced myth this process is reversed: one starts with the human being and then moves to the divine or archetypal level.

Both direct and displaced myth, then, were frequent patterns in nineteenth-century literature, but they were not the only two. The fiction of Théophile Gautier will provide us with some examples of others. In 1844, Gautier wrote a short story entitled "Le Roi Candaule." In this exotic tale he did not subordinate the human to the divine nor, conversely, the divine to the human. He combined the genuinely human and the genuinely divine in roughly equal proportions. This old story, which goes back as far as Herodotus, takes place several centuries before the Christian era in the Eastern portion of the Greek Empire. This location permits Gautier to set up a clash between Eastern and Western values, and because Gautier usually preferred any exotic culture to his own, it is a clash from which the East emerges triumphant.

In Sardis King Candaule, a Greek, has married an Oriental princess named Nyssia. She is so beautiful that he would like his entire kingdom to admire her, but she has been brought up in the Asiatic tradition which cloisters women, and she refuses to go out without a veil or to reveal any part of her body to anyone but her husband. Desperate for someone to share his knowledge of her beauty, he forces the Captain of the Guards, Gygès, who has been secretly in love with the queen, to look upon his wife from a secret hiding place while she is disrobing. Nyssia sees him in hiding but pretends to notice nothing. The next day she forces him to choose between instant death or murder of her husband. If he will kill the king, she will marry him so that it will remain true that no living man except her husband will have seen her body. Gygès kills the king, marries Nyssia, and bribes the Delphic oracles to approve the match in order to quiet the restive populace.

In order to give his narrative a larger meaning, Gautier associates Candaule's desire to show off his queen's charms with the frank openness of Western (Greek) culture, and he equates Nyssia's desire to remain unseen to the hermetically closed harem psychology of the East. The architecture reinforces the cultural opposition. Part of the palace is done in Greek style with delicate columns and open spaces, but the older part has great massive walls, reflecting the closed quality of the more ancient Oriental civilizations.

The two main characters exist, then, as reflections of their cultures; they also are presented as human beings. The husband, although a king, is a man, and pays the price for his vanity. As for Nyssia, she, too, is human. She is a dutiful wife who does not love her husband. The reason for her indifference is clear enough—her husband does not love her, despite all his adulation. When he asks her to pose for him on a tiger skin, he is viewing her not as a person, not even as a sex object, but as an *objet d'art*, and she makes it clear that she resents being dehumanized. Further, her modesty is naturally outraged by her husband's exposing her to Gygès' eyes. So she is not only willing to accept Gygès as her husband, she even promises to love him, for she senses that Gygès truly loves her and will keep her for himself alone.

But Nyssia and Candaule are real on a mythic level as well. Nyssia is more than a woman. We are told that she is made of a "substance idéale," that she is "divine" and that there is something superhuman about her. Although married, she seems to be a cold, aloof statue whose "virginité invincible paraissait défier l'amour." She is a kind of inaccessible goddess, and like one, she has extraordinary powers. She possesses special keeness of vision that enables her to make out Gygès in his hiding place. Gods and goddesses are normally given acute vision as the story of Acteon and Diana attests. This acuity of sight is a metaphor for the total knowledge that a divinity has of the universe over which he or she reigns.

Since she is a goddess, it is natural that she be surrounded and protected by taboos. While the average person may worship from afar, only the true initiate may penetrate into her most intimate presence, and then only in adoration. Nyssia's divine decree is that only her husband may qualify for the ultimate revelation. Candaule fails Nyssia not only as husband but as worshiper. It is true that he is "comme un prêtre ivre du dieu qui le remplit," and that he would like to "répandre son culte sur la terre," but it is the cult of her beauty and not of divinity that he exalts. Worse, to try to use divinity to enhance one's human vanity is sacrilege, and Candaule compounds his evil by forcing Gygès to violate Nyssia's sanctuary. For a mortal to violate a taboo means death, but Gygès is spared because he had not wanted to spy on her, considering such an act to be "un sacrilège." Because Gygès accepts his own inferiority to the goddess, it is Candaule who must die.

Up to this point, it could be argued that despite words like sacrilege, divinity, cult, superhuman, and the like, we have only another case of displaced myth, that Nyssia suggests a goddess but is one only through imagery. But there is another aspect to the narrative: Candaule is not only a king, he is a king literally descended from the gods. On one of the walls of the castle there are bas-reliefs of all his ancestors arranged in a circle. The family line begins with Hercules and shows each generation down to the King. Candaule's own likeness occupies the last place on the circle next to Hercules, leaving room for no more. Fate has decreed the end of this Western man and his Western dynasty, and at the same time the decline of the Western gods. We remember that the Delphic oracles are easily bribed in the story (a sign of their weakness), and Nyssia replaces Candaule as the incarnation of the East and its religions, with all their attendant taboos. Gygès, once loyal to Candaule, is converted and now adores the new divinity.

One can understand the appeal of this type of dual vision where characters are both gods and humans. The scope of the narrative is as large as the cosmos, thanks to the divine dimension, but it is also real and individual and concrete, thanks to the human element. Because of the dual possibilities of this technique, we find some other experiments along these lines during the nineteenth century. Gautier himself tried something analogous in his story "Une Nuit de Cléopatre," and Flaubert gave the form its most fully developed expression in *Salammbô*. In each of these cases, the author has located his narrative in an ancient, exotic culture in order to make the gods convincing, but the very act of avoiding the modern world probably explains why this type of mythic fiction did not become more widespread. It went against the century's desire for contemporary realism in prose.

There is one more type of mythic literature to be considered. We said above that the canons of realism would not permit direct mythic expression within our familiar world of reality, that one could not accept a real Venus walking around a French town. But in fact there is a story that does precisely that. It is Prosper Mérimée's *La Vénus d'Ille* (1837), which introduces us to our final category of the nineteenth-century use of myth, one in which the divine and the human are both present, but not harmoniously fused as in "Le Roi Candaule." I refer to literature of the fantastic, where the lack of fusion of the human and divine worlds can create fear or horror. Mérimée's tale concerns a young French bridegroom who removes his wedding band from his finger and thoughtlessly puts it on the finger of a copper statue of Venus in a garden. That night the statue accepts the implied invitation to the marriage bed, lumbers up to his room, and crushes him in her arms. It is a classic of horror fiction. Indeed, if we are to believe H.P. Lovecraft,[10] horror is a necessary ingredient in fantastic literature. When our comfortable forms suddenly dissolve and unexpected monsters appear, we sense the instability of all apparent orderliness, and fear overwhelms us. But fantastic literature has more to it than evoking horror. Our final text, Gautier's "La Morte amoureuse" (1836) will demonstrate the point.

The story is told in the first person by an old Italian priest, Romuald. As the narrative opens, he is a young man innocent of any sexual experience and about to be ordained. At the ceremony he suddenly notices a very beautiful woman in the church who makes clear by her glances that she wants him to abandon the priesthood and become her lover. Although more than receptive to the idea and feeling that a whole new wonderful world is opening up before him, he finds himself unable to stop the ceremony and utters the fateful words that make him a priest forever. As he leaves the church a hand as cold as the skin of a snake,[11] yet which seems to brand him like a hot iron, touches him, and she says: "Malheureux! Qu'as-tu fait?" A few moments later he receives a mysterious note: "Clarimonde au palais Concini." It turns out that Clarimonde is a notorious courtesan.

At this point the reader stops to ask himself several questions. Has the old priest wittingly or unwittingly deformed the real events of a half-century earlier? Even if he has not, problems remain. Is Clarimonde a live courtesan or a specter of some kind? Is she diabolical, as the cold burning touch would suggest, or does she represent life and love, as the young priest seems to feel? Romuald is aware of the uncertainty as he concludes: "Je ne sais si la flamme qui illuminait [ses yeux] venait du ciel ou de l'enfer, mais à coup sûr elle venait de l'un ou de l'autre. Cette femme était un ange ou un démon, et peut-être tous les deux."

Another priest, Father Sérapion, senses (no explanation is given as to how he learns about it) that Romuald is beset by some temptation and warns him sternly against listening to the devil, but one is uncertain whether to assume Father Sérapion's point of view, even though he announces that dreadful things go on at the Concini palace.

At this juncture Romuald leaves for another town and settles into his clerical duties. One night he thinks he sees a mysterious woman lurking in his garden among the trees. He can find no one and wonders if it was an illusion. Some nights later a mysterious man calls him away to a deathbed. A wild, nightmarish ride of obviously diabolical nature leads to a home with a woman lying dead on a couch. It is Clarimonde. Romuald kisses her, and she responds to his kiss, saying: "Je t'ai attendu si longtemps, que je suis morte; mais maintenant nous sommes fiancés, je pourrai te voir et aller chez toi. Adieu, Romuald, adieu! je t'aime; c'est tout ce que je voulais te dire, et je te rends la vie que tu as rappelée sur moi une minute avec ton baiser." The priest is so overcome that he faints.

When he revives, he is back in his house, and his servant confirms that the experience was not a figment of his imagination, because she saw the mysterious man bringing Romuald home. In fantastic literature it is necessary to establish the sense of reality in order for the fantastic to have much effect. The servant's testimony heightens the reader's apprehension. Then Father Sérapion arrives to inform the younger priest that Clarimonde died the previous night after a week-long orgy, and he suggests further mysteries when he says cryptically that it isn't the first time she has died.

In the final part of the story, Romuald leads the life of an average priest during the day, but at night he dreams with such vividness and precision that he cannot be sure whether the nocturnal experiences are not the true reality and the daytime life the illusion. At night he becomes a handsome young nobleman and the lover of Clarimonde. Their life together is delightful, but Clarimonde begins to weaken and look pale. By chance she sucks Romuald's blood when he cuts his finger, and the color comes back to her cheeks. She realizes that she is a vampire and needs blood to survive. So periodically, she drugs her lover to take a little of his blood. Suspicious, Romuald avoids the drug one night and discovers the truth. But he is touched by the fact that Clarimonde is very gentle and considerate. She takes only enough to restore her health but not enough to hurt him.

Father Sérapion comes to suspect the truth and almost forces Romuald to accompany him to open Clarimonde's grave. Romuald agrees: "J'étais si fatigué de cette double vie.... voulant savoir, une fois pour toutes, qui du prêtre ou du gentilhomme était dupe d'une illusion: j'étais décidé à tuer au profit de l'un ou de l'autre un des deux hommes qui étaient en moi . . . car une pareille vie ne pouvait durer." When the grave is opened, they find her lying there in all her beauty. Father Sérapion sprinkles holy water on her and she crumbles away. That night she makes one last visit to Romuald to tell him that now she must leave him forever, and she does. Romuald ends the story by saying that he regrets achieving peace of soul at such a cost. A final unconvincing moral (no doubt appended to satisfy the censors) warns against looking at women, for, it claims, one's salvation is at stake.

In recent years, critics have been coming to the conclusion that nineteenth-century fantastic literature is much more than entertainment by horror. In a conformist age that had no hesitation in dragging a wayward author into court on charges of immorality, it served to explore in disguised fashion matters that could not be openly discussed. Tzvetan Todorov, for instance, in his *Introduction à la littérature fantastique*,[12] stresses the idea that in the last century fantastic literature served to express taboo or abnormal sexual behavior that a pre-Freudian era could not bring out into the open. Using "La Morte amoureuse" as a case in point, Todorov believes that Romuald's kissing Clarimonde on her deathbed is disguised necrophilia. Perhaps so, but there is another way of looking at the whole manner in which Clarimonde is presented. We are dealing in this story not only with taboo sex but also with a series of ambiguities, the kind of thing that in more complex form John Fowles achieved a few years ago in *The Magus*. In Gautier's tale not only is reality unclear at times, the moral values are also far from simple. Sérapion, the older priest who tries to guide young Romuald, is "good" and Clarimonde, the vampire, is "evil" only up to a point. Underneath the surface one notes that although a priest, and therefore supposedly virtuous, Sérapion is harsh, suspicious, and domineering, whereas Clarimonde, although a courtesan, is considerate and loving. Viewed in this light, Romuald's kiss is not necessarily evil and can be incorporated into the fairy-tale traditions of "Snow White" and "Sleeping Beauty," where kisses are life-giving. Even Clarimonde's vampirism is not really evil. Having drunk her lover's blood, she exclaims in rapture: "Ma vie est dans la tienne, et tout ce qui est moi vient de toi." Here, the vampirism is a metaphor for total love. In short, "La Morte amoureuse" is asking whether asceticism is really more virtuous than ardent physical love, and the answer remains ambiguous to the very end. Obviously, "La Morte amoureuse" has more to it than mere entertainment. The demonic tradition has been used in a new and vital manner.

There are, then, four basic types of mythic expression that one finds in nineteenth-century French literature. The first, direct myth, presents supernatural beings undisguised and gives us human psychology by extension. It survived primarily in poetry. The second, displaced myth, centered on the human and evoked ancient myths through imagery. It was the most original achievement of the four, because it harmonized the exigencies of realism with the eternal truths of myth. To cite only two more examples from major authors: Alfred Engstrom has shown brilliantly that behind the clinical realism of Flaubert's *Madame Bovary*, one may discern a substructure of the three Greek Fates spinning, measuring, and cutting the thread of life.[13] Even the supposedly "scientific" naturalism of Emile Zola did not preclude the presence of myth. Philip Walker has demonstrated that if we are to understand *Les Rougon-Macquart*, we must be aware of underlying mythic patterns.[14] The third type of mythic usage was a mixture of the first two, with directly mythic and truly human traits combined harmoniously in the same characters. As we said above, Gautier's "Le Roi Candaule" was not a unique text. Nonetheless, despite Flaubert's *Salammbô*, this hybrid genre remained somewhat peripheral to the main development of fiction during the past century. Our final category, fantastic literature, shows the supernatural, usually some form of an ancient demonic tradition, violating the serenity and security of our real world, and creating by its intrusion horror and uncertainty. The dislocation of all that is familiar on the surface of our lives permits the exploration of the unconscious and the ambiguities of reality and ethics. Maupassant's "Le Horla" is in this tradition.

It would be interesting to follow these four types of myth into the present century, but that is the subject of another study. As far as the nineteenth century is concerned, we may conclude that even in the positivistic age of Comte, Taine, Darwin, and determinism, an age which tended to see myth officially as only a manifestation of long-dead religions belonging to the superstitious infancy of mankind, myth simply refused to disappear. This persistence of myth is hardly surprising, of course. As we said at the outset, the earliest literature of ancient cultures was myth, and there is little doubt that myth is built into the very fabric of literary structures and will last as long as literature itself.

---

[1] See his *Myth in Primitive Psychology* (New York: Norton, 1926), pp. 19, 91.

[2] *Patterns in Comparative Religion* (New York: World [Meridian Books], 1963).

[3] *Myth: Its Meaning and Functions in Ancient and Other Cultures* (Berkely: University of California Press, 1970).

[4] "Myth" in the *Encyclopedia Britannica* (15th ed.), vol xv.

[5] (Princeton, N.J.: Princeton University Press, 1957).

[6] *Oeuvres complètes* (Paris: Gallimard [Bibliothèque de la Pleiade], 1958), p. 429.

[7] (Oxford: Blackwell, 1941).

[8] Jean-Pierre Richard makes this point in an article, "Hugo" in his *Etudes sur le romantisme* (Paris: Ed. du Seuil, 1970), pp. 177-199.

[9] *Les Travailleurs de la mer* (Première partie, I, i).

[10] *Supernatural Horror in Literature* (New York: Abramson, 1945).

[11] ". . . froide comme la peau d'un serpent."

[12] (Paris: Ed. du Seuil, 1970).

[13] "Flaubert's Correspondence and the Ironic and Symbolic Structure of Madame Bovary," *Studies in Philology*, VI (1945), pp. 470-495.

[14] "Prophetic Myths in Zola," *PMLA*, LXXIV, 4, pt. 1 (Sept., 1959), pp. 444-452.

Texte classique / contexte moderne: L'enjeu des classiques dans la pratique théâtrale entre 1950 et 1970

Laurence Romero
Villanova University

On sait que les classiques dramatiques et leur mise en scène ont toujours eu une importance capitale dans la vie théâtrale française. Il est également clair que les grands classiques n'ont pas eu une existence artistique monolithique et que d'époque en époque on les a montés de façon très différente. Leur place dans le répertoire a également évolué avec le passage du temps et leur interprétation a souvent provoqué débats et polémiques. Sans pouvoir embrasser toute l'histoire de cette progression, il s'agira ici d'en aborder brièvement une partie seulement, celle qui touche à la mise en place centrale des classiques dans les théâtres publics à partir des efforts de décentralisation vers 1950. Ce faisant, on reviendra principalement sur un ou deux metteurs en scène connus, surtout Jean Vilar et Roger Planchon, et sur leurs travaux dans le théâtre dit "populaire" qu'ils ont essayé d'animer. Il faudra rappeler aussi certains aspects du renouveau théâtral entre 1950 et 1970 comme la quête d'un nouveau public, la prise du pouvoir du metteur en scène, et le problème de la fidélité à l'oeuvre classique. En gros donc, il sera question du texte classique et du contexte culturel moderne. Dans le présent essai le terme "classique" s'entend dans le sens d'une grande oeuvre canonisée, provenant *grosso modo* de Shakespeare à Ibsen, soit de 1600 à 1900; ici toutefois on se limitera à quelques mises en scène des classiques français. Globalement on distingue aujourd'hui entre trois groupes de classiques: les classiques anciens de l'antiquité, les classiques dits modernes qui viennent d'être esquissés et qui nous concernent, et les classiques dits contemporains du vingtième siècle dont O'Neil, O'Casey, Brecht, voire Ionesco et Beckett.

L'énorme projet de renouvellement théâtral post-guerre commence dès 1947 par un retour sérieux aux tentatives de décentralisation lancées déjà avant la guerre par le gouvernement du Front populaire. Dans le domaine de la culture ces efforts sont dirigés par le ministre Pierre Bourdan, et pour les beaux-arts et le théâtre, surtout par son adjointe, Jeanne Laurent qui nomme en 1951 Jean Vilar à la direction du Théâtre national populaire (TNP); quatre ans auparavant Vilar et la municipalité d'Avignon avaient fondé ce qui deviendrait le célèbre Festival international. D'emblée Vilar préconisait les classiques comme le fondement même du théâtre public reconstitué après la guerre et animé par une sorte de nouveau contrat social vis-à-vis le public français. "Ce style de théâtre populaire, écrivait-il en 1961, ne pouvait naître que de la présentation privilégiée des classiques, de ces oeuvres-mères d'où tout peut et doit partir, et qui appartiennent à tous... et qui n'ont jamais eu pour effet que de provoquer la réflexion du spectateur. Elles s'adressent naturellement au peuple, et constituent, dans le domaine de la culture, le point de ralliement, au niveau le plus élevé, du plus grand nombre."[1] A peu près au même moment, le jeune Roger Planchon complétait cette attitude en se demandant ce qu'est un classique sinon une oeuvre qu'on a écrite hier.[2] Occupant donc une place primordiale dans l'activité théâtrale que personne ne conteste, la mise en scène des classiques sera comme lieu et moment privilégiés d'une réflexion artistique et historique—comment voir et comment jouer par rapport au passé—une tentative de préciser notre place devant l'histoire, de repenser et de réinventer notre culture dans celle d'hier.

Autour de ces débats aux années 50 et 60 certaines questions de base s'imposaient: qu'est-ce que le théâtre aujourd'hui, qui seront surtout responsables d'assurer sa qualité et sa cohérence artistiques, enfin, pour qui joue-t-on? Pendant la période d'entre deux guerres, à l'époque des grands théâtres privés parisiens dont les salles pleines dépendaient de la seule présence d'une grande vedette, on jouait surtout pour un public bourgeois d'un certain âge et plutôt aisé. Comme M. Jourdain, il est capable de se payer sa culture dont la fonction principale tendait à être le simple divertissement. Or ce public payant cher ses places préfère ne pas être bousculé dans ses moments de détente par des mises en scène trop brusques, compliquées, exigeantes. L'idéal serait nos bons vieux classiques joués par des grandes vedettes déclamant ces beaux vers archiconnus, appris par coeur à l'école. En somme donc, ce fut un théâtre pour l'individu privilégié, le visant dans son privé, un théâtre essentiellement élitaire, intimiste, et sentimental, un lieu de menus plaisirs dans les grands loisirs.

C'était surtout ce genre de théâtre que Vilar, Jean Dasté, Hubert Gignoux, Jean-Louis Barrault, Roger Blin, et dans la suite, Planchon, Marcel Maréchal, Patrice Chéreau, Antoine Vitez et d'autres ont voulu transformer. Dans le cadre de la décentralisation, et pour enfin briser la fascination de Paris comme unique centre des arts en France, on a fondé un peu partout dans l'hexagone des scènes et des troupes. Ce développement est connu: peu après la Libération on commence par neuf Centres dramatiques, puis aux années soixante il y a la création des Maisons de la culture avec des troupes permanentes subventionnées. Dès sa nomination au TNP, Vilar réorganise toute l'entreprise, comme aussi le répertoire, et l'ordre du jour de cette rénovation est l'ouverture. Dorénavant il fallait populariser la culture théâtrale en élaborant un système de scènes subventionnées et ouvertes au grand public, surtout en province où il y avait peu de ressources culturelles. C'était le premier grand pas vers l'utopie rêvée de Vilar, un théâtre-service public, comme le gaz, l'eau, et l'électricité, où toute la Cité se réunissait. Et même si ce rêve n'a jamais été réalisé, il a beaucoup marqué la pratique théâtrale depuis.[3]

Une des premières tâches du renouveau théâtral fut de mettre fin au système du vedettariat où la représentation était centrée autour de la grande star, celle-ci s'occupant surtout de son rôle et de sa carrière. Sans mater leur prestige, Vilar avait su intégrer dans l'ensemble de ses mises en scène ses propres rôles ainsi que ceux de d'autres grandes vedettes jouant pour lui: Maria Casarès (Phèdre), Gérard Philipe (Rodrigue, Lorenzaccio), Daniel Sorano (Sganarelle), Georges Wilson (Créon), parmi d'autres. Cette tendance se prolongera dans les théâtres publics de la décentralisation où surtout à partir de 1970 les metteurs en scène peuvent compter sans question sur des jeunes comédiens professionnels capables de s'intégrer dans la totalité de la mise en scène. Une fois balayée du centre de la scène et de la troupe, la vedette sera remplacée par le metteur en scène (Vilar disait régisseur), et c'est lui qui assurera l'intégrité artistique et la cohérence scénique de la représentation. Non que l'acteur et son travail soient dévalorisés; si un peu moins célébrés qu'avant, les comédiens sont surtout des professionnels disciplinés autour desquels le metteur en scène peut organiser un travail scénique global et intégral. (Souvent, ne l'oublions pas, le metteur en scène est en même temps acteur.) On reviendra plus bas sur la problématique de la prise du pouvoir de ce "personnage douteux" (Planchon, 1985).

Peut-être le projet le plus ambitieux et le plus frustrant du théâtre populaire depuis Vilar fut la grande tentative de recomposition du public, dont on se dispute encore aujourd'hui le succès. On connaît pourtant les efforts considérables surtout de Vilar au TNP et en Avignon, ainsi que ceux de Planchon déjà au théâtre de la Cité de Villeurbanne et ensuite au nouveau TNP, également à Villeurbanne: ils ont fait des enquêtes, organisé des matinées, des débats, des programmes de tous genres pour attirer un public plus mixte et pour briser avec la tradition du théâtre de pure consommation. Depuis lors, on discute les vrais résultats de ces tentatives. Sans revenir sur les détails, rappelons-en certains éléments. D'abord l'idée fantaisiste de vouloir faire venir tout le monde au théâtre n'a jamais été le but des anciens militants du théâtre populaire pour la simple raison que le projet est irréalisable et qu'on était bien trop malin pour s'y laisser prendre. En outre, même dans un cadre plus modeste, la question du public théâtral dépasse largement le domaine du théâtre, même de la culture proprement dite. Inévitablement elle touche à la politique, à la sociologie, à la démographie, à l'économie, à la psychologie, etc. Qu'on le veuille ou non, il s'agit bien d'un phénomène socio-politique si large qu'il est impensable de vouloir refondre en profondeur un public théâtral sans avoir refait au préalable toute la société qui l'entoure. Alors le but de Jean Vilar était d'animer un vrai théâtre populaire, c'est-à-dire, un théâtre public et ouvert où, dans la mesure du possible, toutes les classes et tous les âges de la société française soient représentés, y compris les gens qui d'habitude ne venaient pas au théâtre. Car, comme on le sait trop bien, l'avenir du théâtre est souvent entre les mains de ceux qui n'y vont pas. Dans la perspective historique et avec un peu de recul, il semble bien que les conséquences de la décentralisation (surtout la prolifération des théâtres partout en France) et les efforts de Vilar, de Planchon, et d'autres ont sûrement apporté des modifications, même légères, dans la composition du public théâtral français d'après-guerre. Comparés au grand public parisien d'avant-guerre, les nouveaux spectateurs sont plus jeunes et plus hétérogènes, comptant parmi eux des lycéens, des étudiants, des cadres et des employés des grandes entreprises. Dans certains théâtres, dont celui de Planchon à Villeurbanne vers 1960, il y a eu environ 5 à 6% d'ouvriers (on se dispute ce chiffre); mais enfin la composition du nouveau public importait plus que sa dimension.[4] Et, résultat heureux de ces modifications, les nouveaux spectateurs étant moins soucieux de leur simple divertissement, ils s'attendent à un spectacle plus ambitieux, exigeant, et expérimental, permettant une renaissance dans l'ensemble du travail théâtral. En fin de compte, dès le début de la rénovation des années cinquante et soixante, il fallait à tout prix promouvoir un théâtre en voie d'ouverture vers un programme culturel de base large et variée, le tout animé par des professionnels-bêtes-de-théâtre voués à l'innovation et dévoués à leur public: ceci, pour activer un "public potentiel" (Jeanson) ayant dorénavant davantage d'accès à des spectacles plus abordables et répondant plus aux goûts et aux intérets de la Cité. Voilà donc schématiquement le cadre historique général dans lequel la mise en scène des classiques va occuper une place décisive.[5]

Dans un des premiers rapports statistiques importants après la guerre, *l'ATAC-Informations* (Association technique de l'action culturelle) a publié les chiffres suivants portant sur l'activité des théâtres publics de la décentralisation (les théâtres nationaux n'y figurent pas) entre 1947 et 1972 et qui montrent bien la position prioritaire des classiques dans les répertoires. Plus de 85% des mises en scène de cette période sont des classiques modernes, dont 136 de Molière, 84 de Shakespeare, 36 de Musset, 34 de Marivaux, 26 de Racine, et 24 de Corneille.[6] (La table statistique de l'ATAC répertorie environ 415 spectacles.) Ce goût marqué des classiques a entraîné une certaine interrogation sur sa nature. Pour Vilar et sa génération, est classique toute oeuvre du passé qui par la qualité et le poids a eu une répercussion intellectuelle et artistique—dans l'esprit et sur la scène—parmi nous aujourd'hui chez soi et/ou à l'étranger. (L'influence énorme de Brecht en France après sa visite en 1954 a beaucoup fait pour ouvrir l'activité théâtrale aux oeuvres étrangères.) Mais l'identité même du classique n'a pas changé radicalement depuis 1950. Bien sûr, de pays en pays ce corpus a tendance à s'engrossir par la découverte de nouveaux auteurs obscurs ou d'oeuvres de maîtres peu jouées avant hier. En France on a redécouvert des auteurs comme Lenz et Panizza. En même temps on a commencé à jouer des textes peu goûtés jusqu'alors: *George Dandin*, *La Seconde surprise de l'amour*, *L'Ile des esclaves*, *L'Héritier du village*, et le *Périclès* de Shakespeare. Ces trouvailles ont certainement agrandi l'héritage commun des lettres sans pour autant avoir changé la conception maîtresse du classique: une oeuvre qui persiste à projeter bien au-delà du temps de sa création une vision du monde susceptible de provoquer ou d'émouvoir.

Si la définition du classique n'a pas été mise en question, ce que le metteur en scène en fait lorsqu'il monte sa pièce a été sujet de controverse. En gros, pour la plupart des hommes de théâtre de l'époque nous concernant, le classique n'est plus le véhicule d'une vérité universelle et dont la mise en scène ne serait que la simple répétition d'une tradition scénique. Aussi le classique n'est plus un produit culturel à consommation générale favorisant une mise en scène matériellement opulente mais banale dans son contenu intellectuel, un pur spectacle à plaisir. (A cet égard, on rappelle ici la mise en scène travestie et hautement comique et satirique de Planchon au théâtre de la Cité en 1969: *Contestation et la mise en pièces de la plus illustre des tragédies françaises 'Le Cid' de Pierre Corneille, suivies d'une cruelle mise à mort de l'auteur dramatique et d'une distribution gracieuse de diverses conserves culturelles*.) La conception principale du classique qui a animé beaucoup de mises en scène depuis Vilar, c'est avant tout d'une oeuvre organique qui se doit de changer, de s'adapter, de se renouveler selon le passsage du temps et les inévitables modifications du monde dans l'histoire. Le classique s'ouvre à notre modernité, quitte parfois même à l'absorber. Il n'est plus bloc de marbre de tous les temps, mais miroir fragile recomposant une double histoire, celle de son passé reflétée à la lumière de la nôtre. Bien montée à la scène, l'oeuvre permet alors une double appréhension: à travers la description scénique du moment historique du classique, une vision du monde contemporaine confronte le passé, le critique, et par là, se révèle lui-même. Ainsi conçue, la mise en scène de l'oeuvre classique ne projette pas une image de l'homme universel dans son unique vérité, mais à travers le scepticisme régnant, propose plutôt *des* images de l'homme dans l'histoire et *des* significations possibles émergeant d'une analyse moderne du texte et de son temps; c'est projeter parallèlement une réflexion sur le temps de l'auteur dramatique ainsi qu'un commentaire sur notre moment historique en montrant comment celui-ci peut concevoir celui-là.[7] En voici quelques exemples. Dans sa mise en scène de *Tartuffe* (1962, 1973), Planchon part d'un soupçon que les liens qui rattachent Orgon à Tartuffe sont d'ordre sexuel et son interprétation et le décor de René Allio montrent la distinction fragile entre la sensualité et une dévotion religieuse pousée à l'extrême, phénomène connu à l'époque de Molière. Dans la remise en scène de 1973, Planchon insiste sur l'aspect de transition: une classe de riches bourgeois qui monte en voie parallèle à l'ascendance d'un jeune roi puissant et ambitieux. Un rappel enfin, que nous sommes dans *Tartuffe* encore sous l'ancien régime où la police royale secrète (qui s'organisait alors) détient un pouvoir considérable. A ne pas confondre donc: l'Exempt et ses Gardes ne sont en réalité que le Super-Flic et ses petits agents.[8] En montant *Bérénice* en 1970, Planchon pose le problème de l'ambition politique et du carriérisme flagrant de Titus que celui-ci tourne en prétexte-à-devoir pour abandonner la tendre Bérénice dont il est d'ailleurs devenu fatigué. Cela n'étant qu'un aspect de l'interprétation de Planchon, il montre bien pourtant comment une sensibilité moderne peut pénétrer l'oeuvre classique.[9] En général, le travail théâtral de Planchon indique clairement que la mise en scène actuelle des classiques doit dégager la tradition du conformisme scénique accumulé et aussi, dans la tournure de Gabriel Garran, que "artisan ou partisan, à partir d'un certain niveau d'interrogation, le théâtre cesse d'être innocent, et toute interprétation est une prise de position." La mise en scène toute récente (1987) de *L'Avare* atteste, si besoin est, la forte présence de Roger Planchon dans l'activité théâtrale actuelle.[10] De sa part, Patrice Chéreau jette un oeil critique sur le noble traître à sa classe tout en profitant de ses privilèges, dans son interprétation de *Dom Juan* en 1969 à Lyon. Et c'est là justement l'hypocrisie de Dom Juan. Ce casse-tout de l'époque encore féodale veut se libérer de toute entrave et surtout de celle de la classe nobiliaire soutenue par une pensée et une présence religieuses encore plus tyranniques que l'ordre civil. Evidemment Chéreau en vient à critiquer aussi Dom Juan, son caractère indiscipliné et frivole, son égoïsme dévorant, son arrogance. En somme Chéreau montre le dilemme de l'homme libre—mais nullement idéal—qui confronte une société-machine-à-tuer-les-hommes. Cette interprétation fut très influencée par Brecht, le marxisme, et les événements de mai 1968.[11]

Inévitablement ces mises en scène innovatrices et peu conventionnelles ont beaucoup provoqué les spectateurs et surtout les critiques dont certains criaient contre les soi-disant abus des metteurs en scène prétentieux et si puissants qu'ils pouvaient faire fi de l'opinion publique. En fait, les débats les plus acerbes et qui persistent encore aujourd'hui concernent l'avènement du metteur en scène comme maître absolu de la production théâtrale, c'est-à-dire du texte et de l'écriture scénique. Celle-ci, dont le metteur en scène est le seul créateur, représente le composant matériel (scénographie) ainsi que le gestus (expression corporelle des joueurs), pour accompagner et élucider—voire interpréter—le texte dramatique. Devant ce phénomène du nouveau metteur en scène qui commence à se manifester avec force pendant les années soixante, la critique est divisée. Alfred Simon ne voit que misère en scène depuis l'élévation au pouvoir de cet "Arlequin trismégiste." Pour Simon, tous les aspects majeurs du spectacle sont compromis par la tyrannie du metteur en scène snob obsédé par une ambition délirante: "L'importance du texte diminue dans l'exacte mesure où celle du metteur en scène augmente. ...Réducteur du texte, le metteur en scène est aussi un maître du jeu qui ravale l'acteur au rang d'outil, de marionnette, de robot.... La maîtrise du metteur en scène trouve son achèvement dans la mise en condition d'un public réduit à la consommation passive d'images... quand la mise en scène prend la forme d'un phantasme qui s'interpose entre le corps ludique de l'acteur et la conscience spectatrice du public."[12] Encore récemment dans *L'Express* (no. 1864, p.66), Simon s'impatientait devant des spectacles "qui souffrent des excès de la mise en scène."

Pour sa part, Bernard Dort est plus tolérant. Ce critique voit la prise du pouvoir du metteur en scène dans son évolution historique européenne à partir d'Antoine, en passant par Otto Brahm en Allemagne, par Stanislavski, pour aboutir à la génération de Vilar et les hommes de théâtre français de post-guerre. Dans cette perspective large Dort voit l'émergence du régisseur liée à d'autres mouvements d'émancipation importants dans le théâtre moderne: "Le pouvoir du metteur en scène, sa royauté ou sa tyrannie, pourrait bien n'avoir été qu'un stade de transition vers une émancipation des autres facteurs, des autres pratiques et praticiens du théâtre."[13] Dans un autre texte en anglais, Dort s'explique: "It may be that the rise of the director and the acceptance of the performance as the actual site of meaning (not as the translation or decoration of a text) represent only the initial phase of this transformation. I shall call it the progressive emancipation of the elements of the theatrical performance—the abandonment of an organic unity laid down in advance, and the choice of a meaningful polyphony open to the spectator."[14]

Entre Simon et Dort, Raymonde Temkine voit le metteur en scène pris entre le trop et le trop-peu: "...s'il n'est véritable créateur, il dévalorise le texte en ne l'exploitant pas assez, ou le phagocyte si c'est trop."[15] Elle avoue que beaucoup de metteurs en scène abusent de leur autorité absolue, "mais reconnaissons que beaucoup d'auteurs dramatiques gagnent à être ainsi violés;" mais enfin, "l'auteur prend sa revanche—il espère du moins—par la pérennité possible de son texte. Le metteur ne dispose que de son temps de vie pour gagner la partie... même si l'avenir appartient en dernier recours à l'auteur, je privilégie le metteur en scène, comptable de l'avenir du théâtre, dans le moyen terme."[16]

Ceci dit, il faut constater que, bon gré mal gré, le metteur en scène s'est imposé au théâtre surtout après 1960 et que sa domination reste peut-être le trait le plus marqué dans l'activité théâtrale en France depuis la guerre. Rappelons enfin que même si Jean Vilar n'est pas lié aux abus de la prise du pouvoir du metteur en scène, c'est bien lui, déjà en 1946 et "sans s'en réjouir," qui avait signalé l'apparition de ce personnage qui allait bientôt dominer la scène française: "Les vrais créateurs dramatiques de ces trente dernières années ne sont pas les auteurs mais les metteurs en scène."[17]

Qu'elle se range sous l'indice de l'abus ou non, une conséquence importante de l'emprise du metteur en scène est d'avoir tranché net la vieille question de la fidélité à l'oeuvre. Le fait que le débat en est beaucoup moins intense à l'heure actuelle en dit long sur le travail scénique convaincant des metteurs en scène depuis Vilar, travail qui a gagné peu à peu l'approbation de bien des spectateurs, sinon de tous les critiques. Ainsi, avouons-le, la tolérance devant l'innovation et l'inattendu a été approfondie, au théâtre comme d'ailleurs dans tous les arts. Voilà aussi une partie importante et légitime du travail du metteur en scène qu'on appelle former son public. Néanmoins, avec la prééminence des textes classiques aux années cinquante et soixante, la question de la fidélité à l'oeuvre classique se reposait avec urgence. Liée à un certain esprit libéral devant les grands textes du canon dramatique français, cette interrogation suivait les traces d'une autre libéralisation plus vaste qui fut celle de l'explosion sociale, économique, et historique en France juste après la guerre. Partout il y avait ouverture: accroissement important dans la population, tout le pays un grand champ de reconstruction, refondation de toutes les institutions: culturelle, scolaire, bancaire, législative, juridique, etc. Dans cette ambiance de rénovation et de réinvention, comment le théâtre—l'art le plus social—aurait-il pu s'en échapper, pourquoi au fond y résister?[18] Inévitablement tout le travail théâtral à cette époque, y compris l'attitude devant les textes, a été coloré par une certaine mentalité que l'on pourrait caractériser de pluraliste et sceptique. Or, là où il n'existe plus une seule signification à chercher, là où l'ancienne vision monolithique de l'homme a été transformée en une mosaïque d'aspects divergents et contradictoires, alors devant ce nouveau terrain de possibilités, l'action culturelle confronte sa propre libéralisation. Au théâtre c'était en créant une nouvelle mode, parfois radicale, de monter les classiques que les jeunes metteurs en scène se sont d'abord imposés comme maîtres de la scène. Selon Planchon, "Le surgissement des classiques entraîne la naissance d'un personnage douteux... On peut le déplorer, mais les choses sont liées: la naissance des classiques donne le pouvoir aux metteurs en scène."[19] Dans l'ambiance de l'après-guerre, que disent alors les metteurs en scène de la fidélité à l'oeuvre classique? D'abord qu'il n'y a plus une fidélité aux classiques, mais des fidélités, car ces textes-miroirs vont refléter chaque génération de producteurs et de spectateurs. Les textes de Molière et de Racine n'étant plus sacrosaints, on peut les dépouiller sur la scène et les rendre plus clairs pour le public d'aujourd'hui. Lorsque Planchon fait venir l'Exempt et les gardes en uniformes de la CRS, même stylisés, cela éclaircit leur langage et leur présence; lorsque ce même metteur en scène fait jouer à Samy Frey un Titus littéralement obsédé de sa consécration au pouvoir par le sénat romain, cela aussi donne une dimension spéciale à son discours. Plus près de nous, lorsque Jérome Savary fait à M. Jourdain déclamer de la prose, cela révèle avec lucidité et humour la fatuité du bourgeois gentilhomme. Dans tous ces cas, on peut dire que le metteur en scène est fidèle à la fois au texte classique et à son public pour qui le langage parfois opaque du dix-septième siècle est pénétré et éclairci. A côté de la vision du monde de Molière et Racine, les voies de pénétration de la mise en scène révèlent aussi nos propres préoccupations devant l'état policier, l'ambition et l'égoïsme effrénés, et l'opportunisme excessif. L'écriture scénique, c'est-à-dire l'ensemble des codes d'interprétation, fonctionne alors comme médiation entre sens historique and signification actuelle. Evidemment, nous n'insistons ici que sur une partie de la nouvelle mise en scène des classiques et dans une perspective très limitée. Sans doute qu'il y a eu des excès et on les a cités et commentés avec vigueur; malgré leurs points de vue divergents, par exemple, B. Dort, A. Simon, et R. Temkine n'ont pas manqué de protester contre certains aspects contestables de la mise en scène depuis 1950, souvent liés à la question de la fidélité à l'oeuvre classique. Mais ce qu'il y a de plus justifiable dans l'attitude très libérale des metteurs en scène c'est la liaison qu'ils font entre la fidélité au classique et à leur public. Cela paraît donc normal qu'aujourd'hui la fidélité artistique d'un homme de théâtre devant l'oeuvre classique ne va pas exclusivement aux divines paroles du texte mais tient compte aussi de la culture à laquelle le théâtre participe. Dans une perspective plus large, n'oublions pas non plus que la question de la fidélité aux classiques ne s'est pas posée uniquement au théâtre de la décentralisation entre 1950 et 1970. Elle est en fin de compte composant permanent de la pratique théâtrale et elle restera toujours ouverte. Chaque génération d'hommes de théâtre y répondra à sa guise, et cette réponse toujours provisoire sera ajustée à la mesure et à la nature du moment historique et du climat social et culturel où elle est proposée.

Que l'on soit enfin partisan ou adversaire du travail théâtral de la décentralisation, il faut tout de même admettre que la période 1950 à 1970 fut riche en énergie, originalité, et conviction que le théâtre devait forger une place centrale dans l'action culturelle post-guerre. Polémiques mises à part, les hommes de théâtre ont lutté avec la meilleure volonté pour jeter de nouvelles bases à la culture théâtrale moderne et pour relancer le théâtre public dans des voies ouvertes et généreuses. A l'avenir, l'histoire du théâtre prendra sûrement note des efforts sans précédents pendant cette période à former un nouveau public grand et mixte et à faire venir au théâtre le maximum de gens pour le plaisir et la satisfaction. Car le rêve démocratique des animateurs d'alors c'était de mettre fin au privilège culturel en offrant un théâtre privilégié à tout le monde.

[1]Jean Vilar, *Théâtre service public* (Gallimard, 1974), p. 236; cité aussi dans Bernard Dort, "L'Age d'or ou, la mise en scène des classiques en France entre 1945 et 1960," *Revue d'histoire littéraire* (novembre-décembre 1977), p. 1004. A voir aussi, D.J. Fisher, "The Origins of the French Popular Theatre," *Journal of Contemporary History*, vol. 12 (1977), pp. 461-497.

[2]A l'origine Planchon avait écrit dans ses notes du livret-programme pour la mise en scène de *George Dandin* à Villeurbanne (Théâtre de la Cité) en 1960: "Nous aimons cette pièce car elle a été écrite le mois dernier, c'est pour nous la définition d'un classique." Depuis lors l'expression a évolué d'une boutade inspirée à un dicton populaire.

[3]Pour une information plus ample, voir: Guy Leclerc, *Le T.N.P. de Jean Vilar* (Editions 10/18, 1971); Phillipa Wehle, *Le Théâtre populaire selon Jean Vilar* (Avignon: Ates Sud, 1981); Yvette Daoust, *Roger Planchon Director and Playwright* (N.Y.: Cambridge University Press, 1981); Alfred Simon, *Dictionnaire du théâtre français contemporain* (Larousse, 1973); enfin, les travaux de B. Dort, d'Emile Copfermann, ainsi que les nombreux articles de La Nouvelle Critique et surtout ceux de la revue *Théâtre populaire*, parsemés parmi les 54 numéros entre 1952 et 1964.

[4]Voir mon interview avec B. Dort: "La pratique théâtrale actuelle ou, la nostalgie des grandes formes," *Feuillets* (Fribourg), vol. 5 (Mai 1983), pp.61-70; le même en anglais: "Remembrance of Things Past: French Theatre Praxis Today," *Modern Drama*, vol. CXV, no. 3 (September 1982), pp. 387-398.

[5]A ce sujet voir: B. Dort, *Théâtre public* (Le Seuil: 1967), chapitres I, V, et VI; Philippe Madral, *Le Théâtre hors les murs* (Le Seuil: 1969); Denis Gontard, *La Décentralisation théâtrale en France* (SEDES, 1973); F. Jeanson, *L'Action culturelle dans la cité* (Le Seuil, 1974); Jean Jourdheuil, *L'Artiste, la politique, la production* (Ed. 10/18,1976); André Tissier, "Le Public français face au renouveau théâtral après la seconde guerre mondiale," *Revue d'histoire littéraire* (novembre-décembre 1977), pp. 957-967.

[6]Cité dans B. Dort, "L'Age d'or...," *op. cit.*, p. 1002.

[7]Parmi d'autres, lire: E. Copfermann, *Théâtres de Roger Planchon* (Ed. 10/18, 1977); Richard Demarcy, *Eléments d'une sociologie du spectacle* (Ed. 10/18,1973); B. Dort, "L'Age d'or," et "Un Nouvel Usage des classiques," *Théâtre public, op. cit.*; Alain Girault, "Pourquoi monter un classique?," *La Nouvelle Critique*, no. 69 (décembre 1973), pp. 78-80; J. Jourdheuil, *L'Artiste..., op. cit.*; Gilles Sandier, *Théâtre et Combat* (Stock, 1970), pp. 151-196.

[8]Voir surtout: *Tartuffe*, dans la mise en scène de Roger Planchon, présenté par Alfred Simon (Ed. de l'Avant-Scène—Collection Classiques/Aujourd'hui, 1972); aussi, *Le Tartuffe*, texte présenté par P. Brunet dans la mise en scène de Roger Planchon (Hachette, 1967); E. Copfermann, *Théâtres..., op. cit.*; Y. Daoust, *Roger Planchon..., op. cit.*

[9]Copfermann et Daoust, *supra*.

[10]Molière, *L'Avare*, Préface de Roger Planchon (Livre de Poche: 1986).

[11]Patrice Chéreau, "Notre dossier sur *Dom Juan*," *Approches* (publication de la Compagnie du Cothurne: Lyon), no. 10 (janvier-février 1969); *Tartuffe* dans la mise en scène de Patrice Chéreau, présenté par Gilles Sandier (Ed. de l'Avant-Scène—Collection Classiques/Aujourd'hui, 1970).

[12]Alfred Simon, *Le Théâtre à bout de souffle?* (Le Seuil, 1979), pp. 42-44.

[13]Interview Dort,/Romero, *op. cit.* p. 67.

[14]Bernard Dort, "The Liberated Performance," *Modern Drama*, vol. XXV, no. 1 (March 1982), pp. 63-64; le texte original n'était pas disponible au moment de la rédaction du présent essai: "La Représentation émancipée," in J. Féral, et.al., *Théâtralité, Ecriture, et Mise en scène* (Québec: Eds. Hurtubise, 1983).

[15]Raymonde Temkine, *Mettre en scène au présent*, vol 1 (Lausanne: L'Age d'homme, 1977), p. 7.

[16]*Ibid.*, p. 8.

[17]Jean Vilar, *De la tradition théâtrale* (L'Arche, 1955), p. 71.
[18]Entre autres, lire B. Dort, "Les nouveaux théâtres à l'heure du choix," *Théâtre public, op. cit.*; "Une Propédeutique de la réalité," *Théâtre réel* (Le Seuil, 1971); "Le Théâtre public en France," *Théâtre en jeu* (Le Seuil, 1979).
[19]Molière, *L'Avare, op. cit.*, p. 7.

L'essai, ou l'anti-genre dans la littérature française du XXe siècle

Edouard Morot-Sir †
University of North Carolina

La situation de l'essai dans les littératures modernes depuis le 16ème siècle est aisément définissable: il est toujours et partout présent, mais subordonné aux grands genres, à peine reconnu comme un genre à cause de ses expressions multiples. Il suppose un art difficile et sans loi; ses réussites donnent une impression de perfection énigmatique. L'exemple de Montaigne, aujourd'hui comme hier, se dresse comme une interrogation double, métaphysique et rhétorique. Si l'on considère que le *je* ultime des *Essais* est celui-là même qui est responsable de cette écriture, le fameux "que sais-je?" déborde les frontières de l'épistémologie; il est un "que suis-je?" sémiotique et existentiel. Faut-il dire alors que, pour quatre siècles, la production variée des essais a été un effort pour répondre à cette question: "que suis-je comme parole vivante et hors cadre?" Le genre, quel qu'il soit, est, au contraire, une solution préalable. Il détermine les conditions d'existence d'un mode littéraire. L'essai serait donc l'anti-genre chronique—refus du genre et de ses codifications, refus de laisser le langage enfermé dans des définitions et des règles opératoires, revendication de liberté, signe d'une anarchie endémique qui dériverait de l'invention même des langues. Dans un article récent, Jacques Derrida observe que "depuis toujours le genre en tous genres a pu jouer le rôle de principe d'ordre."[1] Il parle de lui comme d'un "espace normé" à l'intérieur duquel seulement peuvent se produire "toutes les transgressions sophistiquées, toutes les subversions infinitésimales qui vous fascinent" (p. 192). Derrida pense aux modifications internes qu'un écrivain fait subir à la loi du genre et que le critique a le plaisir de reconnaître. Je crois qu'il faut pousser un peu plus loin cette idée. Il y a une transgression qui n'est pas la conséquence d'un ordre préétabli, mais qui préexiste à cet ordre: c'est l'anarchie primitive des langues, dont l'essai serait, de façon toujours imprévisible, la manifestation, signe d'un besoin de liberté antérieur à la fabrication des signes.

L'essai serait-il alors condamné à un succès d'estime accompagnant des réalisations exceptionnelles et inclassables? Ce fut le cas pour quatre siècles du travail que les langues modernes ont exercé sur elles-mêmes. Au XXe siècle, il me semble que la situation a changé, et telle est l'hypothèse que je voudrais "essayer": l'essai a envahi les genres institués, au point même que les genres établis sont devenus des *essais polarisés*, et que la production littéraire dans sa totalité est un immense laboratoire d'essais en toutes directions. Mon analyse se développera sur deux plans: 1) identification des formes profondes qui constituent la compétence (et dans certaines perspectives, l'incompétence) du langage de l'essai, quelles que soient ses expressions; 2) identification des principaux traits qui caractérisent la prise de possession du travail littéraire par l'essai en notre siècle. J'emploie délibérément le mot "travail," non pour donner un écho marxiste à mon hypothèse, mais pour écarter la métaphore du jeu, dont on abuse aujourd'hui en critique littéraire et dans la philosophie du langage.

I

Pour procéder à cette identification des formes profondes de l'essai au XXe siècle, il est naturel de faire appel au vocabulaire de la philosophie. Non pas que l'essai implique fatalement une philosophie, ou qu'il ait le langage philosophique pour domaine privilégié. En fait, il en va de la philosophie comme de la littérature: l'une et l'autre ont été pénétrées par l'essai dès le début de notre modernité; celui-ci refuse la forme du traité ou du système, comme il s'oppose au dogmatisme des genres. Il ne prétend pas s'emparer de la littérature au nom de la philosophie. Sa compétence, en tant qu'elle est immanente à toutes les manifestations linguistiques et culturelles, est une sorte de virtualité sémantique qu'on a appelée autrefois le génie ou l'esprit des langues. Je crois que les langues modernes sont dominées par trois forces ou intentionnalités, à l'intérieur desquelles, et parfois contre lesquelles l'infini des expressions linguistiques s'organise: l'*agnosticisme*, le *subjectivisme*, le *nominalisme*. Ces intentionnalités de langage sont irréductibles les unes aux autres: et il serait naïf de chercher à les déduire les unes des autres. L'histoire des pensées et cultures modernes décèle leur existence comme conditions et corrélations fondamentales de l'essai. Je me borne donc à les prendre comme donnés culturels, sans examiner leur causalité historique et structurelle.

Le terme "agnosticisme" a été créé par T. H. Huxley et il désigne, selon le *Vocabulaire de la philosophie* de Lalande soit la condamnation de toute métaphysique, soit les doctrines, fort variées, qui admettent l'existence d'un Inconnaissable. Il s'agit de deux aspects d'une même tendance qui a souvent servi à justifier la science moderne contre la métaphysique et la pensée religieuse. Mais cette définition, pour exacte qu'elle soit, est purement doctrinale; elle néglige les dimensions linguistiques prises par l'agnosticisme contemporain qui condamne, non seulement des options théoriques, mais, plus encore, un certain langage philosophique: être agnostique, c'est écarter le système comme état linguistique idéal et, en conséquence, la totalisation systématique comme fonction de rassemblement verbal et de cohérence; c'est dénoncer comme illusoire l'espoir d'enfermer les mots dans une unité conceptuelle faite de déductions ou de liaisons dialectiques; sans même aspirer à un langage ouvert, c'est accepter l'incomplétude essentielle des entreprises intellectuelles; on parlera ainsi d'oeuvre inachevée, de pluralisme irréductible, et même de littérature d'échec. Il eût été contradictoire de développer des pensées agnostiques dans un langage dogmatique et de les agencer en systèmes! De là dérive le besoin, qui est devenu une mode et souvent même un procédé, de la *fragmentation* du texte, avec le patronage de Nietzsche, qui a inventé pour l'agnostique la forme du discours tragique et révolté. Est-ce accident si Pascal hante tous les grands écrivains de notre siecle? Il est le modèle à imiter ou à rejeter, et toujours le maître du style pour la prose française abstraite qui trouve dans les *Pensées* sa forme indépassable. Pascal n'a-t-il pas justifié, avant les théories romantiques de l'essai, le discours fragmenté, quand il dénonce la vanité de la métaphysique, et qu'il souligne le caractère irréductible, inconciliable des principes premiers de la pensée?

Cependant l'agnosticisme contemporain a donné un ton nouveau au dialogue pascalien de la raison et de la foi. D'abord, même pour le croyant, il a rendu impossible l'espérance de l'unité de la connaissance par la théologie. Le mot "dieu" n'est plus la base du discours, ni sa fin; l'idée d'une ordonnance unique, linéaire, systématique, du langage est reconnue fallacieuse. Le langage devient un étrange palais où l'on peut entrer et sortir par n'importe quelle ouverture disponible. Il a cessé d'être un ordre classique ou baroque; il n'est plus temple, ni même cathédrale; il est la foire sur la place, cirque sans chapiteau. C'est dans ce milieu, je crois, que nous vivons, recevons et parfois créons nos langages. Il n'est certes pas interdit d'employer les mots "Dieu" et "Absolu," loin de là! Mais, quand ils interviennent, ils n'ont plus la fonction architecturale pour laquelle ils ont eté inventés. Ils évoquent la nostalgie d'une unité extra-linguistique, d'un au-delà, d'un in-dicible, au sens littéral du mot, de quelque chose qui ne peut pas être dit.

Ce sens d'un au-delà du langage n'était que latent chez Montaigne ou chez Pascal, ou encore chez les grands essayistes anglais. Aujourd'hui l'agnosticisme a prolongé la suspension sceptique du savoir par un doute radical sur le langage comme pouvoir de connaissance. Etre agnostique, ce n'est plus seulement restreindre les ambitions démesurées de la connaissance, ni retailler le système à la mesure de l'homme, ni organiser des permissions de cohérence, c'est être vraiment, littéralement, a-gnostique, refuser aux langages le pouvoir de connaissance que les cultures precédentes lui ont arrogé; c'est lui accorder, au contraire, un certain pouvoir d'être, c'est le comprendre comme complément d'être—non plus miroir clair ou déformant, mais produit de l'art, invention de signes et de sens. Les langues ne sont pas faites pour dire ce qui est; elles sont faites pour permettre à l'homme d'essayer de devenir ce qu'il dit. Si Montaigne a pressenti cette fonction du langage d'essai, l'essayiste contemporain a compris que son texte, avant d'être savoir, est invention.

Le doute vécu, parfois sceptique, parfois méthodique, du langage sur lui-même et sur sa prétention gnoséologique, conduit à la conscience de la *subjectivité* insurmontable de ses produits linguistiques. Depuis deux siècles les philosophes se sont évertués à construire toutes sortes de subjectivismes reconnus sous le nom d'idéalismes, dont la variété même—idéalismes phénoméniste, transcendantal, positiviste, absolu, phénoménolgique, etc.—suffit à dénoncer le rêve impossible, contradictoire, de mettre la subjectivité en langage théorique. Une philosophie comme celle de Sartre essaiera en vain de réserver l'aveu des tentations de son idéalisme subjectif et existentiel à l'intérieur du confessionnal marxiste. Or les débauches des idéalismes philosophiques se retrouvent chez les linguistes eux-mêmes qui ont fait de la subjectivité un caractère essentiel du langage. Ce n'est pas par hasard que la Nouvelle Critique a orchestré les déclarations de Benveniste: la subjectivité est "l'émergence dans l'être d'une propriété du langage."

Ces perspectives philosophiques et scientifiques sont-elles ellesmêmes les indices d'une attitude profonde du langage dans notre culture moderne? D'abord, reconnaître la subjectivité du signe créé par l'homme, c'est écarter le vieux rêve de la mimesis, tel, par exemple, qu'il s'exprime dans la formule thomiste: la vérité est l'adéquation du concept et de l'être, de l'esprit et des choses. Le discours moderne ne prétend plus à une telle adéquation, ni même à l'aveu de l'inadéquation. On a cru, et ce "on" désigne surtout les poètes d'avant le Surréalisme et, avec eux, des romanciers et des dramaturges, qu'il devrait être possible de faire de la subjectivité à la fois la matière et la forme de la littérature, en tant que celle-ci s'oppose à la science. Peu à peu nos langages ont rejeté cette solution. C'est ainsi que peut s'expliquer, pour notre siècle, le désarroi de plus en plus fort des genres et, parallèlement, leur envahissement par l'essai.

Le subjectivisme a entraîné une conséquence encore plus sérieuse pour la pratique du langage. Il s'agit de cette découverte: le caractère subjectif du langage réside dans sa *réflexivité*. Descartes sans doute avait été le premier à systématiser cette propriété du langage en essayant de fonder l'édifice entier du savoir sur la conscience de soi. Son langage d'alors avait inauguré une longue ère de psychologie métaphysique. Aujourd'hui un tel langage a cessé d'être vivant, et l'écrivain s'est aperçu que, pour affronter l'exigence de subjectivité, il devait trouver une solution technique à la réflexivité d'un discours qui n'est plus miroir des choses, mais miroir de lui-même: le visage réfléchi du Narcisse valéryen est le reflet de ses propres signes en lesquels il se perd: il se noie dans sa propre transparence. Marcel Proust est, je crois, le premier à avoir reconnu, dans sa portée pratique, le fait de la relation entre les caractères subjectif et réflexif des langues. Son oeuvre, qui montre mieux que tout autre comment l'essai prend possession du roman et qui ne s'appelle roman que dans un sens très relâché, est la solution du problème de l'expression du sujet par son reflet linguistique; elle est la réponse à l'exigence de réflexivité des signes retournés sur eux-mêmes. Un texte de *La Prisonnière* prouve que Proust a été conscient de l'originalité de sa découverte pratique et de sa portée historique. Se tournant vers les grands écrivains du XIXe siècle, il observe que Wagner et les écrivains ont produit des oeuvres qui sont "bien que merveilleusement—toujours incomplètes," et il juge que le XIXe siècle est celui "dont les grands écrivains ont manqué leurs livres, mais, se regardant travailler comme s'ils étaient à la fois l'ouvrier et le juge, ont tiré de cette auto contemplation une beauté nouvelle extérieure et supérieure à l'oeuvre, lui imposant rétroactivement une unité, une grandeur qu'elle n'a pas."[2] "Les plus grandes beautés de Michelet, il ne faut pas tant les chercher dans son oeuvre même que dans les attitudes qu'il prend en face de son oeuvre, non pas dans son *Histoire de la France* ou dans son *Histoire de la Révolution*, mais dans ses préfaces à ces deux livres" (p. 160). L'oeuvre ne doit donc pas être conçue comme un bloc de suffisance monolithique, comme "le calme bloc ici-bas" mallarméen; elle a besoin de se réfléchir, d'être à la fois en elle-même et hors d'elle-même. Avec la fabrication proustienne, l'un des aspects les plus significatifs de cette réflexion consiste dans l'insertion de la pensée théorique à l'intérieur du tissu narratif. Ce qui veut dire que pour Proust, l'universalité intemporelle de la pensée assure la transposition des événements remémorés. On parle souvent du cercle proustien, du reploiement de l'oeuvre sur elle-même. En fait, l'oeuvre s'ouvre sur son commentaire; la narration d'une genèse est doublée d'un essai sur la nature humaine. Et le problème technique de cette réflexivité du discours est une affaire de fragmentation et de rapports entre les fragments de l'oeuvre. Après ses remarques sur Michelet le narrateur proustien revient à Wagner et le loue pour savoir insérer un élément imprévisible dans une unité déjà constituée. C'est l'occasion de blâmer "tant de systématisations d'écrivains médiocres" et de condamner une littérature qui serait "le développement artificiel d'une thèse" (p. 161). Le jugement de Proust sur la littérature et les arts qui le précèdent nous fait comprendre la corrélation entre l'essai et la conscience subjective du langage qui, par sa pratique, est un exercice de réflexivité.

L'agnosticisme et le subjectivisme mettent en question la définition traditionnelle du vrai comme adéquation. L'un et l'autre s'accordent à voir dans les langues des créations autonomes de signes et de sens, et non une imitation, si habile soit-elle, de la réalité. Le dogmatisme de la connaissance et de l'art est ébranlé. Le genre logique cesse d'être modèle épistémologique ou esthétique. Une troisième attitude vient renforcer les deux précédentes; je propose de l'appeler *nominaliste*. L'histoire des idées enseigne que le nominalisme est un aspect récurrent des cultures et philosophies occidentales depuis le IVe siècle avant J.-C. Selon la tradition nominaliste, l'idée générale, avec son caractère d'essence universelle, de modèle platonicien ou de forme aristotélicienne, n'existe pas; il n'y a que des signes référés à des expériences individuelles. Avec le développement de la pensée scientifique, cette attitude philosophique a désigné toutes les théories de la science qui dénoncent le caractère artificiel, conventionnel, des principes. Or, au XXe siècle, le nominalisme a pris une nouvelle allure; il ne dit plus naïvement, avec Condillac, "l'art de raisonner se réduit à une langue bien faite" (*Logique*, ch. V); il dit que tout problème de pensée, théorique ou pratique, est d'abord un problème de langage, que la santé et les maladies des cultures humaines sont d'ordre linguistique, que le signe n'est pas instrument de pensée, mais production, fabrication, et qu'ainsi la science de l'homme qui est la plus générale et qui englobe toutes les autres est la sémiotique.

Cette perspective a eu de multiples répercussions intellectuelles et artistiques. L'une des plus frappantes a conduit, en littérature, a une quasi-obsession de la théorie de la littérature et des genres, au moment même où l'existence de l'une et des autres est mise en doute: le roman devient théorie du récit, et le poème, une doctrine de la poésie. L'essai fournit alors le mode d'expression qui donne satisfaction au besoin de théorie, et à plusieurs titres: d'abord, le problème n'est plus de trouver les règles de vérité dans l'usage des signes. Il s'agit de concevoir leur efficacité, leurs modes d'application dans telles ou telles circonstances; le savoir devient un savoir-faire qui ne dépend que de ses intuitions. Reconnaître la nécessité de l'intuition, c'est renoncer à l'organisation du langage en système, et accepter l'essai comme moyen de communication et d'expression. Selon les goûts, celui-ci sera mis au point provisoire d'un état de connaissance ou d'un état de choses, perspective à compléter par d'autres perspectives, un discours toujours à suivre, toujours à finir, et hanté par son propre fonctionnement. Ensuite le nominalisme conduit à l'idée du langage comme expérimentation. Montaigne a compris et illustré cette attitude mieux que quiconque. Cependant il resta attaché à l'idée de vérité, si élusive soit-elle. En suspendant l'exigence de vérité, l'essai moderne prend conscience de ses propres pouvoirs linguistiques. En ce sens il est sa propre expérimentation, mais les critères au nom desquels il exerce sa pratique linguistique sont mal définis. On parle beaucoup de *cohérence*, de nos jours. Je ne doute pas que le besoin de cohérence ne soit critère de l'essai, mais de façon superficielle. Il est d'autres critères auxquels la critique ne s'est pas encore intéressée, et qui appartiennent à la créativité des signes. Enfin, l'esprit nominaliste, qui garde la nostalgie des grands dogmatismes, ne peut s'empêcher de déprécier le langage au moment même où il l'exalte; il fait de la pensée un exercice de liberté ludique et ironique. La peur d'être dupe conduit à des rêves de destructions sémiotiques, à un sado-masochisme de l'écriture; la fragmentation du discours se transforme en mutilations joyeuses, en jeux de dissonnances intellectuelles. L'essai excelle en ces entreprises verbales où le discours sérieux s'achève en mots d'esprit, en pirouettes, dirait Valéry, et où les profondeurs de l'abstraction sont transmuées en fantaisies légères. L'essai se charge ainsi de toutes les paroles, de toutes les écritures: n'ai-je pas trouvé dans un *TV Guide* la définition suivante de l'essai "familier": "a casual, personal meditation, on a topic minuscule or cosmic—whatever happens to tickle or tick off the writer at the moment"; il se fait encore poème-énigme: la descendance nietzschéenne du fragment, concentré ou dilaté, est innombrable!

II

Voici maintenant quelques signes et preuves spécifiques de l'envahissement de notre espace-temps culturel par l'essai. Par cette analyse je n'espère pas épuiser la question. Quelques témoins sont convoqués; quelques états significatifs sont explorés; et ils se retrouvent à des degrés divers à travers toute notre production littéraire. Il me semble ainsi que notre culture agnostique, subjectiviste, nominaliste, a entraîné quatre révisions radicales dans notre conscience littéraire et, par voie de conséquences, dans la conscience des genres; je les désigne ainsi: 1) *la conscience de l'oeuvre à faire par delà les genres institués*; 2) *l'idée du langage comme contestation de la réalité*; 3) *la crise du porte-parole*; 4) *l'antinomie de la praxis et de la vision littéraires*.

1. L'écrivain a toujours été conscient d'une oeuvre à accomplir, et conscient d'un public, présent ou futur, connu ou inconnu, à qui il la destine. La tradition littéraire et ses "arts" successifs lui préparent en quelque sorte le terrain: les genres dessinent, délimitent, codifient les modes d'expression possibles. On peut ainsi choisir d'être poète, romancier, dramaturge. L'oeuvre rentre sagement, ou en rechignant, dans des cadres préétablis devant lesquels elle s'efface. Le doute sur la valeur de cet encadrement est corrélatif d'une nouvelle conscience de l'oeuvre comme transcendante aux genres en qui elle s'incarne. Les genres cessent d'être des fins pour devenir des moyens relatifs qu'il convient d'essayer les uns après les autres, parfois simultanément. Alors l'essai prend une revanche éclatante. Il n'est plus refoulé dans les genres dits mineurs. La qualification d'essayiste, tant soit peu méprisante ou au minimum protectrice, tend à disparaître. L'oeuvre toute entière, comprise comme unité immanente à la variété de ses manifestations, sera un immense essai—non plus forme statique du langage, mais dynamique de l'oeuvre, esprit du texte. Les conséquences pratiques de cette mutation

littéraire seront plus ou moins sensibles, selon la qualité révolutionnaire de l'écrivain. Elles se produiront de deux façons inverses: les genres établis, tout en conservant leur masque habituel, s'offriront comme des essais; l'essai lui-même, en tant que maîtrise du lexique abstrait, tiendra une place capitale, de telle sorte que la division traditionnelle entre philosophie et littérature s'estompera. Les philosophes eux-mêmes revendiqueront une place dans le panthéon littéraire, cependant que les écrivains, dociles aux genres, tenteront des incursions philosophiques et joueront avec les concepts les plus abstraits. André Gide et Albert Camus offrent deux exemples typiques d'un tel changement.

Gide s'est "essayé" dans tous les genres, les remettant sans cesse en question, corrigeant tout élan poétique par un contrôle critique, détruisant la narration par son commentaire, soutenant la fragmentation de ses oeuvres par la continuité d'un *Journal* qui les relativise et les nie au moment même où il les justifie. Et il arrive à son oeuvre le destin que Proust attribue à celle de Michelet: le lecteur s'adresse au *Journal,* au miroir, pour comprendre le sens final de l'oeuvre. Les éditeurs de la Bibliothèque le la Pléiade assemblent en un volume toutes les oeuvres de Gide sous le titre "Romans, récits, et soties, oeuvres lyriques," et ce volume s'oppose humblement aux deux volumes du *Journal.* Ils n'ont pas tort, ces éditeurs, mais ils n'ont pas raison! Le titre général d'Essai eût mieux convenu pour les trois volumes. Par exemple, des ouvrages tels que *L'Immoraliste, La Porte étroite,* sont à la surface des récits fort élégamment composés; en réalité, ils sont des essais moraux que la narration a pour fonction d'illustrer, à la manière de Platon offrant ses mythes pour agrémenter ses abstractions. Et que dire de *Paludes* ou des *Faux-Monnayeurs*, vrais chefs-d'oeuvre de sadisme romanesque? Cette fameuse "mise en abyme" qui hystérise la linéarité syntagmatique de l'écriture est l'écho de la réflexivité agnostique du langage contemporain. On a parlé à juste titre de "récit spéculaire," pour désigner ces emboîtements réciproques du récit et du récit de récit. Mais, derrière ce besoin de transformer le texte en un jeu de miroir, il y a une exigence plus profonde: si Gide se tortille ainsi et s'il ne peut dormir tranquille dans le lit d'un genre, c'est qu'il ne peut fondre en un seul texte l'événement et la réflexion morale. Son oeuvre, vue dans son ensemble, est la mise en abyme de l'essai dans le récit, l'un reflétant l'autre. Quant au *Journal*, il est le contraire d'un espace bien ordonné; il est une entière disponibilité de langage—pas même essai, simplement "essayage." Et l'on aimerait appliquer à l'oeuvre gidienne la formule de Valéry: elle est essai, en tant que *comédie de l'intellect.*

La formule est transférable à l'oeuvre de Camus, mais cette fois, il s'agit, en intention et en réalité, d'une *tragédie de l'intellect.* Camus a refusé les subtilités du texte mis en miroir, et son instinct d'écrivain l'a fait commencer par les textes de *L'Envers et l'endroit,* qu'il considère comme des essais, et qui sont à mi-chemin entre la méditation morale et l'anecdote vécue. L'essai et le récit y glissent l'un vers l'autre et forment une alliance qui est la marque de l'écriture camusienne. Dans la préface à la réédition de ces premiers "essais," en 1954, Camus a souligné à la fois la maladresse et la valeur "pour moi considérable" de ces textes; et il nous fait cet aveu: "Si, malgré tant d'efforts pour édifier un langage et faire revivre des mythes, je ne parviens pas un jour à récrire *L'Envers et l'endroit*, je ne serai jamais parvenu à rien, voilà ma conviction obscure." On sait que dans les phases de son oeuvre, qu'il dit "même pas commencée" en 1954, il a abandonné la fusion des genres qu'il avait spontanément réalisée dans les premiers essais. Il explore simultanément thèmes et images de l'absurde et de la révolte à l'aide des moyens distincts de l'essai, du roman et du théâtre. Quand il meurt, le même projet doit s'appliquer au mythe de la limite et de la mesure, au mythe de Némésis. Mais, sans jouer sur les mots, la séparation des genres opérée par Camus a été incomplète: toutes ses oeuvres—qu'elles se rattachent en surface au domaine du roman ou du théâtre, sont des essais; non pas des oeuvres à thèse, mais des pensées mythiques, des abstractions vécues en images, si bien que la différence entre des langages comme ceux de *La Peste*, des *Justes* et de *L'Homme révolté* n'est pas dans le genre. Les exigences du langage de l'essai transforment la narration et la dramatisation en expressions mythologiques. Toutefois il serait faux de dire que Camus a mis le roman, la nouvelle et le théâtre au service de l'essai, car il respecte cette "gauchissure" qui fait que le récit ou la tragédie ont leurs lois propres de création. En sens inverse, l'essai camusien emprunte au roman et au théâtre leur dynamique dramatique. Il est construit et vécu comme une tragédie de l'intellect. C'est dans cette perspective, me semble-t-il, qu'il est légitime de dire que, grâce à l'essai, le sens de l'oeuvre a transcendé les genres; la différence entre les genres devient relative, et parfois, négligeable.

2. Singulière coïncidence qui est l'indice d'impérieuses exigences culturelles, entre 1942 et 1943 paraissent trois essais dont l'effet continue à se faire sentir aujourd'hui—*Le Mythe de Sisyphe, L'Etre et le Néant, L'Expérience intérieure*. Le tumulte créé autour des deux premières oeuvres a empêché le public de reconnaître l'importance au moins égale du livre de Georges Bataille. Il y a sans doute d'autres raisons. L'auteur de *L'Expérience intérieure* était aussi celui de *Histoire de l'Oeil*; et les lecteurs ont souvent mal fait le lien nécessaire qui, pour Bataille, unissait mystique et pornographie. Jean-Paul Sartre, dans une étude consacrée à Bataille en Décembre 1943, a montré qu'il avait reconnu la signification exceptionnelle de ce texte qu'il désigne comme un "essai-martyre." Il rapproche Bataille de Pascal. Cependant il ne saisit pas l'originalité du nouveau langage introduit par l'auteur; il constate que l'essai est toujours à la recherche de son style, alors que, selon lui, le roman a déjà trouvé le sien. Ce qu'il manque de reconnaître, c'est que, pour Bataille, le

langage, lieu de communication, doit être, comme tel, *exigence incessante de contestation et de révolte*. Et telle est la fonction de l'essai: conduire le langage vers son au-delà, vers des expériences-limites extra-linguistiques par lesquelles il se perdra dans sa propre violence. Bataille cite cinq expériences excessives: d'abord et surtout, le rire-fou et l'érotisme; aussi, mais à un moindre degré, le sacrifice, la poésie et la méditation. Toutefois, chacune de ces expériences, originale par elle-même, se situe aussi par rapport à celle du langage, comme destructrice du système et, avant tout, de la théologie. Nietzsche est le modèle de pensée, l'inspirateur d'écriture. L'essai devient la forme nécessaire d'une pensée nouvelle par laquelle le langage entre en contestation éperdue avec lui-même. Georges Bataille appelle cette discipline intellectuelle "athéologie." Elle enseigne, non pas l'athéisme vulgaire, mais l'absence de Dieu, ou, plus justement, l'homme placé devant l'absence de Dieu. L'essai luttera donc contre les glissements insidieux de nos cultures vers les cristallisations théologiques de toutes espèces. Bataille compare le langage courant, dans sa pratique, à un enlisement continuel, contre lequel l'essai a pour fonction de résister: "la contestation demeurerait, à la vérité, impuissante en nous si elle se bornait au discours et à l'exhortation dramatique. Ce sable où nous nous enfonçons pour ne pas voir, est formé des mots, et la contestation, devant se servir d'eux, fait surgir—si je passe d'une image à une autre différente—à l'homme enlisé, se débattant, et que ses efforts enfoncent à coup sûr."[3] Ne haussons pas les épaules, en soupirant: voilà encore une de ces plaintes chroniques contre le langage! L'essai ne consiste ni à dire, ni à constater, mais à faire. Il est la vie même de la contestation, une sorte d'*amok* linguistique,[4] une tragédie de l'intelligence, faites d'explosions poétiques, de destructions logiques, de décristallisation athéologique, auprès desquelles la déconstruction de Derrida, qui pourtant en descend, paraît un peu fade et pédantesque. L'*acte du langage* est l'essai, avec ses trois principales fonctions, poétique, romanesque et méditative. C'est la Folie de la Croix dont Pascal parle, mais délivrée de sa protection scolastique; c'est la *nudité* de la croix du langage. Un texte de l'Avant-propos à *Bleu du ciel* montre comment se fait le passage de l'essai au roman: "Un peu plus, un peu moins, tout homme est suspendu aux *récits*, aux *romans*, qui lui révèlent la vérité multiple de la vie. Seuls les récits, lus parfois dans les transes, le situent devant le destin... Le récit qui révèle les possibilités de la vie n'appelle pas forcément, mais il appelle un moment de rage, sans lequel l'auteur serait aveugle à ces possibilités excessives. Je le crois: seule l'épreuve suffocante, impossible, donne à l'auteur le moyen d'atteindre la vision lointaine attendue par un lecteur las des proches limites imposées par les conventions."[5] Parmi les romans qui se prêtent à cette expérience suffocante, Bataille cite *Wuthering Heights, Le Procès, L'Idiot, Le Rouge et le Noir, Sarrazine*. La rage du récit commence par la révolte des abstractions.

3. N'est-ce pas reconnaître le caractère irréductible du roman par rapport à l'essai? A la surface, oui. Mais en profondeur, le récit est commandé par l'essai qui détient le pouvoir décristallisateur du sens. Il possède encore un autre pouvoir: *il met en question le porte-parole*, et ainsi, le droit de créer par le langage, des êtres autres que l'écrivain lui-même. Ici deux problèmes sont liés dont le XXe siècle a pris conscience dans ses oeuvres: qui est le porte-parole qui prend en charge mes paroles? Qui est "je"? Un tout autre problème que le "qui suis-je?" et quelle est la relation entre ce porte-parole et ces êtres auxquels un auteur essaie de donner vie par des mots? Descartes a fait la théorie d'un "je" nécessaire, en attachant toute pensée à un "je" substantiel qui en assume la responsabilité: moi qui médite et écris des méditations métaphysiques, j'existe comme réalité, une par-dessous la diversité de ses modes. L'écrivain aurait alors le droit de dire "je." La source de ces textes et de ces paroles serait fondée. Plus tard le Romantisme a vu dans ce "je" une puissance créatrice, un démiurge-maître de la production romanesque. Cependant ces actes de foi substantialiste et subjectiviste contenaient en eux-mêmes leur négation. Le roman ne sait plus aujourd'hui ce que signifie la création de caractères et de héros. Il s'absorbe dans ses propres techniques et devient essai sur la production du roman. L'essai lui-même, abandonnant les méthodes de l'historien et du critique qu'il appliquait scrupuleusement, mais qu'il cachait derrière un rideau de parade intellectuelle, se complaît aujourd'hui dans l'arbitraire prophétique qui unit la polémique et la poésie: comme vous l'avez deviné, je pense surtout ici aux essais récents des "nouveaux philosophes." Deux livres inclassables marquent deux moments significatifs dans cette tragi-comédie du porte-parole (est-il besoin de souligner que je prends cette expression dans son sens littéral: celui qui porte la parole, et en est aussi le vicaire): *Monsieur Teste* (1896) et *L'Innommable* (1952). Le héros valéryen est l'image de la frustration du porte-parole. Tout au long de la vie de son auteur, il a une existence récurrente, et fait des apparitions sporadiques. Cela commence par une soirée à l'Opéra, continue par une lettre d'authenticité douteuse (dit Valéry), celle d'Emilie Teste, se prolonge par des extraits d'un log-book, qui sont des aphorismes sans lien apparent entre eux, et finit, au moins provisoirement par une lettre du narrateur qui ne parle plus de son héros, mais de la scène littéraire parisienne. *Monsieur Teste*, qui pourrait porter en sous-titre: de l'impossibilité de créer un personnage qui soit votre propre masque, est l'histoire d'un échec. Paul Valéry découvre que le héros de la Comédie de l'Intellect dont il rêve, un nouveau Faust, en qui se réincarnerait Léonard de Vinci, Descartes et M. Dupin, le détective du conte d'Edgar Allan Poe, ne peut être qu'un porte-silence, qui condamne l'imaginaire littéraire et qui a pour idéal la prose abstraite. Est-ce alors l'idée d'un joueur d'abstractions, perdu dans la poursuite de combinaisons formelles

et vides? Par instant, oui: mais l'intention profonde est ailleurs, et elle est grave. On peut certes jouer à creer des personnages, émissaires et contre-émissaires du Je. Mais personne n'est dupe. La littérature devient passe-temps pour l'auteur comme pour le lecteur. Il ne faut donc pas dire "Je est un Autre" car "je" n'est ni moi ni l'autre; il est illusion. Et telle est encore la fonction de l'essai: rendre les genres conscients d'un échec radical: le mariage de l'abstrait et du concret est l'utopie littéraire par excellence. En pénétrant et dissolvant les genres, l'essai permet leur subsistance. Ce qui donne au roman et à la poésie de nouvelles fonctions de serviteurs de l'essai: non pas roman ou poésie philosophiques, mais roman ou poésie-essais. Quant à l'essai lui-même, tel que par exemple Paul Valéry le pratique, il est exercice ironique d'une intelligence qui ayant la pudeur du vrai, s'évade dans le mot d'esprit. Cinquante ans plus tard *Monsieur Teste* se métamorphose dans *L'Innommable* beckettien. Ce livre est la fin d'une trilogie romanesque et annonce la fin de l'écriture romanesque. "Je" congédie ses vicaires. Le porte-parole littéraire est impossible. La parole devient un drame pour société anonyme. Peut-être perçoit-on dans cet appel au silence, et sous le ronflement verbal qu'évoque Proust, dans le texte cité plus haut, l'exigence nouvelle de l'essai-drame. Derrière toutes les apparences de drames divers, il n'y a qu'une unique tragédie—celle de la nature du langage comme signe. Les genres ont pour fonction de faire oublier ce péché originel des mots. Mais en vain! C'est le sens de la prise de possession de la littérature par l'essai; c'est le sens de ces oeuvres qui se comportent à la fois comme arrêts de justice et comme peines subies. Devant l'incapacité de nommer et de créer ce qu'on nomme, seul subsiste l'essai qui est la mise en traitement de nos maladies sémantiques.

    4. Les genres ont donc été les gardiens du sens de nos langues; par leurs règles et leurs usages, ils ont canalisé les mots et servi d'intermédiaires efficaces à des philosophies de l'homme. En ébranlant les genres, l'essai a provoqué peu à peu la disparition de ces humanismes auxquels il semblait destiné. Il est encore associé à une autre crise de notre époque. L'homme est devenu conscient de lui-même comme culture, et aujourd'hui le mot "culture" sert à désigner une vision du monde dans la lumière de laquelle les hommes sentent, pensent et agissent. Les cultures sont étudiées par les anthropologues, et sont alors objets de science. Mais elles sont aussi objets de littérature: en témoignent, en notre siècle, le succès de tous ces livres qui évoquent l'âme d'un pays, d'un peuple, et l'orientation des historiens vers l'histoire culturelle, dont on peut se demander si les oeuvres sont des monographies scientifiques ou des essais. Est-ce la raison pour laquelle André Malraux, dans *L'Homme précaire et la littérature,* déclare que Oswald Spengler est le plus grand essayiste de notre siècle? Je crois que Malraux a raison s'il a voulu dire par là que l'essai est le seul moyen par

lequel l'intelligence humaine puisse se faire visionnaire et s'absorber dans la vision d'elle-même comme culture. On pressent aussi que le mot "culture" est devenu le substitut du mot "Dieu" dans un univers agnostique. A ce titre l'oeuvre d'André Malraux, prise dans sa totalité entre l'imaginaire de récit et l'imaginaire de l'art, est exemplaire. *La Tentation de l'Occident* répond au *Déclin de l'Occident*. L'opposition entre les deux oeuvres est technique avant d'être théorique. Spengler s'efforce de contenir son lyrisme visionnaire dans les cadres d'un discours spéculatif qu'il croit être le seul langage objectif possible, quand l'homme se prend pour objet de connaissance. André Malraux, moins d'une genération après, comprend intuitivement que l'essai ne peut singer l'objectivité scientifique. Il n'a pas pour charge de parler sur les cultures, de les décrire et de les expliquer. L'essai est le moyen d'expression et de création culturelles, comme à d'autres époques, ce fut la sculpture, la peinture, le roman. Il est aujourd'hui l'homme se généralisant et se prophétisant. Il est le sens de l'éternité humaine dressée contre le flux des métamorphoses de l'histoire. Inspiré par cette intuition culturelle, Malraux choisit dans son essai deux porte-paroles à peine caractérisés, un Français et un Chinois: ils échangent des lettres qui d'ailleurs ne se répondent guère. Deux perspectives, l'une historisante, l'autre éternisante, mesurent leurs différences; elles s'affrontent sans se combattre. La lettre impose à l'essai une fragmentation naturelle et écarte les problèmes de commencement et de fin d'écriture. Evénements et faits sont réduits au minimum. On assiste à des élaborations successives de grandes catégories philosophiques, telles que temps, éternité. mort, liberté, création, devenir, etc. Ces élaborations révèlent l'impossibilité d'une cohérence culturelle: non plus déclin de l'Occident, mais déclin de toute culture! Telle est la conclusion inévitable. Et pourtant, avec Malraux encore, l'essai a gardé une nostalgie de théologie: si les cultures sont plurielles, en elles-mêmes elles offrent la possibilité d'une vision unifiante, en quête de laquelle Malraux s'est lancé, avec ses romans et ses études sur l'art. Le langage malraucien croit encore à la possibilité de son expression théorique. Après Malraux, l'essai prend conscience de son impuissance tragique à être vision. Quand il invente un langage, il ne peut plus prétendre voir le monde qu'il crée. Presque un demi-siècle après *La Tentation de l'Occident* en 1970, *L'Empire des signes* de Roland Barthes prouve que le pouvoir visionnaire de l'essai est limité par le langage même. La vision est brouillée, parcellaire; les abstractions confessent leur incommunicabilité; seul subsiste le geste unique du langage, dans le haïku, où l'essai et le poème ne se distinguent plus, dans une chance de vision qui est une chance de pensée. La brève introduction que Barthes donne à son essai, enregistre l'échec de l'écriture. Elle annonce que la double expérience du texte et des images est à la fois "une sorte de vacillement visuel" et "une perte de *sens*": l'une avec l'autre assurent l'échange des signifiants, et dans cet échange il faut "lire le recul des signes." Pouvons-nous lire davantage et dire qu'en 1970 l'essai abandonne son vêtement de sens et son espoir de vision? Il n'est plus qu'un langage où le signe a renoncé à devenir autre que lui-même. L'autre du signe est encore un signe. Alors, le recul des signes annonce-t-il le déclin de l'essai au moment même de son triomphe?

Il serait vain de jouer au prophète. Quel que soit son avenir, l'essai qui a toujours exprimé la vie des idées abstraites échappées des camps retranchés de la science et de l'idéologie, trouvera toujours le moyen de se manifester, par éclairs, par fragments, par dispersion sans cesse reprise. Pour terminer ces réflexions qui rejettent toute conclusion, je propose une définition fonctionnelle de l'essai, car s'il est légitime de dire que l'essai défie sa propre histoire et est prêt aujourd'hui à renoncer à son avenir, il serait trop commode de le juger indéfinissable; et la définition que je risque a pour objet d'inviter à de nouvelles analyses: après un effort de compréhension historique, comme celui que je viens de tenter, il serait profitable de méditer sur la nature du signe abstrait, sur ce pouvoir d'abstraction qui, je crois, est responsable des avatars de l'essai pendant quatre siècles. En bref l'essai est une *exigence stylistique d'abstraction*; il est une *systématisation relative et locale d'idées abstraites saisies intuitivement et en liberté, gardant leur nudité conceptuelle ou cherchant l'enveloppe charnelle des images.*

---

[1] "La loi du genre," *Glyph. Textual Studies 7* (Baltimore: The John Hopkins University Press, 1980), p. 200.

[2] *A la Recherche du temps perdu* (Paris: Gallimard [Bibliothèque de la Pléiade]), III, 160-162.

[3] *Œuvres complètes*, tome V, p. 26.

[4] Cf. *Tel Quel*, No. 10, p. 11.

[5] *Œuvres complètes*, tome III, p. 381.

French Literary Criticism (1945–1975): An Overview

Laurent LeSage
Pennsylvania State University

I had misgivings about accepting an invitation to speak on contemporary trends in French criticism because of the most recent involvement in linguistics, a field where I do not easily follow. The new criticism that I had written about in a book of the sixties has been, as you know, superceded by the new new criticism, and I was already uncomfortable enough with the former, now called thematic, hermeneutical, or phenomenological. The new new criticism with its jargon and its charts seemed far more baffling and tedious. In the recent little essay of Roland Barthes, ironically, I suppose, entitled *Plaisir du texte*, I have copied out a whole page of expressions that might give one pause. There are technical words drawn from rhetoric such as anacoluthon and asyndeton, from sociology such as potlatch, fractured citations such as "semina aeternitatis," "eppur si gaude," playful exploitations such as "doxa-paradoxa," zen words "mushotoku," words invented or recast—"imprévision, scripteur, trivialismes citationnels, hétérologie par plénitude, groupusculaire." Ordinary words are given special meanings. As for charts, in Jean Ricardou's recent work on the new novel, there is a curious one demonstrating the erotic significance of the title of his *Prise de Constantinople*, a line drawing of a female nude, the whole constituting a modern blazon on the level of "Oh, Calcutta." I decided, however, that if I felt a bit outside it all, many others might feel the same, that, for an over view, an outsider might be as useful as an insider, that a veteran teacher of literature and of French, with no cause to further other than to present France to Americans, might initiate a discussion of the subject in relation to our own pedagogy and our own scholarship. French literature today has become increasingly élitish—in poetry, the novel, the theater, as well as in criticism—and requires initiation and reorientation. Whether French teachers abroad conventionally trained can cope with it or whether literature can function as in the past, to be the chief means of introducing foreign students to French culture is open to question. I should like to return to this matter in closing. Let me first review with you the successive developments of French criticism leading up to the present situation; starting with the first advance-guard after World War II.

At that time Jean-Paul Sartre emerged as the intellectual leader of youth. The Existential generation read his condemnation of Giraudoux for his Aristotelianism, Mauriac for his authorian control over his characters, Faulkner for denying his characters a future. The technical implications of Sartre's literary criticism would be exploited later. What Albérès, Picon, Simon, Boisdeffre heard was the philosophic message. Trying to orient themselves in the postwar world, preoccupied with "engagement," such critics were seeking in literature a concept of life, answers to the questions of how to live and why. They reported the death of the humanistic ideal and the birth of the tragic vision. Man, as they composed his picture from the authors in vogue, is an anguished being in a hostile universe and the hero is he who never permits himself any self-delusion nor shirks the responsibility for his own life or for another's. What happened to these critics who sought in literature moral and metaphysical lessons, which they often expounded in impassioned prose? They went on to accept directorships, university chairs, and positions in important journals. Today Albérès and Boisdeffre continue to survey the literary scenes, but with less emotion, they have become historians. Their place as young Turks was taken by another generation in the latter 1950s, a generation interested not in what a work says but how it came into being.

Although this new school of criticism exhibited a marked change in interest, what came to be known as "la nouvelle critique" was more, actually, an outgrowth of the immediate postwar criticism than a contrary movement. The two had in common a fundamental opposition to the major critical traditions that preceded them. The classical method, with its rules and emphasis upon value judgment, was too restrictive. The impressionistic method was not serious enough. The nineteenth-century deterministic or scientific method rested on philosophical postulates discredited by Existentialism. Both schools were in Sartre's debt, the first reflecting his metaphysical and ethical ideas, the second following his lead in psychology and its implications for literature. It is worth recalling that one of Sartre's earliest books was an essay on the imagination, the processes of which constitute the principal study of the new critics. Moreover, his studies of Baudelaire and of Jean Genet developed the techniques of existential psychoanalysis, which provided the new "phenomenological" critics with a method. Yet, although Sartre deserves the most important place among the precursors of the new school, its members preferred to acknowledge other masters, namely Marcel Raymond and Albert Béguin, both professors in Switzerland and authors, so to speak, each of a single book.

Marcel Raymond's book *De Baudelaire au Surréalisme* claimed to repudiate the objective method, to have traced the history of modern poetry not by influences and conscious borrowings but by inner affiliations and relationships. Albert Béguin's *L'Ame romantique et le rêve* emphasized the role of the unconscious in artistic creation and thus paved the way for all the "thematic" studies that would follow. Before his death in 1957 he had the opportunity of giving his blessing to the new school and named Gaston Bachelard and Georges Poulet, plus some young writers like Jean-Pierre Richard and Roland Barthes, as critics of particular interest.

Gaston Bachelard, who died in 1962 at the age of 78, was a Sorbonne professor of the philosophy of science. Through his successive studies on the poetic imagination we may follow his gradual loss of faith in the basic assumptions of science (causality, etc.) and his conversion to phenomenology. Phenomenology, imported into France along with Existentialism, had won great favor with the young intellectuals of the 1950s and has made itself felt in all the developments in French literature since, especially in the novel and in the successive styles of criticism. Serge Doubrovsky in "La Critique comme phénoménologie" says "l'étude des structures littéraires relève d'une phénoménologie propre, c'est-à-dire de la description d'une organisation, mieux, d'une organicité interne de l'oeuvre." The present-day advance-guard is also phenomenological because it criticises itself while criticising. Bachelard had adapted the language of psychoanalysis to his phenomenological investigations of the images created by art but his method and his aim concerned the work of art and not the artist. The same is true of Poulet, whose analysis of French literary classics centered on the works themselves. Dealing with manifestations of the concepts of time and space, Poulet exemplifies the type of subjective, creative criticism that replaced moral lessons or external description of the literary work. Poulet's academic career stretches from Edinburgh, where he first published his studies on time in literature during the fifties, through a stint at Johns Hopkins (which, incidentally, has since remained in close contact with prominent French critics) through Zurich to Geneva. He is, one may say, the dean of thematic criticism.

Such were the professors of literature who inspired the critics of the 1960s. The new critics were critics of the unconscious, as Sarah Lawall has called them, phenomenological or descriptive critics if one thinks of the German tradition and of Heidegger whose influence, as I have indicated, has spanned several generations, thematic critics, since they sought in the work of an author patterns of his imagination, his complexes, personal symbols, drives, and phobias. They are now often called hermeneutic critics. Like their elders they are professors of literature. Jean-Pierre Richard declared himself to be a disciple of Poulet and of Bachelard in his analyses of the creative imagination. He showed us a Stendhal dominated by a duality or an ambivalence expressed symbolically in his work in terms of geography and society, a Flaubert reduced to a voracious appetite and a weak liver—he dreamed of life and of exotic dishes, but he could tolerate only the diet of Croisset! Jean

Rousset dedicated to Georges Poulet his *Forme et Signification*, in which he attempted to show how the message of a work is bound up in its compositional patterns. Jean-Paul Weber ferreted out Alfred de Vigny's obsession with clocks and demonstrated the symbolic expression of this obsession proliferating throughout Vigny's works. Jean Starobinski showed how imagery of looking (*le complexe du regard*) translated in literature various drives that he discerned in the authors. René Girard established triangular patterns involving motivation in works from *Don Quixote to Madame Bovary*. This theory of the referred good caught the attention of Lucien Goldmann, a Marxist critic, who exploited its sociological implications. The bridge between sociology and psychoanalysis was the achievement of Charles Mauron in analyzing Molière's audiences.

We have noticed how frequently these critics borrow techniques and vocabulary from psychoanalysis without, however, pledging full allegiance to Freud or his colleagues. They are literary critics not doctors, although Starobinski actually does have a medical degree. A Sartre who would explain an author by an early "choice" or a Barthes who ransacks the bedchamber have little in common with the professionals like Baudouin or Bonaparte. Likewise the sociological critics like Goldmann belong more to literature than to science, those who look for the intimate structure of the work in the "zeitgeist" rather than in the "erlebnis" of the author, to use the terms of Wilhelm Dilthey, a German critic who has been rediscovered by the present generation. Marxism is represented by critics of various tactics and beliefs from the relative orthodoxy of Goldmann to the free and theoretical interpretation of Althusser or Pierre Macherey, passing by occasional borrowings by critics from Sartre to Kristeva. But even an enemy of the bourgeoisie like François Vernier (*L'Ecriture et les textes*, 1974) does little more than plead for a knowledge of social background as a means of understanding a work. One might best understand the relationship of criticism to Marxism as a "mining" operation rather than as party allegiance. As a mining operation, the relationship to psychoanalysis since critics follow the unorthodox readings of Jacques Lacan. As a mining operation, the relationship between criticism and linguistics. When specialists like Georges Mounin point out that the critics' concept of linguistics is superficial or out of date, they are answered with a shrug. Possibly it is best to see criticism in relation to other disciplines somewhat like Balzac or Zola in relation to the positivistic sciences of their day—catalyst, no more, or figure of speech. Thus the distinction that has been made between pure literary analysis and that involving something else is in most cases unreal or unimportant.

The heyday of thematic criticism was the mid-sixties when, as the "nouvelle critique," it obtained wide notoriety through its quarrel with the objective literary historians of the Sorbonne, particularly Jean

Pommier and Raymond Picard. Pamphlets were written, insults exchanged, conventions convened. But already their successors were making ready to take over. This time there were no noisy recriminations, no diatribes. The thematic critics simply faded out of prominence. Goldmann and Charles Mauron died, likewise the champions of the university. Critics like Richard have gone on writing, but, although still dealing with thematics, show the influence of more recent developments in criticism. An explanation for the coup d'état without bloodshed is the continuous, unifying presence of Roland Barthes, who has consistently moved with the times, from the early days of the "nouveau roman," through psychoanalytical and archetypal criticism to structuralism and semiology. Roland Barthes is surely the contemporary critic with the widest span. We remember him first as Boswell to Robbe-Grillet, explaining what the "nouveau roman" was trying to do. The articles collected in Le *Degré zéro de l'écriture* established him as a theorist of importance, with a new emphasis and expression. Existentialist emphasis on message shifted with Barthes to code; the message that interested him was the one implicit in the code, sociological and political in nature rather than humanistic and metaphysical. In a sense all Barthes was here already in this first book—and all of the "Nouvelle nouvelle critique," for that matter. Each successive publication of Barthes since is just an unfolding, making manifest what was latent in the first book. Thus the *Michelet* impinges on psychoanalysis, *Racine* on archetypal analysis, *Mythologies*, etc. anthropology and structuralism.

Structuralism came into vogue in the latter half of the 1960s. Michel Foucault's *Les Mots et les Choses* took a place occupied twenty years earlier by *L'Etre et le Néant*. It opposed to the diachronic approach to literary history the synchronic and, on the basis of the relationship between sign and referent, presented European culture since the Renaissance in separate culture blocks or systems, "epistemé." Lévi-Strauss studied primitive peoples not from the point of view of living condition or historical development but from myth, taboo. Jacques Lacan reinterpreted Freud, Louis Althusser reaffirmed Marx. What brought together these leaders of different disciplines was the importance given language. As Emile Benveniste stated in *Problèmes de linguistique générale*, one cannot think without language. In repudiating empiricism in favor of abstract science they turned to linguistics. Roland Barthes joined them and brought literary criticism with him. In *Critique et Vérité*, after citing Lacan and Lévi-Strauss for having broken with the traditional methods of their disciplines, he declared that it was now the turn of literary criticism. Psychoanalysis and structuralism had shown language to be a system of signs instead of an instrument. He called for a science of literature and alluded to Naom Chomsky. In accounting for the appeal of the thematic as well as the structuralist approach one must think first of the appeal of coherence over fragmentation, then the appeal of scientific status for something once thought of as only the adventure of a man of culture among his books. Structuralism replaced causality by relationship; linguistics offered method and terms tempting for literary analysis.

As we know, Barthes' summons did not fall on deaf ears. From his post in the Ecole des Hautes Etudes and his place on editorial boards of journals, by his lectures, seminars, and articles, Barthes became a sort of guru for young French intellectuals. The magazine *Tel Quel*, founded at the beginning of the sixties emerged as the first rallying point for the new new critics. The novelist editor Philippe Sollers had surrounded himself with a group of young novelists, poets, professors, who gradually formed the new advance-guard in French literary criticism. Their point of departure was structuralism and one of the group, Gérard Genette, explained that the critic's work is "bricolage" in the sense Lévi-Strauss defines the process for anthropology— making something new out of old pieces. Through the several volumes of his collected articles, *Figures*, one may follow the attempt of critics to situate their work in the structuralist frame and, by digging out the old rhetoric manuals buried for 150 years, lay the foundation for a new scientific rhetoric. Its application can be seen in Genette's own studies appearing in these volumes, the latest one being devoted to Proust. His procedures are perhaps easier to follow in a shorter study such as one on Robbe-Grillet, in which he presents a narrative pattern as a basic theme with echoes, parallels, modulations. His terminology suggests grammar and rhetoric however, instead of music. Another member of the group, Jean Ricardou used Robbe-Grillet also to demonstrate one of his basic contentions—that writing is an autonomous system, not a vehicle for thought. *La Jalousie*, the word, generates the story. In his *Problèmes du roman* he would demonstrate over and over again that fiction is not the writing of a story but the story of a writing. Like the others, Ricardou praises Paul Valéry for his emphasis on art as creation of things. A favorite quote is "La littérature est et ne peut pas être autre chose qu'une sorte d'extension et d'application de certaines propriétés du langage." Sollers, Ricardou, and Jean Thibaudeau have frequently used their own writing as illustration. We speak of all three as novelists but Thibaudeau's remark that the difference between a poem and a novel is only one of length points up the general tendency of critics to abandon distinction between genres to consider just creative writing and ultimately just writing as such, just texts.

J. P. Faye was with Ricardou and Thibaudeau an early confederate of Sollers. As a critic this novelist gained notoriety for his *Récit Hunique*, witty and erudite commentaries on new criticism and the new novel. His position in the Structuralist controversy was against Sartre, although he felt some personal sympathy. In 1968 Faye broke with Sollers and founded *Change*. The story of this squabble, chiefly political, is recorded in *L'Esprit Créateur* as told by Faye to Mary Ann Caws. If the new novel was tied to the publishing house of Minuit, the new criticism is tied to Seuil, which supported for several years *Change* as well as *Tel Quel* and the more recent *Poétique*. In its volume publication it gives generous emphasis to critical studies, suggesting that criticism is highly salable in France today. *Communications* and *Littérature* are directly connected with the university, but I assume that the other periodicals are commercial. The phenomenon of the Editions du Seuil publishing long critical monographs and supporting periodicals engaged in internecine conflict is a curious one viewed from this country where even our underwritten university presses have an eye for figures. Like *Tel Quel*, *Change* appeals to leftish intellectuals and persons not offended by five-letter words. It is interested in the United States, accepting contributions from Americans and reporting on personalities like Angela Davis and Naom Chomsky. The thrust is linguistic, transformational analysis of literature. Faye's most recent volume deals with language, following the pattern set by Barthes in exposing the propaganda hidden in language. *Tel Quel*, which had gradually become overtly political, veered from Russian to Chinese communism by the end of the sixties. Ricardou and Thibaudeau refused to follow Sollers and, like Faye before them, broke with *Tel Quel*. I do not know the details of the differences between Sollers and his associates, but all are political to a degree. The young writers, without being "engaged" in the old-fashioned Sartrian sense, are quite conscious of the ideological commitment implied in any form of art. Faye has accused Sollers of being fundamentally reactionary and self-contradictory.

Tel Quel's novelists have shared space with poets and philosophers. Michel Deguy, professor and editor of a poetry magazine, blends poetry and criticism of poetry in his articles. He too has been interviewed by Mrs. Caws. Jacques Derrida, philosophy professor at the Ecole Normale and this year visiting at Johns Hopkins, theorizes about writing, for him so broad a word (language is only one aspect of writing) that it is tantamount to symbolification. Derrida's articles have been collected in *De la grammatologie* and *L'Ecriture et la différence*, both major texts in the recent history of literary criticism in France. We might note that if the first new critics seem associated with Geneva, the present group constitutes a Paris school. Ecole Normale, Ecole Libre des Hautes Etudes, the various branches of the new Sorbonne define its geographical limits. In Derrida's theory philosophy and grammar mingle and their terminology is interchangeable. Grammatology and ontology are synonyms; other critics make the same association between ontology and rhetoric. Derrida has explained himself on many occasions, but notably with Julia Kristeva a few years ago. He has since broken with Sollers and *Tel Quel*, presumably on political grounds.

The conversation between Derrida and Kristeva is recorded in *Positions*, an important source of documentation that dates from 1972. Its mention brings us to one of the most remarkable of the new new critics and collaborators of *Tel Quel*, Julia Kristeva, now Madame Sollers. She was born in 1941 in Bulgaria and has a background in philosophy. In her numerous articles and books she has preached and practiced literary analysis as a branch of semiotics. There is no more question of author or of esthetic consideration. Structuralism and generative grammar now taken for granted as approaches to literature, Kristeva has sought to add the diachronic dimension by recourse to Marxism as a means of integrating the work into history. Like her colleagues she takes from Marx, as from Freud, only theory—in this case the dialectical process. I believe that this is the newest development in criticism, the move away from the taxonomy that characterized structuralism as it developed in the sixties. Otherwise the seventies seem reaffirming and consolidating positions taken in the 1960s. To be sure techniques of analysis have been refined and elaborated. Patrick Brady, who promises to deal generally with the subject in a forthcoming *Structural Perspectives in Fiction Criticism*, has already begun, in articles, a classification—the actantial sort with Greimas which studies the patterns made by the characters, the modal with Todorov particularly concerned with narration, etc. Professor Brady groups the techniques under the general title of functional analysis, functional kernels being the term which has been applied to the units of narrative meaning.

Julia Kristeva's first work dealt with fiction: *Le Texte du roman*, "approche sémiologique d'une structure discursive transformationelle." The subject is the medieval monument *Le Petit Jehan de Saintré*, the fictional patterns of which she sees in terms of generative grammar. The subject of the book is treated as the subject of a sentence, the story development in terms of predicate of a sentence and of deep and surface structure. Other critics will describe structural relationships in fiction in terms of voice and mood of verbs. Kristeva's analysis is not strictly linguistic but something of a mixture with elements of Hegelian philosophy and symbolic logic. In the more recent *Révolution poétique*, in spite of the title, the concerns are more sociological and historical than literary. Her subject is the innovative poets of the late nineteenth century—Mallarmé, Rimbaud, Lautréamont, who seem to Kristeva to have brought to a crashing halt a two-thousand year old civilization. Her evidence involves what seem far-fetched analogies and unnecessarily complicated and pedantic terms. Most arresting is the yoking of phonetics with psychiatry as follows: "the frequence of the non-voiced dental (s) indicates a urethral phallic tension."

Tzvetan Todorov is another young émigré from Bulgaria. More than anyone else Todorov is responsible for making known in France the Russian formalist group of which Roman Jakobson, who has long been in America, is the prominent surviving member. Taking up Jakobson's concept of "literarity" as the subject of literary criticism, Todorov offers an alternate word, poeticity. On this basis Todorov entitled a book *Poétique de la prose* and a magazine *Poétique*, which he founded in company with Genette and the novelist and Joyce scholar Hélène Cixous. Todorov's poeticity is conceived of as a closed system, susceptible to transformation like grammar, definable in terms of rhetorical figures. Had not Jacques Lacan suggested that tropes translate structures of the mind? A quote from Jakobson that turns up frequently in the new new criticism is to the effect that literary criticism without linguistics is unthinkable just as linguistics is unthinkable without literature. Todorov reiterates the mutual benefits to be derived from collaboration.

One should not want to dispute such a contention. Particularly if the term literature is stretched to mean more than what used to be thought of as literature, more than belles-lettres, the material of our literature departments. The new critics who declare their indifference to subject and to expression in so far as it concerns talent or genius, who have sociological or political interests, would seem to be oriented towards the "literature" that Roland Barthes dealt with in *Le Système de la mode*, that is "para-literature," an anonymous language phenomenon with all the denotations, connotations, implications that are varieties of metonymy. Whether expressed in terms of rhetoric or of linguistics (signified, signifier, sign), the process studied by the new critics is that of symbolification, a basic human faculty best shown in language. It is usually associated in this country more with sociology or speech departments than with literature. Paradoxically the subjects that the French have been using for their study are, in the main, the monuments of belles-lettres—and the most remote, the most recherché. Kristeva with *Le Petit Jehan de Saintré*, Genette with Sponde or DuBellay, Todorov with medieval and Renaissance authors, Ricardou with the "nouveaux-romanciers"—outside an extremely narrow group of professors, such work has really no public at all. One might suspect a big spoof, a "canular." For literature in its traditional narrow sense is simply not important enough any more to be treated as if it were a great power to be reckoned with in a culture. Can Kristeva really believe that a world came to an end with Mallarmé? For a group that has taken up the Surrealist slogan that literature is to be created by everyone, their choice of revered masters is odd, being restricted to a few mandarin or mad poets and if, as Léon Roudiez has direly intimated, their goal is, as was the Surrealists', to change the world, with banner bearing the names Rimbaud, Sade, Artaud, Mallarmé, their attack could only capture a fashion-conscious intellectual élite, the sort of élite that would be titillated by the precious and pedantic essays that these critics write. Periodicals like *Tel Quel, Change, Poétique, Communications, Littérature* can scarcely have readers beyond the initiated. Unreadable themselves and dealing chiefly with the unread, the semiological critics would seem to have a very slight revolutionary potentiality.

Yet, one might object, this is part of a general development in the arts, and literary criticism is actually a late comer. In the plastic arts, in music, in poetry, the novel, the theater, formalism has long been an accomplished fact and the combination élitism and revolutionary involvement taken for granted. If the immediate public is small, it acts as teacher and guide to the general public; gradually a new orientation becomes a conventional approach. Moreover, with time, claims and repudiations become less violent and a revolution becomes a modification and an enrichment of the art. Even a movement denying historicity can be integrated into history. What seem like absurd overstatements today may be seen more properly as new emphasis, lighting from a new angle. Too long, form in art had been ignored in favor of content. It was only a healthy reaction to present a piece of literature as a verbal construct with its independent laws and generative powers. Nothing more natural than to have involved linguistics, the new science. But synthesis seems ultimately inevitable, if only through recognition of the complicated interplay of form and content. My optimism is a good example of the pacification process that Léon Roudiez has warned against and called "récupération universitaire."

It may be just a minor vexation to have to struggle through a welter of jargon and murky prose to arrive at the obvious. (Genette has appended a glossary to his latest *Figures*.) Too often the new essays seem arsenals of platitudes camouflaged by language. Problems of denotation and connotation, figurative language, possibilities of paronomasia, parallels, opposites, the contiguous have always, I suppose, been mulled over. The relation of language to thought is a subject as old as language; one need not be a specialist in psychology, being a simple foreign language teacher is enough to know that Aristotle's thinking had something to do with the fact that his language was Greek. Or to know that Barthes' lumping Chinese and Japanese thinking on the basis of language indicates an extremely summary knowledge. Exactly to what extent language informs thought might well be left to psycholinguists. The implications for literature as stated by our critics are not unknown to us—that in writing, frequently the pen takes over, the vehicle drives itself, that description can even "generate" plot. It is not new to read that literature is patterned, as we learn from Todorov regarding the novels of James. Barthes' analysis of what makes a writer write seems to take him (via Wittgenstein, I suppose) back to the "spieltrieb" esthetic propounded by Schiller. His rhetorical display to establish the distinction between language and style takes him directly back to Buffon. To interpret a text as a galaxy of signifiers sounds like what used to be referred to as levels of ambiguity, even implied in the old phase universality. When Deleuze and Genette consider Proust's novel as Marcel's initiation into signs, we know what they mean because they are merely stating what we knew already, but in a metaphor that captures the attention and focuses it upon an essential feature. If the borrowing from other disciplines like linguistics can be considered just metaphorically, it is of course easier to accept; we can get used to it just as we have accepted for literary criticism terminology borrowed from architecture, geography, needlework, etc. But most critics, we feel sure, would not agree to such an interpretation. Yet they are not clear as to how exactly the linguistic method is to be applied. Now literature is to be thought of as a semiological system that a work can demonstrate, now it is the work itself that conducts the investigation.

But it may be an indication of growth and development that inconsistencies and incompletions can be detected in arguments. Todorov followed Greimas in classification of substantives for his analysis of *Liaisons dangereuses*; for Boccaccio he replaces hero, etc. for proper names. In her attempt to break out of the ideology box, Kristeva argues for a shifting norm, as the only concept admissible as basic for poetic analysis, a "genotype" that is a sort of historical composite. This dissolves the notion of a fixed meaning behind the signifier, with the signifier thereby assuming the role of the signified. This freedom so heady for Kristeva and Derrida is somewhat illusory as long as there is a possibility of rejection of some interpretation. Freedom depends then upon barriers and one is still a prisoner of an ideology. Such speculations lead to affirmations without proof, paradoxes, theory without material support. Derrida asks us to pretend that we are out of the box although he admits we cannot be. Either I do not understand his meaning, or it is verbal play, or it is rephrasing of the old "an sich/fur sich" dichotomy. When Michel Foucault announces that the self is a rather recent invention, he seems original only in phraseology; the cultural history of individualism and egocentrism is familiar to anyone who has had a survey course in the Romantic movement. Of course Roland Barthes is the model for all this thrust into ontological speculation. Already in *Le Degré zéro* we had trouble as the sense of the title seemed to change during the course of the exposition. In *Le Plaisir du texte* we find that his line of argument is still a sort of legerdemain: "On dit couramment 'idéologie dominante'. Cette expression est incongrue. Car l'idéologie, c'est quoi? C'est précisément l'idée *en tant qu'elle domine*: l'idéologie ne peut être que dominante. Autant il est juste de parler d'idéologie de la classe dominante parce qu'il existe bien une classe dominée, autant il est inconséquent de parler d'"idéologie dominante' parce qu'il n'y a pas d'idéologie dominée..." If Barthes set the example of specious reasoning, he also created a model for hairsplitting distinctions and private definitions so that style, language, text, literature must be constantly redefined and words like logocentric, phonocentric, metalinguistic guessed at.

A recent book by an English scholar, Jonathan Culler (*Structuralist Poetics*), carefully follows the reasoning of these critics and points out quite convincingly where they seem to go astray, make an unauthorized short cut or go off the deep end. His overall assessment that their potentiality is probably greater than their accomplishment seems fair enough. The Americans and the Germans, already used to close reading techniques, have viewed the French phenomenon with interest and general approval. The editor of *Diacritics* reviews Kristeva's work perceptively and with genuine admiration. Not only criticism coming out of our French departments, but Anglo-American criticism in general may be heading in the French direction. David Lodge ends his book *The Novelist at the Crossroads* by declaring that the novel, like the poem, is a verbal creation. And in German Manfried Birwisch applies the principle of transformational grammar to the study of literature.

The French reaction has of course been mixed. Whereas techniques used by the new critics have spread throughout the study and teaching of literature, they have met strong opposition. Albert Léonard of Montréal is suspicious of Marxist critics, formalists, scientists, and argues for old-fashioned humanism. Linguists like Georges Mounin do not seem to take the new critics very seriously, colleagues like Meschonnic are generally hostile to individuals and have a system of their own to propose. In his three volume *Pour la poétique*, other than the recognition that linguistics is important and that a poem must be treated as a whole, rather than "pour" there is a great deal "contre"—against Jean Cohen, the thematic critics as well as the linguists. André Niel, in *L'Analyse structurale des textes*, considers that structural explications are too mechanistic and ignore vital elements of a work such as emotional appeal. Michael Riffaterre considers the *Tel Quel* group guilty of wild flights of interpretation and proposes study of poetic structure instead of linguistic. Rousset objects to the abandonment of individual genius as a consideration in criticism, Doubrovsky warns against sterility. François Vernier points to the necessity of history and sociology in approaching a work of literature. Lagarde and Michard are more the target in *L'Ecriture et les textes* than the linguists, but it is clear that all criticism for Vernier must start from Karl Marx. In one way or another they frequently seem to be calling for what Pierre Daix has described as a science of literature distinct from the others—"c'est à partir de cette science seulement qu'ils sauront quoi demander à la sociologie, à la linguistique, à la psychanalyse, à la sémiologie" (*Nouvelle Critique et art moderne*). Unfortunately there is little specific description of what such a science would be and no general agreement as well. The newspaper critics are satirical, although the Nouvelle Critique has not occasioned so many polemics as the Nouveau Roman. The merit of the French comment on the semiological critics is that it offers means of tempering their practices or adding new dimensions. Foreign commentators have not done that, but scholars like Culler and Robert Scholes have the advantage of objectivity and have presented undistorted pictures for their countrymen. Scholes' appraisal summarizes the position of an enlightened and receptive critic: "Certainly some structuralist critics are engaged in taxonomic games of dubious interest, but I am convinced that the whole enterprise is not only sound but essential, that useful work will be done and is currently being done under the structuralist aegis." What Scholes said a few years ago in this article for *Novel* is surely true today, and the work of advance-guard critics is in itself no cause for great alarm. We may feel that it is interesting and even important to see why generative analysis is abandoned in favor of transformational, what the implications are for considering semiology bigger than linguistics or vice versa; one may be willing to admit that common sense and the syllogism are probably not the only way to truth.

My greater worry concerns the implication of trends in criticism for French departments in our American universities. Once upon a time, in the humanistic framework of long ago, it was well and good to use literature as a key to a foreign culture. But gradually the fragmentation into the various groupings of history, sociology, economics, etc. which left literature merely belles-lettres made the continued emphasis on literature dubious pedagogy. Why should literature (or literary history) rather, than, say, art history be the key to a culture? Yet in the foreign language departments literature has continued to be the main emphasis in work beyond the language skill level. The repudiation in France of literary history in the old-fashioned sense makes our bad situation worse. If we go on teaching literary history and the history of ideas, we are not in step with the time; if we teach literature as structure and semiotics, we are not teaching French. We can scarcely maintain an archaic discipline, continue to train students along the lines of Lansonian scholarship; yet the new approaches to literature seem scarcely suitable to present a civilization to foreigners. These approaches have become so specialized that it would seem to exclude many students, especially those not interested in literature of any sort. What sort of training would be required to make a student feel at home in the type of literary criticism practiced today? Maybe Greek and Latin authors studied as classical rhetoric and poetics, modern German philosophy, semiology, political science, anthropology, speech, linguistics, symbolic logic. Even before feeling at home, I imagine, without this type of grounding, we are already busy in our language departments converting to the new practices. The papers read at the national meetings this winter and the articles in our journals reflect the new fashion, course offerings have been modified, and in general students and scholars have again risen nobly to the challenge. I am not sure this is all to the good and feel that before we get further involved we might decide that this was the right time to reexamine the aim of the language departments and the means of accomplishing it. We might, as professors of French, decide to abandon our competition with professors of literature in France or with professors of literature in our English departments in favor of a general commitment to what we are really expected to do and what we can do best— interpret the foreign culture to our compatriots and prepare our graduate students, especially the PhD candidate, professionally in this, our unique rôle. I have no blueprints ready for a new program. But the one I should endorse would not be just more courses in language and civilization as such but one involving interdepartmental cooperation and staffing based on competences other than areas of literary history. The philosophy of our teaching has inspired discussion on a number of American campuses in recent years and some experimentation has been undertaken. Nothing much in the way of change has come about, I fear. Perhaps semiological criticism will drive us to it.

Period Style in the Light of Structuralism, Semiotics, and Catastrophe Theory

Patrick Brady*
Rice University

French Critics and French Literary Mannerism, Baroque, and Rococo

Whereas the diachronic mode of holistic criticism, namely genre theory, dates at least as far back as Aristotle's *Poetics*, the synchronic mode, which we term "period style," is much more recent, and scarcely antedates Wolfflin's famous essay on the Renaissance and the Baroque entitled *Kunstgeschichtliche Grundbegriffe* (1915). Oscar Walzel tried to apply Wolfflin's art-historical categories to literature, and the "Great Baroque Debate" was on. In the domain of French literature, period style work properly includes Henri Peyre's work on the concept of "Classicism," and of course we all refer to the work of a comparatist like René Wellek on the concepts of "Romanticism," "Realism," and so on. But when we talk of period style as a critical domain with its own history, we normally refer to the great and continuing controversy firstly over the distinction between Renaissance and Baroque, then over the distinction between Baroque and Mannerism, and most recently over the distinction between Baroque and Rococo on the one hand and between Rococo and Enlightenment on the other. In other words, the battle concentrates on the period which separates the Renaissance of the 16th century from the Enlightenment of the 18th. There are of course other important period style concepts, like those of romanesque and gothic, but they have yet to be developed in any systematic way, so that the bloody finger of controversy has not yet left its mark upon them. The focus of interest is clearly indicated by the title given to the international congress on period style terms held in Rome in 1960, namely: *Mannerism, Baroque, and Rococo*.

The study of a particular style reappearing at various periods in history is a contraction in terms, as a style is always to some extent historically determined, and a historical environment never recurs in an absolutely identical form. Nevertheless, examples of this questionable approach abound. In the 1840s, Burckhardt proposed rococo as a recurrent style ("Es gibt ein romisches, gothisches und so weiter Rokoko") and a few decades later Brunetière accused Edmond de

Goncourt, that great admirer of the 18th century, of being "rococo" like Crébillon fils—or even "Japanese," the latter apparently being considered a superlative of "rococo." Sacheverell Sitwell declares that "the Baroque and Rococo are recurring phases in aesthetics." Studies of Prévost, Baudelaire, Delacroix, Claudel or Butor as "baroque" provide further examples, as does the celebrated Curtius conception of Mannerism. But if a particular style may not reappear, a style-type may certainly recur, and such recurrence is well worth studying. A good example of a diachronic study of a style-*type* is René Bray's work on *préciosité*, which deals with a single "famille d'esprits" from Thibaut de Champagne to Jean Giraudoux. Similarly, there is a return to the rococo in the latter part of the 19th century in France, led by the Goncourt, Verlaine, Renoir, Debussy; the result, however, is not rococo but impressionism.

As the subject of period style research is vast, we must find ways to limit our discussion. One is suggested by the terms of the present meeting: we shall exclude scholars like Leo Spitzer and Helmut Hatzfeld, who, while they have done significant work on mannerism, the baroque, and the rococo, and in relation to French literature, are not themselves *French* critics. Secondly, we shall exclude French criticism devoted to other literature than the French. On the other hand, we shall include scholars whose native tongue is French even when their native soil is not; indeed, to exclude the Swiss and the Belgians would leave us slim pickings. And this may be our first critical *constatation*: that period style, so readily accepted and developed as a critical tool by German scholars and almost as readily by the Italians, has been viewed with skepticism and used with reluctance by the English and the French.

In terms of the French-speaking tradition, period style may be classified, historically, in three stages: that of the *Nouvelle Critique*, that of structuralism, and that of semiotics.

The "Nouvelle Critique" and the Development of Sets of Criteria

Unlike Anglo-American "New Criticism," with its immanent orientation, the French intellectual movement known as the *Nouvelle Critique* is essentially ideological in character, and traditionally divided into four chief recognized strands: the Marxist, the Freudian, the Existentialist, and the Structuralist. However, those critics usually associated with the *Nouvelle Critique* who have taken the greatest interest in the period style approach are not very obviously classifiable in any one of these categories. I am thinking of Marcel Raymond and Jean Rousset, representatives of the so-called "Geneva School" which also includes Jean Starobinski and Georges Poulet. (It is true that Raymond, like Spitzer, has some affiliations with the psychoanalytical tradition, but these are not evident in the period style work of either of these scholars.) Not that Raymond and Rousset are the only French critics to use such notions: the concept of baroque style in literature was used more than thirty years ago by Raymond Lebègue, followed by André Chastel and Antoine Adam. But Marcel Raymond entered the lists many years earlier, and Rousset has the distinction of having written the most generally accepted and influential study of the concept.

Rousset, who sets out from a study of baroque architecture and theatre and then proceeds to a study of literature, concludes that the characteristic traits of the baroque are: "l'instabilité, la mobilité, la métamorphose, et la domination du décor."[1] Raymond, who has reservations about the somewhat broader conceptions developed by such non-French scholars as Imbrie Buffum and Philip Butler, largely accepts that proposed by Rousset, with the following two additions: "(1) l'idée d'expansion dynamique, liée à celle de dramatisation, l'une et l'autre exigeant un accroissement des moyens d'expression; (2) au-delà des notations de couleur même, la luminosité, le scintillement, le rayonnement des images."[2]

These additional criteria enable Raymond to distinguish the baroque from mannerism, of which he writes: "Le maniérisme, au moins sous sa forme 'lipsienne,' est reserrement, abstraction; la métaphore y tourne au symbole et à l'emblème. En outre, s'il complique et déplace les lignes, s'il multiplie volontiers les plans, on n'y observe rien qui s'offre à la catégorie wolfflinienne du pictural, pas de ces images scintillantes ou rayonnantes qui semblent caractériser la plupart des écrivains baroques du XVIIe siècle."[3]

When we come to the rococo, however, we find the remarks of Raymond and Rousset both superficial and mutually incompatible. Rousset simply identifies it with *préciosité*, while Raymond sees it as a form of late baroque, referring to "ce mouvement qui mène au baroque amenuisé, d'une vitalité plus médiocre, plus chiffonné et désireux d'apporter au spectateur, dans l'immédiat, le plus de plaisir possible, qu'on appelle le style rocaille, ou rococo."[4] Whereas Raymond thus confuses the rococo with the baroque, Roer Laufer confuses it with the Enlightenment. While I myself combatted the Laufer heresy,[5] that of Raymond was laid to rest in 1966 by Philippe Minguet, whose study of German religious architecture (from which he subsequently extrapolates to French literature) clearly distinguishes the rococo from the baroque. Dealing with construction, Minguet finds an "équilibre constructif dans l'art classique et renaissant" and continues: "Les baroques ne renoncent pas à l'effet tectonique, mais ils relâchent la maîtrise à des fins expressives. Le rococo joue à dissimuler l'effort constructif." With regard to space, he evokes the "unité rationnelle de l'espace classique," the various "facteurs de multiplicité dans l'architecture baroque," and remarks: "Le rococo vise une homogénéité synthétique." Finally, under the heading "expression," he contrasts "la félicité classique et l'inquiétude baroque" with "la suavité rococo."[6]

Let us add that during this period it was also affirmed that period style research must take account of a concept's origins in the realm of art criticism[7] and avoid the fallacy of claiming similar aesthetic affiliations for all works of a given period.[8]

Soon a new and deeper interest in the theoretical framework of period style perspectives was provoked by the advent of the era of structuralism.

Synchronic structuralism, arbitrary "ruptures" or discontinuous process, and catastrophe theory

Period style has recently been termed "synchronic stylistics" by Richard Ohmann, an American structuralist.[9] Bishop Hurd's tendency towards a period style approach has been described by Geoffrey Hartman as structuralist.[10] However, while structuralism provides a theoretical framework which helps us to understand the nature of period style, it also, in its more "classical" (that is, synchronic or static) form, brings up certain problems. These may usefully be discussed in connection with the implications of the work devoted by Michel Foucault to the periodization of history.[11]

Foucault is a specialist in the history and philosophy of science. He describes the world-view of Renaissance thought, in which, although the *signifiant* no longer is the *signifié* (the Word no longer is the Thing, as it was in Adamic language), at least it is a Symbol of the Thing (that is, the relationship between *signifiant* and *signifié* is natural or inherent). And he evokes the subsequent change to the world-view of Cartesian Classical thought, in which the *signifiant* is reduced to a mere Sign of the *signifié* (that is, the relationship between signifiant and signifié is arbitrary). He suggests that the Baroque period (turn of the 16th and 17th centuries) may represent a transitional stage between Renaissance and Classical world-views. Now, the contrast between the two systems of thought evoked by Foucault appears in fact to correspond to the distinction between metaphor and metonymy developed by Jakobson. But whereas in the realm of ideas the Renaissance is apparently metaphorical, the Baroque transitional, and Cartesianism metonymic, when we look at the aesthetic manifestations of the principles we have been discussing we find that the Baroque is metaphorical (e.g., *L'Astrée*: pastoral), Classicism is transitional (e.g., *La Princesse de Clèves*: historical), and the Rococo is metonymic (e.g., *La vie de Marianne*: contemporary). Thus there appears to be a time-lag between the change in world-view and the change in aesthetics—if Foucault's analysis is accurate.

Foucault takes a radically static view of history based on a structuralist view heavily dependent on the Saussurian distinction between diachrony as the dynamic perspective of linguistics and synchrony as the static perspective. The static or synchronic character of structuralism has led to problems in the reconciliation of the structuralist and historical approaches to the study and presentation of phenomena—notably, the reconciliation of the structuralist and dialectical interpretations of history. Two criticisms of Foucault's method deserve our attention.

(a) One criticism made of the Foucault view is that it imposes an artificial (and superficial) exclusion of conflict and contradiction from the picture in order to strengthen its static quality. Such a distortion would represent a highly sophisticated version of the error which at other times expresses itself in the form of the fallacy of monolithic period style. It leads to the systematic neglect of major figures in general and of artists in particular. With regard to the displacement of stress from major figures to minor ones (to lend coherence to the picture, the major figures being harder to classify because of their tendency to contest the conventions and go beyond the accepted limits), the question is whether this distortion is an inevitable concomitant of the structuralist method. The answer, of course, is no: it is a valid objection not to structuralism in general but only to an excessively unified conception of it. Foucault also excludes artists from a study of cultures, apparently considering that "l'art échappe à la structure."[12] Revault d'Allonnes, while opposing the neglect of aesthetics, agrees with this conception of art, saying of the relationship between the artist and structures: "Il les fait, les défait, les refait sans cesse."[13] This, however, is directly opposed to the structuralist view, according to which structures are unconscious and ineluctable. The exclusion of artists from a structuralist analysis of period style is both unnecessary and unjustifiable.

(b) Foucault is also criticized for adopting an approach whose static thrust leads him to minimize both evolution and internal conflict. Thus he is attacked for insisting on a conception of structures virtually devoid of transformation and process. Now, even the most rigorous synchronism is so hard to maintain that its status is extremely precarious. Once the term "structure" is applied to any part of the historical sequence, the diachrony-synchrony problem arises. No matter how small the period of time taken, the temporal dimension is present. The linguist may choose not to study the development of the French language diachronically from, let us say, 1800 to 1900, but rather to study it synchronically as it exists in the year 1900. That year, however, is a year of twelve months, involving time-lapse, change, transformation. And even if he reduces the time-span from a year to a day or a second, he would only be *reducing* the diachronic dimension, not eliminating it. The only way to eliminate it is mentally: by choosing to examine the phenomenon *as if* no diachronic dimension were involved, that is by ignoring those aspects connected with the diachronic dimension and its effects. In other words, a "structure" is a hypothesis: it is merely a useful way of looking at things.

Just as language, which cannot exist in reality outside the historical dimension, can nevertheless be looked at synchronically (that is, "structurally"), so any historically situated phenomenon can be looked at in the same way. As for the passage from one structure to another, to speak of such a passage as existing in reality is meaningless—or rather erroneous; it assumes that structures exist in historical reality, instead of having purely hypothetical status within the mind. The passage may be from the hypothesis (structure) 1600-1700 to the hypothesis (structure) 1700-1800, thus deluding people into thinking it is analogous to the passage from one historical period to another; but it may just as easily be from the hypothesis 1600-1700 to the hypothesis 1600-1800. Such a passage is not real and historical, as implied, but purely mental: heuristic, speculative. Thus the so-called problem of reconciling structuralism with history (or dialectics, or Marxism) is not a real problem at all but a mistake, based on confusing two different but entirely compatible (if never co-existent) mental perspectives: structuralism does not claim that there is no movement in history, no dialectic—it merely claims that it is possible to look at the phenomena involved in this movement not only diachronically but also synchronically.

In other words, if the answers have eluded those who have sought to answer this question: "How can we reconcile structuralism and history?" it is because the question is incorrectly formulated in the first place. To attempt to reconcile structuralism with history is like trying to reconcile night with day, or a telescopic view of reality with a microscopic view, or a view through a blue-tinted lens with a view through a red-tinted one. The two, in each case, are very different, perhaps in some ways even antithetical, but in no way mutually contradictory.

Foucault's approach is questionable not because of its excessively static premises but because of its mixture of synchronic and diachronic perspectives. This may seem paradoxical, in that his critics blame him on the contrary for the radical exclusion of the diachronic; however, their objections are in fact valid only in so far as the diachronic perspective is present (as well as the synchronic), at least by implication. And it *is* so present, in the guise of the sequence in which his three culture-periods are arranged. It is significant that when pressed to explain the passage from one episteme to another Foucault postulates arbitrary *ruptures* (analogues to the quantum leaps between successive cultural paradigms postulated by Thomas Kuhn), although his method allows for no such postulates. Obviously, there are adjustments and transformations (that is, modes of evolution) within the rococo culture, society, period, for example; but consideration of these, while both valuable and valid, cannot take place within the framework of synchronic structuralism. For such considerations, we must go either to the genetic structuralism of the great Swiss psychologist and theoretician Jean Piaget, and specifically to his notion of "operational structures" (to which he attributes three chief properties: relational, transformational, and self-adjusting),[14] or to a recent development in mathematical analysis (initiated by René Thom) known as "catastrophe theory." A branch of the mathematical discipline of topology, catastrophe theory is devoted to the description and analysis, and ultimately the prediction, of processes which are "abrupt" or discontinuous. Although it is still in its infancy, it already suggests very strongly that the *ruptures* termed "arbitrary" by Foucault in his rather lame defense of a weakness or lacuna in his system are not really arbitrary but rather merely infinitely (or, to be more precise, indefinitely) complex.

We thus have, even within this very incomplete discussion of structuralism as relating to period style theory, at least four distinct variations, which may be represented roughly as follows:

1. structuralisme synchronique pur (Foucault I)

2. structuralisme synchronique honteux (Foucault II: ruptures [discontinuité inexplicable] ou structuralisme pseudo-synchronique arbitraires)

3. structuralisme transformationnel simple ou systématique (Piaget)

4. structuralisme transformationnel complexe ou discontinu (Thom) [discontinuité expliquée]

Semiotics and the Analysis of Verbal and Verbal Sign-Systems

The term "semiotics" was introduced into philosophy some three hundred years ago by John Locke,[15] and more recently disseminated by the work of Charles Pierce in the field of logic. Semiotics, which may be defined as the general science of signs, was divided by Charles Morris in 1938 into three branches of natural language: syntax, semantics, and pragmatics.[16] As far as France is concerned, we may mention the names of semioticians like Michel Arrivé, Jean-Claude Coquet, and to some extent Julia Kristeva.

What is disturbing about much of this semiotic work is that it seems scarcely to differ from what was called structuralism a very short time ago, and there is no apparent reason at all for using the term "sémiotique" rather than the term "structuralisme" in the title of the volume entitled *Sémiotique narrative et textuelle* published by Larousse in 1973 and presenting work by Barthes, Bremond, Greimas and others who were the structuralists of the sixties. Julia Kristeva at least tries, in her doctoral thesis entitled *Révolution du langage poétique*,[17] to incorporate the three recognized dimensions of semiotics as defined by Morris—which theoretically would be an improvement on the work of the Russians Lotman and Uspensky, who had been castigated for neglecting the pragmatic aspect of literature.[18] But pragmatics takes the form in her work of what she calls the "genotext," apparently in an abusive extrapolation from the term "genotype" used in such fields as biology and psychology. In point of fact, there is nothing "textual" at all in the phenomena studied by Kristeva under the heading of the "genotext."

If I feel so negative about contemporary semiotics, why bring it up at all? The reason is that I believe that, if properly conceived, it can provide a basis for the comparison of artworks of varying type, seen as constituting clusters of literary, plastic, or musical signs which, in the case of any given period style, represent variegated modes of expression of a current *Zeitgeist* or *Weltanschauung*. Instead of being limited to literary analysis, as it is at present, French semiotics must reorient itself to take in the visual signs as well as the verbal if it is to make the rich contribution of which it is capable to the more rigorous period style research of the future.

Conclusion

Derrida considers Rousset to be structuralist, even "ultra-structuralist," but he is not only not structuralist, he is not even ideological in the way other Nouveaux Critiques are—he is not Marxist, not Freudian, not existentialist. Indeed, his unease about all holistic thinking is well illustrated by the fact that he has apparently now renounced his early research using period style concepts. Be that as it may, such early work represented a valuable pioneering stage in the development of a comparative aesthetics. The next stage, that of structuralism, taught us to understand some of our problems a little more clearly. It now remains for semiotics to help us to develop a language capable of analysing with depth and with rigour the various formal systems through which the various arts convey the stresses, needs, and desires of given periods and cultures. This will enable us to transcend conventional modes of comparatism and ultimately to elaborate a formal history and psychology of societies and civilizations, which is the rich promise that has been held out to us from the beginning by the young but rapidly growing discipline of period style research.

---

*Professor Brady currently holds the Shumway Chair of Excellence at the University of Tennessee.

[1] J. Rousset, *La Littérature de l'âge baroque en France: Circé et le paon* (Paris: Corti, 1954), pp. 181-182.

[2] M. Raymond, "Le Baroque littéraire français," in *Manierismo, Barocco, Rococo* (Rome: Accademia dei Lincei, 1962), p. 117.

[3] *Ibid., loc. cit.*

[4] *Ibid.,* p. 126.

[5] Review published in *Studi Francesi,* anno VII, no 3, fasc. 21 (settembre-dicembre 1963), pp. 511-514.

[6] These and the preceding quotations are taken from Ph. Minguet: *Esthétique du rococo* (Paris: Vrin, 1966). See our review in *Studi Francesi,* anno XIII, no 2, fasc. 38 (maggio-agosto 1969), pp. 306-309.

[7] E.g., see our "Rococo and neo-Classicism," *Studi Francesi,* anno VIII, no 1, fasc. 22 (gennaio-aprile 1964), pp. 3449.

[8] E.g., see our "Rococo Style in French Literature," *Studi Francesi,* anno X, no 3, fasc. 30 (settembre-dicembre 1966), pp. 428-437.

[9] R. Ohmann, "Generative Grammars and the Concept of Literary Style," in M. Steinmann: *New Rhetorics* (New York: Charles Scribner's Sons, 1967), p. 136.

[10] G. Hartman, "Structuralism: The Anglo-American Adventure," *Yale French Studies,* vols 36-37 (October 1966), p. 150.

[11] M. Foucault, *Les Mots et les choses* (Paris: Gallimard, 1966).

[12] See Auzias et alii: *Structuralisme et marxisme* (Paris: Union Générale d'Edition, 1970), p. 20, note.

[13] *Ibid., loc. cit.*

[14] See our "From Traditional Fallacies to Structural Hypotheses," *Neophilologus,* vol. LVI, no 1 (January 1972), pp. 1-11.

[15] It had previously been used for the medical theory of symptoms.

[16] The inclusion of pragmatics distinguishes semiotics from metalogic, which is limited to the study of syntax and semantics of formal languages and systems.

[17] (Paris: Seuil, 1974)

[18] See the reviews of their work by St. Zolkiewski entitled "Des principes de classement des textes de culture," *Semiotica,* vol. VII, no 1 (1973), pp. 1-18, and "Poétique de la composition," *Semiotica,* vol. V, no 3 (1972), pp. 205-224.

III. THEMES AND MOTIFS:

FROM

SOCRATIC IRONY TO "TITROLOGIE"

Ironie socratique, ironie romanesque, ironie poétique

Jean-Pol Madou*
Université de Nimègue, Pays-Bas

Trait d'esprit, figure de rhétorique, stratégie du discours et technique de persuasion, l'ironie est devenue avec Socrate la compagne du philosophe dans sa quête de la vérité. C'est en effet l'ironie socratique qui, à l'aube de la pensée, ouvre le champ de la dialectique, lui fournissant d'entrée de jeu toutes les armes de la ruse et de la séduction. Nul ne l'a mieux compris que S. Kierkegaard qui réinterpréta dans sa thèse de doctorat en 1841 toute l'histoire de la philosophie, de Platon à Hegel, à la lumière du seul concept d'ironie.[1] Apparemment tout oppose l'attitude ludique et frivole de l'ironiste au travail laborieux du dialecticien. L'ironie se dissimule dans le clair-obscur de la conscience; la dialectique, en revanche, s'expose au grand Midi de la Pensée. L'ironie et la dialectique ne sauraient assurément se confondre, mais elles sont chez Socrate si intimement et subtilement mêlées qu'on ne saurait dire avec exactitude si la dialectique est la systématisation de l'ironie, ou si, inversement, cette dernière est une forme particulière de la dialectique. Que serait en effet la dialectique sans l'ironie si ce n'est une mécanique implacable, et l'ironie sans la dialectique si ce n'est un jeu vain et stérile qui, indifférent au vrai et au faux, tourbillonnant de paradoxe en paradoxe, se dissiperait comme autant d'ombres évanescentes et mensongères de l'Apparence et du Non-Etre. Aussi l'ironie dialectique ne saurait-elle être mensongère. Dissimulatrice, elle se distingue du mensonge en ce qu'elle n'existe que pour être démasquée. L'ironie ne trompe pas pour tromper mais pour qu'on devine qu'elle trompe.

La dissimulation n'est ironique que si elle se révèle par quelques signes discrets voire initiatiques comme un jeu d'apparences et d'allusions. L'ironie est un faux mensonge qui, ne fût-ce qu'en soulevant déjà le coin du voile, laisse voir en creux la vérité qu'elle occultait. Tout se passe dès lors comme si la vérité ne pouvait se lire que dans le renversement des signes, comme si le savoir ne pouvait se constituer que par la feinte de l'ignorance. Cette fausse humilité qu'affecte l'ironiste s'avère d'autant plus simulée qu'elle vise en fait à extorquer de la bouche de celui qui indûment prétend savoir l'aveu de sa non moins réelle ignorance. L'ironie socratique est une technique de l'aveu. Elle se fait un point d'honneur de ne pas réfuter l'erreur. Elle fait en sorte que celle-ci, prise comme une araignée dans ses propres filets, dépose les armes et, essouflée, se réfute elle-même.

Ce jeu de simulation et de dissimulation où "tu as raison" signifie en fait "tu as tort" n'est évidemment pas la vérité mais la condition de possibilité de sa manifestation. La conquête du savoir vrai présuppose un dédoublement dont seul l'ironiste a véritablement le secret. Aussi Kierkegaard définit-il l'ironie socratique comme un "rien mystérieux" qui au coeur de notre liberté permet de nous dédoubler et qui nous révèle, à la faveur de ce dédoublement, notre divine *disponibilité*: "L'ironie est un point de vue qui s'annule constamment lui-même, elle est un rien qui dévore tout, et un quelque chose impossible à saisir qui est et n'est pas tout à la fois."[2]

L'ironie nous permet ainsi de nous identifier *fictivement* aux choses afin de mieux pouvoir nous en distancier *réellement*, et de faire apparaître à la faveur de cet écart, si minime soit-il, la plénitude de l'Idée. C'est grâce à ce jeu d'identification pédagogique et de distanciation satirique—identification *imaginaire* du maître au disciple et de distanciation *réelle* du disciple par rapport à lui-même—, que l'ironie socratique constitue le "ressort" du raisonnement dialectique qui sous-tend le mouvement ascendant de l'âme vers le Souverain Bien. Gilles Deleuze l'a admirablement résumé: "L'ironie est le jeu d'une pensée qui se permet de fonder la loi sur un Bien infiniment supérieur."[3] C'est sans doute ce qui distingue le raisonnement dialectique du raisonnement géométrique. Celui-ci part d'une hypothèse et, descendant infailliblement une chaine de déductions, débouche sur une conclusion qui, démonstration faite, aura désormais force de loi. Mais, une fois la boucle de la démonstration refermée, la pensée retombe à son point mort. L'opération géométrique ne dispose pas de "ressort," de ce principe de renouvellement dont l'ironie fait don au raisonnement dialectique lui permettant ainsi de rebondir toujours plus haut et d'ouvrir des cercles toujours plus vastes. Comme l'écrit René Schaerer: "L'emploi sérieux de la démarche descendante ne conduit, selon Platon, qu'à une illusion et à un point mort; car la réalité qu'on atteint ainsi n'étant connue qu'en fonction d'elle-même, ne porte aucun principe de renouvellement. Le vrai dialecticien ne pratique pas la géométrie, il en joue; de même d'ailleurs qu'il joue de la littérature, de la poésie et de l'histoire pour les transformer en un genre nouveau, le mythe, qui se situe et se définit lui-même."[4]

Que Platon ait songé à faire de l'ironie un genre littéraire nouveau lui offrant en quelque sorte ses *Dialogues* comme premiers chefs-d'oeuvre, semble une idée contestable quand on sait par ailleurs le sort peu enviable que le philosophe réservait aux poètes et aux artistes dans *La République*. La fin du *Banquet* devrait cependant retenir toute notre attention. En effet, ce grand discours sur l'Amour inspiré, chef-d'oeuvre de Platon, se termine d'une façon bien singulière voire ironique. Les convives de Socrate se sont endormis sur place après avoir passé la nuit à boire et à discuter. Seuls trois d'entre eux demeurent éveillés, Aristophane, le poète comique, Agathon, le dramaturge, et Socrate, l'ironiste. La conversation s'engage sur le point de savoir si l'on peut être à la fois un poète comique et un poète tragique. Le narrateur malheureusement ne nous en dit pas plus long puisqu'il prétend tenir le récit de la bouche d'Aristodème qui à ce moment se trouvait déjà dans un état de demi-somnolence. "De ces propos, au reste, Aristodème disait ne pas se souvenir, n'en ayant pas entendu le commencement et ayant en outre la tête lourde de sommeil. L'essentiel en était cependant que Socrate les forçait de convenir qu'il appartient au même homme de savoir composer comédie et tragédie et que celui qui est, avec art, poète tragique est aussi poète comique. Eux, ils s'y laissaient forcer sans trop bien suivre, et en laissant tomber leur tête. Ce fut Aristophane qui s'endormit le premier, puis Agathon, alors qu'il faisait jour déjà. Là-dessus Socrate, les ayant endormis comme des enfants, se leva et partit."[5]

Nous aurions sans doute aimé en savoir plus long sur les rapports de la tragédie, de la comédie et de l'ironie. Mais ce n'est pas, croyons-nous, sans raison que Platon a laissé tomber le rideau sur cette fin de partie inachevée. A peine résumé, réduit à son argument le plus élémentaire, le récit exprime d'autant mieux son intention allégorique. Toujours aux aguets dans un monde livré à la somnolence, l'ironie socratique seule est capable de déjouer les dilemmes, de transcender les oppositions qui structuraient l'éthique et l'esthétique grecques, celles de l'idéal et du réel, du tragique et du comique. Ecriture ironique que cette fin de Banquet. Tout s'y passe en effet comme si le discours avait épuisé toutes ses possibilités d'expression face à la Transcendance ineffable du Bien Souverain et, dans un mouvement de reflux sur lui-même, n'était désormais plus capable que d'en recueillir l'éclat dégradé. Mais l'ironie est d'autant plus subtile qu'il revient précisément à un récit, transmis par un narrateur somnolent et reproduit dans le style indirect le plus elliptique, d'évoquer une dernière fois la souveraine lucidité de l'ironie socratique qui, seule, permet d'accéder à la vision du Vrai, du Beau et du Bien. La somnolence n'est-elle pas un obstacle à la révélation du Bien suprême? N'est-elle pas cet état limite entre le sommeil et la veille où viennent affleurer à la surface d'une conscience assoupie les rêves et les phantasmes comme autant de vapeurs du délire et de la mélancolie? Le sommeil n'est-il pas, pour reprendre une expression d'Homère, cette "porte d'ivoire" dont se méfiera plus tard cet autre grand ironiste que fut Gérard de Nerval au seuil d'*Aurélia*? L'ironie consiste à se jouer de l'obstacle et à en faire, par une mise en scène savamment calculée, le *signe négatif* de ce qu'il occulte et obscurcit. L'ironie socratique confirme la toute-puissance de l'Idée et la défaillance du langage. Et la division du discours en genres renforce cette impuissance. Aussi Socrate ne semble-t-il pas trop s'intéresser à ce qui différencie le genre comique du genre tragique pour ne retenir que ce qu'ils pourraient avoir en commun. L'ironie est ainsi l'ombre portée ici-bas d'un Bien infiniment supérieur. Aussi l'ironie ne relève-t-elle pas seulement d'une pure rhétorique de la persuasion. D'instrument pédagogico-satirique elle se transforme dans le texte de Platon en une *allégorie* mystique et allusive.

Liée à la naissance de la philosophie, l'ironie socratique marquera le destin de la pensée occidentale. Aussi est-ce un hasard si Frédéric Schlegel, fondateur du mouvement romantique, se réfère explicitement à l'ironie socratique pour définir l'ironie romantique comme l'exercice d'une liberté qui se découvre infinie. C'est aux dialogues socratiques qu'il fait écho lorsqu'il écrit: "Die Philosophie ist die eigentliche Heimat der Ironie, welche man logische Schönheit definieren möchte."[6] La philosphie est la terre natale de l'ironie, laquelle peut être définie comme une beauté logique. Cette expression accouple deux termes qui pour Schlegel sont contradictoires. La "logique" évoque l'ordre du discours, la beauté évoque, quant à elle, l'ordre de la Transcendance ineffable qui excède la mesure du dicible de tout logos.

Cette "beauté logique," Schlegel en capte le reflet, non plus dans la dialectique serrée des dialogues socratiques mais dans le miroir éclaté d'une écriture aphoristique. Systématisant la pratique de l'aphorisme, il se raccroche ainsi à la tradition des moralistes francais (Chamfort, La Rochefoucauld, Pascal, voire Montaigne). Mais alors que l'ironie socratique mêlant la raillerie de l'apparence et le sérieux de l'intention, se tourne contre un interlocuteur afin de le prendre à partie, l'ironie romantique, en revanche, se tourne contre elle-même afin de conquérir dans ce "rapport à soi" une liberté supérieure. C'est ce qui distingue l'ironie romantique de la rhétorique ironique du XVIIIe siècle. "Tandis que Voltaire fait de l'esprit, écrit J. Starobinski, l'ironiste romantique se voudra tout esprit, en opposition générale et indéfinie à tout ce qui n'est pas esprit."[7] Alors que l'ironie socratique n'est jamais qu'un moyen, l'ironie romantique s'avère être une fin en soi. A l'aube du XIXe siècle l'ironie est l'exercice d'une liberté qui se découvre infinie: "L'ironie est la plus libre des licences, écrit Schlegel, car elle permet de se dépasser soi-même, mais elle est aussi la plus contraignante, car elle est d'une absolue nécessité."[8]

Infinie, absolue, la liberté ne se découvre telle que dans la mesure où elle s'impose des limites et des contraintes dont elle jouera en toute souveraineté. Et c'est bien ce que Hegel reproche à l'ironie romantique. Elle n'est que la vanité coupable dans laquelle se complaît une subjectivité vide qui n'a d'autre loi que celle de sa propre jouissance stérile: "Je suis le maître souverain de la loi et de la chose, dont je joue à mon gré et dans cet état de conscience ironique dans lequel je laisse s'abîmer le plus élevé, je ne jouis que de moi."[9] Se réfléchissant indéfiniment sur elle-même, la conscience romantique se joue de toutes ses contradictions ouvrant ainsi un vertigineux jeu de miroirs où toute création s'avère destruction, toute destruction création. Et si la vérité pour Platon demeurait hors jeu—l'ironie n'étant jamais qu'un moyen et non une fin—pour le romantique, en revanche, elle est le Jeu même du Monde oscillant indéfiniment entre l'autocréation et l'autodestruction, synthèse toujours mouvante, sans cesse défaite, sans cesse renouvelée, de l'idéal et du réel, du dit et du non-dit, de l'être et du non-être.

C'est toute la philosophie de Platon qui vient à vaciller dans ce jeu de miroirs lorsque Schlegel écrit dans l'un de ses aphorismes: "Une idée est concept accompli jusqu'à l'ironie, une synthèse absolue d'absolues synthèses, l'échange constant, et s'engendrant lui-même, de deux pensées en lutte."[10] Que l'ironie trouve ainsi en elle-même sa propre finalité ne signifie pas qu'elle se dépense et se dissipe dans un jeu gratuit, comme le croit Hegel, mais qu'elle devient, à la faveur de cette infinie réflexion du sujet sur lui-même, le miroir même de l'Univers dans le jeu mouvant de ses contradictions, tragédie du Destin et comédie des masques. Seule l'ironie le peut puisqu'elle est à la fois toute raillerie et tout sérieux, "naïvement sincère et profondément dissimulée," et nous éveille à l'insoluble contradiction de l'absolu et du relatif, de l'inconditionné et du conditionné ainsi qu'à "l'impossibilité et la nécessité d'une communication complète."[11] Aussi l'ironie se voit-elle dans le même aphorisme schlégélien défini à la fois comme *souffle divin et bouffonnerie transcendantale.*[12]

En effet la figure du bouffon ainsi que celles du mime, du fou, du jongleur, du saltimbanque, n'ont cessé de hanter l'imaginaire romantique et toute la littérature du XIXe siècle. Que l'on se rappelle le Fantasio de Musset, le fou du *Roi s'amuse* de Hugo, les funambules chers à Gautier et et à Th. de Banville, la Fanfarlo, Fancioule, le vieux saltimbanque de Baudelaire, le pitre châtié de Mallarmé, les Pierrots lunaires de Jules Laforgue, et plus près de nous, l'Arlequin trismégiste de Guillaume Apollinaire. Les bouffons et les clowns, comme l'écrit J. Starobinski, "sont les meilleurs emblèmes possibles de la griserie propre à l'*ironie romantique*: ce sont les hauts faits d'un esprit qui affirme sa liberté par le refus éperdu de la contingence imparfaite."[13] Mais les bouffons qui de leurs bonds aériens, défiant les lois de la pesanteur, "roulant dans les étoiles," ouvrent un espace de rêve et de liberté, ne s'avèrent en définitive que les doubles inversés de ces princes mélancoliques qu'ils s'évertuent mais en vain à guérir. Aussi dans la seconde moitié du XIXe siècle l'emblème de l'ironie deviendra de plus en plus une allégorie de la mort. Tels sont "les bouffons qui bouffonnent si bien la mort." Et c'est bien aussi ce que Kierkegaard reproche à l'ironie romantique, à savoir de n'être qu'une dialectique négative, une abstraction sans contenu, un jeu du vide avec le vide qui en définitive révèle une fascination de la mort et du néant. Ce piège que nous tend l'ironie Kierkegaard le décèle déjà au coeur de l'ironie socratique. Et c'est sans doute la raison pour laquelle il en arrive à prendre *au sérieux* les railleries d'Aristophane qui dans sa comédie *Les Nuées* présenta Socrate comme un bouffon charlatan, un vagabond désoeuvré, une sorte de clown suspendu dans une corbeille entre ciel et terre.

Qu'est-ce à dire sinon que l'ironie ne saurait être une Rédemption? Illusion suprême, elle ne nous arrache à la mélancolie que pour mieux nous y replonger. L'ironie et la mélancolie sont comme la double face du dieu Janus, l'envers et l'endroit d'un même Mal. Cet échec de l'ironie s'inscrit dans l'Azur mallarméen:

> De l'éternel Azur la sereine ironie
> Accable, belle indolemment comme les fleurs
> Le Poète impuissant qui maudit son génie
> A travers un désert stérile de Douleurs.[14]

La fascination de l'Azur est l'attrait d'un gouffre.

Par l'ironie le sujet se retranche du monde pour mieux le néantiser et se le réapproprier vidé ainsi de toute résistance. Mais en en faisant l'objet d'une négation infinie, le sujet ne se réapproprie le monde que dans l'espace du rêve et de l'Imaginaire. Car l'ironiste romantique rêve de réconcilier tout ce que la pensée des temps modernes a réussi à séparer: le sujet et l'objet, l'individu et le monde, la praxis et le discours, bref la "totalité de la vie" dont l'unité s'était exprimée et épanouie dans le monde de l'épopée et dont le *Don Quichotte* de Cervantès avait sonné le glas. Mais ce que l'épopée fut pour les Grecs, le roman l'est pour l'époque moderne. Mais alors que l'épopée célébrait la totalité d'un monde et le destin d'une collectivité, le roman n'est désormais plus que l'encyclopédie spirituelle d'un individu dont le *Wilhelm Meister* de Goethe est pour la génération romantique le paradigme incontesté.

Parallèlement aux réflexions sur l'ironie, les *Fragments* de l'*Athenaeum* poursuivent une réflexion sur la théorie des genres, et plus particulièrement sur le discours romanesque qui plonge ses racines lointaines dans la satire latine, le roman grec et les dialogues socratiques. "Les romans sont les dialogues socratiques de notre époque," lit-on dans ces mêmes *Fragments*. Est-ce à dire que le "roman" serait, plus que tout autre genre, à même d'ouvrir cet espace de fiction tout imprégné de "souffle divin" et de "bouffonnerie transcendantale"? La liberté avec laquelle le romancier se dédouble, se projette, se multiplie en autant de personnages qu'il y a de désirs qui l'habitent, n'est-elle pas par excellence l'exercice d'une souveraine ironie, celle d'un Dieu qui, comme l'écrit Flaubert, demeure dans son invisibilité même présent dans la moindre parcelle de sa création? L'exercice de la narration romanesque ne serait-elle pas intrinsèquement ironique? Le roman est à peine un genre. Mélangeant les genres, le discours romanesque ne permet-il pas en effet au narrateur de multiplier sa perception du monde en autant de points de vue qu'il y a de personnages, et de disperser sa voix, comme dans un jeu d'échos, en autant d'instances narratives qu'il y a de points de vue. Le roman n'est-il pas souvent une polyphonie simulée par une voix solitaire?

Le roman, disions-nous, n'est pas un genre. Mélangeant les genres, il trouve son origine dans cette case demeurée anonyme de la poétique aristotélicienne. On se rappelle que la théorie aristotélicienne avait engendré quatre genres fondamentaux au moyen de deux critères, à savoir—deux modes d'énonciation, le narratif et le dramatique,—et deux tonalités, l'une sublime l'autre grotesque. Le dramatique supérieur définit la tragédie, le dramatique inférieur la comédie. Le narratif supérieur définit l'épopée. Le narratif inférieur, quant à lui, demeure mal défini. Refusant même de lui donner un nom, le condamnant en quelque sorte à l'anonymat, Aristote y relègue pêle-mêle comme autant de scories et de déchets du discours poétique toutes les oeuvres qui ne se plient pas aux lois des trois genres précédents, entre autres, cités en vrac, "les mimes, les épopées bouffonnes, les parodies et les dialogues socratiques."[15]

Et c'est précisément aux dialogues socratiques et à la théorie platonicienne qui s'y déploie, que les Romantiques de Iéna se réfèrent comme au fondement de leur théorie du "livre romantique." Schlegel et ses disciples n'ont en effet cessé d'être hantés par la création d'un Livre, d'une Oeuvre pure où la fusion des genres servirait de support à l'union de la poésie et de la philosophie, de l'Art et de la Science. "Cette philosophie, écrit Schlegel, oscillerait entre l'union et la séparation de la philosophie et de la poésie, de la praxis et de la poésie, de la poésie en général et des genres et espèces, et s'achèveraient avec leur union totale. Son début donnerait les principes de la poétique pure, son milieu la théorie des genres poétiques modernes, le didactique, le musical, le rhétorique au sens élevé, etc. Une philosophie du roman, dont la théorie politique de Platon contient les premiers fondements, en serait la clé de voûte."[16] Ce Livre romantique dans lequel se recueillerait la totalité de l'être, microcosme de l'Univers, serait à l'image de l'épopée, mais d'une épopée traversée et portée par le souffle divin de l'ironie: "Elle seule, pareille à l'épopée peut devenir miroir du monde environnant, image de l'époque. Et cependant c'est elle aussi qui, libre de tout intérêt réel ou idéal, peut le mieux flotter entre le présenté et le présentant, sur les ailes de la réflexion poétique, porter sans cesse cette réflexion à une plus haute puissance, et la multiplier comme dans une série infinie de miroirs. Elle est capable de la plus suprême et universelle formation."[17] Cet esprit, flottant entre l'idéal et le réel, porté par un jeu d'ailes, n'exprime-t-il pas tout l'enjeu de l'ironie romantique qui se voit ainsi promue au rang d'opération transcendantale destinée à fonder une métaphysique de la création poétique? Mais le Livre, rêvé par les Romantiques de Iéna, ne verra jamais le jour. Il n'aura jamais été écrit si ce n'est sous la forme de fragments comme plus tard le sera le Livre de Mallarmé sous forme de feuillets dispersés, à moins qu'il n'ait fait naufrage dans le poème du

Coup de dés où très singulièrement le mot "ironie" apparaît au coeur même du texte:

> *Une insinuation*
> *au silence*   simple
>   *enroulée avec ironie.*[18]

L'ironie s'inscrit ainsi au coeur même de la problématique de la création littéraire. Dès le début du XIXe siècle elle permet d'énoncer cette passion de l'Oeuvre pure dont Flaubert et Mallarmé seront, dans la seconde moitié du XIXe siècle en France, les plus lucides et désespérés artisans. Car la Beauté qu'ils s'efforceront de capter dans les rets de leur écriture s'avérera une allégorie de la Mort et du Néant. C'est bien cette passion de l'Oeuvre pure qui anime tout le projet romanesque de Flaubert. Ne rêva-t-il pas d'écrire un "livre sur rien?" Cette passion de la forme pure aspirée par son propre vide Flaubert l'attribue à son tempérament, à sa nature profonde toute transie d'ironie et de mélancolie. Aussi, comme l'atteste sa *Correspondance*, Flaubert s'est souvent identifié à la figure archétypale du bouffon parce que celle-ci, comme l'écrit Sartre, lui permet de disqualifier le fini par l'infini, l'être par le néant.[19] "Le fond de ma nature est, quoi qu'on en dise, le saltimbanque, écrit Flaubert à Louise Colet le 6 août 1846. J'ai eu dans mon enfance et ma jeunesse un amour effréné des planches. J'aurais peut-être été un grand acteur si le ciel m'avait fait naître plus pauvre. Encore maintenant ce que j'aime par-dessus tout c'est la forme, pourvu qu'elle soit belle, et rien au-delà."[20] Soulignons aussi qu'à l'époque où il acheva la rédaction de *Madame Bovary*, le "livre sur rien," Flaubert conçut avec la complicité de son ami Bouilhet le livret d'une pantomime destinée à être représentée sur la scène du Théâtre des Folies Nouvelles: *Pierrot au sérail, pantomime en six actes, suivie de l'apothéose de Pierrot dans le paradis de Mahomet.*[21] Pierrot incarne ce jeu du sublime et du grotesque, du rien et de l'au-delà, du "rien au-delà."

Un livre sur rien, sans sujet, réfléchissant la beauté parfaite de sa forme dans le miroir que lui tend un langage épuré, est un livre qui tient uniquement par la force de son style, la rigueur de son architecture et la souplesse de son phrasé musical. Aussi Flaubert se réfère-t-il à la théorie des nombres qui, dans la tradition platonicienne, fait communiquer le monde de la mathématique avec celui de la musique. "La poésie, écrit-il, doit être aussi précise que la géométrie." Cette rage de la précision s'exprime chez Flaubert par la recherche du mot juste. Mais le mot juste, loin d'être le trait descriptif purement réaliste, est avant tout le mot musical. Dans une lettre à Georges Sand datée du 3 mars 1876 Flaubert écrit: "Pourquoi y a-t-il un rapport nécessaire entre le mot juste et le mot musical? Pourquoi arrive-t-on toujours à faire un vers quand on resserre un peu trop sa pensée? La loi des Nombres gouverne donc les sentiments et les images."[22]

Tout l'effort de Flaubert consiste donc à relever le roman de sa déchéance—le roman n'est-il pas le genre hybride par excellence?—à le transfigurer en ressourçant le langage de la fiction à son origine musicale: "La prose est née d'hier, écrit-il, voilà ce qu'il faut se dire. Le vers est la forme par excellence des littératures anciennes. Toutes les combinaisons prosodiques ont été faites, mais celles de la prose tant s'en faut."[23] Tel est l'enjeu de la notion de *style* chez Flaubert. Tout se passe comme si la phrase parfaitement rythmée pouvait parler à l'âme indépendamment même de son sens. Le style n'est pas seulement une façon particulière d'écrire. Il désigne plus profondément chez Flaubert le soliloque de l'âme éprise de Beauté: "Je me souviens d'avoir eu des battements de coeur, d'avoir ressenti un plaisir violent en contemplant un mur de l'Acropole, un mur tout nu (celui qui est à gauche quand on monte aux Propylées). Eh bien, je me demande si un livre, indépendamment de ce qu'il dit, ne peut pas produire le même effet. Dans la précision des assemblages, la rareté des éléments, le poli de la surface, l'harmonie de l'ensemble, n'y a-t-il pas une vertu intrinsèque, une espèce de force divine, quelque chose d'éternel comme un principe? (Je parle en platonicien)."[24]

Le mot musical est le mot qui, délesté de son opacité matérielle, relevé de sa stéréotypie, se rendrait par son ajustement rythmique au coeur de la phrase, transparent aux jeux de l'Idée, de la Beauté immatérielle. Aussi Flaubert définit-il le style comme *une façon absolue de voir les choses*. Mais cette vision, qui est celle d'un Dieu, se voit qualifiée singulièrement de "blague supérieure," de bouffonnerie suprême. L'impersonnalité dont on a tant parlé dans la critique et qui caractérise l'énonciation flaubertienne de la voix romanesque, n'est pas l'expression d'une "ataraxie" ou d'une "apathie" stoïcienne mais le retrait simulé de la voix narrative qui, s'effaçant ironiquement au moyen du style indirect libre, en arrive à parasiter toutes les fausses perspectives suscitées par le miroir de la fiction. Car toutes les perspectives chez Flaubert sont fausses. La perspective d'Emma Bovary n'est pas plus vraie que celle de Charles, ou celles de l'abbé Bournisien ou du pharmacien Homais, autant d'incarnations de la Bêtise universelle. Le point de vue du Dieu flaubertien, très différent en cela de celui de Balzac, se présente en creux comme l'*intégrale* ironique de toutes les fausses perspectives suscitées ironiquement par le Destin, la Bêtise universelle.

L'outil grammatical et stylistique qu'utilise Flaubert est celui du style indirect libre. Dès lors, qui parle dans les phrases rédigées au style indirect libre? Le narrateur? Le personnage? En vérité ni l'un ni l'autre, ou mieux encore l'un et l'autre à la fois. Brouillage des voix, le style indirect libre marque à la fois la suprême ironie de l'Auteur et la syncope d'un narrateur divin au coeur de sa Création. L'indirect libre ouvre ces espaces des phrases improoprononçables, ce que Ann Banfield appelle "unspeakable sentences," phrases dont aucun sujet ne saurait assumer l'énonciation et dont seules les ruses de l'écriture tiennent lieu.

L'écriture flaubertienne est ainsi l'ombre portée de l'incommunicable sur le langage comme elle est aussi l'ombre portée d'une Beauté immatérielle sur un monde laid et défiguré. Bouvard et Pécuchet ne sont-ils dans l'oeuvre de Flaubert les derniers porte-parole? Ces deux cloportes qui recopient dérisoirement penchés sur leur pupitre toute l'histoire de la Philosophie et de la Science, n'annoncent-ils pas les bouffons tragico-grotesques de Samuel Beckett?

---

* Professor Madou presently teaches at the University of Miami.

[1] S. Kierkegaard, *Le concept d'ironie*, dans *Oeuvres complètes*, tome 2, traduit du danois par Paul-Henri Tisseau et Else-Marie Jacquet-Tisseau (Paris: Ed. de l'Orante, 1975).

[2] S. Kierkegaard, *Le concept d'ironie*, p. 120.

[3] G. Deleuze, *Présentation de Sacher-Masoch* (Paris: Ed. Bourgois, Coll. 10/18), p. 82.

[4] R. Schaerer, "Le mécanisme de l'ironie dans ses rapports avec la dialectique," *Revue de Métaphysique et Morale* (1941), p. 204-205.

[5] Platon, *Oeuvres complètes* (Paris: Bibl. de la Pléiade, Gallimard), p. 764.

[6] Schlegel, *Lycée*, 42.

[7] J. Starobinski, "Ironie et mélancolie," *Critique*, 228 (1966), 294-295.

[8] Schlegel, *Fragment du Lycée*, traduit par R. Ayrault dans *La Genèse du romantisme allemand* (Paris: Aubier, I 970), III, 168.

[9] Hegel, *Principes de la philosophie du droit*, 140.

[10] Schlegel, *Fragment de l'Athenaeum*, 121; voir *L'Absolu littéraire* de Ph. Lacoue-Labarthe et J.L. Nancy (Paris: Ed. du Seuil, 1978), pp. 113-114.

[11] *Ibidem*

[12] *Lycée*, 42. Voir R. Ayrault, *Genèse du romantisme allemand* (Paris: Aubier, 1969), III, 170.

[13] J. Starobinski, *Le portrait de l'artiste en saltimbanque* (Paris: Skira, Coll. des sentlers de la Création), p. 40.

[14] Mallarmé, *Oeuvres*, Ed. de Yves-Alain Favre (Paris: Garnier, 1985), p 38.

[15] Aristote, *Poétique*, 1447 b, trad. de J. Hardy (Paris: Les Belles Lettres[réimpr.], 1969).

[16] Schlegel, *Fragment* 252, dans *L'absolu littéraire*, p. 135.

[17] *Op. cit.*, Fragment 116, p. 112.

[18] Mallarmé, *Un Coup de Dés jamais n'abolira le hasard*, dans *Oeuvres*, p. 427

[19] Sartre, *L'Idiot de la famille* (Paris: Gallimard, 1970), p. 1216

[20] Flaubert, Lettre à Louise Colet, 6 août 1846, dans *Correspondance* (Paris: Gallimard, 1973), I, 278.

[21] Flaubert, *Oeuvres complètes* (Paris: Ed. du Seuil, 1964), II, 418.

[22] Flaubert, *Correspondance Flaubert-Sand* (Paris: Flammarion, 1981), p. 528.

[23] Flaubert, Lettre à George Sand, le 3 avril 1876.

[24] *Ibidem*.

The Spirit of Erotic Wit in French Literature

Benjamin F. Bart †
University of Pittsburgh

The subject of eroticism in French literature appears in anticipation to be one which any healthy person should be able, effortlessly, to treat, if not with elegance and aplomb, then at any rate with ease and gusto. The event, however, has proved to be other than I had anticipated, and this fact in itself has led me to certain reflections, which I should like to discuss with you.

As an initial proposition, I suggest that the word "eroticism" covers so much territory as to be all but unmanageable. *Madame Bovary*, for instance, was brought before the law courts on a charge of "attentat aux moeurs," French legal jargon for our topic, "eroticism." And at the opposite end of the scale, a district in my home city of Pittsburgh is resplendent with large signs proclaiming the availability of "erotic" books, pictures, films, and the like, among which I imagine one would seek in vain for a copy of *Madame Bovary*.

At one extreme, then, "erotic" is a euphemism for "pornographic." This sense for the word is well established and has its useful place in debates about censorship. But it can only obscure the points I wish to make, for when the erotic slips down into pornography, it is no longer literature. Yet a failure to capture the ecstasy, the sublimity, or—at the very least—the excitement of the erotic leaves us drifting aimlessly through the anodyne into banality. Eroticism that bores us by its ordinariness is not literature, either.

I propose, then, to use the word "erotic" in a narrower compass than is customary. I shall be seeking a middle ground for it, which stops short of sex-as-pornography but, I surely hope, lies beyond sex-as-banality. Eroticism thus defined has a comfortably traditional structure. The erotic conceived as a mean between the dull and the dirty reminds us—I hope not too irreverently—of Aristotle's structures in the *Nicomachaen Ethics* and the *Poetics.*

But eroticism is not so easily disposed of, as more than a century of quarrels about it have displayed, for individual sensibilities here vary widely. What bores me as an account of sexuality may titillate you. Or what is to me a charming piece of erotic impudence may for some of you be pornography on a scale such that you would feel constrained to leave the room, were I to begin reading it aloud. One man's meat is another man's poison here. The writings of, for instance, a George Sand raised the issue for Victorian readers in England and began the long-lived reputation of the "dirty French novel" in that country and in America.[1] Balzac, de Maupassant, and a host of other French authors enshrined the notion so firmly amongst the canons of popular criticism in England and America that our analysis must take account of it.

To take a precise example, Balzac lavishes erotic touches on his portraits of Mme Marneffe in *La Cousine Bette*:

> Valérie était délicieusement mise. Sa blanche poitrine étincelait serrée dans une guipure dont les tons roux faisaient valoir le satin mat de ces belles épaules des Parisiennes qui savent (par quels procédés, on l'ignore!) avoir de belles chairs et rester sveltes. Vêtue d'une robe de velours noir qui semblait à chaque instant près de quitter ses épaules, elle était coiffée en dentelle mêlée à des fleurs à grappes. Ses bras, à la fois mignons et potelés, sortaient de manches à sabots fourrées de dentelles. Elle ressemblait à ces beaux fruits coquettement arrangés dans une belle assiette et qui donnent des démangeaisons à l'acier du couteau.[2]

Balzac has ingeniously shifted back and forth between the nude and exciting flesh of his heroine and the clothes which partially cover, partially reveal, her body. We sense that body and start to react in ways that would take us out of the scene and into our own physicality; but at once Balzac shifts to the dress, to the fact that he does not know how Parisian women do it, to the ingenious suggestion that even the steel of the knives is getting itchy. For all but Victorian readers, for whom such passages were entirely new experiences of reading, the description retains its qualities as literature.

Later, Mme Marneffe is putting the final touches on her costume for dinner:

> Valérie se planta le plus joli bouton de rose au milieu de son corsage, en haut du busc, dans le creux le plus mignon. C'était à faire baisser les regards de tous les hommes au-dessous de trente ans.
> —Je suis à croquer! se dit-elle....[3]

It is surprising how many different ways Balzac found to indicate where Mme Marneffe placed this *bouton de rose*. Noting that it took all the assurance of a man of thirty to stare at it was the touch of an experienced as well as an imaginative writer. Making Mme Marneffe look attractive enough to eat linked two primal senses and needs. And having her state it makes it even more sensual. I propose that we agree that Balzac can write very sensually, that we can understand the difficulties the Victorians had, and that we can rejoice that we do not share them.

What will explain this variation among judgments of examples of writing which are variously seen as anodyne or scabrous to people in different ages? Or, had we other examples, of differing reactions among people of the same period but differing sensibilities? One of several key elements is certainly esthetic distance, the distance from his subject at which the author's presentation places us or, at any rate, suggests we stand.

Any passage we call erotic must relate to one aspect or another of making love. Suppose I phrase this as "They spent the night together" or (since it is French literature we are discussing, "Ils ont couché ensemble"). In this quiet example, the esthetic distance from which we view the scene is so great that the reader is left totally unmoved by the blank, factual tone of the utterance. The exciting physical reality of what took place in that bed is all but dissipated into the near nullity of the statement.

In opposite fashion, I could refer to the same event and begin in a louder tone and with a more rapid delivery, "And then he took her. . ." But unlike Agnès, I shall not tell you what he took. However, had my sentence gone on to include a powerful, effective account which did offend some tastes, it would be because for them the esthetic distance had narrowed to the point where they found themselves closer to the event than was comfortable under the circumstances. Language—and not the palpitating events—would still be alone at issue. Nevertheless, the signified would be so close as to impose itself. For a parallel example of signifier approximating to signified, consider the moment at which appropriate words are just about to persuade the lady to accede to the gentleman's wishes. Signifier and signified can come perilously close and, even in literature, the distance can narrow until for some it becomes inadequate to protect the literary status of the utterance.

If esthetic distance is a permissible analytic approach here, then the problem of responses which vary from one person to another is no more than the familiar experience that the threshold of tolerable esthetic distance is not fixed, but rather changes with persons and with periods. Dickens' *Christmas Carol* is typical in this respect. For some, the work escapes the sticky clutches of sentimentality. For others, Tiny Tim cloys.

The proper esthetic distance involves arousing our interest while not overwhelming us and thus moving beyond literature. One way to achieve this, if one is an adequate artist, is through powerful mastery of a chaste use of language. While even chaster in language than Balzac's account of Mme Marneffe, Flaubert's seduction scene in *Madame Bovary* is equally clear about the level of Emma's arousal.[4] Here we shall see how the writer's craft may maintain esthetic distance, even though at the end Emma will fall fainting into Rodolphe's all-too ready arms. The scene begins, you will recall, as Emma and Rodolphe ride off together into the woods:

> Dès qu'il sentit la terre, le cheval d'Emma prit le galop. Rodolphe galopait à côté d'elle. Par moments ils échangeaient une parole. (p. 162)

They are off in the shared exhilaration that two horses can provide their riders when they are galloping side by side. Emma and Rodolphe hardly speak, lost in the rhythm of the horses' movement. This much all readers can sense.

The remaining sentence of the paragraph requires readers with some experience of horseback riding, an awareness almost all of Flaubert's readers would have possessed. To begin with, horses are herd animals and will tend to adjust their pace readily to one another. Additionally, and much more importantly, as a horse breaks into the gallop, his rider has a very simple choice of alternatives. Either he adjusts to the horse's rhythm. . .or he falls off. There is no intermediate state. As Emma adapts herself to the gait of her mount, Flaubert's phrasing and rhythms bear the meaning:

> La figure un peu baissée, la main haute et le bras droit déployé, elle s'abandonnait à la cadence du mouvement qui la berçait sur la selle.

As Emma gave herself to her horse, "s'abandonnait à la cadence du mouvement," her horse was also moving in concert with Rodolphe's. Her body and her would-be lover's were already at one and the seduction was already taking place.

Rodolphe now raised the level of the tensions. A well-trained horse knows that being given his head is a signal to break into his fastest gait. He responds at once:

> Au bas de la côte, Rodolphe lâcha les rênes; ils partirent ensemble, d'un seul bond. . .

The immense physicality of the description links the two mounts in a powerful physical union. Horses and riders race madly up the hill as one being, exulting in the wild rush of feeling. At the top of the rise, exaltation reaches its peak of tension. . .and then finds release:

> puis, en haut, tout à coup, les chevaux s'arrêtèrent, et son grand voile bleu retomba.

In microcosmic form and through riding their horses as surrogates, Emma and Rodolphe have already made love. It will remain only to consummate it directly, without the intervening role of the horses.

The next pages are skillful, as Flaubert slowly takes from the already aroused Emma all those familiar forms of time and space which recall and reinforce conventional morality. From atop the hill, they can see Yonville, "et jamais ce pauvre village où elle vivait ne lui avait semblé si petit." The atmosphere is "tiède," she is a bit "étourdie" (p. 163). And then, with care not to hurry her, Rodolphe, biding his time, seduces her, and we return to the verb which first marked her giving herself to her horse's gait:

> —Oh! Rodolphe!....fit lentement la jeune femme en se penchant sur son épaule.
> Le drap de sa robe s'accrochait au velours de l'habit. Elle renversa son cou blanc, qui se gonflait d'un soupir; et, défaillante, tout en pleurs, avec un long frémissement et se cachant la figure, elle s'abandonna. (p. 165)

The seduction, begun two pages earlier around the departure on horseback, has now moved from its symbolic to its actual consummation.

* * * *

The erotic is here high literature. As we read this deftly handled scene and move from symbol to act, we are seduced with Emma, we know why she gave in, for we have felt the cadences to which she abandoned herself. The careful, sensitive artistry in the short excerpts we have read lies in part in the chasteness of the language Flaubert used to indicate sexual union. The dynamism of a rider giving herself to her galloping steed stands in for Emma's giving herself to the imperious demands of her lover and lets us experience the oneness of the sexual communion before Emma and Rodolphe carry it out. Their intercourse can then take place in the blank space before the next paragraph.

In that fashion, Flaubert's readers experience what he wished them to know in a guise which they do not find inacceptable. The chasteness Flaubert felt must characterize literature was fully protected: riding a horse, and not a sexual embrace, is the overt, manifest subject. When it comes time to recount the sexual union of lover and mistress, we can rely on the union of riders and horses for our experiencing of the scene, and the recurrence of the verb *s'abandonner* serves as the touchstone, the verbal link between the two acts. Long custom had drained this verb of any emotive sexual directness: it was an entirely accepted euphemism, to which Flaubert had restored its vitality by his first use of it. Esthetic distance was preserved.

If we were to require this level of virtuosity in all writing on erotic subjects, we would have almost no examples and literature would be the poorer. Fortunately, *l'esprit gaulois* can also serve this purpose and is a rich and full component of French literature. We shall now examine some of these less exalted examples, to see how they are handled.

The problem of esthetic distance still remains central, of necessity. But in these examples, we shall not have authors with Balzac's clever ability to flirt with dangerous subjects or with Flaubert's sensitivity or his ingenuity in finding appropriate correlatives for the sexual feelings and acts to be portrayed. Other authors had to find other means. Fortunately, there are many ways for them to maintain the delicately balanced stance of acceptable eroticism. In all of them, nevertheless, readers must still be kept at a sort of middling distance from sexuality if the author is neither to bore them nor to press his subject too close to them and thus make them lose the awareness that they are reading literature rather than being stimulated by pornography. One method in particular, however, dominates French handling of this problem, the deft use of wit, the delightful play of *l'esprit* to keep *l'esprit gaulois* literary.

L'esprit is everywhere in French erotic passages and we shall shortly have a quick look at samples from many different authors. But a charming nineteenth-century wit, Paul de Kock, could, more than most authors, spin out an erotic tale over several hundred pages as he played one variation after another on the sex act, its approaches, its frustrations, its accomplishment, and its after-effects. His heroes and heroines live for their single, consuming passion. If you are unfamiliar with them, it makes no difference. You can think of his novels as *Tom Jones* reduced to the bedroom scenes. Paul de Kock's ready wit allows him to present sexuality constantly, but always just sufficiently distanced from us so that we chuckle or giggle, laugh or guffaw. We could not be offended, unless our sensibilities were so delicate that the entire topic had to be kept from our ken.

Consider *Monsieur Gustave, ou le mauvais sujet* (1842).[5] The title already sets the tone: we know where we are before we open the book. Of plot, there really is very little. Episodes, though, we do have, endless changes on the same little play. In my first example, her name happens to be Julie, she happens to be married, and she is of the upper class. That is all we need to know, for as with Tom Jones, no woman resists Monsieur Gustave. He and Julie develop a passion for billiards. Why not? But gradually we acquire the feeling that the signifier "billiards" is being allied to a new signified. The transition paragraph is brief:

> Gustave, à force d'amour, avait calmé les craintes, les soupirs, les pleurs, les remords de Julie. Ils jouaient tous les jours au billard; ils y jouaient le matin, le soir, et je crois même dans le petit bois, dans la grotte, dans le labyrinthe. (p. 35)

The signified here are not what you think, however. They prove to be direct and not euphemisms and this is not where trouble begins. Rather, the dark grotto is so real that this is where Julie's husband stumbles upon her and Gustave in the Stygian darkness. The poor husband, who has heard his wife's voice, struggles blindly forward into the grotto:

> Le cher époux ne voyait rien....

The quiet irony of "le cher époux" sets us off pleasantly.

> Le cher époux ne voyait rien; il s'embarrasse les pieds dans quelque chose...Il tombe...roule...et se trouve sur Gustave, qui, je ne sais pourquoi, était alors à genoux près d'un banc de verdure.

Gustave, however, does not lose his presence of mind for even an instant. He speaks at once:

> Quoi! c'est vous monsieur? j'allais au devant de vous.... Permettez que je vois aide à vous relever....
>
> —Comment c'est toi, mon ami!, dit Mme de Berly [Julie] en s'éloignant très vite du banc de gazon.

Thus far, we have only a simple bit of tomfoolery engineered by the lovers to befuddle the dull-witted husband, whose role derives from ancient comedy. But Paul de Kock, who denied us double meanings for the wood, the grotto, and the labyrinth, now lets us enjoy them. The husband responds:

> —Sans doute, c'est moi...Peste soit de votre idée de jouer sans lumière!....Je crois que je me suis fait une bosse au front..."

If Gustave notes that the husband has thus proclaimed his own cuckoldry, the young man courteously refrains from pointing it out and instead replies:

> —Mais, monsieur, il ne fait nuit que depuis un moment...nous allions faire allumer...—Parbleu! vois êtes bien habiles de jouer comme cela!....Vous ne deviez pas trouver les trous...—Pardonnez-moi, monsieur.

This is all the response that Gustave risks. The husband continues:

> —Sans la voix de ma femme je ne serais pas entré!...Mais je l'ai entendue qui poussait une exclamation de joie...—Ah! c'est que madame venait de mettre dedans. (p. 36)

With that only slightly obscure allusion, we may take our leave of this scene, secure in the knowledge that the next will be like it.

A bit later and driven from his happy billiards and the lovely Julie, Monsieur Gustave is stumbling about a farmyard with his servant in the middle of the night; they have awakened every one and pandemonium reigns. Gustave enters the house, hungry and hoping to find some one to give him food. It is pitch dark again:

> il écoute...il entend du bruit; il ouvre une porte qui n'était fermée qu'à peine; on pousse un cri...Gustave a reconnu la voix d'une femme; il s'avance...il trouve un lit...il tâtonne...il s'assure que quelqu'un est couché là...ce quelqu'un est une paysanne sans doute; mais cette paysanne a des appas fermes, des formes rondelettes, et elle se laisse tâter si complaisamment! "Ma foi," dit Gustave, "je vais essayer de l'attendrir; peut-etre obtiendrai-je ensuite qu'on me fasse une omelette. p. 47)

It is hard to be very severe about a young man so earnestly seeking the favors of a young lady. . . so that she will perhaps then make him an omelet. Distance has been ensured, but sex has not been banished.

Chaos is not over for the night, however. The peasants, milling about in the dark, realize that Marie-Jeanne, the servant with whom Monsieur Gustave is parleying to get his omelet, has the flint and tinder up in her room to strike up a light. By now all are persuaded that the devil is loose in the house and the qui-pro-quo can reign unhindered.

> On arrive devant la porte de Marie-Jeanne; on entend des plaintes, des soupirs, des gémissements étouffés. "Ah! morguenne," dit la mère Lucas, "v'la le diable qui s'empare de Marie-Jeanne!"
>
> Les paysans n' osent pas ouvrir la porte: ils se serrent les uns contre les autres.
>
> "Dis donc, Marie-Jeanne," crie la paysanne, "est-ce que le diable est entré dans ta chambre?" "Oui...oui...mais laissez-moi faire. . .j'saurai ben le combattre tout seule... — Prends garde qu'il n'entre dans ton corps. . .il prend toutes sortes de formes; retiens ben ta respiration!....—Il est déjà entré trois fois, mais il ne reste pas! ...J'savons ben le chasser...Tenez, c'est fini...le v'la qui sort...." (pp 50 51)

The next morning, the prudent Marie-Jeanne calms every one by assuring them that it had all been a bad dream on her part. But Monsieur Gustave did not get his omelet, and we had best leave him before he finds his way into another bed.

* * * *

To cover a greater range of possibilities for wit as the distancing element in erotic passages, I turn now to briefer examples. A surprise ending often saves the day:

> Vous êtes un infame, vous avez lâchement abusé de moi pendant mon sommeil... —Vous m'en voulez donc?... —Oui, parce qu'il fallait attendre que je fusse réveillée.[6]

Or, with the dubious aid of faltering *ri...es e...brassées*:

> Si j'cède à tes beaux discours,
> C'est parc'que tu m'cass' la tête,
> Car avec un' fille honnête
> On n'couch' pas avant huit jours.

Another example of the surprise ending uses the slang term "giberne," normally the cartridge pouch slung about the hips but here used for what we decently label the

> Elle a une crâne giberne, ton adorée, faut lui rendre justice. Tout est-il à elle, dis?

Such unflattering jibes are the stock in trade and common property of all lesser wits. This one recurs in a caricature by Henri Monnier, for which you will easily imagine the expression of the mother, as her daughter explains to a visitor:

> Petite maman s'est fait des nénais avec du coton.

The basic scene recurs in *L'Assommoir,* where Zola adopts the language of his characters to explain that,

> Nana ne se fourrait plus des boules de papier dans son corsage. Des nichons lui étaient venus....[7]

Elsewhere, a mock seriousness may provide the distancing wit. Thus a courtesan is termed a "professeur femelle de philosophie horizontale." Vaudeville was the home for much material in this vein, often rhymed (I cannot bring myself to call the results verse):

> Péters, dis-moi, par amitié,
> Pourquoi que l'usage réclame
> Qu'à Paris on nomme moitié
> Ce qu'au village on nomme femme,
> —C'est que Paris est un pays
> Où se prodiguent tant les dames,
> Que là, les trois quarts des maris
> N'ont que la moitié de leurs femmes.

To even the score, we need only note that the fractions would be even worse, if we were discussing the men.

Not only do these authors exercise their saving wit on routine dubious situations such as the *nichons de Nana*; stock figures also play a central role in many of these shorter pieces, as they have since the Greeks. The kept woman is a standard butt of wit, as is the man who keeps her, for he undertakes to,

> Se charger de son existence, à la condition qu'elle se chargera de votre jouissance, et que vous aurez le droit de coucher avec elle — quant cela lui plaira.

Men are no better than women, for a *maison de tolérance* is a,

> bordel, que non seulement la préfecture de police tolère, mais encore qu'elle autorise pour la satisfaction des besoins du public célibataire — et surtout marié.

Henri de Pène discusses the role of the mistress in more even-handed and more complex terms. The mistress is, he reports, a

> Fille ou femme dont on est le maître, — quand on n'en est pas l'esclave battu, cocu et content; épouse illégitime à laquelle on est plus fidèle qu'à l'épouse légitime et qui se moque de vous tout autant que celle-ci....

The last idea brings the wife more fully to de Pène's attention. He now shifts to her and entertains himself and us by reversing his initial position. Paradox, complete with its logical *donc*, here ensures the light tone of distancing wit. Of married women, he reflects that,

> Le *maître* de quelques-unes, c'est leur mari, espérons-le, pour l'honnour de la morale; le *maître* d'un plus grand nombre, c'est leur caprice; le *maître* de toutes, c'est leur luxe... Quant à l'amant, il n'en saurait être question ici... D'ailleurs, quand une femme a un amant, elle est sa *maîtresse*: ce n'est donc pas lui qui en est le *maître*.

A number of devices from the rest of the literary tradition appear readily enough when an author needs wit to keep his erotic elements under control. Thus the sexual casualness of both men and women is the target in my next example when, at the end, the Parthian arrow finds its mark. An *amant de coeur* is a

> Greluchon, maquereau, homme qui, s'il ne se fait pas entretenir par une femme galante, consent cependant à la baiser quant il sait parfaitement qu'elle est baisée par d'autres que lui: c'est, pour ainsi dire, un domestique qui monte le cheval de son maître.

Sophie Arnould, the singer and wit of the eighteenth century celebrated by the Goncourt brothers, also applies her devastating tongue to the same endlessly new topic of infidelity:

> Une femme aimable est un anneau qui circule dans la société et que chacun peut mettre à son doigt.

* * * *

Like all comic genres in France, erotic literature delights in mocking the classics. One example will suggest the possibilities. The elevated reference at the end of my quotation satirically relieves the stronger language and cruder thought in the earlier phrasings, while at the same time it denigrates the lofty tone of the close itself. "What is it to enjoy oneself?" asks a wit. He responds easily enough:

> Passer sa jeunesse à baiser les filles, quand on est un homme, et à se faire baiser par les hommes, quand on est fille. C'est le *Aimons [-nous]! aimons [-nous]!* de M. Alphonse de Lamartine.

In another area, as in the English tradition, French erotic wit may occasionally drift into black humor:

> Une femme sensible se décide difficilement à laisser pendre un homme pour qui elle a eu des bontés.

Word-play is another commonplace of all forms of wit, the erotic included. Thus "Viticulture" is explained as "la culture des vits." And a well-known anecdote circulated concerning the princesse Mathilde:

> On lui avait recommandé un jeune auteur d'avenir...Celui-ci se présente au jour qu'elle avait fixé pour le recevoir.
> —Ah! c'est vous, dit-elle, Monsieur...Monsieur *Lévy*, je crois?
> —Madame, je me nomme Lépine.
> Oh! mon dieu, reprend la princesse, c'est la même chose. Il me semblait bien aussi qu'il y avait un *vit* ou une *pine* au bout de votre *Lé*.

Eroticism offers endless possibilities for word-play describing sexual acts by other terms. Voltaire's example in Candide is familiar.

> Un jour Cunégonde en se promenant auprès du Château, dans le petit bois qu'on appelait parc, vit entre des broussailles le Docteur Pangloss qui donnait une leçon de physique expérimentale à la femme de chambre de sa mère, petite brune très jolie et très docile. Comme Mademoiselle Cunégonde avait beaucoup de disposition pour les sciences elle observa, sans souffler, les expériences

réitérées dont elle fut temoin; elle vit clairement la raison suffisante du Docteur, les effets & les causes: & s'en retourna toute agitée, toute pensive, toute remplie du désir d'être savante; songeant qu'elle pourroit bien être la raison suffisante du jeune Candide, qui pouvait aussi être la sienne.[8]

The idea, famous and simple enough to copy, recurs in the nineteenth century: Thus,

> La belle en train de bien apprendre,
> Serrait Lucas, qui, las de besogner,
> Par un air abattu lui fit assez comprendre
> Qu'on ne peut toujours enseigner.

Sometimes the word-play is so rapid that it is gone before one realizes it. Referring to venereal disease, one potential victim consoles himself for having risked it by urging that,

> Si j'attrape quéque chose, au moins j' l'aurai pas volé.

Or Lorédan Larchey, in his *Dictionnaire historique d'argot...*, after defining "fouailleur" as "libertin," adds:

> Un T de plus dans le corps du mot livre son étymologie.[9]

Perhaps the most entertaining examples, with which I shall finish, are those where the expression is entirely decent in its direct meaning and can, indeed, be so taken by those who wish. But others will see that the author had another idea in mind, as well. The thought that some readers will miss it adds to our pleasure. Consider a first example:

> Il lui enseigna la danse du loup, la queue entre les jambes.

Or this little scene from the *bal Mabille*, in which the lady turns the remark around herself for our benefit:

> La Dame—Finissez donc, monsieur, vous chiffonnez mon mouchoir!...
> Le Monsieur—Madame c'est pour voir votre chiffre.
> La Dame—Mon *chiffre*, c'est cent francs.

More complex and permissible only because it does disguise its sense under anodyne words is the following:

> Des autres perroquets il diffère pourtant,
> Car eux fuient la cage, et, lui, il l'aime tant,
> Qu'il n'y est jamais mis, qu'il n'en pleure de joie.

And a similar though more familiar shift in meanings:

> Comment pensez-vous qu'on puisse garder une serrure, à qui toutes sortes de clefs sont propres?

* * * *

As I close and we turn our thoughts toward the reception and the dinner to follow, I offer a final example of wit saving the erotic by defusing it through a veil of language, which, here, is surely no more than culinary:

> Le four est toujours chaud, mais la pâte n'est pas toujours levée.

---

[1] See Patricia Thomson, *George Sand and the Victorians* (New York: Columbia University Press, 1977).

[2] I am citing from the edition by Maurice Allen (Paris: Garnier, 1962), p. 165.

[3] *Ibid.*, p. 208. It was drawn to my attention at the Colloquium that *croquer* can also mean "to sketch" but the dictionnaire of the Academy of 1877 gives the sense of "to bite into, eat, etc.," and that seems to me to be the sense here, but the reader may make his own choice.

[4] I am citing from the edition by Mme Gothot-Mersch (Paris: Garnier, 1971), p. 5.

[5] (Paris: Barba)

[6] Except as otherwise indicated, all the remaining illustrations are drawn from Alfred Delvau, *Dictionnaire érotique moderne*, Nouvelle Edition (Bale: Schmidt, 1871).

[7] Edition de la Pléiade (Paris: Gallimard, 1968), p. 709.

[8] I am citing from the edition of André Morize, Societé des textes français modernes (Paris: Droz, 1931), pp. 6-7.

[9] Eighth edition (Paris: Dentu, 1880).

The Problematics of Embedded Poems, from *Aucassin* to Artaud

Laurence M. Porter
Michigan State University

To consider the role of lyrics within longer works is to consider an intratextual problem of the relationship of part to whole that presents itself throughout Western literature from the early Middle Ages to the present, from Boethius's *The Consolation of Philosophy* in the sixth century to John Ashbery's *Three Poems*. One's first impression of such lyric and narrative hybrids is variety. Many different genres may be mixed together, or only two. The same work may contain both prose and verse narration; verse may serve both lyric and narrative functions; and one encounters a wide range of relationships between lyric and narrative sections. So far as the history of lyric and narrative hybrids is concerned, certain individual intertextual linkages can be established, such as those between Boethius and Dante or between Guillaume de Lorris (who uses two embedded poems) and Guillaume de Machaut. But the generic origins of the lyric and narrative hybrid are unclear, as has been demonstrated by the controversy regarding the models for *Aucassin et Nicolette*. Moreover, lyrics can be found embedded in narratives from the beginnings of Western literature, for example in Andromache's elegiac lament for Hector in the *Iliad*, or in the Bard's song in *Beowulf*. Since most narrative is essentially polyphonic, as Plato and Bakhtine have established, lyric embedding is a natural if not inevitable consequence of narration. What generalizations about it, however, can be made?

First of all, I believe that embedded lyrics are dissimilar to internal reduplication. When I attempted to offer a strict constructionist definition of *mise en abyme* in narrative a few years ago, in the context of a general typology of the relations between part and whole in literary works, I proposed five criteria. The *mise en abyme* must be of the same genre as the text in which it is embedded; it must treat the same topic as the framing text; it must be less than half as long as the framing text; it must be introduced by a main character; and it must move the plot. Examples in a different genre or concerning a different topic I call metaphorically displaced internal reduplication; examples that are not introduced by a main character or do not move the plot I call metonymically displaced. All four of these imperfect types of internal reduplications are forms of digression, a term referring to a part of a text experienced as discontinuous with the whole.[1]

Prima facie, any lyric embedded in a narrative is metaphorically displaced. Since the primary illusion of narrative is metonymic enchainment, and the primary illusion of the lyric is metaphoric transformation, the tropological nature of the shift from narrative to lyric is congruent with the tropological texture of the new genre, of the lyric, into which one is shifting. To embed a lyric in a narrative, then, is to create a metaphor of metaphor. One thus automatically signals code-switching, whereas within a lyric itself, as I have suggested elsewhere, embedding of a secondary lyric must be signaled by an identifiable introduction of a new voice or a new audience, by topographical artifice, or by a combination of these devices.

Within an individual work, a shift from narrative to lyric foregrounds the latter, which is recognizable through a greater density of repetitions or rhythms, sounds, or words, or through a combination of these features. Such a transformation represents a form of code-switching analogous to that which can be signalled by a change of language, of stylistic level, or of typographical presentation of a message. In and of themselves, however, shifts like these are empty signs. Depending on the context, they may reflect a totalizing impulse that makes each of two successive messages, like the two terms of a metaphor, refer to a single, overarching truth; they may instead create the dialogic interaction of a tonal dissonance; or they may even connote psychic disintegration, as they do in Patchen or Artaud.

Code-switching in turn implies a recognition that both of the two codes in question are arbitrary. It deconstructs the illusion of a unitary social nexus. It readily associates itself, then, with self-consciousness, of which at least two forms appear to be associated with embedded lyrics. First, a foregrounding of the extradiagetic situation involving author, message, and audience, a shift from the message in the text to the message of the text; second, a representation of a contrast between an unacceptable former implied author, and an emergent, positively transformed implied author. In other words, the implied author no longer is experienced as uniform, but rather as discontinuous.

So great is the variety of possible examples that generalization is difficult. Embedded lyric, however, does interrupt the forward progress of the metonymic chain of cause and effect that constitutes the primary illusion of narrative. It may serve to contrast the subjective with the objective, the general with the particular, or the eternal with the temporal. It may create a sense of closure by accentuating the fictive status of what has preceded, as in the intermezzi and concluding scenes of many of Molière's later plays. An examination of some individual narrative/lyric hybrids may help to bring out their great variability, which is that of polyphony itself.

There appear to be two major polyphonic traditions emerging from the Latin Middle Ages: the allegorical tradition of Prudentius, in which abstract conceptions of personality traits are personified,[2] and the prose-poetry mixture of Boethius, where concrete manifestations of personality are rendered abstract by being presented in the form of different genres. In his sixth-century *The Consolation of Philosophy*, which was greatly to influence Dante's *La Vita nuova*, Boethius alternates prose and verse regularly; both prose and verse address the problem of evil in a didactic manner, with the prose often consisting in a quasi-Socratic dialogue between the author and the personified figure of Philosophy, while the verse provides a monologic restatement and reinforcement of the lessons of the prose. The verse often points to the conclusions that should be drawn from the preceding prose passage or generalizes. Roughly speaking, the prose appears to represent the timebound world of experience, and the verse, the timeless world of wisdom. The prose corresponds to *chronos* or human time, and the verse to *kairos* or eternity as manifested as a chink in the armor of material appearances. As Philosophy explains in the sixth prose section of the fourth book, Providence resembles the artisan's vision of a finished work, whereas Fortune resembles the vicissitudes of the execution of that work over time. Virtuous individuals who suffer, one might add, are like the wood that is sawed, planed, filed, and nailed, and which lacks a vision of the final, perfect work of which it will form part. In other words, we need to learn to be able to see the imprint of *kairos* on *chronos*. Boethius's alternation of verse with prose does not represent the embedding of identifiable lyric genres within a narrative, however, and the distinction between the two forms is not so rigid as the foregoing discussion might suggest. The alternation serves, rather, to enliven a lengthy exposition of theodicy, while also serving as a metaphor for the contrast between our human insight and the divine viewpoint *sub specie aeternitatis*.

A more overt rendition of authorial self-consciousness, however, comes to be associated with a verse-prose alternation in *Aucassin et Nicolette*, which may date from around 1200.[3] Here it is still not a question of embedded lyrics; the verse sections consist in assonating *laisses* of seven-syllable lines. Each *laisse* concludes with a four-syllable line that assonates with the other concluding lines but not necessarily with the host *laisse*. The communicative situation is foregrounded by a *captatio benevolentiae* in the first *laisse*. It promises to cure the hearers of their sorrow and fill them with joy, so that the diegetic situation of the lovers' reunion, curing their lovesickness, corresponds to the extradiagetic situation of the audience. Notations directing the performers to *conter* or to *canter* precede each section, and the ending is formally announced. The versified sections function variously to present a subjective reaction to external events, to retell events already related in prose, or to continue the prose narrative from where it left off.

Metaphorically displaced internal reduplication occurs when Nicolette flees an unwelcome marriage, and arrives at Aucassin's court disguised as a minstrel. She sings him a ballad about Nicolette's undying devotion to Aucassin; in response, he attempts to reestablish the connection between the ideal world of verse and the real world of prose, asking "Biax dous amis, savés vos niént de cele Nicolete, dont vos avés ci canté?" She confirms the story in prose, and then, not having recognized her, Aucassin sends her off as a messenger to fetch herself from abroad. The strain of self-consciousness is reinforced in a second, earlier episode where Aucassin becomes the audience of his own story. Seeking Nicolette in the woods, he overhears some shepherds singing praises of her generosity. Hoping to learn of her whereabouts, he asks them to repeat the song. One answers: "je ne vos canterai mie, car j'en ai juré. Mais je le vos conterai, se vos volés." The wordplay with the apophany *conter / canter* suggests that the author considers the change of medium to be rather arbitrary. As a recent critic has explained, "the text's multiple patterns of reversals [e.g., between Christian and Saracen, male and female, valor and uxoriousness] and its dialogic emphasis throughout allow it to call into question the neatness of the very Self-Other distinction overtly and structurally created in the *chantefable*... the broadest 'lesson' of the text [is] that relations between outer form and inner substance [are] arbitrary."[4] Certain of the lyric sections express the conventions and ideals of courtly love, but these are clearly mocked by the incongruous prose settings. It would be an oversimplification to say of *Aucassin et Nicolette*, as it would of Boethius, that prose stands for time and verse stands for eternity. In Boethius, the verse gloss often consolidates the insights for which the prose has been struggling; in A*ucassin*, the prose often debunks the verse; and in Dante's *Vita nuova*, for example, the retrospective prose glosses of earlier verse reveal an additional spiritual meaning that can emerge only from the interaction of verse and prose.[5]

In *Aucassin* the hero's martial prowess proves ineffectual, whereas it is the heroine's authorial potency that makes things happen and brings the lovers together so that, in a sense, life imitates art. In Guillaume de Machaut's *Le Voir Dit*, with its oxymoronic title, further layers of self-consciousness are added. The triumphant author, a celebrated master, becomes seduced by the fantasies of ideal love in his own verse. When he as a bourgeois and archetypical *amant couart* attempts to act out the aristocratic ideal of *fin'amors*, however, he only makes a fool of himself. As the remembered ecstasy of sexual intimacy fades to be replaced by mistrust, *Le Voir Dit* becomes increasingly the story of its own composition and announces the prospective consummation of its integration into the author's complete works.

Le Voir Dit narrates in prose and octosyllabic couplets. The prose includes letters between the lovers, plus some specific comments on how those letters have been editorially abridged. Both the letters and the narrative include poems by each of the lovers (several attributed to the heroine Toute-Belle were demonstrably written by Machaut years earlier), sometimes presented as the result of laborious elucubrations and sometimes as part of a spontaneous, improvised conversational exchange. That two poems in the same rhyme scheme and form often appear juxtaposed as statement and response betrays the specular nature of the love illusion as the implied author's "découverte amoureuse de soi," all the more so since Toute-Belle as poet is an apprentice, being formed in the male protagonist's image. In a further circular movement, the narrative sections and quoted letters serve to make the love experience celebrated in the verse seem real, while at the same time the esthetic demands for realism give rise to the non-lyric sections: in other words, the prose sections are both the cause and the effect of verisimilitude. Since Machaut relates the same events in three different modes, in lyric, octosyllabic couplets, and prose, the three accounts provide each other with intratextual corroboration.[6] The referential status of the narration becomes confused because it depicts both human and allegorical figures in interaction with the narrator, and both he and the narratee Toute-Belle appear to consider the allegories as real as the people. The formal embedded verse functions variously as a subjective reaction, an episode in Toute-Belle's apprenticeship as a poet, or as a dialogic exchange that moves the plot. But above all, as later in Villon and in Rimbaud, the prose serves as a frame for an anthology of the verse. The first appearance of lyric *formes fixes* embedded in an "autobiographical" monument of French literature corresponds to a high point in the development of artistic self-consciousness: Machaut was "the first poet in French to arrange his *Oeuvres complètes* in manuscript form and to be conscious of his opus as a unity," and the first French poet to compose a long narrative whose subject was the craft of writing.[7]

Artistic self-consciousness becomes much more diffuse in the flamboyant masterpiece of François Villon. Villon's *Testament* is both literally and figuratively an anatomy. It comprehends a wide and incoherent variety of subjects, and it derives from the medieval tradition of parodic testaments in which an animal would bequeath parts of its body to various human notables. Villon often uses ballade-like *huitains* for narration and then launches into ballades without the warning of a presentation formula, *incise*, or title, so that only when we encounter the refrain repeated and therefore identifiable at the end of the second stanza, and the shorter stanzaic unit of the *envoi* with its formal apostrophe at the beginning of the fourth stanza, do we realize that we have been reading a poem. The frame is a speech act of renunciation and farewell; the bequests include prayers, entreaties, insults, praise, advice, and generalizations. All three temporal registers are present: the personal present and the timeless aphoristic present; retrospective memories and the *ubi sunt* topos; and prospective visions of life after death. Form does not follow function: whereas Machaut, for example, modulates from *serrmo mediocris* in his embeded poems. More strikingly, Villon creates internal dissonance of tone within the lyrics, when he makes the ballades' refrains—a formal element that evokes timelessness through its unvarying repetition-clash with their stanzas. Pungent aggression is juxtaposed with humble contrition, for example, in the "Ballade de Merci":

> Au fort, pour éviter rïottes,
> Je crie à toutes gens mercis.
> Qu'on leur froisse les quinze côtes
> De gros maillets forts et massis,
> De plombées et tels pelotes!
> Je crie à toutes gens mercis. (vv. 1990-95).

In the "Double Ballade" warning against "folles amours," on the other hand, it is the refrain which is playful, and the Biblical, historical, and mythological allusions of the first four of six stanzas which are solemn, contrasting with the dismissive "Bien heureux est qui rien n'y a!" (vv. 625-72). Artistic self-consciousness appears in many details other than the tonal dissonance: an imaginary secretary taking dictation, the anagrammatic signatures, and the frequent suggestions of oral communication such as self-correction and appeals or prolepsis (anticipation of objections) directed to a personified audience. Despite the irreverence of tone and the scatology and obscenity found throughout, the sixteen embedded ballades do seem to relate to the timeless and the narrative frame to the topical—not because the ballades are necessarily more elevated or dignified, but rather because they are more general and accessible to future readers other than an audience of close friends.[8]

After Villon the predominant function of embedded lyrics shifts from autobiographical and intratextual to impersonal and intertextual. In Rabelais's burlesque epic (references will be given in the form Book, chapter) verse itself undergoes carnivalization, often being reserved for some of the most obscene (II, 22; III, 6), scatological (I, 13; IV, 44), and nonsensical moments (I, 42; II, 5, 27; III, 21, 47; V, 12) rather than for tender or solemn ones. The encyclopedic tendencies of the Renaissance, and the heteroclite contents of such a Menippean satire or anatomy as Rabaelais's weakens the concept of authorship. He includes at least two poems by Mellin de Saint-Gelais (I, 58; IV, prologue), one by Catullus (IV, 52), and one by Hugues Salel (II, prefatory), and cites many proverbial couplets throughout. The composition and transmission of verse no longer constitutes a major subject of the longer work within which it is embedded, as it did for Machaut or Villon. The embedded poems that represent high points of comic wisdom—the inscription over the doorway of the Abbey of Thélème (I, 54), the sibyl's prophecy (III, 21), and the poem of the Dive Bouteille (V, 44)—are anonymous or attributed to episodic figures, once again distinguishing the implied author from the protagonists. Conspicuous owing to its typographical arrangement, rhyme, and rhythm, verse in Rabelais serves not only as a sign of formality that is subverted by its glaringly informal content, but also as a framing device whose artificiality underlines the fantasy of what it contains. Poems open the first three books, and some verse is introduced at the beginning of each of the last two. In such initial position it functions as part of the *captatio benevolentiae*, like a greeting ritual that establishes initial contact between the author and the readership on a formal plane before the author allows himself to become jocular and familiar. Books I, III, and V (in the second and third-to-last chapters) end with poems as well, moving us out of the temporal progression of the narratives into the timeless interchange between Rabelais and his successive generations of readers. In the interior sections of the narrative, the use of verse foregrounds the suspension of metonymic progress on behalf of playfulness.

The same function for embedded verse as a vehicle for frolicsome intrusions of popular culture persists nearly a century later in Agrippa d'Aubigné's neglected satiric novel, *Les Avantures du baron de Faeneste* (1617-1630). D'Aubigné contrasts the eponymous character, a Gascon Catholic braggart warrior whose name etymologically means "paraître," with the *eiron* Enay (etymologically, "être"). The seventeen short embedded poems are "recited," never written, by the three main characters, as part of the public domain. In the dialogic base inspired by Rabelais the shared poems form a common ground, especially so since Faeneste does not realize when he himself would have reason to take offense at them; they are not problematized as they were in the medieval authors.

At about the same time, however, Honoré d'Urfé's *L'Astrée* (1607-1627) offers a more richly self-conscious use of embedding. Most of the lyrics it contains are unremarkable Petrarchan restatements of love motifs from the pastoral tradition, echoing the attitudes already expressed in the narrative, the *cour d'amour* debates, and the epistolary sections, creating a pseudo-polyphony. The poems themselves remain perilously close to plagiarisms of Desportes and Tasso. Like *Le Voir Dit*, *L'Astrée* functions in part as an anthologizing repository for the author's lyrics: only twelve poems elsewhere attributed to D'Urfé do not appear here.[9] But the Twelve Tables of the Laws of Love, inscribed in octosyllabic *sixains* at the base of the painting in Astrée's temple, present in the form of an anonymous, authoritative revelation the pastoral Platonism that is the official ethos of the work. Silvandre, the main spokesperson for this ideal, admires them; but Hylas, who consistently advocates autonomy and immediate gratification over dependency and commitment, promptly sets out to subvert the official code. He steals back into the temple unobserved and radically alters the commandments of love with slight word changes that reverse their meaning (one thinks of Lautréamont's *Poésies*). Outside the temple again with his friends, he agrees to swear to obey the commandments if they will do the same; they are confused and disconcerted by the new version. At last when the parchments are held up to the light, the palimpsest and Hylas's forgeries are discovered, and he is forced to restore the original (II, 181-201). But his action, and his friends' difficulty in detecting it, calls into question the absolute, supernatural origination of the commandments by emphasizing how much they depend upon their physical existence as text. Much later in the work Hylas's own counterstatement, the Twelve Conditions of Love, is enunciated (in prose, naturally), but it was his friend Corilas rather than Hylas himself who wrote them. Their aim, paradoxically, is not to ensure independence, but rather to unite Hylas with a compatible woman by articulating a contract to which both partners can agree. And Silvandre has the last word, adding the *reductio ad absurdum* of a Thirteenth Condition: we shall remain free to observe none of the first Twelve (III, 490-94). The presence of two contrasting codes, both subverted, makes morality in love become relative to personality and problematizes human relationships.

The common element in all the verse-prose hybrids we have cited from the sixteen and the seventeenth centuries (along with Théophile de Viau's otherwise unremarkable adaptation of Plato's *Phaedo*) is Platonism, with its contrast between essence and appearance. I would not claim that verse corresponds to essence and prose to appearance in these works, but rather that the authors' awareness of a two-tiered Platonic model of reality is reflected in their combination of two different generic modes. In and of itself each mode in these authors proves to be an empty sign like the sun and the moon in the corpus of cosmological myths described in Claude Lévi-Strauss's "Le Sexe des Astres."[10] It is their conjunction that signifies.

Neo-Platonism again makes its appearance in La Fontaine's *Psyché* (1669). His ostensible reason for mingling prose and verse, however, is that he didn't know which medium to choose: prose was too plain for the *héroïque* element of his story, and verse was too ornate for the *galant* main plot. Besides, he hoped that variety would be pleasing.[11] He uses verse for narrating certain occasions where the gods are involved ("il ne siéroit guère bien à la prose de décrire une cavalcade de dieux marins," pp. 46-47); for descriptions; and for a few lyrical effusions. During the time of composition, in the 1660s, the polyphonic structure of the comic, burlesque, pastoral, and heroi-sentimental novel was giving way to a monophonic structure that reflected the imposition of social and political absolutism by *le roi soleil*. *Psyché* represented a compromise between monophonic and polyphonic modes, between classical and baroque. Among the four friends in the narrative frame, Acante wants an elegy, Ariste wants a tragedy, Gélaste wants a comedy, and Polyphile, the narrator of the Psyche story, seeks an equilibrium of forms. Even more so than in *L'Astrée*, verse here has lost its contestatory vigor and comes increasingly to resemble prose, with which it will nearly become confused during Neoclassicism.[12] La Fontaine, who still felt loyal to the disgraced Fouquet but who depended now on the patronage of Louis XIV, preserved some subtle traces of his former attachment in this poem. Certain verses were taken from *Le Songe de Vaux* praising Fouquet's magnificent residence; the orange grove that is celebrated in the opening poem (pp. 29-30) had been transplanted from Vaux-le-Vicomte, as La Fontaine was keenly aware; and he appears to "split the ambivalence" he felt toward the Sun King by depicting his magnificent aspect in Jupiter, and his jealous, spiteful aspect in Venus who feared and envied the beauty of Psyche. Such indirect opposition was of course doomed to be ineffectual.[13]

After La Fontaine two hundred years will elapse before we again encounter a prominent example of lyric and narrative hybrids, although we find embedded poems in Racine's *Esther* and *Athalie* once he has stepped out of the courtly game; in obscure works like Charles Nodier's "Mes Rêveries," or as exotic flavoring in, for example, Chateaubriand's *Atala*. Goethe's *The Sorrows of Young Werther* embeds translations of Ossian rather than original works. The Renaissance revival of classical genres remained dominant till 1830; combined with political absolutism (which persisted in one form or another until the same date), it appears to have militated against the creation of new lyric and narrative medleys.

It was the creation of the prose poem insofar as it effectively deconstructed the dichotomy of prose and verse as a distinction without a difference, that encouraged the creation of new hybrids. The first of these to become well-known in France was Rimbaud's *Une Saison en enfer*. There seven poems are formally presented within the prose of the section "Délires II—L'Alchimie du verbe," but retrospectively, as a form of expression Rimbaud was preparing to abandon. "Depuis longtemps je me vantais de posséder tous les paysages possibles, et trouvais dérisoires les célébrités de la peinture et de la poésie moderne....Cela s'est passé. Je sais aujourd'hui saluer la beauté."[14] The speech act of renunciation remains infelicitous for the implied author; owing to the full quotation of the embedded poems, renouncing them has the same effect vis-à-vis the empirical reader as bequeathing them had in Villon and Machaut. Like *Le Voir Dit*, *Une Saison en enfer* tells the story of its own composition, and the revisions of the inserted poems, which had been composed earlier, make them more self-reflexive than before.[15] The preceding section of that work, "Délires I," told of a misguided search for self-definition through love. "Délires II. Alchimie du verbe," relates the same search effected through writing. The juxtaposition and echoing titles of these two quests reveal Rimbaud's awareness that language is merely another form of the Other. Involvement with it inspires the debasing desire to be loved, or read, understood, and tempts one to compromise one's integrity. Rimbaud alters the poetic practice of his medieval precursors: the prose frame is no longer a gallery for spectators, counselors, or pupils, but rather a way in which the poet can introduce himself into the text as his own self-deprecating audience. Self-mockery protects him from the dangers of the quest—insanity—and rationalizes the cowardice of abandoning it.[16] Despite the intense anxiety of influence apparent in his work up to and including *Une Saison en enfer*, however, Rimbaud does not evade a Baudelairean matrix. His repeated assertions in *Une Saison en enfer*, that he is damned, together with his rhetoric of lucidity surpassing his past, lyrical self, echo Baudelaire's "la conscience dans le mal." The difference between the two poets is that what occurs in two separate movements in Baudelaire—lyrical effusions and self-critical prose poems reworking the former—has been condensed into one synthetic, hybrid text, so that Baudelaire's intertextuality has been transformed into Rimbaldian intratextuality.

Machaut, Villon, and Rimbaud all emerge as anthologists of themselves. Villon is at once strikingly modern and strikingly medieval in presenting an anatomy, whose tonal dissonance is justified because a dying man has the right to say anything. Machaut and Rimbaud, however, remain tainted with nostalgia for those very past selves that are being forsworn, and since their embedded lyrics remain the focus of their nostalgia, lyric preserves its privileged claim on our attention.

The lyric's pretensions to be the signifier of transcendence can more effectively be undermined by altering the relationship in which the prose appears as ground or framework and the poem as figure. This can be accomplished by multiplying the number of identifiable literary genres that appear alongside the lyric within a single text. In Artaud's *L'Ombilic des limbes*, for example, the variety of genres deployed—playlet, narrative, letters, intimate journal, essay, and lyric—deemphasizes lyric per se. Moreover, the three poems in *L'Ombilic des limbes* are completely disconnected from their context. The first poem describes the cosmos with a code conventionally reserved, since the Middle Ages, for Hell, and also evokes both earth like an abscess on God's body, and Hell like a spreading infection beneath the skin of earth. Minus the melodramatic posturing, we still are close here to the de-euphemization of metaphor found in Lautréamont,[17] an example of the code-mixing of Romanticism advocated, for example, in Victor Hugo's "Préface de *Cromwell*," and enacted on a larger scale by the hybridization of lyric and prose. Self-definition and the search for a self-image in painting then forms a transition between Artaud's vision of universal chaos in his first poem and his lyrical self-portrait, "Poète noir." But in the third poem the image of the poet becomes multiple and anonymous; the ceaseless, restless movement in this last lyric, combined with a totalizing discourse, evokes a desire that can never be satisfied. The fixation on oral sexuality in all three lyrics implicitly links the poet's verbalization to his desire; his frequent changing of genres is the objective correlative of his dissatisfaction, and the recurring imagery of abortion figures his frustration as well as his failure to sustain creation. The prose section that follows, via free association, does provide a gloss to Artaud's schizophrenic apocalypse: "J'imagine l'âme sentante et qui à la fois lutte et consent, et fait tourner en tous sens ses langues, multiplie son sexe, — et se tue....une sorte de souffrance froide et sans images, sans sentiment, et qui est comme un heurt indescriptible d'avortements."[18] Artaud abandoned lyric poetry the year after he published *L'Ombilic des limbes* in 1925.

As part of a medley of forms, lyric now functions to show what the intimate journal constituted by the medley tells, the drama of psychic disintegration. Artaud's use of the embedded lyric was not unique. It recurs, for example, in Kenneth Patchen's brilliant but often overlooked *Journal of Albion Moonlight* (1941).[19] Albion, an avatar of William Blakes' Everyman, explains that "If the mind does not function in a logical way, by what right do we demand ordered thinking?...If there can be no logic outside the mind, and if the mind rejects logic, is not the desire for logic a form of madness?"[20] Patchen mixes journal, novel, notes, Whitmanesque lyrics, ecphrasis (of drawings), and tables of contents of prospective works. The narrative of universal murder, inspired by the outset of the Second World War, enacts death in order to kill it. Within this framework, the embedded lyrics appear to represent prophetic affirmations of life. The first of them, for example, declares:

> He was the Word that spake it;
> He took the bread and brake it
> And what the Word did make it,
> I do believe and take it.

After a time Albion Moonlight stops inserting lyric poems into his journal, but the realization of lyricism is replaced by the symbol of lyricism in the form of anaphoric repetitions extending throughout long passages during which narrative progress halts. When narrative resumes it appears in a right-hand column competing with the anaphoric litany in the left-hand column. As the litany reaches a crescendo in an enumeration of "the duty of the artist," the narrative shrinks to a tiny marginal poem:

> I am the love
> I am the hate
> I am the pain
> I am the tears.

A final lyric entitled "The Stallions of Blood" is followed by a dramatization of artistic potency in the form of the tables of contents of prospective works. These, of course, will be interrupted. The journal resumes, and near the end of it the protagonist literally crawls back into his mother's womb. Artaud and Patchen both oppose the hubristic optimism and cult of genre-bound craftsmanship that characterized Modernism during L'Entre-Deux-Guerres.

To use the prose framework to depict a retreat from lyric affirmation is not to achieve the ultimate antilyrical statement, however. Such a statement was made by Vladimir Nabokov's novel *Pale Fire* (1962). There the humdrum versified experience of a North American academic with a moderate amount of imagination is overwhelmed and finally absorbed by the mad visions of the exiled king or pseudo-king of Zembla who is teaching incognito in a foreign language department in order to hide from his pursuers. His commentary, six times as long as the eponymous poem itself, is guided by the delusion that psychiatrists call "ideas of reference," by his notion that everything he observes refers to himself.

The embedded lyric can function variously, then, as a parody of collective ideals, e.g. of the code of chivalry in *Aucassin*; as part of a system for representing a two-tiered Platonic model of reality, as in Rabelais, D'Urfé, or D'Aubigné; as a parody of one's own ideals, as in Rimbaud; as a form of self-aggrandizement, as in Machaut and Mallarmé's "La Déclaration foraine"; or as part of a self-destructive artifact that calls any form of difference into question, as in Patchen, Artaud, and Nabokov. Even the self-aggrandizing modes, however, are associated with self-parody—Machaut's lyric self is the classical *amant couart*, an impotent, timid, easily influenced old man who foolishly strives to ape the chivalric courtly lover; and Mallarmé as the respected but incomprehensible poet must provide a plain prose rendering of his sonnet to convince his paying audience that they have received something worthwhile. Such ineradicable irony suggests that embedding allows the otherwise monologic lyric, the expression of a unified subjectivity, to participate in a polyphonic structure akin to that of the novel. Whereas a poet like Villon's contemporary Charles d'Orléans, for example, who attempts to extend the monophonic lyric so that it may absorb the polyphonic mode of allegory inherited from the psychomachia, encountered a dead end.

Any text, as Roland Barthes has pointed out, is an oppositional text. To be recognizable as a text, it must present itself as different from its context. The hybrid forms of the middle ages, nineteenth and twentieth centuries, however, foreground opposition *intra*textually by means of a medley of genres, whereas the genre-based literary expression of the sixteenth through the mid-nineteenth century tends toward allowing oppositionality to be inferred from its *inter*textual relationships.

[1]On internal reduplication see Laurence M. Porter, "Literary Structure and the Concept of Decadence: Huysmans, D'Annunzio, and Wilde," *Centennial Review* 22, ii (Spring 1978), 188-200; "From Chronicle to Novel: Artistic Elaboration in Camus' *La Peste*," *Modern Fiction Studies* 28, iv (Winter 1982-83), 589-96; and "Internal Reduplication in Lyric Poetry," pp. 192-98 in Claudio Guillén, ed. *Poetic Theory* (New York: Garland [International Comparative Literature Association, X, *Proceedings*, vol. II] 1985).

[2]On the allegorical tradition see Michel Zink, "The Allegorical Poem as Interior Memoir," *Yale French Studies* 70 (1986), 100-126.

[3]In "Precursors and Progenitors of *Aucassin et Nicolette*," *Studies in Philology* 74 (1977), 1-19, Tony Hunt claims the *prosimetrum* of late Antiquity (e.g., in Boethius) and the insertion of sung lyrics into vernacular narrative by Jean Renart as the main literary precedents of the *chantefable* form. The use of assonating *laisses*, however, clearly suggests that *Aucassin* antedates Renart.

[4]Maria Rosa Menocal, "Signs of the Times: Self, Other and History in *Aucassin et Nicolette*," *Romanic Review* 80, iv (November 1989), 497-511 (505 and 507). See also Kevin Brownlee, "Discourse as *Proueces* in *Aucassin et Nicolette*," *Yale French Studies* 70 (1986), 167-82; and Rudy S. Spraycar, "Genre and Convention in *Aucassin et Nicolette*," *Romanic Review* 76, i (January 1985), 94-115, esp. 106-112.

[5]Two important counterstatements to the conventional views of *Aucassin* that I have presented here are offered by Tony Hunt and by Eugene Vance. In "La Parodie médiévale: le cas d'*Aucassin et Nicolette*," *Romania* 100, iii (1979): 341-81, Hunt rehabilitates Aucassin as a *preux chevalier* and strongly opposes the notion that the *chantefable* is a parody featuring gender role reversal in the eponymous couple. In "*Aucassin et Nicolette* as a Medieval Comedy of Signification and Exchange," pp. 57-76 in *The Nature of Medieval Narrative*, ed. Minnette Grunman-Gaudet and Robin F. Jones (Lexington, Ky: French Forum, 1980), Vance argues ingeniously that *Aucassin* is not quite polyphonic: "I would suggest that this text remains within the realm of a monologism at its most 'liberal,' that is, one whose model is that of a law which allows for transgressions of itself." Nearly all great thirteenth and fourteenth-century poets were tempted by an "essentially carnivalesque" dialogism, but "these impulses tend to be eclipsed by totalizing impulses that allow themselves instead to be tempered with irony" (p. 74).

On Dante's *La Vita nuova* and authorial self-consciousness see Susan Noakes, *Timely Reading Between Exegesis and Interpretation* (Ithaca, N.Y.: Cornell University Press, 1988), pp. 69-87.

[6]See Kevin Brownlee, *Poetic Identity in Guillaume de Machaut* (Madison: University of Wisconsin Press, 1984), pp. 15-18, 94-156.

[7]William Calin, *A Poet at the Fountain: Essays on the Narrative Verse of Guillaume de Machaut* (Lexington: University of Kentucky Press, 1974), p. 245.

[8]See David Fein, *François Villon and his Reader* (Detroit, Mich: Wayne State University Press, 1989), pp. 18-23, 58-84, 94, and 105.

[9]The edition cited is Hughes Vaganay's (Lyon: Pierre Massin, 1925-28), 5 vols. References are to volume and page. For a capable overview of formal and generic questions regarding this work, see Louise Horowitz, *L'Astrée* (Boston: Twayne, 1984), pp. 126-40.

[10]Claude Lévi-Strauss, "Le Sexe des Astres," in *To Honor Roman Jakobson*. I am indebted to Guido Saba and G. Buford Norman for pointing out the presence of embedded poems in Théophile, La Fontaine, and Racine.

[11]Jean de la Fontaine, *Psyché*, in his *Oeuvres*, ed. Henri Regnier (Paris: Hachette, 1883-[92]), VIII, 3-234; pp. 19-24.

[12]See M. Jeanneret's informative "*Psyché* de La Fontaine," Bayley and Dorothy Gabe Coleman, eds., *The Equilibrium of Wit: Essays for Odette de Mourgues* (Lexington, Ky.: French Forum, 1982).

[13] Concerning La Fontaine as an oppositional author see the chapter devoted to him in Ross Chambers's *Room for Maneuver* (Chicago: The University of Chicago Press, 1991).

[14] Arthur Rimbaud, *Oeuvres*, ed. Suzanne Bernard and André Guyaux (Paris: Garnier, 1981), pp. 228, 234.

[15] See Danielle Bandelier, *Se dire et se taire: L'écriture d'"Une Saison en enfer" d'Arthur Rimbaud* (Neuchâtel: la Baconnière, 1988), pp. 12, 144.

[16] For a fuller discussion see Laurence M. Porter, *The Crisis of French Symbolism* (Ithaca, N.Y.: Cornell University Press, 1990), pp. 230-35.

[17] See Laurence M. Porter, "Modernist Maldoror: The De-Euphemization of Metaphor," *L'Esprit Créateur* 18, iv (Winter 1978), 25-34.

[18] Antonin Artaud, *Oeuvres complètes* (Paris: Gallimard, 1956), I, 72-73.

[19] For a helpful overview see Richard G. Morgan, "The Journal of Albion Moonlight: Its Form and Meaning," pp. 152-80 in Morgan, ed., *Kenneth Patchen: A Collection of Essays* (New York: AMS Press, 1977). Morgan unfortunately ignores all the embedded lyrics.

[20] Kenneth Patchen, *The Journal of Albion Moonlight* (New York: New Directions, 1961), p. 148.

"J'ai regretté toute ma vie d'être femme":
Madame Palatine féministe?

Dirk Van der Cruysse
Université d'Anvers

On s'étonnerait à juste titre de voir apparaître une princesse allemande dans un colloque de littérature française. Elisabeth-Charlotte von der Pfaz, née dans le Palatinat en 1652, ne devint française qu'à l'âge de dix-neuf ans, lorsque sa famille lui imposa contre son gré un mariage avec le duc Philippe d'Orléans, le frère homosexuel de Louis XIV, appelé "Monsieur" à la Cour de France. Le demi-siècle que la duchesse d'Orléans, appelée "Madame," passa en France ne put faire d'elle une princesse française. On sait qu'elle resta farouchement allemande dans ses modes de penser et d'écrire, et qu'envahie d'une incurable scribo-manie, elle bombardait ses parents et amis allemands d'innombrables lettres allemandes dans lesquelles revivent côte à côte son passé allemand et l'actualité de la Cour de France. Mais on ignore, aussi bien en Allemagne qu'en France, que Madame Palatine est aussi une épistolière française, et qu'elle a écrit des milliers de lettres dans sa langue adoptive qu'elle maniait avec beaucoup de grâce. Selon des calculs très prudents, elle a écrit au moins 60.000 lettres, rédigées pour les deux tiers en allemand et pour un tiers en français. Ainsi, des témoignages précis permettent de conclure que Madame a écrit au moins 7.000 lettres françaises à sa confidente la comtesse de Beuvron. Parmi ses autres correspondants français réguliers, on peut citer sa fille la duchesse de Lorraine, Etienne Polier de Bottens, trois reines d'Espagne, la reine de Prusse, la duchesse de Savoie, Mme de Ludres, etc... De cette montagne épistolaire, environ 4.500 lettres allemandes nous sont parvenues. Me préparant à publier les lettres françaises, j'en ai localisé jusqu'à présent plus de sept cents. Les organisateurs de ce colloque eurent donc bien raison d'ouvrir la porte à Elisabeth-Charlotte, épistolière bilingue, témoin irremplaçable de la société louis-quatorzienne, épouse peu comblée, mère de deux enfants qu'elle adorait mais qu'on éduquait loin d'elle, et princesse très mal à l'aise dans sa peau de femme.

La petite Elisabeth-Charlotte, qu'on appelait Liselotte, manifesta très tôt qu'elle était d'une toute autre trempe que son frère timoré. Turbulente et préférant les épées et fusils de bois de son frère Karl à ses propres poupées, elle se dit souvent dans ses lettres *Rauschenbattenknecht*, mot intraduisible qui suggère un gamin remuant comme une feuille qui bruit au vent. "Je suis un *Rauschenblattenknecht*, écrit-elle en 1706 à sa tante Sophie; je ne me suis jamais demandé si je suis belle ou laide, et je n'ai jamais aimé faire ma toilette."[1] Ce garçon manqué entendit parler un jour de cette Marie Germain mentionnée par Montaigne et Ambroise Paré, qui s'était transformée en garçon pour avoir fait un saut démesuré.[2] Elle confie en 1718 à Caroline, princesse de Galles: "Toute ma vie j'ai préféré les épées et les fusils aux poupées. J'aurais tellement aimé être un garçon que cela a failli me coûter la vie. J'avais entendu dire que Marie Germain était devenue un homme à force de sauter. Cela m'a fait sauter si énergiquement, qu'il est un miracle que je ne me sois pas cassé cent fois le cou."[3]

Voilà donc une jeune princesse qui s'accommode fort mal de sa féminité, pas coquette du tout et visiblement travaillée par la convoitise du pénis. Elle glissera après trente ans de mariage cette confidence dans une lettre de 1701 à sa demi-soeur Louise: "J'ai regretté toute ma vie d'être femme, et, à vrai dire, être électeur m'eût convenu mieux qu'être Madame. Mais il est inutile d'y penser, puisque ce n'était pas la volonté de Dieu..."[4] Profondément providentialiste et fataliste, elle considère son sexe comme inscrit dans son destin. "Chacun a sa destinée": cette constatation revient régulièrement comme un leitmotiv désabusé dans ses lettres. Elle n'aurait pas désavoué cette double prière juive citée par Simone de Beauvoir et Betty Friedan, et omniprésente dans la littérature féministe: "Béni soit Dieu notre Seigneur et le Seigneur de tous les mondes qu'il ne m'ait pas fait femme," disent les Juifs dans leurs prières matinales, pendant que leurs épouses murmurent: "Béni soit le Seigneur qu'il m'ait créée selon sa volonté."[5] Madame ne met pas en cause la supériorité masculine puisqu'elle est voulue par Dieu, mais ne peut s'empêcher de rêver en soupirant d'être homme et de bénéficier de cette situation perçue comme immuable et incontestable.

Cette résignation douloureuse, qui n'exclut point des expressions de regret, nous conduit fatalement à la question si une femme qui aurait préféré être un homme peut être considérée comme féministe. Disons tout de suite que les rêves d'émancipation et de libération qui animent le mouvement féministe eussent été impensables dans la société fortement hiérarchisée de l'Ancien Régime. Les textes du 17e siècle alignés par Carlo François dans son anthologie *Précieuses et autres indociles* révèlent des plaintes et des protestations plus ou moins étouffées, mais aucune velléité sérieuse de contestation ou de transgression des interdits d'une société phallocratique.[6] Les personnages féminins de Molière ne tentent pas de renverser un ordre établi qui leur est défavorable, mais de le contourner par la ruse.

Madame, elle, ne ruse pas, mais toute sa correspondance—parole de femme, parole d'exil—est l'expression continue des limitations qui pèsent sur son existence. Attendre autre chose d'elle serait pécher par anachronisme. N'oublions pas que même une femme libérée comme Mme de Staël, qui vécut un siècle plus tard, écrivait encore à ses débuts: "Un homme doit savoir braver l'opinion, une femme s'y soumettre."[7] Exploiter l'ample discours préféministe qui s'articule dans la volumineuse correspondance d'Elisabeth-Charlotte dépasserait bien sûr les limites d'une communication. Force nous est donc de nous borner aux trois aspects majeurs de l'existence brimée de Madame qui considérait sa féminité comme un bagne, et de lire les contraintes qui pesaient sur sa vie de femme, d'épouse et de princesse.

Tous les contemporains ont souligné les façons masculines de Madame qui, avec ses allures sportives, avait horreur des modes féminines compliquées, des bijoux et des maquillages. Adorant la chasse, l'équitation et la marche à pied, elle préférait un costume de chasse semi-masculin qu'elle ne quittait qu'à contrecoeur, composé d'une ample perruque d'homme, d'un tricorne, d'une grosse cravate, d'un gilet et d'une jupe traînante. Saint-Simon n'exagérait certainement pas en écrivant que "Madame tenait en tout beaucoup plus de l'homme que de la femme."[8] Il lui arrivait effectivement de parler en homme. Ainsi ose-t-elle reprocher à Louvois en décembre 1688 l'occupation française du Palatinat décidée par Louis XIV. "Mais Madame, s'étonna le ministre, c'est pour défendre les propres intérêts de Votre Altesse que nous agissons..."—"En ce cas, Monsieur, répliqua-t-elle, qu'on me mette à la tête des armées et me laisse traiter moi-même mes affaires..."

Est-ce à dire qu'elle avait une piètre opinion de son propre sexe? On la voit consoler d'innombrables fois ses correspondantes de n'avoir donné naissance qu'à une fille. Elle écrit ainsi en 1720 à la reine de Prusse Sophie-Dorothée qui venait d'accoucher d'une fille: "J'avoue que j'ai eu un peu de peine de ce que je n'ai pu faire mon compliment au sujet d'un prince. Il faut espérer, Madame que ce sera pour la première (=prochaine) fois."[9] Si Elisabeth-Charlotte préférait voir naître des garçons plutôt que des filles, ce n'était pas parce qu'elle estimait que les femmes étaient inférieures ou moins utiles, mais parce qu'elle les savait presque inévitablement vouées au malheur. Elle observe en 1702 dans une lettre à sa demi-soeur Amelise: "Je ne m'étonne pas que les femmes, qui sont habituellement plutôt malheureuses, ne se préoccupent point de la mort."[10]

Nous avons la chance de posséder l'inventaire complet de la bibliothèque bien fournie de notre Princesse.[11] Parmi les 1.454 titres représentant plus de 3.000 volumes, on peut relever un certain nombre d'ouvrages que l'on pourrait qualifier de préféministes: *L'excellence des femmes au-dessus des hommes*, *Le caractère des femmes*, *Louange des femmes*, et *L'honnête femme*, essais dont les auteurs ne sont pas encore identifiés. Deux volumes de *Secrets de la beauté des dames* révèlent des préoccupations qui étonnent chez une princesse plutôt hommasse qui répète son aversion du maquillage, des mouches et du rouge.[12] Si aux yeux de Madame l'excellence des femmes ne fait point de doute, leur situation malheureuse dans un monde sexiste dominé par les mâles avec la bénédiction de Dieu lui paraît pour le moins aussi évidente.

Le lecteur moderne des lettres d'Elisabeth-Charlotte a parfois de la peine à comprendre son acceptation inconditionnelle des conventions qui permettent aux hommes toutes les débauches possibles, et qui interdisent en même temps le moindre écart aux femmes. C'est qu'elle considère l'inconstance des hommes comme inscrite dans leur nature et donc inévitable, alors que l'inconduite féminine risque de compromettre la pureté de la transmission dynastique. Lorsque son cousin Georg Ludwig de Hanovre, le futur George I d'Angleterre qui entretenait plusieurs maîtresses au nez de son épouse, répudie et enferme celle-ci pour avoir aimé plus que de raison le beau comte von Königsmarck, Madame n'éprouve aucune sympathie pour celle-ci. Elle attaque en 1695 dans une lettre à sa tante Sophie la mère de la coupable: "Quel seigneur trouve-t-on au monde qui n'aime que son épouse sans avoir en outre d'autres affections, que ce soit pour des maîtresses ou des garçons? Si son épouse devait vivre aussi mal que lui pour cette raison, personne (...) ne serait plus certain que les enfants dans sa maison sont ses véritables héritiers. Cette duchesse ne sait-elle donc pas que l'honneur des femmes consiste à n'avoir rien à faire avec personne d'autre que leurs maris, et que ce n'est pas une honte pour les hommes d'avoir des maîtresses, mais sûrement d'être cocus?"[13] Puisqu'il en est ainsi, il lui arrive de rêver d'une existence féminine moins malheureuse, loin des hommes et de leurs injustes privilèges. Elle soupire en 1705 dans une lettre à sa demi-soeur Amelise: "Le monde a été ainsi depuis toujours, et restera bien de même jusqu'à la fin. Païens ou chrétiens, où il y a des hommes, il y a de la débauche. Celle qui peut vivre sans homme n'est pas la plus malheureuse."[14] La même idée rejaillit en 1709 dans une lettre à Sophie: "Pour se rendre utile dans cette vie, on devrait être son propre maître et ne dépendre de personne."[15]

Ce rêve d'indépendance féminine sous-tend tout le discours conjugal qui s'articule dans la correspondance d'Elisabeth-Charlotte. Lieu privilégié de l'affrontement des sexes, le mariage lui inspire des réflexions désabusées qui visent presque toutes l'intolérable dépendance des femmes de leurs maris—dépendance qui les empêche de se réaliser pleinement. Elle s'en plaint souvent. "Ici en France, dit-elle en 1699 à Sophie, il n'y a que la volonté du maître de la communauté qui compte..."[16] Si Madame, en ses moments de sérénité, est prête à accepter cet asservissement (elle écrit en 1692 à Sophie: "on se soumet avec joie à ceux à qui l'on doit de l'obéissance,"[17] il lui arrive plus souvent de protester. Lorsqu'une grande querelle concernant l'éducation de leurs deux enfants l'oppose en 1689 à son mari monté contre elle par ses mignons, des plaintes amères lui échappent dans une lettre à Sophie: "Quand on n'a pas à dépendre de ceux qui veulent vous chagriner (...) on peut se sauver en les méprisant, mais quand ils sont votre seigneur et maître et qu'on ne peut pas faire un pas dans sa vie sans dépendre d'eux, alors la chose n'est pas aussi aisée qu'on pourrait se l'imaginer. Si mes enfants dépendaient de moi, ils me procureraient une grande joie, mais quand je pense [qu'on les soustrait à mon influence], alors je dois avouer que les enfants apportent plus de chagrin que de joie."[18]

On ne s'étonnera donc pas d'apprendre que, dans l'esprit de Madame, le célibat féminin est de loin préférable aux chaînes du mariage qui sont en plus inconciliables avec l'amour, si amour il y avait le jour des noces. Elle cite plusieurs fois ces vers tirés de l'*Alceste* de Lully et Quinault:

> L'hymen détruit la tendresse
> il rend l'amour sans attraits.
> Voulez-vous aimer sans cesse,
> amants, n'épousez jamais!

Elisabeth-Charlotte résume sa façon de voir en 1694 dans une lettre à sa demi-soeur Louise restée célibataire faute de dot convenable: "Que l'état célibataire devient si à la mode est peut-être dû au fait que les femmes deviennent plus intelligentes et préfèrent vivre seules plutôt que de se choisir des seigneurs et maîtres qui deviennent très souvent des tyrans. Dans mon esprit, il vaut mieux être raillée comme vieille fille que plainte comme femme mariée."[19] Elle revient deux ans plus tard, dans une lettre à Sophie, sur le penchant masculin au despotisme. Comme très souvent, ses propos sont marqués au coin du bon sens: "Les hommes veulent toujours faire sentir leur autorité, que ce soit dans des choses grandes ou petites, et ils ne se rendent pas compte que la vie serait plus agréable pour eux-mêmes et pour leurs épouses, s'ils pouvaient vivre en bonne amitié comme de vrais, bons amis. On ne se comprend pas assez dans ce monde pour se rendre heureux, et c'est pourtant ce qu'il faudrait faire puisque, malheureusement, la vie humaine est si brève."[20]

L'éloge de l'état célibataire est un thème familier dans les lettres de Madame. "Les bons ménages sont rares, écrit-elle en 1719 à Louise; mais j'en ai vus beaucoup qui s'étaient mariés par pur amour et qui se sont haïs ensuite comme le diable, et qui se haïssent encore. Heureux qui n'est pas marié. Que j'eusse été contente si on avait voulu me permettre de mener une bonne vie de célibataire et de ne pas me marier!"[21] Le cri vient du fond du coeur. Six mois plus tard, elle confie à Louise: "Si j'étais restée mon propre maître, je ne me serais pas plus que vous mariée, chère Louise!"[22] On comprend que son expérience pénible de trente années de mariage avec un prince efféminé, homosexuel et profondément égoïste ne lui ait laissé aucune illusion sur le mariage. Elle soupire en 1696 dans une lettre à sa demi-soeur Louise: "Il arrive que des mariages réussissent, mais c'est rare, et sur des milliers il n'y en a pas deux d'acceptables. (...) Les bons mariages font penser à ce qu'on dit du Phénix: on n'en trouve qu'un par siècle."[23]

Sa réaction est caractéristique lorsque sa demi-soeur célibataire Amelise, qui frisait la quarantaine, se vit proposer le mariage en décembre 1701. Elle écrivit en panique à Elisabeth-Charlotte veuve depuis six mois, pour solliciter son avis. Elle reçut en janvier cette réponse qui résume la philosophie conjugale de la duchesse douairière d'Orléans: "Il me semble qu'il faut considérer deux points essentiels quand on veut se marier. Le premier, si l'homme a la situation et assez de moyens pour vivre selon sa condition; l'autre si sa personne n'inspire pas trop de répulsion. (...) Il faut encore faire une réflexion, notamment si vous pouvez vous résoudre à avoir la patience qu'il faut dans le mariage et à vous soumettre à un homme, acceptant patiemment ses faiblesses et les supportant avec patience. Sans cela, jamais le bonheur ne sera possible dans le mariage. Si vous pouvez prendre ces résolutions, chère Amelise, je vous conseille de vous marier. (...) Les mariages qui se font par raison sont souvent beaucoup plus heureux que ceux qui se font par amour, car l'amour (J'entends être amoureux) et l'hymen vont et restent rarement ensemble..."[24]

Aux limitations que lui imposait son sexe et aux contraintes conjugales s'ajoutait pour Madame une dernière servitude. En sa qualité de membre de la famille royale, elle dépendait autant, sinon plus, de son formidable beau-frère Louis XIV que de son époux le duc d'Orléans. Le Roi décide en maître absolu de ses moindres déplacements, de ses chasses, des charges à attribuer dans sa maison, de sa présence ou de son absence dans l'intimité du cabinet royal après le grand couvert, de ses rapports avec ses parents allemands, du mariage de ses enfants. Lorsqu'il contraint le fils de Madame et Monsieur, le futur Régent, d'épouser une bâtarde royale, infligeant à sa belle-soeur qui abhorrait la bâtardise la plus grande humiliation de sa vie, celle-ci ne peut que s'incliner en murmurant douloureusement: "Quand Votre Majesté et Monsieur me parlerez en maître, comme vous faites, je ne puis qu'obéir..."[25] Chose curieuse, cette femme qui accepte d'être dominée et brimée par son beau-frère et son mari, regimbe lorsqu'une autre femme, en l'occurrence Mme de Maintenon, veut régenter son existence. Ayant pâti pendant quatre ans de la redoutable influence et des coups fourrés de l'épouse morganatique de Louis XIV, elle soupire en 1688 dans une lettre à sa tante Sophie: "Obéir au Roi et à Monsieur me paraîtrait en fin de compte assez supportable, mais dépendre de toutes les vieilles femmes qui gouvernent maintenant (...) cela me paraît très dur..."[26]

Les apparences de grandeur qui l'entouraient ne sauraient lui faire oublier la liberté qu'on lui refuse dans cette cage dorée qu'est la Cour. "... La vie des princesses est fort contrainte, écrit-elle en 1721 à Louise; qui est habitué à la liberté allemande a de la peine à s'y faire."[27] Et de citer ces vers tirés de l'*Isis* de Lully et Quinault:

> S'il est quelque bien au monde,
> c'est la liberté.

Le thème de la servitude et de la liberté hante la correspondance d'Elisabeth-Charlotte qui confie en 1682 à Sophie: "Je préférerais mille fois servir un seigneur qu'on estime et admire, oui qu'on aime vraiment, à avoir seulement les apparences de la grandeur sans pouvoir faire quoi que ce soit, car ceci est plus proche de l'esclavage que de la liberté."[28] Et en 1710, toujours à Sophie: "Je préférerais être un riche comte souverain de l'Empire ayant sa liberté, plutôt qu'un enfant de France, car nous ne sommes en effet rien d'autre que des esclaves couronnés." Et elle ajoute: "J'aurais étouffé si je n'avais pas dit cela..."[29] Comment ne pas penser ici, devant ces propos libérateurs, à ces lignes profondes de Béatrice Didier notant dans *L'Ecriture-femme*: "Je veux bien que toute écriture soit transgression, et qu'écrire soit pour l'homme aussi enfreindre un interdit. Disons simplement que la transgression sera double ou triple chez la femme. Il s'agira non seulement de transgresser l'interdit de toute écriture, mais encore de le transgresser par rapport à l'homme et à la société phallocratique."[30]

Qu'on n'aille surtout pas penser que Madame profitera de la régence de son fils pour s'attribuer une influence politique quelconque. Elle avait décidé dès les premiers jours de la Régence qu'elle ne se mêlerait de rien. Début novembre, elle formule catégoriquement sa philosophie de la non-ingérence dans une lettre au roi Friedrich IV de Danemark: "Je me suis imposé comme règle de conduite de ne pas me mêler d'affaires d'Etat. La France n'a été malheureusement que trop longtemps entre les mains d'une femme, c'est pourquoi je veux donner l'exemple à l'épouse et aux filles [du Régent], oui à toutes les femmes de France, de ne pas se mêler d'affaires d'Etat."[31]

Une déclaration presque identique apparaît en 1716 dans une lettre à Caroline de Galles. Manifestement, Madame ne croit pas que les femmes puissent jouer un rôle politique quelconque: "Je vous dirai franchement pourquoi je ne veux me mêler de rien: je suis vieille, j'ai plus besoin de repos que d'être tourmentée. (...) Je n'ai jamais appris à gouverner; je n'entends rien à la politique ni aux affaires d'Etat, et je suis beaucoup trop vieille pour apprendre des choses aussi difficiles. Mon fils a, Dieu soit loué!, la capacité pour mener les choses sans moi. (...) Je voudrais donner un bon exemple à la femme et à la fille de mon fils, car ce royaume a, pour son malheur, été gouverné par des femmes vieilles et jeunes. Le temps est venu qu'on laisse faire les hommes; j'ai donc pris le parti de ne me mêler de rien. Que les femmes règnent en Angleterre, mais en France, pour que tout aille bien, il faut que les hommes gouvernent seuls."[32] Ce propos est d'autant plus frappant quand on sait que Madame, si elle était restée protestante, aurait pu être reine d'Angleterre, car elle descendait d'une grand-mère Stuart.

La correspondance d'une princesse louis-quatorzienne qui se dit une "esclave couronnée" ne pouvait, on s'en doute, articuler un discours féministe au sens moderne du terme. On ne la voit pas militer en faveur de l'*Equal Rights Amendment* par exemple. Victime d'une servitude dorée dont elle était très consciente, Elisabeth-Charlotte propose à ses correspondants une description à la fois douloureuse et courageuse des contraintes qui empoisonnaient sa vie de femme, d'épouse et de princesse. Du courage, il en fallait, car elle savait que le cabinet noir ouvrait la plupart de ses lettres et en faisait des extraits pour Louis XIV et Mme de Maintenon. On sait que les libertés épistolaires qu'elle se permettait lui ont valu à plusieurs reprises des semonces royales. Les contemporains n'ont pas eu tort d'admirer son courage. Saint-Simon la dit "forte, courageuse, allemande au dernier point, franche, droite, bonne et bienfaisante, noble et grande en toutes ses manières,"[33] et le marquis de Sourches loue sa "fermeté au-dessus de son sexe" (compliment de mâle qui prête à réfléchir...) et conclut, ayant décrit la "constance admirable" avec laquelle elle subit quelques coups de lancette: "cette princesse, qui avait un coeur de héros, soutint ces douleurs avec un courage invincible."[34]

Vivant dans un contexte social et politique qui lui interdisait jusqu'à l'idée de contestation et d'émancipation, elle ne pouvait que regretter son sexe et chercher dans l'écriture un défoulement qui lui permettait de survivre et de porter haute sa tête de femme. "J'aurais étouffé si je n'avais pas dit cela..." Le résultat est la description émouvante et détaillée des injustices commises par une société phallocratique à l'égard des femmes, fussent-elles princesses. On aurait tort de la considérer comme une féministe avant la lettre, mais il faut voir dans sa correspondance l'un des documents les plus courageux de l'ère préféministe.

---

[1] E. Bodemann (éd.), *Aus den Briefen der Herzogin Elisabeth Charlotte von Orléans an die Kurfürstin Sophie von Hannover* (Hannover: Hahn 1891, 2 vol.), I, 134 (16 mai 1706). Abrégé ci-après Bod. I, Bod. II.

[2] Montaigne, *Essais*, I, 21 et *Journal de voyage* (éd. Pléiade), p. 1118-1119; A. Paré, *Oeuvres* (éd. de 1607), p. 1017.

[3] H. Helmolt (éd.), *Elisabeth Charlottens Briefe an Karoline von Wales* (Annaberg:Graser, 1909), p. 218 (18 août 1718). Abrégé ci-après Hel.

[4] W.L. Holland (éd.), *Briefe der Herzogin Elisabeth Charlotte von Orléans* (Stuttgart/Tübingen, 1867-1881, 6 vol.), I, 225 (15 mai 1701). Abrégé ci-après Hol. I ... Hol. VI.

[5] S. de Beauvoir, *Le Deuxième Sexe* (Paris: Gallimard, 1986), I, 22; B. Friedan, *The Feminine Mystique* (Penguin Books, 1965), p. 96.

[6] C. François, *Précieuses et autres indociles* (Birmingham, Alabama: Summa Publications, 1987).

[7] Mme de Staël, *Mélanges de Madame Necker*.

[8] Saint-Simon, *Mémoires*, éd. Boislisle (Paris: Hachette, [Grands Ecrivains de la France]), XLI, 117.

[9] H. Helmolt (éd.), *Briefe der Elisabeth Charlotte von Orléans an Sophie Dorothée von Preussen*, in: *Historisches Jahrbuch*, 29 (1908), p. 834 (5 sept. 1720).
[10] Hol. I, 299 (22 juill. 1702).
[11] Paris, Archives Nationales, 300 AP 1751: *Inventaire de S.A.R. Madame*.
[12] *O.c.*, 167 v°, 171 r°, 208 r°, 235 r°, 241 r°.
[13] Bod. I, 208 (13 févr. 1695).
[14] Hol I, 419 (5 nov. 1705).
[15] Bod. II, 200 (7 févr. 1709).
[16] Bod. I, 378 (23 sept. 1699).
[17] Bod. I, 145 (12 avr. 1692).
[18] Bod. I, 107 (20 mai 1689).
[19] Hol. VI, 522 (7 nov. 1694).
[20] Bod. I, 252 (23 août 1696).
[21] Hol. IV, 363-364 (28 déc. 1719).
[22] Hol. V, 180 (20 juin 1720).
[23] Hol. I, 56 (11 févr. 1696).
[24] Hol. I, 264 (8 janv. 1702).
[25] Bod. I, 143 (10 janv. 1692).
[26] Bod. I, 97 (2 août 1688).
[27] Hol. VI, 172 (10 juill. 1721).
[28] Bod I, 55 (24 nov. 1682).
[29] Bod. II, 253-254 (17 août 1710).
[30] B. Didier, *L'Ecriture-femme* (Paris: P.U.F., 1981), p. 16-17.
[31] J. Elias (éd.), *Briefwechsel zwischen Elisabeth Charlotte von Orléans und Christian Wernicke*, in: *Romanische Forschungen*, 5 (1890), p. 297 (2 nov. 1715).
[32] Hel., 216 (22 sept. 1716).
[33] Saint-Simon, *Mémoires* (éd. Boislisle), XLI, 117.
[34] Sourches, *Mémoires* (éd. Cosnac), II, 140,147.

Marceline Desbordes-Valmore:
ni poésie féminine, ni poésie féministe

Christine Planté
Université de Paris

Je voudrais dans cette étude interroger les notions de *poésie féministe* et de *poésie féminine* à partir de la lecture d'une oeuvre poétique de femme, celle de Marceline Desbordes-Valmore (1786-1859). Le point de départ de cette réflexion m'a été fourni par l'absence de Desbordes-Valmore dans l'anthologie de poèmes féministes français récemment publiée par Domna Stanton.[1] Cette absence n'est pas commentée en tant que telle, mais soulignée de façon explicite, et on peut déduire ses motivations de celles qui justifient, aux yeux de D. Stanton, l'exclusion de Louise Labé du volume, puisque ces deux poètes appartiennent à une même série d'"exclues" célèbres, avec Marie de France et Anna de Noailles. D. Stanton explique que le cas de Louise Labé a été pour elle l'objet d'une longue hésitation, puisque la préface en prose à ses poèmes adressée à Clémence de Bourges est "décidément féministe selon les critères de cette anthologie," alors que les sentiments exprimés dans ses sonnets d'amour à un homme diffèrent considérablement. Et elle ajoute ce commentaire:

> Labé's passionate and tortured verse is not "feminist" in content (the level of the signified), although an analysis of the subtle ways in which she reworks Petrarchan conventions (on the level of the signifier) could provide the basis for a feminist reading.[2]

Je reviendrai plus loin sur cette tension contradictoire entre le point de vue de la "qualité poétique" et celui de l'"idéologie." En ce qui concerne Desbordes-Valmore en tout cas, le jugement implicitement porté coïncide avec celui de Daniel Armogathe et Maïté Albistur[3] dans leur *Histoire du féminisme français*, qui ne voient chez elle "nulle trace de lutte des sexes"; et ce rejet est, logiquement, l'envers de l'appréciation assez élogieuse de son oeuvre par les écrivains et poètes de son temps. Les motifs de sa "condamnation féministe," si on cherche à les expliciter et les développer, seraient à peu près les suivants: les *thèmes* de l'oeuvre—poésie amoureuse, sentiment maternel, célébration intimiste—impliquent une image de la femme soumise à ses fonctions traditionnelles, et soumise à l'homme; le *personnage* de Marceline Desbordes-Valmore, autour duquel s'est bâtie toute une légende édifiante, coïncide fâcheusement avec l'*Eternel féminin*, et avec des modèles normatifs; elle fut reconnue comme poète, voire comme *grand poète*, de son temps, et figure encore—même dans une place mineure—dans l'histoire littéraire: c'est donc qu'elle aurait plié aux conceptions esthétiques dominantes, et aurait composé avec l'idéologie patriarcale et ses valeurs. Il y a tout de même quelque chose de gênant à voir ici l'appréciation féministe se contenter de reproduire—en inversant la polarité des valeurs—le jugement de la tradition critique. Le premier pas, élémentaire me semble-t-il, dans la (re)lecture '"féministe" d'une femme poète serait *de la lire*, si possible sans les préventions héritées d'ouvrages de seconde main. Le second, de la lire *comme poète*, c'est-à-dire sans réduire son oeuvre à des "thèmes" ou à un contenu idéoloique, et sans la rapporter d'emblée à un féminin supposé. C'est dans cette visée que je proposerai ici brièvement deux ordres de remarques:

1) Sur Marceline Disbrodes-Valmore elle-même, dont la reconnaissance littéraire a le plus souvent été une méconnaissance, faite de distorsions de lecture et de malentendus. On peut tout aussi bien la dire moins "féminine" et plus "féministe" que ne l'a voulu la tradition, mais ces caractérisations ont, je crois—dans son cas au moins—, peu d'intérêt et peu de sens. D'où ma deuxième série de réflexions;

2) Sur la pertinence historique et critique des notions de *poésie féminine* et de *poésie féministe*, qui tendent à fonctionner dans un système d'opposition, commode, mais très discutable. De quel point de vue ces critères opèrent-ils, et dans quelle mesure peuvent-ils rendre compte de l'historicité propre des discours et des pratiques poétiques?

1. La reconnaissance comme méconnaissance.

L'image et la légende de Marceline Desbordes-Valmore telles qu'elles se sont bâties dans les discours critiques et dans l'histoire littéraire reposent sur une lecture partielle et hâtive de l'oeuvre, et sur une information partielle, voire erronée, quant à la biographie. Revenir sur le pourquoi et le comment de ce travestissement, commencé dès le vivant de l'auteur, et auquel elle-même, puis son fils, ses amis, ont, délibérément ou non, collaboré, exigerait de longs développements,[4] dont cette contribution n'est pas le lieu. Je tenterai simplement d'y montrer comment, à partir d'une lecture attentive de l'oeuvre et de la correspondance, et d'une information moins incomplète sur sa vie, on peut déjà la dire à la fois moins '"féminine" et plus "féministe," ce qui vise moins à la "réhabiliter," qu'à montrer les limites de telles notions dans l'approche d'une oeuvre poétique.

Moins féminine: l'amour passionné que l'on retient surtout dans ses poèmes, qui a prêté à tous les clichés de la femme abandonnée (nouvelle version de la religieuse portugaise) et de la pécheresse repentie, a été rapproché à la fois de son dévouement conjugal envers Prosper Valmore, que l'on a souvent voulu plus médiocre et grincheux que de raison, et du sentiment religieux, pour composer un tableau moral exemplaire. Or sa vie même comporte quelques traits peu compatibles avec cette image exemplaire: elle a été actrice, elle a eu plusieurs amants, dont l'un *pendant* son mariage, et a mis au monde deux enfants naturels; vis-à-vis de ses amants comme de son mari, elle a su faire preuve d'indépendance morale—et économique; son intérêt pour les problèmes politiques et sociaux, s'il ne s'ancre pas dans une analyse bien cohérente et rigoureuse, n'est ni superficiel ni épisodique, ni "tout en discrétion" comme l'écrivent Armogathe et Albistur; sa vie conjugale comporte, à côté du dévouement domestique que les critiques ont si bien mis en exergue, une certaine inversion des rôles sexuels: elle écrit et publie, elle est connue, admirée, et amie avec les artistes célèbres de son temps, elle gagne, grâce à sa pension et à ses publications, une partie de l'argent du ménage, elle conseille, encourage, et protège dans sa carrière un mari plein d'admiration pour elle, conscient de sa propre infériorité, et poursuivi par l'échec dans sa carrière théâtrale. Surtout, dans ses poèmes d'amour, c'est elle qui célèbre l'aimé, et cette inversion-là, dans une période où l'amour romantique assigne à la femme le rôle d'inspiratrice et de dédicataire silencieuse du poème et de la passion, n'est certes pas indifférente. L'humilité dont elle a fait preuve dans les rapports conjugaux et sociaux, et dans ses déclarations sur son oeuvre, est à confronter à tous ces éléments et à examiner alors de façon plus critique: comme l'attitude qui lui permettait de poursuivre sa voie propre, sous la protection paradoxale de sa place et de son image de femme. Plutôt que de la comparer (à partir du plus superficiel, du plus anecdotique—et du plus faible—de ses poèmes: thèmes sentimentaux, images gracieuses, métaphores banales, syntaxe répétitive et peu rigoureuse) à la poésie féminine de son temps, il me semble intéressant de voir en quoi ses écrits, à la différence de tant d'autres qui nous apparaissent aujourd'hui comme un illisible et larmoyant ron-ron, ont gardé la force d'une voix originale, et ont contribué à ouvrir le chemin d'une modernité poétique à laquelle Verlaine, Rimbaud, Mallarmé ont rendu hommage—et cela peut-être pas seulement en raison de machiavéliques et phallocratiques intérêts.

De l'ambiguïté de l'humilité et de sa position d'énonciation poétique, je prendrai pour exemple le poème, célèbre et souvent cité, intitulé *Une Lettre de femme*, qui commence par ces vers:

    Les femmes, je le sais, ne doivent pas écrire;
    J'écris pourtant,
    Afin que dans mon coeur au loin tu puisses lire
    Comme en partant.[5]

Immédiatement, y apparaît la tension entre le générique *les femmes* et le *je*, l'antagonisme entre la norme et la pratique singulière du sujet étant affirmée et délibérément soulignée, par *je le sais* et *pourtant*; par l'opposition (*Les femmes,*)/(*Je...,*) en début de vers, avec une ponctuation forte entre les deux, accentuant l'opposition métrique alexandrin/tétrasyllabe, alors que celle-ci est au contraire atténuée par la continuité syntaxique aux vers 3 et 4, consacrés au mouvement vers le *tu*. Mais voilà justement le coupable aux yeux de la critique féministe: ce *tu*, un homme, origine et finalité du poème, pesamment soulignée par l'*afin que*, et décevante raison de la transgression de l'interdit, encore faut-il voir que ce *tu* au fur et à mesure que l'oeuvre se développe, désigne de moins en moins un homme précis et réel, ce qu'il n'a d'ailleurs jamais fait de façon univoque, au profit d'une pluralité de sens (soi-même, Dieu, tout autre et tout lecteur...), syntaxe de l'altérité, de l'élan et du dialogue organisatrice de toute une poétique. Il n'en demeure pas moins qu'il est ici ce qui permet à la parole de naître, ou plutôt d'être dite, et la déception d'une lecture féministe ne peut que s'aggraver devant la strophe suivante et son amoureuse humilité:

> Je ne tracerai rien qui ne soit dans toi-même
> Beaucoup plus beau:
> Mais le mot cent fois dit, venant de ce qu'on aime,
> Semble nouveau.

Cette déception, toutefois, ne saurait provenir que d'une réduction du poème à son "message": une femme amoureuse dit "je t'aime," et par ailleurs éprouve "le complexe de la femme de lettres,"[6] dans une ignorance de son *dire* et de son faire, et de son dispositif très particulier, titre compris. Car *Une Lettre de femme*, par l'utilsation de déterminants indéfinis, que l'on retrouve dans d'autres titres de Marceline Desbordes-Valmore éloigne ce qui suit de l'anecdote ou de la confidence strictement personnelle, pour le tirer vers une portée plus universelle, et situe la position d'énonciation comme marquée par la conscience du statut de femme, qui détermine aussi l'attaque du poème, statut à la fois assumé (vis-à-vis des autres femmes, et lectrices éventuelles, commes vis-à-vis du destinataire, réel ou fictif), et transgressé par le langage et l'écriture. Quant à l'idée même de la *lettre*, elle crée l'amorce d'une fiction qui situe les conditions d'énonciation du poème, et tend par là à abolir, comme c'est fréquemment le cas dans le reste de cette oeuvre, une série d'oppositions: récit/poésie lyrique; langage de la communication ordinaire/langage de l'écriture poétique; prose/poésie; écrire/dire. Elle joue de ces oppositions pour instaurer l'ambiguïté, et par là les abolir, ou les déplacer: que l'on voie l'extrême ambivalence d'*écrire* dans *ne doivent pas écrire* (de la littérature, de la poésie?), et j'*écris pourtant* (une lettre, mais aussi un poème). Elle modifie le statut et le sens du poème en l'actualisant, en en faisant un dire, ce que souligne encore la deuxième strophe, qui oppose la banalité du *cent fois dit* à la *nouveauté* de son énonciation au sein du discours de l'aimé: le sens est dans le *dire*. Il importe alors de considérer que, quel que soit son "contenu" amoureux et idéologiquement peu progressiste, le poème soit là, et soit poème, et justement pas lettre d'amour de Madame Desbordes-Valmore à Monsieur X..., poème faisant exactement ce qu'il dit: créant du nouveau avec les mots les plus ordinaires et les images les plus banales, et demeurant dans la tension ambiguë imposée par ces deux termes: être femme et écrire.

Plus féministe aussi que ne l'ont dit ceux qui en ont chanté les louanges, cette oeuvre l'est probablement ne serait-ce qu'en raison de cette insistance sur la condition de femme de son auteur, avec toutes les contradictions et les difficultés qui en résultent. Je passerai rapidement sur le sens d'une solidarité féminine qui découle de cette conscience, très manifeste dans la vie et dans l'oeuvre de Marceline Desbordes-Valmore, parce qu'il peut être jugé extrêmement ambivalent par l'installation, voire la complaisance qu'il entraîne dans la déploration de la souffrance et de l'état des choses, qu'il peut parfois finir par conforter, et que ceci nécessiterait donc de plus larges analyses. Il en va de même pour le type de relation entre expérience et écriture qui sous-tend l'ensemble de l'oeuvre, faite d'une réciproque transformation de l'une par l'autre, qui peut prêter à des interprétations et des appréciations contradictoires: pour le jugement négatif et restrictif de la critique littéraire du XIXe siècle, il faut voir là surtout le signe d'une incapacité féminine à s'élever jusqu'à la création véritable, et à faire autre chose que parler de soi et raconter sa vie sous des formes plus ou moins déguisées. Je me limiterai donc ici à mentionner tout ce qui peut amener à rapprocher Marceline Desbordes-Valmore du féminisme au sens strict—si tant est que l'emploi de ce mot ait un sens pour cette période: en 1833, alors qu'elle est un poète célèbre, elle publie à plusieurs reprises dans *Le Conseiller de femmes*, journal lyonnais d'Eugénie Niboyet, une ancienne saint-simonienne. Elle fut amie de Louise Crombach, saint-simonienne aussi, et citée comme témoin de la défense à son premier procès, à propos duquel elle écrit à une amie: "J'ai vu une fois de près un tribunal d'hommes. Ce n'est pas ainsi que je comprends la lumière et la justice"[7]; de Pauline Roland, par qui elle sera amenée à collaborer à la *Démocratie pacifique* de Victor Considérant en 1843, et qui l'inscrira sur son testament rédigé lors de son second emprisonnement sous le Second Empire. Elle souscrivit à l'*Union ouvrière* de Flora Tristan, puis à la collecte organisée pour lui ériger un monument après sa mort. Elle admirait George Sand, en particulier *Indiana* et *Lélia*, sans toutefois sympathiser avec la femme, et fut très liée avec Marie d'Agoult (Daniel Stern).

Tout ceci, dira-t-on, ne constitue pas une dimension féministe de l'oeuvre—et on aura raison: ces rappels ont simplement pour but d'arracher Desbordes-Valmore à une certaine image faite d'ignorance de l'histoire et d'un conformisme niais. Quant à sa poésie, qui en effet n'est pas féministe, il faut pour mettre ce jugement en perspective rappeler deux éléments. D'abord, sa date de naissance: 1786; elle a vingt ans de plus que les femmes qui composent, dans les années 1830, le premier mouvement collectif français d'affranchissement des femmes. Née avant la Révolution, commençant à écrire sous l'Empire et à publier sous la Restauration, elle est marquée par ce contexte, à la fois historique et littéraire, où le moins que l'on puisse dire est que la dlfférence des sexes n'occupe pas le premier plan des débats; d'une certaine façon, elle vient de l'Ancien Régime, et de la province, et reste attachée à des formes de sociabilité dont elle a vu le bouleversement. Il y a par là quelque anachronisme à lui faire reproche de son non-féminisme, et il faudrait bien plutôt s'étonner de l'ouverture dont elle a su faire preuve dans l'accueil des femmes et des oeuvres que je viens d'évoquer, rencontrées alors qu'elle avait entre quarante et cinquante ans. Un tel anachronisme est un effet des classifications et périodisations de l'histoire littéraire, qui situent en général Desbordes-Valmore dans les "petits romantiques" ou "romantiques mineurs" et ne s'embarrassent pas d'autres précisions, ce qui fait qu'on la situe vaguement dans les années 1830, écrivant à l'imitation et à la remorque des grands du romantisme. Or son premier livre paraît la même année que les *Méditations* de Lamartine, quand Hugo est un tout jeune journaliste qui d'ailleurs fait l'éloge de cette oeuvre et, quelles que soient les critiques que l'on puisse lui adresser, force est de voir qu'elle est plus largement novatrice qu'imitatrice, méritant plutôt d'être classée—s'il faut absolument des classifications et des périodisations—dans ce que le poète Jean Tardieu a proposé d'appeler un "premier romantisme."[8] Par ailleurs, même à la rapporter aux critères politiques et historiques de la période dans laquelle elle publie la majeure partie de ses poemes, cette caractérisation de non-féminisme ne va pas sans problèmes.

Car les motifs idéologiquement répréhensibles aux yeux de la critique féministe d'aujourd'hui, que sont l'exaltation de la passion amoureuse, de la maternité, des qualités de coeur et d'âme des femmes sont aussi présents, quoiqu'articulés très différemment dans le féminisme de 1830,[9] et centraux dans le féminisme de 1848,[10] où ils servent à une stratégie de la demande de reconnaissance, de la part des femmes, décidément ancrée dans les attributs et rôles traditionnels de la féminité. Le seul "reproche" que l'on pourrait lui adresser serait donc de n'avoir pas fait état explicitement des antagonismes de sexes dans ses poèmes, et de n'y avoir pas demandé l'égalité des droits. Mais y aura-t-il beaucoup de *poètes féministes* à ce compte, et ces questions ont-elles un sens? Ceci conduit en tout cas à une interrogation plus générale des caractérisations de *féminine* et de *féministe*.

2. Ni féminine, ni féministe.

Bien entendu, cette réflexion pourrait s'appliquer à l'écriture en général, mais il me semble que les questions soulevées par l'emploi des adjectifs *féminine* et *féministe* s'adressent avec une acuité particulière à la poésie. D'abord parce qu'il y a moins de femmes poètes, cette remarque constitue un lieu commun de la critique littéraire du XIXe siècle (globalement antiféministe ou, au mieux, paternaliste), comme de la réflexion féministe du XXe siècle. Woolf, dans *A Room of One's Own*, commentant longuement la multiplication des romancières, attribue l'absence de femmes poètes à la difficulté pour les femmes d'écrire sans rage et sans amertume, à l'impossibilité que la poésie jaillisse d'elles en toute liberté et sans obstacle. Son analyse se fonde surtout sur la littérature de langue anglaise; en adoptant son point de vue pour envisager l'oeuvre de Marceline Desbordes-Valmore, on pourrait dire que celle-ci a pu être poète justement parce que sa poésie n'est pas le lieu d'expression d'une revendication féministe. Gilbert et Gubar, dans *Shakespeare's Sisters*, Domna Stanton elle-même, dans l'introduction à l'anthologie citée, reviennent sur cette dissymétrie dans le rapport des femmes à la poésie et à la prose, et sur la nécessité de définir la spécificité des pratiques poétiques des femmes. Or choisir comme mode d'approche de ces pratiques l'étude—ou même simplement la redécouverte—de la poésie féministe implique dès le départ une difficulté, si ce n'est une impossibilité, dans les termes. En effet, *féministe* renvoie dès le départ, au signifié, ou au "message" du poème, alors que le terme même de poème devrait imposer la prise en compte de l'écriture, du rythme, et du mode d'énonciation. Cette contradiction se tranche en général au profit d'un absolu primat du "contenu," qui aboutit à ne pas retenir, dans une anthologie, les poèmes de Desbordes-Valmore, mais à sélectionner, à la même époque, ceux d'Amable Tastu et de Louise Colet. Je peux éventuellement comprendre un tel choix d'un point de vue idéologique—politique—encore que dans les trois cas cités l'appréciation soit très discutable, et Amable Tastu comme Louise Colet plutôt suspectes au regard de critères féministes intransigeants, mais il s'agit là de jugements de valeurs inhérents à tout projet d'anthologie, qui, comme tels, peuvent se discuter. En revanche, je ne peux comprendre quelle conception de la poésie est mise en oeuvre pour procéder à la sélection des textes, lorsque je vois retenus ceux de Constance Pipelet ou de N. Clifford-Barney, le premier, indiscutablement féministe, n'ayant de "poétique" que le fait d'être écrit en alexandrins, le second, avec un "contenu" lesbien et subversif, relevant d'une lourde rhétorique, qui dément à chaque vers le propos du poème, qui est, paraît-il, de refuser la rhétorique et d'opposer aux mots la vie et l'amour. Que l'on me comprenne bien: il ne s'agit pas ici de la question, déjà longuement débattue, de la relativité des valeurs esthétiques et des hiérarchies littéraires, et du fait que ces poèmes seraient "mauvais" alors que ceux de Louise Labé et de Desbordes-Valmore seraient "bons" et "beaux." Il ne s'agit pas non plus de réduire cette difficulté, que Domna Stanton elle-même a bien vue et commentée, à une opposition dualiste du signifié au signifiant, du contenu idéologique aux moyens littéraires plus ou moins heureux utilisés: ce serait là se situer dans une théorie dualiste et instrumentaliste de la poésie—et par delà, du langage, dans laquelle la critique littéraire féministe a tendance à se laisser enfermer. Or les femmes auraient d'autant plus intérêt à interroger ce dualisme[11] qu'il participe d'une vision d'un monde et d'un mode de théorie dont elles-mêmes sont les victimes. Ce que je veux dire simplement, c'est qu'il me semble qu'alors, il n'y a pas de conception théorique de la poésie, c'est-à-dire qu'il y en a une, la plus superficielle et traditionnelle qui soit: celle qui oppose les vers à la prose, le poétique au langage ordinaire de la communication, et fait de la poésie une sorte de supplément ou d'ornement esthétique, un moyen parmi d'autres, plus joli et plus difficile que d'autres, de faire passer un contenu. Car il me paraît impossible d'avancer qu'une théorie féministe de la poésie pourrait se résumer et se contenir dans le terme de féministe, qui implique un point de vue *politique*, mais ignore le mode de rapport qui s'établit dans l'écriture entre féminisme et poésie, entre le dire et le dit. S'il s'agit simplement de dire par là qu'on va s'occuper de textes féministes écrits en vers, c'est se compliquer bien inutilement la tâche (mieux vaudrait peut-être proposer un choix de textes plus larges, pour faire entendre des voix féministes du passé), et c'est une définition un peu courte de la poésie, et peu admissible en 1986. Mais faisant abstraction quelque temps de cette contradiction fondamentale à mes yeux, je voudrais revenir sur tout ce qui met en cause la pertinence des qualificatifs *féministe* et *féminine* dans l'usage d'une critique littéraire, y compris de points de vue historique et politique.

Poésie féministe fait problème dans la mesure où la définition et le référent de cet adjectif en France ne vont pas de soi. Il est évident qu'on ne peut restreindre l'étude de la littérature féministe à la seule période où le mot existe (fin XIXe, où il est d'abord utilisé par des hommes, Faguet et Dumas fils), et à des mouvements se réclamant explicitement de cette appellation. Pourtant, un mot n'est jamais rien qu'un mot, et le fait qu'il n'apparaisse pas auparavant renvoie à un état autre des rapports et des mouvements sociaux. L'utiliser pour désigner des phénomènes— politiques, sociaux ou littéraires—antérieurs implique donc des distorsions et une pratique de l'anachronisme délibéré: encore faut-il en définir les critères et les limites. En France, selon le point de vue et les historiens, la limite antérieure pourra être 1789, 1830 (autour de laquelle se fait le plus large accord), ou 1848, et le critère le plus généralement retenu celui de la revendication de l'égalité des droits.[12] Critère sujet à discussion politique, puisqu'il met l'accent sur l'égalité, et non sur l'identité-différence, ce qui constitue déjà une interprétation du féminisme, et à discussion historique et lexicologique, puisque le mot même d'égalité, et l'exigence de l'application de son principe, sont peu ou pas présents dans les argumentations politiques des années 1831-1850 qui demandent cependant une plus large place sociale pour les femmes. Quelle que soit la définition retenue, on voit qu'elle impliquera donc que le *féminisme* réside dans le point de vue critque, et non (seulement) dans les mouvements ou les textes étudiés. Ce qui signifie aussi que nous sommes amenées à considérer comme relevant de pratiques féministes des femmes, et peut-être des hommes, qui ne se disent pas eux-mêmes féministes et dont l'action politique collective n'est pas le propos (comme peuvent faire des critiques pour Dickinson, par exemple)— l'inverse étant aussi à envisager. Et cela à partir d'un point de vue nécessairement extérieur et non immédiat aux textes, qui établit un rapport entre des enjeux politiques (d'aujourd'hui), les écrits eux-mêmes, leur confrontation à d'autres écrits littéraires, théoriques, normatifs ou critiques contemporains, d'hommes ou de femmes, et le propre métadiscours des auteurs. Si l'on veut tenir tous les éléments de ce rapport il devient alors beaucoup moins évident et facile de déclarer *féministe* un poème, ou quelque oeuvre littéraire que ce soit. Parler de "pratique poétique déviante," comme le fait Stanton, est une formule qui soulève plus de problèmes qu'elle n'en résoud: s'il s'agit de pratiques poétiques qui, comme elle le dit, désignent "les institutions qui perpétuent l'oppression des femmes," on se trouve une fois encore ramené au contenu, la déviance est dans le propos; c'est en outre s'enfermer dans le débat sans fin de la norme et de l'écart, avec cette difficulté supplémentaire que transgression de la norme sociale et transgression de la norme littéraire ne coïncident pas nécessairement; c'est enfin supposer toute une étude de l'historicité des discours et des pratiques poétiques intégrant une pensée de la différence des sexes. Une telle étude, si elle existe, n'en est qu'à ses balbutiements. A moins que la "déviance" ne consiste simplement dans le fait d'écrire, en particulier des poèmes, ce qui voudrait dire que tout poème écrit par une femme est féministe. Sur ce point du moins, il y a un large accord des critiques et féministes contemporaines pour rejeter une telle définition comme insuffisante et confusionniste. Et pourtant, ce *consensus* est peut-être à interroger, car, à se reporter aux discours normatifs du XIXe siècle, il se pourrait bien qu'il y ait effectivement une dynamique de remise en cause à la fois sociale et subjective dans le simple fait qu'une femme écrive des poèmes—si toutefois ce sont vraiment des poèmes, et non des conseils didactiques, moraux, domestiques, voire des considérations politiques, arrangés en alexandrins. Je suppose toutefois que D. Stanton caractériserait au contraire comme "déviante" toute pratique poétique qui s'oppose à ce qu'il est convenu d'appeler *poésie féminine*, celle-ci confirmant les images traditionnelles de la femme, celle-là les subvertissant.

Mais qu'appelle-t-on au fait *poésie féminine*? Les implications que Stanton associe à ce mot, se référant aux travaux de Jeanine Moulin, sont essentiellement négatives: sentimentalité, conformisme, fadeur, banalité, délayage et épanchement. Telles sont en effet les associations que ce syntagme appelle presque automatiquement en français, un peu de la même façon que le substantif féminin de *poétesse*. Est-ce une raison pour reprendre ce qualificatif comme tel, et pour le faire fonctionner dans une opposition à féministe, ce que fait non seulement Stanton, mais Elaine Showalter lorsqu'elle propose une périodisation de la littérature des femmes en trois phases: "feminine/feminist/female"?[13] J'y vois plusieurs obstacles: d'abord, qu'on le veuille ou non, ce mot contient, outre la connotation "sensibilité larmoyante," la dénotation "de femme"; c'est-à-dire qu'il renvoie à la fois au donné biologique et au construit historique, social, et idéologique; au sexe et au genre—et le maintien de la confusion est fâcheux, puisqu'il reproduit le piège même et la limitation obligée dans lesquels les femmes se sont vues au XIXe enfermées par la critique littéraire. Car l'emploi de ce mot implique une histoire, et de se situer par rapport à elle, et à la tradition qui a érigé les canons littéraires du féminin; là encore, que les reproches, implicites ou explicites, que contient le mot de "féminine" dans son opposition à "féministe" coïncident avec ceux qu'adressaient aux femmes écrivains les critiques porte-parole des institutions et des valeurs littéraires devrait nous amener à faire fonctionner ces catégories de façon plus circonspecte. Autre source de confusion: dans l'acception même de *féminin* comme construction idéologique-historique, l'adjectif renvoie à la fois à des éléments thématiques (amour, maternité, sensations, notations intimistes), et à des éléments formels (genres mineurs et "privés," constructions discontinues et peu rigoureuses, lexique concret, syntaxe peu soucieuse de la logique et de la grammaire), alors que féministe, on l'a vu, renvoie essentiellement à des éléments idéologiques-thématiques, sans qu'il soit possible de dégager un paradigme, même large, des traits d'une *écriture féministe*. En effet, lorsque la réflexion féministe critique contemporaine a voulu désigner des pratiques d'écriture de femmes rompant avec les canons de la féminité comme avec les normes des institutions littéraires, elle a eu recours, en France en particulier, au syntagme d'*écriture féminine*. Et voici *féminine* ici devenu éminemment novateur, subversif, *féministe* même, de péjoratif et réactionnaire qu'il était, accolé à poésie: ce qu'il désigne dans les deux cas est-il si radicalement différent? L'oeuvre de Marceline Desbordes-Valmore présente de nombreux traits qui figurent dans les différentes évocations de l'écriture féminine. Ceci montre la difficulté de ces caractérisations, leurs limites, leur non pertinence, me semble-t-il, dans l'analyse littéraire. Et suffit du moins à montrer que le couple féministe/féminine ne peut fonctionner, ni pour désigner une opposition dans les pratiques d'écriture, ni pour instaurer une périodisation littéraire. On pourrait bien sûr imaginer une savante combinaison des deux critères, qui aboutirait à une typologie à quatre cases: féminine/féministe, féminine/non-féministe, etc... Il faudrait de surcroît y intégrer le critère de l'originalité poétique proprement dite, encore une fois évacué du précédent tableau. Que gagnerait-on à ces savantes taxinomies? Peut-être une certaine clarification des ruptures historiques et des enjeux politiques, car là l'opposition féminine/féministe, et l'étude du rapport des deux termes, peuvent prendre leur pertinence; on le voit dans la périodisation que propose Showalter, qui fait intervenir comme repères et facteurs de rupture des événements extra-littéraires et sociaux. Mais bien peu de choses dans la lecture concrète d'oeuvres singulières: imaginez qu'il faille faire entrer dans les cases d'une telle typologie les oeuvres de Desbordes-Valmore, ou de George Sand, d'Elisabeth Barret Browning ou d'Emily Dickinson: féminines, non-féminines? féministes, non-féministes? Cela peut se discuter à l'infini, selon le moment de l'oeuvre envisagé, selon le point de vue et la situation historique des lectures. En tout cas, pas réductibles à ces catégorisations, qui ne nous en apprennent pas tout, et certainement pas l'essentiel de leurs écrits, si on veut les traiter comme oeuvres, dans leur propre cohérence et la systématique interne de leurs valeurs et de leur langage—ce qu'il est bien banal d'accorder aux oeuvres d'hommes. Définitions, périodisations, catégorisations prenant pour critère le féministe et le féminin ont un sens politque, et une visée stratégique: selon une formule désormais classique, rendre les femmes à la littérature (à l'histoire), et rendre la littérature (l'histoire), aux femmes. Elles valent pour faire surgir des massifs oubliés ou méconnus, pour redessiner des paysages, contester des ruptures et des frontières admises—et toutes ces métaphores spatiales, récurrentes dans le métalangage de la théorie et de la critique féministes, disent combien c'est là affaire de stratégie. Mais quelle est la place des écritures singulières dans cette guerre de positions? A vouloir rendre visible le féminin pour que cesse de se perpétuer la confusion du masculin et de l'universel, à vouloir y renvoyer les femmes dans leur écriture et dans leur langage (cette expression, il faut le noter, s'emploie rarement au pluriel), il y a le risque toujours reconduit de les y enfermer, et, les rapprochant sans cesse des autres femmes du présent ou du passé, dans un *continuum* de leurs textes, de reproduire, au nom d'une solidarité nécessaire et enfin conquise, le déni d'individualité, de subjectivité, de créativité, qui leur a dans l'histoire été constamment infligé par les hornmes et par la critique littéraire. La reconnaissance et la considération de chaque oeuvre poétique, de chaque oeuvre littéraire comme telle, me paraît donc devoir constituer une des premières exigences d'une théorie féministe critique de la littérature. A cette reconnaissance de la femme comme individu et comme sujet, il n'est pas certain d'ailleurs que perdent le politique et la stratégie.

[1]*The Defiant Muse. French Feminist Poems from the Middle Ages to the Present. A Bilingual Anthology* edited and with an introduction by Domna C. Stanton (New York: The Feminist Press at the University of New York, 1986).
[2]Introduction, p. xxiv-xxv.
[3]Maïte Albistur et Daniel Armogathe, *Histoire du féminisme français du moyen-âge à nos jours* (Paris: éd. *des femmes*, 1977), p. 264. L'appréciation "nulle inspiration proprement féministe" est visiblement principalement fondée sur des ouvrages critiques, et non sur une lecture de l'oeuvre. La tradition provient donc d'abord de jugements masculins: Sainte-Beuve, Baudelaire. Cette démarche, et la "condamnation" de Desbordes-Valmore qui en résulte, sont compréhensibles compte tenu du projet de l'ouvrage (une histoire du féminisme), et de la date à laquelle il a été écrit, faisant alors une sorte de travail premier de défrichage. Il me semble plus gênant qu'elles soient reproduites dix ans plus tard, et dans une anthologie dont le domaine et le propos sont aussi la poésie. De Albistur et Armogathe, voir aussi *Le Grief des femmes. Anthologie de textes féministes du moyen-âge à nos jours*, 2 vol. (Paris: Ed. Hier et Demain, 1978).
[4]Tous les éléments concernant la biographie qui figurent dans cette partie proviennent du récent ouvrage de Francis Ambrière, indispensable sur la question, et qui met fin à un certain nombre de mythes: *Le Siècle des Valmore. Marceline Desbordes-Valmore et les siens* (Paris: Seuil, 1987). Sur la question de l'humilité, du conformisme, de l'usage qu'elle a fait de sa position de femme, voir les analyses plus détaillées que j'ai développées dans: "Marceline Desbordes-Valmore: une femme poète—les silences dans la voix", *Actes du Colloque Marceline Desbordes-Valmore et son temps* (Douai: Mémoires de la société d'agriculture, sciences et arts, 1986); "L'art sans art de Marceline Desbordes-Valmore," *Europe* (Paris: mai 1987, n° 697),164-176; "L'autobiographie indéfinie," *Romantisme* n° 56. *Images de soi: autobiograhpie et autoportrait au XIXe siècle* (Paris: CDU-SEDES, 2e trim. 1987), 47-58.
[5]Marceline Desbordes-Valmore, *Oeuvres poétiques*, éd. établie et commentée par Marc Bertrand, 2 vol. (Grenoble: Presses universitaires de Grenoble: 1973), tome II, p. 506.
[6]L'expression est de Albistur et Armogathe.
[7]Cité par Francis Ambrière, *Le Grief des femmes*, II, p. 119.
[8]Jean Tardieu, "Pré-romantisme ou premier romantisme," *Cahiers du Sud*, n° 302 (2e sem. 1950, t. xxxii, 37° année), 7-19.
[9]Sur les contradictions et les ambiguïtés du féminisme saint-simonien, voir l'étude de Valentin Pélosse "Symbolique groupale et idéologie saint-simonienne," dans: Claire Démar, *Ecrits sur l'affranchissement des femmes (1832-1833)* (Paris: Payot, 1976); Maria Térésa Bulciolu, *L'Ecole saint-simonienne et la femme* (Pisa: Goliardica, 1980); Christine Planté, "Les féministes saint-simoniennes: possibilités et limites d'un mouvement féministe en France au lendemain de la révolution de 1830," *Regards sur le saint-simonisme et les saint-simoniens*, sous la direction de J.R. Derré (Lyon: Presses Universitaires de Lyon, 1986).
[10]Voir Michèle Riot-Sarcey, Eléni Varikas, "Feminist Consciousness in the Nineteenth Century: The Consciousness of a Pariah," *Praxis International: Feminism as Critique* (Oxford, 1986, vol. 5 n° 4), 443-465, en particulier la partie intitulée "Feminism as the Art of the Possible," p. 457.
[11]Un exemple historique: cette forme de dualisme, particulièrement présente dans les oppositions qu'établit le saint-simonisme: esprit/matière, homme/femme, païen/chrétien, Ancien/Nouveau Testament (même s'il les travestit habilement en organisation et rhétorique "ternaires, ou se donne pour vouloir renverser les hiérarchies existantes au profit du terme méprisé ou opprimé dans ces couples duels), éclate de façon particulièrement claire dans sa théorie du langage. Celle-ci, en effet, jetant le masque du renversement des valeurs et du dépassement des oppositions, reprend l'antagonisme classique de l'esprit et de la lettre, au profit, bien sûr, de "l'esprit." L'analyse du maintien de la théorie traditionnelle sur ce point permet, très

tôt, d'envisager et de comprendre les limites de ce mouvement, et son évolution vers une conservation de l'état des choses, dont les femmes, comme les ouvriers, feront les frais.

[12]Ce critère de l'égalité est celui qui a été retenu pour l'élaboration d'un dictionnaire biographique du féminisme français, projet entrepris dans le cadre du CNRS, sous la direction de Laurence Klejman, Michelle Perrot, Michèle Riot-Sarcey et Florence Rochefort.

[13]Elaine Showalter, *A Literature of Their Own: British Women Feminists from Brontë to Lessing* (Princeton, N.J: Princeton University Press, 1977); "Toward a Feminist Poetics," *The New Feminist Criticism: Essays on Women, Literature & Theory*, ed. Elaine Showalter (New York: Pantheon Books, 1985), 125-143.

Exotisme et vie quotidienne:
le cas de la "littérature d'évasion"

Claude Javeau
Université Libre de Bruxelles

Les propos qui suivent ne laissent pas de trancher assez singulièrement sur ceux, imprégnés de la plus estimable des éruditions, que tiennent la quasi-totalité des autres intervenants de ce colloque sur l'exotisme littéraire. En effet, je ne vais pas présenter l'un de ces grands auteurs dont s'enorgueillit (ou devrait s'enorgueillir, si l'on en croit ce qui a été dit de Loti) la littérature française. Mon corpus de référence sera constitué par l'une des cases du "second rayon" prisé par les amateurs de littérature populaire, en l'occurrence les romans que l'on a longtemps dits "pour midinettes." En second lieu, je ne m'intéresserai guère à la production elle-même des textes, envisagée sous l'angle du rapport entre l'auteur de l'oeuvre et l'oeuvre elle-même, mais bien à leur *consommation*, c'est-à-dire à l'attribution de sens à laquelle procède le lecteur de tels ouvrages lorsqu'il s'absorbe dans cette activité sociale — au sens wébérien du mot[1] — qu'est la lecture. Toute activité orientée vers autrui est en effet porteuse de sens, autrui, pour la circonstance étant la constellation d'êtres peu ou mal définis (je vais y revenir) qui a permis que le livre arrive un jour entre les mains du lecteur.

Je crois utile de préciser que la tradition sociologique à laquelle j'entends me rattacher ici est le courant phénoménologique, illustré par Alfred Schütz (1899-1959), disciple d'Edmund Husserl, et par sa nombreuse descendance, dont en particulier Peter Berger et Thomas Luckman.[2] Selon cette tradition, le "social" se construit à partir des interactions significatives que nouent entre eux des individus autonomes, nantis d'un bagage cognitif que le procès de socialisation a fait "sédimenter" en eux. La sociologie issue de la phénoménologie husserlienne accorde beaucoup d'importance au sens commun, au monde tel qu'il apparaît (aux yeux des acteurs) comme allant-de-soi, dans l'objectivité d'une évidence entretenue par le commerce même qui s'établit entre les individus, pris isolément ou en groupes. Cette sociologie opère aisément sa jonction avec les conceptions wébériennes, ainsi que l'a très brillamment montré Robert Williame.[3] Weber, on se le rappellera, se préoccupe avant tout du sens que les acteurs accordent à leur actions. Schütz reprend la question là où Weber l'a laissée et s'inquiète de la constitution de ce sens même et de ses modes d'attribution. C'est dans cette direction que j'entends engager la suite de cet exposé. Mais, auparavant, permettez-moi de rappeler quelques évidences relatives aux pratiques culturelles dans les sociétés techniquement très développées.

Les moments des pratiques culturelles

L'étude sociologique des pratiques culturelles, au sens d'activités spécifiques reposant sur la constitution et l'appropriation d'objets, matériels ou non, que l'idéologie commune des sociétés de type occidental désigne comme "culturels," repose sur la prise en considération de trois moments essentiels au moins. Nous distinguerons donc entre:

1) le moment de la *création* de l'objet culturel (chanson, poème, tableau, cathédrale, spectacle télévisé, livre, etc.);

2) le moment des *médiations institutionnelles* dont la fonction est de mettre l'objet culturel en contact avec un public: c'est en réalité le vrai moment de la production culturelle;

3) le moment de la *consommation* de l'objet culturel par un public, étendu ou restreint, peu importe.

Il convient de remarquer que le moment médian, celui des médiations institutionnelles (marché de l'édition, musées, conservatoires, radio-télévision, etc.), s'il médiatise l'"offre" en direction de la "demande," joue également le rôle inverse, en médiatisant la "demande" vers l'"offre," en faisant connaître à celle-ci, de manière "objective" ou non, les attentes supposées du public. Il va de soi que ce schéma n'est harmonieux qu'en apparence, de nombreuses perturbations pouvant affecter le moment médian, telles que censure étatique, pénuries de matières premières, monopoles de production et/ou de distribution, etc. Certains cas de figure, à la limite, échappent au schéma de la médiation,[4] comme par exemple la confusion des moments de la création et de la création dans les activités dites, en Europe, d'"animation culturelle." D'autres ressortissent à une pure logique de marché. D'autres encore renvoient à un ensemble de pratiques bureaucratiques, comme dans les pays totalitaires, où le monopole de l'Etat en matière culturelle est lié à l'absence d'une authentique "opinion publique."

Me concentrant sur le troisième moment, celui de la consommation des objets culturels, l'"exotisme" dans des productions littéraires, pour aborder l'objet de notre rencontre, apparaît bien comme relevant à priori d'une médiation fonctionnant de manière bilatérale. Vers l'aval, on trouve la proposition d'une thématique particulière—en l'occurrence celle de l'*ailleurs*—à un public potentiel de lecteurs, elle-même tributaire du système d'intérêts d'auteurs à un moment donné. Lequel système d'intérêts n'est pas indépendant, en amont, de la représentation que se font ces mêmes auteurs des attentes du public qu'ils visent, partant de leurs propres "chances de succès." Encore une fois, il s'agit ici d'une construction idéale-typique (au sens wéberien du terme). Certains cas de figures échappent complètement à ce modele, qui, comme tout idéal-type, n'est en rien normatif. Par exemple, la poésie composée et diffusée en "cénacle" implique la quasi-absence de médiation institutionnelle. De son côté, la production en série de livres de faible valeur marchande, basée sur les résultats d'études de marché plus ou moins poussées (ce que l'on pourrait appeler le "marketing littéraire"), réduit à peu de choses le système d'intérêts autonome des auteurs. En réalité, il se réduit au seul appât du gain. Notons que ces remarques, cela va de soi, valent pour d'autres thématiques que l'exotisme.

La littérature[5] de "grande consommation," qui prit la succession des feuilletons du siècle dernier, répond à cette dernière figure. Les auteurs, s'il est encore possible d'en distinguer, sont réduits à un rôle d'exécutants obéissant aux prescriptions du marketing de la maison d'éditions. Dans certains cas, ces auteurs reçoivent même, dans des espèces d'"écoles d'écriture" spécialement instituées à cette fin, une formation spécifique qui doit les rendre capables de respecter ces prescriptions. Dans ce domaine de la littérature, la triade des moments se réduit en fait à la dyade "médiations institutionnelles-public," avec une prépondérance sensible du premier terme.

Littérature d'évasion et stock de connaissances

La littérature d'"évasion," telle que je vais la définir, correspond à ce dernier schéma. Notons au passage qu'il s'agit d'une littérature destinée avant tout à un public féminin,[6] qui encourt dès lors presque certainement le risque d'être d'emblée taxée de "frivole" et de porter tous les stigmates de l'absence de sérieux qui sont généralement attribués aux productions féminines ou adressées aux femmes. Il s'agit là d'un aspect important de notre objet sur lequel je ne m'étendrai pas mais qu'il est bon de garder à l'esprit. Par "littérature d'évasion," j'entendrai un produit culturel imprimé, largement diffusé et à prix réduit (notamment dans les magasins à grandes surfaces), présentant un récit généralement situé dans un cadre exotique et dans lequel la passion amoureuse joue un rôle primordial. L'exemple de cette littérature est donné, en langue française, par la collection Harlequin, diffusée en France et les autres pays de langue française par la maison parisienne Edimail.[7] Cette collection, qui se subdivise en neuf séries, a pour slogan: "Tout un monde d'évasion." Elle propose au public populaire des ouvrages traduits de l'américain (ce qui accentue l'effet d'exotisme). Il ne fait pas de doute que les livres de cette collection (et d'autres semblables) sont largement diffusés et lus. Ce qui m'intéresse ici, ce ne sont pas les "motivations" des acheteurs-lecteurs de tels livres, largement sollicités par une publicité sans doute fort efficace. Le plus souvent, les motivations reconnues à divers groupements d'acteurs sociétaux ne sont rien d'autres que des catégories de sens commun utilisées par les praticiens du marketing en guise de principes explicatifs. Bien au-delà des motivations, ce qui constitue pour moi le vrai problème sociologique, c'est celui de la recherche du *sens* que les contenus de ces livres prennent dans l'univers des représentations de leurs lecteurs, tel qu'il s'exprime dans le "stock de connaissances disponibles" (stock of knowledge at hand) dont traite Alfred Schütz. Selon cet auteur:

> Man in daily life...finds at any given moment a stock of knowledge at hand that serves as a scheme of interpretation of his past and present experiences, and also determines his anticipations of things to come.[8]

En termes husserliens, ce stock résulte de la "sédimentation" des significations, elle-même produit de la socialisation, au cours de l'histoire personnelle des individus. Ces derniers, il faut le rappeler, ne doivent pas être comparés à des atomes isolés, mais bien à des fragments difficilement isolables de groupes plus ou moins étendus (familles, groupes de pairs, tribus, classes sociales, groupes ethniques, castes, etc.), au sein desquels fonctionnent des modes identiques de captation (moment précédant la sédimentation) et de sédimentation des éléments cognitifs signifiants.

Selon la définition que j'ai proposée de la littérature d'évasion, les deux éléments les plus importants que nous devons prendre en considération sont, d'une part, l'histoire d'une passion amoureuse, et de l'autre, le décor exotique dans lequel elle se déroule. Comment l'un et l'autre de ces éléments sont-ils "captés," d'abord, et "sédimentés," ensuite par des groupes spécifiques (correspondant à ces "cibles" relativement précises dans la stratégie de marché des éditeurs de ce genre de littérature)? Il est évident que le procès de captation-sédimentation sera d'autant plus intense que les éléments en question, dans le système de représentation des groupes concernés, apparaîtront davantage porteurs de sens. Pour le membre d'un groupe qui ne consomme guère une telle littérature, un livre de la collection Harlequin sera faiblement porteur de sens (autrement dit, en termes schüziens, ainsi que nous le verrons plus loin, sa relevance sera réduite) et constituera tout au plus un objet de curiosité, à moins, évidemment, qu'il ne devienne objet d'investigation scientifique.

Deux hypothèses de base

Pour ce qui est de la capacité de ces deux éléments structuraux à "faire sens" (c'est-à-dire à engendrer la capacité à s'en voir attribuer par les lecteurs), j'avancerai deux hypothèses:

1) Pour les consommateurs de la littérature d'évasion, la passion amoureuse est vécue sur le mode de l'extériorité. Par passion amoureuse, j'entendrai ici l'expression aiguë d'un grand désordre des sentiments. Parler d'"extériorité," c'est supposer que de tels récits sont considérés comme ressortissant à d'autres moeurs, d'autres modes de vie que ceux des catégories sociales où se recrutent les lecteurs de ces récits.

2) Pour ces mêmes consommateurs, l'exotisme est un lieu imaginaire de dissidence. Par dissidence, j'entendrai l'introduction d'une distance entre l'apparente évidence du monde et le jugement porté sur ce monde, cette distance restant de l'ordre du caché, du non explicite ou encore du "souterrain." En fait, "dissidence" se conjugue ici avec "duplicité": on feint d'adhérer à l'ordre du monde, ce qui est, en dernière analyse, une manière d'y adhérer—un ordre étant toujours considéré comme nécessaire.

Pour ce qui est de la première hypothèse, il conviendrait tout d'abord de s'interroger sur le mode de socialisation à l'amour en usage dans les divers groupes sociaux. Ici encore, je me hasarderai à une hypothèse: dans les classes populaires, principale "cible" de la littérature d'évasion (et par "classes populaires," j'entends à la fois la fraction "installée" de la classe ouvrière, la strate des petits employés et petits fonctionnaires, les artisans et les petits commerçants), l'articulation "amour-mariage" implique un ancrage dans la durée, correspondant à un projet conforme d'existence à deux, faisant l'économie de tout débordement érotico-amoureux. Les classes populaires sont généralement opposées au désordre individuel, même si une fraction d'entre elles, le prolétariat et les couches qui lui ont succédé, a parfois préconisé le désordre collectif (dans le respect, il est vrai, d'une certaine discipline). D'où leur méfiance à l'égard de la passion amoureuse, acquise conjointement avec une certaine respectabilité, elle-même obtenue, en même temps qu'une substantielle amélioration des conditions matérielles, à la suite des durs combats pour l'émancipation du siècle dernier et de la première moitié de celui-ci.[9] Certes, l'affection réciproque est inscrite dans le modèle des relations amoureuses en usage dans les classes populaires, mais celle-ci est exclusive de la passion, au sens romantique ou romanesque du terme. La vraie passion appartient à l'ensemble des attributs constituant l'apanage des classes supérieures, notamment de ceux qu'Edgar Morin appelle les Olympiens. Ces classes possédant la richesse matérielle, celle-ci sert de garant à la réparation inéluctable de tout grand désordre social (comme la passion amoureuse, désordre par excellence). Remarquons toutefois que, dans la littérature d'évasion, la passion dévorante se conclut généralement par un retour à l'ordre, c'est-à-dire le mariage ou la promesse de mariage. Le mariage fait partie de l'ordre normal du monde. Son exaltation correspond à un profond souci de dignité, cultivé par décalque des habitus bourgeois et surtout petit-bourgeois.

Dans le stock de connaissances, la passion amoureuse figure, en tant qu'attribut typique des classes aisées, dans le second cercle des connaissances, celles qui, tout en étant familières, ont été acquises par procuration.[10] Parmi les voies de procuration, figurent la littérature (d'évasion ou non: on peut avoir lu, à l'école, *Le Rouge et le Noir* ou même *La Princesse de Clèves*), le cinéma, les feuilletons télévisés, les chansons, les rubriques des faits divers des journaux, les magazines spécialisés dans les faits et gestes des Olympiens, etc. Il est permis de penser qu'il est assez rare, dans les classes populaires, que les individus aient une connaissance directe de passions amoureuses (par exemple, dans l'entourage immédiat), sinon assorties d'un commentaire péjoratif. La "captation" de ce contenu cognitif s'opère donc par la rencontre avec l'un des médias que je viens de citer, véhiculant un "message" en relative dissonance avec le système de règles-normes-valeurs en usage dans le groupe social récepteur. Cette dissonance suscite l'intérêt et met en branle le procès de projection-identification bien connu des psychologues sociaux, pourvu, bien entendu, que le retour à la normalité (l'apaisement de la passion dans une fin morale, à savoir le mariage) soit garanti de manière suffisamment explicite.

Exotisme et dissidence

Le rôle de l'exotisme (nous verrons plus loin ce qu'il convient ici d'entendre par ce terme) doit être envisagé sous l'angle du concept de dissidence (ou encore de duplicité), illustré par divers travaux du sociologue français Michel Maffesoli.[11] Introduisons-le de la manière suivante. L'existence sociale des individus se construit autour de deux pôles, l'un majeur, celui de l'ordre social, imposé par l'appareil de légitimation du système social, et l'autre mineur, constitué par les diverses formes de résistance à cet ordre, et source de dissidence, soit réelle (dans des pratiques secrètement illégitimes: fraude, adultère, toxicomanie, sabotages divers), soit imaginaire. Ces deux poles gouvernent la *texture paradoxale* du social: sous l'ordre auquel les individus donnent toute apparence de souscrire, prolifèrent les "plages" de désordre, manifestant la perversité polymorphe, pour reprendre la célèbre expression freudienne, des populations les plus soumises en surface. L'ordre, il est vrai, s'efforce bien de récupérer ce feu couvant du désordre, notamment dans la fête (que la théorie sociologique classique, depuis Durkheim, identifie à la mise en scène collective du chaos originel, dont doit resurgir le système ordonné et contrôlé qu'est la société), mais le désordre lui tient toutefois bon, tant sont imprévisibles et multiformes ses avatars. J'insiste bien sur le caractère consubstantiel à tout ordre de ces dissidences, qui ne doivent être réduites à de simples réactions à l'aliénation figurant, par pétition de principe, au coeur de ce qu'Henri Lefebvre a appelé la quotidienneté.

Si l'on entend (j'y arrive) par *exotisme* tout "lieu autre" pouvant figurer un espace de liberté par rapport aux contraintes jugées normales de la vie quotidienne, ce lieu apparaît comme support imaginaire de dissidence, c'est-à-dire de rupture plus ou moins accusée avec les règlements sociaux découlant de cette normalité: respect des horaires, souci d'économies financières, primat du travail salarié, modération des sentiments, etc. "Imaginaire," au demeurant, ne signifie pas "faux," "factice" ou "mensonger," mais bien "cadre d'images." Les individus, du reste, ne sont pas dupes du caractère imaginaire de cette dissidence, et s'ils s'y aliènent éventuellement (en poussant un peu loin l'identification aux héros des récits exotiques), ce n'est pas, si l'on peut dire, à leur raison défendante. L'imaginaire—on devrait sans doute mieux dire: l'imaginal—est une dimension intrinsèque de la socialité, de l'"être-ensemble" intersubjectif. En tant que lieu imaginal de dissidence, l'exotisme plante un décor à l'histoire d'amour passionnelle, c'est-à-dire à un comportement attribué, en principe, à d'autres classes sociales, considérées généralement comme "supérieures" ("la haute"). Un nouveau paradoxe est ainsi mis en évidence: le lieu de dissidence encadre une manière de soumission à l'ordre social, dans la mesure où il consacre les distinctions entre classes et les distances que ce même ordre établit entre elles. Il en est ainsi, d'ailleurs, de toute dissidence, sauf lorsqu'elle éclate en révolte contrepoint de l'ordre social, elle ne met pas celui-ci en cause, mais se contente de le colorer d'une certaine façon, ce qui contribue à conserver à la vie quotidienne son caractère essentiellement mensonger,[12] comme Goffman, en étudiant les rites d'interaction, l'a si bien vu. Ainsi l'ordre social maintient-il, voire renforce-t-il, sa légitimité, celle-ci résultant alors, fût-ce partiellement, d'une adhésion volontaire, et non plus de la simple contrainte mécanique ou organique, comme le pensaient, par exemple, les durkheimiens.

Du point de vue cognitif, l'exotisme apparaît dès que se révèlent à l'individu d'autres milieux—*Mitwelten*—que le sien, que cette altérité se rapporte au temps (exochronie) ou à l'espace (exotopie). Ainsi conçu, l'exotisme mène aisément à l'utopie ou à l'uchronie, mais il s'agit toujours, cependant, de lieux ou d'âges de "nulle part" qui gardent quelques liens de familiarité. Si la passion amoureuse, argument du récit, se déroule dans une île du Pacifique, ce lieu autre est, en fait, un lieu de nulle part, aucune véracité documentaire n'étant exigée de l'auteur, qui peut aller jusqu'à inventer le nom et la position géographique de l'île. Il convient seulement que le décor, décrit en très larges touches, ne déroge pas à un stéréotype des îles du Pacifique. On parlerait alors d'utopie typique. Le lecteur (re)fait l'expérience des "ailleurs," qui entrent ainsi dans le second cercle de son stock de connaissances, celui des connaissances familières par procuration (à moins que de fréquents voyages à l'étranger ne lui aient rendu les lieux exotiques directement familiers, auquel cas il s'agirait alors du premier cycle du stock de connaissances: les lieux de vacances, cependant, n'offrent le plus souvent de l'exotisme qu'une version édulcorée et rassurante), tout comme c'était le cas pour la passion amoureuse.

Quant à la dissidence, elle me semble inscrite au coeur même de l'expérience de l'altérité des partenaires sociétaux. Si autrui se révèle toujours comme ouverture sur l'interaction, et non comme simple instrument, l'échapée qu'il inflige à Ego mène à l'idée de duplicité, car l'ordre social, qui prétend régir souverainement les rapports entre les acteurs, se trouve dénoncé comme mensonger. En termes plus simples, la simple présence d'autrui, qu'Ego ne pourra jamais, même dans le rapport amoureux le plus intense, "absorber" complètement, introduit du désordre dans l'ordre. D'où l'idée de ruse, de piège tendu à autrui pour inventer une vérité en contrepoint du mensonge. Le paradoxe (encore un) veut évidemment qu'autrui se dérobe aussi au piège de la vérité. D'où l'éternel recommencement de la dissidence. En la situant imaginairement dans un ailleurs qui se présente comme l'envers de l'expérience quotidienne commune, la dissidence conjure le danger de sa propre dissolution par le rétablissement de l'irréductibilité d'autrui à toute manipulation, même symbolique. "Ailleurs," autrui peut être figé dans une relation qui, pour être mensongère, peut être néanmoins acceptée (provisoirement, le temps d'une lecture) comme véridique. On rejoint ici la fonction *constative* de toute littérature—celle qui fait dire, par exemple, que le monde des livres est "plus réel" que le monde de l'expérience commune.

L'exotisme figure donc un lieu de conjuration de la dérobade d'autrui, où la dissidence sert surtout à la réconciliation avec l'altérité. L'autonomie des protagonistes du récit fonde leur hétéronomie dans l'imaginaire du lecteur. Dans la vie quotidienne, l'hétéronomie des acteurs fonde l'autonomie de l'ordre social, qui n'a de comptes à rendre à personne. A la fin du livre, l'opération se solde par un résultat nul: autonomie et hétéronomie sont à nouveau confondues, au profit de l'ordre. D'où la profonde normativité de cette littérature d'évasion. Les classes populaires sont généralement éprises d'ordre, et les tactiques de dissidences, inscrites au coeur de toute existence collective, n'ont pour but que de rendre l'ordre plus attrayant.[13] Ainsi, une démarche phénoménologique aboutit à la conclusion politique souvent énoncée, selon laquelle la littérature d'évasion, comme d'autres formes d'expression destinées au public populaire, servent avant tout à "défendre et illustrer" l'ordre social.

Relevances

Dans les termes de la sociologie compréhensive de Schütz, toute lecture ou autre acte d'appropriation d'un message esthétique quelconque est figuré par le concept de relevance *thématique*. Ce type de relevance implique que l'intérêt de l'individu vise à prendre un objet pour thème, tandis que d'autres intérêts moins importants *hic et nunc* constituent l'horizon. Chaque thème possède un horizon spécifique: l'étrangeté de la portion du monde qui se révèle problématique est atteinte sur un fond non-problématique. Dans le cas qui nous occupe, l'horizon est constitué par la vie quotidienne, perçue sous l'angle de sa banalité intrinsèque (à quoi d'ailleurs elle ne peut être entièrement réduite).[14] La portion problématique est celle de la passion amoureuse dans un cadre exotique. Le premier problème qui se pose au lecteur est: "à quoi la passion aboutira-t-elle?". Ici, le passage à la dissidence consiste à feindre que la question reste ouverte, alors que la réponse est connue: jeu de dupes où le dupé est volontaire. Le deuxième problème peut s'énoncer comme suit: "comment se dessiner un décor exotique qui, par définition, tranche avec le décor familier?". A ce stade intervient un autre mode de relevance, à savoir la relevance *interprétative*, par laquelle l'acteur—en l'occurrence, le lecteur ou, plus souvent, la lectrice—superpose à l'expérience actuelle d'un objet problématique le souvenir d'expériences passées semblables. Il ne peut s'agir, le plus souvent, que d'expériences types, car le monde est nécessairement typifié. Ceci signifie que, hormis les cas où les interactants se sont trouvés en congruence prolongée de flux de consciences (comme dans des relations intimes), les expériences dont les significations ont été sédimentées dans la conscience de l'individu se rapportent toutes à des *types* préalablement constitués et légués à celui-ci comme tout l'arsenal cognitif, par les agents de sa socialisation. Les lieux exotiques, à cet égard, n'échappent pas à la règle de la typification. Certes, il peut arriver que le lecteur ait connu lui-même, pendant un temps assez long, des endroits qui devraient passer à ses yeux pour exotiques. Mais la familiarité, précisément, risque fort de les dénuer de tout exotisme; en réalité, ce qu'ils conserveraient d'exotisme proviendrait de la possibilité de les rapporter à un type bien ancré dans le stock de connaissances de l'individu.

La *culture* d'un groupe, au sein d'une société globale, fournit à tous les membres du groupe un catalogue de types (d'acteurs, de situations, de lieux, d'activités, etc.), qui fonctionnent comme des marqueurs de territoire cognitif parcouru pour l'individu. Dans la culture "populaire," les lieux exotiques sont ainsi typés à l'avance: lieux de fuite et de nostalgie anticipative, de dissidence et de réaffirmation de l'ordre du monde, ils jouent un rôle non négligeable dans les procès de *régulation* que les individus mettent en oeuvre dans leur univers quotidien. A cet égard, la littérature d'évasion et les productions culturelles connexes, quoi qu'on pense de leur valeur esthétique, constituent l'un des piliers d'une culture sensiblement plus complexe, j'espère l'avoir montré, que les lettrés pourraient le penser au premier abord.

---

[1]"Nous entendons par 'activité' (*Handeln*) un comportement humain (...), quand et pour autant que l'agent ou les agents lui communiquent un sens subjectif. Et par activité 'sociale,' l'activité qui, d'après son sens visé (*gemeinten Sinn*) par l'agent ou les agents, se rapporte au comportement d'autrui, par rapport auquel s'oriente son déroulement." M. Weber, *Economie et société* (Paris: Plon, 1971), I, 4.

[2]P. Berger L. et Th. Luckmann, *The Social Construction of Reality* (Harmondsworth: Penguin Books, 1979).

[3]R. Williame, *Les fondements phénoménologiques de la sociologie compréhensive: Alfred Schutz et Max Weber* (La Haye: Martinus Nijhoff, 1973).

[4]Pour ce qui est des productions littéraires, une très belle analyse a été proposée par J. Dubois, *L'institution de la littérature* (Bruxelles: Nathan/Labor, 1978).

[5]Dans ce texte, j'entends le mot "littérature" en dehors de toute appréciation de qualité; il s'agira donc de toute production imprimée sous forme de livres et mis en vente dans des circuits normaux de commercialisation.

[6]J'ai introduit cette remarque à la suite d'une intervention très pertinente d'une participante à la conférence, notre collègue de West Virginia Universlty, Janice Spleth.

[7]Edimail, S.A., 53, avenue Victor-Hugo, F - 75016 Paris.

[8]A. Schutz, "Tiresias, or our knowledge of future events," *Collective Papers* (La Haye: Martinus Nijhoff, 1971), I, 283.

[9]Ceci est vrai du moins par la fraction—importante—de la classe ouvrière qui a vu son sort matériel s'améliorer considérablement et dont le mode de vie s'est rapproché de celui des couches inférieures de la petite-bourgeoisie traditionnelle, laquelle a servi en quelque sorte de modèle, que cela plaise ou non aux "ouvriéristes."

[10]Les "cercles" ou zones des connaissances sont reprises par Schütz à W. James, qui distingue quatre d'entre elles, depuis celle des "connaissances approfondies" jusqu'à la part inconnue, mais connaissable, du monde.

[11]Voir notamment M. Maffesoli, *La conquête du présent* (Paris: PUF, 1979). Egalement, du même: "Dynamique de la dissidence," *Cahiers Internationaux de Sociologie*, 64 (1978); "Résistance et socialité," *Actions et Recherches Sociales* (Mars 1984), 62-73.

[12]Voir Cl. Javeau, "Huit propositions sur le quotidien," *Sociétés* 3 (1985), 7-9.

[13]Ce qui n'implique pas que l'ordre doit rester immuable. En fait, ce qui prime réellement, c'est l'idée même d'un ordre, quel qu'il soit.

[14]Voir Cl. Javeau, "Les symboles de la banalisation," *Cahiers Internationaux de Sociologie*, 75 (1983), 343-353.

Ravel's
Trois poèmes de Stéphane Mallarmé

Robert Gronquist
Simmons College

> "Music revives the recollections it would appease."
>
> —Madame de Staël
>
> "There are so many things to be considered in a single note."*
>
> —His Holiness Gyalwa Karmapa

That in 1913 both Debussy and Ravel would independently set three poems by Mallarmé, with two of their three selections turning out to be identical, was, in Debussy's phrase, "a phenomenon of autosuggestion worthy of communication to the Academy of Medicine."[1] Knowing of Debussy's frequent attendance at the famous *mardis chez Mallarmé* and of Ravel's instinctive sympathy with the more private and esoteric forms of art, we are not surprised that each musician would be drawn to Mallarmé's magical weavings of suggestive sound and elusive symbol;[2] but indeed we may well be intrigued by the coincidence of both composers having set in the same year "Soupir" and "Placet futile" in that order, differing only in their choice of a third poem: whereas Debussy chose the *vers de circonstance*, "Eventail,"[3] Ravel added the yet more abstruse "Surgi de la croupe et du bond."

Clearly the coincidence of both composers' increased interest in Mallarmé is probably due to the growing acclaim for the poet signaled in 1911 by Albert Thibaudet's *La Poésie de Stéphane Mallarmé*,[4] the first major study, and by the third edition of *Les Poésies de Stéphane Mallarmé* which was published in 1913.[5] But no final explanation can be given for the choice and ordering of the song settings; while each composer chose a later poem for his third song, the earlier two songs are arranged neither by the poems' dates of origin nor by their order of appearance in the 1913 collection.[6] Each composer seems to have been attracted by the principle of beginning with a poem of relative clarity and directness of poetic content and style (the almost Romantic "Soupir") and moving towards the highly abstract *alchimie du verbe* of the late poems. We will see this evolution marvelously amplified in Ravel's settings.

Arbie Orenstein's excellent biography, *Ravel: Man and Musician*, relates details concerning the rather strained personal relationship which had come about between the two composers by 1913:

> Ravel completed his songs before Debussy and asked Dr. Edmond Bonniot, Mallarmé's son-in-law, for permission to utilize the poet's texts. The men were on friendly terms and the required authorization was granted immediately. A short time later, when Dr. Bonniot was approached by Jacques Durand with a similar request, he agreed to the publication of "Eventail," but refused "Soupir" and "Placet futile," whose rights had just been granted to Ravel. The imbroglio was mentioned in a letter to Roland-Manuel: "We will soon witness a Debussy-Ravel match. The other day, our publisher sent me a desperate letter, because Bonniot had refused the authorization for "Soupir" and "Placet futile" which Debussy had just set to music. I have settled everything." Ravel secured the publication of Debussy's songs by begging Dr. Bonniot to grant Durand the required authorization, a gesture typical of his probity and good will. (67)

As to the genesis of the Ravel songs, the story has frequently been told of how, early in 1913, Diaghilev commissioned Ravel and Stravinsky to complete and reorchestrate Mussorgsky's opera, *Kovantshina*, for a Paris production; how Ravel, joining Stravinsky at Clarens on Lake Geneva, discovered his colleague's *Poèmes de la lyrique japonaise* with their instrumentation derived from Schönberg's recent *Pierrot Lunaire*; and how Ravel grew fascinated with the coloristic possibilities of such a scoring (voice, piano, string quartet, piccolo, flute, clarinet, and bass clarinet).[7] On April 2, 1913, he wrote enthusiastically to Madame Alfredo Cassella suggesting a "concert scandaleux" to consist of (a) *Pierrot Lunaire*, (b) Stravinsky's Japanese lyrics, and (c) his own two Mallarmé songs. The third song was not yet projected.[8]

It was at Clarens, too, that Ravel first saw the score of Stravinsky's new *Le Sacre du printemps*, a work whose first performance he predicted would be "as important an event as the premiere of *Pelléas*."[9] Returning to Paris, he witnessed the chaotic premiere of *Le Sacre* on May 29 and soon after was summering at Saint-Jean-de-Luz where "Surgi de la croupe et du bond" was completed.

When the three songs were finally performed the following January, they evidently were met with favor, and, when heard in London a year later, were judged by the *Daily Mail* as being "among the most recent and interesting examples of modern song. The tiny orchestra is handled with utmost delicacy and intimacy of expression. ...Mr. Thomas Beecham conducted and Mme Jane Bathori-Engel sang the very difficult vocal part with great insight and expressiveness." In the *Westminster Gazette* a markedly different, yet equally credible tone prevailed: "An attentive audience listened in absolute bewilderment to some of the strangest exercises in ultramodern cacophony which it would be possible to imagine. ...Now and then the divergence between the voice part and the accompaniment seemed so pronounced as almost to suggest that Mme Bathori-Engel was singing one number while the instrumentalists were playing another.[10]

Strange as the songs may have seemed to early audiences, for musicians of today the *Trois Poèmes* are supreme examples of Ravel's compositional art, difficult to perform and too seldom heard, but among his most original, subtle, and recondite achievements.

As Pierre Boulez informs us in his essay, "Trajectories: Ravel, Stravinsky, Schönberg,"[11] Ravel had been inspired by the idea that Stravinsky verbally gave him of *Pierrot Lunaire*. "The imagination, operating through a like mechanism with the two composers, took the place of actual study of the score, which was not engraved until 1914" (Boulez, p. 243), and the influence of Schönberg's work came as intervals, instrumental dispositions, coloristic possibilities, i.e., external procedures and devices transposed with great precision into Ravel's already formed musical language. Boulez further observes "that even in the use of the instrumental ensemble, the influence of *Pierrot Lunaire* resides above all in the nomenclature. For whereas Schönberg's use of various elements—which he *chose*—proceeded from a need to express himself contrapuntally, that is, by individualization of each instrumental component, Ravel made use of a like formation—in some degree imposed—as a restricted orchestral apparatus. ...In the Mallarmé songs, one again encounters that apparatus of sound presentation, more studied than ever, which proceeds from doubling, superimpositions, sound effects that have nothing to do with *Pierrot Lunaire*, but result from a certain 'mechanics' of orchestration—the refined outcome of classic orchestration" (pp. 245-246).

Indeed, as Ravel no doubt intended, the songs have little to do with Viennese expressionism and its attendant musical techniques and very much to do with Symbolist aesthetics, being, first and foremost, perfect vessels for that "préciosité pleine de profondeur si spéciale à Mallarmé" to which he specifically refers.[12] What this brief study may achieve is some insight into Ravel's conception of the poems and his consequent elaboration of them.

Before looking more closely at the songs, we will speak of the composer's literary interests. That Ravel read widely, was proud of the French language, and wrote in a style characterized by clarity and ease is generally acknowledged. His personal library at his country house, Le Belvedère, contains a wide variety of works including the complete Molière, La Fontaine, Hugo, Balzac, and Proust, among many others. As his friend, Ricardo Viñez, wrote, he was fond of "poetry, fantasy, precious and rare, paradoxical and refined,"[13] and, indeed, he once referred to himself as "the little symbolist."[14]

Early in his career Ravel composed settings of poems by Verlaine, Leconte de Lisle, Verhaeren; and as early as 1896, when he was 21, he set Mallarmé's "Sainte" for voice and piano. Its dedication to Madame Edmond Bonniot, Mallarmé's daughter, suggests that he may have been acquainted with the poet himself. One thing is certain—and the *Trois Poèmes* offer further proof—Ravel's approach to composition was thoroughly adaptable to Mallarméan hermeticism. It was criticized the year after "Sainte" by his conservative teacher, Fauré, as "too recherché" and "overly refined."[15]

Yet, one might argue, will not any composer run that risk when seeking to create musical analogues to Mallarmé's intentional ambiguities? Can one imagine straightforward and ingenuous songs which utilize poems of a man who admitted that, for him, creative invention "has to do with nothing else than the musicality of everything?"[16] Certainly, listening to Ravel's songs, the listener readily senses that Theodor de Wyzewa's words about Mallarmé's poems are equally applicable to the music: "Each one of his lines was intended to be at once a plastic image, the expression of a thought, the enunciation of a feeling, and a philosophical symbol" (Michaud, p. 4).

1. Soupir

Mon âme vers ton front où rêve, ô calme soeur,
Un automne jonché de taches de rousseur
Et vers le ciel errant de ton oeil angélique
Monte comme dans un jardin mélancolique,
Fidèle, un blanc jet d'eau soupire vers l'Azur!
—Vers l'Azur attendri d'Octobre pâle et pur
Qui mire aux grands bassins sa langueur infinie
Et laisse, sur l'eau morte où la fauve agonie
Des feuilles erre au vent et creuse un froid sillon,
Se traîner le soleil jaune d'un long rayon.

Arthur Symons' version of "Soupir" may be an appropriate vehicle by which we can enter Mallarmé's poetic world of richly ambiguous, suggestive, and intellectually refined beauty:

My soul, calm sister, towards thy brow, whereon scarce grieves
An autumn strewn already with its russet leaves,
And towards the wandering sky of thine angelic eyes,
Mounts, as in melancholy gardens may arise
Some faithful fountain sighing whitely towards the blue!
Towards the blue pale and pure that sad October knew,
When, in those depths, it mirrored languors infinite,
And agonizing leaves upon the waters white,

> Windily drifting, traced a furrow cold and dun,
> Where, in one long last ray, lingered the yellow sun.[17]

We observe readily "the same melancholy atmosphere, the same visual imagery," and "that continuous movement from the first line to the last"[18] which in the original attracted Ravel and Debussy.

Fittingly, Ravel dedicated his first song to Stravinsky, whose later words on rhythm and structure are appropriate for an understanding of Ravel's conception: "Music is a *chronologic* art... (It) presupposes before all else a certain organization in time.... Composing... is putting into an order a certain number of... sounds according to certain interval relationships."[19]

Ravel begins "Soupir" as if *without* time, or like time halted. With the static, shimmering effect of the strings in harmonics and glissandi, he creates for the entire first half of the poem an aural suggestion of the timeless "white fountain" which "sighs towards the azure." Harmonically just an E minor eleventh chord with flatted 7th,[20] the effect is a marvelous intimation of Mallarmé's intended *état d'âme,* of a state of syn-aesthetically variable sense and multidimensional significance so important to his poetry. Through that chord (made so ineffable by the instrumental coloring) sound the first five lines of the text, composed as an exquisitely controlled melody, always quiet, in the transposed Dorian mode from E. It alone provides a sense of movement—the inhalation of the "soupir." As it gradually ascends, however, the piano at pianissimo introduces increasingly lower notes of the chord—fountain-like, mirroring the melody—which finally settle "au fond" on a low E and B just as the voice mounts to its key word, "Fidèle." Subtly Ravel permits the line itself to settle, echoing an octave lower on "l'Azur," and the Same D—F$^\#$ of the highpoint. And a yet more remote echo of the same two pitches is heard instrumentally a bar later, as the shimmering sounds and mist of figurations, as it were, evaporate.

At the start of the second half of the poem, Ravel suddenly delineates a restrained atmosphere, the picture of dead leaves on the water, harmonically in marked contrast to the brighter cascades of the opening. The mood is now of "langueur infinie," and though that autumnal mood prevails until the last three measures when there is a suggestion of the color of the opening bars (and also a final settling in the bass on E again) the music establishes structural antipodes paralleling those of human feeling implied in the text.

Arthur Wenk comments on the mirror effect of the syntactical structure of the poem: "The first half contains all the forward movement—the subject and the verb. The second half is only an extended prepositional phrase, a release of the tension built up in the first half. 'Vers l'Azur' is the center of symmetry for this reflection, just as it is the apex of the up-and-down motion" (Wenk, p. 248). Ravel, however, utilizes the lines "Vers l'Azur attendri d'Octobre pâle et pur / Qui mire aux grands bassins sa langueur infinie" as the center section of the song, to stop that motion and to suggest the static midpoint of a sigh before the expected shorter exhalation. The composition implies in the last section an antithesis to the first: measure 26, marked "1er Mouvt," utilizes for the voice part the notes of the earlier enriched minor triad now transposed to D# with the text, "Et laisse sur l'eau morte...."

For the two lines preceding, the center section of the song, Ravel had explored in six bars the entire pitch range thus far utilized, touching often on E, melodically highly angular for the voice, but avoiding the important F# which climaxed the first section. That pitch is saved, along with an equally crucial harmony*, for the start of the downward motion of the last section where, in a wonderfully controlled chromatic line, Ravel completes the voice part of the song (bars 26-35) in a melody whose prominent notes fall from the high F# to B, the last and lowest vocal pitch of the song.

Harmonically stable as the concluding three-bar coda is, a structurally important complex of pitch relationships** has been set up which remains important for the next two songs as well. While Orenstein is correct in describing "Soupir" as tonal in its harmonic language, the use is anything but "traditional" (Orenstein, p. 181). Rather, Ravel has elected to build the piece on a mere six principle harmonies***, each of them lingering, often to recur and then dissipate gradually a measure or two later. Mirrorlike, again, he utilizes a motive**** of the instrumental parts at both the slowing termination of the first section of the song (meas. 13-16) and the parallel closing three bars (35-37).

*Ex. 1

**Ex. 2

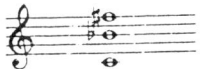

***Ex. 3

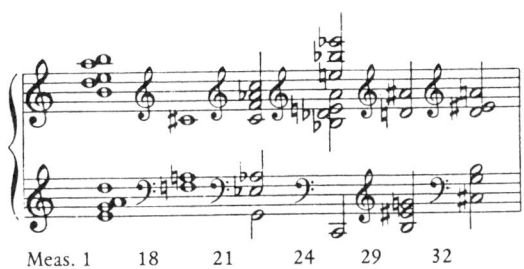

****Ex. 4

2. *Placet futile*

Princesse! à jalouser le destin d'une Hebé
Qui poind sur cette tasse au baiser de vos lèvres
J'use mes feux mais n'ai rang discret que d'abbé
Et ne figurerai même nu sur le Sèvres

Comme je ne suis pas ton bichon embarbé,
Ni la pastille, ni du rouge, ni jeux mièvres
Et que sur moi je sais ton regard clos tombé
Blonde dont les coiffeurs divins sont des orfèvres!

Nommez-nous…toi de qui tant de ris framboisés
Se joignent en troupeaux d'agneaux apprivoisés
Chez tous broutant les voeux et bêlant aux délires,
Nommez-nous…pour qu'Amour ailé d'un éventail
M'y peigne flûte aux doigts endormant ce bercail,
Princesse, nommez-nous berger de vos sourires.

Described by Mallarmé as an evocation of a painting by Boucher or Watteau, "Placet futile" is reminiscent of 16th-century French emulators of Plato and Petrarch, and of the court poets of the 17th century. In the poem we are struck by what Wallace Fowlie calls the "verbal ornateness of (Mallarmé's) imagination."[21]

"I fully realize the great audacity of having attempted to interpret this sonnet in music," wrote Ravel. "It was necessary that the melodic contour, the modulations, and the rhythms be as precious, as properly contoured as the sentiment and the images of the text. In spite of that, it was necessary to maintain the elegant deportment of the poem. Above all, it was necessary to maintain the profound and exquisite tenderness which suffuses all of this. Now that it's done, I'm a bit nervous about it."[22]

Elegant deportment. Profound and exquisite tenderness. Better terms could scarcely be found to describe the song's mysterious and masterful reinforcement of Mallarmé's poetic control. "Le hasard était nié par le grimoire."[23]

Creating a musical fabric wherein tempo is frequently altered and lyrical effusions evaporate into simple line, Ravel builds the song on several melodic motives, the three most important being:

Ex. 5

Throughout, the voice is treated more instrumentally, more as a member of the ensemble than in "Soupir," and is given unusually angular lines amidst a harmonic language of unusually intricate chromaticism. Yet, as in Example 6, the vocal part is perfectly in keeping with natural speech inflections. With the concluding line of the text we see three of the vocal part's principle melodic gestures combined, an example of Ravel's predilection for joining thematic ideas earlier presented separately:

Ex. 6

As in the first song, we also find examples of modal formulation, like the following in transposed Dorian:

Ex. 7a

Nommez-nous   toi de qui tant...

and, as in both other songs, a traditional tessitura and absence of virtuosity.

Structurally "Placet futile" has a tripartite form like "Soupir," additionally articulating in that form the two-part symmetry of the concluding tercets of the sonnet: parallel to the beginning of the first tercet (Ex. 7a) is the following:

Ex. 7b

Nommez-nous pour qu'Amour. . .

Although there is a tonal orientation throughout most of the song, Ravel ingeniously suspends that sense of tonality, delaying the arrival of the tonic F for eight bars in order to let it coincide with the subject and verb of the text. Even then, avoiding any sense of stable tonality, the section soon cadences— by means of a sequential vocal line against a pentatonic instrumental melody—on a simple, yet distinct E major triad.

In the pentatonic instrumental fragment (which we may assume is intended to trigger resonances of China and the Orient in our musical subconscious) we see one of Ravel's more apparent methods of linking music with poem: this is the line that refers to Sèvres porcelain. As Mallarmé sought to make each poem, each word even, a meeting place, a point of encounter, so, too, Ravel musically elaborates that network of metaphors to help make each poem a still richer crossroad in an essential liaison with the rest of the world. Multiple connections link in our minds with segments from the totality of our experience.

334 **Twenty Years of French Literary Criticism**

One recalls Mallarmé's remark in a letter of 1864: "I am inventing a language that must necessarily spring from a very new poetics, which I could define in these words: to paint not the thing but the effect it produces. The poetic line should be composed not of words but of intentions, and all the words should efface themselves before sensations."[24]

Throughout the song one detects echoes and reapplications of important ideas and effects. The downward shifting of the F harmony to the E at the end of the first quatrain recurs at the corresponding moment in the second quatrain, as A minor to G#.

A more fascinating linkage is with the opening song, "Soupir." We hear at that same G# arrival the same ringing octaves of the piano that, in the first song, were on the important F#. They are now a whole-step above on G#.

Ex. 8

I shall return to this linkage later.

As Mallarmé in his *Réponse à Jules Huret* stressed the importance of evoking little by little an *état d'âme*, Ravel little by little prepares the arrival of the exquisite third section of "Placet futile." The long, lyrical vocal flights which thus far have never repeated themselves but rather consist of constant expansion and variation of the basic musical materials—these now come to focus: first tentatively, then, as in the text itself, more conclusively on the languid and quietly sensuous lines we have already seen, "Nommez-nous...."

Parallel to the stepwise shifting to a lower harmony that marks the end of the first two quatrains, the two tercets of this third section are also delineated by a downward shift (via some extraordinarily rich, bitonally-conceived harmonies, Example 9 from C# minor (meas. 19) to B minor (meas. 22).

Ex. 9

Bm.　II　　V

Such formal correspondences as the instrumental material of the first quatrain (bars 8-9) returning in the second (bar 16) and the expressive "Princesse" of the opening reintroduced (at the climaxing vocal pitch) near the end (Example 6) are but obvious instances among the many ways in which Ravel seems to have inferred from Mallarmé's poetic style the technique of almost constant structural transformation and suggested relationships.

That technique, as well as new uses of instrumental color and the free juxtaposition of phrases and other rhythmic units, which all serve the poetry so well in "Placet futile," are applied even more experimentally in the last song, "Surgi de la croupe...."

> *3. Surgi de la croupe et du bond*
>
> Surgi de la croupe et du bond
> D'une verrerie éphémère
> Sans fleurir la veillée amère
> Le col ignoré s'interrompt.
>
> Je crois bien que deux bouches n'ont
> Bu, ni son amant ni ma mère
> Jamais à la même chimère
> Moi, sylphe de ce froid plafond!
>
> Le pur vase d'aucun breuvage
> Que l'inexhaustible veuvage
> Agonise mais ne consent,
> Naïf baiser des plus funèbres
> A rien expirer annonçant
> Une rose dans les ténèbres.

> "...the contemplation of objects, the image flying out of reveries inspired by them, that is what song is."
> —Mallarmé[25]

Seldom if ever has poetry sought to parallel so precisely the suggestive power of music, its ability to skirt the domain of conceptual, nondescriptive thought. Here is verbal calculation possessing extraordinary affinities with music and dreams; "the image or symbol has become vestigial; rather the words are self-contained images, used not in logical relationships but as notes that form a chord" (Balakian, p. 98).

When the thread of logical discourse is thus abandoned, traditional approaches of literary criticism bring no satisfactory explication. (And certainly Rollo Myers contributed no understanding when he wrote: "This famous example of Mallarméan obscurity defies translation, but is devoid of any very profound significance, being merely an evocation of a vase empty of flowers" [p. 141].) This is poetry of a man keenly aware that the mind cannot apprehend reality when separated from it. Knowledge is possible only when subject and object are united. "Knowledge is consciousness, the true aim of poetry, but consciousness in our time is no longer a Cartesian entity, but a kind of Bergsonian continuous becoming."[26] Words come to be seen by the poet not as firm receptacles of fixed awareness but rather as suggestions of transient and fleeting experience with minimum reference to logical meaning. "They will be, as much as words can stand it, what they are in themselves, the organic notations of an experience. In two respects, in respect of fleetingness and transience and in respect of being essentially themselves, they resemble musical notes, which, at best, should be what they are and nothing else. The new way of presenting the poetic experience also resembles music in the fact that structural rhythm plays an essential part in suggesting the poetic experience and the emotion which underlies it" (Chiari, pp. 38-39). As a case in point, "Surgi de la croupe..." can be read quite definitively as a poem of the poetic experience and of Mallarmé's particular emotions accompanying it.[27]

Ravel's setting of the poem is a perfect distillation of the poet's "music of silence" and is paradigmatic of the text's cancellation of rhetoric, eloquence, and formalism. Weirdly evocative of a shadowy mood and of the nondiscursive verbal conjurations, the music seems to move by opaquely dissonant harmonic shapes surrounding ambiguous melodic lines. Yet careful listening reveals that nothing is haphazard in the scoring.

An upward rush of notes arrives on a lengthy high A (played by the flute) which connects in the ear with the same A sustained by the violin at the end of the previous song. The second bar introduces the principal motive with its haunting effect:

Ex.10a

It is soon altered to:

Ex 10b

It is one of the two principal elements in the song. Measures 3-6 have repetitions of the motive, first with the same simple chordal accompaniment, then with the rushing figure out of which emerges, in bar 5, the vocal line for the first quatrain. Harmonically, measures 7 and 8 provide a cadential effect in $F^\#$ minor,[28] significant first for its identification as the crucial $F^\#$ of which we have spoken, second for the fact that these two bars alone are all that prevent the composition from being totally without suggestion of tonality, and third because simultaneously is introduced the bell-like octave on $A^\#$ (bar 7) and $E^\#$, (bar 8) in the piano.

We have, of course, observed in both previous songs these occasional bare octaves struck with the right hand, and left vibrating like strokes of a deathknell in the void. They occur first prominently amidst the icily autumnal evocation of "Soupir" (ringing on $F^\#$), next, more briefly, at an important moment in "Placet futile" (on $G^\#$). And how they function as the second principal element in "Surgi de la croupe et du bond," starting on the next whole step up, $A^\#$, and supplanting the above mentioned melodic motive (Ex. 10). It dominates the musical texture through all of the second quatrain (enharmonically changed) as the essential B^b (see Ex. 2) in polarity with F (bars 9 and 10). Bitonally, they ring against a conflicting harmonic polarity of D major and A major chords, like an image (or symbol?) of overlapping levels of reality. Aurally, the composite effect leaves a prominent B^b in the ears of the listener, an effect reinforced by the accented B^b's in the instrumental parts of bars 16-18:

Ex. 11

The climactic arrival of the voice part at the word "agonise" brings a return to the principal melodic motive (Ex. 10b) with its reiterative B^b's and bell-like F's sounding in the glassily shimmering texture. The last four lines of the poem are set by Ravel with harmonies almost spectral in effect and motivically with a gyrelike pattern of descent leading to the last and lowest vocal pitch, B^b—"A rien expirer annonçant / Une rose dans les ténèbres."

* * * * *

How does one summarize Ravel's utilization of the complex symbolism of Mallarmé's profoundly connotative poetry? I have endeavored, in my descriptive passages which deal with the music, to imply directions for more intensive analysis, a pursuit which can only vastly extend one's appreciation of the composer's rigorously refined art. Ravel was a man whose passion, as Léon-Paul Fargue once observed, was "to offer the public works which were 'finished,' polished to the ultimate degree."[29] Yet description is but a paltry shadow beside the palpable work of art. The poetry and the music are what truly speak.

Having chosen to work with cryptic poems which themselves aspire to a musical ideal, Ravel settled upon a vastly increased norm of harmonic dissonance and evolved a subtle and ingenious web of instrumental sound against which the voice declaims the text. Formally, there is ample evidence of a tripartite conception with strikingly clear relationships among the songs. There is also a psychologically disturbing movement, seen in text, harmonic vocabulary, and mood, away from "L'Azur" towards the "gouffre," evoking finally only a mirage of meaning in an absurd universe. Poetically and musically the *Trois Poèmes de Stéphane Mallarmé* are records of journeys of discovery across various *états d'âme*, all linked by that direction of *décadence*.

Art is a special mode of apprehending reality, a symbolic system different from that of science and pragmatic manipulation, but equally valid and with its own rights. As the referential content of a poem is only a small part of its multivalent totality, the supplementary "musicalizing" which can be achieved by a composer of the stature of Ravel only adds to that totality, intensifying its moods, clarifying its structure, linking its suggestive powers to still other verbal and aural configurations, and generally extending the often overwhelming impact of intellectually refined beauty.

Together the poet and the composer sing desparingly of "le Glorieux Mensonge" (as Mallarmé wrote in the now famous letter to his friend Cazalis in 1866) and "glorify it as the only testimony and sublime product of our consciousness and our invention."[30]

---

*Quoted by Peter Crossley Holland in "The Music of the Tantric Rituals of Gyume and Gyuto," recording notes for *The Music of Tibet* (Anthology of the World's Music AST—4005).

[1] Quoted by A. Orenstein, *Ravel: Man and Musician* (New York: Columbia University Press, 1975), p. 67.

[2] Arthur Wenk's recent study, *Claude Debussy and the Poets* (Berkeley: University of California Press, 1976), documents very effectively the impact of poets and writers on the composer. Nothing of comparable nature exists for Ravel.

[3] Debussy's title; Mallarmé entitled the poem "Autre éventail."

[4] (Paris: La Phalange, 1911).

[5] (Paris: Editions de la Nouvelle Revue Française, 1913).

[6] "Soupir," the first song, initially appeared in *Le Parnasse contemporain* (May 12, 1866), and is found on page 24 of the 1913 collection. "Placet futile" is the earliest poem chosen. It dates from 1862 (under the title "Placet") in *Le Papillon* (February 25) and is on page 18 in the 1913 collection. "Surgi de la croupe et du bond," Ravel's third poem, first came out in the "Sonnets" of *La Revue Independante* (January, 1887). It is found on page 148 of the 1913 collection. Debussy's third choice, "Autre éventail," appeared in the *Revue critique* of 1884. It is on page 93 of the 1913 collection. Of further importance for Mallarmé studies are the "Deux lettres à Albert Thibaudet" from Paul Valéry, also of 1913. They can be found in *Ecrits divers sur Stéphane Mallarmé* (Paris: Editions de la Nouvelle Revue Française, 1950).

[7] A version for voice and piano alone was also done. Musical examples in this paper will be drawn from that scoring due to spacial limits.

[8] Ravel's letter is partially in Chalupt and Gerar, *Ravel au miroir de ses lettres* (Paris: Robert Laffont, 1956), p. 97. The concert did take place the following year but *Pierrot Lunaire* had to be substituted by Maurice DeLage's *Quatre Poèmes Hindous*.

[9] From a letter dated March 3, 1913, to his friend, Lucien Garban. Quoted by Rollo Myers, *Ravel: Life and Works* (New York: Thomas Yoseloff, 1960), p. 47.

[10] *Daily Mail and Westminster Gazette*, March 18, 1915. Quoted by Orenstein, p. 68.

[11] *Contrepoint*, Autumn, 1949 (Paris, ed. Richard-Masse). Later included in *Notes of an Apprenticeship* (New York: Knopf, 1968), pp. 242-267.

[12] Roland-Manuel, "Une Esquisse autobiographique de Ravel," *La Revue Musicale* (December, 1938), p. 22.

[13] Ricardo Viñez, "Des Souvenirs d'enfance et d'adolescence," *La Revue Musicale* (December, 1938), p. 165. Viñez was a brilliant pianist who premiered a number of Ravel's and Debussy's works.

[14] In an unpublished letter to Madame de Saint-Marceaux, summer, 1889. Quoted by Orenstein, p. 20.

[15] From a progress report at the Paris Conservatoire. Quoted by Orenstein, p. 27.

[16] From the lecture, "La Musique et les Lettres," given at Oxford and Cambridge, 1892. Quoted by G. Michaud, *Mallarmé* (New York: New York University Press, 1965), p. 44. Translation by M. Collins and B. Humez.

[17] Arthur Symons, *The Symbolist Movement in Literature* (London: Heinemann, 1899).

[18] Ruth Z. Temple, *The Critic's Alchemy* (New Haven: College and University Press, 1953), p. 167.

[19] Igor Stravinsky, *Poetics of Music* (Cambridge: Harvard University Press, 1947), pp. 28, 37.

[20] It is also recognizable as notes of a pentatonic scale from G, the $F^{\#}$ being an appogiatura to the E.

[21] Wallace Fowlie, *Mallarmé* (Chicago: University of Chicago Press, 1953), p. 18.

[22] From an unpublished letter to Roland-Manuel dated October 13, 1913. Quoted by Orenstein, pp. 128-129.

[23] From *Igitur*. Quoted by Fowlie, p. 196.

[24] Quoted by Michaud, p. 32.

[25] Quoted by Anna Balakian, *The Symbolist Movement* (New York: Random House, 1967), p. 85.

[26] Joseph Chiari, *Symbolism from Poe to Mallarmé* (London: Rockliff, 1956), pp. 36-37.

[27] Wallace Fowlie's *Mallarmé* and Robert Greer Cohn's *Toward the Poems of Mallarmé* (Berkeley: University of California Press, 1965) are both very helpful in assisting the reader to comprehend the particular complexities of the poem. James Lawler's *The Language of French Symbolism* (Princeton: Princeton University Press, 1969), provides excellent commentary on the "Glorieux Mensonge" of the early letters and its importance as background to the "Chimère" of later works like "Surgi de la croupe et du bond."

[28] It is interesting to observe also that the accompanying vocal line in these bars establishes a major rather than minor mode, thereby drawing attention to the conflict between $A^{\#}$ and A natural. The motive of Examples 10a and 10b does the same.

[29] Emile Vuillermoz, et al., *Maurice Ravel par quelques-uns des ses familiers* (Paris: Editions de Tambourinaire, 1939), p. 160.

[30] Quoted by Michaud, p. 44.

The Enchantment of Orpheus: Music and Words in Contemporary French Fiction

Roland A. Champagne
University of Missouri-St. Louis

> "Why should not a modern literature be as unsparing and as direct as song?"
> —James Joyce

During the last several decades, the phenomenon of "écriture" has arisen around the example of the French writer Roland Barthes. This "écriture" is a literature of imaginative creativity in contradistinction to J. P. Sartre's dictum of a *socially* committed literature. The traditional parameters of time, place, and character development appear useless as formal principles by which to evaluate "écriture." However, the critical investigations of a rediscovered science called "semiotics" (the science of signification) do give us the means for understanding the formal unity of some exponents of "écriture." Specifically, Claude Lévi-Strauss, Pierre Boulez, and Umberto Eco have examined the links between words and music. Their theories can help us to understand some of the formal unity in the works of such writers as Marguerite Duras, Michel Butor, and Philippe Sollers. The musical properties of melody, harmony, and serial structure transposed into a verbal narration provide formal adhesion within such texts as Sollers' *H* (1973), wherein the absence of sentence and paragraph structure defies a grammatical analysis of the plot.

In the late nineteenth century, the composer Claude Debussy was especially intrigued by the transposition of words into music. His musical scores for nineteen of Paul Verlaine's poems are testimonies to the intercommunication of words and music. As we examine the present day fixation with such an intercommunication, the words of a Debussy contemporary, Théodore de Banville, are worthy of reflection: "(La Poésie) est le seul art complet, nécessaire, et qui contienne tous les autres, comme elle préexiste à tous les autres."[1] Banville's observation may very well be substantiated by the present-day "écriture" which is drawing music and words together into a poetic marriage. Let us then examine the constituents of such a "poetics" as those musical criteria called melody, harmony, and serial structure.

The musical scale do-re-mi provides a parameter for evaluating the relative values of notes as representatives of melody. Melody has sometimes been recognized as the horizontal axis of music in that it relates musical notes to their context on a horizontal line of a succession of pitches and intervals. Even modern music, which claims not to be subject to melody, is often drawn into that axis, because as Friedrich Nietzsche once observed: "hearing something new is embarrassing and difficult to the ear; foreign music we do not hear well—when we hear another language we try involuntarily to form the sounds we hear into words that sound like home to us."[2] In this respect, music becomes a function of what Roman Jakobson called the "syntagmatic" axis, that is, a poetic cohesion implemented by the metonymic function of direct association. Similarly, the language of "écriture" in contemporary fiction operates according to the principle of melody. The fragmented dialogues in Marguerite Duras' work (e.g. *Moderato Cantabile*, 1958; *Détruire Dit-elle*, 1969) provide horizontal cohesion to her works by giving rhythm to the work in a songlike fashion. It is a poetic rhythm which organically unites the dialogues of her characters into clusters of sense. These dialogues are the melody of her prose style in that they give a horizontal structure to the obviously fragmented presentation. As George Springer pointed out in his basic study of language and music, prose can also contain musical features: "apart from poetic language there exists in ordinary prose a category of meaning reminiscent of the purely formal meaning which characterizes music."[3] And such a feature of ordinary prose is being investigated and employed by contemporary French writers of fiction.

The Debussy experience offers some commentary on this situation. Debussy had found some common intersections of words and music which could be developed to enhance both entities. He was particularly eager to imitate Verlaine's transcendence of the codes imposed upon verbal poetry by Banville. Hence, Debussy devised musical scores which transgressed the barline. His arabesques were invented so that a whole-tone scale could poetically present the obscurity and vast depths of the sea as Debussy transformed the gray colors and vertigo of Verlaine's poems so that, as Arthur Wenk recently observed, "with no intrinsic allegiance to a particular center, the whole-tone scale obscures the musical train of thought like a tonal fog."[4] The effect of such music is to displace the center of structure away from the barline, that is the measure, in order to achieve an atmosphere which transcends the succession of notes in a melodious sequence. The flute of *L'Après-midi d'un faune* is an especially good example as it recreates the sun-sparkled shelter of Mallarmé's forest.

Likewise, contemporary French fiction suggests, through associative word-patterns, that the center of verbal communication must be displaced. Philippe Sollers—with his *Lois* (1972), *H* (1973), and *Paradis* (1975)—tries to demonstrate that fiction has been too logocentric—that is, constrained by recoverable messages, grammatical structure, sentence organization, and dictionary meanings. Instead, his texts propose forms that defy content-retrieval and project neologisms, associative word patterns, and an internal organicism. As Eric Taylor once told us about Debussy, however, "merely to explain what the ideas of Debussy were is to leave the task unfinished: however interesting they may be in themselves, what really matters is how and to what extent they affected the music, and this after all is ultimately a matter of orchestration, harmony, rhythm, melody, and the like."[5] Indeed, such formal liberties as found in the texts of Sollers affect the orchestration of the *verbal* components of fiction. Just as musical melody is concerned with the relative duration of pitches and the intervals between them, so is the horizontal or syntagmatic axis of fiction concerned with tonal emphasis upon certain key words rather than others as well as with the intervals of silence in a dialogue (so crucial to many of the texts by Marguerite Duras). For example, in *Moderato Cantabile*, Chauvin and Anne use silence to communicate their distress at re-creating the murder that occurs at the beginning of the narrative while their words are assurances of their mutual interdependence. With the arrival of the *ciné-roman*, words can be appreciated within the context of visual, oral, olfactory, tactile, and other means to communicate a story. It now becomes important to consider what are the syntagmatic ties of a story. In Duras' *India Song* (1973), the geographic pattern of the story is readily described as musical: "Les noms des villes, des fleurs, des états, des mers de l'Inde ont, avant tout, ici, un sens musical."[6] This piece of fiction is subtitled text, theater, and film; it therefore is concerned with the semiotic, metalinguistic context of verbal fiction. Such a context is provided by the musical aura of Duras' work which suggests a metalinguistic significance to the words. Nicholas Ruwet once isolated such a significance in a study of the relationship between the words and music of song wherein "...la fonction, de loin la plus importante, qui soit dévolue au matériel sonore dans le language, est la fonction distinctive."[7] Specifically, changes in musical pitch indicate shifts of emphasis and tone in a story to complement the points of geographical or temporal location recalled by language. For example, again in Duras' *India Song*, Oriental music provides an atmosphere of otherness to an Occidental rendering of the words which specify the text to a particular hotel or *in* chronological development. Beyond the words, a fluid narrative takes the reader on an associational journey wherein recurring motifs such as light and dark, whispering and silence, the rushing of ocean waves, and the steady rhythm of the rain provide au aura which cannot be hemmed in by the conventions of time and place. In Duras' *Détruire Dit-elle*, a tennis match is constantly being heard beyond the walls within which a story is being narrated. The constant rhythm of the tennis ball acts as a musical counter-point to the narrative in that the ball seems to be bouncing by itself, thus playing the game without players. In contradistinction, the words of that text appear to predicate the characters of a sanatarium through their dialogue. Hence, the bouncing tennis ball may be telling us that there is a hint of madness in our use of words which do not convey what we desire from them. It was Pierre Boulez who had pointed out the use of counterpoint as a technique which developed polyphonic music in Western civilization.[8] Likewise, in the fiction of Duras, counterpoint is often introduced through a recurring image such as the pounding surf, a tennis ball, etc. to produce polyphonic strains within the monophonic plane of a verbal narrative.

By introducing polyphony into narrative, Duras has also made a case for a vertical axis in contemporary French fiction. Musically, harmony achieves a similar effect in contradistinction to melody. Hence, musical backdrops to language provide a horizontal and vertical grid-pattern by which the form, rather than the content, of the text controls the reader. Harmony, as a pattern of intervals and notes sounded together, can achieve either consonance or dissonance as timing produces different paradigmatic results. Claude Simon, in his *Triptyque* (1973), projects a visual simultaneity which approaches consonance, that is, normality or repose. In Robbe-Grillet's *Glissements progressifs du plaisir* (1973), a *ciné-roman*, the figure of Nora recurs to give harmonious concordance to the text. By contrast, Butor's *La Modification* (1957), produces a discordant musical pattern as Paris and Rome are contrasted and past, present, and future become mixed in order to portray the disturbance and tension which transcend the voyager's words.

Some contemporary fiction imitates the intoxicating and ecstatic effects of music and thereby escapes the grid-pattern of melody and harmony. Just as William Barret remarks that the "dramaticules" of Beckett are similar to contemporary atonal music in their common dissolution of form,[9] the primitivistic gropings of Beckett's characters may be imitations of a primitive sense of nonverbal music. Siegfried Nadel tells us in his study of the origins of music that "we find special evidence in support of the opinion that music was a product of man's purpose to create for his own use a 'peculiar' magic language of invocation and exorcism.[10] Such a magic element is implemented in fiction similarly to serial music which ties singularly distinct sounds together in a perpetually expanding code. Jean Paris evokes the literary series in what he calls "generative criticism" (*Change*, No. 16-17) which establishes an architectural framework by which repetition produces serial thought and links together heterogeneous parts of a verbal narrative. In his *La Structure absente* (1972), Umberto Eco develops arguments for serial thought as a cause for the historical evolution of communicative codes by relating heterogeneous axes of messages. Likewise, serial music has become the model for much contemporary fiction. Whereas "during the Renaissance the forms of vocal music were to a great extent determined by the words...,"[11] the words of contemporary French fiction are determined by an organic music wherein naming destroys the pleasure of language. This fiction is a fiction of allusion. For example, Duras' *La Musica* (1965) alludes to the suffering of two wedded partners about to be divorced through the silence which interrupts their words to one another. That silence functions as a generating element in the serial structure of the text. Pierre Boulez defines such a musical series as "le germe d'une hiérarchisation fondée sur certaines propriétés psychophysiologiques acoustiques, douée d'une plus ou moins grande sélectivité, en vue d'organiser un ensemble FINI de possibilités créatrices liées entre elles par des affinités prédominantes par rapport à un caractère donné."[12] The musical series is thus a generating catalyst of a hierarchical structure or formal entity. Within contemporary fiction such a technique helps to orchestrate the apparently diverse and disparate themes and events of many individual works. For example, Michel Butor's *Portrait de l'artiste en jeune singe* (1973), is united by the incantatory chateau which recurs throughout the text as the setting for images of the medieval occult and which generates a "finite whole" of images to constitute the text. The effect of serializing this chateau in successive clusters of images is to exemplify Thomas Munro's insight that "shifting clouds of musical, obscurely suggestive words and cryptic metaphors blur all definite outlines of thought and action, as impressionist painting obscures the contours of solid objects in a shimmering haze of light."[13]

Both Michel Butor (in *Portrait*) and Marguerite Duras (in *Moderato Cantabile*) have been fascinated by the infinite musical possibilities which Diabelli inspired in Beethoven. Likewise, Butor and Duras employ a plot which constantly replays the same scene with changing details. This musical technique of variations on a theme has a mesmerizing effect on the reader of fiction. Similar to Orpheus who enchanted the sirens so much with his lyre that he transformed them into rocks, the texts of contemporary fiction control their readers with a symphony of musical sounds. For example, such texts as Philippe Sollers' *H* and *Paradis* are constructed by words structured like sound waves and are read by readers whose consciousness blends with those sound waves in a perfect weaving of writing and reading as synonymous activities. Lévi-Strauss in *Le Cru et le cuit* (1964), had noted that "... of all human products, music strikes me as being the best suited to throw light on the essence of mythology."[14] Specifically, the mythology of narration is being revealed by current experiments with the formal ties between music and words. Pierre Boulez recreates Mallarmé's verbal poetry in a symphony of sounds. Michel Butor and Henri Pousseur are extending the verbal frontiers of narrating with their studies of the mutual influences of words and music. It was Butor himself who, as early as 1964, announced the exciting potential for a "new literature" which could learn from music:

"Si le roman est le laboratoire du récit, la musique n'est-elle pas l'antre où peuvent se forger les armes et instruments d'une littérature nouvelle, le labourage du terrain sur lequel cette moisson pourra mûrir?"[15] And we patiently look forward to such a "harvest" which will yet produce an operatic text that will truly be enchanting to read.

---

[1] Théodore de Banville, *Petit traité de poésie française* (Paris: G. Charpentier, 1888), p. 3.

[2] Friedrich Nietzsche, *Beyond Good and Evil*, trans. Walter Kaufmann (New York: Random House, 1966), p. 105.

[3] George P. Springer, "Language and Music: Parallels and Divergencies," in *For Roman Jakobson*, ed. Morris Halle *et al.* (The Hague: Mouton, 1956), pp. 508-509.

[4] Arthur B. Wenk, *Claude Debussy and the Poets* (Berkeley: University of California Press, 1976), pp. 80 ff.

[5] Eric Taylor, "Word and Music; Debussy: The Early Years," *Month*, 215 (1963), 34.

[6] Marguerite Duras, *India Song* (Paris: Gallimard, 1973), p. 9.

[7] Nicolas Ruwet, "Fonction de la parole dans la musique vocale," *Revue Belge de Musicologie*, 15 (1961), 15.

[8] Pierre Boulez, *Relevés d'apprenti* (Paris: Le Seuil, 1966).

[9] William Barrett, *Time of Need* (New York: Harper & Row, 1972), p. 258.

[10] Siegfried Nadel, "The Origins of Music," *Musical Quarterly*, 16 (1930), 542.

[11] Edward T. Cone, "Words into Music: The Composer's Approach to the Text," in *Sound and Poetry*, ed. Northrop Frye (New York: Columbia University Press, 1963), p. 4.

[12] Pierre Boulez, *La Musique Aujourd'hui* (Paris: Gonthier, 1963), p. 35.

[13] Thomas Munro, *Toward Science in Aesthetics* (New York: Liberal Arts Press, 1956), p. 346.

[14] Claude Lévi-Strauss, *The Raw and the Cooked*, trans. John and Doreen Weightman (New York: Harper & Row, 1969), p. 27.

[15] Michel Butor, *Répertoire II* (Paris: Minuit, 1964), p. 35.

Déictique, énonciatrice et poétique: les fonctions du titre

Serge F. Bokobza
University of Alabama—Birmingham

La problématique d'une science des titres a été soulevée à propos de nombreux domaines. Déjà on peut dire que pour les arts de la figuration l'ouvrage de Michel Butor, *Les Mots dans la peinture*,[1] est devenu un classique. Le moins sérieux, mais quelquefois ingénieux travail de Christian Moncelet, *Essai sur le titre en littérature et dans les arts*,[2] enquête même dans le domaine musical. L'importance du titre a aussi été repérée en histoire de l'art. Un spécialiste du Moyen Age allemand, Jean Wirth, a ainsi souligné qu'il y a souvent autour du titre de certaines oeuvres un enjeu idéologique et que, puisque la fadeur de certains titres ne pouvait s'expliquer que par la peur de nommer la réalité, une lecture idéologique qui voudrait analyser l'esthétisme en rapport avec une situation historique précise devra aussi dégager le "vrai" titre d'une oeuvre.[3] Quant à l'historien Jean-Louis Flandrin, il a montré dans son étude comparative des titres du XVIe et du XXe siècles, "Sentiments et civilisations: sondages au niveau des titres d'ouvrages," comme le titre est riche, témoin d'une consience (ou d'une insconscience?) collective: "au niveau des titres, on retrouvera les notions qui s'affichent... les notions les plus valorisées par la civilisation."[4] Enfin l'article du Groupe Mu, "Rhétoriques particulières (Figure de l'argot, Titres de films, La clé des songes, Les biographies de *Paris-Match*," analyse plus particulièrement le titre de film dans ses constituants, mais aussi dans les relations qu'il entretient avec les autres titres.[5]

Cette question du titre se pose aussi dans bien d'autres domaines que celui de la littérature, de l'histoire de l'art ou du cinéma. On pourrait par exemple, considérer les titres de journaux, les slogans publicitaires ou politiques, enfin tous ces énoncés courts qui fonctionnent comme des titres sans texte.[6] Essayer de dégager une théorie générale sur la fonction des titres, qui rendrait compte de tous les titres et dans tous les domaines, serait non seulement au-dessus de nos moyens mais produirait également une théorie trop vague pour rendre compte efficacement des problèmes de titrologie romanesque qui seuls vont nous intéresser ici. Même si certaines de nos remarques pourraient également s'appliquer—mutatis mutandis—à d'autres genres, nous nous sommes limités dans cette étude à la fonction du titre dans le roman.

La critique a généralement négligé l'étude des titres de roman, plus précisément, elle a pratiquement toujours sous-estimé leur rôle dans le processus de la création et de la connaissance romanesque. On ne peut pas dire que le titre ait été systématiquement ignoré de tous, mais si le rapport d'un titre et d'un roman a quelquefois été analysé, l'efficacité du procédé commence seulement à être décrite et étudiée. Il y a donc matière à investigation. Mais ce serait un sujet trop vaste que de travailler sur tous les titres d'une manière exhaustive, puisque le titre s'apparente à tous les romans. Ce serait également une tâche inconcevable que de rechercher tous les titres qui font problème. On ne demande jamais non plus aux romanciers les raisons qui les ont poussés à choisir tel ou tel titre, plutôt qu'un autre; et si la problématique du titre appartient à tous les écrivains, seuls quelques-uns ont cru devoir se justifier, comme Balzac dans son "Avant-Propos" à la *Comédie humaine*. En fait, tous les soins, toutes les justifications que les romanciers apportent à leurs titres, ne se trouvent jamais—ou presque jamais— dans le texte même de l'oeuvre. Il est rarissime de lire dans les premières pages d'un roman l'explication du titre que porte ce roman, comme l'a fait de nos jours Michel Tournier dans son roman *Les Météores*. On trouve plutôt ce genre de préoccupation dans la correspondance, et surtout dans certains remaniements du manuscrit. Ces hésitations et ces discours sur les titres ne sont finalement amenés à la connaissance du public, et donc des lecteurs, qu'accidentellement et sous forme de notes et préfaces. Ce qui tend à renvoyer tout intérêt aux titres et à la titrologie romanesque à une sorte de goût pour le travail de bibliothèque, à cheval entre l'érudition et la "petite" critique. Enfin, si certains titres ont traditionnellement attiré l'attention de la critique, c'est toujours dans la mesure où ceux-ci ne respectaient pas une des clauses de ce que l'on pourrait appeler "le pacte de la titrologie," c'est-à-dire, et le plus souvent, celle de la fonction énonciatrice du titre. C'est toujours quand la critique a pensé que le titre ne "traduisait" pas l'oeuvre, qu'il ne renseignait pas ou peu sur le contenu du roman qu'il nommait, qu'elle s'est intéressée à lui.

L'histoire du titre n'est pas mystérieuse, l'étymologie du mot non plus. Titre vient du latin "titulus," dont les sens étaient multiples: rang, affiche ou étiquette. Utilisé dans ce dernier sens, le "titulus" servait à faire connaître le nom de l'auteur et la matière traitée dans le "volumen" sans avoir à dérouler celui-ci. Ruban pendu au "volumen," le "titulus" correspondait d'abord à un besoin pratique de connaissance et de classement. Avec l'apparition du livre se développe l'habitude de placer le titre aux premières pages, enfin le livre imprimé lui consacre une pleine page. Mais jusqu'au XVIIIe siècle, les libraires vendaient des livres tout reliés et la couverture était muette. C'est la Révolution de 1789 qui entraîne la vente de livres brochés sans couverture, puisque le cuir coûtait trop cher. C'est non seulement l'invention de l'imprimerie, mais aussi et surtout la transformation du livre en marchandise populaire et bon marché et plus particulièrement l'avènement de l'âge du roman qui voient la naissance du titre tel que nous le connaissons.

Signe de la transformation en marchandise d'un ouvrage, le titre n'en a pas moins de multiples fonctions. Tous les critiques qui se sont intéressés aux problèmes de la titrologie ont repéré certaines de ces fonctions. Léo Hoek dans son essai, *Pour une sémiotique du titre*,[7] en relève deux qu'il appelle: "identificationnelle" (quelquefois aussi nommée "référentielle") et "énonciatrice." Charles Grivel dans un excellent chapitre, intitulé "Puissance du titre," de son ouvrage sur le roman, divise en trois les fonctions du titre: "appellative" qui désigne l'ouvrage, "désignative" qui désigne le contenu, et "publicitaire" pour mettre en valeur.[8] Claude Duchet dans son article, "*La Fille abandonnée* et *La Bête humaine*: éléments de titrologie romanesque," décompose également en trois les fonctions du titre: "référentielle," "conative" et "poétique," respectivement centrées sur l'objet, le destinataire et le message.[9] Si nous n'avons pas de texte de Barthes qui traite exclusivement des problèmes de titrologie, il a ébauché le sujet de manière brève et décisive dans *S/Z* ainsi que dans son "Analyse textuelle d'un conte d'Edgar Poe."[10] Pour Barthes, le titre a toujours et sumultanément une double fonction: "énonciatrice" et "déictique."

Il importe peu de souligner la variation du nombre des fonctions du titre entre ces différents critiques, puisque souvent on découvre les mêmes rôles sous des noms différents, ou encore des fonctions différentes sous des noms identiques. L'important sera seulement de bien délimiter les fonctions et ensuite seulement de les nommer.

La première fonction du titre sera d'annoncer "qu'un morceau de littérature va suivre (c'est-à-dire, en fait, une marchandise)" ("Analyse," p. 33). A la suite de Barthes, nous appellerons cette fonction du titre, la fonction déictique, qui sert à désigner, à montrer. Cette fonction nomme l'ouvrage et permet de le rendre unique; centrée sur le roman, elle le transforme en objet:

> Pour qu'un texte soit reconnaissable de l'extérieur comme texte et classifiable par rapport aux autres textes circulant dans une société, le titre est cet élément dont la fonction classificatrice permet de saisir dans un coup d'oeil à quel genre de texte on a affaire. (Hoek, 1)

> Le roman est montré "roman" dès son titre; la spécificité du livre est précisée à tel point qu'à la seule perception du livre...la catégorie même s'en trouve déjà affirmée; le titre réunit en lui-même de quoi réussir cette identification. (Grivel, 169)

Mais il y a une ambiguïté car si le titre se réfère bien au texte qui le suit, les mots du titre comprennent d'abord les sens régulièrement enregistrés par le dictionnaire, mais ils vont aussi inclure un certain nombre de sens par connotations successives et ainsi élargir le sens commun.[11] Cet élargissement de sens ne sera pas issu du dictionnaire, mais il guidera quand même la lecture. Le titre devient alors un signe à contenu "flottant" qui ne prend sens que par rapport à une situation concrète de discours. De ce point de vue, le titre—phrase a-grammaticale et non-définie sémantiquement par le dictionnaire—se rapproche encore une fois, sur le plan linguistique, du nom propre. Comme lui, il commence par une majuscule; de même que le nom propre inaliénable, le titre devient propriété privée et fonctionne comme le nom propre de l'oeuvre désignant tout le texte de l'ouvrage. Enfin, comme le nom propre, le titre ne peut être que dénué de sens, surtout au début, puisqu'il sert seulement à marquer les repères entre le texte et le hors texte:

> L'intitulé n'assigne donc pas la capitale d'une écriture, il en assure le suspens; et le contour, la bordure et le cadrage. Il donne un premier pli et dessine autour du texte une sorte de blancheur matricielle.[12]

Dans l'optique de cette fonction déictique, le titre d'un roman ne renvoie pas à un référent qu'il semblerait dénoter, il renvoie au roman qui porte ces mots comme titre et le montre en tant que marchandise:

> Le titre du livre (tel que nous ne le lisons pas comme titre) désigne ce qui le remplit (comme l'homme qui se vit comme signe est censé remplir son nom), comme si l'objet livre devait être considéré comme une forme (définie par le genre), vide qui se remplisse à volonté d'une marchandise mise en circulation par le demi-grossiste (l'auteur), vendue sous une étiquette qui ne trompe pas son monde (le titre) et acheté selon les besoins du consommateur (le lecteur).[13]

On peut donc affirmer que la fonction déictique du titre est sa fonction première et primaire: elle sert à identifier une masse de pages. L'auteur, ou dans certains cas l'éditeur, décide de réunir un paquet de feuilles sous une étiquette commune: le titre.

Dans cette relation entre le "demi-grossiste" et le "consommateur," le titre-étiquette représente le premier lien. Mais dans ce rôle la fonction du titre sera double, raconter le sujet de l'oeuvre et appâter le lecteur éventuel, comme l'exprimait déjà Baillet dès 1725:

> Le titre d'un livre doit être son abrégé, et il en doit renfermer tout l'esprit autant qu'il est possible... Je n'entends pas le titre d'un livre, donc ce titre ne vaut rien; parce qu'il est censé n'être pas bon dès que les plus simples et les plus grossiers ne l'entendent pas. Et je ne suis point tenté d'acheter et de lire un livre sous ce titre, comme je ne le suis pas d'acheter une marchandise dont l'étiquette et la montre me sont inconnues.[14]

En suivant la terminologie de Barthes qui nous paraît la plus précise, nous appellerons cette deuxième fonction, la fonction *énonciatrice* du titre: "ce qu'il énonce lié à la contingence de ce qui suit" ("Analyse," p. 33). De par cette fonction, le titre devient l'abstraction du texte, sa métaphore ou sa métonymie puisqu'il symbolise ou raconte le texte. Autre façon pour un auteur de forcer l'attention du public sur son ouvrage, le titre se transforme en clé.

Selon le canon "classique" de la titrologie exprimé par Baillet au XVIIIe siècle, le titre doit si bien exprimer le sujet du livre, qu'en retour on doit pouvoir dire de chaque partie de l'oeuvre, ce qu'en est le titre général: "il [le titre] doit être le centre de toutes les paroles et de toutes les pensées du livre, de telle sorte qu'on n'y en puisse pas même trouver une qui n'y ait de la correspondance et du rapport" (p. 163). C'est là bien évidemment une proposition utopique. Si le titre est d'abord le moyen de désigner, une fois pour toutes, un ensemble de pages qui forment un roman, il ne peut jamais répondre d'avance à aucune exigence interne du texte qu'il précède. Un titre ne peut nous paraître juste et nécessaire qu'a posteriori.[15] Une oeuvre peut d'ailleurs changer de titre, ou même être publiée concomitamment sous deux titres différents (cf. *Les Possedés*/*Les Démons*).

Comme le titre veut aussi, et simultanément, mettre en valeur l'ouvrage qu'il nomme, il doit également se soumettre aux lois du marché et de la compétition. Alors, si certains auteurs ou éditeurs cherchent ou abusent de titres extraordinaires, clinquants et provocateurs, c'est bien dans le but de stimuler la curiosité du public, de l'allécher pour lui donner envie de lire le roman. Il s'agit simplement d'être différent. Ce qui est la règle élémentaire de la publicité. Pour le lecteur, ce titre énonciateur devient, dans tous les sens, le hors-d'oeuvre de l'oeuvre: "La couverture c'est, préparant de l'extérieur le lecteur à l'oeuvre, une sorte de hors-d'oeuvre."[16]

Or, si le titre fonctionne réellement et uniquement dans le but de la vente et de la réclame, les conclusions à en tirer sont bien plus graves que nos prémisses: le titre est extérieur à la création romanesque. Il fonctionne comme une simple pièce rapportée qui n'a rien à voir avec une quelconque poétique. Ensuite, puisque le titre est aussi quelquefois imposé à l'auteur par l'éditeur, voire par les pouvoirs publics, il ne peut pas prétendre à être la clé du texte. Il serait donc parfaitement légitime d'ignorer le titre d'un roman, non pas seulement parce qu'il est le signe imposé par les développements d'une société marchande, mais surtout parce qu'il serait extérieur à la création littéraire.

Doit-on alors subir le titre, sans plus? Sûrement pas. Le titre est à lire et doit être lu. Certes, les fonctions déictique et énonciatrice servent toujours d'appât pour transformer le public en lecteur, c'èst-à-dire en chaland: "Un beau titre est le vrai proxénète du livre ce qui en fait faire le plus prompt débit" disait Furetière.[17] Mais comparé à l'ampleur et à la richesse du roman, le titre est bref, pauvre, laconique. Pour dominer le texte, il sera obligé d'opérer une condensation, une abstraction, un emboutissement, d'où la nécessité pour l'auteur d'allier sa subjectivité d'écrivain à la nécessité de trouver un titre, qu'il espère sera compris et aimé avec facilité par un lecteur indéterminé.

Nommer un livre, donner un titre, ce sera alors créer un intérêt et développer un manque. Ce sera aussi promettre de satisfaire cet intérêt et ce manque par la lecture du roman, donc par là même encore, se créera la nécessité de l'acheter. Pour inciter donc à l'achat, la fonction énonciatrice ne sera pas complètement respectée. Le titre ne doit pas tout dire, en fait il ne doit jamais exprimer complètement l'information qu'il est supposé divulguer. Au contraire, le titre doit jouer le rôle de point d'interrogation à l'énoncé littéraire, qui à son tour lui sert de réplique. Le titre prend valeur d'incipit puisqu'il est lié à l'allusion qui suit. Le texte n'est que le produit du titre et le titre bien plus qu'un énonciateur devient un conducteur de texte, ce que J. Derrida a joliment appelé un archonte:

> Mallarmé prescrit de suspendre le titre qui, comme la tête, le capital, l'oraculeux, porte front haut, parle trop haut, à la fois parce qu'il élève la voix, en assourdit le texte conséquent, et parce qu'il occupe le haut de la page, le haut devenant ainsi le centre éminent, le commencement, le chef, l'archonte. (204)

Chez certains auteurs cette valeur de conducteur du texte peut être hypertrophiée, au point de devenir même et réellement l'incipit du texte: le titre pré-existe au texte même du roman et en devient sa matrice. Dans ce cas, c'est vraiment le texte du roman qui sert à expliquer le titre déjà trouvé:

> Si j'écris l'histoire avant d'avoir trouvé le titre, elle avorte généralement. Il faut un titre, parce que le titre est cette sorte de drapeau vers lequel on se dirige: le but qu'il faut atteindre c'est expliquer le titre. (...) Au début, c'est purement typographique, c'est purement un dessin, je vois le titre sur un livre, je vois le titre sur la page, je vois
>
> Les Deux Cavaliers
>
> Je vois de quelle façon ils se placent, typographiquement. Dès que cette typographie du titre est suffisamment alléchante pour moi, pour qu'elle mette en branle mon appareil créateur, à partir de ce moment-là, je ne cesse pas de penser à une histoire possible, sous ce titre que je vois.[18]

Si ce type de création romanesque ne semble pas répandu par le biais de cet aveu de Giono, nous pouvons avancer que la fonction énonciatrice du titre est déjà un point de vue sur l'oeuvre. L'auteur choisit d'énoncer, d'isoler et de souligner un élément de signification. Le titre annonce bien ce que le roman exprime, mais aussi et surtout ce que le romancier considère comme esentiel dans son texte, même si la raison principale du choix du titre n'est pas toujours claire et se trouve plutôt au niveau de "l'inconscient de l'écriture," comme l'explique Michel Butor:

> En général le livre est déjà très avancé avant que je lui donne vraiment un titre. Je le désigne pour moi-même d'une certaine façon mais le titre lui-même peut arriver très tard et d'ailleurs changer au cours du travail un grand nombre de fois. L'inconscient de l'écriture joue pour les titres autant que pour le reste, c'est-à-dire que je peux des années plus tard, grâce à un critique sensible par exemple, ou à une rencontre, tout à coup découvrir pour quelle raison principale j'ai employé ce titre-là.[19]

Ainsi, si au niveau de sa fonction énonciatrice le langage du titre renvoie au contenu, ce troisième niveau va conceptualiser. Le titre va structurer tout le roman, tout en privilégiant un élément fonctionnel qui sera un complément d'information à la volonté de l'auteur de sursignifier son texte, mais aussi du même coup l'appauvrir, car l'auteur choisit de réduire à une seule unité, et la diversité et la richesse de son texte: "[le titre] subsume et dissimule, par l'unité de sa proposition, l'immense diversité du texte dont il se veut l'annonce" (Ricardou, p. 61).

Pour le lecteur, le titre est donc déjà un discours sur le texte à venir, qui veut non seulement dévoiler un contenu, mais aussi et simultanément mettre en relief les éléments porteurs d'intérêts. Le titre et le texte se trouvent bien en rapport de complémentarité, et le titre indique alors autant l'esprit de l'oeuvre que son sujet: "J'ai souvent désiré que... tout auteur fût contraint de faire préjuger par le titre qu'il adopte, et la thèse qu'il soutient, et l'esprit dans lequel il la développe" conclut Balzac dans un article de critique.[20]

Pour reprendre une métaphore stendhalienne, le titre serait un miroir placé devant un texte par un auteur ou un éditeur, qui en réfléchissant une nature du texte doit conduire le lecteur au type de lecture que l'auteur ou l'éditeur veut imposer au texte. Marque d'un jugement, expression d'un idiosyncracisme, point de vue sur l'oeuvre, le titre participe alors au phénomène littéraire par excellence, la valorisation du mot, le travail sur la lettre, "ce support matériel que le discours concret emprunte au langage."[21]

Ensuite, si le titre constitue bien le premier contact entre le public, les lecteurs et un énoncé romanesque, tout en se constituant aussi comme premier niveau de manifestation du roman, le phénomène littéraire ne sera pas seulement le texte du titre, mais aussi les rapports de ce texte avec les lecteurs, la relation entre un signe et ses interprétants:

> On peut distinguer les systèmes où la signifiance est imprimée par
> l'auteur à l'oeuvre, et les systèmes où la signifiance est exprimée
> par les éléments premiers à l'état isolé, indépendamment des
> liaisons qu'ils peuvent contracter. Dans les premiers, la signifiance
> se dégage des relations qui organisent un monde clos, dans les
> seconds elle est inhérente aux signes eux-mêmes.[22]

Pour l'étude des titres ces deux systèmes vont se mélanger: rendre compte de la production de sens et son interprétation exige la compréhension des relations qui existent entre les signes et leurs référents.

En somme, le titre de roman aura une triple fonction: 1) de projecteur; 2) de projecteur chargé d'attirer les regards; 3) de créer le relief: changer l'éclairage ce sera aussitôt changer la profondeur et la forme du relief. De ce point de vue, le titre qui accompagne le roman devra être analysé, non seulement en fonction des relations qu'il entretient avec le contenu même de l'oeuvre (auteur), mais aussi face à sa position vis-à-vis du public (lecteur). Cette fonction de médiateur entre d'une part le texte et l'écrivain, et d'autre part le texte et le lecteur, ne sera pas gratuite, ni anodine, ni innocente, elle produira un effet que nous appellerons la fonction *poétique* du titre: c'est cette fonction qui va permettre de réinscrire la pluralité en injectant ces petites différences qui introduisent le romanesque, et c'est toujours grâce à cette fonction poétique que le titre pourra dépasser le dénotatif pour devenir une nébuleuse de signifiés.

Contrairement aux titres des autres genres, les types et les fonctions du titre de roman ont été en grande partie déterminés par les conditions économiques et techniques, principalement par l'invention de l'imprimerie, mais aussi et surtout par la diffusion du roman à des milliers d'exemplaires, ce qui lui a permis d'accroître sa force. Il fait maintenant l'objet de soins jaloux de la part des auteurs et surtout des éditeurs, car même si certains auteurs ne considèrent pas toujours le titre comme partie intégrante de l'oeuvre, les éditeurs ont très vite compris son rôle commercial. A leurs yeux le titre a acquis une importance majeure par l'influence (réelle ou supposée) qu'il exerce sur la masse des acheteurs potentiels qui doivent céder à son leurre. Cette puissance du titre devrait jouer seulement pour les jeunes romanciers privés des avantages d'une réputation établie, et elle devrait décroître à mesure que l'audience de l'écrivain augmente. On pourrait espérer aussi qu'un roman, même desservi par un titre médiocre ou jugé tel, ne soit pas entravé longtemps et que tôt ou tard les qualités profondes de l'oeuvre devraient lui assurer le succès. Ensuite, le roman est devenu un tel produit de consommation que même la célébrité d'un écrivain ne lui garantit pas souvent l'entière responsabilité quant au choix de ses titres. C'est toujours au niveau de ce choix que l'éditeur garde le plus souvent un droit de regard et de pression. Ce qu'on appelle pudiquement une collaboration fructueuse.

Mais choisis par l'auteur ou par l'éditeur, tous les titres de roman relèvent quand même de ces trois fonctions: déictique, énonciatrice et poétique. Seule pourra changer l'emphase placée sur telle ou telle fonction, selon le groupe de pression victorieux: de l'auteur dont la notoriété augmente le pouvoir de décision, ou de l'éditeur qui croit connaître ce qui fait vendre, le goût du public et la mode du jour.[23]

Même si les pouvoirs signifiants d'un titre de roman sont toujours en équilibre entre les lois d'un marché et la volonté d'un créateur, le titre sera capable de réveiller dans chaque lecteur un imaginaire différent, en rapport avec son vécu. Parce que le titre ne change pas, il est un point de repère sur lequel l'imaginaire de chaque lecteur peut se projeter. Le titre va commumquer avec la culture, le savoir, l'histoire, et c'est à travers lui que le roman va nous pénétrer. Avec sa culture, son expérience, chaque lecteur va aborder le texte du roman de différentes manières, ce que le lecteur va lire prendra un sens nouveau et parce que le titre passera à travers le texte du roman, quelque chose en lui pourra s'y éveiller. Le titre de roman va exprimer à la fois la contingence initiale de l'invention mais aussi la graduelle nécessité que lui confère le roman qui se condense autour de lui. Il n'y a donc pas de bonnes ou mauvaises significations du titre: il y a celles qui affaiblissent la compréhension du roman et celles qui en renforcent la prospective cohésionnelle. Au niveau de la critique, on ne pourra simplement que vérifier la cohérence interne d'une explication, ainsi que ses sources. En dernière instance, le choix final ne peut être que celui du lecteur. Comme à notre époque la distorsion des lectures est accentuée par l'extension et l'hétérogénéité du public, selon sa chronologie et ses codes culturels de références, ce lecteur ajoutera ou retranchera des éléments de significations.

---

[1] (Paris: Skira, 1970).

[2] (Le Cendre: Editions BOF, 1972).

[3] A propos d'unt gravure de Dürer appelée "Le Chevalier, la nuit, la mort," J. Wirth avance que cette gravure devrait s'appeler "Le Rêve du cavalier." Si "cavalier" est devenu "chevalier," c'est que ce terme est plus noble; quant à "rêve," s'il disparaît, c'est justement parce que ce mot n'est pas considéré noble... Aux problèmes que posent les titres dans l'iconographie médiévale allemande, J. Wirth croit que la meilleure justification d'un titre serait encore la répétition de ce titre par l'auteur. Jean Wirth, *La Jeune fille et la mort* (Genève: Droz, 1979), p. 94.

[4] *Annales* (Economies, Sociétés, Civilisations), 5 (1965), 939-66. Pour J.-L. Flandrin, "cette étude laisse l'impression d'un renforcement de l'interdit sur l'usage des relations génitales et sur les mots qui peuvent y faire des allusions trop réalistes... Les titres indiquent seulement les notions qu'une civilisation ose afficher" (p. 961).

[5] *Communications*, 16 (1970), 70-125. Voir également le travail collectif, sous la direction de J. Molino, "Sur les titres des romans de Jean Bruce," *Langages*, 35 (1974), 87-116.

[6] Le linguiste M. E. Buyssens dans sa sémiologie, classe ensemble dans le second type, l'art, la publicité, la politesse, le geste, l'enseigne. Cf. *Langages et discours*, p. 37, cité par S. Ullmann, *Précis de sémantique française* (1952; Berne: Editions A. Francke S. A., 1975), p. 24.

[7] Cf. Léo Hoek, *Pour une sémiotique du titre*, Documents de travail et pre-publications, Centro Internazionale di Semiotica e di Linguistica, Università di Urbino, No. 20/21, genn-

febbr. (1973), série D. Dans ce travail, Léo Hoek fait appel à la grammaire générative et transformationnelle, élaborée par Noam Chomsky et ses épigones, qui distinguent deux niveaux de structures dans la langue, la structure profonde et la structure de surface. Léo Hoek suppose ainsi qu'en profondeur "il existe pour tout titre une phrase explicite performative qui doit avoir la forme suivante: 'je déclare à toi que ce texte s'appelle X.' A la surface nous ne retrouvons que X." Dans cet essai axé sur les titres romantiques, la deuxième partie s'intitule: "Haut-parleurs romantiques, essai de description structurale du récit des titres à l'époque romantique (1830-1835)," Léo Hoek s'attache à élaborer une sémiotique du titre, "une science qui s'occupe de l'étude des titres en tant que signes" (p. 2). Dans un autre article intitulé: "Description d'un archonte: préliminaires à une théorie du titre à partir du Nouveau Roman," in *Nouveau Roman: hier, aujourd'hui*; I. *Problèmes généraux* (Paris: U.G.E., 1972), pp. 289-306, Léo Hoek a tenté de dépister comment s'institue la relation du titre avec le texte dans le cas précis des ouvrages du Nouveau Roman. Il propose également une structure inhérente à tous les titres. Cet article, issu d'une communication au Colloque de Cerisy (1971), est suivi d'une discussion particulièrement intéressante, et plus précisément d'une féroce attaque de la part du romancier Alain Robbe-Grillet contre les méthodes et les conclusions de Léo Hoek.

[8]Charles Grivel, *Production de l'intérêt romanesque* (la Haye-Paris: Mouton, 1973), p. 129.

[9]*Littérature*, 12 (1973), 49-73.

[10]Roland Barthes, "Analyse textuelle d'un conte d'Edgar Poe," in Claude Chabrol, *Sémiotique narrative et textuelle* (Paris: Larousse, 1973), p. 34. Dès les premières pages de son célèbre essai sur la nouvelle de Balzac, *Sarrasine*, Barthes écrit: "Sarrasine, qu'est-ce que c'est que ça?" *S/Z* (Paris: Seuil [Points], 1970), p. 24.

[11]La dénotation se produit entre le signe et le référent, elle renvoie à l'existence objective d'une chose ou d'un être défini, c'est-à-dire dans le cas le plus facile à imaginer, un objet réel. Ce n'est plus la séquence sonore ou graphique qui se lie au sens mais les éléments permanents du sens par rapport aux valeurs subjectives variables qui constituent la connotation: "tout ce que ce terme peut évoquer, suggérer, exciter, impliquer de façon nette ou vague chez chacun des usagers." André Martinet, "Connotations, poésie et culture," in *To Honor Roman Jakobson*, II, 1288. Voir également Barthes: "les connotations sont des sens qui ne sont ni dans le dictionnaire, ni dans le français dont est écrit le texte." *S/Z*, p. 15. La connotation entraînerait une littérature datée du signifié?

[12]Jacques Derrida, "La Double séance," *La Dissémination* (Paris: Seuil, 1972), p. 205. On trouve chez Proust un exemple de ce pouvoir attirant et matriciel des titres: "Elle avait pris *François le Champi* à qui sa couverture rougeâtre et son titre incompréhensible donnaient pour moi une personnalité distincte et un attrait mystérieux.... Tous les changements bizarres qui se produisent dans l'attitude respective de la meunière et de l'enfant... me paraissaient empruntés d'un profond mystère dont je me figurais volontiers que la source devait être dans ce nom inconnu et si doux de 'Champi' qui mettait sur l'enfant qui le portait sans que je susse pourquoi, sa couleur vive, empourprée et charmante." *Du côté de chez Swann* (Paris: Livre de Poche, 1954), p. 51.

[13]Marcellin Pleynet, "La Posie doit avoir pour but...," in *Tel Quel*, *Théorie d'ensemble* (Paris: Seuil, 1968), p. 101.

[14]Adrien Baillet, *Jugemens des savans sur les principaux ouvrages des auteurs* (Amsterdam: aux dépens de la Compagnie, MDCCXXV [1725]), I, 163. Le chapitre intitulé "Préjugés des titres" (pp. 163-83) est certainement le premier texte de l'histoire littéraire sur le sujet des titres.

[15]"Quand le livre marche, dit simplement Jacques Peuchemaurd, directeur littéraire chez Laffont, on peut dire que son titre est bon." Cf. Gilles Pudlowski, "Le Baptême des livres," *Les Nouvelles Littéraires*, 16 Juin 1980, pp. 24-25.

[16]Jean Ricardou, "Naissance d'une fiction," in *Nouveau Roman: hier, aujourd'hui*; II. *Pratiques* (Paris: U.G.E., 1972), p. 381. Pour le narrateur de *Du côé de chez Swann*, hésiter entre

deux titres, c'est hésiter entre deux desserts...: "cherchant à approfondir successivement le titre de l'une et le titre de l'autre, j'arrivais à me représenter avec tant de force, d'une part une pièce éblouissante et fière, et de l'autre une pièce douce et veloutée, que j'étais incapable de décider laquelle aurait ma préférence, que si pour le dessert, on m'avait donné à opter entre le riz à l'impératrice et la crème au chocolat" (p. 89).

[17]Furetière, *Le Roman bourgeois* in *Romanciers du XVlle siècle* (Paris: Gallimard, 1958), pp. 1082-85.

[18]Jean Giono, in Robert Ricatte, "*Les Deux cavaliers de l'orage* de Jean Giono. Etude de genèse," *Travaux de linguistique et de littérature* publiés par le Centre de Philologie Romane de l'Université de Strasbourg, VII, 2 (1969), 223-24. Est-ce le titre ou la première phrase du roman qui est le plus difficile à trouver pour un auteur? Voire qui engendre le roman? Nous avons la réponse de Giono, mais pour Aragon, c'est la première phrase qui déclenche l'écriture du roman (cf. *Je n'ai jamais appris à lire ou Les Incipit* [Genève: Skira, 1969]). Quant à Jean Ricardou, le vertige du signifiant entraîne le titre à engendrer le roman. "La naissance d'une fiction" s'élabore à partir de la couverture du livre, du nom de l'auteur, de l'éditeur, etc., pour arriver à la *Prose/Prise de Constantinople*. Cf. Ricardou, pp. 386-87. Dans son article "Paranomase et signifiance," M. Riffaterre démontre comment le titre de Baudelaire "Alchimie de la douleur" contrôle l'engendrement du texte entier: "douleur" à cause de l'article défini devient un abstrait de sens général et par métonymie il représente un sens plus général encore: la condition humaine. Dans le même article, lire aussi l'analyse du titre de Breton *Poisson soluble.* Cf. *Sémiotext(e),* II, I (1975), 15-30. Sur le dialogue entre l'incipit et le texte, voir l'article de Victor Brombert, "Opening Signals in Narrative," *New Literary History,* 11 (1979-1980), 489-502. Cet article sur les "ouvertures" ne s'intéresse pas à proprement parler aux titres, mais les analyses sur l'importance de l'incipit débordent souvent le cadre des "premiers mots" puisque comme, l'écrit avec justesse V. Brombert: "Literally speaking, even if in a subliminal manner, the first word of a text remains longest with the reader along the textual trajectory, and by this virtue alone acquires a privileged status. The same, a fortiori, is true of titles and epigraphs. It is this textual memory—conscious and unconscious—that structures the linear into a simultaneous order" (p. 495). Enfin sur les titres surréalistes voir les travaux de Ruth Amossy et Elisheva Rosen, *Les Discours du cliché* (Paris: S.E.D.E.S., 1982), lire en particulier le chapitre intitulé 'Le Titre cliché surréaliste," pp. 126-137.

[19]Michel Butor,"Ecorché vif,"in *Colloque de Cerisy* (Paris:U.G.E., 1975), p. 447.

[20]Honoré de Balzac, *Oeuvres diverses,* I, *Oeuvres complètes* (Paris: Conard, 1935), XXXVIII, 638.

[21]Jacques Lacan, "L'Instance de la lettre dans l'inconscient ou La Raison depuis Freud," *Ecrits* (Paris: Seuil [Points], 1966), I, 251.

[22]Emile Benvéniste, "Sémiologie de la langue (2)," *Sémiotica,* I, 2 (1969), 120.

[23]Yves Velan, écrivain suisse francophone, vient de publier un roman intitulé: *Soft Goulag.* Ce titre jure singulièrement par rapport aux titres de ses précédents romans: *Je* et *La Statue de Condillac retouchée,* allusions littéraire et philosophique. Le titre de *Soft Goulag* est issu de l'actualité. Ce titre est incontestablement déterminé par des considérations publicitaires et politiques, mais aussi poétiques. Le premier titre du roman était: "Une Thèse sur le droit des naissances," titre bien meilleur au niveau de la fonction énonciatrice, puisque ce roman se présente comme une thèse de doctorat sur la régulation des naissances dans une Amérique future. En choisissant pour titre définitif *Soft Goulag,* c'est bien sur la fonction poétique du titre que le romancier joue. D'abord, il renforce l'impression de "roman" que le premier titre n'avait pas; ensuite le titre *Soft Goulag* a un sens plus large, une polysémie référentielle très moderne ("software," "softcore," "G.O.U.L.A.G.") à la fois tape-à-l'oeil, mais en même temps horrible. Comme le titre français de l'ouvrage de H. Miller, *Le Cauchemar climatisé,* le titre-oxymoron *Soft Goulag* est à lui seul un jugement politique sur le contenu du roman et reflète en plus, et dans sa langue même, la division du monde et l'absence de choix. Ce titre retrouve, et exprime à l'envers, le même dilemme que la *Statue,* celui de l'analogie et de l'altérité. Enfin, certains titres

peuvent avoir une fonction énonciatrice volontairement pervertie par l'auteur. Ainsi le roman de Boris Vian intitulé *L'Automne à Pékin* ne se passe ni à Pékin... ni pendant l'automne... Ce titre ne peut que signifier la volonté d'un auteur de trahir le "pacte de la titrologie," et au niveau de la création romanesque, cette volonté est signifiante.

Index

Adam, Antoine, 243
Adam, Jean-Michel, 101, 104, 106n. 1
Aesop, 126, 132
Albérès, R.-M., 228
Albistur, Maïthé, 303
Alembert, Jean d', 154, 155, 156-159, 161-162, 164, 166
Althusser, Louis, 230, 231
Ambrière, Francis, 311n.4&7
Amossy, Ruth, 357n.18
Amyot, Jacques, 112
Aneau, Barthélemy, 112
Antoine, André, 207
Apollinaire, Guillaume, 45
Apuleius, 127
Aragon, Louis, 22, 28, 33, 34, 64n.5, 357n.18
Aristotle, 43, 44, 104, 140, 144, 236, 241, 259, 263
Armogathe, Daniel, 303
Arnauld, Antoine, 150n.6
Arnould, Sophie, 273
Aron, Raymond, 22
Aron, Robert, 29
Arrivé, Michel, 247
Artaud, Antonin, xxxiii, 59, 235, 286, 287-288
Ashbery, John, 277
Asselineau, Charles, xxvi
Assouline, Pierre, xxiii
Astruc, A., 6
Aubignac, François d', 138, 140-144
Aubigné, Agrippa d', 154, 187, 283, 288
Augustine, Saint, 118
Aulagnier-Spairani, P., 64n.14, 65n.27
Aurbach, Erich, xxiii, 43
Ayrault, R. 262n.12
Bachelard, Gaston, 229
Baillet, Adrien, 356n.14
Bajomée, D., 76n.3
Bal, Mieke, 99, 106n.1
Balakian, Anna, 336
Ballanche, Simon, 187

Balzac, Guez de, 123
Balzac, Honoré de, xxiv, 35, 36, 45, 48, 80-82, 87, 164, 166, 185, 230, 264, 265, 268, 327, 348, 353
Bandelier, Danielle, 290n.15
Bandy, W.T., xxvi
Banfield, Ann, 261
Banville, Théodore de, 257, 341, 342
Baraz, Machaël, 119
Barbey d'Aurevilly, Jules-Amadée, 82
Barrault, Jean-Louis, 202
Barret, William, 344
Bart, Benjamin, xxxiii, 263-275
Barthes, Roland, xvi, xviii, xxiv, xxxiv, xxxvii, 35, 42n.2, 59, 64n.3, 64n.9, 99, 104, 107n.8, 108n.22, 227, 229-237, 248, 341, 349, 351, 356n.10
Bartholi-Engel, Jane, 326
Basil, Saint, 116
Bataille, Georges, xxiv, 55, 60, 64n.11, 76n.11, 221, 222
Baudelaire, Charles, xviii, xxvi, 228, 242, 286, 312n.3, 357n.18
Beauvoir, Simone de, xxii, 6, 8, 11, 15n.4, 18, 20, 22, 27, 298
Beckett, Samuel, xx, xxiv, xxxvii, 68, 201, 223, 224, 262, 344
Beecham, Thomas, 326
Beethoven, Ludwig van, 345
Belaval, Yvon, 60, 62, 64n.1, 64n.19
Béguin, Albert, 228
Benvéniste, Emile, 231, 357n.22
Berger, Peter, 315
Bernanos, Georges, 28, 30
Bersani, Leo, xxiv, 64n.4
Beuvron, comtesse de, 291
Birwisch, Manfred, 238
Black, John B., 108n.9
Blake, William, xxxiv
Blanchot, Maurice, xxiv, 42n.2, 53, 60

Blin, Roger, 202
Bloom, Harold, xx
Boccaccio, Giovanni, 237
Boethius, xxxiv, 277, 279
Bogue, Ronald, xxiii
Boileau, Nicolas, 114, 123, 135, 141, 143-144, 148, 154, 155
Boisdeffre, Pierre de, 228
Bokobza, Serge, xxxii-xxxviii, 347-358
Bonheim, Helmut, 102, 107n.15
Bonniot, Mme Edmond, 328
Booth, Wayne, 107n.5, 107n.7
Borgerhoff, E.B.O., 135n.1
Bossuet, Jacques, 147-148
Boswell, James, 231
Bottens, Etienne Polier de, 291
Boucher, François, 165
Bouchier, Jean-Jacques, 60, 64n.2, 65n.55
Bouhours, Dominique, 139
Boulez, Pierre, xxxvii, 327, 341, 344, 345
Bourdan, Pierre, 201
Bourges, Clémence de, 301
Bower, Gordon, 108n.19
Brady, Patrick, xv, xx, xxvii, xxxi-xxxii, 234, 241-249
Brahm, Otto, 207
Brasillach, Robert, 30, 33
Bray, René, 242
Brecht, Bertolt, 201, 204, 206
Brée, Germaine, xv, xix, xx
Bremond, Claude, 107n.16, 248
Breton, André, 357n.18
Brochier, J., 65n.29
Brody, Jules, 135n.1
Brombert, Victor, 357n.18
Brooks, Peter, 104, 107n.21&23
Browning, Elisabeth Barret, 311
Brownlee, Kevin, 289n.4&6
Brunetière, Ferdinand, 241
Brückner, P., 65n.40
Budé, Guillaume, 116
Buffalo Bill, 8
Buffon, comte de, 236
Buffum, Imbrie, 243
Bulciolu, Maria Térésa, 311n.9
Burnier, Michel-Antoine, 16n.21
Butler, Philip, 243
Butor, Michel, xv, xxi, xxxvii, 26, 46, 47, 242, 341, 344, 345, 346n.15, 347, 353
Buyssens, M.E., 355n.6

Calin, William, 289n.7
Camilli, C., 65n.28
Camus, Albert, xxv, 26, 27, 30, 87, 99, 187, 220-221
Carter, Nick, 8
Casarès, Maria, 203
Cassella, Mme Alfredo, 326
Castex, Pierre, 88n.3
Castro, Fidel, 176
Catullus, 282
Caws, Mary Ann, 233
Céline, Louis-Ferdinand, xxiii, 19, 25, 28, 30, 31, 33
Cervantes, 230, 258
Chagall, Marc, 19
Chambers, Ross, 104, 290n.13
Chamfort, Sébastien de, 256
Champagne, Roland, xxxvii, 341-346
Champagne, Thibaut de, 242
Champigny, Robert, xv, xxv, 89-95
Chapelain, Jean, 123
Charles IX, 115
Charles, II, 161
Chastel, André, 243
Chateaubriand, François-René de, xxx, 11, 185, 188, 191-193, 285
Chaucer, Geoffrey, 277
Chénier, André, 187
Chéreau, Patrice, 202, 206, 210n.11
Chiari, Joseph, 336
Chocheyras, J., 121n.5
Chomsky, Naom, 231, 233
Cicero, xxvii, 114, 116, 117, 125, 137
Cixous, Hélène, 235
Clarac, Pierre, 135n.1
Claudel, Paul, 242
Cléopâtre, 93
Clifford-Barney, N., 307
Cohen, Jean, 238
Cohn, Robert Greer, 340n.27
Colet, Louise, 260, 307
Collot, M., 76n.1
Commager, H.S., 184n.30
Comte, Auguste, 199
Condillac, Etienne, 218
Cone, Edward T., 346n.11
Considérant, Victor, 305
Contat, Michel, 6-7, 14, 15n.6, 16 n.11
Copernicus, 186
Copfermann, Emile, 210 n.3,7&8
Coquet, Jean-Claude, 247

Index

Corneille, Pierre, 93, 141-144, 147, 148, 204, 205
Crant, Phillip, xi
Creuzer, Georg, 186
Crébillon fils, 241
Crépet, Eugène, xxvi
Crépet, Jacques, xxvi
Crétin, Guillaume, 114
Crocker, Lester, xv, xix, xx, xxvi, xxix, 64n.12, 169-184
Crombach, Louise, 305
Culler, Jonathan, xvi, 238-239
Dacier, Anne, 155
Daix, Pierr, 238
Dante, xx, 187, 277, 279
Daoust, Yvette, 210 n.3,8&9
Dardigna, A.M., 65n.33
Darwin, Charles, 199
Dasté, Jean, 202
Daudet, Alphonse, 82
Davidson, Hugh, xv, xxvi, xxviii, 135 n.1, 137-151
Davis, Angela, 233
Day, James, xv
Dällenbach, L., 76n.16
Debussy, Claude, xxxvi, 242, 325, 329, 341-343
Delacroix, Eugène, 242
DeLage, Maurice, 339n.8
Deleuze, Gilles, 35, 42n.2, 64n.13, 237, 254
Delmont, Léon, 46
Démar, Claire, 311n.9
Demarcy, Richard, 210n.7
Democritus, 157
Denoël, Robert, xxiii
Derrida, Jacques, xvi, xxiv, xxxvi, xxxvii, 35, 42n.2, 213, 222, 233-234, 237, 352, 356n.12
Desbordes, Valmore, Marceline, xxi, xxxv, 301-313
Descartes, René, xxviii, 145-146, 49, 161, 162, 216, 223
Desné, Roland, xv
Diabelli, Anton, 345
Diaghilev, Serge de, 326
Diaz, Furio, 182
Dickens, Charles, 265
Dickinson, Emily, 309, 311
Diderot, Denis, xxix, 158-161, 163-166, 169-170, 176-184
Didier, Béatrice, 297
Dilthey, Wilhelm, 230
Docherty, Thomas, 102, 107n.15
Dolezel, Lubomír, 108n.19
Dolle, J.M., 184n.27
Dort, Bernard, 207, 209, 210n.3,4, 6,13&14, 211n.18
Doubrovsky, Serge, xvi, 229, 238
Doyle, A. Conan, 94
Dreyfus, Alfred, 36, 86
Drieu La Rochelle, Pierre, xxiii, 25-34
Drykoningen, F., 76n.10
Du Bellay, Joachim, xxvii, 113-114, 117-120, 235
Du Bos, Jean-Baptiste, 162
Duchet, Claude, xxxviii, 349
Dumas, Alexandre (fils), 308
Dumas, Alexandre (père), 3
Duncan, Philip, xv
Duras, Marguerite, xxiv-xxv, xxxvii, 67-76, 341-345
Dürer, Albrecht, 355n.3
Durkheim, Emile, 321
Eco, Umberto, xxxvii, 341
Edmiston, William, xv
Einstein, Albert, 186
Eliade, Mircea, 186
Ellison, David, xxi, xxiv, 35-42
Engstrom, Alfred G., 87n.1, 88n.4, 198
Erasmus, 117, 118
Erickson, John, xv
Euclide, 47
Faguet, Emile, 308
Fain, M., 65n.27
Falconet, Etienne, 165
Fargue, Léon-Paul, 338
Faulkner, William, 228
Fauré, Gabriel, 328
Faye, J.P., 232, 233
Fédida, Pierre, 64n.15
Fein, David, 289n.8
Fielding, Henry, 268
Finkielkraut, A., 65n.40
Fisher, D.J., 210n.1
Flandrin, Jean-Louis, 347
Flaubert, Gustave, xviii, xxx, xxxiii, 9, 15n.6, 76n.11, 82-83, 87, 99, 195, 198, 229, 230, 260-262, 263, 265-267
Fontenelle, Bernard Le Bovier de, xxviii, 147, 154, 156, 165
Foucault, Michel, xvi, xxiv, 65n.33, 231, 237, 244-246
Fouquet, Nicolas, 285
Fowlie, Wallace, xix, 340 n.21&27

France, Anatole, xxv, 86-87
François, C., 298n.6
Frazer, James, 186
Frederick the Great, 160
Freud, Sigmund, 40, 59, 230, 231, 234
Friday, N., 65n.52
Fry, Samy, 209
Frye, Northrop, 104, 187
Gadoffre, Gilbert, 119
Gaillard, F., 64n.24
Galles, Caroline de, 292, 297
Garnier, Robert, 119
Garran, Gabriel, 206
Gautier, Théophile, xviii, xxx, 185, 188, 193-195, 196-198, 257
Genette, Gérard, xvi, xxvii, 42n.1, 42n.3, 49, 99, 100, 107n.7, 232, 235, 236, 237
Genêt, Jean, 22, 228
Gentis, R., 64n.21
George I, 294
George, Albert J., 87n.2, 88 n.3
Gerassi, John, 16n.13
Gerig, John L., 121n.5
Germain, Marie, 292
Gide, André, xxv, 33, 50, 87, 220
Gignoux, Herbert, 202
Giono, Jean, xxiii, xxxviii, 352, 357 n.18
Girard, René, 230
Giraudoux, Jean, 106, 228
Girault, 210n.7
Glenn, Christine, G., 107n.2
Godard, Jean 119
Godenne, René, 88n.3
Goethe, Johann W., 258, 285
Goldmann, Lucien, 230, 231
Goncourt (frères), 48, 242
Goulemot, J. M., 65n.41
Grant, Richard B., xv, xxx, 185-199
Greimas, A.J., 102, 107n. 18, 234, 237, 24
Griffin, Robert, 12n.3
Grivel, Charles, xxxviii, 349
Gronquist, Robert, xxxvi-xxxvii, 325-340
Guers-Villatte, V., 76n.14
Hamon, Philippe, 43, 44, 47, 102, 107n.15
Hannover, Sophie von, 292, 294
Hardee, Maynor, xi, xv
Hart-Nibbrig, C.L., 65n.46
Hartman, Geoffrey, 243
Hatzfeld, Helmut, 242
Hawthorne, Nathaniel, 88n.7
Hegel, Georg, 104, 253, 256, 257
Heidegger, Martin, xx, 229
Heliodorus, 112
Hemingway, Ernest, 76n.13
Hénault, Anne, 106n.1
Heyndels, Ralph, xv, xxiv, 53-66, 76 n.3
Hoek, Léo, 349, 355, 356n.7
Holland, Peter Crossley, 339*
Hollier, Denis, 16n.22
Homer, xxvii, xxviii, 99, 112, 113, 116, 117, 125, 153, 155, 156, 158, 255, 277
Horace, 114, 116, 125, 126, 128, 140, 143
Horowitz, Louise, 289n.9
Hough, Robert L., 88n.7
Hubert, René Riese, xv
Hugo, Victor, xxx, 94, 188-191, 257, 286, 306, 327
Huizinga, Johan, 111, 114, 115, 120
Hunt Herbert, 187
Hunt, Tony, 289n.5
Hurd, Bishop, 243
Huret, Jules, 334
Husserl, Edmund, xxxv, 315
Huxley, T.H., 214
Ibsen, Henrik, 201
Ingarden, Roman, 68
Ionesco, Eugène, 201
Iser, Wolfgang, 68
Jakobson, Roman, 234-235, 342
James, William, 324
Jameson, Fredric, 107n.2
Jaucourt, Louis de, 155, 157
Jauss, Hans-Robert, 42n.9
Javeau, Claude, xxxv-xxxvi, 315-324
Jeanneret, M., 289n.12
Jeanson, F., 204, 210n.5
Jodelle, Etienne, 122n.29
Jodogne, Pierre, 121n.4
Johnson, Theodore, 42n.8
Jollivet, Simon, 8, 12
Jolson, Al, 17
Jourdheuil, Jean, 210 n.5&7
Joyce, James, 46, 341
Kahn, M., 64n.17
Kant, Emmanuel, 47
Kierkegaard, Sören, 253, 254, 257
Klossowski, P., 65n.42, 65n.50
Kock, Paul de, 268-270
Kotin, Armine, xx

Index

Königsmarck, Hans Christopher, 294
Kristeva, Julia, xvi, 76n.5, 230, 233-235, 237, 238, 247, 248
Kuhn, Thomas, 246
Labé, Louise, xxxv, 301, 308
Laborde, Alice M., 59, 62, 65n.32
Lacan, Jacques, xvi, xxiv, 64n.6, 65 n.53, 230, 231, 235, 357n.21
Lacoue-Labarthe, Ph., 262n.10
Lacy, Norris, xv
La Fayette, comtesse de, 320
La Fontaine, xii, xxvii-xxviii, xxxiv, 123-135, 140, 284-285, 327
La Forgue, Jules, 257
Lamartine, Alphonse de, 185, 273, 306
Lammert, Eberhart, 107n,7
La Mothe, Charles de, 119
La Motte-Houdar, Antoine, 154, 156
Lanser, Susan Sniader, 104
La Rochfoucauld, François de, 133, 134, 256
Laubriet, Pierre, 88n.5
Laufer, Roer, 243
Laurent, Jeanne, 201-202
Lautréamont, comte de, 234
Lawall, Sarah, 229
Lawler, James, 340n.27
Lebègue, Raymond, 242
Le Boulch, Dr, 65n.30
Lecarme, Jacques, 16n.14
Leclaire, S., 58, 62, 64n.22, 65n. 26
Leclerc, Guy, 210n.3
Leconte de Lisle, Charles Marie, 328
Lefebvre, Henru, 321
Leiris, Michel, 22
Lejeune, Philippe, xxi, 3-16, 42n.1
Lely, G., 65n.54, 107n.3
Lenz, Jakob, 205
Léonard, Albert, 238
Lesage, Alain, 160
LeSage, Laurent, xvi, xxxi, 227-240
Lévi-Strausse, Claude, xxxvii, 98, 186, 231, 232, 284, 341, 345
Lévy, Benny, 16n.16
Lewis, Robert, 87n.2
Leymarie-Mathias, Geneviève, xxi, 23n.2
Lichtenstein, H., 64n.7
Locke, John, 162, 247
Lodge, David, 238
Longinus, 144
Loraine, duchesse de, 291

Lorris, Guillaume de, 277
Loti, Pierre, 315
Lottmann, Herbert, xxiii
Louis XIV, 123, 160, 285, 293, 296
Louis XV, 160
Lovecraft, H.P., 196
Luckman, Thomas, 315
Lukáks, Georg, xxiii
Lull, Ramon, 116
Lully, Jean-Baptiste, 295, 296
Lyttleton, George, 155
Machaut, Guillaume de, 277, 280-281, 282, 285, 286, 288
Macherey, Pierre, 230
Madou, Jean-Pol, xxii-xxxiii, 253-262
Madral, Philippe, 210n.5
Maffesoli, Michel, 320
Malbranche, Nicolas de, xxviii, 146, 149
Malherbe, François de, xxix, 123, 128, 129, 130, 139, 143, 153, 155
Malinowski, Bronislaw, 186
Mallarmé, Stéphane, xxxvi, 76n.11, 234, 235, 257, 258, 259-260, 288, 303, 325-340, 342, 345, 352
Malraux, André, 11, 25, 28, 29, 34, 93, 224, 225
Maréchal, Marcel, 202
Margolin, Uri, 102
Marie de France, xxxv, 301
Marino, Giambattista, 126
Marmontel, Jean, 164
Marot, Clément, 113, 128, 154
Martinet, André, 356n.11
Marx, Karl, 234, 238
Mathias, Bernard, xv, xxi, xxii, 17-23
Mathieu-Colas, Michel, 107n.11
Maupassant, Guy de, xxx, 84-86, 106, 199, 264
Mauriac, Claude, 11
Mauriac, François, 99, 228
Maurois, André, 36, 37, 42n.4
Mauron, Charles, 230, 231
Maurras, Charles, xxiii, 31
McDougall, J., 64n.8
Mendel, G., 64n.18
Menocal, Maria Rosa, 289n.4
Mérimée, Prosper, xxv, 77-88, 195
Merleau-Ponty, M., xxiv, 7, 46, 64n.8
Meschonnic, Henri, 238

Metz, Christian, 107n.2
Michaud, G., 328
Michelet, Jules, 217, 220
Miller, Günther, 49, 51
Miller, Henry, 357n.23
Minguet, Philippe, 243
Mitchell, W.J.T., 107n.5
Molière, xxxi, 123, 133, 147, 158, 204, 205-206, 209, 230
Molino, Jean, 59, 64n.10, 65n.25
Moncelet, Christan, xxxvii, 347
Monnier, Henri, 271
Montaigne, Michel de, 19, 146, 216, 218, 256, 292
Morgan, Richard G., 290n.19
Morot-Sir, Edouard, xxxi, 213-226
Morris, Charles, 247, 248
Moulin, Jeanine, 310
Mounin, Georges, 230, 238
Munro, Thomas, 345
Musset, Alfred de, 204, 257
Mussorgsky, Petrovich, 326
Myers, Rollo, 336
Nabokov, Vladimir, xxxiii, 288
Nadel, Siegfried, 344
Nancy, J.L., 262n.10
Napoléon I, 93, 230
Nerval, Gérard de, 255
Newcomb, Anthony, 107n.2
Newton, Isaac, 154, 161, 186
Niboyet, Eugénie, 305
Nicole, Pierre, 148, 150n.6
Nietzsche, Friedrich, 33, 215, 222, 342
Nizan, Paul, 7
Noailles, Anna de, 301
Noakes, Susan, 289n.5
Nodier, Charles, 285
Norman, Buford, xv, 289n.10
Nuiten, Henk, xv
O'Casey, Sean, 201
Ohmann, Richard, 244
Olds, Marshall, xv
Ollier, Claude, 46
O'Neill, Eugene, 201
Orléans, Charles d', 111, 288
Orléans, Philippe d', 291
Ornstein, Arbie, 326
Ovid, 125, 126
Palatine, Madame, xxi, xxxiv, 291-299
Panizza, Oskar, 205
Pappas, John N., xxviii-xxix, xxx, 153-167
Paré, Ambroise, 292
Paris, Jean, 344
Pascal, Blaise, xxviii, 146-147, 148, 215, 221, 222, 256
Pasquier, Etienne, 114
Passerat, Jean, 118
Patchen, Kenneth, xxxiii, 287-288
Pavel, Thomas, 102, 103, 104, 106n.1, 107n.17, 108n.19&21
Peletier du Mans, xxvii, 112, 113, 116, 117
Petrarch, 332
Peyre, Henri, xix, 145n.1, 241
Pélosse, Valentin, 311n.9
Pétain, Philippe, 26
Pène, Henri de, 272
Peuchemaud, Jacques, 356n.15
Phaedrus, 126
Philipe, Gérard, 203
Piaget, Jean, 247
Picard, Raymond, 231
Pichois, Claude, xxvi
Picon, Gaëtan, 228
Pierce, Charles, 247
Pipelet, Constance, 307
Planchon, Roger, xxx-xxxi, 201-206, 208-211
Planté, Christine, xxi, xxxv, 301-313
Plato, xx, xxiv, xxix, 43, 116, 118, 125, 153, 154, 155, 157, 253-256, 259, 284, 332
Pleynet, Marcellin, 356n.13
Poe, Edgar Allan, 87, 88n.7
Pommier, Jean, 231
Porter, Laurence M., xv, xxxiii, 277-290
Poulet, Georges, 49, 229, 230, 242
Pousseur, Henri, 345
Poussin, Nicolas, 81
Prendergast, Christopher, xxiii
Prévost, Antoine-François (l'abbé), 163, 242
Prince, Gerald, xxv-xxvi, 97-108
Propp, Vladimir, 98, 102, 107n.3
Proust, Marce, xxiv, 35-42, 51, 216, 220, 232, 327, 356n.12&16
Prudentius, 41
Prussen, Sophie Dorothée von, 293
Pudlowski, Gilles, 356n.15
Quinault, Philippe, 295, 296
Quinet, Edgar, 187
Quintilian, 137
Rabelais, François, xxxiv, 118, 121, 126, 283, 288

Index 365

Racine, Jean, xxxi, 123, 128, 134, 147, 155, 162, 204, 209, 285
Ragache, Gilles, xxiii
Ragache, Jean-Robert, xxiii
Rahner, Hugo, 122n.24
Rapin, René, 144-145
Ravel, Maurice, xxxvi, 325-340
Raymond, Marcel, 88n.4, 115, 228, 242-243
Raynal, Guillaume, 164
Reck, Rima Drell, xv, xxiii, 25-34
Renart, Jean, 289n.3
Renoir, Jean, 36, 37, 242
Ricardou, Jean, xxxviii, 35, 107n.8, 227, 232, 233, 353, 356n.16, 357n.18
Ricatte, Robert, 357n.18
Richard, Jean-Pierre, 199, 229, 231
Richelet, César, 139
Ricoeur, Paul, xxiii, 101, 107n.12
Riffaterre, Michael, xvii, 238, 357n.18
Rigolot, François, xv
Rimbaud, Arthur, xxxiv, 19, 153, 164, 234, 235, 285-286, 288, 303
Riot-Sarcey, Michèle, 311n.10
Robbe-Grillet, Alain, xxxvii, 26, 45, 68, 76n.11&15, 106, 231, 232, 344
Robertet, Jean, 111
Rohan, Chevalier de, 160, 165
Roland, Pauline, 305
Romero, Laurence, xxx, 201-211
Ronsard, Pierre de, xxviii, 114, 115, 119, 126, 154, 155
Ronzeaud, Pierre, xv
Rosen, Elisheva, 357n.18
Rosset, Clément, 65n.49
Roth, Phillip, 19
Rousseau, Jean-Jacques, xx, xxix, 17, 18, 157, 158, 160, 161, 162, 165, 169-177, 181-184
Rousset, Jean, 47, 230, 242-243
Rubin, David, xv
Ruwet, Nicholas, 343
Ryan, Marie-Laure, 102, 103, 105, 107n.17&18, 108n.19
Saba, Guido, 289n.10
Sachs, Murray, xv, 77-88
Sade, Marquis de, xxiv, 53-66, 235
Saint-Gelais, Mellin de, 282
Saint-Lambert, Jean de, 161
Saint-Marceaux, Mme de, 339n.14

Saint-Simon, duc de, 293, 298
Sainte-Beuve, Charles, 155, 312n.3
Salel, Hugues, 112, 116, 117, 282
Saliat, Pierre, 112
Sand, George, 260, 263, 305, 311
Sandier, Gilles, 210n.7&11
Sarraute, Nathalie, 22, 26
Sartre, Jean-Paul, xx, xxi, xxii, xxv, xxx, 3-16, 18, 22, 25, 27, 30, 45, 87, 185, 221, 228, 230, 231, 232, 262n.19, 341
Saussure, Nicolas de, 43
Savary, Jérome, 209
Schaerer, R., 262n.4
Schilder, P., 65n.34
Schiller, Friedrich, 236
Schlegel, Friedrich & Wilhelm, 256-258
Scholes, Robert, 239
Schönberg, Arnold, 327
Schütz, Alfred, 315, 318
Sedaine, Michel, 163
Ségur, Comte de, 164
Seneca, 146
Serail, Jean, xv
Sérant, Paul, 29, 32
Shakespeare, William, 91-92, 158, 201, 204, 205
Showalter, Elaine, 313n.13
Simon, Alfred, 207, 209, 210n.3
Simon, Claude, xxxvii, 46, 344
Sitwell, Sacheverell, 242
Smith, Barbara Herrnstein, 107n.5
Smith, Maxwell, 87n.2
Socrates, xxxii-xxxiii, 33, 153, 253-258
Sollers, Philippe, xxxvii, 64n.23, 232, 233, 341, 342-343, 345
Sorano, Daniel, 203
Sourches, marquis de, 298
Spariosu, Mihai, xxiii
Spengler, Oswald, 224, 225
Spitzer, Leo, 242-243
Spleth, Janice, 324
Sponde, Jean de, 235
Spraycar, Rudy s., 289n.4
Springer, George P., 346n.3
Staël, Madame de, 298n.7
Stanislavski, Konstantine, 207
Stanton, Domna, xxxv, 301, 307, 308, 309, 310
Stanzel, Franz, 107n.7
Starobinski, Jean, 230, 256, 257
Stein, Nancy, 107n.2

Steiner, Wendy, 107n.2
Stendhal, 11, 43, 229, 320
Stern, Daniel, 305
Stone, David, xv, xxvi, xxvii, 111-122
Stravinsky, Igor, xxxvi, 326, 327, 329
Stuart, Mary, 115
Suarez, Georges, xxiii
Symons, Artheu, 328
Taine, Hippolyte, 199
Tardieu, Jean, 311n.8
Tastu, Amable, 307
Taylor, Eric, 343
Temkine, Raymonde, 207, 209, 211 n.14
Temple, Ruth Z., 340n.18
Terence, 125
Tertullian, 146
Teste, Emilie, 223
Thibaudeau, Jean, 232, 233
Thibaudet, Albert, 339n.6
Thom, René, xxxi, 247
Thomas, Jean-Jacques, xviii
Tissier, 210n.5
Tobin, Ronald, xv
Todorov, Tzvetan, xvi, 43, 107n.8, 197, 234, 235, 237
Tonelli, F., 65n.35
Tournier, Michel, 348
Trahard, Pierre, 88n.3
Tristan l"Hermite, xii
Tuve, Rosemond, 121n.16
Urfé, Honoré d', 283-285, 288
Valéry, Paul, 65 n. 47, 124, 223, 224, 232, 339n.6
Vallès, Jules, 21
Valmore, Prosper, 303
Van den Heuvel, Pierre, xxiv-xxv, xxxvii, 67-76
Van den Hove, Mariska, 76n.8
Van der Cruysse, Dirk, xv, xxi, xxxiv, 291-299
Vance, Eugene, 289n.5
Varikas, Eléni, 311n.10
Varsava, Jerry A., xxiv
Vaugelas, Claude de, 123, 139
Vegetius, 116
Velan, Yves, 357n.23
Verhaeren, Emile, 328
Verlaine, Paul, 242, 303, 328, 341, 342
Vernier, François, 230, 238
Védrine, Louise, 5
Vérard, Anthoine, 115, 116
Vian, Boris, 358n.23
Viaud, Théophile de, 284
Viegnes, Michel, xxi, xxiv, 43-52
Vigny, Alfred de, 191, 230
Vilar, Jean, xxx-xxxi, 201-205, 207-211
Villey, Pierre, 119
Villiers de l'Isle-Adam, Philippe de, 82
Villon, François, xxxiv, 111, 281-282, 286, 288
Viñez, Ricardo, 327
Virgil, 125, 126, 127
Vitez, Antoine, 202
Voiture, Vincent, 126, 128, 129, 140
Volaterranus, Raphael, 122n.19
Voltaire, xxix, 155, 156, 158, 162, 162, 165, 166, 256, 273
Vuillermoz, Emile, 340n.29
Wadsworth, Philip A., xi-xvi, xix, xx, xxvi, xxvii-xxviii, 123-135
Wagner, Richard, 217
Walker, Philip, 198
Walzal, Oscar, 241
Warhol, Robyn, 104
Weber, Jean-Paul, 230
Weber, Max, xxxv, 315
Wehle, Phillipa, 210n.3
Weinrich, Harold, 49
Welek, René, 241
Wenk, Arthur, 329, 342
Whitman, Walt, 62
Williame, Robert, 315
Williams, John R., xvi
Wilson, Edmund, 37-38
Wilson, Georges, 203
Winnicott, W., 64n.20
Wirth, Jean, 347
Wittgenstein, Ludvig, 44, 236
Woolf, Virginia, 43, 307
Wyzewa, Théodore de, 328
Zola, Emile, xxxii, 83-84, 88n.6, 230, 271
Zoran, Gabriel, 102, 107n.15
Zsuppan, C. M., 121n.5

Tabula gratulatoria

(* Philip A. Wadsworth Scholarship contributor)

Claude & Marcia Abraham*
Stephen & Dorothy Ackerman*
Serge Bokobza
Germaine Brée
Horace & Eleonor Byrne*
Roland Champagne*
Ilona Chessid
Marie-Magdeleine Chirol
S. Douglas Cornell*
Philip Crant*
William F. Edmiston*
David R. Ellison*
T. Bruce Fryer*
Christian Garaud
Perry J. Gethner
Richard B. Grant
Marcel Gutwirth
A. Maynor Hardee
Eglal Henein
Freeman & Alexandra Rowe Henry*
Elizabeth G. Joiner*
A. Curtis Lafrance*
J. Patrick Lee*
Wolfgang Leiner
Jean-Pol Madou
Georges May*
Rob Roy McGregor*
Lucille Mould
Buford Norman*
Laurence M. Porter
Christine McCall Probes*
William Roberts
Laurent Romero*
Mary Madeleine Rowan
Murray Sachs*

Marie-Odile Sweetser*
Alex Szpgyi
Ronald W. Tobin
Michel Viegnes
Marie Wegimont

Papers on French Seventeenth-Century Literature , Tübingen, Germany*
Willam B. Perkins Library, Duke University
Princeton University Library
Z. Smith Reynolds Library, Wake Forest University
University of South Carolina Libraries
Southern Oregon State College
Madeleine Clark Wallace Library, Wheaton College